W9-AUU-019

THE ENGLISH CIVIL WAR

THE ENGLISH CIVIL WAR

Papists, Gentlewomen,
Soldiers, and Witchfinders
in the Birth of Modern Britain

DIANE PURKISS

BASIC
BOOKS

A Member of the Perseus Books Group
New York

Copyright © 2006 by Diane Purkiss
Published in the United States by Basic Books,
A Member of the Perseus Books Group
Published in the United Kingdom by HarperCollins*Publishers*

All rights reserved. Printed in the United States of America. No part
of this book may be reproduced in any manner whatsoever without
written permission except in the case of brief quotations embodied
in critical articles and reviews. For information, address Basic Books,
387 Park Avenue South, New York, NY 10016-8810.

Books published by Basic Books are available at special discounts for
bulk purchases in the United States by corporations, institutions, and
other organizations. For more information, please contact the Special
Markets Department at the Perseus Books Group, 11 Cambridge Center,
Cambridge MA 02142, or call (617) 252-5298 or (800) 255-1514, or
e-mail special.markets@perseusbooks.com.

Maps of Great Britain by John Giles

A CIP catalog record for this book is available
from the Library of Congress.
ISBN-13: 978-0-465-06756-5
ISBN-10: 0-465-06756-5
United Kingdom: ISBN-13: 978 0 00 715061 X; ISBN-10: 0 00 715061 X
06 07 08 / 10 9 8 7 6 5 4 3 2 1

942.062
PuR

CONTENTS

PICTURE CREDITS

The following photographs are reproduced courtesy of:

Frontispiece from the Scottish Prayer Book of 1637. (The Trustees of the National Library of Scotland.)

Old London Bridge from an *Album Amicorum*. (Edinburgh University Library/Bridgeman Art Library.)

Charles I when Duke of York by Robert Peake the Elder. (Bristol City Museum and Art Gallery/Bridgeman Art Library.)

'Laud's Dream' by unknown English artist. (Ashmolean Museum, University of Oxford/Bridgeman Art Library.)

Oliver Cromwell, aged two, by unknown English artist. (The Trustees of the Chequers Estate/Bridgeman Art Library.)

Portrait of John Hampden, attributed to Robert Walker. National Portrait Gallery, London.

Anna Trapnel, from a 1660 engraving designed to show her as a witch.

Lucy Percy Hay, Countess of Carlisle by Sir Anthony van Dyck. (Private Collection/Bridgeman Art Library.)

Inigo Jones' sketch of a costume for Henrietta Maria at her masque of *Chloridia*. (Chatsworth Settlement Trustees and Chatsworth House Trust.)

Henrietta Maria and her dwarf Sir Jeffrey Hudson by Sir Anthony van Dyck. (Private Collection/Bridgeman Art Library.)

The Short Parliament assembled at Westminster in April 1640. (Museum of London/Bridgeman Art Library.)

The execution of Thomas Wentworth, engraving by Wenceslas Hollar. (Bibliotheque des Arts Decoratifs, Paris/Bridgeman Art Library.)

Pamphlet sketch showing the nightmares of the Ulster rebellion: a 'Papist riping up a wife with childe'. (Private Collection/Bridgeman Art Library.)

John Pym, engraved by George Glover. (Private Collection/ Bridgeman Art Library.)

A threatening letter sent to John Pym, depicting the quelling of a riot in Westminster Hall. (British Library, London/Bridgeman Art Library.)

Brilliana Harley by unknown artist.

James Graham, 1ˢᵗ Marquess of Montrose, after Gerrit van Honthorst. (National Portrait Gallery, London.)

Key figures of the Civil War, in a contemporary engraving by an unknown artist. (British Museum/Art Archive.)

Charles I in armour by Sir Anthony van Dyck. (Collection of the Earl of Pembroke, Wilton House/Bridgeman Art Library.)

The Kingdom's Monster Uncloaked. A woodcut from *c.*1640–43. (Private Collection/Bridgeman Art Library.)

Portrait of Oliver Cromwell by Robert Walker. (Leeds Museums and Galleries/Bridgeman Art Library.)

Woodcut made *c.*1645–8: *To him, Pudel . . . bite him, Peper.* (Private Collection/Bridgeman Art Library.)

Descent from the Cross by Sir Peter Paul Rubens. (Art Archive/ Antwerp Cathedral/Joseph Martin.)

Portrait of Sir Ralph Verney by C. Jansen. (Claydon House, Buckinghamshire/ Bridgeman Art Library.)

Anne Harrison, Lady Fanshawe by Catherine Maria Fanshawe. (National Portrait Gallery, London.)

Philip Skippon by R.S. after unknown artist. (National Portrait Gallery, London.)

Prince Rupert Hiding in a Field, July 1644. (Private Collection/ Bridgeman Art Library.)

The Siege of Oxford, June 1645 by Jan Wyck. (Art Archive/Private Collection.)

Charles I and Thomas Fairfax at the Battle of Naseby. (Art Archive.)

'The Vindication of Christmas'. (British Library, London/Bridgeman Art Library.)

John Milton by unknown artist. (National Portrait Gallery, London.)

Frontispiece of *Areopagitica*. (Private Collection/Bridgeman Art Library.)

Frontispiece of *The Queene-like Closet*. (British Library, London.)

Frontispiece from *The Closet of Sir Kenelme Digbie*. (Printed by E.C. for H. Brome at the Star in Little Britain, 1669.)

Matthew Hopkins, the Witchfinder General. (Private Collection/ Bridgeman.)

The Declaration and Standard of the Levellers. (Private Collection/ Bridgeman Art Library.)

A New-Yeers Gift for the Parliament and Armie. (Private Collection/ Bridgeman Art Library.)

The World turned upside down. (British Library, London/Bridgeman Art Library.)

Front page from *Mercurius Civicus*. (Private Collection/Bridgeman.)

Front page from *Mercurius Politicus*. (Private Collection/Bridgeman.)

Prince Charles as a boy by Pieter de Jode II, after Sir Anthony van Dyck. (National Portrait Gallery, London.)

Prince James in 1640, by Wenceslaus Hollar. (National Portrait Gallery, London.)

Princess Elizabeth and Princess Anne painted by Sir Anthony van Dyck. (Scottish National Portrait Gallery/Bridgeman Art Library.)

John Bradshaw after unknown artist. (National Portrait Gallery, London.)

The hat of John Bradshaw. Ashmolean Museum, (University of Oxford/ Bridgeman Art Library.)

Execution of King Charles I from contemporary broadsheet. (Art Archive.)

LIST OF MAPS

LONDON

SAINT PAULS

The large circuit of multitude of streets besydes the beautifull & stately buildings in this shyre, and most famous Citie LONDON: can nowise be demonstrated in soe little compasse, as here I am inforced to shewe. But as Hercules his bodie might be measured by his foote, and the universall Globe drawe in a smale circle: Soe in this other conceit the magnificent theweof in mynde, even curiously seeke satisfaction by the sight whole pleasant situation, beautye, and rich blessings both for soyll and sea equals, yf not exceeds, any Citie under Heaven. The trew plott whereof I purposely reserve to a further leasure & larger scale. And

Described by Iohn Norden, Augmented by I. Speed Solde in Popes head alley against the Exchange by George Humble

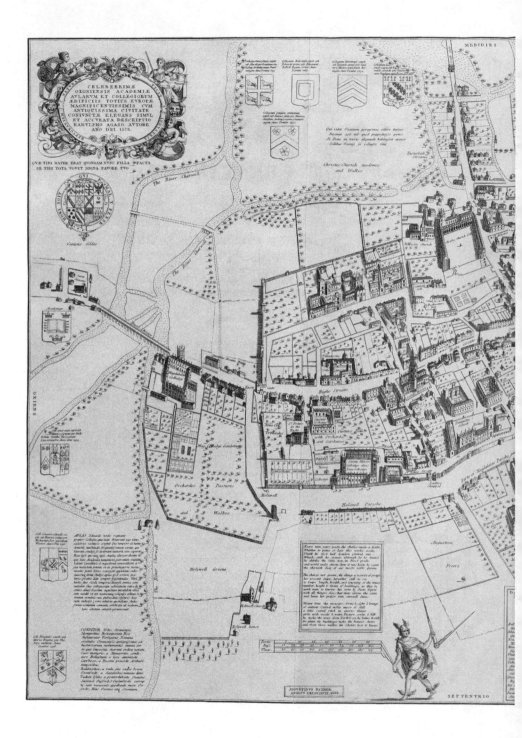

N

W — E

S

ATLANTIC
OCEAN

ULSTER

IRELAND

Drogheda

Dublin and
the Pale

Carnarvon

IRISH
SEA

Launceston

Kingdom of England,
Scotland and Ireland

0   50   100 miles

NORTH
SEA

SCOTLAND

Inverness

Aberdeen

Dundee

Stirling

Glasgow Edinburgh

ENGLAND

Ludlow Holdenby House

Manningtree

Burford Ware Maldon

LONDON
Syon House
Hampton Court
St George's Hill

Carisbrooke

English Channel

FRANCE

Civil War Battle Sites

N
W E
S

NORTH
SEA

Perth
Inverkeithing
Stirling
Falkirk
Glasgow
Linlithgow
Queensferry
Edinburgh
Leith
Musselburgh
Dunbar
Berwick
Philiphaugh

Marston
Moor
York
Preston
Lathom House
Barthomley
Nottingham
Coventry
Naseby
Norwich
Worcester
Brampton
Bryan
Gloucester
Edgehill
Colchester
Cirencester
Faringdon
Oxford
Newbury
Rochester
Bristol
Salisbury
Turnham
Green
Canterbury
Basing
House
Taunton
Exeter
Lostwithiel

0   50   100 miles

THE ENGLISH
CIVIL WAR

An Epistle to the Gentle Reader

If this were truly a seventeenth-century book or pamphlet, it would be likely to include an epistle to you, the reader. In the seventeenth century, with which this book is concerned, authors and readers approached each other more formally and courteously than is now customary. A book usually began with a polite letter to the gentle reader, a letter which asked for the reader's attention, apologized for the book's shortcomings, and explained what benefits patient perusal of the work might offer. The tone was often self-deprecating, and it was usual to deprecate the book itself as 'my poor book'. The poet Robert Herrick thought his book was likely to be used as toilet paper when his readers were tired of it; Milton repeatedly asked God to fix his awful weaknesses. In addressing the reader as 'gentle', the author invited him or her to be so; to be courteous and polite in turn. Gentle also has a class meaning; it implies wealth, and with it education, power and discernment.

I hope it is not too self-conscious for me to emulate this charming tradition and thus to offer a tribute to it. In reviving a good custom and addressing you, gentle reader, my chief purpose is to welcome you to a story that greatly concerns you.

Frankly, I am in hopes that you may be among those to whom the words 'The English Civil War' have always stood for an unsolved mystery. The Civil War is perhaps the single most important event in our history, but for rather complex reasons many of the very intelligent readers who abound in these isles know little of it. The great battlefield sites of Edgehill, Marston Moor, and Naseby are difficult to find and poorly marked. The siege sites of Basing House and Donnington Castle are ruins dotted with picnickers rather than sacred memorials to heroic endeavour and ideas. We have no Fourth of July, no Bastille Day to commemorate our own heroic struggle to define and enact freedom, even though on it depended the ideas that were later to lead to those two other revolutions. Self-deprecation can go too far, and as a nation we are perhaps too good at it, so good that it becomes a species of forgetting.

So it is that in these pages I would like to introduce you – gently – to the war and the men and women who fought in it. In this book I invite you with all respect to make the acquaintance of what we call The Civil War – the series of battles and campaigns fought on the field and also in people's hearts and minds between 1642 and 1649, culminating in the judicial execution of a king and the creation of the only English Republic to date.

You, dear courteous reader, will come to know more anon. You will not come to know everything worth knowing from my poor book alone, but it may make you feel well enough acquainted with its subject to pursue the men and women it sketches through other books, to see them in the streets of your own town or city.

To some of you I should not presume ot offer such an introduction. For some of you, the civil war is an old friend, and I welcome you too to these pages. Among your number are doubtless the formidable amateur experts who also dot our landscape; those who know far more than I about the siege of Gloucester or the range of a demi-culverin, those who could draw an accurate sketch of the battle lines at Newbury, those who have an especial hero among the fighting men and women whose stories burst from the pages of history – Fairfax, Cromwell, Charles I. I bow to you and apologize in advance for any errors you may discern. But I also beg you not merely to indulge your passion, but to make the acquaintance of persons whose stories you may not have considered important, especially the stories of non-combatants, the stories of those for whom war was not battle but privation or writing or ideas.

Finally, I address you, discerning and erudite readers, academic historians, colleagues. Not all of you will agree with what I have done here. So it must be, for I hope we might at least unite in stating that no history of this war has ever commanded universal acclamation. It may be that some of you may think, for instance, that cookery writers should not elbow parliamentary debates aside as they do here, for the reason that the latter have more serious influence on the lives of ordinary men and women. But do they? The democratization of simple knowledge is part of the *political* story of these years. And unlike the form of government, this reform is lasting. Bear with me, tolerate me, and you may find some profit in it.

I also want to say this to you, as an apology for my poor naked book; once upon a time, our courteous readers enjoyed academic history because it was grounded, as was the novel, in a drama of character. Macaulay and Carlyle were read and loved because their version of history was a guide to human nature. For complex and very good reasons, their approach has been largely abandoned by professional historians; indeed, for many a focus on individual character in history is now an irredeemable sign of the amateur. In all my work I am trying to seduce the academy into taking this human approach back, reviving it, and thus giving its revived force to the subjects of our ruminations. If the past is not to be dry, then it must live, and so must its people. I hope I may be forgiven much that is faulty or imperfect for my attempt to return to a moment when history was a vital part of the nation's idea of who and what human beings are.

I also gratefully greet those of my profession who have made the present book possible by their tireless, often unrewarded and unrecognized attempts to labour through unread and grimy manuscripts and smudged public records in search of those most elusive of all historical personages, the ordinary man and woman. May we all, author and readers, unite in their name. And I commend this my poor book to you above all.

Your very humble servant,

THE AUTHOR
Oxford

February 2006

I

The Last Cavalier?

One night in 1712, a man named Thomas Neville lay dying in his own bed, surrounded by family and friends. He was an ordinary gentleman, but in his lifetime he had been among those who had seen the Middle Ages finally disappear, and the modern era emerge. He had seen wonders, and had even made them happen. But the changes he had witnessed were accompanied by violence and terror unmatched in the history of his country. Thomas Neville was the last man to remember that turmoil, the last surviving field officer from a once-great but defeated army, the army of King Charles I.

Thomas Neville had had better reason than most to join the king's army. He had seen his rich father ordered to give up the house he had grown up in and had heard him say that 'rather than yield to dishonourable persons, I will make my house my grave'. His enemy – the Parliamentarian Lord Grey of Groby – stormed the house and took his father prisoner; the building was burned to the ground. From then on Thomas Neville and his elder brother William were at war, whether they wished to be or not. In 1644, they fought at Newark; in 1646 at Ashby de la Zouch. Both brothers survived the war, but William was dead by 1661. Thomas survived to tell his stories of dashing Cavalier Prince Rupert galloping to the rescue to his children and grandchildren.

By the time Thomas Neville closed his eyes in death, the war he had fought in had become distant even for his grandchildren. In the decades that followed the war, throughout Britain, people began to make efforts to write down the Civil War stories that their grandfathers had told.

Those who had fought themselves had spent the Restoration years writing down their experiences, fighting old battles again. And grandmothers wrote too, for grandchildren who would never know their grandfathers because they lay buried at Edgehill, at Newbury, at Marston Moor or Naseby, or by lesser towns or streams where short sharp engagements had been fought. Some wrote for the God for whom they had shed their blood; others for the Good Old Cause, and still others for the kings living and dead whom they had served. Some recounted their war experiences in the hope of a disability pension, or to explain to a sceptical community exactly what they had done. All of them wrote because they knew they had lived through a time like no other.

Their descendants kept their letters, their diaries, their memoirs faithfully, knowing that in those pages lay a link to a time fast passing from memory into history. Others sought to scrabble together the storm of paper the war had produced; George Thomason tried to collect every pamphlet, newspaper and ballad printed during the war, while Samuel Pepys put together ballads and Edward Hyde and John Aubrey wrote down soldiers' and survivors' recollections. Those who had been children when King Charles raised his standard recorded their memories of the lost king; those who had been youths when Cromwell held court at Westminster wrote down what they had seen. Between them all, they kept alive what all history needs: the stories of the people who lived it.

Those who kept these careful records were right about the importance of what they had seen to the lives of the men and women of the future. We owe our state of government to the English Civil War, but most of its beneficiaries have little idea who fought whom or when or why. Nor do most of us care; what little we know seems remote and difficult to grasp, with stiff figures on battlefields and stiffer constitutional debates. Yet actually, the English Civil War was the making of our country. It made us the nation we are, the countries we are, the people we are. It also created those more permanent revolutions by influence: Thomas Jefferson and George Washington recalled and revered the Good Old Cause against the king's tyranny, and the French revolutionaries had read their Milton. The glories and liberations of that long-ago conflict still benefit us today; so too its failings and limitations are with us, part of our blood, setting the horizon of our expectations. And to understand ourselves, we have to understand the people we were, the people who fought in that war.

This book has two goals: to tell the story of the English Civil War up to and including the execution of the king, and to bring to life the people who fought in it, died in it, and in doing so changed the history of the world for ever.

To do this, I tell the story of the war from the points of view of the people involved. The war is interesting because it was fought by people, men and women. My cast of characters ranges from Charles I himself, disastrous shaper of his own fate, through his most educated and articulate opponents, men like John Milton, and through men and women utterly obscure before the war and glintingly prominent after it, men like Oliver Cromwell, through to what Charles himself might have called 'the meaner sort', men like witch-finder Matthew Hopkins and revolutionary Gerrard Winstanley, godly women like Anna Trapnel. We first glimpse these people before the war, and we see how the war changes them, creates unexpected chances for them to change their lives, overthrows what they thought they could take for granted. When the war ends, when King Charles is dead, we see what all these people have left, what remains of their lives. Mine is not an even-handed portrait. Not all of these people represent something beyond themselves and their individual stories. Some figures that were important do not get as much space as the well-informed reader might expect. But this unevenness was part of contemporaries' experience of the war; they too did not always see a 'big picture', but the small details of a burned barn, a changed pattern of church service, a son lost in battle.

The armed conflict was also a major event in its own right. Estimates suggest that around 800,000 people in the British Isles died during its course, the majority of them in Ireland. One in four of all men served in the armies on one side or the other, which suggests that a majority of able-bodied men was involved. The war was not a clean and tidy affair of sabres and dashing cavalry charges; it was a bloody business largely driven by guns – cannons and muskets and pistols – which at times appears to have combined the worst aspects of the American Civil War and Vietnam. Both sides used soft lead bullets that did terrible damage to flesh. For years afterwards, the London streets were full of one-legged beggars. Cities and castles were razed to the ground.

There were atrocities involving civilians, again especially in Ireland. The war was expensive, and individual families were ruined – or made – by its sweeping hand. And so people came to see change all around them. They thought that the world had been transformed for ever, for them and for their families. Because they thought that, some of them began questioning many taken-for-granted aspects of life, looking in new ways at the purpose of women, the purpose of government and of its leaders, and at the purpose of human beings. Some of what they invented still governs our lives: universal male suffrage, promotion on merit, women's involvement in politics, the ordinary man's need for a home and food.

Isabella Twysden's Civil War diary illustrates the way big events look to small people. In her journal, however, a big event could be personal or political; she gave equal weight to the birth of a new baby, or King Charles's capture by his enemies in the Parliamentarian army. She tried to chronicle her own life and the life of the nation, with no anxiety about the disparity of scale, because to her both kinds of events were important.

   She tried to keep a record of news, a daily chronicle. She didn't write down what she felt, but only what happened. Her first three entries for 1645 read:

> The first of Janua. Mr John Hotham was beheaded on Tower Hill.

> The 2nd of Janu Sr John Hotham (father to Mr Hotham) was beheaded on Tower Hill.

> The 10 of January My Lord of Canterbury was beheaded on Tower Hill and was buried at Barking Church

Interspersed with the doings of the great she recorded events crucial to her:

> The 8 Feb I came to Peckham great with child, and ride all the way a horseback, and I thank God had no hurt

> The 6 of March [1645], between one and two in the morning I was brought to bed of a boy, the 7 he was christened and named Charles, the gossips [godparents] were my brother

Charles and Francis Twysden and my Lady Astley [wife of Jacob Astley]

The 11 of March there was the terriblest wind, that had been known since ever the like, it did a great deal of hurt

The 3 of April a little before 3 in the morning my sister Twysden was brought to bed of a girl at Maling, it was christened the 5 and named Ann, without gossips . . . the new way.

It might seem incongruous that Isabella recorded this mass of detail about her baby's christening and her niece's christening in a war diary, but she did so because domestic details like this had themselves become battlefields. In particular, the baptism of babies had become caught up in the political divisions the war had created. Many families of traditional views were made miserable by the difficulty of getting vulnerable infants baptized by their preferred rite. As George Thomason amassed a collection of over a hundred tracts on the question of infant baptism, worried parents tried to do their own homework, anxiously poring over the Bibles and pamphlets much as modern parents might agonize over vaccination. In 1646, when their child was born, John and Lucy Hutchinson took some time to decide, but eventually chose not to have the new baby baptized, whereupon, Lucy wrote, they were reviled as sectarians. The Directory of Public Worship, which replaced the prayer book in 1645, dispensed with the sign of the cross, and the minister was told bluntly to sprinkle the child's face 'without adding any other ceremony'. Godparents were also ruled out firmly, and instead the child was presented by its father. Some people accepted this philosophically. Still others rejoiced at the opportunity to choose adult baptism, and found names for themselves that reflected their faith. But the diarist John Evelyn loathed it, and had his babies christened at home, according to the old rite, while he continued to act as godparent for friends who felt the same.

This is how war and other such large events are experienced: Isabella juxtaposes Fairfax's capture of 4000 soldiers at the pivotal battle of Naseby in 1645 with worries about the money owed to the baby's monthly nurse, who is leaving for London. For her, the personal and the political are well blended. My intention is to achieve the same mix in this book. This method has its drawbacks, as Isabella's diary shows; the stories that result can seem to jump about, and strict chronology is sometimes sacrificed to the writer's interest in particular events. But it is truer to how this war was felt. There was not one Civil War, but thousands, different for each person involved.

So large impersonal changes such as constitutional reforms are important but only because they are eventually experienced by people. I found Charles Stuart much more interesting than absolutism, Oliver Cromwell more compelling than Puritanism. And neither man is helpfully summed up by a list of his beliefs, because both were also feeling human beings, inconsistent and emotional, and so were all those who fought alongside them.

II

The Meek-Eyed Peace

The story of the Civil War begins with the world before the cataclysm. The group of people who were to play great roles in the enormous events to come were in 1639 leading lives that seemed to them normal. There were political struggles, there was murmuring and discontent, but these disputes were well within the realm of normality. True, there had been a war with Scotland, and matters there were still not settled. But there had been such wars before. There was nothing to suggest that the nation was about to be violently torn in pieces by the most costly armed conflict in its history. Even the two protagonists, Charles and Cromwell, could have no inkling of what was coming.

By focusing on a morning in the late winter of 1639, we can catch a glimpse of those last moments of unthinking normality. On that morning Charles I was hunting. The king loved hunting on horseback, and loved it far more than the tedious obligations that came with rule. When on a progress, a tour to meet his subjects, Charles would sneak off to the chase rather than remain to shake the lord mayor's hand. On a cold morning, a winter's morning, the horse and the freshly killed game both steamed lightly, the heat of their bodies drowning out the scent of trodden leaves. For Charles, his horse was more interesting and less demanding company than his subjects; it did not rush up to him with importunities he did not understand, did not beg for his touch to heal it of nauseating diseases. It served him and knew its place – and so did those who rode with him. Through hunting Charles could feel connected with his father, James I, who had also loved the chase, but who had not very greatly loved Charles. And he could feel absolute

– absolutely confident that the still-vast royal forests belonged to him and no one else. In those forests were deer that had been bred by his royal predecessors, Henry VIII and Elizabeth I, as well as his father. The forests were also still dangerous, full of wild boar. In their leafless and endless embrace, Charles need not fear having to treat with anyone. He ruled all he saw. And at just a year short of forty, his grip on power had become tight and remorseless.

His future foe, Oliver Cromwell, loved to hunt on horseback too, and like Charles, a winter morning in 1639 might have found him at the chase. We can picture both, then, crouched over the carcass of a slain deer, ceremoniously dividing the venison for various people: their fellow-hunters, those who were due a gift, the hunt servants. This picture to us suggests mess, but to Charles and Cromwell it would have meant order, the comforts of ritual. Bloody and dangerous as hunting could be, it was a moment for all gentlemen to feel in control of the world, like God looking over his creation on the seventh day of rest. An important metaphor for Cromwell, for ever since his extreme depression in his middle twenties, religion had become his reason for living. Now a man of forty, he had put his turbulent youth firmly behind him. But he still loved the chase. The experience of hunting yoked the gentry to the aristocracy; it made gentlemen feel like rulers.

Middle-class town dwellers like John Milton had other interests. Milton loved books. On a winter's morning in 1639, he would have been at his desk or in his library, reading, writing, thinking. He liked to get up early, working or studying until dawn. He had only the slender light of a candle to illuminate and warm his small dark parlour. He did not order a fire, despite the cold; Milton was not a poor man, but he was not a rich one. At thirty-one, he did not have what his father might have called a proper job, and by 1639 he had published only one poem. But he already knew that he would be the greatest English poet in history. His Latin was so good that he could, literally, write like Horace and Ovid; he knew the epics of Homer and the tragedies of Euripides by heart. Now he had just come back to England after a Grand Tour of Italy, and was writing an elegy in Latin for his only real friend, who had just died. During the war, Milton would have many associates, but no real intimates; the conflict would both further and thwart his passionate ambition.

Nehemiah Wallington might have been reading, too, if he had not had to work so hard at his trade of woodturning; like most ordinary Londoners, his day was dominated by work, to which he was called by the many London bells which tolled the hours of daybreak and dark. He liked to follow theological debates when his job allowed, and he especially loved the bestselling work *The Plain Man's Pathway to Heaven*; much of its homespun wisdom found its way into the journal Nehemiah was keeping, recording his spiritual life. At forty-two, he couldn't help but be conscious that his life might well be drawing to a close. So Nehemiah liked sermons too, and preaching of all kinds. That was lucky, because a sermon from a very godly preacher could easily last two hours, sometimes longer, and on a Sunday Nehemiah and hundreds like him would be in the congregation, absorbing every word. It was people like Nehemiah who hated the Anglican Church's swerves towards what they thought was treacherous popery, and provided most of the unrest before the Civil War itself began. It would not take much for them to blame the king for it, and his little Catholic queen.

If Nehemiah went to his favourite church, though, he could pass the theatres it denounced on his way, and sometimes even feel tempted to enter them. If he had ever given in to temptation, he would have seen thrillingly innovative new scenery that looked from a distance like the real world, and in 1639 might have been adorning plays like Henry Glapthorne's *Argalus and Parthenia*. A Caroline play could be perverse and tragical, climaxing in a huge pile of corpses, or a sharp and salty comedy that made fun of the people in the next street. Nobles, on the other hand, could see a very different kind of production, a masque, a four-hour extravaganza presented by the most beautiful and alluring ladies of the court; in one scandalous production they wore topless costumes, baring their breasts. This was doubly scandalous, because these were real women acting, and speaking lines as well – not professional actresses, but the queen and her ladies. A man named William Prynne had recently lost his ears for writing that women actresses were notorious whores, in a manner that plainly insulted Queen Henrietta. But to a man like Wallington, the queen's activities were a clear temptation to providence, and a sign that London was no city for the godly, but rather a portal of hell.

For better-off children, the country could be a delicious place of play. In 1639, some who would rise to prominence in the war were still close to a childhood of wild unsupervised games. The eleven-year-old John Bunyan might have been holed up somewhere with his favourite book, no Bible, but the racy – and sexy – adventures of a superhero called *Bevis of Hampden*. And thirteen-year-old Richard Cromwell, Oliver's son, was still slogging his unenthusiastic way through grammar school, unaware that he was to be – briefly – ruler of England. The young Matthew Hopkins shows what terrible pressures could be created inside the good seventeenth-century child. As a boy, Matthew is said to have 'took affright at an apparition of the Devil, which he saw in the night'. As the son of a godly vicar, whose will insists firmly on salvation through faith alone, Hopkins was like most godly children; he was terrified of the powers of hell, which he believed might claim him. And yet in maturity Hopkins liked to invent different childhoods for himself. He told William Lilly that he came from a line of school-masters in Suffolk, 'who had composed for the psalms of King David'; there was indeed a John Hopkins, an English hymn-writer, but he didn't have a son called Matthew. Hopkins told Lady Jane Whorwood that he was really named Hopequins and was the grandson of an English Catholic diplomat, Richard Hopequins, a much grander back-ground than he could really claim. These alternative identities suggest a profound wish to hide from something or someone, perhaps from the Devil.

Among all those relishing peace were the two men who were to be the chief protagonists in the coming wars. The man who was to be the only king ever executed by the English people was born a privileged little boy, but one whom nobody particularly wanted. Charles Stuart spent a childhood ill and in pain, bullied by those he loved, and he grew into a disabled and often unhappy adult. In the same calendar year, another boy was born, a boy who was to become the only man not of royal blood ever to head the English state. Oliver Cromwell was welcomed into a family of struggling East Anglian gentry, the adored and long-awaited only boy in a family of girls. The boost to his self-esteem was lifelong.

When Charles was born on 19 November 1600, he was his parents' third child, and they had a fine son already, destined to rule in Edinburgh one day. Charles was nobody's favourite, nobody's problem. He was first assigned a noblewoman to be his foster-mother, in the manner usual for those of his class; her name was Lady Margaret Ochiltree. Charles cared enough about Lady Margaret to be angry when her pension fell into arrears in 1634. But of course she didn't do the child-care herself; Charles also had a wetnurse, and a rocker who was supposed to rock the cradle, but was also a general nurserymaid, and other nursery nurses. Like other upper-class children, his closest bonds were therefore with servants, and hence precarious because servants could come and go. A child was supposed to be attached to his natural parents, but when he was only two, Charles lost his parents to England; James left Scotland in April to take the throne of England after Elizabeth I died in March 1603, and was followed a month later by Anne, with her eldest children, Henry and Elizabeth. With astonishing insensitivity, or perhaps with a desire to begin Charles's princely training, the royal couple also moved him to a new household, that of Alexander Seton, Lord Fyvie, who had nine surviving daughters and a son.

Installed in this overflowing family, Charles does not seem to have flourished. Reports sent on him spoke of his longing to be with his parents. There was another problem, too, one that would overshadow Charles's relations with his parents still further. Fyvie sent bullish reports on Charles to the court, but read carefully they contained alarming news. In April 1604 – when Charles was three – Fyvie said that Charles was 'in good health, courage and lofty mind' but added that he was 'weak in body'. Most ominously of all, he confided that Charles was 'beginning to speak some words'. If Charles was really only beginning to speak at the age of three, it points to severe disability. Fyvie added 'he is far better of his mind and tongue than of his body and feet'. This report alarmed Charles's parents, for James sent Dr Henry Atkins to examine the prince. Arriving on the night of 12 May 1604, he reported to the king that he had found the young duke 'walking with an ancient gentlewoman his nurse in the great chamber ... although he walked not alone but sustained and led by that gentlewoman's hand'. Atkins said that Charles evaded an examination by 'calling for music to one of his servants ... desiring several kinds of measures ... and would imitate the instrument with the sound of the true tune with his high tender voice'. But the next day he was duly examined, and Atkins reported that he was in reasonable condition but for the joint problems, 'the weakness of his legs', diarrhoea said to be caused by teething, and a desire to drink often. Tellingly, Atkins couldn't examine Charles's teeth because 'his Highness would not permit any to feel his gums'. Despite his fairly reassuring report to the king and queen, Atkins wrote more frankly to Secretary of State Robert Cecil that 'at my coming the duke was far out of order'. To the king he announced that the duke would begin a journey south under his supervision. Charles had difficulty standing and walking because 'he was so weak in his joints and especially ankles, insomuch as many feared they were out of joint' and of the 'joints of his knees, hips and ankles being great and loose are not yet closed and knit together as happeneth to many in their tender years which afterwards when years hath confirmed them proves very strong and able persons'.

The lonely little boy had rickets. This childhood illness was a dominant factor in the development of his personality. The victims of rickets suffer low height and weight, and painful decayed teeth. The spine and breastbone are affected, long bones are shortened and deformed, the ligaments are loose, and fractures are common. Rickets gives bow legs and a pigeon chest, visible deformities. Rickets may also have caused lowered resistance to other diseases, including measles, diarrhoea and whooping cough. But perhaps most significantly, modern studies of rickets suggest that it affects the personality, making for apathy and irritability, and this was noted in Charles's case. His guardian wrote to James, saying that 'the great weakness of his body, after so long and heavy sickness, is much supplied by the might and strength of his spirit and mind' – which might be a diplomatic way of calling the small duke a headstrong child. A toddler in pain is a difficult toddler.

Unfortunately, Charles was not especially lucky in his parents' response to his illness. If we compare it with that of Buckinghamshire gentleman Ralph Verney, we can see that the royal family were not only careless but callous. Mary Verney wrote of her son: 'for Jack his legs are most miserable, crooked as ever I saw any child's, and yet thank God he goes very strongly, and is very straight in his body as any child can bee; and is a very fine child in all but his legs' . . . And she too blamed diet. 'Truly I think it would be much finer if we had him in ordering, for they let him eat anything he has a mind to, and he keeps a very ill diet.' Ralph Verney's response was anxious and sympathetic:

'truly the crookedness of his legs grieves my very heart, ask some advice about it at London, but do not tamper with him'. What he meant by this is dismally clear. When Charles arrived in London on the heels of Atkins's report, fresh stories of his illness flew about, and those eager to act as guardians to him melted away. 'There were many great ladies suitors for the keeping of the duke; but when they did see how weak a child he was, and not likely to live, their hearts were down, and none of them was desirous to take charge of him.' Kind Richard Carey took Charles on, though he reported that 'he was not able to go, nor scant stand alone, he was so weak in his joints, and especially his ankles, insomuch as many feared they were out of joint'. Carey's first move was to surround Charles with his own servants; another change of personnel for the little boy. Even more disturbing is his account of his wife's struggles with James I's plans, as Richard reported:

> Many a battle my wife had with the King, but she still prevailed. The King was desirous that the string under his tongue should be cut, for he was so long beginning to speak as he [the king] thought he would never have spoke. Then he [the king] would have him put in iron boots, to strengthen his sinews and joints, but my wife protested so much against them both, as she got the victory, and the King was fain to yield.

These cruel treatments, contested by Charles's new foster-mother, may have had their origins in James's own separation from his mother and his own lack of security. Mary Queen of Scots fled to England without James before his first birthday, leaving him with foster-parents. James himself did not walk until he was about five, and like his son he too had childhood rickets. Also like his son, he compensated for his difficulty in walking by taking up riding and then hunting with especial vigour. When James was around four, he was moved from the woman's world of the nursery to the schoolroom; this was three years earlier than normal, and it reflected his status as king, but it was hard on him. He loved books, but his tutor George Buchanan was a hard man who hated Catholics, and Mary Queen of Scots most of all. James grew up with his ears ringing with stories of his mother's wickedness. Buchanan thought she was a witch, a whore and a murderer. On one occasion, he beat the king severely. James may also have been alarmed at seeing his own disabilities reflected in his son. James had very noticeable physical problems: his tongue was too large for his mouth, which made him dribble, and he had only imperfect control over bodily functions and a profound dislike of bathing. When thwarted, he would fling himself furiously about, sobbing or screaming, as his son did.

Historians have tended to portray Charles's rickets as shortlived, but this may betray the influence of Stuart propaganda. Richard Carey was afterwards keen to tell the world that he had performed a miracle cure. 'Beyond all men's expectations so blessed the duke with health and strength under my wife's charge, as he grew better and better every day.' Royal astrologer William Lilly said Charles overcame his physical weakness by running and riding and hunting, and that his success made him stubborn in endeavour. Similarly, Philip Warwick reported that 'though born weakly yet came [he] through temperance and exercise to have as firm and strong a body as that of most persons I ever knew'. And all his life he walked breathlessly fast. But on 6 January 1605, when Charles was created Duke of York, all his robes and other vestments had to be carried by an attendant gentleman, and Charles himself was held in the arms of the Lord High Admiral, the Earl of Nottingham. On 15 September 1608 he was too weak to go to a christening, and it was said that he was 'exceedingly feeble in his lower parts, his legs growing not erect but repandous [crooked] and embowed, whereas he was unapt for exercises of activity'. As late as 1610 his movements were clumsy, and his part in a masque had to be specially contrived to hide his legs – a circle of children surrounded him as he danced. Finally, Charles's father and his son, the future Charles II, were both tall, but Charles remained small, further evidence of the severity of his rickets. His brittle bones impeded his growth severely, so that he only reached 5' 4", or in other accounts 4' 11". (5' 4" is based on a surviving suit of armour.) The Court portrait painter, Van Dyck, used devices such as a flight of steps, the presence of a dwarf, and a raised throne to make Charles look bigger. In the case of the mounted figure of Charles created by Hubert le Sueur the sculptor was explicitly told to make the figure six feet in height. By contrast, both his older siblings Henry and Elizabeth were relatively tall – Henry was 5' 8" at the age of seventeen – and also healthy.

The disparity led to rivalry, and James made matters worse by telling Henry that he would leave the crown to Charles if Henry did not work harder. This sort of cruelty, together with the characteristically violent and competitive early modern boys' culture, led Henry to bully his smaller, weaker, less capable brother, and to taunt him, explicitly, about his disability. One day, as the two were waiting with a group of bishops and courtiers for the king to appear, Henry snatched the Archbishop of Canterbury's hat and put it on Charles, saying that when he was king he would make Charles primate, since he was swot and toady enough for the job and the long robes would hide his ugly legs. Charles had to be dragged away, screaming with rage. Like many a victim of bullying, Charles tried to win his brother over by extreme submissiveness: 'Sweet, sweet brother,' he wrote, desperately, when he was nine, 'I will give everything I have to you, both horses, and my books, and my pieces [guns], and my crossbow, or anything you would have. Good brother love me . . .' The pathos of this letter can scarcely be exaggerated. In late 1612, however, Henry was dead, aged eighteen. He died of typhoid fever after a hard game of tennis. His last request was for his sister Elizabeth to visit his bedside; there was no mention of his brother. Diarist and MP Simonds D'Ewes recorded that 'Charles duke of York was so young and sickly as the thought of their enjoying him [as king] did nothing at all to alienate or mollify the people's mourning'.

King James wrote textbooks to edify his children, but was less enthusiastic about spending time with them. He preferred his male companions, especially his lover and favourite George Villiers Duke of Buckingham. Buckingham, beautiful as a hunting leopard, supernaturally brilliant at divining the psychic needs of the powerful and supplying them, became after Henry's death the elder brother Charles had always wanted, one who loved and accepted him. Like all brothers, Charles and Buckingham fought for mastery, and Charles usually lost. Charles bet Buckingham a banquet on a game of tennis – he lost – and another on which of two footmen could run fastest – he lost again. The disastrous Spanish marriage negotiations of 1623 were a similar game, designed to show the boys in a romantic, daredevil light. Fancying himself in love with the Spanish Infanta, whom he had never seen, Charles impetuously decided to sweep her off her feet. Adopting a disguise was part of the fun; all his life he loved theatricality. In this case he donned a false beard and a false name, John Smith, and set out, accompanied by a similarly attired Buckingham, who was travelling as 'Tom Smith'. The disguises were so poor that they were arrested as suspicious characters in Canterbury. The boys bought better beards over the Channel, and visited the court of Louis XIII; they rustled some mountain goats in the Pyrenees, and in March they walked into the British embassy in Madrid and declared that they were taking control of the marriage negotiations. To show his love, Charles climbed over the wall of the garden where the Infanta liked to walk. As he leapt down, the Infanta fled, screaming for her chaperone, and Charles had to be let out by a side door. Charles also made many concessions to the Spanish in the negotiations. But when Philip began to insist that Elizabeth's eldest son would need to marry a Hapsburg before Spain would help the Palatinate, Charles balked. This gave Philip the excuse to pack off his guests by pretending that Charles's threat to return home to his ageing father was a farewell. The boys slunk home. Charles may have been miserable and humiliated, but London was overjoyed – the people had not warmed to the idea of a queen from Spain.

And yet Charles's lifelong quest for the love he lost as a child did evoke a response in some of those closest to him, most of all in his future wife, who had herself been a lonely little princess. When Buckingham was removed by an assassin in late August 1628, Charles and his till-then neglected bride fell abruptly but permanently in love, and what had been a miserable forced marriage became blissful domesticity. Gradually, encircled by his wife's warm regard, Charles built up a retinue of trusted retainers who could help him to feel safe, conceal his deformities, and support him. He made an idyll and then resisted anything that came to disturb it. The loyalty Charles commanded was personal and protective. All his life, Charles would be loved by those who saw him every day, hated only by those who saw him from a distance. James Harrington, one of those appointed by Parliament to attend on the king during his captivity, 'passionately loved his Majesty, and I have oftentimes heard him speak of King Charles I with the greatest zeal and passion imaginable, and that his death gave him so great a grief that he contracted a disease by it; that never anything did go so neer to him'. Sir Philip Warwick wrote that when he thought of dying what cheered him up was the thought that he would meet King Charles again. Warwick also praised the dignity of his deportment, a contrast with his father's uncontrolled excitability: 'he would not let fall his dignity, no not to the Greatest Foreigners that came to visit him and his court'. Clarendon was personally devoted to the king whose decisions he criticized. The Duke of Ormonde, passed over for promotion by Charles, lost his son in 1680, but wrote to a well-wisher that 'my loss, indeed, sits heavily on me, and nothing else in the world could affect me so much, but since I could bear the death of my great and good master King Charles the First I can bear anything else'.

Historians have long agreed that 'the man Charles Stuart' was one of the principal causes of the war. The king's small and painful body was a picture in miniature of the divisions that were also to rive his people. Charles's love of codes and disguises and his longing to make the monarchy independent of any hurtful criticism proceeded from the bullied child he was. He wanted to put the past behind him, but that longing itself chained him to it. His odd and fatal mixture of indecision and stubbornness is typical of a victim of bullying. All his life, Charles needed love. He set his people test after test, and they could not love him enough to heal the wounds inflicted in the past. By 1639, Charles was keeping the peace by deafening himself to any signs of conflict. His need for tranquillity had become one cause of the coming war.

Oliver Cromwell was born on 25 April 1599, in the High Street of Huntingdon. He was the last of a long family; he had six sisters, and three siblings who died in infancy. Like Charles I, he had an older brother named Henry, four years older than Oliver, who died before 1617; another boy, named Robert, died in 1609, shortly after his birth. Cromwell had an unusually close, tender and long-term relationship with his mother for whom he soon became the main patriarch and protector. For most male children in Tudor and Stuart England, the early years were split in two by the onset of formal schooling or training around the age of seven. Before that, they were at home under the care of mothers and servants. Schooling represented a violent repudiation of infancy, and with it the world of the mother; it also symbolized a tussle with the father's authority. It was a chance for boys to be different from their fathers, to do something their fathers had never done, to climb an inch or two further up the social ladder than their fathers had. And their fathers were not always overjoyed about it.

The grammars were a wide crack in the invincible hierarchy of the class system in more respects than this. The master was compared to an 'absolute monarch', 'a little despotic emperor'. It may be that many grammar schools bred suspicion of such absolutism. What reinforced these feelings of misgiving and dislike were the beatings; it is hard for us to imagine what these were like, or to understand the fear and horror they generated. Both John Aubrey and Samuel Hartlib still dreamed of school beatings twenty years after leaving. Bulstrode Whitelocke, who hated them, understood them as 'a severe discipline', that would lead boys to 'a greater courage and constancy'. The experience of this schooling was shared by all the men who became Charles's principal foes, though it was also common enough among Royalists. Oliver Cromwell attended the free school just down the road from his home, which offered a grammar-style education, preparing him for entry to Sidney Sussex College, Cambridge. Many not very reliable and Royalist accounts of Cromwell's childhood describe him as distinctly rowdy in late boyhood and early adolescence; taking hearty exercise, behaving with noticeable boisterousness, scrumping apples and stealing pigeons, getting into fights ... All this may well be untrue, but the stories convey the perception that Cromwell was energetic and dynamic, a force of nature difficult to control.

Cromwell described himself as 'by birth a gentleman, living neither in any considerable height, nor yet in obscurity'. Actually, even this simple statement was defensive rather than descriptive. He was the eldest surviving son of the younger son of a knight. Cromwell's grandfather lived the life of a gentleman in a brand-new manor house, built on the site of a former nunnery, and with a second hunting house in the fen, on the site of a former abbey. Oliver's father Robert could manage only a town house in Huntingdon, and a modest income of £300 a year, nothing like the £2000 a year that his father enjoyed. His grander relatives had a mansion at Hinchinbrooke, built from the ruins of three abbeys, a nunnery and two priories. The manor was splendid enough to entertain James I. Oliver could only be a poor relation of all this substance. Oliver was so badly off that he paid tax *in bonis*, on the value of his moveable goods, and even that was only four pounds a year, suggesting an income of a hundred pounds a year or less. When he moved to St Ives in 1631, essentially he was there as a yeoman, not a gentleman; he had slipped from the gentry to the rank of the middling sort. His circumstances improved somewhat in 1636, but he nevertheless continued to lead a life more like that of those just below the gentry. He lived in a town, not a manor, he worked for his living. He had only a few household servants, no tenants or dependants. When he declared his enthusiasm for the 'russet-coated captain that knows what he is fighting for', he was not condescending; he was describing the men among whom he had spent his life as an equal, the men of his own class – he was describing himself. And when as Protector he likened himself to a good constable rather than to a justice, he was expressing the same class allegiance.

Eight of Cromwell's children survived infancy, but his eldest son Robert suffered an accident at school in Felsted in May 1639 and was buried there, at seventeen. Recalling this twenty years later, Cromwell recalled that 'when my eldest son died, [it] went as a dagger to my heart'. It was this sympathy with parents who had lost a child which led Cromwell to write so warmly to the bereaved during the war. And yet Cromwell's son's death draws our attention to the troubled aspects of his childhood and youth. Because early modern men were supposed to see themselves as their fathers over again, for a son to be truly adult, he had to somehow push his father aside in order to take his place. The death of a father or of a son could induce an identity crisis. This sounds abstruse, but it is exactly the kind of question encouraged by the work of Thomas Beard, Cromwell's schoolmaster, whose book *The Theater of Gods Judgements* proposed that reprobates are punished for their sins in this life as well as the next. Struck down by bolts of lightning on their way home from church, the sinful begin their sojourn in hell and act as an example to the living.

Cromwell's mother Elizabeth Steward was thirty-four when Oliver was born. Before she married Cromwell's father, she had been the wife of John Lynne of Bassingbourn, and had a daughter called Katherine who died as a baby. From the Lynnes she inherited the brewing-house whose association with Cromwell later writers found so rib-ticklingly funny. Her father was a solid gentleman-farmer who farmed the cathedral lands of Ely. Clarendon called her 'a decent woman' and an ambassador praised her as 'a woman of ripe wisdom and great prudence'. Cromwell, as the only surviving son, was forced to abandon his Cambridge college and return to the household on his father's death. But he returned not as a child, to be under his mother's governance, but as *head* of that household, effectively usurping his father's place. Elizabeth Steward Cromwell formally combined her household with her son's in the late 1630s, along with his youngest sister Robina. She never left him again, and remained such a key part of his circle that everyone who knew him knew her too. During the war, when Cromwell was desperate for money and reinforcements, his mother wrote, crossly, to a cousin: 'I wish there might be care to spare some monies for my son, who I fear hath been too long and much neglected.' When he moved from his London lodgings to Whitehall as Protector, she went with him. Elizabeth Cromwell Senior did not enjoy the palace; its splendours did not impress her. She was more concerned about her son; musket fire made her tremble for him, lest it be an assassin's bullet. She did not die until she had seen her son become Lord Protector. Elizabeth Cromwell was eighty-nine at her death late in 1654. Her health had been failing for some time, and Cromwell put off a visit to Richard Mayor: 'truly', he wrote, 'my mother is in such a condition of illness that I could not leave her'. Thurloe recorded her last blessing to her son: 'The Lord cause his face to shine upon you and comfort you in all your adversities, and enable you to do great things for the glory of your most high God.' She was given a funeral at Westminster Abbey, illuminated by hundreds of flickering torches.

A mix of frustrated social ambition and a longing for absolution, together with the strain of being thrust early into the role of family carer and provider, may explain the spiritual crisis which overtook Cromwell towards the end of the 1620s. Although such crises were commonplace, this was because stories of reprobation and salvation were among those most available to people trying to negotiate complex feelings. Cromwell's emerged out of a period of black depression. Sir Theodore Mayerne, the prominent London physician, treated Cromwell for *valde melancholicus* at the time of the 1628/9 Parliament. Melancholy and mopishness were common accompaniments to a religious conversion. Cromwell's doctor Dr Simcotts of Huntingdon said that he had often been called out to Cromwell because he believed himself to be dying. Simcotts also said that he was 'a most splenetic man and hypochondriacal'. This may be what contemporaries classed as spoiling, too. Of his conversion, Cromwell himself wrote: 'You know what my manner of life hath been. Oh, I lived in and loved darkness, and hated the light. I was a chief, the chief of sinners. This is true: I hated godliness, yet God had mercy on me. Oh the riches of his mercy! Praise Him for me, pray for me, that he who hath begun a good work would perfect it to the day of Christ.'

When Royalists talk about Cromwell's wildness 'which afterwards he seemed sensible of and sorrowful for', and the Puritan Richard Baxter says he was 'prodigal', this implies that Cromwell may have been fond of telling his life story as the story of the Lord's prodigal, a sinner in youth, converted in a sudden crisis to godliness and a repudiation of his former life. All godly people thought of themselves as repentant sinners. Being godly did not mean being gloomy and sad; Cromwell liked food, music and dancing, but not as forms of religious practice. His oft-repeated conversion should not lead us to imagine that Cromwell's sins were especially great, but it does suggest that he saw himself as distinct from the godly prior to his conversion. Bishop Burnet said Cromwell led a very strict life for about eight years before the war; being a Scot, he probably meant the Bishops' Wars, which would put Cromwell's conversion in 1631 or thereabouts. What godly people like Cromwell wanted was to complete the work of Reformation, which meant both reforming the liturgy and Church calendar and reforming behaviour.

It was Charles, who had had the more difficult and painful childhood, who was the first to think differently about the state. He wanted a new kind of kingdom. But this wasn't a long-held dream; it was an angry response to what he felt as intolerable bullying. When the 1628/9 Parliament tried to assert its own sovereignty over his, when it began making demands on him rather than acting according to his direction, when it failed him – as he saw it – in a manner that compromised his honour in his dealings with his enemies abroad, then – and only then – Charles recalled that the Bourbons were phasing out their ancient assembly, that the Spanish had never needed one. Why go on summoning

Parliament, that dated institution? The events that were ultimately to lead to the Civil War were set in motion by a royal tantrum.

The idea of 'personal rule' did not occur to Charles all at once. Indeed, in his proclamation dissolving what turned out to be his last Parliament, he affirmed his enthusiasm for the institution. But he resolved to do without it, and do without it he did, in an ad hoc and improvisational manner. The process was scarcely trouble-free, and the biggest problem was supply. From the king's point of view, Parliament existed to generate revenue. Without it, the king could only use his prerogative, as it was called. It meant he could raise money through reviving some archaic taxes – more of this in a moment – and enforce policy mainly through the courts – the Star Chamber, and the High Court. The Star Chamber was a kind of distillation of the Privy Council, which met in the room so named at the Palace of Westminster; it became a court that focused its gaze on political and public order cases, which made it a natural political instrument of repression.

Even before Charles began trying to rule without Parliament, he faced a mountain of debt generated by successive and entirely unsuccessful wars with France. But the astounding thing was that he cleared it without coming anywhere near alienating the vast majority of his subjects. By 1635, after six years of peace, royal finances were in reasonable shape. The economy had improved, and so the king was able to earn extra money from customs. Charles also dug deeply into his nobles' purses, finding tiny revenue-raisers like fining gentlemen who could have become knights for failing to do so at his coronation. These were petty, but no one much minded about them.

Historians have tended to see Charles's other big moneyspinner as significantly more controversial. This was the so-called Ship Money. Ship Money was a hangover from the days when the English navy was a dignified name for a bunch of privateers. The king would conscript ships that were owned by nobles or gentlemen for the duration of a particular campaign, and then give them back, along with any plunder or any valuable prisoners, at the end of the campaign in question. Because of revolutions in ship design, such privately-owned ships no longer made for a powerful navy by the 1630s, so Charles began to fear that the French and Dutch would gain control of the English Channel and the North Sea. He could have done the orthodox thing, called

Parliament to pass legislation authorizing a tax to finance the navy. Instead, he twisted the medieval system into a means of financing a standing, professional fleet.

Popular notions of the Civil War give this tax much prominence, as the tyrannical extraction of monies without 'representation', as the American revolutionaries were to put it nearly one hundred and fifty years later. When the payments were first demanded, the nation grumbled a bit – taxes are never popular – but it paid up. Much of the discontent was about the unevenness of methods of assessment; in some areas, quite different standards were used to assess near neighbours, and this was just as popular as one might expect. But until 1638 returns hovered around the 90% mark. As time went on the mutterings did increase in volume, as it dawned on people that this occasional levy had somehow become a permanent seasonal item, coming round as regularly as Christmas. But for most of the 1630s, the nation grumbled but it paid the tax.

A Buckinghamshire gentleman called John Hampden sought to change this state of discontent into something more substantial. He was the son of an outstandingly godly man, whose will had roundly announced, 'I know my soul to be sanctified.' This holy, inspirational figure died when John was only a toddler, and his mother harboured political ambitions for him. The family was not a great one, but was solidly prosperous. John Hampden was soon drawn into a political circle that became immensely powerful in its criticism of Charles's policies. He had been very active in the 1628 Parliament, collaborating with John Pym, and in the key debate of 5 June 1628, he made a speech that a contemporary summarized as follows:

> Here is [firstly], an innovation of religion suspected; is it not high time to take it to heart and acquaint his Majesty? Secondly, alteration of government; can you forbear when it goes no less than the subversion of the whole state? Thirdly, hemmed in with enemies; is it now a time to be silent, and not to show to his Majesty that a man that has so much power uses none of it to help us? If he be no papist, papists are friends and kindred to him.

This speech may have been the reason that the king chose to try Hampden of all the Ship Money refusers, rather than the godly peer

Lord Saye and Sele, who had also been noisily refusing to pay in the hope of bringing matters to a head. Hampden was determined to secure a ruling that called the king's taxation into question. He deliberately failed to pay just one pound of what he owed, meekly anteing up otherwise. The judges treated Hampden's case with a procedure reserved for the most significant disputes. Instead of being heard in the Court of Exchequer, normally responsible for collecting revenues, it was referred to the Court of Exchequer Chamber, a special body dating from 1585, in which all twelve judges in England took part, and the Court of Exchequer was to follow the advice it received from a simple majority of the twelve. The trial began in November 1637. On Hampden's side the case was argued by a member of the group critical of the king, the Earl of Bedford's client Oliver St John. St John was an obscure young lawyer who was to make his name out of the case, just as Hampden did. He argued not that the king had no power to command his subjects to provide a ship, but that he could only exercise this power in an emergency, such as the invasion of the realm. Because no such emergency existed at the time the king called for the money, he was required to call Parliament to levy it as a tax; hence Ship Money was an unparliamentary tax. The king's solicitor and representative Sir Edward Littleton replied for the Crown, arguing that the circumstances had not permitted the time-consuming summoning of Parliament. Hampden's second lawyer, Robert Holborne, replied, and in his submission the fundamental issue was carefully stated: 'by the fundamental laws of England, the king cannot, out of parliament, charge the subject – no, not for the common good unless in special cases', even if he thought the danger was imminent. The subject's right to his property occluded the king's right to decide that danger was immediate. (Unfortunately, Holborne's delivery was marred by some kind of speech impediment.) The fat was in the fire, and the king's representative Anthony Bankes began talking of principles instead of narrow micromanaging. He made a ringing and poetic defence of the king as 'the first mover among these orbs of ours . . . the soul of this body, whose proper act is to command'. No one could criticize the king's exercise of his powers because there was no valid place or position from which to do it.

When the judges finally considered their verdict, they had a complex body of issues to address. Four of them made strong claims for the prerogative, following the lead given by Bankes. Two took a firm stand against any such claims, and one of them – Croke – argued flatly that only Parliament could allow the king to charge a subject. But the others stuck doggedly to the legal technicalities and tried to close their eyes to the wider issues, debating whether the king could act alone if he merely apprehended national danger, and whether he had used due means. This last point was really about whether Ship Money was a tax or a form of military service; none of the judges was very sure what to decide, but eventually two key judges said that since Hampden was being tried for unpaid debt then he could not be seen as required to provide a service, and they ruled against the king. This led them to decide for Hampden. The eventual result was that the king won, but with a narrow majority; because of divisions among the judges, bystanders could not even agree on what, exactly, the majority was, but many thought it just seven over five. The nation had been following the case so passionately that curious bystanders couldn't get into the court even by rising at dawn. The case turned Hampden into a hero; it might have been better for Charles if he had lost, since winning made him seem more of a tyrant. From then on, more people began to refuse to pay Ship Money.

But the hearing did nothing directly to unseat Charles. It gave a brief voice to resentment, but resentment is not revolution. The main result was that for the sheriffs and constables forced to collect trifling sums such as a penny from the poorest men, life became nearly unbearable. Administrative nuisances, however, did not threaten the regime in and of themselves. There was no chance of personal rule being truly disturbed by tax protests. The sense of grievance was confined to a small minority; but it was an articulate minority with good connections, increasingly an *organized* minority, drawn from exactly the class the House of Commons existed to represent. It was becoming obvious that if Charles ever did call Parliament, he could expect trouble from it.

Personal rule was not, however, sunk solely by finance and taxes, but by the fact that the king made another, larger group of enemies. Or rather, this second group of enemies were made for him by his Archbishop of Canterbury William Laud and his queen, Henrietta Maria.

Again, these enemies probably never amounted to a majority of the nation. But they were exceptionally motivated, as religious minorities are apt to be, articulate, superb at using the printing press to spread their ideas, and they increasingly overlapped with the first group, the erstwhile MPs. They were godly Protestants who feared popery; they ranged from sectarians who wanted complete reform to Presbyterians who would have no bishops, to conservatives who supported the Anglican Church of Elizabethan England.

If there was simmering discontent in the 1630s, it was not so much with Ship Money as with Archbishop Laud, eagerly bringing ceremonial back to the Church of England in the form of altar-rails and reverence for the Eucharist, and as eagerly denouncing and suppressing 'Puritans', or the godly, as they called themselves. Worst of all, Laud was dismantling the central doctrine of Calvinism, predestination. In Calvinist predestination, every person is already bound for heaven or hell. Human beings are so sinful that they can only understand God's message and achieve faith if he gives them grace to do so. This happens suddenly if it happens at all. God chooses who will be saved and who damned, regardless of merit or desert. God emerges as not unlike a capricious monarch, electing some to bliss, dropping others into woe. But Laud and his followers were Arminians (though Laud tried to stay neutral in public), and this meant they believed that faith grew slowly together with a person's chosen and willed virtue.

So from a godly point of view, the Church of England was being run by an emissary of hell, and the king was doing nothing to stop him. People began to wonder if Charles's personal rule risked running the kingdom into the arms of Rome. In the Stuart era, religion led, and political questions followed. The result was to stir up constant questions about what might previously be taken for granted.

Whatever the godly thought, Laud saw himself as a stout Protestant, doughtily fighting the encroachments of Rome and the godly alike. For him, the Church of England was a shambles. He was especially upset by Old St Paul's in London, the nave of which had become a place to see and be seen, to sleep rough, or to do a little business. There were adverts plastered on the walls and pillars. The noise was intense and irreverent: 'like that of bees, a strange humming or buzz mixed', thought the horrified prelate. For Laud, the church should be hallowed, special. It wasn't that he believed in the Real Presence; he just thought, not too eccentrically, that churches ought to be different from markets, and that it wouldn't hurt to bring beauty and order to them.

But it did hurt. The Church of England, then as now, was an awkward coalition of quite diverse groups. With much bickering, its members had come to tolerate the white walls and bare wood of the Elizabethan church settlement, the spareness of its services. Some wanted still more reform – was not a church itself a kind of icon? – but were willing for it to take place gradually, through local effort. Some still enjoyed church ales – a kind of beery parish sale-of-work – and maypoles, and defended them robustly. But in most places everyone felt that though far from perfect the church did offer something to them.

Laud's reforms destroyed everyone's optimism. The moderate middle were comfortable with a reduced number of icons, but not happy to see them going up instead of coming down. As for the very godly, they viewed Laud's alterations with utter horror. William Prynne wrote furiously of those 'who now erect crucifixes and images in our churches, contrary to our articles, injunctions, homilies'. And these fears and horrors were not baseless. Bristol alone spent almost £200 on its high cross, which now included statues of James I and Charles I. The link between images of the Stuart kings and icons was ultimately to prove very unfortunate, but also indissoluble. New stained-glass windows were put in, especially in Oxford and Cambridge colleges and at Durham and Lambeth. And there was a new service order. Ministers had to wear full clerical robes; they had to bow at the name of Jesus, use the cross to baptize and recite the full Book of Common Prayer service with no omissions and additions.

And while personal rule might be forgotten for months on end, Laud's innovations were on constant display in every church. Laud had said, for example, that the altar 'is the greatest place of God's residence on earth': 'yea, 'tis greater than the pulpit, for there 'tis *hoc est corpus meum*, this is my body. But in the pulpit 'tis at most but *Hoc est verbum meum*, This is my word.' For a godly churchwarden, this was a direct attack – on his authority, and on that of God Himself. To keep the altar sacred, the churchwarden was supposed to erect railings, which were to mark the space around the altar as sacred, and hence keep out of it everyone from the churchwarden keen to use it as a table for his account books to schoolboys using it as a place to store hats and satchels. Boys were apparently especially inclined to take a quiet nap under it at sermon time, and dogs sometimes nipped in and took the consecrated bread, to Laud's very particular horror; a woman in Cheshire was unpopular because she held her dancing baby over the table and afterwards someone spotted a lot of water on the table itself. Laud concluded sensibly that it might have been worse. But the new arrangement also kept the congregation away from the sacred, implying that it was not for the likes of them. In Suffolk people complained that the new rails and table meant that 'not half of the people can see or hear the ministration'.

This is one of the moments where the interlacing of politics and religion becomes obvious: the rails and table, harmless though they sound, were experienced as creating an entirely artificial hierarchy, reserving the priest as sacred and the altar as a sacred space where he presided (not unlike the inner rooms at court). Because that new church hierarchy seemed so specious, other hierarchies began to seem equally open to question.

Laud and his altar-rails were in part an attempt to prevent an upper-class drift to Rome. Fear of this had begun when Charles married Henrietta Maria, and was realized when the queen's Jesuit chaplains and courtiers managed a spectacular wave of conversions among the aristocracy. To grasp this dread and its power, we might begin on a day in July 1626, when the then-new queen made an unusual pilgrimage, as one of those who disliked her reported in horror:

> Some say the queen and a group of her followers were strolling through the royal parks around St James's palace, and happened to stop for prayer for the Catholics who had died on Tyburn Tree.

Others say the queen made it an almost official pilgrimage: barefoot, she walked while her confessor rode, as if to imitate the martyrs' routes to the scaffold. At the gallows, she fell to her knees with a rosary in her hand.

> Nay their [the priests'] insolences towards the queen were not to be endured; for, besides that these bawdy knaves would, by way of confession, interrogate her how often in a night the king

had kissed her; and no longer ago than upon St James's Day last those hypocritical dogs made the poor queen walk afoot (some say barefoot) from her house at St James's to the gallows at Tyburn, thereby to honour the saint of the day in visiting that holy place where so many martyrs forsooth hath shed their blood in defence of the Catholic cause. Had they not also made her to dabble in the dirt, in a foul morning, from Somerset House to St James's her Luciferian confessor riding alongside her in his coach? Yea, they have made her to go barefoot, to spin, to cut her meat out of dishes, to wait at the table, to serve her servants, with many other ridiculous and absurd penances; and if they dare thus insult over the daughter, sister, and wife of so great kings, what slavery would they not make us, the people, to undergo?

For this reporter, not only was Henrietta's pilgrimage an outrage to Christendom, it was also an affront to royal dignity. What was the background to this extraordinary event, unprecedented – and for that matter, unrepeated – in the annals of English monarchy? For Henrietta, what was being visited was a sacred site, a wailing wall, a place holy to her people because sanctified by their blood. Tyburn, with its Triple Tree, was not any old gallows; it was the place where men and women had died bravely for the Catholic faith.

Henrietta held to a belief for which material objects – people, places – were important. Catholicism was not something that happened in the head; it involved the vital and willing body in strenuous acts of faith to other bodies, beginning with Christ's own bleeding body, and ending with those of the martyrs. Visiting Tyburn, she would have felt something of what we might feel visiting the site of Auschwitz – awe, pity, fear, and passionate indignation – and a little of the fear might still have felt pressing and personal, for the laws of England allowed people to be hanged for being Catholic, for doing no more and sometimes rather less than Henrietta's marriage treaty allowed her to do. Only two years after the treaty was signed, two Catholics were hanged at Lancaster. Henrietta's family were Catholic, as were her friends, and she was personally devout. Events like the hangings were utterly baffling for her, and hardly added to an already imperilled sense of security.

Catholics had been feared since the 1570 papal edict against Elizabeth I, but what aroused a new kind of anxiety was the perceived influence of Catholics at court. The powerful Duke of Buckingham's wife and his mother had both converted to Catholicism in 1622. Catholic icons were still being imported into the country. One member of the 1621 Parliament reported that rosaries, crucifixes, relics, and 'papistical pictures' were flooding in, and that in Lancashire they were made and sold openly in the streets. In *The Popish Royal Favourite*, William Prynne claimed that Buckingham's 'Jesuited mother and sister' influenced him and through him the kingdom. Henrietta's marriage treaty guaranteed her the right to practise her own religion, and her household servants to do the same. This was by itself enough to terrify. But her behaviour made matters worse. Henrietta was strongly, passionately, vehemently Catholic. The English were inclined to read this as rather tactless. They hadn't been unduly pleased by the previous queen Anne of Denmark's Catholicism, but at least she had shown the good taste to keep it decently under wraps. Henrietta was a woman of real conviction, which meant she didn't and couldn't. She was also a girl in her late teens, not very experienced in politics or used to compromise. Half Bourbon, half Medici, she had not learnt much about giving way from her mother. She stoutly refused to attend her husband's coronation, because it was a Church of England ceremony.

Henrietta's fervour had much to do with fashion. To a godly critic of the queen, Catholicism was part of a deadly and poisoned past, but to the queen herself it seemed the future. Catholicism fitted with court fashions; the court loved ritual and drama, colour and the baroque. The Laudian idea of 'the beauty of holiness' was one that Catholicism could accept, even if Laud himself was eager to maintain boundaries. When the aestheticization of faith became the goal, England could only lope awkwardly behind Rubens's Antwerp or Bellini's Rome. Both Charles and Henrietta did not want to trail in last in the aesthetic revolutionary army; they wanted to march in the front ranks. Precisely because the godly were not keen on images, pagan or Christian, those vanguards were dominated by Catholics.

As well, Henrietta wanted to be Esther, freeing her people through her influence. She was called to save English Catholics from the savage prejudices of their fellow-countrymen. Henrietta had been asked by the pope himself to promote Catholicism in her new kingdom. She went about it with characteristic verve and taste.

The centrepiece of her campaign was the building of her hated chapel. She wanted to create a new kind of place of worship, employing the most avant-garde and brilliant architect, Inigo Jones. The foundation stone was laid on 14 September 1632, and the chapel opened 8 December 1635, the feast of the Immaculate Conception of the Virgin Mary. One French envoy claimed that it had taken a long time because Inigo Jones was a Puritan and did not want it done. However, like many a godly soul, Jones was not averse to commerce, and after he had been given some additional monies, the work was completed.

The old chapel, which had existed since Anne of Denmark's day, had been unpopular enough. Apprentices talked of pulling it down in 1634. The new one became a symbol of all the terrors the queen's very existence came to evoke. It was plain outside; inside it was exuberant, rich, fanciful. There were the gold and silver reliquaries. There were ciberia, chalices, embroidered stoles. There were paintings, statues, even a chapel garden, a tribute to the queen's interest in all things that grew green. It was, observers thought, 'quite masculine and unaffected' on the outside. But inside it was splendid, with an elaborate altarpiece made up of a series of seven oval frames containing angels sitting on clouds. A delicate carved screen on fluted and gilded Doric columns marked the entrance to the queen's closet. And the opening celebrations were more splendid still.

As George Garrard observed tartly, 'the ceremonies lasted three days, massing, preaching and singing of litanies, and such a glorious scene built over their altar, the Glory of Heaven, Inigo Jones never presented a more curious piece in any of the masques at Whitehall; with this our English ignorant papists are mightily taken'. The king visited it three days after the opening, and told Father Gamache that he had never seen anything more beautiful or more ingeniously contrived. It had one feature which would strike some modern Catholics as surprising, and which horrified Protestant contemporaries. An eminent sculptor named François Dieussart 'made a machine, which was admired even by the most ingenious persons, to exhibit the Holy Sacrament, and to give it a more majestic appearance'. The resulting spectacle deserves a full description, even though it is tiring; the ceremony itself must have been even slower:

It represented in oval a Paradise of glory, about forty feet in height. To accommodate it to the hearing in the chapel, a great arch was supported by two pillars towards the high altar, at the distance of about eight Roman palms from the two side walls of the chapel. The spaces between the pillar and walls served for passages to go from the sacristy to the altar . . . Over each side appeared a Prophet, with a text from his prophecy. Beneath the arch was placed outside the portable altar, ten palms in height . . . Behind the altar was seen a paraclete, raised above seven ranges of clouds, in which were figures of archangels, of cherubim, of seraphim, to the number of two hundred, some adoring the Holy Sacrament, others singing and playing on all sorts of musical instruments . . . all conceiving that, instead of the music, they heard the melody of the angels, singing and playing upon musical instruments . . . In the sixth and seventh circles were seen children with wings . . . like so many little angels issuing from the clouds . . . In the eighth and ninth circles appeared cherubim and seraphim among the clouds, surrounded by luminous rays . . . All these things were covered with two curtains. It was the 10th of December, in the year 1636, that the queen came with all her court to hear Mass. As soon as she had taken the place prepared for her, the curtains being drawn back, all at once gave to view those wonders which excited admiration, joy, and adoration in her Majesty and in all the Catholics . . . Tears of joy seemed to trickle from the eyes of the queen.

This magic chapel was the height of fashion, but in essence not unique. Before the Reformation, such contraptions were not uncommon, and they were not, of course, intended to fool anyone, but to add a dramatic element to sacred ritual. In the 1433 York Domesday pageant, there was 'a cloud and two pieces of rainbow of timber array for God' and a heaven with red and blue clouds, an iron swing or frame pulled up with ropes 'that God shall sit upon when he shall sit up to heaven'. At Lincoln Cathedral, a series of ropes and pulleys allowed the Paraclete to descend at Pentecost. The grail romances sometimes described similar contrivances. Reincarnating and refurbishing such sacred dramas, Henrietta had not meant to trick anyone, any more than she thought people would take her for a goddess when she appeared before Inigo

Jones's painted scenes, so lifelike in their three-dimensionality. What she did intend to convey was sophisticated knowledge, spectacle, and perhaps fun.

She liked jokes. She once managed to inveigle Charles into gambling with her for a golden crucifix. The king won, and was placed in the embarrassing position of having to decide whether to keep it or not. The Catholic Elizabeth Thorowgood thought that the king was sympathetic to Catholics because of his wife, but Mary Cole, also a Catholic, thought the opposite. She wondered how the queen could stand it.

She could stand it best by making and enlarging her own brilliant Catholic world, lit and sculpted with the very latest. And Henrietta wanted London to know it was there; in 1638, she even planned a procession to Somerset House to celebrate the birth of the dauphin. She made a new and very Catholic festive calendar for it; in 1637, there was a special Christmas Mass, attended by her flock of recent converts, and at Worcester House, in the Strand, there was a display of the Holy Sepulchre during the 1638 Easter season. But on Holy Thursday 1638, the Spanish ambassador shocked London by processing through the streets, crucifixes and torches held aloft, from the queen's chapel to his own residence. There was a minor riot, and he was warned by the king.

So neither Henrietta nor her allies were content to hear Mass in a private fashion. It was not only that she felt she had nothing to be ashamed of. She was not even trying to revive Catholic England, that medieval past that had been violently rocked to sleep by Elizabeth and James and by her husband. She was trying something much more ambitious. She was attempting to bring *modern* Catholicism to England, and with it the eye-popping glories of the Catholic baroque that had fuelled the Counter-Reformation with their beauty and exoticism. She was hoping to seduce the English aristocracy with the brilliant modernity of a Church that was part of a rich aesthetic future. This was a far riskier project. It was also doomed to ultimate failure.

But not at first; initially it succeeded brilliantly. When the Earl of Bath attended Catholic Mass for the first time, he wondered aloud why Protestants were deprived of the many splendid aesthetic consolations offered by Rome. There were multiple conversions among Henrietta's ladies, and Rome became quite the fashion, especially when Lady Newport converted, despite her husband's godliness. The centre of much of the bustle was the household of Olive Porter, niece of Buckingham; she had been miraculously prevented from dying in childbirth in February 1638. 'Our great women fall away every day', wrote one of Strafford's less sanguine correspondents. One of the horrors was that it was all so . . . feminine. But there were men involved too – social historian Lawrence Stone speculates that in 1641 something in the order of a fifth of the 121 peers were Roman Catholics. Historian Kevin Sharpe suggests that not only were there more Catholics in the 1630s – and more visible Catholics – but that overall numbers may have reached 300,000. The papal envoy George Conn reported happily that while in the past Catholics would only hear Mass in secret, now they flocked to the queen's chapel and the embassy chapels. When one of the king's favourites, Endymion Porter, abruptly silenced a French Huguenot for criticizing the papal agent, the court knew the prevailing wind was blowing from Rome.

Inigo Jones, of course, was the name that connected the chapel with other activities at Somerset House; as well as building the chapel, he was also constructing a theatre there from 1632, and the connection was not lost on men like William Prynne. The new theatre was to be the venue for a new kind of play, a French pastoral by Walter Montagu. It was called *The Shepherd's Paradise*, it lasted for seven hours, and was in rehearsal for four months. It was about love. It was about faith. It was about four hours longer than the audience was used to.

For William Prynne, the problem with such work wasn't that it was long and exceedingly moral and rather dull; anyone who thought Montagu's playtexts on the long and wordy side had only to sample Prynne's prose to find Montagu positively crisp and succinct. No, for Prynne the problem was that it was all far too terribly exciting, so that *Tempe Restored*, another drama of the same sort, was for him a 'Devil's mass', a Catholic ritual. In this masque, there is a kind of confession, and a scene of absolution: Tempe is cleansed of the evil beasts of Circe.

Everyone at court took the hint, though not all were willing to act from expediency. They could see that the tides of fashion were flowing in the queen's favour. Laud, who hated Rome because he was somewhat seduced by it himself, stridently issued a proclamation against those resorting to Mass, and the queen as belligerently responded by holding a special midnight Mass for all converts. Endorsements of the Virgin Mary, including *Maria Triumphans*, an anonymous work dedicated to defending the Virgin, linked Henrietta – Queen Mary – with Mary the Queen of Heaven: 'She whom [the book] chiefly concerns, will anew become your patroness, and thus will Mary, the Queen of Heaven for a great queen upon earth, the mother of our Celestial king for the mother of our future terrene king. And finally, by your protecting and pleading for it, the immaculate virgin will (in a more full manner) become an advocate for you, her Advocate.'

This was not the wisest move the queen could have made. It arose from her name: the king liked to call her Maria, and the English did call her Queen Mary, a name that now sounds positively stuffy and cosy, but which at the time had a dangerous ring. England had had a Queen Mary, and a Catholic one at that. She had also narrowly missed another in Mary Queen of Scots. 'Some kind of fatality, too,' wrote Lucy Hutchinson waspishly, 'the English imagined to be in her name of Marie.' When Marian devotion was constantly evoked, so too were the queen's dismal predecessors, Mary Tudor and Mary Queen of Scots. It did offer the queen an opportunity to knit together the Platonic cult of devotion to her, evoked by many sighing sonnets, and the cult of the Virgin Mary, so that she and the Virgin could be understood in the same way; as intercessors, whose special grace it was to plead with the king ... of earth, of heaven. It made the tiny queen feel important. Being Mary's votary involved (again) touches of theatre; one could be Mary's bondslave, for instance, and wear a length of chain to show it.

But it was the sheer flagrant unapologetic visibility of Henrietta's Catholicism and its proximity – in every sense – to the centre of monarchic power that really alarmed those who hated and feared popery. We might detect a trace of defiance in Henrietta's openness, a trace, therefore, of fear. But to the godly, she seemed a shameless emissary of the Whore of Babylon. Her attempts to secure the religious toleration of Catholics seemed to many a sinister plot. When she and her helper Conn tried to facilitate Catholic marriages (then illegal) and to obstruct a plan to take into care the eldest sons of all Catholic families to bring them up as Protestants, she was thwarting the godly.

The fact that the godly were witnessing the happiest royal marriage in English history only made them more miserable, for what might the emissary of the Whore do with the king? Everyone knew how close they were, and for anyone who doubted it, there was the long row of children to prove it. Lucy Hutchinson thought, with many, that Charles was more in love with his wife than she with him, describing him as 'enslaved in his affection towards her'. She was, thought Hutchinson, 'a great wit and beauty', which only made matters worse. Just as ordinary women could persuade their husbands to buy them pretty dresses while cosily tucked up between the sheets, thought one pamphlet, so the queen might incline the king to popery: note the connection between popery and feminine frills and furbelows. 'Some say she is the man, and reigns', said *Mercurius Brittanicus* more bluntly and much later (15–22 July 1644). When Parliamentarians said 'evil counsellors', it was often the queen they meant. Surely, they felt, it was only a matter of time before Henrietta managed to persuade the king to greater toleration – or worse . . . In fact, perhaps, even now . . . The dreads represented by the queen were knitted together and became suspicion of the king. At one London house in May 1640, a woman named Mrs Chickleworth told all she knew: 'the queen's grace, she said, went unto the communion table with the king, and the queen had asked your grace [Archbishop Laud] whether that she might not be of that religion which the King was – yes or no? Whereupon his Grace answered her Majesty "you are very well as you are, and I would wish to keep you there." And now the King goes to Mass with the queen.' The story spread, and was retold in the same London neighbourhood later that year, this time (optimistically?) by a Catholic. The king, she said, 'was turned to be a Papist'.

Actually, this was unlikely to the point of impossibility. Charles was horrified by the rate of conversion the queen's efforts had made possible, just as Laud was. In 1630 he ordered his subjects not to attend Mass at Denmark House, and he repeated the ban the following year. Laud was even less enthusiastic. In particular, he was dismayed by the ructions in the Falkland family. Lady Newport and Lady Hamilton converted. Elizabeth Cary, Viscountess Falkland, had not only converted to Catholicism, but managed to persuade her daughters to it as well, and Laud was alarmed. It was partly because he so feared the new waves of conversion that Laud thought it sensible to readmit the beauty of holiness to the simplicity of the Church of England. The queen's favourite, Walter Montagu, had also converted, and when he returned to England from France the only people who would receive him were the earls of Holland and Dorset. Charles ordered his subjects not to attend embassy Masses, and ticked off the Spanish ambassador for going so openly to Somerset House. But suspicion continued to rise, and as Laud tightened his grip on ordinary worship, people formed simple equations: altar-rails, popery, the queen, the king. What it amounted to was that England, elect Protestant nation, was believed to be in danger from its own sovereign.

Nevertheless, despite all these doubts and difficulties, the terrifying thing about Charles's personal rule is not that it was bound to fail, but that it nearly succeeded. There were tensions, there were fears, even panics; there was also opposition. But these things were common, and had accompanied the Tudor reforms of the monarchy, too; indeed, Elizabeth I was threatened with far greater outbursts of popular dissent than Charles faced before 1642. The Civil War was not bound to occur; it would take a special, exceptional set of circumstances to make it happen.

Like all those keen to redefine their powers by extending them, Charles eventually stretched his arm too far, and only in this sense was he 'doomed' to failure. But had he managed to avoid this characteristic tendency to test the limits one more time, he might well have succeeded in transforming the English monarchy at any rate from a leadership role amidst a system of checks and balances to something that would look to history like the rule of the Bourbons in France. Such absolutism might have produced a comparable cultural renaissance. Certainly this would have suited Charles; without the restraints of the implied need for consultation, he might even have endorsed something like Catholic toleration, and equally probably a more determined attempt to confine and restrict Calvinist Protestantism. After all, these became the settled policies of both his sons when they eventually succeeded him.

And we should not assume too blithely that the sequel would therefore have been a more violent and more total repudiation of the monarchy at some later date. But it would also have had an immeasurable impact on the history of the world. If there had been no English Civil

War, would there have been an American or a French Revolution? It may be that Charles could have redefined government in autocratic terms for the whole of Western civilization, almost indefinitely. The result might well have been a British Empire that looked a good deal more like the Roman Empire, with concomitant court corruption and rivalry. Charles's good characteristics – taste, refinement, elegance, sophistication, complexity – would have flourished. But we would altogether have lost Cromwell's virtues – common sense, pragmatism, simple hard work, honesty. We would be a different nation in a different world.

III

Two Women:
Anna Trapnel and Lucy Hay

The key to the kingdom in 1639 was London, and it was mush-rooming from town to megalopolis. At the beginning of the sixteenth century it was as small and compact as a provincial town in modern Britain. Now it was growing rapidly, and its growth imposed structural change. The old ways of life in London had to alter to accommodate the city's new immensity. It was possible to begin to think new thoughts – political, religious, social – in this new space.

The old city had been hugger-mugger since the days of the Romans, and all through the Middle Ages the rich lived cheek-by-jowl with the poor. An aristocrat could be deafened by the hammering of a black-smith next door. This created a kind of unity. There was just one London, whoever you were. Now the capital was breaking down into many cities, as Jacobean and Caroline London began sorting itself into zones. Industry was slowly being exiled from the city, and was always excluded from the new, pretty residential areas for the better-off. Increasingly, the suburbs were the site of manufacturing industries – pewterers in Billingsgate and Bishopsgate, for instance. Immigrants were crucial to the development of new industries: London's first fine glass came from the Broad Street Glasshouse, run by an emigrant from Venice originally, and later by Englishmen who learned his skills. This influx created further divisions; some industries were different cul-turally and linguistically from one another and from their customers.

The result of the new industrial suburbs and the new residential areas, taken together, was a city that was divided, at least to some extent, by social class: the rich lived mostly in the newly built West End, in beautiful regular buildings, while the poor lived around the walls of the old city and by the river, and – increasingly – in the expanding, wild, unregulated 'East End'. It would be wrong to equate the West End with Royalism to come, and the emerging East with Parliamentarianism, or to see in that sharp class division the inevitable, bloody division of a nation. But it would also be wrong not to, because the East End did declare all but unilaterally for Parliament. A concomitant West End support for the king did not emerge, however, and the East Enders' Parliamentarianism proceeded less from class hatred than from the much more subtle expression of social class in religious difference. Getting to know two women, Anna Trapnel from the East End, Lucy Hay from the West End, will help to show why matters were complicated.

We need to recall that both the West and East Ends were reacting against a sturdy, ageing centre; in the seventeenth century, the aristocracy could be as innovative as the workers, and as eager to extend its power. Between those two extremes, the old city of London still stood, walled against attack as it had been in the now-vanishing Middle Ages. The great gates in its walls could be closed against invaders: and had been, as recently as the reign of Elizabeth. It was a city preoccupied with two things: religion, and work. It was the home of churches, and of the trade guilds that ruled men's lives and professions. There were so very many churches, hundreds of tiny intricate parish boundaries: All Hallows, Honey Lane, All Hallows the Great, All Hallows the Less, St Benet Sherehog, St Faith Under St Paul's, a parish church actually inside the great cathedral, St Laurence Pountney, with its tall spire. And the guildhalls clustered round them, bakers and silversmiths and chandlers and shoemakers, civil and ecclesiastical authorities knitted together in the twisting, weaving, narrow streets. It was a city governed by hierarchy which constrained enterprise, but because it was a boom city enterprise still managed to flourish there.

One such enterprise was the West End itself, new-built estates run up by nobles. Far more of the West End that Lucy Hay knew is still visible; Anna Trapnel's East End was all but erased by the giant hands of industry and the Blitz. There are some constants, though, most of all the street plan. If Anna Trapnel were blindfolded, her feet could still trace the way along the length of Poplar High Street to St Dunstan's church, Stepney. And the church that was the centre of her world is still standing, though smudged and blurred by Victorian 'restoration'.

Anna Trapnel was nobody in particular. She was one of many nobodies given a voice by the war. She came from the world of radical religious outlaws, the independent sects, and in it she became – briefly – a well-known figure. Then she faded, and we do not even know how or when she died. But she left writings behind which open something of her life to us. Anna Trapnel tells us that she was born in Poplar, Stepney, in the parish of St Dunstan's. There is no record of her baptism, and this might mean that she wasn't baptized as a baby, suggesting very strong godly views on her parents' part. She also tells us that she was the daughter of William Trapnel, shipwright.

'Shipwright' is a vague term. It could mean anything from a master designer who could keep in his head complex and secret plans that allowed a ship to be buoyant and able to manoeuvre, to a man with an adze – but even a man with an adze was a man of remarkable skill. Shipwrights were among the most skilled workers of their day, trained to assemble large and heavy timbers into a vessel which would withstand the enormous stresses both of the sea and wind and of a heavy cargo, or guns. On their skill many lives depended. A master shipwright was also a manager, controlling huge teams of workers. And yet as one expert on the seventeenth-century navy remarks, a shipyard at that time must have been a pretty dangerous place. It was, necessarily, full of inflammable materials – wood, tar, cordage. As in later shipyards, heavy weights would have been slung on relatively rickety sheers, using vegetable cordage, tackles and capstans. And everywhere, fires: fires for steaming timbers into flexibility, fires to melt pitch, to mould iron. There were sawpits too, and other dangers: the mis-swung adze or axe. It would have seemed nearly infernal to a young girl, with its brilliant red fires and smoking tar.

The Poplar shipyards were created to be outside the jurisdiction of the shipwrights' guild which governed shipbuilding at the London docks. It was outside the walls of custom and law. Independency in trade perhaps encouraged Independency in religion. For St Dunstan's Stepney, the East End church, was one of the most staunchly godly and anti-Laudian churches of the time. This was in part because its congregation included a high proportion of Huguenot refugees from the wars of religion in France, men and women who could tell many stories of how papists persecuted the people of God.

It was industrial, cosmopolitan, but also rural. Poplar obtained its name from the great number of poplar trees that grew there. Poplar High Street was open to fields on both sides; Poplar Marsh raised cattle, and its grass was esteemed. An eighteenth-century visitor noted the mix of rural and urban: 'Part of this marsh is called the Isle of Dogs, although it is not an island, nor quite a peninsula. It is opposite Greenwich in Kent; and when our sovereigns had a palace near the site of the present magnificent hospital, they used it as a hunting-seat, and, it is said, kept the kennels of their hounds in this marsh. These hounds frequently making a great noise, the seamen called the place the Isle of Dogs.' Anna could have heard the royal hunters, and they in turn could have heard the hammer of the shipyards. Poplar High Street was lined with shipwrights' houses, but it was also a sailors' town, so these were interspersed with pubs: the Green Man, the Spotted Dog, the Black Boy, the Green Dragon. Dragonish indeed to the godly: freedom could become lawlessness. Poplar saw many sailors' riots.

Later, when Anna Trapnel had moved inside the walls of the City of London, Poplar became an industry town, even a boom town. Within the parish of St Dunstan's were huge new shipyards at Blackwell (for the East India Company), Limehouse, Wapping and Ratcliffe. The East India Company – in a manner almost anticipating Ford and Microsoft, and limping in the footsteps of landowning gentry – began to build its own amenities for its employees, including a chapel, which was erected in the year 1654 by a subscription of the inhabitants.

As London divided into better and worse areas, where Londoners lived began to make a difference to how long they lived. Slums like Bridewell and Blackfriars suffered much more from the 1636 plague than the richer central areas. Stepney's burials outnumbered baptisms by 80%, though this statistic may mislead us as it may be due to godly reluctance to baptize. Some 90,000 people lived east of the City, in the parishes of Poplar, Stepney and Hackney. John Stow said these people inhabited what he called 'base tenements', which may simply reflect Stow's prejudice against new build. And houses *were* smaller and more cramped. In Shadwell and Tower Liberty in the 1650 survey, 80% of houses were one or two storeys with an average of four rooms each, compared with 6.7 rooms in the West End. And the East End houses were mostly of timber and boards, not brick, and only one-third had gardens (often crucial economically) compared with 42.9% in the West End. Already, too, the East End had more constables.

Housing design, even for the rich, was in a state of flux. In this period domestic architecture was moving from what are called hall houses to the organization of separate chambers. The hall house was a large room with many smaller rooms built onto it. The hall had a central hearth. In the hall, communal male activities took place, while the private chambers were occupied by women and children. But in the sixteenth century houses changed, a process which had begun much earlier but now became commonplace. Segregation by sex was replaced by segregation by class, with servants cut off from everyone else. Upstairs and downstairs assumed their significances. As a result, great houses became disconnected from those whose economic activity supported them – farms, quarries and the like were separated from houses by distance. Finally, domestic surroundings became increasingly elaborate – more and more windows had curtains, more tables were encased in cloths, more floors were covered in carpets and rugs. This inspired plenty of shopping, and shipping to fill the new shops with exotica, and to that end London acquired its first shopping mall, the Royal Exchange.

The kind of house Trapnel probably knew best was multipurpose, a dwelling and also a business. Houses above or with a shop often used the ground floor exclusively for business purposes, and the family rooms were on the upper floors. But the 'shop' would also be a manufacturing place – a workshop – and so it could be noisy or dusty. Many businesses needed kitchen facilities, so households would have to share their kitchen with the dairying or laundry. We can get a glimpse of this kind of house from probate inventories. When Daniel Jeames, a chandler from Middlesex, died in 1663, shortly after the tumultuous events described in this book, his house contained the following:

Kitchen: Sixteen porringers, two great flagons, nine little flagons, two pewter candlesticks, six chamber pots, one brass kettle, one brass pot, one fire shovel and tongs, and five forks, four spits and dripping pan, one gridiron, one chopping-knife, one iron pot, one iron kettle, and a jack, two cupboards, one table, three chairs and three stools.

In the shop Butter and cheese and other commodities

In the room over the shop seven chairs, two tables, one form, one set of hangings, one chest, one cupboard

In the room over the kitchen six pairs of shoes, two dozen of napkins, three table clothes, one dozen of towels, one Featherbed, two Featherbolsters, one Flockbed, one drawbed, one green rug, one Trundle bedstead mat, one Feather pillow, two blankets, one jug, one table, three chairs, two stools, a little trunk with some other things

In the garrett two featherbeds, one bolster, a set of striped curtains and valance, one table one cupboard and one old sawpot [?] with some other lumber

Item two Bibles and a Testament

Item two silver bowls and two silver drinking cupes

Item in ready money iiii pence

Item his apparel

It all seems pitifully little, if we imagine how extensive our own inventories might be. The stress on bedclothes, too, is alien to us; before washing machines, to own a lot of bedlinen was an important source of comfort. For ordinary tradespeople like the Trapnels, home was still a bare place, about warmth and family rather than interior design. But the few possessions needed to make it livable were doubly precious.

Paradoxically, at exactly the moment people demanded more space, and more privacy, housing in London and in some other fast-growing towns like Bristol was getting hard to find; so scarce that most people lived in lodgings or took in lodgers. The family of John Milton shared a house with five other families. Anna Trapnel, when she moved to central London from Poplar, lived with two different landladies. They may have been her employers, too, for everyone but the very poorest also had servants. Servants were vital assistants in the constant struggles for food, warmth and cleanliness, which all centred on the hearth and the fire. Later eras have sentimentalized the phrase 'hearth

and home', but in the kind of house Anna Trapnel lived in, the maintenance of a good fire involved much vital, risky and backbreaking work,
wrestling not only with heavy, dirty fuel but with extreme heat, red-hot
implements, and boiling liquids.

While Anna Trapnel's father struggled with hot metal in the shipyard,
or with bubbling tar, she grappled with blistering cauldrons at home.
The difference between industry and cooking – in smell, risk, filth –
was much less marked than it later became. Despite women's efforts,
inadequate fires meant that houses were not comfortable. Most bed-
rooms had no fireplaces, and even the biggest houses, with fifteen or
more rooms, had on average only a third of them heated. Innovations
were beginning to change this, and with the developments in heating
came social changes. Just as the city was dividing into rich and poor
districts, so the house itself was increasingly marked off into different
areas.

Though Poplar was outside the walls, Trapnel was still a Londoner,
an inhabitant of by far the largest and most important city in the
British Isles. Between 1600 and 1650 the population grew from 200,000
to 375,000, despite outbreaks of bubonic plague. If this book were to
attempt the impossible task of writing about the Civil War experience
'representatively', then most of those it studied would need to be
Londoners. In 1642, London stretched for five miles from Stepney to
Westminster, and south five miles more to Rotherhithe. One of the
main sights of the old city was London Bridge, with its eighteen solid
stone piers which rested on piles that forced the current into narrow
and swift channels; the boatmen couldn't shoot the bridge on a flood
tide, and it was also dangerous on an ebb tide. Many people avoided
the danger by getting out at Old Swan Stairs, on one side of the bridge,
walking down Upper Thames Street, and getting back into boats at
Billingsgate Stairs. Fifty watermen or so died every year trying to shoot
the bridge, usually by drowning.

While the East End was being built, rich landowners were arriving
in town for what came to be known as the season. They also needed
housing, and it was for them that the West End was built. The new
city catered for the rich, and for their new power to shop. For a
gentleman like Sir Humphrey Mildmay, the whole day could be spent
shopping. When you had promenaded down Paul's Walk, the middle

aisle of St Paul's, which was also a shortcut that saved walking around the cathedral itself, you could say that everyone important had seen your new clothes. Or you could go to an ordinary, or eating house, which were graded according to cost. They served good simple food. Servants could eat at a threeha'penny ordinary. Around St Paul's too were the London booksellers and the tobacconists. In Cheapside there were the goldsmiths' shops, the nearest London came to actually having streets paved with gold. The menagerie in the Tower was another spectacle.

But Trapnel may not have done any of these things. They were part of a richer, more leisured life than hers. Her focal point was the church. As she herself wrote:

> When a child, the Lord awed my spirit, and so for the least trespass, my heart was smitten, and though my godly mother did not see me offend, that she might reprove me, which she was ready to do, being tender of the honour of her beloved Saviour, even the least secret sin, that the world calls a trifle, though I thought it nothing, yet still the all-seeing eye watched my ways, and he called to me, though I knew it not . . . a child of wrath as well as others.

We don't know how old Trapnel was when she wrote this, but she was part of a local community which felt the same. In 1641, Stepney produced the first call to allow parishes to appoint their own lecturers, visiting speakers, often not in holy orders, who might preach for hours. Many disliked their way of speaking, which was to allow themselves to say anything prompted by the Spirit. *Ex tempore*, thought one critic, excludes the *pater noster*. One lecturer was Jeremiah Burroughs, suspended by Bishop Wren and later chaplain to the Earl of Warwick, a defender of popular sovereignty; another was William Greenhill who established a gathered church in 1644.

Greenhill was a man who had been in trouble for refusing to read *The Book of Sports*, the Stuart guide to maypole building and hock-carts which had upset godly people up and down the country. He was the afternoon preacher to the congregation at Stepney, while Jeremiah Burroughs ministered in the morning, so that they were called respectively the 'Evening Star' and the 'Morning Star' of Stepney. In 1643, he was to preach before the House of Commons on the occasion of a public fast, and his sermon was published by command of the House, with the title 'The Axe at the Root', a title which suggests his strong independent opinions. His later career shows his ability to reach children: after the death of Charles, he became Parliament's chaplain to three of the king's children: James, Duke of York (afterwards James II); Henry, Duke of Gloucester; and the Princess Henrietta Maria, and he dedicated a work on Ezekiel to Princess Elizabeth, at that time a little girl.

To us it is difficult to imagine that sermons could be exciting or radical, and comparisons with political meetings or public lectures do little to convey the mixture of shivering tent-revival rapture and sharp thought which they produced. But to the average Protestant, and especially to the godly, all individuals – and the nation itself – were always understood to be trembling on the brink of an abyss, the pit of hell, from which they could be snatched to safety at the eleventh hour by the strong words of an heroic preacher. This was just the sort of drama – a kind of endless, high-emotion soap – likely to attract an adolescent girl whose circumstances were otherwise obscure. Anna herself describes her eager response:

> When I was about fourteen years of age, I began to be very eager and forward to hear and pray, though in a very formal manner; Thus I went on some years, and then I rose to a higher pitch, to a more spiritual condition, as I thought, and I followed after that Ministry that was most pressed after by the strictest Professors, and I ran with great violence, having a great zeal, though not according to knowledge, and I appeared a very high-grown Christian in the thoughts of man; . . . providence ordered that I should hear Mr Peters speak . . . though I thought myself in a very good condition before, yet now it seized upon my spirit, that surely I was not in the covenant . . . I then went home full of horror, concluding myself to be the stony ground Christ spoke of in the parable of the sower; I apprehended divine displeasure against me . . . I ran from minister to minister, from sermon to sermon.

Anna Trapnel's religious background supported her notion that she was worthless, while feeding her longing for compensation through being specially chosen by God. This drama had its dark side. During a prolonged spiritual depression, Anna contemplated murder and suicide, but on New Year's Day 1642 she heard John Simpson preaching at All Hallows the Great, and there was an immediate (and joyful) conversion. The godly typically went through these periods of joy and misery; they were an intrinsic part of Calvinist salvation.

Simpson was relatively young, in his thirties, and another of the St Dunstan's lecturers. A man of passionately independent views, he was removed from his lectureship in St Aldgate in 1643, and banned from preaching. He was soon in trouble again for asserting, allegedly, that Christ was to be found even 'in hogs, and dogs, or sheep'. In 1647 Simpson became pastor of the gathered congregation at All Hallows the Great. He was also to fight against Prince Charles at Worcester in 1650. Unlike many radicals, Simpson placed no trust in Oliver Cromwell as the instrument of God. He reported visions in which God had revealed to him Cromwell's lust for power and his impending ruin. He became a leader of the Fifth Monarchists, a group who believed themselves the elect and the end of the world near. Many contemporaries were bewildered by Simpson's volatile and passionate nature and thought him mad. But everyone recognized his power as a preacher. In the heady atmosphere of freedom from guild restraints, immigrants bringing novel ideas, the wildness of the East End, and the religious adventure of St Dunstan's, the unthinkable was soon being thought, and not only by Trapnel. Joan Sherrard, of Anna Trapnel's parish, said in 1644 that the king was 'a stuttering fool' and asked passionately 'is there never a Fel[t]on yet living? [Felton was the man who had assassinated the Duke of Buckingham.] If I were a man, as I am a woman, I would help to pull him to pieces.' It was the kind of thing one housewife might shout at another in a noisy high street. It was unimaginable at court, only a few miles distant.

The world was an altogether different place for noblewoman Lucy Hay. West End, not East End; magnificent houses, not wooden terraces; shopping, not working; the court, not the pulpit – though Lucy was religious, and militantly Protestant at that. Lucy Hay was England's *salonnière*, a beautiful woman who enjoyed politics, intrigue, plots, but also intellectual games, poetry, love affairs (intellectual, and probably occasionally physical), fashion, clothes and admiration. She was one of Henrietta Maria's closest and most trusted friends, but also her competitor and sometime political enemy. Her world was more introverted than Trapnel's, with the obsessive cliquishness of an exclusive girls' school. But like many a pupil, Lucy struggled not only to dominate it, but also to find ways to widen it.

Her success was founded on her face. She was such a beauty that when she contracted smallpox, the whole court joined forces to write reassuring letters to her husband, telling him that she was not in danger of losing her looks. She asked for and received permission to wear a mask on her return to court, until her sores were entirely healed; when she removed it, people said that she was not only unblemished, but lovelier than ever.

Lucy Hay came from an extraordinary family, the Percys, Earls of Northumberland, a family of nobles always powerful in dissent. Her great-uncle was a leader in the Northern Earls rebellion, beheaded for it in 1572, and her father was imprisoned in the Tower for suspected involvement in the Gunpowder Plot. The Percys were a noble family inclined to see the monarch of the day as only *primus inter pares*, and to act accordingly. Lucy's father was known as 'the wizard earl' because of his interest in magic, astronomy and mathematics – he was so interested in numbers that he kept three private mathematicians at his side. Hard of hearing, remote of bearing, and often shy, he was also a passionate gambler, and his contemporaries found him difficult to understand. His wife, Dorothy Devereux, was the sister of the Earl of Essex who was Elizabeth's favourite late in her life, and Dorothy, too, was loved by the queen. But like the Percys, the Devereux found it difficult to accept the absolute sovereignty of the monarch. They had their own power and they wanted it respected.

Within the marriage this mutual strong-mindedness did not make for harmony. The couple separated, and after Elizabeth had brought about a reconciliation which produced a male heir, fell out again. There was no divorce, but they lived apart. Henry Percy did not take to James I. He disliked in particular the many Scots James had brought with him and may have seen their promotion to the nobility as a threat to established families like his own. In the autumn of 1605, he retired to Syon House to think more about numbers and less about politics. His choice of retreat points to the way the Percys had come to see themselves as a southern family; there was no question of a retreat to the north, to the family seat at Alnwick.

This mathematical pastoral was, however, threatened in two ways. First, the Gunpowder Plot exploded, and Northumberland's kinsman Thomas Percy, four years his elder and one of the chief conspirators, had dined on 4 November with Northumberland at Syon House. Though not a papist, Northumberland was a known Catholic sympathizer, who had tried to secure the position of Catholics with James when he became king. Although he had few arms, horses or followers at Syon, and had known none of the conspirators excepting Percy, he was sent to the Tower on 27 November. He tried to excuse himself in a manner which reveals the Percy attitude to affairs of state: 'Examine', he said, 'but my humours in buildings, gardenings, and private expenses these two years past.' He was not believed. On 27 June 1606 he was tried in the Court of Star Chamber for contempt and misprision of treason. At his trial, he was accused of seeking to become chief of the papists in England; of failing to administer the Oath of Supremacy to Thomas Percy. He pleaded guilty to some of the facts set forth in the indictment, but indignantly repudiated the inferences placed upon them by his prosecutors. He was sentenced to pay a fine of 30,000 pounds, to be removed from all offices and places, to be rendered incapable of holding any of them hereafter, and to be kept a prisoner in the Tower for life. Voluntary exile had become forced imprisonment. The hand of royalty was heavy.

Northumberland protested to the king against the severity of this sentence, but his cries went unheard. Much more significantly, and perhaps more effectively, his wife Dorothy appealed to the queen, Anne of Denmark, who took a sympathetic interest in his case. This may have been where Lucy learned that women have power, that one can work through queens where kings are initially deaf. The king nevertheless insisted that 11,000 pounds of the fine should be paid at once, and, when the earl declared himself unable to find the money, his estates were seized, and funds were raised by granting leases on them. Northumberland did pay 11,000 pounds on 13 November 1613. He and his daughter had learnt an unforgettable lesson about royal power and nobles' power.

Typically, Northumberland tried to recreate his private paradise inside the Tower. Thomas Harriot, once Walter Ralegh's conjuror-servant, Walter Warner, and Thomas Hughes, the mathematicians, were regular attendants and pensioners, and were known as the earl's 'three magi'. And Northumberland had Walter Ralegh himself, also in the Tower, as an occasional companion. Nicholas Hill aided him in experiments in astrology and alchemy. A large library was placed in his cell, consisting mainly of Italian books on fortification, astrology and medicine; he also had Tasso, Machiavelli, Chapman's Homer, *The Gardener's Labyrinth*, Daniel's *History of England*, and Florio's *Dictionary*.

During her stay in the Tower, did Lucy read them? An intelligent girl might have been expected to do so. Another Lucy, Lucy Hutchinson, recalled her own intensive education:

> By the time I was four years old, I read English perfectly, and having a great memory, I was carried to sermons, and while I was very young could remember and repeat them exactly . . . I had at one time eight tutors in several qualities, languages, music, dancing, writing and needlework; but my genius was quite averse from all but my book, and that I was so eager of, that my mother thinking it prejudiced my health, would moderate me in it. Yet this rather animated me than kept me back, and every moment I could steal from my play I would employ in any book I could find, when my own were locked up from me. After dinner and supper I still had an hour allowed me to play, and then I would steal into some hole or other to read. My father would have me learn latin, and I was so apt that I outstripped my brothers who were at school, although my father's chaplain, that was my tutor, was a pitiful dull fellow.

Lucy Hay never became an eager reader, as Lucy Hutchinson did. Instead, she whiled away her time in exactly the way any adolescent girl would: she fell wildly in love with someone her father thought very unsuitable, the king's Scottish favourite James Hay. But Lucy was also still a daughter in her father's house. As dutiful daughters, Lucy and her elder sister Dorothy paid their father a visit in the Tower. In Lucy's case duty was not rewarded. After he had given her sister a few embraces, Northumberland abruptly dismissed Dorothy, but instructed

Lucy to stay where she was, asking her sister to send Lucy's maids to her at once. 'I am a Percy,' he said, 'and I cannot endure that my daughter should dance any Scottish jigs.' The Percys who had been keeping the Scots out of England for several hundred years were speaking through him.

'Come, let's away to prison', Northumberland might have said to his errant Cordelia, hoping that they would sing like birds in the cage. However, since he snatched Lucy away from an exceptionally lavish party put on just to impress her by her very passionate suitor, it seems unlikely that she was pleased. In any case, all her life, Lucy wanted anything but retirement. She wished to be at the centre of things. And her choice of partner was a sign of her lifelong brilliance at spotting just who was able to open secret doors to power.

To Northumberland, imprisoning his daughter along with him, and thus depriving the king's favourite of his desires, might have seemed a nice and ironic revenge on the king who had unfairly locked him away. Revenge apart, however, Northumberland loathed James Hay. First, he was a Scot, and there was great resentment among English courtiers and nobles against those Scots brought south by James Stuart. Secondly, he was a favourite of the king who had just punished and shamed Northumberland. But more than all this, the antipathy seems to have been personal. On reflection it is hard to think of two more dissimilar men. Northumberland was intellectual, shy, proud, private, and above all of an ancient family. James Hay was a social being. If Northumberland loved books, James Hay loved banquets and parties.

Especially, he loved giving them. When he held a banquet, Whitehall hummed with servants carrying twenty or twenty-five dishes from the kitchens to the banqueting hall. It was James Hay who invented the so-called antefeast: 'the manner of which was to have the board covered, at the first entrance of the guests, with dishes, as high as a tall man could well reach, and dearest viands sea or land could afford: and all this once seen, and having feasted the eyes of the invited, was in an manner thrown away, and fresh set on the same height, having only this advantage of the other, *that it was hot*.' Hay's servants were always recognizable because they were so richly dressed. Or because they were carrying cloakbags full of uneaten food: 'dried sweetmeats and comfets, valued to his lordship at more than 10 shillings the pound'. Once a hundred cooks worked for eight days to make a feast for his guests. The party he had put on to impress Lucy involved thirty cooks, twelve days' preparation, seven score pheasants, twelve partridges, twelve salmon, and cost 2200 pounds in all. John Chamberlain thought it disgustingly wasteful, an apish imitation of the monstrous ways of the French. But it was exactly the ways of the French – elegance, taste, fashion – that made James Hay so personable, so modern. He also liked elegant clothes, court socials and courtly pursuits, especially tilting. He introduced Lucy to the pleasures of the court masque, a musical drama which combined the attractions of amateur theatricals, drawing-room musicmaking, and a costume ball. His wedding to Honora Denny had been accompanied by a masque by Thomas Campion, and in 1617, the year of his courtship of Lucy, he sponsored a masque subsequently known as the Essex House Masque. He also funded a performance of Ben Jonson's *Lovers Made Men*.

Hardest, perhaps, for Northumberland to bear, Hay was the son of a gentleman-farmer of very modest means. He was on the make, charmingly and intelligently. He was no fool: he spoke French, Latin and Italian, and one of the reasons he liked to live at a slightly faster pace was that he had spent his youth in France learning about food, wine and pleasure. His choice of Lucy Percy as a bride was astute and sensible, too; he must have spotted her as a future beauty, and of course her family credentials were good, or would be when he had wheedled Northumberland out of gaol.

Lucy was abandoning her father's world and its values in choosing James Hay. He must have fascinated her, enough to make her put up with virtual imprisonment to get her way, but it was not his looks that made him so appealing. Surviving portraits bear out Princess Elizabeth's nickname for him, which was 'camelface'. Encumbered with a notoriously shy and distant father, it may have been James's easy charm that Lucy found irresistible. And she was only a teenager; though used to magnificence, she was not used to courtly sophistication. James exuded the suavity of French and Italian courts. He knew all about how things were done in those foreign places, then as now redolent with associations of class and chic. And coming from a difficult, even tempestuous marriage between two people of equal rank, she knew that nobility in a partner was no passport to married bliss. Most of all, and all her life, Lucy was alert to power – who had it, who did not, who was in, who out.

Finally, banquets and masques and feasts and court life offered Lucy a chance to take centre-stage. Northumberland was never going to offer her that. He thought great men's wives existed 'to bring up their children well in their long coat age, to tend their health and education, to obey their husbands . . . and to see that their women . . . keep the linen sweet'. Or so he wrote to his sons, at the very time when Lucy was incarcerated with him. He added that if wives complained, the best idea was to 'let them talk, and you keep the power in your hands, that you may do as you list'.

Northumberland may have thought he had power, but as many men were to find when the Civil War began, the women in his family knew exactly where real influence lay. About this his daughter was wiser than he. Eventually she wore her father down. He began using pleas rather than force. He offered her 20,000 pounds if she publicly renounced James Hay. Lucy declined; she probably knew that he didn't have the money, encumbered as he was by fines. Instead, she escaped from the Tower, and fled straight to James, who as Groom of the Stool was resident in the Wardrobe Building. Alas, he was in Scotland with the king, but he knew his Lucy. He left a fund of 2000 pounds for her entertainment while he was away.

James, on his return, worked sensibly on and through Lucy's mother and sister, winning them with the same charm that had dazzled Lucy. Finally, in October 1617, the old earl gave in. He blessed the pair. Perhaps he was tired of seclusion in the Tower and knew Hay could procure his release. Perhaps Northumberland was forced to recognize what his daughter had noticed long before, that power had passed to a new and very different generation.

Lucy and James were married in November 1617. It was a quiet wedding by James's usually ebullient standards, costing a mere £1600, but it was well attended: the king, Prince Charles, and George Villiers, later the powerful Duke of Buckingham, were among the guests. James Hay, in order, apparently, to overcome Northumberland's prejudice against him, made every effort to obtain his release. In this he at length proved successful. In 1621 King James was induced to celebrate his birthday by setting Northumberland and other political prisoners at liberty. The earl showed some compunction in accepting a favour which he attributed to Hay's agency.

James's lightheartedness concealed a tragic past, however. His first wife, Honora Denny, was an intelligent and kind woman who had received dedications from Guillaume Du Bartas, one of John Milton's role models. But she had died in 1614. Her death was the result of an attempted robbery; she had been returning from a supper party through the Ludgate Hill area when a man seized the jewel she wore around her neck and tried to run off with it, dragging her to the ground. Seven months pregnant, the fall meant she delivered her baby prematurely. She died a week later. Her assailant was hanged, even though Honora had pleaded that he be spared before her own death. It was a moment in which the two almost separate worlds of peerage and poor met violently; the meeting was fatal to both.

Despite this saintly act, Honora Denny Hay was no saint. Either James Hay's taste in women was consistent, or his second wife modelled herself closely on his first. Honora Denny was a powerful figure because she was a close confidante of Anne of Denmark. Rumour said that she had used her position as the Queen's friend to make sure a man who had tried to murder one of her lovers was fully punished. Lucy, the wilful teenage bride, was to become one of the most brilliant, beautiful and sought-after women in Caroline England, following her predecessor's example studiously and intelligently. And if Honora Denny Hay had lovers, and got away with it, Lucy could learn from this too.

James Hay's career was as glittering as she had predicted. Retaining his position as the king's favourite without any of the slips that dogged the careers of Somerset and Buckingham, he did a good deal of diplomatic work which took him far from home. In 1619 he was in Germany, mediating between the emperor and the Bohemians, and paying a visit to William of Orange on the way home. William scandalized Hay by offering him a dinner in which only *one* suckling pig was on the table. On his next mission to France in 1621, James cheered himself by having his horse shod with silver; every time it cast a shoe there was a scramble for the discard. But it was not only the old-fashioned who might have preferred William's solitary pig to James's extravaganzas. The disapproval of courtly colleagues like Chamberlain symbolized the difficulty facing the Hays as they tried to get on in society.

This society was unimaginable to Anna Trapnel, as her world was to them. It was a milieu full of new and beautiful *things*, new ideas. The court was their world, headed by a king who came to own the greatest art collection in the history of England, while in Stepney people ate black bread and died daily in the shipyards that built trading vessels to bring his finds to England.

A Van Dyck portrait of Henrietta Maria with her dwarf Jeffrey Hudson painted in 1633 shows fragments, symbols of her court. The monkey is a representative of Henrietta Maria's menagerie of dogs, monkeys and caged birds, while the orange tree alludes to her love of gardens. Van Dyck deliberately downplays regality; gone are the stiff robes and jewels of Tudor portraiture, and here is a warmer, more relaxed figure who enjoys her garden and pets and is kind to her servant.

Lapped in such care, the queen and Lucy were encapsulated in the jewel case of the royal household, which included everyone from aristocratic advisers and career administrators to grooms and scullions. At the outbreak of the war, it comprised as many as 1800 people. Some of these were given bed and board, others received what was called 'bouge of court', which included bread, ale, firewood and candles. The court also supported hordes of nobles, princes, ambassadors and other state visitors, who all resided in it with *their* households, such as Henrietta's mother Marie de Medici, and her entourage.

The household above stairs was called the chamber (these were people who organized state visits and the reception of ambassadors); below stairs it was called simply the household (these were the people who did the actual work, the cooking, cleaning and laundering). Supporting the household accounted for more than 40% of royal expenditure. Many servants had grand titles, rather like civil service managers now: the Pages of the Scalding House, the Breadbearers of the Pantry. There were unimaginable numbers of them. The king had, for example, thirty-one falconers, thirty-five huntsmen, and four officers of bears, bulls and mastiffs. The queen had her own household, which included a full kitchen staff, a keeper of the sweet coffers, a laundress and a starcher, and a seamstress. There were over 180, not including the stables staff.

Charles's court was divided into the king's side and the queen's side,

horizontally. It was also very strictly divided vertically, with exceptionally formal protocols to enforce these divisions. Charles insisted on the
enforcement of these protocols far more firmly than his father had.
Only peers, bishops and Privy Councillors could tread on the carpet
around the king's table in the Presence Chamber, for example. All these
labyrinthine rules had to be learnt and kept. The king's chambers were
themselves a kind of nest of Chinese boxes; the further in you were
allowed, the more important you were. The most public room was the
Presence Chamber; beyond it was the Privy Chamber, which could be
entered only by nobles and councillors; beyond that was the Withdrawing Chamber and the Bedchamber, reserved for the king and his
body servants, and governed by the Groom of the Stool.

Charles actively maintained seven palaces: Greenwich, Hampton
Court, Nonesuch, Oatlands, Richmond, St James's and Whitehall, and
he also had Somerset House, Theobalds, Holdenby (in Northamptonshire), and Wimbledon, the newest, bought by Charles as a gift for
Henrietta Maria in 1639. There were also five castles, including the
Tower of London, and three hunting lodges, at Royston, Newmarket
and Thetford (the last was sold in 1630). All were to be touched by the
war. Many were ruined.

Whitehall was the king's principal London residence, a status recognized by both the Council of State and Cromwell, who chose it as the
principal residence themselves. It was a warren, a maze of long galleries
that connected its disparate parts in a rough and ready fashion, and it
was cut in two by the highway that ran from London to Westminster,
and bridged (in a manner reminiscent of Oxford's Bridge of Sighs) by
the Holbein Gate. Set down in the middle of the medieval muddle, like
a beautiful woman in a white frock, was the Inigo Jones Banqueting
House: icy, classical perfection. The long, rambling corridors and rooms
of Whitehall were full of tapestries, paintings, statues (over a hundred)
and furniture; it illustrated the idea that a palace was about interiors
and personnel, not architecture. In that, it was oddly like the houses
Anna Trapnel knew.

But Charles and Henrietta tried to alter this muddle. Dedicated and
knowledgeable collectors, they eagerly acquired and displayed beautiful
art. St James's had an Inigo Jones sculpture gallery in the grounds that
had been built to house the astounding collection of the Duke of

Mantua; a colonnaded gallery ran parallel to the orchard wall, whose roof was cantilevered over the gardens so the king could ride under cover if the weather was wet. Somerset House had belonged to Anne of Denmark, and now it became Henrietta Maria's. There were thirteen sculptures dotted about its garden, some from the Gonzaga collection. In the chapel, some thirty-four paintings were inventoried during Parliament's rule, some described in the angry terms of iconoclasm: 'a pope in white satin'. (In a hilarious irony, this was where Oliver Cromwell's body was displayed to the nation in 1658.) Hampton Court chapel had 'popish and superstitious pictures', later destroyed.

Among their other hobbies, Charles and Henrietta were eager gardeners – though neither picked up a spade. But they were both keenly interested in the visual and its symbolic possibilities. The garden, for the Renaissance, was not just an extra room, but an extra theatre, the setting for masques, balls and parties. But it was also a place to be alone and melancholy. It symbolized aristocratic ownership and control of the earth and its fruits. Like other visual arts, garden fashion was changing. As portraits became more realistic, gardens assumed a new and striking formality: mannerist gardens, with grottoes and water-works, gave way to the new French-style gardens, which were all about geometry and precision, and acres of gravel on which no plant dared spread unruly roots. André Mollet, a French designer whose ideas prefigured Le Nôtre's Versailles, created gardens at St James's and at Wimbledon House for Charles and Henrietta. It was not for nothing that this style became associated with the absolutism of the Bourbon kings, and Louis XIV in particular. Such baroque planting in masses seemed richly symbolic of the ordered world of obedient and grateful subjects beyond the garden gates. It symbolized their mastery over the realm; every little dianthus, in a row, identical, massed, smiling. No weeds.

But Charles and Henrietta were not just buyers of pictures and makers of gardens. They wanted to be great patrons, like the Medici. One of the first seriously talented artists that Charles managed to lure to England was Orazio Gentileschi, now best-known as the father of Caravaggio's most brilliant follower, Artemisia Gentileschi. Orazio arrived in England in October 1626, perhaps as part of the entourage of Henrietta's favourite Bassompierre. He came to England directly from the court of Marie de Medici. Orazio was so much Henrietta's painter that he was buried beneath the floor of her chapel at Somerset House when he died, an entitlement extended to all the queen's Catholic servants. She may have liked him because, like her beloved husband, he always wore the sober, elegant black of the melancholy intellectual. He was also small and slight, like Charles.

His greatest commission was probably Henrietta's own idea; nine huge panels for the ceiling of the Queen's House at Greenwich. Greenwich itself, referred to as 'some curious device of Inigo Jones's', was also called 'the House of Delight'. The house was elegant, smooth, very feminine – seventeenth-century minimalism, but with curves, with grace. The paintings added colour and fire. The white-and-gold ceiling was augmented with the brilliant colours of a sequence that was to be called *Allegory of Peace and the Arts under an English Crown*. The so-called tulip staircase is a misnomer, but a felicitous one, since it conveys the long elegant lines of the curling flights. And like the tulip craze, the palace's glory was shortlived, for its mistress did not enjoy it for long. Its post-war fate was to become a prison for Dutch seamen, a victim of Parliament's iconoclasm.

In the seventeenth century, artists often worked with family members; in acquiring Orazio's services, Charles and Henrietta also gained those of his brilliant daughter. Artemisia almost certainly helped her father with the sequence, while the plague raged through London and the armies gathered reluctantly for the Bishops' Wars. Orazio's two sons played a crucial role in Charles's activities as a collector, going to the Continent to advise King's Musician Nicholas Lanier when he was negotiating to buy the Duke of Mantua's collection, the biggest single picture purchase by an English sovereign. Lanier also bought Caravaggio's astounding and magnificent *Death of the Virgin* for Charles secretly in Venice. And the melancholy, artistic Richard Symonds suggests a closer relationship between these two exceptionally talented royal servants; in describing Lanier, Symonds calls him '*inamorato di Artemisia Gentileschi: che pingera bene*' (lover of Artemisia Gentileschi, that good painter) while Theodore Turquet de Megerne says Nicholas Lanier knew artistic techniques that were Gentileschi family secrets; they could have met in Rome or Venice, via Artemisia's brothers. If so, this was an affair between two of the most talented people at Charles and

Henrietta's court. However the country felt about them, the king and queen had created a world in which such talent could flourish, and find an echo in the mind of another.

And the royal couple could be influenced by this cultural world of their own making. Artemisia says something in one of her letters that is very reminiscent of remarks Henrietta makes about herself during the war: 'You will find that I have the soul of Caesar in a woman's heart' (13 November 1649). Henrietta was to call herself a she-*generalissima* in similar fashion.

Other schemes came to nothing. Henrietta had ordered a Bacchus and Ariadne from one of her favourite artists, Guido Reni of Bologna, whose *Labours of Hercules* was one of the paintings Charles had acquired from the Duke of Mantua. It was never sent to London because Cardinal Barberini thought it too lascivious. A cut-price deal was done to ornament the withdrawing room with twenty-two paintings by Jacob Jordaens, a pupil of Rubens, bound to charge much less than the master himself. Balthasar Gerbier tried to get the job for Rubens, promising that the master would not seek to represent drunken-headed imaginary gods, but that he was 'the gentlest in his representations'. Nonetheless, the royal couple chose the cheaper pupil, with instructions not to tell Jordaens who the clients were, in case he raised his price. He was also firmly told to make his women 'as beautiful as may be, the figures gracious and svelte'. Gerbier kept on pushing to get the commission for Rubens, but on 23 May, he had to report the failure of his hopes with Rubens' death. Eight of Jordaens's paintings were duly executed; like many another artist in the service of Charles and Henrietta, he saw only a small portion of his promised fee, £100 of £680.

The might of the court, its self-absorption and glory, is best glimpsed in the way it displayed its own world to itself. The court masque was like a mirror, gleaming, shining. It was also like an insanely elaborate production of *A Midsummer Night's Dream* at a well-endowed school; big sets, but amateur actors.

Shrovetide 1630 was a festivity from the seventh Sunday before Easter till the following Tuesday (now called Shrove or Pancake Tuesday). The idea was to eat up all the meat, eggs, cheese and other foods forbidden in Lent. But Shrove also meant shriving or confession of sins, and the gift of absolution from them. The godly didn't like it much; it was 'a day of great gluttony, surfeiting and drunkenness', thought one godly minister, and it was also a day for football and cockfights. In choosing it for her first big masque, called *Chloridia*, and telling the story depicted in Botticelli's *Primavera*, Henrietta was trying to tame festivity, to make it her own, and to combine fun with the shriving of sin, with redemption. The masque's preface recorded the splendour of the event:

> The celebration of some Rites, done to the Goddess Chloris, who in a general counsel of the Gods, was proclaimed Goddess of the flowers, according to that of Ovid, in the *Fasti*. The Curtain being drawn up, the Scene is discovered, consisting of pleasant hills, planted with young trees, and all the lower banks adorned with flowers. And from some hollow parts of those Hills, Fountains come gliding down, which, in the far-off Land-shape, seemed all to be converted to a River. Over all, a serene sky, with transparent cloudes, giving a great lustre to the whole work, which did imitate the pleasant Spring. When the spectators had enough fed their eyes, with the delights of the Scene, in a part of the air, a bright Cloud begins to break forth; and in it is sitting a plump Boy, in a changeable garment, richly adorned, representing the mild Zephyrus. On the other side of the Scene, in a purplish Cloud, appeareth the Spring, a beautiful Maid, her upper garment green, under it, a white robe wrought with flowers.

The resemblance to a mythological painting by an Italian or Flemish master is clear. Inigo Jones, the creator of its visual aspects, carefully borrowed books about continental wedding pageants from the Cotton library. He suggested a costume for Henrietta herself, 'several fresh greens mixed with gold and silver will be most proper'. This was Ben Jonson's last court masque, and he made the most of it. Attendance was by invitation, and those not among the called and chosen had little hope of getting in; boxes were overflowing with richly dressed ladies as it was. They wore shockingly low-cut dresses, too, thought the Venetian embassy chaplain: 'those who are plump and buxom show their bosoms very openly, and the lean go muffled to the throat'. There were feathers, and jewels, and brightly coloured dresses. One of the scantily-clad dancers was Lucy Hay. The masque began at about 6 p.m., and afterwards the king attended a special buffet supper for the cast. At the end of the evening the supper table would be ceremoniously overthrown amidst the sound of breaking glass, so dear to the upper classes, as a kind of violent variant of James Hay's double feasts.

Charles and Henrietta were good at the visual, and they also had in Nicholas Lanier a fine musician. Their pet poets were less distinguished. Here is William Davenant: 'How had you walked in mists of sea-coal smoke,/ Such as your ever-teeming wives would choke/ (False sons of thrift!) did not her beauteous light/ Dispel your clouds and quicken your dull sight?'

Shakespeare it isn't, but it is fascinating testimony to the returning traveller's first impression of London; coal fires – whoever you were. Coal, and its black dust, linked Henrietta and Lucy to Anna Trapnel's Stepney.

And Lucy Hay, too, had to instruct her maids to get the coal dust off the new upholstery. The first years of Lucy's marriage were difficult. She fell ill, so seriously that she nearly died, and perhaps as a result of this illness, she suffered the tragic stillbirth of the only baby she would ever carry. Having married a man with no money of his own, dependent on the king for favours, Lucy was in an oddly vulnerable position. She and her husband needed her efforts to survive James I's death in 1625 without loss of position. And they had a tremendous stroke of luck early in the new reign. Exasperated with Henrietta Maria's French ladies-in-waiting, Charles literally threw them out on 7 August 1626. James Hay may have been among those who urged this; Buckingham certainly was. The list of replacements included Lucy. But Henrietta didn't want her – hers was the name which made the young queen balk.

It is easy to understand the queen's difficulties. Henrietta was young, and rather daunted by England and the English court. Lucy was beautiful and clever and seems to have struck every man who met her as a kind of goddess. What queen consort in her senses would want her footsteps dogged day and night by somebody so very desirable, so charismatic? Henrietta wanted to lead; she didn't want to follow. And Lucy's sexual reputation had begun its nosedive. It was widely assumed that she was the mistress of that most glittering, most hated upstart of all, the Duke of Buckingham, and that Hay and Buckingham both hoped to use her to gain power over the young queen. Henrietta was quite intelligent enough to resent this. And she hated Buckingham, and detested his power over her husband.

Her mixed feelings about Lucy might have had another, darker cause. It may be that James Hay and Buckingham were both hoping that Charles might become infatuated with Lucy, that they might be able to control the king through his mistresses. This was not a stupid idea: the strategy was to pay rich dividends with Charles's son, after all. And even the rumour cannot have endeared Lucy to the young, insecure queen, who believed passionately in marital fidelity.

And how might Lucy have felt about these plans? The self-willed girl, who chose her own husband? Perhaps the sense of being used and ordered in and out of bed bred a curious solidarity between Lucy and the queen, since in these unpromising circumstances Lucy somehow triumphed. By the summer of 1628, she had become Henrietta's best friend and closest lady-in-waiting. As James Hay had taught her, she used dinners and entertainments: Bassompierre, the French ambassador, reported on Lucy's cosy supper parties 'in extreme privacy, rarely used in England, and caused a great stir, since the Queen rarely associates with her subjects at small supper gatherings'. This was high fashion, exciting, vivid, very faintly transgressive. It was women-only, too. Bassompierre noted that the king 'once found himself in these little festivities ... but behaved with a gravity which spoiled the conversation, because his humour is not inclined to this sort of debauche'. The kind of games which may have been played are exemplified by Lucy's doglike and ambitious follower Sir Tobie Mathew, who wrote a character of her; it can be read as nauseatingly fulsome or very double-tongued indeed. Those who saw it as flattery agreed that it was 'a ridiculous piece'. In his character, Mathew praises her ability to turn aside her followers' wooing by seeming not to understand them. What Lucy liked was the idea of love, love as a game: a solemn Platonic game, yes, but one that could at any moment be deflated by sharp satire.

It was typical of Lucy that she could bring triumph even out of the disaster of serious and disfiguring illness. When she developed smallpox in the hot summer of 1628, it coincided very neatly with the death of the Duke of Buckingham, who had come to be James Hay's rival and enemy. Buckingham's death left an enormous gap at the very centre of

power, a gap which James and Lucy Hay raced to fill. Everyone wrote
to James, who was in Venice, urging him to return to England at once,
even urging Lucy's illness as a good excuse. In fact, though, James was
both too late and not needed. The person who stepped into Buckingham's position of power and influence over Charles was in fact his
queen, Henrietta. And Lucy had assiduously cultivated her. Henrietta
loved Lucy so much that she could hardly be restrained from nursing
her personally. When Lucy began to recover, Henrietta rushed to her
side.

But despite these glowing moments, the relationship had its ups
and downs. Tobie Mathew could report in March 1630 that Lucy and
Henrietta were not as close as before, and by November William, Lord
Powys could inform Henry Vane that Lucy was back in full favour
again. The problem sometimes seemed to be that Lucy was not very
good at being a courtier: her natural dominance sometimes over-
powered her political instincts. Powys remarked that 'she is become a
pretty diligent waiter, but how long the humour will last in that course
I know not'. And although she and Henrietta had much in common,
they were very different in inclination and temperament. Lucy's rather
Jacobean liking for fun, frivolity and parties was not altogether shared
by Henrietta, who liked her parties too, but preferred them to have
serious moral themes. When another of Henrietta's advisers lamented
that the wicked Lucy was teaching the queen to use makeup, he was
complaining that she brought some Jacobean dissoluteness to the prim-
ness of the new court. Henrietta had moods in which she found this
fun, and moods in which it made her feel shamed and guilty, particularly since Lucy could not share the great passion of her life, her Roman
Catholic religious zeal. Finally, as Tobie Mathew remarked, Lucy was
really a man's woman: 'She more willingly allows of the conversation
of men, than of Women; yet, when she is amongst those of her own
sex, her discourse is of Fashions and Dressings, which she hath ever so
perfect upon herself, as she likewise teaches it by seeing her.'

She liked admiration and she also liked politics and intrigue. Her
main interest in Henrietta was almost certainly centred on the access
the queen gave her to her own powerful court faction, and Henrietta,
like anyone, may sometimes have resented the fact that she was never
liked for herself. And both women were locked in the competition that

court society imposed on them, an unspoken, deadly scramble for notice, importance, power, access, which neither could ever truly win. Henrietta was always ahead because of her position, but like most people, wanted to be loved for her own qualities, and there Lucy could outdo her in wit, charm and beauty. It was easier for Henrietta to blame Lucy for her occasional eclipse than to question why her husband's nobles so resented her influence; it was easier for Lucy to triumph over and rival Henrietta than to ask herself why her role in affairs always had to be a minor one.

Lucy and Henrietta were also frustrated because no one really took them seriously. They were both encased in a role which compelled them to be sweet and wise and self-controlled in public. Though women were often seen as emotionally and sexually uncontrolled, *behaving* that way led to social ostracism. They were not allowed to display or even to have feelings of competitiveness, anger, and frustration, which meant that those feelings raged unexpressed and unchecked. Composing *bons mots* of detraction, laughing at adorers, and slighting each other gave those feelings temporary release. What they both truly wanted was to have an impact on policy.

So, late in the 1620s, Lucy was a trifle bored. It all seemed so easy. At first the new monarchy of Charles I appeared a little dull and straitlaced: 'If you saw how little gallantry there is at court,' Lucy complained, 'you would believe that it were no great adventure to come thither after having the small pox, for it is most desolate and I have no great desire to return.' But this is the carelessness of success. A 1628 painting shows her translated to the centre of feminine power at court, transformed by masque costume into a goddess. The Duke of Buckingham, as Mercury, leads a procession of the arts to the king and queen, Apollo and Diana; the countess can be seen directly behind the queen's shoulder, handily placed for whispering in her ear. Such allegorical names could be codewords, too; the countess's brother-in-law referred to himself as Apollo, Walter Montagu as Leicester (a name that hinted at his role as the queen's favourite, and perhaps implied something about their relationship). Lucy sponsored a performance called *The Masque of Amazons*, and danced in other masques. She was on top of her own small world.

But then it all fell apart. For reasons about which we can only speculate, Lucy declined a personal invitation to dance in William Davenant's *The Temple of Love*, in 1634. And she never danced again in a court masque. Her absence from court was also noted by Viscount Conway in 1634: 'now and a long time she hath not been at Whitehall, as she was wont to be, which is as when you left her: But she is not now in the Masque. I think they were afraid to ask and be refused . . . What the Words [quarrel] were, I know not, but I conceive they were spoken on the queen's side, where there will never be perfect friendship. For my Lady of Carlisle . . . will not suffer herself to be beloved but of those that are her servants.' Conway's diagnosis was that Lucy was spoiled, could not bear to play second fiddle to the queen any longer, but it's notable that he attributes the final unforgivable words to Henrietta.

While James Hay was accomplishing his gorgeous dash through Europe, Lucy was pursuing her own interests with equal vim and excess. With her customary adaptability and nose for fashion, she picked up from France the one role that would allow a woman in her position exactly the kind of power that her father had declared to be impossible. She was a *salonnière*, which meant something more than an influential hostess. A *salonnière* was a woman who was married or widowed, beautiful, sought-after, enormously literate and well-informed, fun to talk to, and interested in politics. Her salon consisted of her followers, chosen (like guests at a dinner party) with both business and pleasure in mind – a mix of poets and politicians. These followers played a half-joking, half-serious amorous game, presenting themselves as devoted to their lady, writing sonnets and letters to her, composing love games for her. Yet the focus was on wit and skill rather than merely on sex; the game of courtship provided a thrilling occasion for exercising power and talent. In particular, the goal was to find new ways of praising the *salonnière* herself – and new extremes of praise, too. So when Edmund Waller assured Lucy that in her presence all men 'ambition lose, and have no other scope,/ Save Carlisle's favour, to employ their hope', William Cartwright could trump him by telling Lucy that any jewels she wore could only darken her lustre. And it was not only professional poets, perhaps hungry for advancement, who wrote. Courtiers and nobles addressed verse to her too. The Earl of Holland wrote love poems. Lucy's sister Dorothy thought they were awful, 'he is more her slave than ever creature was', she wrote disgust-edly, 'many verses he hath lately writ to her, which are the worst that ever were seen'.

But then, Dorothy was biased. Like Lucy, Dorothy was ambitious and intelligent, but unlike Lucy she was married to a quiet, mild-mannered nobleman with strong principles, a member of the Sidney family with little interest in making a place for himself at the centre of the Caroline court. That did not stop Dorothy intriguing for him night and day, though. Her letters to and about Lucy burn with a frustrated ambition that allows us to see how galling it must have been for other women to witness Lucy's success. But she was admired by men. Perhaps her effect was most eloquently summarized by the ageing Earl of Exeter:

> The night is the mother of dreams and phantoms, the winter is the mother of the night, all this mingled with my infirmities have protracted this homage so due and so vowed to your ladyship, lest the fume and vapours so arising should contami-nate my so sacred and pure intention. But much more pleasure it were to me to perform this duty in your lodgings at Court when you see your perfections in the glass adding perfection to perfection approving the *bon mots* spoken in your presence, moderating the excess of compliments, passing over a dull guest, without a sweet smile, giving a wise answer to an extravagant question . . . Were I young again, I should be a most humble suitor.

It sounds idyllic. But for her critics, and for the critics of salons and their female patrons in general, the salon was a nightmarish space full of horribly spoiled women whose caprices could unfairly influence national policy.

For a while, Lucy did not care, and could afford not to. But the game of love toyed with the deadly serious game that Lucy and James were also playing: advancement. For James Hay, whose power had been based on James I's favour, the transition to Charles's reign was a struggle, and though he kept his hand in, he was never quite so central again. Charles made him Governor of the Caribbees in 1627, and a Gentleman of the Bedchamber in 1633. But he died relatively young, on 20 April 1636, when he was only fifty-six, and he did it, like everything else, with character and in style. 'When the most able physicians and his own weakness had passed a judgement that he could not live many days, he did not forbear his entertainment, but made divers brave clothes, as he said, to out-face naked and despicable death withal.' It was a gallant remark, but one that showed James Hay's limitations. Even facing death, his mind ran along its usual graceful, frivolous paths.

Next time, Lucy would look for someone more serious. Just as she had altered her world spectacularly by marrying James, so she would seek out extreme change again and again. James's death left her a rich, young and beautiful widow, perhaps the ideal position for a woman in the seventeenth century who wanted both power and a good time. No patriarchs and no mental limits would stop her now. And perhaps having had a husband of glorious frivolity is precisely why she then sought seriousness, and sought it before the now-ailing James had died. Political power for Lucy was to come next through Henry Rich, Earl of Holland, one of her most self-abasing followers, but also one of the shrewdest and least disinterested. Holland was an eager member of a faction which included Lucy's brother the Earl of Northumberland, which argued passionately for a French alliance and for movement against the rising power of the Hapsburgs. Henrietta Maria often supported this faction. It was anti-Spanish, bursting with military ambition and rather reminiscent of the Earl of Essex and his followers during the reign of Elizabeth in its dash and impracticality.

Seriousness led to seriousness. She had had troops of frivolous followers, but when Lucy fell in love again, it was not with a gallant cavalier. The man who caught her eye was like her father and her husband in that he was powerful, mobile, and ambitious. But Thomas Wentworth, later Earl of Strafford, was utterly unlike the easygoing and high-living James Hay. He wasn't content with a life of pleasure, as Hay had been. He wanted to rule, and Lucy was a vital part of his political plans.

Wentworth's ambitions had changed radically in the course of his lifetime. He had begun as an ardent defender of Parliament's 'ancient and undoubted right', and in 1627 had eagerly gone to gaol for refusing to pay the Forced Loan. But he always opposed the godly, and attempts to control the king, and these considerations led him to change sides abruptly, a *volte face* which led directly to a barony and elevation to the Privy Council. Victorian historian Thomas Macaulay commented that he was the first Englishman to whom a peerage was 'a baptism into the community of corruption'. Part of the loathing he aroused in contemporaries was caused by dislike of the opportunist turncoat. But he may have sincerely believed that in the all-too-evident split between the king and Parliament, it was the king who was ruling the country. Lucy was part of his plan to ingratiate himself thoroughly with the court.

Wentworth knew the language he should use to approach someone like Lucy, the fashionable vocabulary of literary Platonism, on which he was drafting a short dissertation designed to please the ladies. In a letter to Viscount Conway, as early as March 1635, Wentworth wrote: 'I admire and honour her, whatever her position be at court. You might tell her sometimes when she looks at herself at night in the glass, that I have the ambition to be one of those servants she will suffer to honour her . . . a nobler or a more intelligent friendship did I never meet with in my life.' As a result of drawing the most powerful courtier in Britain into her net, Lucy was confirmed as a source of power – frightening but indispensable. Like a rich relation, she had to be concili-ated and placated. And it went straight to her head – to Wentworth's, too. For him, Lucy was a kind of trophy, a sign that he had made it, to the very top of the world. They exchanged portraits, full-sized ones by Van Dyck; Wentworth could literally hang Lucy on his wall.

But for Lucy it was all part of a pathway to a sterner, fiercer kind of love, the love of God. For she became, and ardently remained, a Presbyterian, an adherent of the Scottish Kirk, one of those who longed to see the achievements of the Scots repeated in the English Church. Perhaps Wentworth had told her stories about Ireland, or possibly she was intimidated by the tight knot of Catholics around Henrietta. Per-haps attaching herself to Wentworth, who was rather Godlike in his own estimation, helped form her views. She was as partisan, as militant, as Anna Trapnel on behalf of God. She never became fanatical – at the end of her life she could still tell ribald jokes about godly Scots – but she was serious. And she was also very practical. Her new admirer could help her protect her property in Ireland from the papists. Women like Lucy used their power to keep their estates intact.

So the streets of London in the late 1630s threaded through radically different worlds. They were stitched together by trade. A piece of silk might have known a wider London than any of those who wore it, for the silk would have come into the country through Poplar docks, new home of the East India Company. Unloaded on a wharf, surrounded by spices and scents from the East, it was also thrown about by hard-working navvies who lived in the sprawling, brawling East End, which was *terra incognita* to the West End that it served. Luxury passed by the life of a poor girl like Anna Trapnel, but did not settle in her hard world. Yet her London was linked to the brighter London of Lucy Hay through a finely spun skein of silk, and both women would be affected by the war.

IV

The Bishops' Wars,
the Three Kingdoms, and Montrose

The immediate cause of the terrible wars wasn't class difference, or resentment of the luxury at court. The gulf between dismal shipyard conditions and the exceptional extravagance of court masques was for the most part endured silently. What triggered the war was a prayer book. It was known as the Scottish Prayer Book, and it was an attempt by Archbishop William Laud to extend to Scotland the reforms that had made many so unhappy in England. The book in question was large, a folio. It was badly printed, with many typographical errors, and it was delayed for months in the press. But these were not the worst of its problems. It came to symbolize many things: the menace of popery, English rule in Scotland, the king's unwillingness to listen to his truest friends.

This little cause of a great war still has its posterity today. Unless you are Roman Catholic, the Lord's Prayer ends with the words 'For thine is the kingdom, the power and the glory, for ever and ever'. These final lines are William Laud's lasting memorial. As Archbishop of Canterbury, he added them to the Lord's Prayer in the new Scottish book. When Charles II created the 1662 Prayer Book, its authors borrowed heavily from Laud's Scottish Prayer Book, and retained the lines, which to this day have something of the ring of ecclesiastical monarchic absolutism.

But the addition to the Lord's Prayer was not why the Scottish Prayer Book was so disliked, though a general antipathy to set prayers rather than extempore devotions was an issue. The controversy brought to a head tensions that were already at work. The crisis reflected the unstable situation between the three kingdoms of England, Ireland and Scotland. It exposed deep fissures and incongruities which were already present. It would be an exaggeration to call them festering grievances. The badly printed book acted as a wake-up call. People suddenly stubbed their toes on differences which they had once been unwilling to see. Charles wanted to extend his father's policy and attempt uniformity of religion between the kingdoms. He wanted order and obedience. He was announcing that he and not the Scots was in charge of the Kirk. And that could not be borne.

Charles's intentions and personality mattered terribly because all that tied Scotland to England was the bare person of the king. James I had tried to unite England and Scotland in more than himself, but had met with ferocious opposition from both sides. The English didn't want smart Scots on the make like James Hay influencing affairs in London. The Scots didn't want to disappear into the identity of their richer, more populous, more powerful neighbour. Their unease was exacerbated when James died and was replaced by his son Charles. Charles sounded much more English than James had, despite having been born in Scotland. The Scots suddenly felt they were being ruled by a king from another country; James, after all, had been their king first.

James had, in fact, been especially the nobles' king. The Scottish nobility knew all about managing the power of a monarch with worrying ideas in matters of religion. They had managed to carry out a Protestant reformation in 1560, against the wishes of their ruler, the Queen Mother, who had been acting as regent for her daughter Mary Queen of Scots while she reigned as Queen of France. Then, in 1567, they had replaced Mary Queen of Scots, the recalcitrantly Catholic monarch, with her newborn son. Of course they had never meant to do away with monarchy itself, only with popery. But they were practised in putting God first and the monarch resolutely second.

But though the nobles had felt James was theirs, they saw that he was lost to them when he went south in 1603 to govern England. The court vanished from Edinburgh, and the Scottish nobility no longer had access to the person of the king. James only revisited Scotland once in his entire reign, so he came to see English ways as natural. This trend intensified under Charles, so that by 1638, the English thought of the king as theirs, with Scotland as a kind of allotment that he might visit and farm in his off-hours, or a small estate, best left to second sons. England's arrogance in this was founded in its undoubted economic superiority; it was richer by far, had almost twice the population of Scotland, Wales and Ireland put together, and had the largest city in Western Europe as its capital.

Ironically, the identity of the Scottish nobility was not only compromised by their absentee landlord, but by their own Anglicization. The Scottish nobility began to demand deference from inferiors in a way that had never before been customary. They also expected a king to require less deference from them than the English norm. The trouble was that Charles failed utterly to convince them that he valued them. A slew of administrative reforms flew past their heads, and Charles did not even make a pretence of consultation. In a world of honour, that stung. The result was that Charles had few friends or allies among the Scottish Lowland nobles.

Through its earlier civil war over Mary Queen of Scots, Scotland came to define itself in terms of religion. It needed a unifying factor, for Scotland was as ethnically split as Ireland. The Lowlands spoke Anglo-Scots, and the Highlands spoke Gaelic. The Lowlands thought the Highlands barbarous, almost like the Irish; after all, they both spoke Gaelic, and the Highlanders were violent thieves in Lowlanders' eyes. The Highlanders thought the Lowland Scots were usurping foreigners who had pushed the Gaels out of the fertile lands. Finally, Highland chiefs liked to ignore the Crown as much as possible, while Lowland chiefs tried to be involved in decision-making and government. But religious differences, though fierce, were less stark. The Lowlands, or the 'radical south-west', was passionately godly, vehemently Presbyterian, but Aberdeen was Episcopalian. Many Highlanders were nominally Catholic, but the Campbells were eagerly Protestant; in fact, despite being Highlanders, the Campbell Lords of Argyll tended to think like Lowlanders, keen to 'civilize' the Highlands.

The Scottish Church was itself a jumble. It had been a Presbyterian, Calvinist Kirk, with strict Church courts imposing tough moral discipline, presided over by ministers and lay elders. James had managed to bolt an episcopate onto it, and while some of its members remained unenthusiastic, the uneasy Jacobean status quo was grudgingly accepted. This disgruntled compromise was symbolized by the Five Articles of Perth, of 1618, which attached to the Kirk such Anglican matters as holy days, confirmation by bishops, kneeling at communion, private baptism, and private communion. But they were often not obeyed by those for whom they stuck in the throat as popish, and at first Charles seemed happy to tolerate this.

It was when it became evident that Charles and Laud hoped to make the Church of England and the Kirk as close to identical as possible that the Kirk grew restive. A small radical party was created within the Kirk just as a godly party formed within the Church of England. Most of the very godliest Scots went to Ulster, to preach there. But some stayed behind because they felt that the Kirk was still God's chosen church. One godly minister, Samuel Rutherford of Kircudbrightshire, wrote of the Kirk as his 'whorish mother', or 'harlot mother'. She might be corrupt, but she still belonged to him.

To understand the Scots, one must understand the way the Kirk fostered a certain idea of collective identity, generating a powerful sense of sin, and then alleviating it with penitence. The Stool of Repentance was a wooden seat, often a kind of step-stool with different levels for different crimes. It stood immediately in front of the pulpit, elevated to where everyone could see it. Those deemed immoral by the Church courts had to sit on it while a sermon was preached. The connection between the trembling example of sin before the eyes of the congregation and the words of the preacher was what made this punishment different from most English methods, in which the sinner was generally displayed by the church door rather than inside the building. In Scotland, words and spectacle were welded together into a single great theatrical event. To emphasize this, the sinner then made a speech of repentance. It was important to cry, and sound truly sorry. If the congregation was convinced, the sinner would be welcomed back into the community with kisses and handclasps; if not, there would be more of the same. Some 'sinners' embraced the drama, and revelled in the opportunity to tell everyone exactly how wicked they had been. The congregation, too, was knitted together by their shared emotions of revulsion and joy at repentance. The ritual created a community which reacted to divisions and differences sternly, with horror and violence.

The Kirk's idea of community became central to Scotland's sense of its national destiny. To reinforce this ideal, the Eucharist was extended into a great festival of togetherness, with everyone sitting at long tables, passing bread and wine, and then listening to very, very long sermons. Advisers tried their best to warn Charles that he couldn't impose the English Prayer Book on Scotland from the first moment they knew a new liturgy was coming. So Charles and Laud listened, and tried to incorporate changes that they hoped would appease the Scots. But their efforts failed to quell rising alarm, which was further spread by the new canons imposed in 1636. These ruled out extempore prayer and insisted that ministers be allowed to preach only in their own locale. Wild rumours circulated in Edinburgh that the new liturgy was going to reappoint abbots to the old monasteries and offer them seats in the Scottish Parliament. Even some Scottish Catholics began to believe the king was gradually restoring the Roman Church. These rumours fomented existing opposition within the Kirk. Implicit in Kirk identity was the idea that Scotland was the chosen Nation of God, the true Israel. Just as the Israelites had suffered enslavement and imprisonment at the hands of tyrants, but had triumphed through the might of God, so they too would succeed through God's power. Their views were given a darkly frightening context by the outbreak of the Thirty Years War in Europe, which pitted Catholic against Protestant. For Protestants, it was the beginning of the struggle against Antichrist, encouraging them to see the fight against Rome as a fight between Good and Evil.

The crunch came in October 1636, when the Scottish Privy Council was ordered to issue a proclamation commanding the use of the new prayer book. By that time, the opposition was ready. The alarm generated by the whole affair was now at a level where some of the Kirk members would not have accepted a prayer book handed down by Moses from Mount Sinai. Accordingly, in April 1637, one of the Kirk's most godly spokesmen, Alexander Henderson of Leuchars, met in secret with a group of Edinburgh matrons, who agreed to lead the protest when the prayer book was first used. Women may have been chosen because it was hoped that they would not be punished savagely.

The prayer book's supporters tried to be ready, too. Those willing to use it decided to begin at the same time, hoping to divide the opposition and to show solidarity. So on the morning of Sunday 23 July 1637, 'that black doleful Sunday to the Kirk and the Kingdom of Scotland', said Presbyterian Archibald Johnston, the two Scottish archbishops, and eight or nine bishops, assembled in St Giles Church Edinburgh, and the dean began to read. Johnston of Warriston was a zealous lawyer who became a Scots commissioner. He deposited his diary in Edinburgh Castle for safekeeping, believing he was living in momentous times, like an Old Testament prophet. Johnston recorded what happened: 'at the beginning thereof there rose such a tumult, such an outcrying . . . as the like was never seen in Scotland'. Women began to shout insults, 'calling them traitors, belly-gods, and deceivers'. Others 'cried Woe! Woe!' and some cried 'Sorrow, sorrow for this doleful day, that they are bringing in popery among us!' and many got to their feet and threw their wooden stools at the bishops. The atmosphere was intimidating, as one observer, minister James Gordon, reported; 'There was a gentleman who standing behind a pew and answering Amen to what the Dean was reading, a she-Zealot hearing him starts up in choler, traitor, says she, does thou say Mass at my ear, and with that struck him on the face with her Bible in great agitation and fury.'

Seeing that the crowd was inattentive, the bishop abandoned his attempt to read from the prayer book, and preached a sermon instead. Some of the most violent protesters had already left, but they hung around outside, making a racket, and finally throwing stones at the bishop when he tried to leave. Other bishops and clerics were also attacked by groups of Edinburgh women. Johnston was pleased. 'I pray the Lord to make his own children with tears and cries to pray against the spiritual plague of Egyptian darkness covering the light of the Gospel shining in this nation', he wrote, fitting words for the man who was to be one of the leaders of resistance himself.

The women involved were described as 'rascal serving-women', and certainly those arrested were indeed servants. Other 'women' were said to be men in disguise, for, said one witness, 'they threw stools to a great length'. The opposition now gathered itself together to organize a campaign to petition the king in London. Petitions came mainly from Fife and the West, and when it began to be obvious that the king wasn't speeding to remove the hated book, many became anxious that war might ensue. The godly Presbyterians had no intention of backing down. There were more riots, and more petitions, and finally Charles responded autocratically, claiming that he had written the prayer book himself (the suppliants had claimed to believe it was the work of bishops). His touchy pride had surfaced again, but so had his wish to be loved; he offered to forgive everyone if they would only go home and do as they were told.

This offered nothing to moderates, and made the intransigent even more certain that they were doing God's work. On 23 February 1638, the nobles chose a committee of lairds, burgesses and ministers to sit with them. This committee created the Covenant. It was based on the old confession of faith signed by Charles's father James in 1581, a textual ancestry that tried to proclaim the committee's loyalty to the Stuart monarch. It vowed to uphold the true religion of the Church of Scotland, and to oppose popery and superstition. It was first signed at Greyfriars Kirk, Edinburgh, on 28 February. Read aloud by Johnston, it was signed by the assembled nobles first, then lairds. Next day three hundred ministers signed it. Then hundreds of people in Edinburgh, then thousands more as it was distributed across the nation by its original signatories.

Later, support for the Covenant came to mean resistance to tyranny, but that was an evolution. The original Covenant bound its signatories to uphold true religion and to support the king. It neglected to specify which injunction was more important if there should be a conflict between them.

The Scots invented the Covenant as a form of resistance to rule from Westminster. Those who took the oath were required to oppose the recent innovations in religion. Loyalty was reserved for a king willing to defend true Protestant religion. The Covenant was with God; if the king failed to defend the reformed tradition in the Kirk, the people were morally required to resist him because to do so was to keep faith with God. But the oath also included a declaration of allegiance and mutual association which became a definition of nationhood. Scotland, under a covenanted king, had a divine role to play in overthrowing popery and thus bringing about Christ's rule on earth. Perhaps one day every nation was to be part of the Covenant, under Scotland's leadership.

Charles still failed to act. It was becoming clear that he was not in control of the situation. Like many men with problems, his were made worse by a visit from his mother-in-law, who came for a prolonged stay in 1638. A contemporary engraving of her progress shows a sumptuous procession down a Cheapside lined with slender, pointed Jacobean gables. A brilliant patron of the arts, a flamboyant presence, a Medici to the core, Marie de Medici cut a swathe through London's crowds. Her vast entourage, which she expected Charles to support, included six coaches, hundreds of horses, monks and confessors in handfuls, peers and princesses, dwarfs and dogs. Dash was a strong point. Tact was not. She told everyone that she was hoping for Charles's conversion to the one true Church. He, so quiet, so shy, so unwilling to express public opinions, must have felt uneasy with her bounce and verve. Laud, too, had grave doubts about the boisterous Marie's impact on her daughter and so on the king. When Henrietta called for English Catholics to fast on Saturdays and to contribute the money to the army sent against the wholesomely Protestant Scots, she linked the expedition in the mind of the public with her own faction. She was also known to be contemplating a Spanish match for her daughter, who was seen attending Mass as the army marched.

In London, Charles and his advisers had begun to evolve ambitious plans for Scotland. Wentworth was determined to carry out the policies he had introduced in Ireland; he wanted an English deputy, and probably English law, too. The Scots, who had ears in the king's circle, probably got wind of this line of thinking. It made them more determined to hang on. By now, Charles was convinced that the only way to solve his problems in Scotland was by force of arms, and he spun out the negotiations only to give himself time to arm, a pattern of behaviour he was to repeat in England later.

In June 1638, Charles finally sent Hamilton to mediate with his fellow-Scots. By then the Covenanters had grown more confident, encouraged by the widespread support they had received. They asked for a free general assembly and a Parliament to make sure the prayer book could never be reintroduced. Hamilton was only there to stall the Scots until Charles could get his army moving. The Covenanters had created a new system of representation; commissioners from each shire and burgh were to form an elected body and to remain in the capital, being replaced frequently by elected substitutes. This new body was to have a different president every day, so that power was not concentrated in the hands of one man. This idealistic if slightly impractical rule suggests that tyranny was very much a preoccupation. And yet despite all this, the new assembly was window-dressing. Power remained with the strongest nobles, Rothes, Montrose and Loudoun.

On 21 November 1638, a new representative body met, this time representing the Kirk itself. This was the Glasgow Assembly. Huge numbers of people filled Glasgow Cathedral. The new body soon proved unmanageably radical. Hamilton tried to control it, with about as much success as Canute holding back the waves. Having rid itself of Hamilton, the new body began enacting a godly dream of restoring the Kirk to its glory days of full and unmixed Presbyterianism. On 4 December, the new assembly passed an act declaring the six previous Kirk assemblies unlawful, which meant that the Kirk was no longer bound by their decisions. Then on 6 December the assembly condemned Charles's prayer book and canons as replete with popish errors. On 8 December, the assembly abolished episcopacy, and on 10 December it removed the disputed Five Articles of James's reign. This brisk and decisive rate of progress resulted in a Kirk purified of compromise and popery, in less than a month. The Scots were creating God's kingdom, allowing the light of the gospels to shine.

Their decisiveness would prove an example for the English godly party from this time on. The Kirk ensured this by distributing polemics explaining the connection between the restored Kirk and the legitimacy of resisting a tyrant. One of the creators of the Covenant, Alexander Henderson, wrote that 'except we stand fast to our liberty we can look for nothing but miserable and perpetual slavery'. What he meant was liberty in religion, but the heady experience of having that liberty at Glasgow had made him determined to protect it against the prerogative of anyone who sought to take it away. The result of the prayer book crisis was therefore to join religion and political ideology stoutly together by an unbreakable chain.

It was easy to see why men like Alexander Henderson would be Covenanters. Less easy to understand is the position of Highland nobles like Argyll and Montrose. Of these two leading Highland nobles of the Civil War years, it was the ambitious, eager, warmhearted Montrose who was the first to subscribe to the Covenant. He first joined those Covenanters who sought to petition or supplicate the king in November 1637. It seems an odd decision for a Highlander. The Lowlands were suspicious of popery in part because they perceived the Gaelic lands – Ireland and the Highlands – as a hotbed of papists, and this was not altogether paranoia; there had been a significant Catholic revival among the Gaelic lands. Lowlanders also saw the Highlands as barbaric because of the growth and development of its clan structure in the sixteenth century. Later writers infatuated with the romance of old Scotland portray the clans as ancient, even paleolithic, but in fact they were largely a product of the late Middle Ages and the Renaissance. It is difficult to define what a clan was; it came to be seen as a family structure, but in Montrose's time it was a band, or bond, which could be created between equals or between those of different rank. Usually, it was faintly feudal; the clan chieftains offered protection (from other clans) in return for loyalty (fighting when summoned). The result was to set up violent rivalries across the Highlands. Each clan could increase its wealth, honour and fame only by expanding into the territory of another clan, by raiding another clan, or by plunder. The result might be just a few casualties, but it sometimes involved the massacre of whole communities, including women and children. Such bloodshed frightened and horrified Lowlanders, who were inclined to see the Highlanders as barbarians.

The Covenant flourished in an urban world of merchants, professionals and other middling men. These people were all but absent from clan Highland life. So too was the king, and central government in general. Highland chiefs were traditionally not very interested in central government, or even in the making of laws. At home, they made their own. As for the monarch, in theory Highlanders were effusive in their tributes to the Stuart kings, but in practice they recognized few real obligations to them. Highlanders also shared with their royal master King Charles a love of disguise and tricks which is especially manifest in Montrose's generalship and tactics. Montrose would be dependent, too, on men even more monoculturally clannish than he, notably the fighter Alasdair MacColla. Masking, mumming and women dressed in men's clothing doing strange midnight dances were ineradicable parts of the Highland scene, and alien to the Presbyterian Kirk.

But Montrose signed the fierce and rigid Covenant. It is entirely probable that he was swayed by two things: the excitement of the moment which fed his personal ambition, and a very reasonable wish to influence events. He came from one of the oldest and noblest families in Scotland, and held estates in Perth, Stirling and Angus; he was educated richly and fully, in France and Italy as well as Scotland. He was graceful and handsome, with cold, lucid grey eyes. He was also a fine horseman and an excellent archer. He was, said Clarendon, too apt to condemn those he did not love.

He had been at the University of St Andrews, majoring, as it were, in hunting and hawking, in archery and golfing, though he did do some studying. At the age of seventeen, Montrose was married to Magdalene Carnegie, daughter of Lord Carnegie, afterwards Earl of Southesk. In 1633, as soon as he was twenty-one, he left Scotland to travel on the Continent. He had come back to Scotland in 1636, and had been presented to the king in London, by Hamilton, who apparently told Charles that someone as beautiful and charismatic and arrogant as Montrose could only be a menace. So Charles merely extended his hand to be kissed, then turned away. Montrose was bright and proud; he got the message. It has been suggested that the slight to his honour was what impelled him to see the merits of the Covenant. But he himself later wrote:

> This our nation was reduced to almost irreparable evil by the perverse practices of these sometime pretended prelates, who having abused lawful authority did not only usurp to be lords over God's inheritance, but also intruded themselves in prime places of civil government; and by their Court of High Commission, did so abandon themselves to the prejudice of the Gospel, that the very quintessence of Popery was publicly preached by Arminians, and the life of the Gospel stolen away by enforcing on the Kirk a dead service book, the brood of the bowels of the whore of Babylon, as also to the prejudice of the country, fining and confining at their pleasure: in such sort, that trampling upon the necks of all whose conscience could not condescend to be of their own coin, none were sure of life nor estate, till it pleased God to stir up his own instruments, both in Church and policy, for preventing further, and opposing, such impiety.

For Montrose, then, Covenanting was not always an angry response to rule from Westminster; it could also be an angry response to rule from Canterbury. Montrose had been reading not only the Bible, but Foxe and Spenser, and from them he had learned about the global war against the evil Whore of Babylon, popery whether lodged in the so-called Church of England or in Rome. It was that war which he set out to fight. But he set out to fight it *as a Highlander*, and this meant to increase his own power at the expense of other Highland nobles.

He was not the only one. Archibald Campbell, Earl and later Marquess of Argyll, a Highland noble with a huge estate, much of which had been acquired from the MacDonalds by very dubious methods, similarly had an eye to the main chance. He became an ardent Covenanter because the king was willing to employ the Mac-Donalds under the Catholic Earl of Antrim to suppress the 'rebellion'. The new war of religion meant business as usual among nobles and clans who had been enemies for centuries. Meanwhile, veterans from Protestant armies on the Continent were flooding back to Scotland, forming a professional army under Alexander Leslie, who had held a senior command under Swedish Protestant King Gustavus Adolphus.

It was an age that loved plotting and feared the plotting of others, but there may have been a real conspiracy. The Scots' success at doing what some English people longed to do – rolling back the Laudian reforms – struck the English forcibly. There is some evidence of high-level contact between the king's godly opponents in all three kingdoms from the early 1630s. John Pym, the Earl of Warwick, and Lord Saye and Sele actively plotted with their natural allies among the Covenanters to force Charles to call Parliament. Contemporaries thought that the Covenanters would never have dared to rebel without friends in England. We could even think of a kind of cross-border godly culture, with exchanges of publications, and personal contacts sensibly un-marked by treasonable correspondence. Print and pamphlets allowed the godly party in England to connect the terror of Catholicism with their own godly agenda.

This meant Montrose was not alone in his dread of the pope's divisions. He believed firmly in monarchic power, too, but also thought that it must be restrained by law. He was elected to one of the 'tables', committees which also contained representatives of lairds, burghers and ministers, to monitor information which passed between the king and his council.

Opposite the Edinburgh Mercat Cross, a scaffold was erected. 'James,' said John Leslie to Montrose, 'you will not be at rest till you be lifted up there above the rest in three fathoms of rope.'

From England, it all looked very different; so much so that you could be forgiven for thinking you were reading about different events. From London, the conflict did not appear to be a war about who the Scots were, but a war about the Laudian Church. To Charles, the Scots' opposition seemed like a threat, a deliberate and mean attempt to undermine him. It was victory or death. His feelings blinded him to politics. For Charles, the Scots were out to destroy monarchy and impose a republic. 'So long as the covenant is in force,' he declared, 'I am no more in Scotland than a Duke in Venice, which I will rather die than suffer.' He spoke of 'those *traitors*, the Covenanters'. He murmured defensively that 'the blame for the consequences is theirs'. In August he ordered one of their propaganda sheets burned by the public hangman, and a few weeks later proclaimed all Scots invaders traitors whose lives were forfeit.

Charles saw the Covenanters as incomprehensible aliens, not as his familiar subjects even though he had spent his early childhood in Scotland, and may even have retained a very slight Scottish accent. Charles's warm embrace of Europe in the person of his wife, his liking for European fashion and formality in matters of court life and religion, meant that Scottish plainness struck him as boorish and threatening.

Whitehall tried to organize an army under the Earl of Essex to go to Scotland. The godly Essex's appointment was designed to reassure those who feared that the war was a campaign against the godly, since he had fought for the Dutch; however, Henrietta insisted that her ally the Earl of Holland be general of the horse. Holland was never an especially credible military leader, and his appointment convinced some that sinister forces were at work (meaning the queen). In fact Holland was part of a warmly Presbyterian faction at her court, which included Lucy Hay, but the anxiety about popery in high places refused to abate.

A slow-paced mobilization continued. Finally, at the end of March

1639, the king left, at the head of some 20,000 men, many of them notably unwilling. 'We must needs go against the Scots for not being idolatrous and will have no mass amongst them', declared an anonymous news-sheet. There was a shortage of incentives. Scotland was cold and plunder-free. The loyal, brave Sir Edmund Verney wrote to his son Ralph that 'our army is but weak. Our purse is weaker, and if we fight with these forces and early in the year we shall have our throats cut, and to delay fighting long we cannot for want of money to keep our army together.' He also commented that 'I dare say there was never so raw, so unskilful and so unwilling an army brought to fight . . . Truly here are many brave gentlemen that for point of honour must run such a hazard as truly would grieve any heart but his that does it purposely to ruin them. For mine own part I have lived till pain and trouble has made me weary of to do so, and the worst that can come shall not be unwelcome to me, but it is a pity to see what men are like to be slaughtered here, unless it shall please God to put it in the king's heart to increase his army, or stay till these know what they do, for as yet they are as like to kill their fellows as the enemy.'

Verney thought he knew who the mysterious agents behind the war were: 'The Catholics make a large contribution, as they pretend, and indeed use all the ways and means they can to set us by the ears, and I think they will not fail of their plot.' He thought that in part because Henrietta Maria was diligently trying to persuade the English Catholics to prove their loyalty to Charles with lavish donations to the war chest. She wrote individually to Catholic gentry families and especially to women. Some ladies did give up their jewellery, and peers like the Marquess of Winchester contributed four-figure sums. But a mysterious letter purporting to be from the pope urged them not to give. This may have been good advice, whoever it came from, because the main result was to make good, not especially godly men like Verney suspect that a papist plot lay behind the Scottish war. Madame de Motteville, Henrietta's friend and confidante after the war, said Henrietta had told her that Charles was indeed trying to transform Scottish religion in order eventually to restore popery. It wasn't likely, but she may have hoped it was true.

For the raggle-taggle army, it was hot and miserable on the way from Newcastle to Alnwick, thirsty and slow, and Alnwick was in a state of ruin, having been all but abandoned by the Percys for the urbanities of Syon House. The king tried to behave like a good commander. He lived under canvas with his men, he rode up and down to cheer his army, wearing out two mounts. At Berwick the rain set in.

People were, to say the least, sceptical – about the war itself, its causes, the army's chances of success. George Puryer was hauled before the Yorkshire Justices for opining 'that the soldiers were all rogues that came against the Scots, and if it had not been for the Scots thirty thousand Irish had risen all in arms, and cut all our throats, and that the king and queen was at mass together, and that he would prove it upon record, and that he is fitter to be hanged than to be a king, and that he hoped ere long that Lashlaye [David Leslie] would be a king, for he was a better man than any was in England'. This outburst aptly summarized the grievances of those unenthusiastic about the entire campaign, but there was another factor too; in fighting for the wrong side in matters of religion, the people of Stuart England feared not only that they were unjust, but that it might be a sign that they were damned, even a sign that God was deserting the nation.

The First Bishops' War amply fulfilled the worst apprehension of Verney and the nation. The king's army camped outside Berwick in May 1639, and on 3 June the Earl of Holland, too, managed to find in himself an even worse performance than the country had expected. He and his cavalry sprinted ahead of the disordered infantry. Late in a long afternoon, Holland suddenly saw his folly in leaving them behind. Eight thousand Scottish footsoldiers were closing in on him, in a wide sickle, as if his men were grass ripe for cutting. Holland halted, sensing disaster. He and the Scots gazed at each other in a deadly game of chicken. Blustering, Holland sent a trumpeter to ask for the Scots to withdraw. Leslie, the Scottish commander, sent the messenger back, with a cool request that Holland withdraw instead. Holland had his only flash of good sense for the day. He obeyed, and fled, pursued by the Scots' cries of derision. They were in fine fettle after weeks of sleeping rough and singing psalms. The English were miserable; when it wasn't raining, it was hot, and when it was hot there were midges, and what on earth were they doing here anyway?

The commanders were busy. They were not, however, busy safe-guarding the army or doing the king's bidding. Holland and Newcastle were expending their energies fighting a duel over an incident connected with the colours; colourful indeed, and full of musty rites of honour, but quite beside the point.

The king and the Scots managed a kind of peace in June 1639, signing a truce. But even while they were doing so, amicably enough, the first battle of the Civil Wars had begun, between Scot and Scot, between the Gordons, ardent supporters of the king, and the Covenanters under Montrose, at the Bridge of Dee.

The man in charge of the defence of Aberdeen had every reason to dislike Montrose, since Montrose had earlier been responsible for his captivity. Montrose had occupied the town before, on 25 May, but by then the Royalists had melted away. Montrose had marched north to besiege some local lairds, and in his absence the king's ships, captained by Aboyne, had reoccupied Aberdeen on 6 June. By then Montrose had gone south to make sure his foe was not leading another, larger force. Finding this fear to be groundless, he marched north again.

The Dee was brimful of rain, swollen and impassable. The bridge was barricaded with earth and stones. Montrose's guns pounded the bridge from the southern bank, but made no impact; the shot passed over the heads of the defenders. Some women came out with suppers for their men, a cosy domestic event which was to be repeated many times in the wars that followed. The day wore on till nightfall, with nothing done. Montrose knew delay would defeat him. He moved his guns, and next morning the bridge took a real pounding; nonetheless the defenders clung on to the north bank. So Montrose decided on a feint. He led his horse westwards, as if he meant to cross higher up. He set a trap with himself as the bait. The cannons kept up their pounding; one volley of shot took Seton of Pitmedden in the belly, cutting off his torso from his legs. Once enough defenders had been distracted into pursuing Montrose himself, the rest of the Covenanters charged the bridge, and the defenders retreated. Montrose marched into Aberdeen, refused to burn it, but allowed his troops to feast on its salmon and corn. But it was not subdued. As Montrose stood in the town centre, the man standing next to him was shot dead. The bullet was probably meant for Montrose.

For London it was calming and consoling when Charles finally returned from the Scottish wars, on 3 August 1639, but enthusiasm was damped by the fact that he arrived in his mother-in-law's carriage; symbolically this seemed to signify that he was under her thumb. The arrival of a Spanish fleet was rumoured to be an instrument for invasion of Scotland, England, or both. Ballads and newsbooks stressed the Spaniards' amazing wealth; they were said to have fired gold and silver from their cannons when they ran out of ammunition.

So in an atmosphere of fear, the stories and rumours circulated faster and faster in London and its environs. The rumpus over the prayer book was beginning to look to some ardent Protestants like the beginning of a war of Good against Evil. In June 1640, rumour tore through Woolwich and Plumstead that the high constable had searched the house of one Mrs Ratcliff, and found ten beds, still warm from their hastily-departed papist sleepers. The rumour reached the blacksmith, Timothy Scudder, in his shop at Plumstead; he passed it on to his customers, adding that he had heard that forty or fifty men had landed at Woolwich, heading for Mrs Ratcliff's home, called Burridge House. A man named Allen Churchmen was loading his cart with bricks when he saw the men too. Meanwhile the maid at Burridge House had told the wife of the victualler that there was a vault being made at the house; could the missing men from the beds be hidden in it? At the local tavern, too, workmen from the house were questioned by townspeople eager for the latest news. The story flew from person to person, lighting up the social network as it went. As more and more stories of this kind were told, panic and terror spread. Fear is a solvent of social glues.

With the Scottish question unresolved, Charles sent for someone used to pacifying unruly Celts. He summoned Thomas Wentworth.

In the late summer of 1639, Wentworth was still in Ireland, where he had done his best to galvanize the tottering Church of Ireland as an advance unit in the onward march of civilization. Wentworth had managed to impose his own ideas on Ireland, but at the cost of alienating moderate Irish opinion, a policy whose drawbacks would become self-evident very shortly indeed. He had also become very rich through the normal joys of Stuart government: selling offices, taking over customs farms. He was distinctly reluctant to answer Charles's command.

Perhaps Charles was a little afraid of this Yorkshire tough. 'Come when you will,' he wrote, with a mixture of autocracy and timidity, rather as he had once written to his elder brother, 'ye shall be welcome to your assured friend, Charles Stuart.' But Charles knew his man, perhaps informed about him by Henrietta, who in turn was briefed by Wentworth's lover and court patron Lucy Hay. Charles at once granted him the earldom Wentworth badly wanted, so that he became Earl of Strafford; he also gave him command of the army. Wentworth's plan was to use an Irish army to put down the Scots. But the situation was irretrievable. The Scots were all over Northumberland and Durham, and the English forces were the same poorly organized rabble; there was no chance of rounding them up. Wentworth kept hoping that English loathing of the Scots would galvanize them, but he underestimated the extent to which many Englishmen now felt that the Scots were their allies against enemies nearer at hand. So he was sent back to Ireland to raise money and soldiers. All this achieved was to create a panic in the already unruly troops about Catholics in their midst. Mutinies against 'popish' officers became common, and one officer was even set upon and beaten to death. Young Edmund Verney said he had to go to church three times a day to show his men that he was not Irish nor a papist.

In Ireland, there had been forty years of peace after Elizabeth I's forces had finally defeated the Gaelic leaders in 1603. James could and did claim descent from the ancient royal houses of Ireland, which further strengthened London's authority. The population expanded to around two million, and the economy grew too; there was now a small woollen industry, and some ironworks, but still to English eyes the majority of the people lived directly off the land, off bogs and forests. English-style landownership was slowly imported. Yet there were deep tensions. The largest group, three-quarters of the population, was the ethnic Irish, the Old Irish. Little has survived written by them, so it is hard to know how they saw themselves, but we do know that they were Catholic. Then there were the Old English, descendants of medieval settlers, also mainly Catholic but with a few Protestants like James Butler, Marquess of Ormond, mainly settled in the Dublin Pale, Munster and Connaught. Pushed out of high office by the Elizabethan regime to be replaced with Protestants despite their long loyalty to the Crown, they had begun to intermarry with and ally themselves to the Old Irish. The Old Irish were being pushed out, too – evicted from land their families had held for centuries by the Plantation Scheme, which took land from Irish Catholics and handed it over to Protestant settlers. Protestants knew how to farm properly – that is, in an English manner. There were 25,000 or so Scots among the settlers, because the government hoped that by encouraging this it would drive a wedge between the MacDonnells of Ulster and the McDonalds of Clan Ian Mor, both Catholic, both keen to form a single unit. Many Catholic Irish had begun to leave; some had left for foreign military service, and they were soon recruited by Spain to fight the Dutch, where they met the likes of London soldier Philip Skippon over the battlements, while Skippon in turn formed impressions of them, that they were part of a vast Catholic conspiracy to rule the world. Those who had fought against Spain in the Low Countries never forgot this.

When Wentworth had become Lord Deputy of Ireland in 1632, his job was to strengthen royal authority as much as possible. He wanted to civilize Ireland, but without spending any English money on it. He thought Ireland had had far too much English gold poured into it already; look at the fat cats among the Protestant landowners! Thus he alienated his natural allies. He planned a vast, money-raising plantation for Connaught. He also intended to put down the activities of the Presbyterian Scots in Ulster, a bunch of fanatics who stood in the way of Laudian reforms he hoped to spread. He also hated Catholics, and was determined to stop them appealing to the king for mercy over his head. There was a savage series of bad harvests and outbreaks of cattle disease in the 1630s, especially in Ulster. Soon, the only thing that everyone in Ireland could agree on was their loathing of Strafford. The Three Kingdoms were coming apart along the seams.

In the Bishops' Wars, an estimated five hundred men died. Also lost was Charles's personal rule. He had run out of money. He called Parliament on 13 April 1640, at Wentworth's urging; Wentworth needed funds to pay his troops and to equip them. He promised that he could control an English Parliament just as he had Irish Parliaments. This was empty nonsense. Moreover, Wentworth was sick with gout and eye trouble; he had to be carried about in a litter.

Charles had a plan that he believed would help control Parliament. The Scots had written a letter – with Montrose among its signatories – sometime in February 1640 which was addressed to Louis XIII, King of France. It denounced Charles's oppressive rule as the result of Spanish influence and Hapsburg power, and urged France to ally with the Scots against England. Charles was certain that Parliament would be so horrified by the letter that it would at once vote him the monies he needed to bring the renegade Scots to heel. But Parliament was not especially horrified, perhaps because better-informed members of the Commons knew that Louis's adviser Cardinal Richelieu was unlikely to want to support the Covenanters. Stolidly, the Commons insisted on bringing a long list of English grievances to Charles before it would agree to vote him the money for the Scottish wars.

To grasp the transient drama of the Short Parliament it is necessary to understand what Parliament was in the seventeenth century. Although called by the same name and occupying the same site, it was very different from the body we know today. In the first place, a seventeenth-century House of Commons was not democratically elected. MPs were almost always from a particular stratum of society, the gentry or merchant class – the number of the latter among MPs was growing, but not at any breakneck speed – and most elections were not contested; rather, the MP stood before the assembled franchise-holders and was acclaimed. Even this very feeble democratic gesture was confined to men with property, characteristically landed property. Very occasionally a woman property-holder did try to exercise the franchise, but she was usually turned away by outraged males, and generally suffrage and being an MP were entirely landed male affairs. Women, servants and labourers were no more part of it than they were part of the monarchy – less, if anything, for a female ruler was more conceivable than a female MP. Like everything else in the seventeenth-century state, the vote was unevenly distributed, so that in some urban areas maybe as many as one-third of adult men could vote, but this was an atypical peak; in rural areas suffrage could fall below 5%. Then there was the problem of the Celtic kingdoms. Although the Welsh sent representatives, the Scots and Irish did not. Finally, the Commons' powers were always bracketed by the power of the House of Lords, which represented the aristocracy and also the government of the Church of England.

Together with the monarch, the two houses were supposed to form a kind of snapshot of the nation's various social classes, but in fact the result was a portrait-bust, showing the nation only from the chest up.

Secondly, Parliament could only be summoned by the monarch, and each time this happened a different body resulted, which then sat until the monarch chose to dismiss it. Finally, monarchs tended to see Parliaments solely as a way of raising money, while legal experts such as Edward Coke saw Parliaments as much more – vehicles of complaint, guarantees of justice if the courts failed, and – most controversially – sites of ultimate sovereignty, on behalf of the whole people. In fact most Parliamentary time was spent on local issues, often of soporific triviality to everyone outside the locale in question – deepening the River Ouse, for example. Men might become MPs because of an interest in some such local issue, or more simply and far more commonly to prove their status. Because becoming an MP was such a popular way to show yourself a proper gentleman, the number of seats kept increasing. Once elected, MPs tended to race up to London for as short a time as possible, since life in the capital was expensive and they had things to do at home. Divisions (actual votes) were fairly uncommon; mostly the goal was unity, 'the sense of the house', rather as in the elections themselves, where the goal was unanimity, participation, and not choice. Nor was there a great deal of talk or debate. Most country gentlemen were unused to speechmaking; only those who had been at university or the Inns of Court had the right rhetorical training. These were the same men who were charged with maintaining law and order when they got home to their counties – JPs, deputy lieutenants, tax commissioners, commissioners of array. So there were always plenty of other things to occupy time.

Parliament was supposed to act in an ad hoc manner, to fix things that had gone wrong, like a physician. So permanent alliances were rare and parties nonexistent. Parliament was also seen as ancient, part of an older way where the Commons spoke to the king: 'We are the last monarchy in Christendom that yet retains our original rights and constitutions', thought Sir Robert Phelips proudly in 1625. The antiquity of Parliament was reflected in the site where the House of Commons met. The Royal Chapel of St Stephen was secularized at the

Reformation; before that, it had been part of Westminster Abbey, and by 1550 it had become the meeting-place of the Commons, which had previously been forced to cram itself into any old vacant committee room. The symbolism was obvious. The Commons was a true, re-deemed fount of the virtue which the Catholic Church and its denizens had failed to acquire, and hence failed to infuse into the national fabric. Secular authority elbowed out spiritual authority while borrowing its prestige. The overlap between religion and politics was clear.

The chapel was tall, two-storeyed, and had long, stained-glass windows. The members sat in the choir stalls, on the north and south walls. As the number of MPs increased inexorably, these expanded to a horseshoe shape, four rows deep, and then an additional gallery was built in 1621 to house still more seats. It was like a theatre, thought John Hooker. The Speaker's Chair replaced the altar, and his mace rested on a table which replaced the lectern. The antechapel acted as a lobby for the rare divisions; members who wished to vote aye could move out into it, while noes stayed inside. St Stephen's Chapel was the seat of the House of Commons from 1550 until it was destroyed by fire in 1834. Parliament's authority was enhanced by this spectacular setting, and from it the English developed the habit of housing important secular institutions in buildings of medieval Gothic design.

But the temple of democracy was surrounded by a den of thieves. Ben Jonson commented on how disreputable the little city of West-minster was. The Palace was surrounded by shops and taverns; it did not help the area's reputation that the three best-known taverns were called Hell, Heaven and Purgatory. Hell had several exits, to allow MPs to make a quick getaway. The area around the Palace was crowded and crammed with hawkers' stalls. Hoping to catch the eye of MPs and peers, were lobbyists; barristers, clerks, servants, messengers and other employees scurried down the many shortcuts that led from the street to the Thames, from the Commons chambers to the Lords. Printers congregated around the Palace, many specializing in printing petitions to the Commons, others documenting its activities, publicizing the Commons' just discovery of the wickedness of this man, its fairness in helping that struggling local industry. When Parliament was sitting, its 450-odd Commons members, 50–70 peers and handful of bishops created an economic powerhouse for the entire area.

Parliament also had practical functions. It was supposed to make taxes honest. Chronically short of money, the monarchy got its income from rents, court fines, and a mass of funny, quaint revenue-raisers, including customs and excise (tonnage and poundage). What made for shortage was the Europe-wide economic crisis generated by inflation; taxes didn't keep pace with the dropping value of money, and any attempt to make good the deficit by levying more of them led to political trouble. In theory, this grim scenario gave Parliament more power; any group of MPs could withhold money in exchange for concessions on whatever grievances they wanted to air. There were some Jacobean attempts at a settlement involving a fixed royal income, swapping taxes for redressed grievances, but they had always collapsed in the face of James's apparently genetic difficulty in sticking to a budget for his own spending. Charles, sensibly enough, was trying to find a way around the entire creaky machine, a way that would allow him to make the English state modern, like France and Spain, its rivals. But some of the men who felt their local authority depended on Parliament knew they could use the House of Commons to stop him, and they did so without further ado.

They were helped by the fact that the House of Commons was not static. It was changing, evolving. Increasingly, local electors had begun to expect that MPs would deliver local projects; in exchange, they would agree to taxes without too much fuss. Conversely, if pet projects evaporated, they might grow restive. And it is easy to overstate the consensuality of Jacobean Parliaments. There was the particular case of the Petition of Right, produced by the 1628 Parliament, which announced roundly that there should be no taxation without representation, no taxes without the consent of the Commons. It also decried arbitrary imprisonment. As often, these were presented as traditional rights; actually, from the king's point of view they extended Parliament's powers, clarifying what had been gratifyingly murky, and he agreed to the petition only in order to ensure supply (a term which means the provision of money). The same 1628 Parliament, gratified, grew more and more determined to ensure the safety of Protestantism; indeed, its MPs felt they had been chosen for this very purpose. Amidst scenes of unprecedented passion, in which the Speaker was physically prevented from rising by Denzil Holles, who pinned him in his chair, the House condemned Arminians and the collectors and payers of tonnage and poundage as enemies of England, and deserving of death. What followed was dissolution, but the tantrum had its effect. Charles felt sure Parliament was a kind of rabble. It was its behaviour that made him grimly determined never to call one again. And when he did, having avoided doing so for twelve years, it turned out that its ideas had not changed.

Parliament met on 13 April 1640. At once it became apparent that little had changed since 1629; if anything the members were more anxious, more discontented, and more determined to be heard by the king. The personnel were different – one of the reasons for John Pym's prominence was that virtually all his seniors had died in the long interval of personal rule – but their concerns remained the same. The stories of two MPs illustrate how Parliament came to be so intransigent. A member of the old guard from 1628, William Strode was well-known already for his radical activities in that year. Strode had played a major part in resisting the Speaker's efforts to adjourn the House. He explained that 'I desire the same, that we may not be turned off like scattered sheep, as we were at the end of the last session, and have a scorn put on us in print; but that we may leave something behind us'.

Summoned next day to be examined by the Privy Council, Strode refused to appear, and was arrested in the country, spending some time in the Tower after he had doggedly refused bail linked to a good-behaviour bond. He was still in gaol in January 1640, when he was finally released. This was supposed to be a reconciling, peacemaking move. In fact, he was a kind of living martyr for the Good Old Cause before it was properly formed. He was not a maker of policy, but he was exceedingly bitter against Charles. Clarendon calls him 'one of the fiercest men of the party', and MP Simonds D'Ewes describes him as a 'firebrand', a 'notable profaner of the scriptures', and one with 'too hot a tongue'. Strode was also animated by the same sense of godly mission that was motivating the Covenanters themselves. Like their wilder spirits, he was fervently anti-episcopal. It was these godly views that led him to assert Parliamentary authority over prerogatives, the guarantee of religious rectitude and a bulwark against the crafts of popery.

One of the new MPs was Henry Marten, who was joining his father as an MP for a Berkshire seat dominated by the county town of

Abingdon, later to become a godly stronghold during the war. He had already refused to contribute to a new Forced Loan to fund the Scottish wars. Marten was not, however, an obvious or orthodox member of the godly faction led by John Pym and his allies. Indeed, Marten was widely known as a rake and a rascal. Seventeenth-century biographer John Aubrey called him 'a great lover of pretty girls', and he had been rebuked for it by the king himself, who called him 'ugly rascal' and 'whore-master'. Aubrey claims Marten never forgot the insult, and it may have been this which made him different from his much more moderate father and brother-in-law. Marten emerged quickly as a radical voice and was to develop a career as a key man on committees later, but during the Short Parliament he was not an obvious leader. He was, however, one of many MPs who were determined to assert the Commons' 'ancient rights' and restrain the king's attempts to diminish them. He played no role; he made no speeches. But he was there, and his later career shows that he was convinced. The calling of the Short Parliament created an opportunity for men like Strode to win those like Marten to their view of events, and to make them allies. Led by Pym, those concerned about religion were able to do so very effectively.

Hence when the Commons met, and Secretary Windebank read the Scottish Covenanters' letter to Louis XIII, he was met by an MP called Harbottle Grimston, who explained courteously that there were dangers at home that were even greater than those to which the letter referred. The liberty of the subject had been infringed, contrary to the Petition of Right. The king's bad ministers were not giving him the right advice. All this was reinforced when John Pym rose for a two-hour speech in which he explained that 'religion was the greatest grievance to be looked into', and here he focused on what he described as a campaign to return England to popery. 'The parliament is the soul of the commonwealth', the intellectual part which governs all the rest. As well, he said, the right to property had been infringed. It was embarrassingly clear that he meant Ship Money, and when the Commons sent for the records of the Ship Money trials, it became even clearer. Finally, the Commons said firmly that it could give the king nothing until he clarified his own position.

After only a few days, it was evident to most that there was little hope of compromise. Charles offered a last-ditch deal; he agreed to abandon Ship Money in exchange for twelve subsidies for the war. This was less than he needed, but to Parliament it seemed like an enormous amount. MPs wondered about their constituents' reactions. Charles could see there was no prospect that MPs would agree. Pym had been in touch with the Scots, and some whispered that he might bring *their* grievances before the House. Thus it was that by 5 May 1640 Charles had – equally hastily – decided to dissolve Parliament again. The Short Parliament was a sign of Charles's short fuse, and a tactical disaster. The whole grisly mess to come might have been averted if Charles had only managed to endure people shouting critically at him for more than a month. But the insecure boy still alive and well in Charles Stuart simply couldn't do it. He wanted to believe that Parliament would go away if he told it to, as it had in 1629. He wanted to believe that the problem was the rebellious Scots and their co-conspirators in London, and that defeating the former would put an end to the latter. He didn't want to believe that John Pym, MP, had managed to talk others into sharing his own world-view. And so he couldn't get together the money he needed to prosecute the Scottish war again.

But he was determined to try. On 20 August 1640 Charles left London to join his northern army, while the Scots crossed the Tweed and advanced towards Newcastle. The king had managed to scrape up around 25,000 men, but they were untrained, raw. And they were hungry; the army brought no bakeries, no brewhouses. And they were cold; no one except the senior officers had tents. Their pistols were often broken across the butt, making them more likely to explode.

They were explosive in other ways, too. They fired guns through tents, including the king's tent. They were mutinous. They were beggarly. They were more fit for Bedlam (London's asylum) or Bridewell Prison than the king's service. They murdered a pregnant woman in Essex and beat up Oxford undergraduates. And some were vehement iconoclasts, which illustrated the incongruity of the war itself. In Rickmansworth, a quiet Sunday morning service was disrupted when Captain Edmund Ayle and his troop smashed the altar and rails. It was a taste of things to come; so too were the complaints from families whose larders were eaten bare by the hordes of soldiers, families who found themselves playing host to drunken soldiers.

When the hungry, ill-disciplined English clashed with the Scots at Newburn, on 28 August 1640, the Scots easily drove them back, securing their first victory over the English since Bannockburn. To the Scots, it was proof of their divine election. Bishops, thought one Covenanter, were 'the panders of the Whore of Babylon, and the instruments of the devil'.

So when Charles had to call Parliament again, on 3 November 1640, John Pym had his chance, and he also had experience, allies, and knowledge of the system.

V

Pym against the Papists

One of the first things done by the Parliament that opened on 3 November 1640 was to release William Prynne and Henry Burton from prison (John Bastwick came home to London a week later, to similar acclaim). All three had been imprisoned – Prynne first in Caernarvon, which the government hoped would be remote enough to allow the whole matter to be forgotten, then in Jersey when this hope proved vain – because of their vigorous objections to the Laudian Church and their agitation for godly reform. Prynne had first been gaoled for attacking the wickedness of stage plays, with a sly hostile glance at the queen, and from prison had written an angry denunciation of bishops; loathing of the episcopate was Bastwick's and Burton's crime too. All of them had become symbols of the sufferings of true Protestants under the regime of Charles and Laud.

Their release was therefore the beginning of a campaign against the personal rule of Charles, launched with a graphic political message. The release of the three was a sign that England was once more a nation fit for the godly, and that the Commons would keep it so. Prynne, Burton and Bastwick had all been sentenced during Charles's personal rule to be mutilated by having their ears cropped, and then fined, and imprisoned for life for their writings in 1637. Each man, free but forever disfigured, was a walking advertisement for Parliament's clemency and the king's tyrannical cruelty.

They arrived in London on 28 November 1640, after a momentous journey. Their way was strewn with rosemary and bay, and they were greeted by bonfires and bells. It was an unusually warm day for

November, tempting immense crowds out into its golden light. They stopped for dinner in the little town of Brentford, which was to be the scene of fierce fighting later in the war.

So thick was the throng that their progress slowed to one mile an hour. It was, thought some observers, almost like a royal procession. The living martyrs were home at last. In London itself, some three thousand coaches, and four thousand horsemen, and 'a world of foot' awaited them, everyone carrying a rosemary branch. Everyone noticed that the bishops were far from overjoyed. They had every reason for apprehension. Prynne's warning to Laud that his own career was not immune from ruin was about to be as spectacularly fulfilled as the crudest tragedy.

And Prynne, like many a prophet, was himself one of the main causes of what he had cleverly foretold. On 18 December 1640, Laud was charged with high treason, and when he was removed to the Tower in the spring of 1641, Prynne gained access to his private papers, which he promptly published, carefully providing glosses. For Prynne – as for the young, clever John Milton – the bishops were nothing more nor less than 'ravenous wolves'. It is fair to say that in bringing Laud to book, Prynne too was an iconoclast, and Laud an icon whose smash would prove his falsity. Just as early reformers had eagerly exposed Christ's 'blood' of Hailes Abbey in Gloucestershire to be a fake, so Prynne sought to open Laud to public inspection, to provoke healing ridicule and laughter. But there was always the risk that Prynne and Pym would come to resemble the men who, they felt, had persecuted them.

One of the new pamphlet plays, entitled *Canterbury His Change of Diet*, was composed to mark the occasion of the condign punishment meted out to the three. 'Privately acted near the Palace-yard at Westminster', said the title page. 'The Bishop of Canterbury having variety of dainties, is not satisfied till he be fed with the tippets of men's ears.' Laud's love of luxury, his links with the court, are turned into a kind of monstrous cannibalism.

The charges against Laud had to do with profound, deepening, widening dread of popery. It was this fear that animated the man who led the Commons, sometimes from the wings but increasingly from centre-stage. The man was John Pym, and his hour had found him. It was Pym's task not only to reflect but also to whip up anti-popery, to turn headshaking dismay at the queen's antics into shouting alarm. Only by generating a sense of national crisis – England was in danger, about to be swept away – could Pym hope to overcome the English political system's tendency to right itself, to seek consensus and shun division.

The ground for his campaign had already been prepared. John Pym's anti-popery was not unique to him, nor was his use of it in Parliament historically unprecedented. The Parliament of 1621 had been preoccupied with the idea that a Jesuit conspiracy was behind the fall of the Palatinate to the forces of Rome. The Parliament of 1628/9 was anxious that Arminianism was spreading. Arminianism was the belief that men and women could be saved by their own works, and by their own goodness and repentance; the way to heaven was a slow and steady walk, lined with kindness to others. This harmless-sounding idea flew in the face of Calvinism, which held that every person was destined by God to be either saved or damned and could moreover be saved by his grace alone. As Pym's stepbrother Francis Rous put it: 'an Arminian is the spawn of a Papist; and if there come the warmth of favour upon him, you shall see him turn into one of those frogs that rise out of the bottomless pit. And if you mark it well, you shall see an Arminian reaching out his hand to a Papist, a Papist to a Jesuit, a Jesuit gives one hand to the Pope and the other to the King of Spain; these men having kindled a fire in our neighbour country, now they have brought over some of it hither, to set on flame this kingdom also.' Arminianism was seen as a menace because it was believed to prevent the kind of real, passionate soul-searching, with real self-loathing and much anguish, that was needed for true repentance. As a result of heightened anxieties of this kind, becoming an MP came to involve a declaration of religious allegiance. When Richard Grosvenor made a speech in support of candidates in Cheshire in 1624, he roundly announced that they were staunch Protestants, 'untainted in their religion'. The 1624 elections were especially dominated by anxieties about popery in the wake of the Spanish Match and its failure.

This dread of sneaking popery centred on the court, because it was the queen's influence that was feared most. Sir William Bulstrode was horrified by the spectacle of people trooping off to Mass with the queen:

'so that it grows ordinary with the out-facing Jesuits, and common in discourse, Will you go to Mass, or have you been at Mass at Somerset-house? There coming five hundred a time from mass.' In this atmosphere, Pym scarcely had to work hard to rouse fears that were ever-present.

The fear was renewed by Protestant England's consciousness of its own history. John Foxe's book *Acts and Monuments*, known as the *Book of Martyrs*, which graphically described the burning of Protestants during the reign of Mary Tudor eighty years earlier, was widely read and highly influential. The godly iconoclast William Dowsing owned three copies of it for his own personal use. So eager was Ipswich for the book that a satirist invented a maiden who shaped her sweetmeats into figures from Foxe. More recent events also haunted the Protestant imagination. Dread was fanned every year in the fires of the fifth of November. The Gunpowder Plot made papists and Jesuits seem especially the enemies of the Houses of Parliament. The godly Samuel Ward always warned his congregations on 5 November of the terrible danger in which they stood. Every year the celebration of Bonfire Night, in which often the pope and not Guy Fawkes was burned in effigy, reminded everyone that Catholic conspirators might be in their midst, but that God had delivered them. In the 1630s, only Puritans celebrated, but by 1644 the whole nation adopted the festival; even Royalists tried to invoke it by claiming that it was Parliament that resembled the gunpowder plotters. November was, besides, a Royalist month; it embraced Princess Mary's birthday on the fourth, and Henrietta Maria's on the sixteenth, and the king's on the nineteenth. Despite all this, spectacular fireworks displays marked the day in November 1647, celebrating Parliament's victories. The celebrations were themselves a kind of elaborate allegory of popery, and included 'fire-balls burning in the water, and rising out of the water burning, showing the papists' conjuration and consultation with infernal spirits, for the destruction of England's king and Parliament'. They also rang the church bells all over England every 5 November. They grew louder and louder as the 1630s went on, and somehow, in some places, the bells rung for the king's coronation day become softer, less sustained. Catholic courtiers, Catholic nobles, and above all the queen: men and women began to wonder if they were poised to act, to use the king as their tool.

Everyone had noticed how many Catholics eagerly joined the king's army against the Scots. All through the 1630s there were stories of plotting papists: a mole-catcher called Henry Sawyer was examined by the council for saying that when the king went to Scotland to be crowned, the Catholics would rise up and attack the Protestants. It was widely whispered that such campaigns would be led by Catholic gentry, but some suspected involvement at higher levels. The Earl of Bridgewater, the young John Milton's patron, reported worriedly to Secretary Coke that there had been a violent incident; an elderly woman had begged alms of a young gallant on horseback, who had responded by offering her a shilling if she would kneel to the cross on the shilling itself. She refused, and the young man killed her. Terror was increased when the winter of 1638–9 saw freak storms, which contemporaries read as signs. Dennis Bond of Dorset reported in his diary that 'this year the 15 December was seen throughout the whole kingdom the opening of the sky for half a quarter of an hour'. Henry Hastings reported that a vision of men with pikes and muskets had been seen in the sky. Brilliana Harley thought that in 1639 the Antichrist must begin to fall, while the armies themselves quailed at the spectacle of lightning and thunder. 'Many fears we have of dangerous plots by French and papists', recorded Robert Woodforde, while the alarm was such in Northamptonshire that some town marshals in Kettering set up a round-the-clock guard. On further rumours that papists were making ready to set fire to the town, the watch was strengthened. It was becoming clear that Charles couldn't altogether control the situation. People began to wonder if he could guarantee the safety of the English Church and its members from the dreadful dangers besetting them within and without the kingdom. And Charles himself might be a danger.

The man who rose to greatness by exploiting those fears also believed in them; indeed, he was their creation. John Pym came from Somerset, from an estate which had been in the family for three hundred years. His father died when he was only a baby, and his mother married again. Later, Pym's mother believed she was damned, a tragedy which often afflicted Calvinists. Her new husband was a godly gentleman of Cornwall, Anthony Rous, and Pym grew up in the area around Plymouth. In Armada year, he was five years old when Drake set sail, and perhaps he never forgot the fear, the beacons lit from end to end of the land, sending their smoke high up into the sky. Anthony Rous was not the man to let him forget; he was one of Drake's executors, and was himself a red-hot Puritan, running a kind of house of refuge for godly ministers. However, his brand of austere Calvinism had not yet become a source of disaffection; indeed, it was the glue that kept godly left and Anglican middle together in the years of Pym's childhood.

Nevertheless, Pym lived a comfortable gentleman's life – Oxford, and then the Middle Temple. But his time there was disrupted by what might have seemed like a frightening recapitulation of his worst childhood fears; while he was in residence, in 1605, the Gunpowder Plot was discovered, proof that plotting Catholics were here, in England. The gentleman's life resumed, but there was much evidence that it seemed fragile. He never really made headway in Somerset society; his circle of friends was solid but limited, and when drawn to the attention of the Commons, he was styled 'one Pym, a receiver', which meant he was deputed to collect the king's rents, a process that got him involved in supplying timber for the repair of the coastal forts and thus discovering their parlous state for himself, something that horrified the man who had known the menace of the Armada as a boy. His job also involved disafforestation, an operation which meant that ordinary people lost the right to gather firewood in the forest and to pasture animals in it. This was felt as ruthless and unjust by its victims, whose livelihoods were thus destroyed, and though Pym did his best to defend his tenants on at least one occasion he was also the landlord's man, not the tenants' representative. What he wanted was plenty of money in the royal exchequer so that the darkness of popery could be repelled by shot and shell.

As an MP he was serious. He was unresponsive to the House's mood, unwilling to joke and play, and poor at improvisation. He had his own ideas, and he had no wish to modify them. Yet this carried its own conviction in uncertain times. What helped to give credence to his vehement religious opinions and fears was his mastery of facts and figures in the labyrinthine areas of Crown finances. He was also exceptionally dedicated; he wanted his way more than most of the others, who preferred to adjourn and go off to a good ordinary. But he soon became a brilliant manipulator of the House's *amour-propre*. Only the potential power of the Commons offered the frightened little boy that Pym had been safety from the popery he hated and dreaded. So in 1621 he was noticeably anti-Spanish and anti-Catholic, but had also begun to ruminate on Parliament's role in safeguarding England against popery. 'The high court of Parliament is the great eye of the kingdom, to find out offences and punish them', he said. Already he saw the king as an obstacle to this safeguarding: 'we are not secure enough at home in respect of the enemy at home which grows by the suspen[ding] of the laws at home'. He said papists broke the 'independency upon others' which loyal subjects owed, and that the king, by mistaken lenity towards them, was hazarding the state. His position had hardened further by 1624, when he urged a search for recusants who gave away their secret beliefs by their acts; this is anxious, even paranoid, and his subsequent job of hunting down popish schoolmasters increased his anxiety and reinforced his convictions. By 1628 he was in the thick of the campaign for the Petition of Right, and was the chief opponent of Arminianism, which for Pym was a way for the Devil to persuade people that they need not repent.

Like many godly men, Pym was also involved in New World colonization projects, often attempts to build beyond the seas the godly nation which was failing to materialize in the British Isles. Pym was on the Providence Company board, whose very name proclaimed its godliness. This also yielded valuable political contacts. Through it Pym kept in constant touch with his patron the Earl of Bedford, Lord Saye and Sele, and the Earl of Warwick. They met often at Saye's London house. Pym was treasurer, and helped John Hampden prepare his case against Ship Money in 1638.

It was the opening debate of the Short Parliament that made Pym a national hero. It was not his first attempt to energize the nation by articulating its dread of papists, but the Laudian reforms and the Scottish wars meant that the nation had now moved into step with Pym's own terrors. He summarized every grievance against the king, but the focus was on religion. Later, Oliver St John said that Pym and his friends had been determined to ensure that the Short Parliament failed.

When the Short Parliament dissolved, Pym began to negotiate with the Scots, bypassing the king, while during the election campaign for the Long Parliament Pym 'rode about the country to promote the election of the puritanical brethren to serve in Parliament'. Once Parliament met on 3 November 1640, he moved at once to attack Strafford, and called him 'the greatest enemy to the liberties of his country, and the greatest promoter of tyranny, that any age had produced'. In this he was acting for an alliance of English dissidents and the Scots, who knew Strafford had argued for the Anglicization of Scotland as a province of England, and that he had wanted to go on fighting the war after the Scottish victory at Newburn. The Irish, too, loathed Strafford, and in beginning impeachment proceedings, Pym was acting on behalf of interests in all three kingdoms.

During the next few months, Pym created the laws and institutions that were to govern the early Parliamentarian regime: the Militia Ordinance, the Nineteen Propositions, and above all the Committee of Safety. Its very name points to what had been important to Pym all along. He was not a radical; he believed that the Elizabethan constitution was being undermined by a popish conspiracy. In the Church, too, all he wanted was the Elizabethan black-and-white simplicity of his childhood and youth; he did not want anything truly radical. His own paranoia about papists within was widely shared, but partly because he made it so by voicing his fears eloquently and publicly. It was he more than anyone else who persuaded the men of the House of Commons that a popish conspiracy had entangled the king and his chief ministers, and posed an immediate threat. On 7 November 1640, Pym made a speech two hours long, claiming there was a design of papists to alter law and religion. Sir Francis Seymour voiced the ideas central to Pym: 'one may see what dangers we are in for religion Jesuits and Priests openly to walk abroad and particularly what encouragement this is to our Papists. No laws in execution. For papists often to go to mass.' Pym moved that a committee be appointed 'to see that the papists depart out of town'. The committee was duly created on 9 November 1640, and was empowered to supervise and report on any dispensations granted to recusants. The king was regarded as ineffective because so many papists, it was said, were living round about and were protected by Letters of Grace, royal pardons-in-advance. So the committee began drawing up plans to constrain papists more tightly. Why shouldn't the anti-recusancy laws apply not just to known recusants, but also to the secret and crypto-papists infesting the Church and the state? Why shouldn't the laws be extended? Pym even suggested that Catholics should be forced to wear distinctive and recognizable dress, as if they were prisoners. He and the Commons then proposed that the queen should be deprived of all her Catholic servants. 'We ought to obey God rather than man, and that if we do not prefer God before man, he will refuse us', said Pym. This statement shows how radical thinking in religion could come to sound like – and to be – political radicalism. What was odd about Pym was shared by a lot of his contemporaries. They could act and talk radically while their reflexes remained conservative, even reactionary. They backed awkwardly into a revolution they did not intend.

The committee on recusants reported to the House on 1 December 1640. Sixty-four priests and Jesuits had been discharged from prison, on Secretary of State Windebank's authority. Windebank had also written repeatedly to local authorities asking them to halt their proceedings against papists. The House ordered Windebank to appear, to explain himself, and Pym and the future Royalist general Ralph Hopton moved that 'some course might be taken to suppress the growth of popery'. Then two days later the House ordered all JPs in Westminster, London and Middlesex to tell churchwardens to compile a list of known recusants 'so that they may be proceeded against with effect, according to law, at the next session, notwithstanding any inhibition or restraint'.

For Pym, the papists were not only a problem in matters of religion; they had become a political menace as well, because they were organizing a conspiracy 'to alter the kingdom in religion and government'. The country was awash with rumours of papists amassing arms; the House was told of a stabbing carried out by a popish priest because the magistrate in question was about to act against papists in Westminster. They worried that the army commanders were untrustworthy, and agreed to create another committee to look into 'the state of the king's army, and what commanders, or other inferior officers, are Papists'. Sir John Clotworthy, the tirelessly godly Ulsterman and Pym's relation by marriage, reported that eight thousand of Ireland's ten thousand soldiers were papists, 'ready to march where I know not.

The old Protestant army have not their pay, but the Papists are paid.'

The Commons began to take action to protect the realm. It purged itself of papists by deciding that all members must take communion and that the House should also make a confession of faith renouncing the pope. Meanwhile petitions complained that the government was too lenient towards papists. From the counties came stories of planned Catholic risings. John Clotworthy reported that there was a Catholic Irish invasion at hand. Pym told Parliament that divers persons about the queen were plotting a French invasion. In the Grand Remonstrance, too, plots were prominent, among Jesuits, bishops, prelates and popish courtiers. In reply, some hardy souls pointed out that nothing very much had happened yet, but this did not stop Pym or his followers from disseminating their fears. They may never have become majority beliefs, but they did become very widespread. The *Declaration of Fears and Jealousies* was especially fearful about Henrietta Maria, 'a dangerous and ill-affected person who hath been admitted to intermeddle with the great affairs of state, with the disposing of places and preferments, even of highest concernment in the kingdom'.

So widespread was the fear, that 'popery' was coming to mean something close to 'anything in religion or politics that I don't approve of or like', that though it extended itself from actual card-carrying Catholics to those in the Church of England suspected of an over-fondness for ceremony, it remained firmly grounded in a clear if misinformed apprehension of Romish practices. In particular, popery was *foreign*, and especially it was Spanish, and hence cruel, or French, and hence silly and nonsensical. Or, to put it another way, the English – and for that matter, the Scots – increasingly developed their ideas of national identity in response to the perceived menace of popery. To be truly, properly English or Scottish was to stand against Rome, an idea that was promulgated by writers from Edmund Spenser to every grubbing pamphleteer. This was to cast a long shadow for Charles Stuart, for it was thus that he could come to seem a traitor to his own people. The flavour of foreignness was to be intensified by the stories from Ireland later in 1641.

In just the first few months of the Long Parliament, no fewer than five popish plots were reported and discussed. A papist army was thought to lurk in South Wales. In early May 1641, every member of the House pledged to 'maintain and defend the true reformed Protestant religion . . . against all Popery and Popish innovations'. Pym himself was menaced personally, or so one newsbook thought. It reported on 'a damnable treason by a contagious plaster of a plague-sore, wrapped up in a letter and sent to Mr. Pym; wherein is discovered a devilish plot against the parliament, Oct. 25 1641'. Two terrifying menaces to security combined: plague and popery.

Or was it the printer who deserves credit for ingenuity? There was a raging bull market for popish plots in 1641. There was *A bloody plot, practised by some papists in Darbyshire, and lately discovered by one Jacob Francklin.* There was *Matters of note made known to all true Protestants: 1st, the plot against the city of London [&c.]. A most damnable and hellish plot exprest in three letters, against all Protestants in Ireland and England, sent out of Rome to the chief actors of the rebellion in Ireland.* There was *The truest relation of the discoverie of a damnable plot in Scotland.* And *A discovery to the prayse of God, and joy of all true hearted Protestants of a late intended plot by the papists to subdue the Protestants.* And *A discovery of the great plot for the . . . ruine of the city of London and the parliament,* a pamphlet sometimes attributed to Pym himself. There were dozens of pamphlets like these doing the rounds. One was *Gods Late Mercy to England, in discovering of three damnable plots by the treacherous Papists,* printed in 1641. It told a compelling story. On 15 November, a poor man named Thomas Beale lodged in a ditch near a post-house, and while thus concealed, he heard two men planning to surprise and take London for the papists, and to murder key MPs. They and their co-conspirators had been promised ten pounds and the chance to receive the sacrament of the Eucharist if they did so. Beale rushed to the Commons with his story, and the malefactors were arrested, but the author decided that 'we have . . . as just cause to fear the papists in England as they did in Ireland'. The House agreed, and responded with ever-tougher anti-papist legislation. Another pamphlet, *A True Relation of a Plot,* told of Catholics in Derbyshire, amassing supplies of gunpowder – itself virtually a logo for Catholics after 1605 – and also old iron; they had planned to blow up the local church with the worshippers inside.

So readers could learn some simple lessons. For the pamphleteers, Catholics were people with gunpowder, people who plotted; traitors too. They had tortuous, devious minds. They were animated by hatred of the good and godly. And they were at this very moment menacing the country from within: why, any stranger at an alehouse might be a Jesuit in disguise. And from without, too: the Jesuit in the alehouse might be in touch with a vast army ready to sweep into England.

Into this dynamite came a spark. On 1 November 1641, news reached London of a major rebellion in Ulster. Many years later, one of the many Protestants terrorized by it recalled the fear. Alice Thornton was the daughter of Sir Christopher Wandesford, who succeeded his cousin Strafford as Lord Deputy of Ireland:

> That horrid rebellion and massacre of the poor English prot-
> estants began to break out in the country, which was by the
> all-seeing providence of God prevented in the city of Dublin,
> where we were. We were forced upon the alarum to leave our
> house and fly into the castle that night with all my mother's
> family and what goods she could. From thence, we were forced
> into the city, continuing for fourteen days and nights in great
> fears, frights, and hideous distractions from the alarums and
> outcries given in Dublin each night by the rebels. These frights,
> fastings, and pains about packing the goods, and wanting sleep,
> times of eating, or refreshment, wrought so much upon my
> young body, that I fell into a desperate flux, called the Irish
> disease, being nigh unto death, while I stayed in Dublin.

Stories of terrible atrocities committed by the insurrectionists circulated in London as well as in Dublin. This may have been the kind of thing Alice feared:

> they [Irish rebels] being blood-thirsty savages . . . not deserving
> the title of humanity without any more words beat out his
> brains, then they laid hold on his wife being big with child, &
> ravished her, then ripped open her womb, and like so many
> Neros undauntedly viewed nature's bed of conception, afterward
> took her and her Infant and sacrificed in fire their wounded
> bodies to appease their Immaculate Souls, which being done,
> they pillaged the house, taking what they thought good, and
> when they had done, they set the house on fire.

This horrible story may or may not be true: as in the Indian Mutiny in the 1850s, stories like this had propaganda value far in excess of any simple truth. But to a young English girl, fifteen-year-old Alice Thornton, crouching in Dublin, stories like this might seem a direct threat to her in particular. Immediately the news press went into overdrive, and tales of atrocities began to pour forth. There were descriptions of gruesome tortures, especially stories of unborn babies ripped from their mothers' wombs, wives raped in front of their husbands, and girls in front of their parents. The rebels allegedly hanged a woman by her hair from a door; in Tyrone, it was said, a fat Scot was killed and rendered into tallow candles, in a grisly prefiguration of the Holocaust's soap industry. Humble people lost relatives and friends too. Among the dead was Zachariah, the brother-in-law of London woodturner Nehemiah Wallington, though the news did not reach Nehemiah himself until almost two years later, in 1643. The story was horrible: Zachariah had been cut down while his children begged, 'Oh, do not kill my father. Oh, do not kill my father.' Two of those children also died that winter, of cold and exposure, and Zachariah's widow, the sister of Nehemiah's wife, had to scramble along in a desperate plight, so desperate that she eventually took an Irish Catholic as her lover and protector. This horrified Nehemiah, but it was a move born of dire necessity. She sent one of her surviving sons to her sister and to Nehemiah, where he was trained as a woodturner. At least she had managed to get him away.

Nehemiah knew by then just how to interpret Zachariah's last words, which he carefully transcribed into his diary: 'as for the rebels, God will raise an army in His time to root them out, that although for a time they may prevail, yet at last God will find out men enough to destroy them. And as for the king, if it be true, as these rebels say, that they have his commission . . . to kill . . . all the Protestants . . . then surely the Lord will not suffer the king nor his posterity to reign, but the Lord at last will requite our blood at his hands.' They were to be the instruments of God's vengeance. This idea, piled on top of months of anxiety and panic, created a mentality which led people to think that the king needed to be restrained. After the war, clergyman and chronicler Richard Baxter said the rising was one of the main causes of the Civil War: 'the terrible massacre in Ireland, and the threatenings of the rebels to invade England'; Royalist historian Edward Hyde, Earl of Clarendon also thought it a key factor. John Dod told the Commons Committee that 'he saw a great number of Irish rebels whom he knew had a hand in the most barbarous actions of the rebellion, as the dashing of small infants and the ripping up of women and children and the like'. Joseph Lister, a boy of twelve at the time, never forgot his terror that he and other Protestants were about to be set upon as the Protestant Irish had been: 'O what fears and tears, cries and prayers night and day!' he recalled, 'was there then in many places, and in my dear mother's house in particular!'

London still retained some sense about nonsense. In January 1642, a tract entitled *No pamphlet, but a detestation against all such pamphlets as are printed, concerning the Irish rebellion*, denounced the 'many fabulous pamphlets that are set out concerning the rebels in Ireland' as forgeries. But similar accounts of the Thirty Years War made them seem likely. John Erwyn led a party of Scots soldiers to Edward Mullan's house in Ireland on Sunday 2 February 1642. He drew his sword 'and wounded the said Mary Mullan in her head, and forehead, and cut her fingers, at which time she cried out, "Dear John, do not kill me, for I never offended you", repeating this to him two or three times, where-upon he thrust her under the right breast and she gave up the ghost ... And after a time the said Erwyn took a mighty lump of fire and put it on the said Mary Mullan's breast, expecting she was still living.'

Mary's words sound like the desperate self-defences of women accused of witchcraft by violent neighbours. Particularly telling is the test to see if Mary is really dead; it sounds as if Erwyn expects Mary to be impervious to weapons. A pamphlet called *Treason in Ireland* told typical stories, and invited its readers to see the sponsors as traitors of the worst and cruellest kind:

> Henry Orell, when they slew his wife an ancient woman, and ravished her daughter in the most barbarous manner that ever was known; and when they had done pulled her limbs asunder, and mangled her body in pieces without pity or Christianity ... The woman and her maid a brewing, for it was an alehouse, where they brewed their own drink. The maid they took and ravished, and when they had abused her body at their pleasure, they threw her into the boiling cauldron.

The terror in England was almost a panic. On one public fast day at Pudsey the congregation was thrown into turmoil because of reports that the Irish rebels had invaded the West Riding and had reached Halifax and Bradford. 'Upon which the congregation was all in confusion, some ran out, others wept, others fell to talking to friends, and the Irish massacre being but lately acted, and all circumstances put together, the people's hearts fainted with fear.' Fears were not allayed till it was discovered that the supposed rebels were actually refugees. Elizabeth Harding testified that her lodger had remarked, on hearing of the Irish rebellion, that 'the worst of the plot was not yet discovered there, and that the Protestants heels would go up apace'. Devonshire petitioners were terrified when refugees told them of 'their wolvish enemies, that the bounds of that kingdom shall not limit their malicious tyranny'. Many Londoners, like Nehemiah, believed that 'he that will England win/ Must first with Ireland begin'. Wallington added, 'now, all these plots in Ireland are but one plot against England, for it is England that is that fine, sweet bit which they so long for, and their cruel teeth so much water at. And therefore these blood-thirsty papists do here among us in England plot what may be for our overthrow, to bring in their damnable superstition and idolatry among us.' Parliament thought that the English Catholics were to have risen at the same time. The counties that felt especially exposed – North Wales, Cheshire and Lancashire – began asking London for help.

People felt they were already at war, and believed that the rebels would find a fifth column of supporters poised to help them. In Parliament 'new jealousy and sharpness was expressed against the papists', said Clarendon, 'as if they were privy to the insurrection in Ireland, and to perform the same exploit in this kingdom'. Considerable numbers of English Catholics were said to have gone over to Ireland to help the rebels. Jesuits were (as usual) thought to be behind it all. Pym was quickfooted as ever, and managed to make political capital from it all: 'the papists here are acted by the same principle as those in Ireland; many of the most active of them have lately been there; which argues an intercourse and communication of counsels'. One pamphlet revealed a plan to blow up and burn the chief English cities and to land an army. When another plot was revealed in London, 'the poor people, all the countries over, were ready either to run to arms, or hide themselves thinking that the Papists were ready to rise and cut their throats', wrote Richard Baxter. Some counties asked for help in rounding up the local Catholics who were believed to be on the brink of helping to launch an invasion.

There is no evidence that English Catholics had any such intentions, and most of them probably shared their countrymen's dislike and fear of the Irish; one, John Carill, of Harting in Sussex, actually sold lands to raise money for an army to suppress the rebellion, a tactful move to appease his neighbours. But it made little difference. Ardent Protestants saw events in both Ireland and England as signs of a general European Catholic conspiracy to eradicate Protestantism. The worst-case scenario envisaged the Irish landing in England, backed by Spain and France; then they could turn against the Dutch too. It was believed that the pope was behind this, for he had given plenary indulgences to all those who made war on his behalf. As fears of a Catholic invasion spread, England was seen as a tiny, gallant Protestant nation, encircled by conniving Catholic superpowers keen to blot it from the earth.

As with more recent conspiracy theories, the immediate result was loss of civil liberties. Trunks and possessions of suspected persons heading for Ireland were ordered to be searched. Letters were intercepted and read. Even foreign ambassadors' reports came under scrutiny. Irish soldiers returning home from fighting for the kings of France or Spain were detained at the ports and questioned. A register of Irish residents in Middlesex and Westminster was drawn up, and all over England and Wales Irish Catholics and priests were arrested. English and Welsh Catholics found themselves secured and disarmed too. Catholic peers and bishops in the House of Lords came under renewed political attack. And yet another army began to be raised to put down the rebellion.

The question was, could the king be trusted with such an army? What if it were used against the king's critics at home? After all, the rebels themselves unhelpfully claimed to be fighting for the maintenance of the royal prerogative against the Puritans in Parliament. They also claimed they held the king's commission under the great seal. In London the queen and other advisers were openly attacked as the authors of the rebellion; at the beginning of 1642 Pym claimed that the king had granted passes to the rebels. Clarendon claimed in his *History of the Rebellion*, written after his exile from court in 1667, that some chose the Parliamentarian side because they saw the king as the ally of the Irish rebels; he also thought that the idea of the king as a secret supporter of Catholicism was a key factor in dividing the nation. It was not only the godly who were terrified by the Ulster Rising. Royalists were also revolted; Wales, for example, suffered more Irish invasion panics than most areas, but eventually became staunchly Royalist. It seems as if the rebellion in Ireland only galvanized anti-monarchical spirits when added to a premix of godliness, dislike of Laud and anxiety about the Catholics at court. Parliamentarian propaganda sought to link Laud with popery, tyranny and barbarity, while Parliament fashioned itself as the upholder of traditional liberties. For the rest of the war, Parliament would harp on this note, constantly pointing to papists within Royalist circles or forces, asserting that some Irish rebels had been recruited into the king's armies, while Royalist forces were compared with the rebels at the taking of Marlborough, at which the prisoners 'were used after the manner that the Irish rebels used the Protestants in Ireland'.

Late in 1641 and for the first months of 1642, Protestant Irish refugees flooded into England and Wales, seeking aid from relatives, poor relief, or Parliament. Edmund Ludlow noted that everywhere they went they told stories of the brutalities they had endured, sometimes in a bid to gain relief. Many arrived at Chester and Milford Haven, and more in Lancashire and the Isle of Wight in March 1642 and February 1643 respectively. The earlier refugees were mostly women and children. They told their stories to eager, frightened audiences.

One account given by Richard Baxter summed up the intense propaganda appeal of the Ulster Rising:

> This putteth me in mind of that worthy servant of Christ, Dr Teat, who being put to fly suddenly with his wife and children from the fury of the Irish Rebels, in the night without provision, wandered in the snow out of all ways upon the mountain till Mrs Teat, having no suck for the child in her arms, and he being ready to die with Hunger, she went to the brow of a rock to lay him down, and leave him that she might not see him die, and there in the snow out of all ways where no footsteps appeared she found a suck-bottle full of new, sweet milk, which preserved the child's life.

The helpless women and children, at the mercy of their enemies but cared for by God, were truly iconic for all Protestants in all three kingdoms. If anyone who could read was not afraid of Catholic plots in 1640, a diet of this kind of print ensured that they were terrified by 1642.

Part of the Commons' efforts to save the kingdom from being engulfed by popery was the prosecution of Strafford, who had come to seem symbolic of the worst aspects of the personal rule. Loathing Strafford was a way of complaining about Charles. Traditionally, grievances about monarchs expressed themselves as dislike of the monarch's councillors. More importantly, Strafford was the direct enemy of Pym and his supporters. He had tried to get the Commons to impeach them for their correspondence with the Scots Covenanters; now they turned the tables on him.

Pym had thought of Strafford's trial as an obvious case of treason. But treason had to be a crime against the king. It was widely known that Charles had trusted Strafford completely and was still refusing to get rid of him or to back away from his policies. So Pym said that Strafford was guilty of treason not against the king, but against the constitution. Here again, Pym seems to have reversed accidentally into radicalism because of expediency. Strafford sensibly pointed out what a dangerous idea this was, but by then he was so hated that the London crowd simply wanted him dead, and was not over-particular about the means. The case began with Pym's sizzling attack on Strafford's activities in Ireland, another Pym theme. But things didn't quite go to plan. At his trial, Strafford remained brave and calm, and even those who loathed him were moved to grudging admiration. His worst crime, which was to have said that an Irish army might be brought over to reduce Scotland and then England, was poorly evidenced – only Henry Vane the Elder could be got to say that he had heard Strafford actually say it, and the law required two witnesses. Nonetheless, Strafford's indictment allowed the Commons to practise talking as if they and not the king embodied English sovereignty. It was to become an acceptable rather than an unthinkable idea.

Now it was another MP, godly Arthur Haselrig, who had a clever new notion, though not one congenial to Pym, who was hoping for a show-trial. Why not drop the cumbersome impeachment, which

actually required tiresome amounts of proof? Why not simply introduce a Bill of Attainder? All this required was a Commons vote. At first
Pym was against it, but came around to the idea once he saw that it
was the only sure-fire way to bring Strafford to the scaffold. Strafford's
final speech in his own defence, made on 13 April, was a gallant attempt
to rebut the charges in the name of the very traditions the king had
violated: 'I have ever admired the wisdom of our ancestry, who have
so fixed the pillars of this monarchy that each of them keeps their
measure and proportion with each other . . . the happiness of a Kingdom consists in this just poise of the king's prerogative and the subject's
liberty and that things should never be well till these went hand in
hand together.'

It was Pym who stood up to refute Strafford, and he said that 'if the
prerogative of the king overwhelm the liberty of the people, it will be
turned into tyranny; if liberty undermine the prerogative, it will grow
into anarchy'. This scarcely answered Strafford's charge that laws could
not be set aside. Prophetically, he argued that 'You, your estates, your
posterities lie all at the stake if such learned gentlemen as these, whose
lungs are well acquainted with such proceedings, shall be started out
against you: if your friends, your counsel were denied access to you, if
your professed enemies admitted to witness against you, if every word,
intention, circumstance of yours be alleged as treasonable, not because
of a statute, but a consequence, a construction of law heaved up in a
high rhetorical strain, and a number of supposed probabilities'.

Thanks to this powerful appeal, fifty-nine people voted against the
Bill of Attainder at its third reading, and found their names on a list
posted outside the Commons, headed, 'These are the Straffordians, the
betrayers of their country.' Things were turning nasty.

The same mood prevailed in the streets, and newer and more radical
voices emerged from the hubbub. Rude Henry Marten, *certainly* no
Puritan, was among those who produced the Protestation, which was
an imitation of the Kirk's Covenant, and toughly vowed to crush all
who threatened true religion, especially priests and Jesuits, 'and other
adherents of the See of Rome [that] have of late more boldly and
frequently put in practice than formerly'. It did offer allegiance to the
king as well, but like Pym, Marten had come to think the king was the
problem in guaranteeing true religion. As early as 1641 Marten con-

fessed to his friend Sir Edward Hyde that he did not believe that one man was wise enough to rule a whole nation. By 1642 he was identified as a key figure among those Sir Simonds D'Ewes referred to as the 'fiery spirits' who used language disparaging towards the royal dignity. Having proclaimed kingship to be forfeitable he was excluded from pardon for life or estate by Charles I in the same year. Later he was to go further. In support of the Puritan divine John Saltmarsh, the author of a pamphlet proposing the deposition of the king, Marten stated in the Commons on 16 August 1643 that 'it were better one family be destroyed than many'. He was asked who he meant, and at once said he meant the royal family. For this the Commons sent him to the Tower; they were not yet ready to hear what he had to say.

In the meantime, a group of writers had vowed to free Strafford; borrowing a none-too-plausible plot from the stage, they planned to seize the Tower and help Strafford to make his getaway, while bringing the army south. The group included William Davenant, who had long claimed to be Shakespeare's illegitimate son, and the elegant and intelligent Sir John Suckling. Also involved was George Goring, later a Royalist general of notoriously undisciplined troops and himself a wild card. Charles, who always loved a play, was privy to their counsels, but may also have urged Goring to leak it to the Parliamentarian leadership. He was attempting to convince them not to pursue Strafford to death, trying to frighten them off. It didn't work. The Lords passed the attainder by a slim margin, with many bishops and all the Catholic peers missing. An armed mob accompanied those taking it to the king for signature.

And the next day, on Sunday 9 May 1641, after hesitating all evening, Charles signed his chief counsellor's death warrant. He did it to save his wife, who would certainly have been next, and his frightened children. But he never forgave himself. Strafford was to face the executioner's axe on 12 May 1641, before a huge and joyous crowd. 'I do freely forgive all the world,' he said on the scaffold, 'I wish that every man would lay his hand on his heart and consider seriously whether the beginnings of the people's happiness should be written in letters of blood.' But London was glad to have it so, and as Strafford's bloody head was lifted, bonfires flamed across the country, and at dusk candles were lit in windows to celebrate his fall.

It was in this atmosphere of tension and violence that on 7 November 1641 Pym began formally to connect 'the corrupt part of our clergy that make things for their own ends and with a union between us and Rome'. This is close to what Milton wrote in a sudden outburst of passionately anti-Laudian fervour in *Lycidas*: the spineless clergy do not feed their hungry sheep, and so Rome, 'the grim wolf with privy paw' carries off more of them every day. But Pym meant more. For him, increasingly influenced by the Scots, bishops themselves were coming to seem central to the problem. And Parliament was the centre of the solution: 'the parliament is as the soul of the commonwealth, that only is able to apprehend and understand the symptoms of all such diseases that threaten the body politic'. He spoke for two hours. He connected the religious menaces of popery with menaces to Parliament, to property. That afternoon, although this was not obvious to him or to anyone else, Pym created the Parliamentarian cause that was to be disputed so bloodily over the next nine years.

The Grand Remonstrance was Pym's powerful statement of a political credo that demanded reform on a grand scale indeed. The elections to the Common Council a month later, in December, provided a very comfortable majority of Pym's supporters, and from January 1642, the older and more conservative councillors were systematically replaced by those who served Pym. The Grand Remonstrance was not a Declaration of Independence, or a Declaration of the Rights of Man, much less a Marseillaise. It was still couched in the conservative rhetoric of days of yore, asking the king in fulsome terms of grovelling humility to redress grievances. But even that rhetoric had begun to fall away, and some at least of it was addressed to the people, not the king. It was first read on 8 November 1641, and finally passed in the middle of the night on the 22nd. In it Pym's exceptionally vehement anti-popery and his concerns about the state came to seem one and the same issue. It contained long low moans about the Jesuited papists: 'the multiplicity, sharpness and malignity of those evils under which we have now many years suffered . . . and which were fomented and cherished by . . . those malignant parties whose proceedings evidently appear to be mainly for their advantage and increase of popery'. They, it seemed, and not Strafford, were responsible for everything that had gone wrong in the past fifteen years. Like Hitler's anti-Semitism, Pym's anti-popery was both a genuine moral passion and also a card he played to try to bring the public into sympathy with his plans.

The phrase Grand Remonstrance is still used for any rebuke, though few today have much idea of what was in the original. The Remonstrance was a multipurpose affair. It was a discontented history of the personal rule of Charles I, minute and even fussy. Every grievance of the personal rule found a place. But its main concerns were large. Its announced goal was to restore 'the ancient honour, greatness and security of this crown and nation'. It was to expose the 'mischevious designs' that had tried to drive a wedge between the king and his people, forcing them to argue about liberty and prerogative. It was also supposed to expose those who intended to drive Puritans out 'with force' or root them out by violence. It demanded that the king employ only ministers 'as the Parliament may have cause to confide in, without which we cannot give his Majesty supplies for the support of his own estate'. It demanded that bishops be deprived of votes in the Lords, 'who cherish formality and superstition' in what came to seem an 'ecclesiastical tyranny.' It complained of illicit revenue-raising through Ship Money and the Forced Loan. It objected to the imprisonment of members of the Commons. It protested very strenuously at the destruction of the king's forests, a matter near Pym's heart, and to the selling of Forest of Dean timber to 'papists', 'which was the best storehouse of this kingdom for the maintenance of our shipping'. It also tried to reassure everyone that it was not a blueprint for religious radicalism. There would be, if anything, more discipline than before. Similarly, it closed with a ringing avowal, explaining that all its creators wanted was 'that His Majesty may have cause to be in love with good counsel, and good men'.

The debate was the most passionate the House had ever seen. The final exchange, on 22 November 1641, was especially fierce, and here the shadowy outlines of Royalist and Parliamentarian became briefly visible. Many spoke against the Remonstrance. They disliked its peremptory procedure, the refusal of its creators to consult the Lords. Pym and his chums were becoming starkly visible as a powerful clique, and some members of the Commons were not eager to expel one clique in order to have another in its place. Those who disliked the Remonstrance complained that it dragged old skeletons from their graves. Pym retorted that the country's plight was desperate. Popery was about to destroy everything. But some were beginning to wonder if there really were evil Jesuits lurking behind every tree. A moderate group containing future historian and Earl of Clarendon Edward Hyde and the brilliant young humanist Lucius Cary, Viscount Falkland, were among the doubters. They worried, too, that Pym and his faction were encouraging sectarians and godly fanatics. One dissenter was Sir Edward Dering, and his concerns show what was truly radical about the Grand Remonstrance, though not everyone noticed at the time. There was something big at stake here: 'When I first heard of a remonstrance, I presently imagined that like faithful counsellors we should hold up a glass unto his majesty; I thought to represent unto the king the wicked counsels of pernicious councillors; the restless turbulency of practical papists . . . I did not dream that we should remonstrate downward, tell stories to the people, and talk of the King as a third person.'

For Dering, the Remonstrance was radical and entirely unacceptable not for *what* it said, but *to whom* it was said. Parliament was no longer addressing its grievances to the king, but to the people. Sovereignty and the definition of who guaranteed the people's rights had shifted. Pym responded, though, with the glorious plainness which kept him in his place as leader: 'It's time to speak plain English,' he said, 'lest posterity shall say that England was lost and no man dared speak truth.' The debate went on until after midnight, when there was – at long last – a division. Over three hundred MPs were still present. The Remonstrance was carried, on a majority of just eleven votes. This tiny margin helped convince the king that strong action against a little faction would settle things. He was wrong, as the Remonstrance itself showed. But it also showed that the nation's representatives were beginning to divide. So too would the nation.

VI

Stand Up, Shout Mars

Already, as the Commons debated, the city of London was reflecting the turbulence of its governors. Two years of disorder and riots – outbreaks in which those ordinary people who could not speak in Parliament or even in church demanded a voice. Hostile crowds attacked Lambeth Palace in May 1640, demonstrated in large numbers during Strafford's trial in the following spring, and took to the streets in the winter of 1641–2. Conservatives were alarmed by the coincidence of these demonstrations with Pym's assaults in the House of Commons, thinking that the radicals in Parliament were orchestrating the mobs. But Pym and the crowds were engaged in a kind of dance in which neither led, but each responded to a music of discords in Church and state. Huge numbers signed petitions – 15,000 signed the Root and Branch Petition, which urged the abolition of bishops, deans and chapters, tendered in December 1640; 20,000 Londoners signed a petition against Strafford, and 15,000 'poor labouring men' signed a petition complaining about the faltering economy on 31 January 1642. Thirty thousand apprentices – nearly all of those in London – signed a petition presented in the violent demonstrations of Christmas 1641. However, this must be seen in context. London's apprentices had always been inclined to riot. Fisticuffs and shouting were good entertainment for boys.

London was wild with rumour and story. The undercurrent of dread, that sometimes threatened to rise and swamp the city, was the fear of popery. 'Prentices and clubs' became the call. The London apprentices in May 1640 threatened to rise against the Queen Mother Marie de

Medici and Archbishop Laud. They marched, with a drummer at their head. Placards materialized everywhere, calling the apprentices to rid the city of the curse of bishops. Everyone was on holiday for May Day, so when the crowd of apprentices reached St George's Fields, Southwark, it was augmented by sailors and dockhands, idle through lack of trade. They decided to hunt for 'Laud, the fox', and 500 of them marched on Lambeth Palace. The apprentices, balked because Laud had escaped, went instead to break open prisons, and to attack the house of the Earl of Arundel. A rumour swept London that 50,000 Frenchmen were already hidden away in the city's suburbs, ready to spring out and support the king, and overthrow true religion. On 21 May, the judges declared the disturbances were high treason, and John Archer, a glover of Southwark, was brutally tortured before his execution. The justices were hoping to make him an example, but the effect was the reverse of what they had in mind. This did not give the crowds much reassurance about the government's intentions. Finally, the following year, the crowd's hunger for a scapegoat had been rewarded by the spectacle of Strafford's severed head, but this had not so much placated as excited them further.

Since the fall of Strafford, events stood on a knife edge, and were served by rumour, gossip, personal contacts. It is said to have been Henrietta herself who, Lady Macbeth-like, urged her husband to aggression. She is supposed to have told him, 'Go, you coward, and pull those rogues out by the ears, or never see my face more.' And Henrietta may have had reason to fear that Parliament was preparing to move against her, personally. It had removed Strafford; it had attacked Laud. Of its great enemies, only she was left. And Charles may have seen himself in nightmares reluctantly signing her death warrant too.

Charles became convinced that strong action against a tiny band was all that was needed to give him back his life, his court, his rule. He was a knight-errant. He was, it turned out, Don Quixote, living in a world that did not exist. Like other mildly stupid people, he gave no thought to what would happen if his plans went awry and the bold action failed. He only saw the dazzling sun of success.

On 4 January 1642, the king set off at about three o'clock for Westminster. He had decided to arrest his five worst enemies, those wretched fellows, Pym and his *junto*. He had identified the men he thought most dangerous – Pym; John Hampden, his old foe, who had spoken so stoutly for the Remonstrance; Denzil Holles, another Ship Money refuser; young Arthur Haselrig, who had suggested the plan to attaint Strafford, and (unexpectedly) William Strode. They were all men with a history of opposing him, but his shortlist of ringleaders omitted many key figures, including all Pym's supporters in the Lords. Even if his expedition had been successful it would not have silenced all his critics.

Charles knew he could find his quarries in the Commons. Accounts differ as to whether the king advanced on Parliament with his guards, or on his own, but it seems unlikely that even Charles would have set out to face a defiant House with only Prince Rupert for company. Bulstrode Whitelocke says 'the King came, guarded with his pensioners, and followed by about two hundred of his courtiers and soldiers of fortune, most of them armed with swords and pistols'. Whoever he took with him, he was too late. The birds had flown, as he himself later quipped. The phrase shows that he saw himself as a hunter, a role in which he felt at home.

For a moment he could not believe his failure. Charles looked desperately around the chamber for the men he wanted. He called their names, unable to give up hope that they were there. Then he asked the Speaker for his chair, with careful courtesy. It was like Charles to say 'By your leave, Mr Speaker, I must borrow your chair'; the politeness and deference of his words emphasized rather than concealed the gross disregard of the Commons' independence implied in his entry with armed guards. He knew how they might feel: 'I must declare', he said carefully, 'that no king that ever was in England shall be more careful of your privileges', but he went on, 'yet you must know that in cases of Treason no person has a privilege'.

The House was not impressed. As Charles left, in defeat, the Commons roared 'Privilege! Privilege!' The cry was echoed by the London crowds next day.

Historians do not quite like the idea that it was Lucy Hay who warned the Five Members, but this is no mere fantasy invented by romantic lady novelists. There are contemporary voices who believed it to be true. Philip Warwick saw Charles's plans frustrated by the countess personally: 'Yet his coming to the Lower House, being betrayed by that busy stateswoman, the Countess of Carlisle, who has now changed her gallant from Strafford to Mr Pym, and was become such a she-saint, that she frequented their sermons, and took notes, he lost the opportunity of seizing their persons.' Thomas Burton, for example, in his diary of Cromwell's Parliament, quotes Haselrig himself as the source for Lucy's intervention:

> The King demanded five members, by his Attorney-General. He then came personally to the House, with five hundred men at his heels, and sat in your [the Speaker's] chair. It pleased God to hide those members. I shall never forget the kindness of that great lady, the Lady Carlisle, that gave timely notice. Yet some of them were in the house, after the notice came. It was questioned if, for the safety of the house, they should be gone; but the debate was shortened, and it was thought fit for them, in discretion, to withdraw. Mr Hampden and myself being then in the House, withdrew. Away we went. The King immediately came in, and was in the house before we got to the water. The queen, on the King's return, raged and gave him an unhandsome name, 'poltroon', for that he did not take others out, and certainly if he had, they would have been killed at the door.

Similarly, the poet John Dryden remarks that 'Mr Waller used to say that he would raze any Line out of his Poems, which did not imply some Motive to virtue, but he was unhappy in the choice of subject of his admirable vein in poetry. The Countess of C. was the Helen of her country' – as if the war had been fought over Lucy herself. Bishop Warburton called her 'the Erinnys of that time', and claimed that she was the source of information and intelligence 'on his majesty's intentions'.

It was not only Restoration writers who saw Lucy as the chief instrument of knowledge. Henry Neville, republican intellectual, portrayed her as Pym's lover in 1647: 'first charged in the fore-deck by Master [Denzil] Hollis, in the Poop by Master Pym, while she clapped my Lord of Holland under hatches'. Astrologer William Lilly, though he names another party as the direct source of Pym's warning, provides information about leakages from the king's secret councils via the queen's circle: 'All this Christmas, 1641, there was nothing but private whispering at court, and secret councils held by the Queen and her party, with whom the King sat in council very late many nights.'

Lucy was certainly still a visible member of the queen's party, but events show that her heart by now lay elsewhere. Lucy liked and embraced change. While her sister, equally ambitious, married a staid aristocrat of whom her father thoroughly approved, Lucy had married a young man of fashion. Tiring of him, she fell in love with an authoritative statesman of pronounced political philosophy. Neither choice was remotely snobbish; if anything, Lucy seemed particularly attracted by men with more than a touch of the people in their makeup. When her statesman fell, Lucy seems to have fallen in turn for his intelligent foe, John Pym, another change for her. Here was a man who was like her previous lovers in intelligence and power, but who was capable of showing her quite another world, a world to which she was attracted by its very difference.

It is also quite possible that Lucy – just like the rest of Pym's followers, and a strong minority of the nation – was outraged by Charles's behaviour. No Catholic, she disliked the influence exerted by Laud on the Church. Her personal attraction to Strafford may have been strong, but she may not necessarily have sided with him on questions of absolutism, and his fall and the king's willingness to sign his death warrant may have done something to put her off the absolute power of monarchy, as well as forcing her to realize that it was not in fact absolute. This may not have been a matter of direct personal vengeance either. Lucy had just seen a great self-made man struck down by the king. To a woman who had spent years trying to advance herself and her family in the eyes of a monarch, this cannot have been very reassuring. It might have reminded her of her father's fate, or even of the entire history of the Percys, a family struggling to maintain a powerful aristocratic position without monarchic interference, which had seen several members executed for treason. Strafford's death confirmed in Lucy Hay an ideology of monarchy limited by strong Protestantism and aristocratic counsel, an ideology she was to adhere to throughout the Civil War years. And odd as it may have seemed, Pym and the saints offered a more rational path to that goal than did any of those remaining about the king.

Self-preservation, too, was always a central plank in Lucy's motivation. If Lucy knew anything of Pym's plans to impeach the queen, she may have become anxious that she would herself be implicated.

Strafford's death was a warning that no one could escape by virtue of position or rank. It may have seemed sensible to have a foot in both camps. And since she was almost certainly not the only one who disclosed the king's plans, it *was* sensible. Strafford's fall from power was a warning. It might have looked like the beginning of the end for everyone in the king's and queen's immediate circle.

Ironically, too, if Lucy did send a message to Pym, it may suggest that he was more circumspect with her than others had been, for some historians think that Pym lured Charles into the rash invasion of the House, that the whole attempted arrest was a trap. If so, Pym may have been making use of Lucy, knowing only too well that she had a foot in both camps and an eye on the winning side. If Lucy was lurking in Pym's camp to gather information, then he may have used her to leak unreliable information to the queen's circle, even to bait the trap he was setting for the king. Is it significant that it was Henrietta's urgings which sent the king to the House, her interests which prompted him to act so rashly? Perhaps Lucy Hay betrayed her friend the queen not by giving away her plans, but by unwittingly giving her false information. Who was using whom?

Somewhere, Pym and the other members hid while Charles and his men burst into the Commons. Rumour said that they took refuge in the Puritan stronghold of St Stephen's Coleman Street, very near the Guildhall. It was ominous that the new state wrapped itself protectively in the folds of the church, ominous and predictive of what would become a Parliamentarian theocracy of sorts. They were able to enter the Guildhall the next day, to cheers.

These events left Charles and Henrietta thoroughly scared, and after a failed bid to persuade the London aldermen to give up the errant members, on 10 January 1642 they packed their bags and abandoned Whitehall for Hampton Court. It was Charles's second disastrous mistake in under a week. The king and queen knew that when the House reconvened it might go on to impeach the queen as the one who had invited the 'Jesuited papists' who threatened the nation into the country in the first place. They had sensed the mood of London when Charles rode to the Tower the day after his disastrous invasion of the Commons. 'Sir, let us have our liberties,' cried someone in the crowd, 'we desire no more.' The Christmas holidays meant that London's apprentices, always volatile, were available to demonstrate. On 6 January there was a panic in the City as vast crowds thronged public spaces; a fight broke out between the king's supporters and demonstrators at Westminster Abbey, and Sir Richard Wiseman was killed. The demonstrators took up a collection to pay for Wiseman's funeral, though, and the French ambassador commented on how calm the crowds were in comparison with crowds in Paris.

In the Guildhall it was the same. 'Parliament, Privileges of Parliament', shouted some. Others shouted back 'God bless the king'. But there were not enough of them, and – with no military effort at all, without even a show of real opposition – Charles's opponents achieved the tremendous victory of persuading him to vacate London.

In doing so, Charles lost prestige. He lost credibility as the inevitable, the unconsidered government. And he lost the Tower, with its mint and its armoury, and the London militia. Perhaps the capital had become peripheral to him. He had had dreams of a new London that would reflect the order and ceremonial he loved, but it had failed to materialize from the mongrel old city, crowded with unregulated houses of worryingly diverse and muddled shapes. Early in his reign, Charles had grandiose schemes for London; he issued proclamations to regulate new building, enforce the use of better materials, and impose some semblance of town planning. He wanted to rebuild and beautify Whitehall itself, but also the great cathedral of St Paul's, so tumbledown and so given up to profane activities that Charles felt it was unworthy of his capital. He wanted to demolish the existing jerry-built medieval housing to forward these schemes. He wanted London to reflect his own ordered family, his well-regulated court. He disliked the continued residence in London of those who, he felt, should be in the provinces looking after their tenants; the gentry were strictly prohibited from neglecting their estates in the country and the duties they should be performing there by residing in London all year round.

The problem with all this was that the London corporation was unenthusiastic. And as often, when Charles couldn't realize his fantasies, he turned his back. During the period of his personal rule, Whitehall had become just another palace, like Hampton and Oakley and Greenwich. He knew nothing first-hand of the vast activity that surrounded his court – the trade, law, business, finance, the sheer human pressure of what was in a few short years to become the greatest city in Europe. He had always avoided it. He hated the London crowds that reached out to him, hoping his touch would heal their sores. He had not visited the great shipyards at Poplar that had loomed over Anna Trapnel's childhood, nor seen the first ships of the East India Company dropping anchor in Poplar docks laden with luxuries. He had seen only the luxuries. Now this city, invisible to Charles, was to be his downfall. He had refused to see it, and London, not the city to take a slight lightly, never forgave him.

Like all wars, the Civil War was expensive, and the money to pay Parliament's army came from the public. London alone provided between a quarter and a third of all the money spent by Parliament. And yet at the same time business was down; with the court gone the trade in luxuries, which had been booming, collapsed. And with the king away, Parliament at once acted to alter the social fabric of the city. The theatres were closed, the traditional holidays abolished: this threw still more people out of work.

Not everyone was miserable as the conflict deepened. Woodturner Nehemiah Wallington was happy, because his London was a godly city once more. For him, all events were a rich source of moral lessons. This was a man who, when his house was burgled in August 1641, tried to see in it the correcting hand of God's providence: 'because the Lord doth see the world is ready to steal away my heart, therefore, he doth it in love to wean me from the world'. But Wallington, like other godly folk in London, lived in terror that his bounty of spiritual surroundings might be taken from him. He was also a workaholic who adjured himself to wake at 1 a.m. to write, and who decided to miss a spring expedition across the fields to Peckham with his wife and daughter in order to stay at home and worry about 'the sadness of the times'.

Even before the war, London had outgrown law and order – the king's palace at Whitehall, like some manor surrounded by new estates, was now at the heart of a troublespot. The Middlesex suburbs contained a high proportion of the disorderly poor – to the north and west, as well as to the east. The large number of apprentices and other migrants – young, poor, male and single – meant that turbulence within the city was endemic; the rallying cry 'prentices and clubs' symbolizes that threat. London was huge. It was constantly growing. And it was noisy:

its streets resounded with pealing bells, the cries of street traders, the songs of buskers, the news cries of ballad-singers. Some traders made sure they were noticed with bells, horns and clappers. Every time you sat down in a tavern a fiddler and a flautist or two would appear, and expect to be given a fee for cacophonous playing. Alehouses were noisy. But almost all houses in London except the very grandest were right on the street. The clatter of carts, and of water-carriers on cobbles was almost constant. Dogs barked and howled. There were more and noisier birds: rooks and jackdaws were once common in the city. And London talked; from the upper storeys Londoners could eavesdrop on neighbours or shout abuse at them.

It wasn't just the noise of London that a countryman might have found surprising. London was also smelly. If we could travel back in time and sniff the London air, we would be suffocated not by the smell of sewage, but the pervasive acrid reek of coal fires. As the seventeenth century progressed, industry moved into the East End and Southwark, and the smells it produced lessened. When slaughterhouses were moved out in the 1620s and 1630s, the city lost the noise and mess of pigs, cows and sheep driven through the centre. There was also less noise from smithies, tanneries and the like, but the shouts of those advertising bear-baiting and prize-fights went on. So did town-criers, shouting the time, the news, the dead, the 'For Sale' notices. The noise did have a term: there was a curfew, and the nights were much quieter.

In the period of personal rule, Charles had relied on the London money market as well as on his subjects for forced loans, and in the crisis of 1640, when the royal forces' defeat in war coincided with a widespread refusal to pay outstanding taxation, the City's financiers declined to continue to support the regime. Some rich men were ruined in Charles's fall, which may have made the others less keen to bail him out. Once the Scots were seen successfully to resist the king, some of the discontent that had been bubbling beneath the surface in London, repressed by Laud, became visible. After all, in 1637 John Lilburne had been whipped at the cart's tail for publishing an attack on the bishops, and in the 'liberties' outside the jurisdiction of the City, there were separated congregations, church groups that had declared their independence of bishops and priests. Cheaper, open-air theatres staged plays openly critical of the court.

The intermittent swirls of London's rage finally eddied into a new whirlwind of riot over the appointment of a Lieutenant of the Tower. On Monday 27 December 1641, Londoners marched to Westminster, demanding to know what had happened about their Commons petition. Were they to be landed with Charles's unpopular and corrupt appointee Colonel Lunsford as Lieutenant of the Tower? When they heard that he had been removed, they did not go away, but hung about asking what had happened to their petitions on ecclesiastical matters. They made a lane in both Palace yards, 'and no man could pass but when the rabble gave him leave to . . . Soon they set up the cry of "No Bishops! No Bishops!"' There was an undignified tussle between the Archbishop of York and a boy whom he unwisely tried to arrest. A near-riot began when Lunsford himself appeared in Westminster Hall, and he and other citizens tried to drive away the angry protesters with swords: 'then David Hyde began to bustle, and said he would cut the throats of those roundheaded dogs'. With that, Hyde, Lunsford and some others attacked the protesters, 'and cut many of them very sore'. They were driven back by a hail of hurled stones. Then came the indefatigable John Lilburne, with 'about a hundred citizens, some with cudgels, some sailors with truncheons, and the rest with stones'. Under the assault, half the gentlemen fled. The rest fought on, but were finally routed by citizens who fought 'like enraged lions'.

On 28 January 1642 Captain Philip Skippon 'marched very privately when it was dark to the backside of the Tower, and stayed at the iron gate with his men . . . he sent one into the Tower to the serjeant, who commanded the Hamleters, that he should march out of the Tower with his men and come to him. But the Serjeant desired to be excused.' Skippon, snubbingly described by Clarendon as a 'common soldier', was actually the son of a minor Norfolk gentleman, who had fought as an officer for the Elector Palatine and then in Holland against the Spanish – two Good Old Protestant wars, giving him plenty of practice for a third. His toughness as a trainer of troops was vital in moulding the London trained bands into the crucial fighting force they became, and he was to become one of Parliament's most stalwart and sensible soldiers, a major-general of infantry in the New Model Army.

When Nehemiah Wallington described the serjeant's refusal to obey Skippon's order as a plot by 'malignants' to take over the Tower and the City, he saw such incidents as standing in the way of the political and spiritual rebirth of the nation: 'you see many an excellent blessing and mercy in this very birth', he wrote, 'for this honourable parliament (as the Mother) to bring forth, and cannot'. This defined all the conflicts so far as an effort to turn England into a godly nation.

The king's departure left Parliament free to begin to gather troops from Anna Trapnel's East End. A militia committee was established in Tower Hamlets – authorized to assemble and train men and to suppress riot and trouble, and to collect a rate to finance the troops. The Tower Hamlets militia were strongly Parliamentarian, refusing to unite with city regiments whose loyalty to Parliament they suspected. (In 1662 Charles II refused to attend a muster on Tuttle Fields because of a rumour that the Hamleters would shoot at him.) So it came to seem appropriate that at any rate by February 1642, the Tower had come into the hands of the city authorities, its ramparts guarded not by royal troops but by the trained bands of the East End that Charles so hated, the Tower Hamlet bands. Anna Trapnel's world had triumphed, in London, at least.

London was not the only place with unruly crowds. Many other areas saw violence erupt. In the early months of 1642, some rebellious energies were contained by traditional means. The majority of locales drew up and presented petitions to Parliament, opening with fulsome praise of the institution. Many expressed concern about the king's evil councillors, by whom they largely meant Laudians and papists. Still others blamed the universities as nests of papistical and Arminian thought. Most expressed dread of a popish invasion; nineteen counties demanded that all papists be disarmed, while others expressed doubts about strict measures already taken. Oxfordshire begged Parliament to administer oaths to those searching recusant houses for arms to prevent them from concealing what they found. But fear of popery also provoked extreme violence. On 13 May 1642, a year after the London crowd had been gratified by Strafford's death, an Essex village saw a crowd of over a hundred gathered at the blowing of a horn, before marching out to the heath of Rovers Tye, where they tore down a series of enclosures that had been built by the Lucas family. All through Essex, Parliamentarians had rushed to fill the army of Robert Rich, first Earl of Warwick, known as a political activist and as a patron of sermons fervently denouncing popery, just as they had stayed away from the king's army gathered to fight the Scots two years before. Local Roman Catholics were disarmed, and fortifications built around Colchester. Laudian ministers were quickly silenced. But local magnate Sir John Lucas was determined to bring aid to the king. He gathered horse, arms and men at his residence just outside Colchester's walls. But his plans were known to his enemies. A night-watch set by the mayor spotted him as he left his house by the back gate. A musket was fired, the local beacon was lit to alert the villages. The trained bands and the Parliamentary volunteers besieged his estate, even bringing two pieces of ordnance. Men, women and children gathered, forming a crowd of around two thousand all told. The attack on Sir John Lucas's house included an assault on the ladies' chamber. There, tireless collector (and inventor) of atrocity stories Bruno Ryves tells us, a naked sword was set to Sir John's wife's breast. To Clarendon's later horror at the disregard of rank implied, Lucas ended up in the town gaol, and he was glad enough to be there.

Observers thought this outbreak of rage looked exactly like the 'inundation of the vulgar', the rising of the belly against the brain, which had been predicted by the Cassandra-like MP Simonds D'Ewes as the inevitable outcome of civil war. Though the rioters themselves sought to justify their actions by claiming support for Parliament, even Parliamentarians among them spoke of the violence of 'the rude people': 'we know not how to quiet them', muttered the mayor of Colchester, 'we could not repress them if we had five trained bands'. In parts of Suffolk, where there were further disturbances, the rioters were said to have denied any religious motivation, saying they were for the king, and would not be governed by a few Puritans.

The Essex-Stour valley mob initially confined itself to attacking the local Catholic community, but soon everyone got a taste for the fun, and the violence became less discriminating. 'As well Protestants as Papists' were plundered; similar unpolitical incidents involving the 'lewd and disorderly people' were reported in the area in the last three months of the year. 'Forasmuch as at this present there are disorders and distempers . . . and evil affected persons who hunger after rapines and spoilings and plunder of men's houses.' It was an excuse for a spot of vandalism, but it might be premature to assume there was no class distinction behind the plunder of the houses of the rich. There is some shaky evidence from the inexhaustible Ryves that locals picked out as targets families who were already disliked. Ryves shapes his account around the attack on Countess Rivers because it violates codes of honourable conduct in war: 'And you may guess what spiritual men they were, and likewise what danger this honourable person was in, they express themselves in rude unchristian language, that if they found her they would try what flesh she had?'

The Rivers family felt menaced from the beginning. Lady Rivers's sister Lady Penelope Gage wrote anxiously from Hengrave Hall, north of Bury St Edmunds, at the very beginning of 1642, that 'we are daily threatened by the common sort of people'. Living in St Osyth, the Rivers's Catholicism had long made them the object of local suspicion and dislike. Ryves claimed the Colchester attackers began a kind of cat-and-mouse game with the countess. They pursued her as if she were a comic-book villain. The crowd reached St Osyth only a few hours after she had made her escape; they were joined by sailors and what one local Catholic called 'the whole army rout'. At once, wrote a contemporary, they 'enter the house, and being entered, they pull down, cut in pieces, and carry away her costly hangings, beds, couches, chairs, and the whole furniture of her house, rob her of plates and monies'. Her servants were attacked. She made it to her house at Long Melford in Suffolk, but the crowds followed her there, gathering support en route, especially from seamen, a group especially noted for their strong anti-popery. Countess Rivers was understandably afraid. She sent for help to the Earl of Warwick, but he was at sea, Lord Rich was at Oxford, and Charles Rich was out hunting. So Arthur Wilson, steward of the Earl of Warwick, travelled through the Stour valley on his master's instructions during the riots, hoping to rescue the recusant Lady Rivers from the fury of the mob. Wilson was a Puritan and a Parliamentarian, but he thought very little of the crowd:

> With difficulty I passed through the little villages of Essex, where their black bills and coarse examinations put us to diverse demurs. And, but that they had some knowledge both of me and the coach, I had not passed with safety . . . When I came to Sudbury in Suffolk, within three miles of Long Melford, not a man appeared till we were within the chain. And then they

began to run to their weapons, and, before we could get to the market-place, the streets swarmed with people. I came out of the coach, as soon as they took the horses by the heads, and desired, that I might speak with the mayor, or some of the magistrates, to know the cause of this tumult, for we had offended nobody. The Mouth cried out, This coach belongs to the Lady Rivers; and they are going to her, for he had recognised her steward in the coach: and some, who pretended to be more wise and knowing than the rest, said, that I was the lord Rivers. And they swarmed about me, and were so kind as to lay hold on me. But I calmly entreated those many hundreds which encircled me, to hear me speak, which before they had not patience to do, the confusion and noise was so great. I told them, I was steward to the Earl of Warwick, a lover of his country, and now in the parliament's employment. That I was going to Bury [St Edmunds], about business of his. And that I had letters in my pockets (if they would let any of the magistrates see them) which would make me appear to be a friend and an honest man. That said, the Mouth cried out, Letters, letters! The tops of the trees, and all the windows, were thronged with people, who cried the same. At last the mayor came crowding in with his officers: and I showed him my letters . . . The mayor's wisdom said, he knew not my lord's hand; it might be, and it might not. And away he went, not knowing what to do with me, nor I to say to them.

But the town-clerk, whose father was a servant to the Earl of Warwick, 'told them I was the Earl of Warwick's steward: and his assurance got some credit with them. And so the great cloud vanished. But I could go no further to succour the Lady Rivers. For I heard, from all hands, that there was so great confusion at Melford, that no man appeared like a gentleman, but was made a prey to that ravenous crew.' So he left the coach at Salisbury, 'and went a bye-way to Sir Robert Crane's, a little nearer Melford, to listen after the countess'. He thought he was witnessing the actions of an 'unruly multitude . . . the rabble', not those of 'honest inhabitants'. He thought that they only pretended to religious fervour, while in fact 'spoil and plunder were their aim' and that they acted as if 'there had been a dissolution of all government'; he concluded that 'so monstrous is the beast when it holds the bridle in its teeth'.

Countess Rivers's ordeal was not yet over. On Wednesday 24 August, 'a multitude of like disposed persons, threatening her death' nearly caught her; they entered the house 'before she had fully escaped their sight' (perhaps she had been loth to use the 'back gate for beggars and the meaner sort of swains to come in at', noted by James Howell when he visited the house). So the crowds ransacked the house. John Rous reported that 'the Lady Rivers house was defaced, all glass broken, all iron spoiled, all likely places digged where money might be hidden. The gardens defaced. Beer and wine consumed and let out (to knee deep in the cellar) The deer killed and chased out.' She may have been helped to escape by Sir Robert Crane; she sought sanctuary at Bury St Edmunds, thirteen miles away. It shut its gates against her. Eventually she was allowed in, but was forced to flee to London the next day.

The crowds, unsatisfied, moved on to other targets: the Audleys, a Catholic family within the liberties of Colchester, who had already been the subject of a panic in 1640 when it had been said that Catholics were assembling for an insurrection. The family's house and cattle were plundered. On his funeral monument, Sir Henry had written *Non aedes (belli civilis furore diructas)* (He did not rebuild his house, destroyed by the fury of the civil war); the doggy, compressed Latin suggests some haste. A clergyman called Gabriel Honeyfold was set upon by 'a multitude of boys and rude people' who 'throng about him . . . throwing stones and dirt at him'. Another minister, Erasmus Laud, lost his cattle too, and the attackers also took all his wife's spare clothes. He was attacked solely because his name was the same as that of William Laud, the hated Archbishop of Canterbury. All across the east, local Catholic gentry were assailed; the landed Martins whose chapel was itself a provocation; the house of Carey, a steward to the Rivers family. The riots spread to neighbouring locales, including Maldon, where a Catholic landowner named Edmund Church came under attack; 'the poor people of the neighbourhood pulled down and carried away a barn and an oxhouse, declaring that Edmond Church was a papist', and that they would pull down his house if any opposed them. As in other civil wars, people who had been warily tolerant neighbours for years suddenly turned on the minority in their midst. Wherever there was a Catholic family, the crowds gathered: the Petres, the Southcotts.

The trouble only stopped when Parliament implemented a vigorous programme of Catholic-watching and sequestration.

Historians have disagreed violently about whether the rioters were motivated solely by religion, or whether class hatred played a part too. For many in the swirling, angry crowds, the war was, precisely, a war on the papists, and the goal was to prevent them from carrying out the hideous designs they were believed to be nurturing. In its paranoia this enabling narrative of recruitment does strongly resemble Nazi anti-Semitism, and like Nazi anti-Semitism it could easily tip over into corruption, profiteering and simple looting. Unlike anti-Semitism, however, it was elastic, able to embrace people (ultimately including Charles himself) who were clearly not Catholic nor even particularly sympathetic to Catholicism, but who were not godly enough, who did not share the culture and aspirations formed among the godly and the indefatigable tellers of their story, the London press. People who said 'damme me!' or 'sinke me!', people who fought alongside the Royalists or supplied them willingly, could come to be seen as near-papist because they were assumed to be part of a vast and secret conspiracy or else the dupes of that conspiracy. As well, England was swayed by rumours of prominent conversions; Laud was said to have been present when 'Doctor Prince' received extreme unction; an Essex man thought most of the bishops were secret Catholics; Suffolk parishioners began to suspect their ministers of Catholicism. Fears centred on the queen; at Bures a local gentleman said that 'the king hath a wife, and he loves her well, and she is a papist and we must all be of her religion, and that's the thing the bishops aim at'.

But many of those accused of popery were merely Arminian or not sufficiently godly to abhor Laud's reforms. No one even knew how many Catholics there were in the Eastern Association, and as some of the stories above make clear, locals were not always sure about who counted as Catholic; there were probably only 30,000 Catholics in the whole country, in a population of around four million. But prejudice was deaf to statistics. The queen's activism and the Laudian reforms made it *seem* that Catholics were gaining in strength. So did the rising number of Catholic peers: in 1603, there were nine, and in 1625 eighteen; the number of active, visible priests rose too, and Jesuits went from nine in 1593 to around 180 by 1641. The people of Essex and Suffolk had no direct knowledge of these alarming statistics, but they may have picked up a general and accurate sense that Rome was on the rise.

Dreadful as it seemed for Countess Rivers, worse fates awaited others. In Dorchester, in August 1642, two Catholic priests disobeyed a royal proclamation of 8 March 1641 which had tried to placate the public by insisting that all priests leave the country. They were arrested; one recanted, and the other refused to do so. His name was Hugh Green, and he was fifty-seven years old. He had been making for the ports to try to leave the country when he was arrested by a customs officer. He spent five months in gaol, was tried and convicted.

Green was to be executed on a Friday, by his own desire. They brought the furze for the fires to Gallows Hill, outside Dorchester, on Thursday. Green himself was taken to Gallows Hill on 18 August 1642. A crowd was waiting for him. It was eager and hopeful; after the terror of the Irish, after all Pym had said, it seemed obvious to the spectators that traitors like this one were behind it all. Three women were being hanged, too, for various crimes, and two had sent him word the night before that they would die in his faith. He absolved them with a sign, because he wasn't allowed close to them. 'God be with you, sir!' they cried.

Green gave away his things – his beads, his crucifix, his *Agnus Dei*, his handkerchief, his book of litanies. However, he would not apologize for what everyone knew to be his treachery. He made a long speech, denouncing heresy. Sir Thomas Trencher's chaplain, who had once been a weaver, was angry, shouting 'He blasphemes. Stop his mouth!' So the sheriff told Green to stop. Then he prayed instead for unity, for peace, and for the king, and forgave everyone. He called a Catholic woman, Elizabeth Willoughby, to him and she came, and he asked her to say goodbye to his fellow-prisoners, and he blessed her and five others.

He prayed for half an hour. No one could be persuaded to turn the ladder and make him fall. Finally, the hangman, sitting astride the gallows, persuaded a country clown to turn the ladder, and Green dropped. He made the sign of the cross three times. And they cut him down with a knife at the end of a long stick, handed up to the hangman by a constable, 'although', said Elizabeth, 'I and others did our uttermost to have hindered him'. Their courage was wasted. 'The man that was to quarter him was a timorous, unskilful man, by trade a barber, and his name was Barefoot. He was so long dismembering him that he came to his perfect senses and sat upright.' Elizabeth Willoughby managed to write down her horror:

> Then did this butcher cut his belly on both sides, and turn the flap upon his breast, which the holy man feeling put his left hand upon his bowels, and looking on his bloody hand laid it down by his side, and lifting up his right hand he crossed himself, saying three times, Jesu, Jesu, Jesu Mercy! The which, although unworthy, I am a witness of, for my hand was on his forehead . . . all the Catholics were pressed away from him by the unruly multitude except myself . . . Whilst he was thus calling upon Jesus, the butcher did pull a piece of his liver out instead of his heart, and tumbling his guts out every way to see if his heart were not among them; then with his knife he raked in the body . . . Methought my heart was pulled out of my body to see him in such cruel pains, lifting up his eyes to heaven, and not yet dead. Then I could no longer hold, but cried, *Out upon them that did so torment him.* His forehead was bathed in sweat, and blood and water flowed from his eyes and nose. And when on account of the gushing streams of blood his tongue could no longer pronounce the saving name of Jesus, his lips moved, and the frequent groans which he uttered from his inmost heart were proof of the most bitter pain and torture which he suffered.

Hugh Green lingered in the hands of the local barber for half an hour or more. When another Catholic woman pleaded with the sheriff, he was finally put out of his agony. After he had died at last, his heart was cut out and held up on a spear point, then flung into the fire where a minute before, his genitals had been burned. Some Catholic bystanders, including Elizabeth, tried to take the torn body away for burial, but the crowd stopped them, angrily, and it was all Elizabeth could do to get home without being torn to pieces herself.

Then Green's head was cut off, too, and the crowd kicked it about like a football. As a football, in fact; they went on playing till four o'clock – which proved that the man had no power – but since they believed Catholics were in league with the powers of darkness, they put sticks in the eyes, nose, and mouth, and buried the head near the scaffold. They had thought of putting it on one of Dorchester's gates as a trophy and a warning, but they had been put off, Elizabeth said, because a previous priest had been so displayed and God had punished the town with the onset of plague.

Others suffered the same fate. In July 1641, a Douai priest named William Ward who had spent twenty years in prison was suddenly dragged off to be hanged at Tyburn. In December, Parliament wanted to hang another seven priests. Charles refused the petition – courageously, if rashly, given that half the nation was by now wondering if he was not a papist himself – but two more priests were nonetheless executed in January 1642, and another seven in 1642 alone. Parliament, when ruling alone, went on to put to death twenty-four priests between 1641 and the end of the First Civil War, simply because they were priests. Eager claims for Parliamentarian tolerance and enthusiasm for liberty were liable to skate over the horrible deaths of these men, victims of a holy crusade and a paranoid terror that had little to do with liberal values. Rather, the English Civil War would not have occurred without the hysterical dread of popery which provoked the kind of violence Lady Rivers and Hugh Green experienced. Liberty was what had to be defended *from* papists like them, *by* truly godly people. In this way, a nation came to define itself against some of its own citizens. Civil war was bound to follow.

VII

The Valley of Decision

The king had set up his standard before London had begun to gather troops. It was 22 August 1642, as a newsbook reported:

> His Majesty came weary out of Warwickshire to Nottingham, and after half an hour's repose, commanded the Standard to be brought forth, which was carried by a Lord, His Majesty the Prince, the Duke of York, and diverse Lords and Gentlemen accompanying the same, as soon as it was set up, his Majesty called for the printed Proclamation, mended with pen and ink some words misprinted, or not approved of, and caused the Herald to read the Proclamation three times, and so departed.

The same newsbook went on to say, 'They plunder all men's houses whom they please to call roundheads, and bring in cartloads of household stuff and sell them before the court-gate.'

The contrast between the king's standard-raising and the murky behaviour of his troops is clear. What the newsbook writer didn't know was that even the standard-raising was something of a public relations disaster. For one thing, it was pouring. For another, the standard had to be planted in a hole scraped out of the mud with knives and bare hands. Finally, not many had as yet rallied to the king, and the standard was unfurled before a meagre assortment of three cavalry troops and one infantry battalion. Worst of all, the wind blew the standard down into the mud during the night. For a people saturated in Biblical portents, it was a sign of doom. For a man like Charles, to whom ceremony was the vessel bearing the precious liquor of authority, it was ominous. But he was committed, now, to war. Charles longed for military settlement, for a simple battle where he could beat his foes and show them to be traitors, treat them as the rebels they were. 'I am going to fight', he said, 'for my crown and dignity.'

And blood had already been shed. When William Brereton tried to raise troops for Parliament in Chester, he and his men were set upon by an angry mob. The Earl of Bath got a similar reception in Exeter. When Ralph Hopton rode into the small town of Shepton Mallet, he was hoping to recruit more men for the king. It was 1 August. But a thousand or so men turned out to stop any recruitment. Both Hopton and his foes withdrew to gather their forces. Three days later, the two troops met at Marshall's Elm. It was a Royalist victory, and twenty-seven Parliament-men lay dead. Only a skirmish, it was nevertheless the first real fighting of the war.

'Are you for the king, or Parliament?' schoolboys used to cry. In the war years, soldiers stopped all comers and asked them, 'King or Parliament?' But when conflict first began, it did not begin with the choice of sides, but with their formation from much more inchoate and various positions.

Before Charles raised his standard at Nottingham in August, it only became obvious as the months of late summer slid by that there were any sides to take, and even then it was not at once apparent that there were only two; at first there was room for many sides. Caught up in the unfolding events and in the hot tide of feelings running through the three kingdoms, the people did not know that they were about to fight an 'English Civil War'. Some thought that they were beginning a religious war against the Antichrist. A subset of these thought that they were fighting against a vast conspiracy of Catholics who were plotting to subvert Church and state, others that they were fighting to protect Church and state against a vast rebellion against just and legitimate authority. Still others thought the war was merely a simple and obvious matter of honour, which required that obligations to those higher in the hierarchy be observed at the price of blood. Still others thought they were witnessing a kind of rebalancing, where Parliament was about to curb the excesses which had grown upon the king and his counsellors of late. Others thought that what was happening was a chance for regions normally excluded from the processes of government to make their voices heard. Some people thought it an ideal chance to make war on neighbours that they had always disliked. Others thought it a chance to get rich quickly, with plenty of plunder available. A few – not many – thought that England would do better as a republic like Rome or Venice. A very few thought the end of the world was coming.

Because men and women thought in these diverse ways, the 'English Civil War' was not one war, but many; within each 'side', there were ancillary struggles to define that 'side's' purpose. Labels like 'Royalist' and 'Parliamentarian' describe coalitions of difference, coalitions that sometimes broke under pressure. These same pressures would break many men and women, and because choices were often so finely balanced, families broke too.

Two hundred and fifty years or so before the king abandoned London, Geoffrey Chaucer had described a group of pilgrims gathering there, all sorts and conditions of men and women, their various statuses, professions and trades. His diverse men and women were to share a journey to redemption, and exchange stories. In 1642, the social hierarchy and many of the conditions of men he described still existed, though some of the clerical orders had been swept away by the Reformation. But all three kingdoms were still societies of sorts and conditions, societies in which people's choices and tales were shaped by the place they occupied. In 1642, these sorts and conditions of men and women were to share a different and more painful journey, not towards redemption, but to the perdition of war. And they all had stories to tell on the way. Every kind of person in 1642 had to make their own sense of what was happening. Powerful nobles like Lucy Hay, gentlemen like Ralph Verney, tradesmen like Nehemiah Wallington, serving-women like Anna Trapnel – all were united and divided by the terrible choice before them. Like Chaucer, we can ride swiftly past a representative few of those estates and persons, and hear fragments of their stories. But unlike Chaucer, we do not have equal access to every estate. Most – though not all – of those who wrote down their decision-making and its origins were the better-off, with leisure, literacy and ambitions. We do not have anything like as many stories from the lower orders as we would wish, though we have some, and as we shall see, one good effect of the war was to enable ordinary soldiers to find a voice that would be heard. But for now, before the war has begun, we will be hearing mainly from what Chaucer would have called the gentil, the nicely born and bred.

We may begin with The Gentlewoman's Tale, the story of the choices made by Brilliana Harley. The Harley family of Brampton Bryan, Herefordshire, were an especially united family due to their shared beliefs. Brilliana's father was Sir Edward Conway, Governor of Holland and Zeeland during their revolt against Spanish rule in the 1570s, so uncannily predictive of the Civil War in its anti-monarchic violence, iconoclasm, and cries of 'liberty!' Born in 1598, she was in early middle age when the conflicts began, forty-four or so. Anne Fairfax, the wife of Parliament's most important general, was her cousin.

Until the war, Brilliana's life was dominated by family life and religion. Early modern women dreaded infertility because they were usually held responsible for it, and once pregnant they feared miscarriage and stillbirth because they were considered the fault of women too. It was widely believed that the mother's imagination could act upon the child during conception or pregnancy, causing deformities. Looking at a picture of John the Baptist at the moment of conception could create a child covered in hair, while gazing at a hare might cause a hare lip. Birth, too, was dangerous for mother and child. Women feared the death of the child: Alice Thornton dreamt of lying in childbed with a white sheet spread, but drops of blood sprinkled on it. 'I kept the dream in mind till my child died', she wrote. Lady Eleanor Davies was haunted by the image of a dead child which she saw in her dreams. Women also feared that they might die themselves. Elizabeth Joscelin was not the only pregnant woman to compose a loving letter of advice to her unborn child in case she was not available to guide the child in person. In her case her fears proved well grounded, and she died soon after giving birth. Lucy Hutchinson's grandmother lost her wits after a difficult birth.

The ceremony of childbirth was a women's affair. Birth took place in a room from which all light was excluded; most air too. Only women could be present, and the labouring woman's mother was usually with them. All the women, including the one giving birth, drank caudles, often a kind of eggnog with milk, wine and spices. But there was no anaesthesia available, and births did go catastrophically wrong from time to time.

After the birth, the woman remained in the birthing room for ten days, lying on the same linens on which she had delivered. After this time had elapsed, her 'upsitting' occurred; the linen was changed and she sat up and could show off the baby to its father and to other male visitors. But she and in particular the baby traditionally did not leave the home until a month had passed, during which time she would if reasonably off be cared for by a lying-in maid. At the end of the month, she and the baby would go to church for the churching ceremony, though a godly woman like Brilliana Harley might well find the ceremony offensive. Women from lower social strata would then feed their babies themselves. Some better-off women expressed the wish to do so but were sometimes forbidden by their husbands. The frequent remedies for sore and dry breasts in early modern commonplace books suggest that the process was not trouble-free, certainly not pain-free.

Historians used to think – rather arrogantly – that parents in earlier periods minded less about the deaths of children because such tragedies were much more frequent. Recent research strongly suggests that this was not the case. If anything, children were even more valued then than they are today because they represented prosperity and hope for a better future economically. And Brilliana, who certainly didn't need her children's labour, nonetheless adored her eldest son Edward, whom she called Ned. It was Ned who was the centre of her emotional life, not his father Robert. Brilliana sometimes asked Ned to tell Robert things or to ask him for things, but she also relied on him directly for love and comfort.

Brilliana's other emotional centre was her religion. She was a very godly woman, alert and curious within a framework of strong, severe Calvinism. For Brilliana faith, good works and respect for God are not the means to salvation, but outward signs of election. From the beginning of time, God knows exactly who will ultimately join him in heaven, and who will be damned. This cannot be changed. Free will does not exist. So Brilliana wrote in her commonplace book that 'man can not move it [his will] once to goodness, for moving is the beginning of turning to God . . . It is God that first turns our will to that which is good and we are converted by the power of God only, it is God that works in all of us.' This could make life very difficult, for godly people were prone to terrifying bouts of introspection, examining themselves for signs that their faith was adequate enough for election. This was made all the more troubling because even those who were not truly elected could show some signs of faith; Brilliana, quoting directly from Calvin, wrote that 'those that are not elect have some signs of calling, as the elect have, but they never cleave to Christ with that assurance of heart with which the assurance of our election is established, they depart from the church because they are not of the church'.

One of Brilliana's servants, Blechly, decided that she was not saved in May 1640: '[and] has these 2 days been in grievous distress, and is in grievous agony of conscience and despair; she says she shall be damned'. Brilliana urges Ned to ask his tutor to pray for Blechly. Doubt and despair could themselves be outward signs that one was not a member of the elect, which made them even more terrifying. At the same time, complacency was a bad sign as well, so those cast temporarily into despair could revive themselves and experience a new birth of faith. Brilliana reminded Ned of the need for self-examination.

The Harleys made sure the vicar of their local church at Brampton was of their kind. At the end of the 1630s a man called Stanley Gower was the incumbent; on arrival in 1634 he had set about overlooking those regulations of the Laudian Church offensive to the godly. He wouldn't let his parishioners stand during the gospel, nor bow at the name of Jesus; he left the absolution out of the prayer book's service, he refused to rail the altar, still treating it as a movable communion table, and he told his congregation not to kneel in prayer, and not to remove their hats.

Robert Harley was part of the godly power network that was eventually to ensnare the king. He was accused of allowing Gower's offences, harbouring Richard Symonds, a radical separatist who was also his son's tutor, and creating special fasts for his own household, usually a sign of radical Puritanism. Harley was also in touch with that godly powerhouse and *eminence grise* Lord Saye and Sele, a distant cousin, and with his son Nathaniel Fiennes, with whom he exchanged godly books. He was also in contact with Prynne and Burton, visiting Prynne during his imprisonment, and sometimes meeting Burton bound on the same errand. It was Harley who moved at the start of the Long Parliament that all three should be invited to put their case to Parliament, which found in their favour and offered them compensation. During the Short Parliament, Robert Harley urged that bowing to the altar was idolatrous, and, with Pym, wanted it named a crime. At the same time, Brilliana disliked independents like the Brownists; she would not have seen eye to eye with Anna Trapnel. What she and Robert wanted was not innovation, but the retention and modest extension of what she saw as the normal practices of the Calvinist Elizabethan Church.

The Harleys saw the events of the 1620s and '30s as a sign that the final struggle between the people of God and the Antichrist had begun. Brilliana wrote to Ned that 'this year 1639 is the year in which many are of the opinion that the antichrist must begin to fall. The Lord say amen to it.' The Harleys firmly believed in a sophisticated conspiracy of Catholics who manipulated Charles and would eventually convert him. It was against this background that news of the Ulster Uprising broke in November 1641. The belief that the same things could happen at any moment in England was fuelled when a tailor named Beale claimed on 15 November that he had overheard a design to kill 108 MPs, followed by a general Catholic rising. Robert Harley promptly wrote to John Aston: 'look well to your town, for the Papists are discovered to have a bloody design, in general, as well as against the kingdom, as elsewhere'. At Brampton they were all in arms in the castle, 'and took up provisions with them there in great fear', wrote Brilliana.

To keep abreast of the 'real' news, suppressed by the government, the Harleys tried to get hold of printed news-sheets called corantoes and of manuscript news-sheets, called separates, which reported such events as speeches in Parliament and state trials. Sixteen-year-old Ned kept Brilliana supplied with separates during the Short Parliament. But personal letters were still the main source of news. The risk that they might be intercepted encouraged writers to be circumspect, however. Brilliana warned Ned about this risk: 'when you write by the carrier, write nothing but what any may see, for many times the letters miscarry'. Some letter-writers used codes (Charles was especially fond of them). But the practice increased both paranoia and a sense that one was surrounded by spies and foes, plotting. Brilliana was delighted to hear of the abolition of the Court of High Commission, which had been the instrument of silencing many godly ministers, but not everyone in Herefordshire or the Marches was equally delighted to see godliness return. Brampton's own vicar, Gower, reported glumly that 'the vulgar comfort themselves with assured confidence that the bishops will get up again. I tell you but the language of Babel's bricklayers', while Thomas Harley, in Brampton, reported to his brother Ned in London that 'some men jeer and cast forth reproachful words against the Parliament, and others that might forward the work of the Parliament are very backward'.

When Parliament went into brief recess in September 1641 Robert returned to Brampton and tried to enforce the Commons' resolution to remove all crucifixes and images from churches, not only purifying his own church at Brampton, but all those in surrounding villages. At Leintwardine he broke the windows and smashed the glass with a hammer, throwing it into the Teme 'in imitation of King Asa 2 Chron 15:16 who threw the images into the brook Kidron', but at Aymestrey the minister and the parishioners withstood him. Harley wrote angrily to churchwardens in Leominster asking why they had failed to take down the crosses he had seen passing the church.

For most of 1642 to 1644, Robert was away from home, serving as an MP at Westminster. In his absence his wife Brilliana took charge of the Harley estates. She disliked it when he was away because she felt miserably isolated: writing to Ned, she complained that 'now your father is away, you know I have nobody that I can speak to'. But she knew it was her duty. Robert Harley often criticized her management: 'what is done in your father's estate pleases him not, so that I wish myself with all my heart in London, and then your father might be a witness of what is spent: but if your father think it best for me to be in the country, I am well pleased with what he shall think best'. This sounds submissive, but the note of anger is unmistakable.

For Brilliana her connectedness with her son became a way to imagine herself escaping from the dangers that enclosed her more and more tightly. In theory, Oxford was a world that Robert knew and she didn't, a man's world. Robert had been to Oxford, to Oriel College in 1597, graduating with a BA in 1599; his tutor Cadwallader Owen was a powerful godly influence on the young man. Robert was also in charge of the boys' education, searching for a tutor for them in 1631, but they were eventually sent away to school, to Shrewsbury. Ned went up to Oxford in 1638, just before his fourteenth birthday. He went to Magdalen Hall, where the principal John Wilkinson was a solid Calvinist, and where he would be taught by another staunch Puritan, Edward Perkins. Brilliana, however, took a strong interest in Ned's godly tutors. She was worried when William Whately died and his living became vacant; she feared they might lose the services of ·Mr Perkins, too, since 'as soon as any man come to ripeness of judgement and holiness he is taken away, and so they still glean the garden of the ripe grapes and leave the sour ones behind'. She also worried, like any other mother seeing a child off to university, that he would be exposed to moral danger. She wrote in a letter, 'now I fear you will both see and hear men of nobility and excellent parts of nature abandon themselves to swearing and that odious sin of drunkenness'. Robert also wrote that 'the universities do too much abound with such pigs'. The larger world beyond the family was menacing. But it was also enticing. Brilliana's letters betray twin yearnings; to enclose Ned in the safety of family holiness, and to catch a glimpse of his larger world through him. She sent him reams of advice and torrents of home-made medicines:

> 13 November 1638. I beseech the Lord to bless you with those choice blessings of his spirit, which none but his dear elect are partakers of. I have sent you some juice of liquorice, which you may keep to make use of, if you should have a cold.
>
> 17 November 1638. I am glad you find a want of that ministry you did enjoy: Labour to keep a fresh desire after the sincere milk of the word, and then in good time you shall enjoy that blessing again.

She worried all the time about Ned's health and well-being: 'Pray send me one of your socks, to make you new ones by', she wrote; and 'You did well to take some balsam; it is a most sovereign thing, and I purpose, if it please God, to write you the virtues of it'. Sometimes she was tentative: 'Dear Ned, if you would have anything, send me word;

or if I thought it a cold pie, or such a thing, would be any pleasure to you, I would send it to you. But your father says you care not for it, and Mrs Pierson tells me when her son was at Oxford, and she sent him such things, he prayed her that she would not' (14 December 1638). But at heart she was a generous provider. She also kept her husband supplied, writing that 'I have sent your father a snipe pie and a teal pie, and a collar of brawn, or else I had sent you something this week' (December 1640).

She also liked to supply spiritual food. She urged holy books on Ned, as part of their literary discussions: 'I believe, before this, you have read some part of Mr Calvin; send me word how you like him.' With almost every letter a present or a small piece of advice arrives: 'I have sent you a little purse with some small money in it, all the pence I had, that you may have a penny to give a poor body and a pair of gloves; not that I think you have not better in Oxford, but that you may sometimes remember her, that seldom has you out of my thoughts.'

Ned also sent her things, including books. She wrote to thank him: 'I thank you for *The Man in the Moon*. I had heard of the book, but not seen it; by as much as I have looked upon, I find it is some kind of *Don Quixote*. I would willingly have the French book you write me word of; but if it can be had, I desire it in French' (30 November 1638).

The Man in the Moon was an imaginative choice. It was actually an early work of science fiction: the hero, Gonzales, is on his way home from Spain when he falls ill, and is put ashore on a desert island. Here he soon trains a pair of swans to be his servants, and eventually through the use of complex machinery they fly him to the moon, where he finds an ideal society in which there is no war, no hunger, a cure for all illnesses. This society does not lack hierarchy, however; there is a system based on height, and the king is the tallest man. There's an element of Swiftian satire of learning, but also a critique of contemporary politics; if Ned sent his mother this book, it shows that she was herself an adventurous and curious reader, interested in unfeminine topics like political theory. It is also suggestive that Brilliana knew about *Don Quixote*, that great debunking of the chivalrous romances to which Charles and Henrietta and their court were so addicted.

But Brilliana was no bluestocking; she was keen on the emerging commodity culture of the late 1630s, and wanted to furnish Brampton in style. She often asked Ned to shop for her: 'If there be any good looking glasses in Oxford choose me one about the bigness of that I use to dress me in, if you remember it ... All my fruit dishes are broken; therefore good Ned, if there be any such blue and white dishes as I used to have for fruit, buy me some; they are not porcelain, nor are they of the ordinary metal of blue and white dishes' (19 November 1639).

Another fashionable commodity was news: 'I should be glad to hear from you how the King went to Parliament' (23 April 1640). Brilliana didn't only ask for news: she passed it on eagerly, showing that her choices were based on a careful attempt to keep abreast of things. She wrote to Ned about the army gathering for the war against the Scots (3 July 1640). She liked to pass on news from others to Ned; 'The last night I heard from your father. He saw Mr Prynne and Mr Burton come into London; they were met with 2000 horse and 150 Scotch, and the men wore rosemary that met them.' Rosemary for remembrance.

In the end Ned did not stay at Magdalen long enough to take a degree. He left Oxford in November 1640 to witness the opening of the Long Parliament. At first his visit was prolonged because an outbreak of plague in Oxford made it risky to return to Magdalen, and then events in London proved exciting enough to make a return to Oxford seem futile. Imaginatively, and eager to hear his news, Brilliana supported his stay in London. Meanwhile the education of her younger sons became more and more problematic. The other children had a tutor, Richard Symonds, who fell in with a group of separatists in 1639 and left with his wife. They then had a schoolteacher called Mr Ballam, who was sick a good deal, so that the boys 'lose their time very much'. Tom was 'as busy as can be about the Parliament and holds intelligence with all that will give him true notice of things', while Robin was restless 'and cares not to know how it goes in the Parliament'. He preferred the company of the servants, to his mother's dismay. He was also subject to fits, possibly epileptic. Brilliana tried to take the boys' education in hand herself, making them do Latin translation, but managed to persuade them to do 'but a little'. She did try sending them to school with the curate William Voyle, at nearby Llanfairwater-dine, but they had to come home almost at once because the food was uneatable. Eventually, by May 1642 she suggested the boys be sent to Oxford. Luckily, Robert Harley refused, for they would have had a difficult time in what was shortly to become the Royalist capital. Instead, Ned joined the forces of Sir William Waller in May 1643, and persuaded Brilliana to let Robin join too in June. The younger children – Tom, Dorothy, and Margaret, and their cousin Edward Smith – stayed at Brampton Bryan.

Brilliana was delighted by the fall of the bishops, especially Laud: in March 1641 she wrote gleefully: 'I am glad the bishops begin to fall and hope it will be with them as it was with Haman; when he began to fall, he fell indeed.' Brilliana is identifying the Protestant English Church with the Jews, the Chosen People, and perhaps with Esther, their saviour. Odd though it may sound, she may be thinking of embroidery; she was a keen needlewoman, and for many gentry women embroidery allowed a self-expression not really possible elsewhere. Judith, Esther and Susanna were all favourite Civil War subjects; women could see themselves as saviours of their nations. Later she wrote, 'I much rejoice that it is come so far that the bishops and all their train is voted against. I trust in God they will be enacted against, which I long to hear, and I pray God take all those things away which have so long offended' (5 June 1641). When finally reform came to Hereford, she was delighted: 'they have turned the table in the cathedral [so it became a plain communion table turned west–east] and taken away the copes and basins and all such things [Laudian innovations]. I hope they begin to see that the Lord is about to purge his church of all such inventions of men' (17 February 1642). She was also pleased by the fall of Strafford, but thought he 'died like a Seneca [a righteous pagan] but not like one who had tasted the mystery of godliness' (21 May 1641).

Yet despite all this, Brilliana typifies the moderate Parliamentarians who hoped that the king might be persuaded to listen to Parliament. While asking Robert to get some arms and powder for local Puritans (23 April 1642) she also wrote piously that 'the Lord in his mercy make them one, and in his good time incline the king to be fully assured in the faithful counsel of the parliament' (29 April 1642).

Despite her close-knit immediate family, Brilliana's wider circle of kin was divided: her brother-in-law Pelham wrote to her that he had gone to York to join the king. 'I think now that my dear sister was taken away that she might not see that which would grieve her heart', she wrote despondently on 17 May 1642. She was also divided from her locale, which was largely Royalist. Frightening demonstrations began to happen in Herefordshire. 'At Ludlow they set up a maypole, and a thing like a head on it, and so they did at Croft, and gathered a great many about it, and shot at it in derision of roundheads. At Ludlow they abused Mr Buge's son very much, and are so insolent that they durst not leave their house to come to the fast. I acknowledge I do not think myself safe where I am, I lose the comfort of your father's company, and am in but little safety, but that my trust is in God', she wrote on 4 June 1642. At the county fair, where Brilliana had to go to sell some horses, she was again afraid: 'I thank God it has passed quietly, but I was something afraid, because they are grown so insolent. I hope this night will be as quiet as the day has been', she wrote on 11 June 1642. Evidently Robert told her not to worry so, because she wrote obediently (but without agreement) to Ned on 20 June 1642, 'Since your father thinks Herefordshire as safe as any other country, I will think so too; but when I considered how long I had been from him, and how this country was affected, my desire to see your father, and my care to be in a place of safety, made me earnestly desire to come up to London. But since it is not your father's will, I will lay aside that desire.' So far she wrote as Brilliana the good wife, but as she continues she reminds Ned forcibly of the precariousness of her position. Immediately afterwards she tells the story of a godly preacher: 'This day Mr Davis came from Hereford, where he went to preach, by the entreaty of some in the town, and this befell him: when he had ended his prayer before the sermon, which he was short in, because he was loth to tire them, two men went out of the church and cried "pray God bless the King; this man does not pray for the king". Upon which, before he read his text, he told them, that ministers had that liberty, to pray before or after the sermon for the church and state. For all that, they went to the bells and rang, and a great many went to the churchyard and cried "roundhead". In the afternoon they would not let him preach; so he went to the cathedral. Those that had any goodness were much troubled and wept much.'

More fears were aroused by 24 June 1642: 'Mr William Littleton being at Ludlow last week, as he came out of the church, a man came to him and looked him in the face and cried "roundhead". He gave the fellow a good box of the ear, and stepped to one that had a cudgel and took it from him and beat him soundly. They say, they are now more quiet in Ludlow.' And Brilliana knew that some of her neighbours were on the opposite side. The committed Royalist Sir William Croft, she wrote, 'came to see me: he never asked how your father did; spoke slightly, and stayed but a little. I hear that he has commanded the beacon new furnished, and new pitch put into it. I have sent to enquire after it; if it be so I will send your father word.'

Brilliana and her house at Brampton were now alone in increasingly hostile territory, as dislikes deepened into divisions, sides became visible and were chosen. Shropshire and Worcestershire, to the north of Brampton, became by degrees staunchly Royalist, while the Welsh counties in the west were also dominated by the king's supporters. The nearest Parliamentarian garrison to Brampton was Gloucester, and although Brilliana tried to stay in touch with its commander it was too far away to give her much practical help. Parliamentarians in Herefordshire began to seek safety elsewhere. John Tombes felt that his wife and children were no longer safe: 'the barbarous rage and violence of the people so increased'.

Brilliana began to prepare for the trouble she knew was coming. She was especially offended that the people in Herefordshire and Shropshire appeared not to appreciate Robert Harley: 'at first when I saw how outrageously this county carried themselves against your father, my anger was so up, and my sorrow, that I had hardly any patience to stay. But now, I have well considered, that if I go away I shall leave all that your father has to the prey of our enemies, which they would be glad of; so that, and please God, I purpose to stay as long as it is possible, if I live. This is my resolution, without your father contradict it. I have received this night the hamper with the powder and match, but I have not yet the muskets, but will enquire after them', she wrote on 2 July 1642. In two days' time she wrote again to tell Robert by bearer that the king had sent a commission to twelve of the justices to settle the militia. To Ned she wrote despondently that 'Your father they are grown to hate ... My dear Ned, I am not afraid, but sure I am, that we are a despised company.' By 8 July she was reporting still more militia activity: 'they threaten poor Brampton', she wrote, 'but we are in the hand of our God, who I hope will keep us safe'. She packed up the plate to send it to Robert, characteristically putting in a cake for him, too, but on 9 July 1643 she added, 'I do long almost to be from Brampton.' Ned and Robert sent more arms; she sent more plate, carefully telling the carrier it was a cake so it would not be stolen. To get an idea of affairs, she sent Samuel to Hereford. He did not bring back good news: 'they all at Hereford cried out against your father, and not one said anything for him, but one man, Mr Phillips of Ledbury, said when he heard them speak so against your father, "Well", said he, "though Sir Robert Harley be so low here, yet he is above, where he is".' She was worrying again. 'My dear Ned, I cannot think I am safe at Brampton, and by no means I would have you come down.' Even the servant she sent with a letter to Ned on 19 July was a further headache: 'he is such a roguish boy that I dare not keep him in my house, and as little do I dare let him go into the country, lest he join with the company of volunteers, or some other such crew. I have given him no more money than will serve to bear his charges up, and because I would have him make haste and be sure to go to London.' She ordered shot from Worcester, in secret. Her skills as a housewife, dispatching food parcels and ordering supplies, were now turned to martial purposes.

The commissioners of array mustered the trained bands in Hereford, and removed Robert Harley from his position of command. When Robert's name was called 'a great many cried out and wished you were there so that they might tear you to pieces'. But others were more loyal; half of Robert's band defaulted during the Hereford muster.

There was more drama in the parish church at Leominster when Wallop Brabazon, one of the king's most zealous and eager commissioners, tried to force a visiting rector to read aloud one of the king's pamphlets from the pulpit. The rector in question, from nearby Bitterly in Shropshire, refused diplomatically, pointing out that only the local vicar was enjoined to read it, but Brabazon's men began calling him 'Roundhead' and threatening him with their cudgels. Order was restored with an effort. Incidents like this helped Brilliana to feel more alarmed and isolated than ever; she worried that the same Royalists might try to force Stanley Gower to read the same pamphlet in the local church.

By now it was clear that there were two sides in Herefordshire, the godly who felt themselves under attack, and the Royalists, who were vastly in the majority. Brilliana Harley and her family were cast as godly not only by their own choices, but by the perceptions of their neighbours. They could never have been anything else.

Not all gentlemen with strong religious views sided with Parliament, however, as this Tale of Three Gentlemen shows. The first is Cornish gentleman Bevil Grenville, a member of one of Cornwall's greatest gentry families, who was also a brave, intelligent and rather romantic man. He was descended from a celebrated man of action: he was the grandson of Sir Richard Grenville of the *Revenge*, the man who in 1595 had fought on tirelessly alone against an entire Spanish invasion fleet for fifteen full hours. Richard was a potent symbol of English rebuttal of Catholic invasions. But his descendant was not only a warrior, but also a man who said he had devoted so much time to what he called 'the sweet delights' of poetry and history while at Oxford that he had never learnt to manage an estate. His letters to his wife are touching in their devotion:

> My dearest, I am exceeding glad to hear from you, but do desire you, not to be so passionate for my absence, I vow you cannot more desire, to have me at home, than I do desire to be there, & as soon as I can dispatch my business I will instantly come away . . . I hope you will not have the child so soon as you fear. I will be as fast as I can, send down those provisions.

Wherever he was physically, Bevil's mind was on his home and estate:

> I have left no order with any body, for the moorstone windows . . . Make all the haste you can, to thresh out your corn, for fear it be spoiled, & observe how many bushels it is. Let Charles the joiner make a board for the parler [parlour] as soon as you can, as plain and cheap as possible, he can make, only 2 or 3 deal boards fitted together, and tressels to stand on, & so long as to reach from the window to the little door, but not to hinder the going in and out.

When he heard his wife was sick, he wrote in even more heartfelt terms:

> My broken lines express the fracture that these tidings do make in my heart and sinews. Yet they have not so far deprived me, but I can resolve this, that if you cannot send me better news

by this bearer ... then I will be with you by Gods help before
I sleep.

On hearing she was better, Bevil reverted to household planning:
Turkey work stools, damask, diaper tablecloths, the children's shoes,
feathers for a bed, keeping the pigs out of the plant nursery and the
orchard. He filled his letters with this woven fabric of a shared household, with the joys of shopping, and said far less about his lack of
enthusiasm for the Laudian changes in religion. But he warned his son,
'now you are sent abroad into the forest of this world, where so many
wild beasts wait for the devouring of all youths, I mean the depraving
of their manners'. The little world they made was to be ripped apart
by the coming conflict.

It took Bevil almost no time to declare for the king. And yet Bevil
Grenville was not the likeliest choice for a Royalist stalwart and war
hero. He had been a crucial ally of MP Sir John Eliot in his fights
against Charles's favourite the Duke of Buckingham and against the
king's methods of revenue-raising. Eliot was a fellow-Cornishman and
a friend, and the old saying has it that a Grenville was never found
wanting in loyalty. Like many of Charles's fiercest opponents, Eliot was
fiercely anti-Catholic, demanding that laws against them be severely
enforced in the 1620s. Eliot was eventually imprisoned for his refusal
to pay the Forced Loan in 1627, played a major role in the 1628
Parliament, and was one of those responsible for the Petition of Right.
As a result of his activities, he was again arrested and imprisoned in
1630.

Bevil blamed Charles for the problems his friend suffered. Indignation conquered caution, and he wrote furiously in 1628 that 'the
King hath lately sent [Eliot] to the tower, for some words spoken in
the Parl[ia]m[en]t. But we are all resolved to have him out again, or
will proceed in no business.' But Grenville's enthusiasm for opposition
waned when it became apparent that Eliot might die in prison after
his second arrest. His loyalty now led him to urge his friend to compromise and get out of gaol: 'I cannot but out of the fullness of my grief
be very Passionate at your long suffering', he wrote, with the old
indignation. But he also commented that 'more of the honest knot are
fetched away' which he says 'drives me into wonder and amazement'.

But then he grows defensive. 'No man', he declares, 'hath with more boldness declared his resolution in this particular than myself, which nor fire nor torture can divert me from, while in my own heart I am satisfied that it belongs to the duty of an honest Englishman so to do.' Having shown he is no traitor, Bevil proceeds in a separate, undated letter to try to persuade his friend to live rather than die for the cause: 'for your country's sake, your childrens' sake, your friends' sake . . . I say I beseech you be not nice, but pursue your liberty if it may be had on honourable terms. I will not desire you to abandon a good cause, but if a little bending may prevent a breaking yield a little unto it', he urged, adding that this would after all enable Eliot to serve his country later. It was all to no avail. Eliot had developed a lung disease, and he died in prison in early 1632.

Interestingly, Bevil's letters to Eliot do not mention religion as an issue. But when writing to another friend, the future Parliamentarian general Sir William Waller, Bevil showed an interest in the providential unfolding of history not much removed from that expressed by Robert Harley: 'I wonder nothing at what the Divine justice doth threaten the iniquity of the present times with, but I rather wonder (all things considered) that it hath not sooner happened', he wrote gloomily. The man who wrote this letter was not at the time a likely Royalist.

But Bevil was to change, and change radically. As well as his friend Eliot, his father had also died. Sir Bernard Grenville had been a much more conservative thinker than his son, and while Bevil was befriending Eliot and refusing to pay the Forced Loan, Sir Bernard had been obliged to try to collect it. His father was also a Buckingham supporter. This gap between father and son foreshadowed the more dramatic fissures that were to split whole families during the war itself. However, on his father's deathbed in 1635 they were reconciled. This reconciliation seemed to precipitate Bevil into the ardent Royalism that characterized the rest of his career. Determined to join the campaign against the Scots in 1638, he wrote:

> I cannot contain myself within my doors when the King of England's Standard waves in the field upon so just occasion, the cause being such as must make all those that die in it little inferior to Martyrs. And for mine own part I desire to acquire an honest name or an honourable grave. I never loved my life

or ease so much as to shun such an occasion which if I should
I were unworthy of the profession I have held, or to succeed
those ancestors of mine, who have so many of them in several
ages sacrificed their lives for their country.

Then when he served in the Long Parliament, he eloquently and vehemently opposed Strafford's attainder, just as decisively as he had backed
Eliot in 1628. He wrote to his fellow-Cornish MP, Alexander Carew:
'Pray Sir, when it comes to be put to the vote, let it never be said that
any member of our county should have a hand in this fatal business.'
Carew replied back, dryly, that 'If I were sure to be the next man that
should suffer upon the same scaffold with the same axe, I would give
my consent to the passing of it'. Bevil remained adamant.

   With sentiments like this, it is not surprising that Bevil Grenville,
the king's own choice, plunged into the job of commissioner 'for the
peace' or (more bluntly) recruiter for the king's army. At a public
meeting in Launceston, on 5 August 1642, the sheriff read out the King's
Proclamation against the Cornish militia. This call to muster was a
traditional proceeding whenever the king required an army. And yet
recruitment was slow; even eager, committed Bevil Grenville could only
bring 180 men to a muster meeting on 17 August. So a truce was agreed
with the militia from 18 August for 15 days. Everyone was groping for
what to do. But then four days later the king raised his standard at
Nottingham, the brief pause was over, and the splitting into sides
continued. When future Royalist general Ralph Hopton arrived on
25 September, he tipped the balance in favour of the king with a piece
of dash worthy of D'Artagnan. There was a local peace treaty, made in
August, but it was shattered when Ralph Hopton burst in, fleeing
with his horse from the Somerset disaster. Hopton tactfully presented
himself for trial for breaking the peace; the royalists acquitted him and
indicted their opponents for the same offence. Richard Vyvian stood
on the steps of the Town Hall in Truro and demanded that the mayor
call out the trained bands for the king. The mayor refused. Vyvian
appealed to the crowd which had quickly gathered. 'What unlawful
assemblies were gathered in many parts of the country to the danger
of their lives, their wives and their children.' His words had some effect.
On 5 October, the trained bands of Truro were sent out for the king.

   The majority of the Cornish greater gentry declared for the king, but while some, like Bevil Grenville, were eager, others were dragged along reluctantly. Grenville wrote, 'for my part I am impatient (as all my honest friends also are) that we did not march presently, to fetch those traitors out of their nest at Launceston, or fire them in it. But some of our fainter brethren here prevailed so far with the sherriff, as there is a conference agreed on this day between 6 of a side, to see if they can compass matters.'

Oddly, he was as motivated by religion as the Harleys, and just as much a Puritan. He was so strict with his troops that he is reported to have 'wished that his army were all of them as good as his Cause'. He 'disciplined them to piety and strictness', wrote an early biographer, '[and] there were fewer oaths among them than in any army in England'. Like Hopton himself, Bevil was a Calvinist. Bevil had been active against the Scots, however, which might point to a notion of 'king first, God second'. He was also a Cornishman, and the Cornish declared almost *en masse* for the king. The Cornish still spoke a different language in the seventeenth century, and had a long and deep tradition of religious and civil dissatisfaction with decrees from Westminster. They failed to identify with the notion of Englishness that was central to the Parliamentarian cause. In October 1642 the Cornish ejected the supporters of Parliament from the county, out of dislike for their ardent Protestantism; this was promptly denounced by Parliamentarians as a rerun of the popish Western Risings of 1549, and in a way it was, for the Cornish had loathed the vehemently Calvinist Edwardian prayer book as a foreign imposition.

A particularly zealous iconoclast, a man named William Body, had been murdered by the parishioners of St Keverne on 5 April 1548, though the ringleaders were executed promptly by the gentry of eastern Cornwall. In June 1549, when the new and vehemently Protestant prayer book came into use, the West Country congregations forced their priests to revert to the old Latin service, and they rose behind the banner of the Five Wounds, which asked for the restoration of the old Mass, all the icons and the communion service once or twice a year in one kind only. At Stratton, the parishioners took from hiding the images they had carefully kept, and displayed them again; they were removed once more when the rebellion ended. They were led in part by Robert Welsh, a priest born in Cornwall, but who had a parish in the Exeter suburbs. The West Country's loyalty to the old religion continued. Devon and Cornwall provided only one martyr for the Marian fires.

It is a long historical stretch from 1549 to 1642, almost from grandfather to grandson, but it may not be a coincidence that the places up in arms against the very Protestant prayer book were also among those that took up arms first, and most willingly, for the king. By contrast, towns that leapt to be Protestant in 1558, including Coventry, Colchester, Ipswich, Leicester – were Parliamentarian. It wasn't quite as simple as this; as with any rule, exceptions can be found. But it might be that the revolts of 1549 lingered – in Cornwall, at least – as a story, a memory of how false religion could be opposed in arms.

Others in Cornwall were more doubtful, however. Unlike Bevil Grenville, Francis Godolphin was a reluctant belligerent. He spent most of the war working for the king in Oxford or Scilly, and entertained the Prince of Wales on St Mary's in March and April 1646, fleeing with him to Jersey on 16 April. On the surface he seems a pattern of steady loyalty, but his letters breathe doubt. 'I suppose every man ought in this distraction to be provided as well as he can to defend himself and the cause his conscience directs him to defend', he wrote tepidly. He referred often to negotiations. In 1646 he wrote, bitterly, 'how grossly we are all led like sheep to the slaughter . . . All the kings offers or demands are answered by saying the trust reposed in us by the country will not suffer us to admit of such conditions.' Still others supported Parliament, but like Sir William Courtney may never have taken up arms on its behalf: 'out of your wisdom and care of the public good to end these troubles by a treaty and not by force, for by a treaty you may preserve the Commons from ruin the great men and their estates to them and their posterity', he wrote. He dreaded social disorder, 'for I have seen the disposition of men that have arms and strength that they may times make themselves master of their officers and sometimes officers suffer the soldiers to be their masters'. By February 1643, he was gloomily predicting famine, murder and pestilence if a peace were not reached soon.

So it came about that Bevil Grenville declared for the king out of honour and local identity, both of which motivated him more strongly than religion, in which his views paralleled those of the Harleys. It wasn't simply a Holy War, and it didn't seem like one to everyone, not even to everyone holy.

Where a gentleman lived was crucial in determining allegiance and thinking. Sir Thomas Salusbury was a Welsh gentleman and an enthusiastic poet who eventually raised a regiment for the king. He left a letter in which we can see the deliberation process in action, the kinds of issues a man might consider before committing himself.

In Wales, and in Cornwall, strong national identity was marked by language difference. Most Welsh still spoke Welsh, and although the prayer book had been translated into Welsh, very godly reformers hadn't really penetrated Wales. One historian calls the Civil War 'the war of five peoples' – English, Scots, Irish, Welsh and Cornish – and argues that each saw the war differently. But one could also call this war a war of two million people, each with his or her own point of view, a point of view which might be shaped by national and regional identity or religious conviction or social and familial tradition or, simply, personality, luck and experience.

In a letter to his sister Lady Ursula Lloyd, Salusbury outlined the way in which he had come to decide to fight for the Royalist cause. He began by explaining that he had rushed impulsively to York to join the king, 'for that I feared lest discourse with friends of a contrary opinion might have prevailed against my desired undertakings grounded upon so much conscience and reason'. He had to commit himself quickly before someone talked him out of it. Like Brilliana Harley and Nehemiah Wallington, he thought about the coming conflict in Biblical terms, but he came to a different conclusion: 'for mine own part only, and that with Joshuah's resolution, though all Israel should go aside, yet I and my household will serve the Lord, which I cannot do truly unless I serve his anointed also'. He consulted his Bible carefully to try to decide what was truly right: 'Fear God and the King and meddle not with those that are given to change, saith Solomon [Proverbs, chapter 24] Fear God & honour the King saith St. Peter in his 1st Epistle, 2nd chapt. 17 verse. Of the same mind was St. Paul and our Saviour himself commands give unto Caesar the things that are Caesars and unto God those things which belong unto God.'

Thomas was sure of what he said, and this bred an equal certainty that his opponents were wrong: 'Both Testaments are full of positive precepts to this purpose, howsoever the filthy dreamers of these times that defile the flesh, despise dominion, and speak evil dignities are willing to misunderstand and being unlearned and unstable, wrest them as they do other scriptures to their own destruction', he wrote darkly. He probably meant the godly. Despite choosing the opposite side to Brilliana, Thomas also saw himself as isolated because of it: 'I have told you what my conscience leads me to, and how far it hath carried me, and if all the men of the earth were of another opinion in this, I am resolved to live and die.'

Historians have tended to associate Royalists with emotion – loyalty, devotion – and Parliamentarians with reason. But Thomas Salusbury claimed that good sound reason led him to choose to side with the king, and to make that choice in July, a little earlier than most: 'The arguments my reason suggest unto me are grounded upon the diverse inconveniences already grown and the like daily more to increase . . . the multitude of schisms crowded . . . already into the Church, give us too just a cause to fear.' While a man like Nehemiah Wallington might fear papists as a threat to the True Faith, Salusbury dreaded the disunity he felt was sure to follow godliness. Like his opponents, too, Salusbury saw connections between the way the Church was heading and the fate of the polity, writing: 'nor is it to be hoped that ever the cracked peace of this kingdom may be soldered or pieced together if the regal power be rent and divided into so many pieces'. Like William Shakespeare the generation before, Salusbury feared the mob, writing anxiously that 'in one man's breast there can be no faction; in two there may, but in a multitude it is scarce possible but there must as long as men continue to be of several opinions which certainly will not be otherwise in this world.'

He feared, too, that there might be a general collapse of order and as a result foreign intervention in the affairs of Britain: 'Look but upon other places where they have shaken the obedience of their sovereigns as the Low Countries and Germany, whether ever the sword is like to go from their doors. Hath not Holland ever been the stage of war and as it were the cockpit of all Christendom since they withdrew themselves from the obedience of their sovereign the King of Spain, though he were a tyrant and an usurper.' He also felt that rebellion against a monarch could never succeed: 'And doubtless if a King be oppressed by force or the defection of his people it is an injustice that can never be forgotten, and they that force against him have need to be very strong to keep him under by the same force, for they must look for great and frequent attempts which will never be wanting as long as there is any spark left in the hearts of the people of respect to the royal majesty.' The general tone of the letter is strictly abstract. Salusbury professes no personal loyalty and does not even mention Charles by name. But he also felt deeply about the abstractions he considered, especially the principle of monarchy. Salusbury knew his history; his land was a place from which claimants to the throne had often sprung, from Owen Glendower to the Tudors. Hence he wrote that a war against the king 'is like to embroil the kingdom in perpetual war as long as any lives that hath or can pretend a title to the Crown, which certainty will never be shut out from its legal prerogatives more than the sea from those bounds which God hath set it'. This was practical, but it was also a principled defence of monarchy as good order that proceeded from a reasonably pessimistic view of the world. The best that could be hoped for was calm, for 'if it lose in one place it gaineth in another or will be always striving and in distemper while the world endureth'.

Salusbury, who may already have been a professional soldier before the war, shared at any rate the soldier's contempt for the courtier: 'my addresses to the Court have not been out of vanity or ostentation to make large offers, for I have made none, nor out of fashion, but conscience which shall ever lead me till it bring me out of all troubles to eternal peace'.

Salusbury's dark vision of the difficulty of order might have come from the paradox of his nationality. The Welsh were seen in England in terms of stereotypes, though these stereotypes were conflicting. For the godly, Wales was a dark corner of the land, requiring spiritual evangelization, while for others, especially those interested in folklore, Wales was the home of the original and ancient Britons. As historian Lloyd Bacon richly shows, still others showed the Welsh as hilarious buffoons. All three representations are elegantly combined in Shakespeare's brave but foolish Fluellen. The fact that the Welsh spoke a different language helped to put off the ever-insular English. Another Welsh gentleman, John Wynn, wrote to his son Cadwaladr on how to conduct himself at Oxford in the late 1630s – and reminded him not to speak Welsh, not to drink or smoke, and to avoid other riotous Welshmen. Transparently, this advice was meant to help Cadwaladr avoid arousing English prejudices. Wynn himself had aspirations governed by the behaviour of the English gentry. He had just extended and decorated his house with shields of arms over the mantels.

Welsh efforts to assimilate were to falter under the pressure of events. Once the anti-papist panics began in the wake of the Ulster Rising, the Welsh themselves were seen as menacing, possible doorways for popish armies to enter the British mainland. Meanwhile Welsh political aspirations were satirized: did the funny Welsh want their own Parliament, wondered one pamphlet? The result of all this Parliamentarian and godly prejudice was, predictably, to drive the Welsh into support for the king as the only leader who truly represented them and their interests. The Welsh gentry were therefore outsiders in the world of English gentlemen, but they wanted to belong. A strong monarch might have seemed more likely to uphold their point of view than the English gentlemen in Parliament, and Thomas Salusbury had personal experience of what they could and could not do, having himself sat in the Short Parliament. The fact that he did not try to regain the seat when the Long Parliament was summoned showed his feelings.

The general Royalism in Wales then drove a wedge between the people of southern England and the Welsh. The Welsh were told that the English would kill their women and children, the English that the Welsh longed for their fertile land and were coming *en masse* to take it. As in other arenas – religion, class – the war managed to exacerbate divisions that were lying dormant, to break down wary tolerance into open hostility.

The war could also open divisions in families. One family which split in half on the rock of the war was the Verney family, greater gentry whom we have already met briefly: Ralph and Mary, the concerned and gentle parents of a rickety child, and Edmund, chronicler of the Bishops' Wars. Ralph Verney was a Parliamentarian, unlike his brother Edmund and his father Sir Edmund, both of whom were Royalists.

This made for misery. Ralph and his father had stopped writing to each other. Ralph's mother wrote that 'your father I find is full of sad thoughts'.

He saith little to me of it, but saith if the king commands he must go: I dare not say more to him because I would not have him think you said anything to me of it; you I know have serious thoughts concerning your father many ways . . . Your father sent me word that the king has given him leave to stay till he sends for him; I am very glad of it for when he goes I doubt the love of the Parliament he will lose quite, which I fear will make them do any ill office they can. I am sorry to hear the Lords are raising money and horse; truly if they send to my lord we will part with none: I hope they will not for we are poor, and my lord of his estate but tenant for life cannot tell how to pay a debt if we run into it.

Later, Ralph's mother wrote:

Your father like a good servant I believe is much for his master, and so I think we are all; I wish he may keep that power that is fit for him, but I confess I would not have the papists so powerful; the most of them I believe would be glad to see the Protestants of England in as miserable a condition as they are in Ireland, if it was in their power to make them so. In a few weeks now I hope that we shall see all that is intended; I pray daily that we may have no fighting; I hope the king will command your father to stay where he is . . . Since I wrote this letter I received your last . . . I am loath to eat in pewter yet, but truly I have put up most of my plate, and say it is sold, I hope they will send to borrow no money of my lord; if they do we must deny . . . they talk strange things of my Lord of Essex, that he will seek the King to London dead or alive; this is high methinks for people to talk so.

Ralph was advised that if only he and his father could meet 'one discourse or two will make all well again', and 'not to write passionately to your father, but overcome him with kindness'. But Edgehill, the first major battle, intervened. And at Edgehill, Sir Edmund refused to put on armour. Nor would he put on the buff-coat, made of thick hide, which afforded some protection against sabres and bullets. He offered himself as a kind of sacrifice, not the last to do so, as we shall see. Was he in despair? Or did he feel he had to redeem impugned family honour? Neither we nor Ralph can know. But his death at Edgehill was a sad way of resolving his dilemma.

There had been many ominous signs for the Verneys. 'Melancholy men', said Clarendon, a category which may have included Sir Edmund Verney, 'observed many ill presages about this time.' When the royal standard blew down, this seemed another bad omen for Verney as standard-bearer.

Ralph had taken the Oath of Allegiance, and so was directly opposed to the king. 'I long to hear how your father takes your protestation to the Parliament,' wrote a mutual friend, 'I fear he will be much trouble at first, but in a little I hope will make him pass it over. I find by your father's letter you sent me down, he is a most sad man. I pray God he may do well. I fear his troubles together will make an end of him.' Sir Edmund was 'much troubled' by Ralph's choice, but he told a friend that 'he hath ever lain near my heart, and truly he is there still'. Sir Edmund was not a wholehearted, rip-roaring Royalist, but a loyalist who believed he had no choice. 'He is passionate, and much troubled, I believe, that you declared yourself for Parliament . . . maybe he would have the king think he was a little displeased with you for going that way; if you can be absent from the parliament I think it would be very well. I am sure I should think it a very great happiness to be in your company. Now let me entreat you as a friend that loves you most heartily not to write passionately to your father, but overcome him with kindness; good man, I see he is infinitely melancholy, for many other things I believe beside the distance between you.' Ralph felt he did have a choice, and made it.

Next is the Tale of the Noblewoman and her Son, a tale of division and heartbreak. Other families were even more deeply and hurtfully divided.

Susan Feilding, Countess of Denbigh, was the sister of the wily, beautiful and unlamented George Villiers, Duke of Buckingham, favourite of both James I and Charles I. Like her brother, she was clever, beautiful and ambitious. She was at court from the 1620s, and a powerful member of the queen's circle, though she and Henrietta differed in matters of religion, for in 1625 Susan was a Protestant, though she was not godly; she was one of Laud's keenest supporters. She had been a Lady of the Bedchamber since the very early days of the queen's presence in England, along with Lucy Hay and the Duchess of Buckingham. Like Lucy, Susan tried to use her position to influence events, but she was less successful, though also less controversial, than the dashing Lucy. She was godmother to Princess Mary, sharing the post with Lucy herself. And unlike Lucy, she conformed to the queen's requirements in matters of religion, attending Mass with Henrietta in her Oratory, ultimately converting to Roman Catholicism while in exile. Her daughter Mary Feilding, later the Marchioness of Hamilton, had already converted in a blaze of adverse publicity, as did her niece Ann, Countess of Newport. The family's fate was strongly tied to the fortunes of the queen and her circle.

Susan's husband William declared for the king (and was to be killed in 1643). But her eldest son Basil unexpectedly declared for Parliament. He himself said lack of preferment was the immediate cause, but that was after the Restoration, when a passionate declaration of principle would have been very tactless. By June 1639 Basil had been removed from his ambassadorial post in Venice, leaving a trail of debts. He had not been an especially lucky or gifted civil servant, but had been diligent in finding pictures for the king. Susan Feilding found it impossible to accept his decision. In a series of heartfelt but also calculating letters, she implored him to change his mind. One especially impassioned appeal was written in mid-1642, before the shooting war had begun. It began by accusing Basil of something akin to possession by another: 'Methinks you spoke Mr Pym's language, and I do long to hear my dear son Feilding speak once again to me in the duty he owes to his Master and dread sovereign, the master of your poor afflicted mother, banished from the sight of you I do so dearly love.' Unlike Thomas Salusbury, Susan did not use reasoned political argument to try to win Basil to the Royalist cause, but arguments based on feeling and on family ties. She argued that he was making a disastrous career move: 'Let me entreat you to look back upon me and on yourself whose ruin surely I see before my eyes. All that is here does more wonder at you than at all the rest, your fortune being but weak, and the many obligations you and your best friends have to the King and Queen.' Moreover, he was, she felt sure, siding with the losers. She told him firmly that the king was going to win, and that he was choosing the less fashionable, popular side: 'The King is now in a very good condition, and doth daily grow better, his people being every day more and more his. Do not deceive yourself, he shall not want men nor money to do him service. All good men begin to see how he hath been abused, and none are undeceived, and I hope you will be amongst them.'

She reminded him that other powerful men were making more sensible choices and securing their own advancement: 'I hear my lord Paget and many other lords are going to York [to join the king]. Oh that I might be so happy as to hear you were gone too.' And she did not shrink from passionate emotional appeals, melodramatic and even stagey: 'Let my pen beg that which, if I were with you, I would do upon my knees with tears', she wrote passionately, adding 'I want language to persuade with you, though I do not love and reason. Therefore for the great God of Heaven's sake let me prevail with you. Do not let me be made unhappy by you, my dear son. I have suffered grief and sorrow enough already; let me reap comfort from you in this action. Remember it is a loving mother that begs for the preservation of her eldest son.' Her final sentences summed up her twin appeal. She stressed the choice of the fashionable Earl of Holland, who, she says, 'is gone to the King'. Neatly, she turns this news into a fresh appeal: 'I hope the next news it will be you, and so with my blessings to you, and my daughter, I take my leave.'

Susan Feilding is using the private language of motherhood to try to change her son's political allegiance. Like many a mother in Shakespeare's history plays, she is carrying out a powerful political act, called pleading – it sounds weak, but was a vital skill for female courtiers. At its strongest, this could be the appeal of Clytemnestra. At the end of Aeschylus's *Libation-Bearers*, when Orestes confronts his mother, she shows him the breast that suckled him as an argument against his taking vengeance on her. In a similar tone, Susan Feilding wrote that 'I have too great a part in you, that you are cruel to deny me any longer'. How could the familial body be divided? To Susan that unnatural division was symbolic of the unnaturalness of the emergence of a party that opposed the king.

This kind of division troubled all Civil War writers. The whole point of *civil* war is to divide families and other groups that normally – or normatively, ideologically – understand themselves to be united. For Susan, it's almost as if her son choosing a different side impinges on her identity – and so it was perhaps perceived at court. That is why her emotional entreaties are combined with active appeals to ambition and common sense, or – less kindly – an eye to the main chance. She may even have been writing not for Basil's eyes only, but for the queen's, hoping to show her the letter and thus clear herself.

On another occasion she wrote, more flagrantly: 'I am much troubled to hear that the king lay any marks of disfavour upon you, for I desire you should prosper in all things', but at once she segues into a rationale for that discomfort with the split in the family. She says her grief over the division is like a new and painful childbirth: 'I do more travail with sorrow for the grief I suffer for the ways that you take, that the king does believe you are against him, than ever I did to bring you into this world . . .' Susan Feilding is asking Basil to put the claims of the mother who bore him above what would have seemed to the king's foes the sovereign interpretive reason of the individual, to put loyalty to his family above his conscience – or rather, to make that loyalty the governing force of his conscience. It was this enmeshment of the individual in society that people like John Milton were to resist so vehemently with a new, even eccentric notion of individual liberty irrespective of marital or familial ties, a notion of the individual as an island, entire of itself. It was an idea born out of opposition to the cosy entanglings of Royalist rhetoric.

It was not just Susan who was trying to enfold Basil into the unity of the Feilding family. Susan also persuaded her son-in-law James, Duke of Hamilton, to speak to the king on Basil's behalf. Basil's sister Elizabeth also wrote twice to him, telling him 'pray Brother, leave the way you are' since his 'name had grown odious in print' and that if he stayed with Parliament he was risking his wealth and estates, incurring God's wrath, and losing his honour. Elizabeth also told him that there must have been a mist before his eyes when he said that only he and his party were truly for the king. Elizabeth pointed out tartly that 'the intention of a war against him [the king], which is daily spoke of in London' seems likely to remove the mist. She said that she was hopeful that he would go into the country, for after serving the king, she thinks the next best thing 'is to retire from the doing of those actions which are against him'.

We don't have Basil's reply. Elizabeth went on, game, immovable, and like her mother asserting ties of kinship above other loyalties: 'Dear Brother, I can yet call you,' she wrote sweetly, but added, with an unmistakable note of venom, 'since it hath not been in your power to hinder the king from being in a probability of getting what you would so fain have wrested from him.' Like her mother, she dwelt on the probable cost to Basil's career: 'Your harsh proceedings will be a means to hurt yourselves and advance the king's cause,' she wrote tartly, and much more angrily than Susan, she added 'which I infinitely rejoice at, for, seeing you have so willingly thrown away at once, your honour, gratitude, and all that's good, the bare name of brother serves to make me observe the more the losing of these qualities which make you dearer to me than the title.' Elizabeth made it clear that she had no time for treachery; so while her mother wrote submissively, emotionally, lovingly, Elizabeth made it apparent that her brother had lost her good opinion, if not her loyalty. She sounded exasperated rather than pleading: 'Can no consideration move you to be true to the King, neither fear of God, the punishment of what will follow, nor the desire of gaining your lost honour', she asked testily.

Elizabeth had undergone a personal experience which suggested that God was providentially at work in her life. She and her father had a very narrow escape from drowning in the Thames on 6 July 1641 when the royal barge caught against one of the piers of London Bridge and capsized. One woman was drowned, a Mrs Anna Kirke, and the others escaped only with difficulty, 'being also cast away in the Thames were miraculously preserved'. Sometimes a near-death experience makes its survivors reflect on what is truly important, and somehow this piece of ill-luck turned good fortune went along with stubborn commitment to family loyalties and personal relations.

The possibility that Basil might become involved in a shooting war against the king, facing the prospect of firing on his own sovereign, horrified both Elizabeth and Susan, who still believed that it might be possible to change her son's mind. She reminded him that affairs were reaching crisis point: 'I cannot refrain from writing to you and withal to beg of you to have a care of yourself and of your honour, and as you have ever professed to me and all your friends that you would not be against the person of the king, and now it is plainly declared what is intended to him and his royal authority, so now is the time to make yourself and me happy by letting all the world see who have been deluded all this time by them that pretend to be . . . [illegible] . . . of the commonwealth.' She also gives us a helpful notion of what the queen's circle were saying about the growing band of their declared opponents: 'It is now seen what their aim is', she wrote dramatically, probably referring to the impeachment of Laud and the possible risk to the queen. 'I am informed the bishops will be inquisitioned at the beginning of the next week for their votes in the house, therefore I would entreat you to absent yourself at this time, that you may make not the last error worse than the first, to the perpetual grief of the heart of your poor mother.'

Understandably, perhaps, Basil stopped answering his mother's letters, but this hurt her still more. Susan wrote: 'I fear I am forgot of you, or else I believe I should have heard from you in all this time which is no small grief to me.' She was forlorn in other respects, too. 'I have lost all my goods,' she wrote sadly, 'which is and hath been both to me and all that belongs to me a sorrow beyond expression and I do not find this place agrees so well with me and the perpetual fear I am in of hearing worse and worse news of my poor majesty makes me abound with sorrow . . . You may be sure the great God of heaven will not let the just to suffer long and for your part I know more than I did when I saw you last, they do not trust you, take my word. Dear Son, Have a care of my poor little Su [Basil's daughter, called after his mother] and send for her sometimes. I shall never fail to give you the best counsel I can, and I do believe that you will find that your mother has dealt more really with you than any other, and I am sure has suffered more than any other. I hope you will never take arms against the King, for that would be too heavy a burden for me to bear.' But in just a few short weeks, as summer turned to crisp autumn, Basil was to do just that.

This is a long story, but it is Susan's story. Basil's side has not survived, so we cannot guess what considerations made him a Parliamentarian. It may have been because of the long years he spent in Venice, the most admired republic in Europe, though whilst there he had been sent away for having 'monarchical' sympathies. Or – as for so many – it may have been a matter of religion. He had been travelling with a godly chaplain, John Reynolds, in the 1620s, which might imply adherence to a more godly way of thinking than that of his mother. At first he became a moderate, like the Earl of Essex, but later he was passionate and radical, siding with the army in its later struggles with Parliament. It is striking that in families where father and son were divided, the father was most often Royalist and the son for Parliament (though not in every case). For the young, dismay at Charles's innovations in the role of monarchy was not overborne by a sense of personal loyalty and the need to uphold hierarchy, as it was for their fathers. The young man with a father yet living was always especially enmeshed in the drawbacks of hierarchy. Some may have felt, too, that one father was quite enough. Basil's father William was a dullard who owed his position entirely to Susan's power and influence, something that may have made it hard for his son to bear his authority.

A final factor is that Basil had more on his mind than politics in 1641. His wife died on 1 April that year, and just three months later he married Elizabeth Bourchier, daughter of the Earl of Bath. Elizabeth certainly loved him. While he was absent on campaign, she wrote him a letter signed with 'a hundred thousand thousand kisses'. Perhaps with such blazing affection at his side, Basil felt he could do without a loving mother's approval.

These stories could be repeated endlessly, ramified, nuanced, by the many other accounts of the moment of decision that survive. If we know less than we might like about how the literate chose and defined sides, we know less still about the ordinary man and woman of early modern England. A few exceptional people did leave accounts of themselves, but mostly when we do have records of the views of those below the rank of Chaucer's perfect gentlemanly knight, what remains is a fragment; something overheard by a neighbour in an alehouse or at a village well, and reported to the authorities, or an incautious remark in church. What we can glean from these snatches of overheard conversation is that craftsmen and tradesmen, their wives and daughters discussed the affairs of the nation as earnestly as gentlemen. Sometimes, though, we hear from ordinary men and women because they incautiously voiced their political views aloud and thus had them repeated in court. John Troutbeck expressed the feeling of many when he said that 'the king was half French, half German, and that he could live as well without a king as with a king'. He added that if the king did not keep his oath and the laws that he might be deposed. This is a sophisticated argument for a rural tradesman, and one can imagine that John expressed it as part of a heated debate. Such debates must have gone on in every alehouse, every hall, every parlour. Mary Giles of Holborn was charged with having declared her intention to kill the king of England, as did Henry Sutton the same year, 1642. Thomas Aldberry, a gunsmith from East Smithfield, said early in 1643 that 'there is no king' and announced that he would therefore acknowledge no king. Thomas Creed responded rudely to the king's flight from London, calling it 'very great infamy and depravement'. Ansell Powlten said that the king had not a foot of land but that which he must win by his sword, a statement which was repeated by others; it meant that the monarch was not part of the nation, but stood outside it. Roger Moore said that if the king demanded that a man turn papist then that man should 'rise up against him and kill him'.

People could also express themselves through petitions to the king, or to Parliament, and hundreds of these flowed in from every county demanding that Laud's reforms be scrapped. John Waterton, a parishioner in Anna Trapnel's always rebellious parish of Stepney, remarked darkly that 'there were more souls damned [by the new prayer book] than died of the plague', and he offered to fight anyone who disagreed. Conversely, some fiddlers were arrested in June 1642 for singing 'a scurrilous song against the Parliament'. John Scullard, a London labourer, exclaimed 'a pox confound the Parliament' in October 1642, while Edward Jeffery threatened to cut the throats of MPs. The men of Parliament, said a vintner named Nicholas Browne, were nothing but Robin Hoods and Little Jacks; these appellations were not intended to be complimentary, but to tar Parliament as rebels and outlaws.

Sometimes, too, partisans themselves tried to explain why others chose the sides they did, but their accounts are not always reliable. Take Richard Baxter, chaplain, Protestant but no independent, writing many years after the war to defend dissenters against the then-draconian laws being passed against them. For him to be Parliamentarian is to be virtuous:

> And abundance of the ignorant sort of the country, who were
> Civil, did flock in to the Parliament, and filled up their armies

> afterwards, merely because they heard men swear for the
> common Prayer and Bishops, but heard others pray that were
> against them; and because they heard the King's soldiers with
> horrid oaths abuse the name of God, and saw them live in
> Debauchery, and the Parliament's soldiers flock to sermons, and
> talking of religion, and praying and singing psalms together on
> their Guards. And all the sober men that I was acquainted with,
> who were against the Parliament, were wont to say, the king
> hath the better cause, but the Parliament hath the better men.

and also to be oppressed:

> If a man did but pray in his family, or were but heard repeat
> a sermon, or sing a psalm, they presently cried out, Rebels,
> roundheads, and all their money and goods that were portable
> proved guilty, how innocent soever they were themselves ...
> Thousands had no mind to meddle with the wars, but greatly
> desired to live peaceably at home, when the rage of Soldiers and
> Drunkards would not suffer them.

This is plainly special pleading on behalf of dissenters, since by the
time Baxter was writing, his side had lost the peace and was perpetually
on the defensive. Nevertheless, Baxter is describing a world increasingly
divided from itself, and hence a world of fear.

Not everyone made choices. The corporation of Coventry strove at
first to remain neutral, terrified of alienating either side. There were
those who changed sides quickly, under pressure, when one group won
out in their locality. When Coventry eventually became a stronghold
of the godly, some of those who had been neutral hastily became
zealous. In similar fashion, Exeter was initially divided between an
eager godly party who supported Parliament and a loyal party led by
the Earl of Bath. When Bath fled, hounded because of his Catholicism,
the loyal opposition collapsed, and Exeter became a Parliamentarian
stronghold. Some people even waited till one or other army was in
their area before making up their minds. Some unhappily hoped that
they could simply stay out of it and wait for it to blow over. This group
included ordinary people, in North Devon, for instance, where only a
few could be induced to fight for the king even by very diligent recruitment. So as the shooting war began, the nation did divide, but not
evenly or predictably or seamlessly.

VIII

Bright-Harnessed Angels: Edgehill

Edgehill is a ridge, on the border between Oxfordshire and Warwickshire, three hundred feet high above the plain, three miles long. In 1642 it was bare apart from a clump of trees. The king came to it because he was moving towards London. Parliament's forces were dispersed around various garrisons – Worcester, Coventry, Warwick Castle. Essex, their commander, felt defensive. And there was an underlying reluctance to attack the king and his forces. It was still unimaginable, attacking the king. Meanwhile, as the October nights drew in and the cold sharpened, the villages began to experience the long-drawn pains of armies camped or quartered in them; eating their food, wrecking their houses. There were few tents, and fewer supplies.

The Earl of Essex finally lumbered out of Worcester on 19 October 1642. Poor Essex was known far and wide among the Royalists as an impotent cuckold. His wife had annulled her marriage to him on grounds of non-consummation, a subject of many ribald jokes among Royalists. Despite this handicap, he was one of the very few truly great nobles to have sided with Parliament, so he had seemed the obvious choice to lead Parliament's armies. He was a prize to them, proof that they were not the ragtag of tapsters and shopmen that the Royalists said they were. He was also, it would emerge, only a moderately competent commander.

He was opposed by quite a different figure, one who would exemplify the word 'Cavalier': the very young, dashing, and exceedingly potent Prince Rupert, Charles's nephew. Of course, Charles himself was in command of the Royalist armies, but Rupert commanded the cavalry – mostly, when the older men could be persuaded to listen to his ideas. He was the child of war, and had plenty of experience in the Thirty Years War, which had unthroned his father and turned his mother into the Winter Queen. As summer chilled into autumn, he was eager for the fray.

Now, in October, Essex had no idea where the king and his army were, and they were equally ignorant of his whereabouts. Unused to war, the heavy cavalry clung to the army, instead of carrying out reconnaissance. So when the Royalists reached Edgecote, they had no idea that the Parliamentarians were nearby: they had reached the little town of Kineton after dark. As Rupert's quartermasters rode into the village of Wormleighton, they met some Parliament-men, who were also searching for somewhere to spend the night. Rupert took them prisoner and sensibly sent out scouts, who reported that the whole army was nearby.

Typically bold, Rupert wanted to attack immediately, at midnight, but Charles was reluctant, issuing orders for a concentration. With characteristic impatience, Rupert and his men arrived at the meeting-point at Edgehill by dawn. Hours later, the main body of the cavalry arrived, at around ten, and two hours later still, the foot, so that at noon everyone except the rearguard was standing on the ridge, looking down on Kineton, where they could see Essex's army, which had noticed the Royalists at around 8 a.m. and begun collecting itself. In the centre were the foot brigades, supported by cavalry, while on the left were more cavalry, interspersed with musketeers.

Among Essex's troops on the Parliamentarian side were men who would become household names during the war, but who now stood anonymous among their fellows. There were a young captain named Henry Ireton, a cornet called Edward Whalley, and John Okey, and there was John Lilburne, the future Leveller, whose valour would earn him a cavalry troop to command – all future radicals of diverse stripe. There were fifteen men on the field that day whose fate it was to sign the warrant for the death of a king. Among the Royalists were two future kings, Charles II and James II, and the physician William Harvey, said by some to have been in charge of the princes, the man who discovered the circulation of the blood: with admirable detachment, he spent some of the battle reading a book under a hedge until a bullet grazed the ground near him. There too was Thomas Salusbury and the Welsh levies he had raised at the king's command. Opposite Basil Feilding in his place in Essex's forces was his father, William Feilding, Earl of Denbigh, a volunteer in the King's Horse. Despite Susan's pleading, Basil had stuck firmly to Parliament. Now it was to come to bloodshed, though luckily the two Feildings were not actually driven to cross swords. Opposite John Cary, Viscount Rochford stood his father, Henry Cary, Earl of Dover. Doubtless many members of less prominent families were also to find themselves opposed by those of their own blood. Among the king's forces was Henry Lilburne, brother of the radical John Lilburne who stood for Parliament: another divided family.

Meanwhile Rupert was quarrelling with other Royalist commanders. He was trying to get them to deploy in the Swedish manner, which he had learnt fighting under Gustavus Adolphus. The king backed him gamely, and this so offended one of the commanders, Robert Bertie, Earl Lindsey, that he posted himself at the head of his men, directly opposite Essex, hoping to engage him personally. For Lindsey, as for many other Royalists, the war was apt to be seen as a personal quest for honour. He responded to a menace to his image by trying to restore it by a feat of frantic derring-do. This would not be the last time that such considerations swayed Royalist leaders. Meanwhile Rupert commanded the right and the centre was taken by the foot troops. On the left wing were more cavalry.

No one really knew what they were doing. The strict sonata forms of battle on which interesting and subtle arpeggios and variations could be played had not yet been set. The orchestrated armies had come together, but were not used to playing in concert. Some were used to playing with different performers and conductors. Others were picking up their instruments for the first time, and some could not read the music of war at all. Nor was it clear who was in charge.

The result, predictably, was not only chaos, but tentativeness. Everyone in command was following a few simple rules. The battle lines were drawn up; therefore there had to be a bombardment. The Royalists had a good general of artillery, but not many guns. The Parliamentarian gunners were very lucky; there was an unexpected ricochet effect. But on the whole the opening artillery duel taught both sides the relative impotence of the heavy weapons they had lugged so far over thick mud. The guns were weak, misfires were common, and neither side managed to do more than make a lot of smoke.

Dragoons were sent to clear the Parliamentarian musketeers from the wing, and then Rupert ordered his cavalry to advance. Down the hill they trotted. As they moved forward, they went faster, cantering, galloping. Stoically, the Parliamentarian horse waited, stock-still. They should have been on the move, but they did not know it. They were raw, so raw that they committed the classic error of firing while the Royalists were still out of range. Because no Civil War weapons were repeat-firing, this kind of waste happened often. But no one knew that yet, and the Parliament-men were so shaken and uncertain of what to do that they began to run. Rupert's troops rode right after them, attacking the fleeing men, cutting at them with their heavy sabres. Sir John Byron's men shot after the fleeing Parliamentarians, too. It was the same on the left, where the Royalist charge swept Feilding's men aside, and other Royalist troops soon joined in the pursuit, leaving the field. A few Royalist commanders kept their heads and ordered their men back to the battle. But most had been expecting to sweep the reprobate enemy away in minutes, and they had just done so. The lack of control is manifest in the wounding of a woman named Agnes Potter, who later died of her injuries.

The Royalist foot were led forward by Sir Jacob Astley, who had begun the advance with a passionate and commonsensical prayer: 'Oh Lord,' he begged, 'thou knowest how busy I must be this day. If I forget thee, do not thou forget me.' Then he shouted 'March on, boys', and the foot moved forward, slow and heavy. The Parliamentarian foot had seen their cavalry run. Other, bolder men rushed into the gap, just as the ten thousand Royalists crashed into the front line. And now it came to push of pike, that deadly rugby scrum in which men armed with long and savage spears tried to force each other onto their points, an ancient kind of warfare that stretched out bloody hands to the spears of Macedon and Greece. With characteristic self-insight, the nine-year-old Prince James observed intelligently that the result confounded expectations. 'The foot being engaged in such warm and close service,' he wrote later, 'it were reasonable to imagine that one side should run and be disordered, but it happened otherwise, for each as if by mutual consent retired some few paces, and they stuck down their colours, continuing to fire at one another even till night; a thing so very extraordinary, that nothing less than so many witnesses as were there present, can make it credible, nor can any other reason be given for it, but the natural courage of Englishmen, which prompted them to maintain their ground, though the rawness and inexperience of both parties had not furnished them with skill to make the best use of their advantages. 'Tis observed of all nations that the English stick closest to their officers, and 'tis hardly seen that our common soldiers will turn their backs, if they who commanded them do not first show them the bad example, or leave them unofficered by being killed themselves upon the place', he added, showing that he had spent his time at Oxford talking with some old soldiers.

James was almost captured during the battle. He later described the incident himself:

> Sir Will Howard went off with the prince [Charles, later Charles II, then a boy of twelve] and myself and we had not gone above musket-shot off from the place when we saw a body of horse advancing directly towards us from the left hand of the King's foot; upon which sending to see what they were, and finding them to be the enemy, we drew behind a little barn not far distant from them, which was encompassed by a hedge. In this barn several of the king's wounded men were there dressing, but the enemy observing the King's men to be within the enclosure, drew back immediately without engaging them, by which means the Prince and Duke escaped the evident danger of being taken; for had they charged our small party they could not have failed of beating them.

A great historical possibility flashes into view: what if Charles, Prince of Wales had been held by Parliament? The prince might have been willing to make a deal behind his father's back and over his head. Assuming Charles did not escape as his brother was to do, there would have been no reinvasion in 1649/50, and perhaps no Restoration. This may have been one of the war's key turning-points.

If so, it was scarcely visible in the confusion and mess of the battle. Meanwhile two Parliamentarian cavalry regiments were still not engaged, and now they moved forward against the Royalist foot. They crashed headlong into Feilding's brigade, and broke it, capturing its commander and colonels, and surging into the Royalist gun positions. It felt marvellous, but they had no nails with which to spike the guns. 'Nails! Nails!' shouted the commander, like a despairing Richard III turned smith. There were none, however, so they had to be content with cutting the cannons' drag-ropes. After that, they had little idea of what to do, so they suddenly decided to retire to their own lines. Meanwhile, a Parliamentarian force had brilliantly taken to guarding the Parliament guns, which had been abandoned by their original defenders. Though no artillery-men, they had managed to turn and fire at least one piece at an oncoming troop of horse. Unfortunately, the troop in question was their own men, come back from their failed attempt to spike the Royalist guns.

Now Lindsey, the insulted commander who had hoped to grapple Essex hand-to-hand, met the fate he had been seeking. He caught a musket shot in the thigh, and fell to the ground, mortally wounded. And he was not alone. After the battle, Sir Edward Sydenham wrote to Ralph Verney, to tell him some terrible news:

> For all our great victory I have had the greatest loss by the death of your noble father that ever any friend did ... he himself killed two with his own hands, whereof one of them had killed poor Jason [Sir Edmund Verney's bodyservant] and broke the point of his standard at push of pike before he fell, which was the last account I could receive of any of our own side of him. The next day the king sent a herald to offer mercy to all that would lay down arms ... he would not put on arms or buff coat on the day of battle, the reason I know not ... the king is a man of the least fear and the greatest mercy and resolution that I ever saw, and had he not been in the field, we might have suffered ... My humble service to your sad wife. God of his infinite mercy comfort you both which shall be the prayers of your friend and servant.

Ralph was miserable:

> Madam, I never loved to be the messenger of ill news; therefore I forbore to send you this; which is the saddest and deepest

> affliction that ever befell any poor distressed man; I will not
> add to your grief by relating my own deplorable condition,
> neither can my pen express the miseries I am in; God's will be
> done, and give me patience, to support me in this extremity.

His misery only increased as the details were revealed, and it became
obvious that Sir Edmund's body would never be recovered. It had been
buried among the multitude, which the family felt as a dishonour.

Meanwhile Sir Charles Lucas's men charged into Essex's rear; Captain
John Smith took a colour from the foe, and brandished it to show his
fellows, only to discover that he had almost no fellows left; there was
only one man still with him. He prudently decided to trot back to the
king's army, but as he went he noticed a man on foot carrying another
set of colours. A boy called to him sharply, 'Captain Smith! Captain
Smith, they are carrying away the royal standard!' 'They shall have me
with it, if they carry it away!' Smith declared, and cried out to the
Parliament-men, 'Traitor, deliver that standard!' He charged in with
his rapier drawn, killed one man and wounded another, captured the
banner, and freed Richard Feilding, who was being led into captivity
by some Parliamentarian troops.

It sounded like splendid dash. But Edmund Ludlow, a Parliamentarian, told a different, sourer tale: 'It [the standard] was taken by one
Captain John Smith, who with two more, disguising themselves with
orange-coloured scarves, had [the Earl of Essex's colour] and pretending
it unfit that a penman should have the honour to carry the standard,
took it from him, and rode with it to the King, for which action he was
knighted.'

For Ludlow, Smith was a trickster; an early example of the tendency
for the Scarlet Pimpernel self-images of Royalist officers to melt into
a puddle of pomposity and deceit. Or the victim of a vile post-war
calumny? No way to resolve it, but there is one clue; even in his friend's
account, Smith sounds just the man to think of the idea that a secretary
should not have the honour of carrying the king's colours.

The Royalist cavalry were still galloping about after booty until finally
they were so tired, and their horses so blown, that fresh Parliamentarian
troops under MP John Hampden were able to drive them off.

'As the darkness came on, both armies began to draw off, the royalists
to the brow of the hill, and the enemy to Kineton', Prince James noted.

The king spent the night in a barn, reluctant to appear to withdraw. No one could do any more because everyone was exhausted, and baffled. Who exactly had won? No one has been sure since. But historians tend to see Edgehill as a Royalist success; it did clear their way to London. From Charles's point of view, it resolved nothing, though it proved that his subjects were willing to fire on him, and he on them. The newly-formed sides were hardened by the spilling of blood.

Large set-piece battles break down on examination into the piece-meal butchering of many individual men. At Edgehill, many of the soldiers had never seen the face of war before. John Smith's lieutenant William Holles could stand for all those whose inexperienced bodies were shattered on that cold October afternoon. He received a savage wound, as described by his relative Gervase Holles:

> During the fight he received a shot on the face, and came up to me to the head of the brigade bleeding very much. I bid him go and get himself dressed; he replied he was not so ill shot as that he would leave the field whilst I was in it, and notwithstanding the disease his hurt conveyed him. The extremity of his anguish increased by the sharpness of the season and want of present application shut up both his eyes, and swelled his face for some days to a strange deformity.

William could not open his eyes until days later, when he forced them open in order to come to Gervase's aid in commanding a 'forlorn hope', the term for a group deployed in advance of the main army whose job was to harass and disrupt an enemy attack before it could reach the main body of the army. He was to die two years later, near Newark.

For the men who fought the Battle of Edgehill, the aftermath was bewildering. Parliamentarian Edmund Ludlow described the unnaturalness of that night, the loss of normality, the blindness:

> The night after the battle our army quartered on the same ground that the enemy fought on the day before. Nor men nor horse got any meat that night, and I had touched none since the Saturday before, neither could I find my servant who had my cloak, so that having nothing to keep me warm but a suit

of iron, I was obliged to walk about all night, which proved very cold by reason of a sharp frost . . . when I got meat I could scarcely eat it my jaws for want of use having almost lost their natural faculty.

The loss of domestic and local comforts was hard on all the new soldiers:

> We were almost starved with cold that bitter night, our army being in extreme want of victuals; and about 9 or 10 of the clock drew out again into battalia, and so stood 3 or 4 hours, till the enemy was clean gone from the hill, and then we drew again into our quarter, and there have lain this night, and purpose this day, after we have buried our dead, to march to Warwick.

For the wounded, the experience was even more alarming. William Harvey told John Aubrey the story of Sir Adrian Scrope, 'dangerously wounded and left for dead amongst the dead men, stripped, which happened to be the saving of his life. It was cold, clear weather, and a frost that night, which staunched his bleeding, and about midnight, or some hours after his hurt, he awaked, and was fain to draw a dead body upon him for warmth's sake.'

The London diary of John Greene reported at Christmastide, 1642 that 'There are now divers reports of strange sights seen, and strange noises heard at Edgehill where our last battle was fought; in the place where the Kings army stood terrible outcries; where the Parliaments [stood] music and singing'.

A pamphlet recorded:

> portentious apparitions of two jarring and contrary armies where the battle was strucken, were seen at Edge Hill, where are still many unburied carcasses, at between twelve and one of the clock in the morning . . . These infernal soldiers appeared on Christmas night, and again on two Saturdays after, bearing the kings and Parliaments colours. Pell mell to it they went, where the corporeal armies had shed so much blood, the clattering of armes, noise of cannons, cries of soldiers, sounds of petroncls,

and the alarum was struck up, creating great terror and amazement.

The aftermath of this first major battle confronted both armies not with the spectacle of their prowess, but with their helplessness. The exhausted armies sat silently about the field, listening to the groans of wounded and dying comrades, unable to help or even to find friends in the darkness. There were no stretchers and no ambulances. The very circumstances produced dread. The wounded themselves featured prominently in at least one account of the apparitions: 'about Edge-hill and Keinton, there are men seen walking with one leg, and but one arm, and the like, passing to and fro in the night'.

The Battle of Edgehill never really ended in the minds of those who had fought and suffered it. It left marks on families, too. Basil Feilding led the horse on the right of the Parliamentarian line, while his father William, Lord Denbigh was on the Royalist right, among the king's horse; they therefore did not meet, but each was part of a successful cavalry stand. The Feilding family had already suffered loss. A few weeks before Edgehill, Basil's sister Elizabeth's husband had been lost, killed on horseback by a musket shot at the Battle of Liscarroll, fighting for the king against 'the lords and Rebels of Munster' in Ireland. But a greater loss was to come. Basil's father William was wounded the spring after Edgehill, while attacking Birmingham with Rupert; he died a few days later at Cannock. Basil was granted a pass to travel and see his dying father, but he arrived too late. By now, Susan was in The Hague with Henrietta Maria, campaigning and raising money and arms.

From there she wrote to Basil:

> There is none in the world should be more joyed at an accommodation of the King and parliament than myself so that they would humble themselves to the king, and acknowledge their errors, which now we hear the best of his subjects begin to be undeceived and come in to serve him, it is no time to delay for any that loves themselves, for I do assure you the game is changed, and I hope the catastrophe will be the King's. I dare not speak to the queen of any such business as you wrote me of, because I am sure I should be denied, and thought to want wit. I hope we stand upon other terms now, and if you will believe me as I am a tender and loving mother, it is time for

you to run to the king upon your knees and crave his pardon. I dare not write to you what I would, and I really tell you that I do believe your party does not deal fairly with you, for they know they are not so well as they have been, but you think that I shall be the last that shall know of the disorder they are in at this time, believe me this is true.

And when Basil wrote to her to try to comfort her over his father's death, she flashed back: 'I beg of you, my first born, to give me that comfort of that son I do so dearly love, that satisfaction which you owe me now, which is to leave those that murdered your dead father.' Carried away by misery, she wrote angrily: 'O, my dear Jesus, put it into my son's heart to leave that merciless company that was the death of his father, for now I think of it with horror, before with sorrow . . . Before you were carried away by error, but now it is hideous and monstrous . . . Let your dying father and unfortunate mother make your heart relent; let my great sorrow receive some comfort.'

In a final appeal, she wrote: 'My tender and motherly care cannot abstain from soliciting you to go to the king before it be too late. All that party will be able to make their peace, while you will be left out . . . I have so great part in you, that you are cruel to deny me any longer', while Elizabeth told Basil that '[there is] more honour in quitting an ill way than in being constant to it'.

In vain. Basil remained in arms for Parliament throughout the war.

The shooting war, the big battles are all very well. But the principal experiences of war could be very different: less dramatic, and much more personal.

For Sergeant Nehemiah Wharton, the Civil War began in August 1642 with an orgy of plunder and iconoclasm; he does not stress the distinction between them much, and his letters show how one could effortlessly slide into the other. Wharton was an apprentice to George Willingham, who had a merchant's business at the Golden Anchor in St Swithin's Street, but he left to join the trained bands under Denzil Holles. On 16 August 1642, he and his men sallied forth, not to the war as such, but to the house of a suspected papist called Penruddock, 'and being basely affronted by him and his dog, entered his house and pillaged him to the purpose. This day, also, the soldiers got into the church, defaced the ancient and sacred glassed pictures, and burned the holy rails.' For Wharton in 1642, and perhaps for many others, this *was* war. There was no 'front' to define the fighting; it was us against them in every suburb, village, farmhouse, town and city. His account is corroborated by a pamphlet that presents his acts as atrocities, displaying a pathetic picture of the poor victim sitting with tears rolling down his face amidst the ruin of his home, but to Wharton war was about plundering the wrongdoers and attaining righteousness by doing so. He brought to the trained band exactly the mentality that had fuelled the riots of the winter in London. It was an apprentice's mentality, seeing things simply, in black and white, and narrowly, with reduced sympathies. Yet the experiences of travel, of war itself, and of fighting enlarged Wharton, almost against his will. He began to see that war was something more than an opportunity for bullying on a really grand scale.

His education took a while, admittedly. He missed the main opportunities for plunder in Oxford, but managed to find a few surplices and tore them up for bandages. His regiment chopped up the altar-rails at Wendover for firewood, and were incited to further violence by a minister who had himself been robbed by Royalists. But some cracks began to appear in Wharton's godliness. For a godly man, he seemed strikingly fond of swearing, disliking his lieutenant-colonel, and calling him 'a goddamme blade, and doubtless hatched in hell' in a letter to his master, Willingham. In a similarly ungodly manner, Wharton was not averse to a barrel or two of good beer, gleefully describing their discovery of a good barrel of Old Hum outside Coventry. But it was feast, then famine: Wharton and his men got no more to drink but 'stinking water' on their next twelve-mile march. Casually, he notes that on arrival at the next town, the soldiers pillaged the parson and took away his surplice; at the next town [Long Bugby], however, they had no lodgings 'and were glad to dispossess the very swine', while others were quartered in the church. 'This town', says Wharton, 'had been so abused by the rebels, that both men, women and children were glad to leave the town and hide themselves in ditches and corn fields.' But he and his men went out on another fun-filled mission 'and returned in state clothed with a surplice, hood and cap, representing the bishop of Canterbury'. On another trip, he informed his former master, 'our soldiers brought in much venison and other pillage from the malignants about the country'.

By 7 September, Wharton was wondering if his letters were getting through 'because you never yet honoured me with a piece of paper'. By now, he says, the army is getting tired of it all: the foot are on the point of rebellion, because they have not been paid, and because 'the footmen are much abused and sometimes pillaged and wounded'. One of the Five Members, John Hampden, 'tried to appease them, but could not'. By Monday, though, normal service had been resumed, and Wharton and his men could report that all venison belonging to malignants had been destroyed, while they were in pursuit of a 'base priest' who had arms in his house, but on the way he met a servant of Justice Edmonds, who had been pillaged by the bluecoats of Colonel Cholmondeley. Wharton divided his men in three, surrounded the Royalists, and forced them to carry their plunder back to their victim. Unsurprisingly, he was rewarded lavishly with a scarlet coat, 'lined with plush', and (even better) with 'several excellent books in folio of my own choosing', he wrote happily on 13 September 1642.

Wharton was a pillager, but he was no philistine. A relatively poor man who could not normally afford folios, his delight in books is evident. The war was opening doors for him that he could *only* enter as a thief. But on the way back to camp, the biters were bit; Wharton was intercepted by angry Royalists, who 'pillaged me of all, and robbed me of my very sword, for which cause I told them that I would either have my sword or die in the field, commanded my men to charge with bullet, and by divisions to fire on them, which made them with shame return me my sword'.

Incidents like this probably motivated the troops, as did reports of the (rather similar) behaviour of their opponents; when Wharton's groups heard that Prince Rupert 'that diabolical cavalier' was surrounding Leicester and demanding 2000 pounds or else threatening to plunder the town, 'our soldiers were even mad to be at them, but wanted commission'. To us what seems oddest is Wharton's mixture of eager plundering gusto and holiness. Wharton's troop often heard two sermons a day as travelling preachers reached them: John Sedgewick, Mr Marshall, Mr Ash. The contradiction is resolved when it emerges that the sermons were, in fact, exhortations to holy war.

Eventually a letter and parcel reached Wharton from his master, sending him a scarf from his mistress, a hatband, and gold and silver lace. He had a smart suit made. 'And I hope I shall never stain them except in the blood of a cavalier', he wrote, boyishly enough. In his gold lace and scarlet suit, and his scarf, Wharton was not dressed in the manner that a modern costume designer would choose for a godly Parliamentarian. Instead – as with the books – he sees the war as a chance to cut an exceptional dash, even to break some sumptuary laws. And he was not alone. There were many men in the army of Parliament that wore huge hats with feathers, and men in sober black and wideawake hats who fought for the king.

Wharton's letter from his master was so full of exciting London news that he showed it to the captains of his regiment, who were dining with one of the preachers, and returned thanks and greetings. Wharton was still concerned about whether his mail was getting through, though, and added, 'every day you may find a post that serveth our army at the Saracen's Head, in Carter Lane. His name is Thomas Weedon, who is with us once a week constantly.' There was no army mail service, and no Royal Mail either. Wharton and others had to find private individuals, carriers, to take their letters for them. These could be permanent 'posts', like the one Wharton mentions, or personal servants, or just chums who happened to be going to London.

But though there were luxuries, there was also privation. When quartered at Burford, he complained that 'many of our soldiers can get neither beds, bread, nor water'. As they moved on Worcester, the weather worsened, 'such foul weather that before I had marched one mile I was wet to the skin'. Rain, unnoticeable to civilians, became crucial once men were on the march for days at a time. Things went from bad to worse: an engagement with Prince Rupert resulted in the death of some key officers, and 'our wounded men they brought into the city, and stripped, stabbed and slashed their dead bodies in a most barbarous manner'. Rupert's men also met, Wharton says, 'a young gentleman, a Parliament-man, as I am informed, his name I cannot learn – and stabbed him on horseback with many wounds, and trampled upon him'. Stories like this one could circulate as news in London, increasing the city's alarm.

They had another miserable night. War was showing its uglier face to Wharton: 'we abode all night, where we had small comfort, for it rained hard. Our food was fruit, for those who could get it; our drink, water; our beds, the earth; our canopy, the clouds; but we pulled up the hedges, pales and gates, and made a good fire; his Excellency promising us that if the country relieved us not the day following, he would fire their towns. Thus we continued singing of psalms till the morning. Saturday morning we marched into Worcester – our regiment in the rear of the waggons – the rain continuing the whole day, and the way so base that we went up to the ankles in thick clay; and about four of the clock after noon, entered the city, where we found twenty-eight dead men, whom we buried – some of the cavaliers – and those were all that we can find slain upon our side.' On 26 September he wrote, presciently, 'we shortly expect a pitched battle, which, if the cavaliers will but stand, will be very hot; for we are all much enraged against them for their barbarisms, and shall show them little mercy'. He also had a surprisingly good time visiting Worcester Cathedral, delightedly admiring King Arthur's tomb 'but no picture thereon'. He looked forward with more and more excitement and trepidation to the pitched battle, as soldiers do, hoping for something definitive:

> They boast wonderfully, and swear most hellishly, that the next time they meet us they will make but a mouthful of us, but I am persuaded the Lord hath given them this small victory, that they may in the day of battle come on more presumptuously to their own destruction, in which battle though I and many thousand more may be cut off, yet I am confident the Lord of Hosts will in the end triumph gloriously over these horses and all their cursed riders.

To London-born Nehemiah Wharton, Worcester was a foreign city, unlike the world he knew:

> the city is so vile, and the country so base, papistical, and atheistical and abominable, that it resembles Sodom, and is the very emblem of Gomorrah, and doubtless it would have been worse than either Algiers or Malta, a very den of thieves, and refuge for all the hell-hounds in the country; I should have said in the land, but we have handsomely handled some of them, and do cull out the rest as fast as we can.

Like most soldiers, Wharton recorded events in detail, but he also began to note impressions of people and places, like a travel-writer. He recorded the same turbulence in Herefordshire that terrified Brilliana Harley:

> the citizens [of Hereford] were resolved to oppose us to the death, and having in the city three pieces of ordinance, charged them with nails, stones, etc, and placed them against us, and we against them, resolving either to enter the city or die before it. But the Roundheads in the city, one of them an alderman, surnamed Lane, persuaded the silly mayor, (for so he is indeed) that his excellency and all his forces were at hand, whereupon he opened unto us, and we entered the city at Bicesters gate, but found the doors shut, many of the people with their children fled, and had enough to do to get a little quarter.

He added, however, some local observations: 'The inhabitants are totally ignorant in the ways of God, and much addicted to drunkenness and other vices, but principally unto swearing, so that the children that have scarce learned to speak do universally swear stoutly. Many here speak Welsh.'

He also reports the grisly accidents of war, inevitable with so many men armed and not very disciplined: 'This day our companies exercising in the fields at Worcester, one of the Lord General's soldiers shot at random, and, with a brace of bullets, shot one of his fellow soldiers in the head, who immediately died.'

After this, Nehemiah Wharton's letters cease. No one knows what became of him. We know what happened to his regiment, though. At Edgehill, a few short weeks later, Denzil Holles's men were smashed like tinder by Rupert's horse, though 'everyone fought like a lion'. What was left of it re-formed and was destroyed by the Royalists on 12 November at Brentford, killed, captured, or drowned. It was never re-formed. Wharton was probably among its casualties, cut off, like so many, at the very moment when he was learning to think for himself.

The violence done on the battlefield and in families found an echo in a breakdown of neighbourly relations. When Richard Culmer saw a window with a depiction of the *Salvator Mundi* – Jesus as Saviour of the World – in the vicarage house at Minster, near Canterbury, he had no hesitation in breaking it to pieces, even though it was in a private house and not a place of worship. Equally merciless was the young William Springate, who as deputy lieutenant for Kent in the 1640s encouraged his soldiers to break pictures and crosses, and handed out surplices to clothe pregnant women. One day, on a visit to a co-Parliamentarian who helped in a search-and-destroy mission to 'popish' houses, and who had a firmly Puritan wife, Springate caught sight of paintings of the crucifixion and resurrection hanging in the hall. He sliced the pictures out of their frames and presented them, spiked on his sword, to his host's wife in the parlour, from where the paintings had been removed, 'to manifest a kind of neglect of them'. 'What a shame it is', Springate's widow recalled him saying, that 'thy husband should be so zealous a prosecutor of the papists, and spare such things in his own house!'

In the weeks following the Battle of Edgehill, the king was marching on London. The Parliamentarians established a forward post at Brentford; three regiments were placed there, including Denzil Holles's redcoats, and the greencoats of John Hampden. Rupert's men managed to capture the advanced post, but were checked at the barricades, which had been reinforced by artillery. This was to be one of the crunch points of the war, one of the moments which determined events.

The exhaustingly energetic political activist John Lilburne had asked for a troop of horse, having 'showed his valour' at Edgehill, but his Parliamentarian commander the Earl of Warwick begged him to defend London. 'I hope we shall beat him,' he said, 'and the wars will be at an end before thou canst get a troop of horse raised, but if thou leavest me now, I shall think thou art either turned covetous, and therefore would have a troop of horse for a little more pay, or else thou art turned coward, and therefore would leave thy foot company, now when we are going to fight, and I do believe should do it tomorrow.' Warwick saw the coming battle as crucial.

Lilburne rose to the occasion, and said that he would take his horse 'and post away to Brentford to your Regiment and fight as resolutely tomorrow as your Lordship shall'. So he was present when Prince Rupert and his men suddenly materialized from the mist in the early morning of 12 November. They attacked Denzil Holles's Parliamentarian regiment, which suffered heavy casualties and began to fall back on the town. Lilburne managed to galvanize the men around him with a stirring speech, calling upon them to show the gallantry of soldiers and be willing to shed their blood for the good of their country. The Royalist soldiers turned back into Brentford, and ransacked nearby houses for powder and match. They met with the remnant of Holles's shattered forces, who fought desperately and gamely against overwhelming numbers. They faced cannon and musket fire before and on their flanks, and had only a few straggling hedgerows for shelter. Some men were forced into the river, some swimming to safety while others drowned. Lilburne himself was captured, and taken off to Oxford Castle. But Parliament's train of artillery escaped.

The Welsh Royalist soldier John Gwynne remembered:

> The very first day that five comrades of us repaired from the Court at Richmond to the King's royal army, which we met accidentally that morning upon Hounslow heath, we had no sooner put ourselves into rank and file . . . but we marched up to the enemy, engaged them by Sir Richard Wynne's house, and the Thames side, beat them to retreat into Brentford, beat them from the one Brentford to the other, and from thence to the open field, with a resolute and expeditious fighting, that after one firing suddenly to advance up to push of pikes and the butt-end of muskets, which proved so fatal to Holles his butchers and dyers that day, that abundance of them were killed and taken prisoners, besides those drowned in their attempt to escape by leaping into the river. And at that very time were come a great recruit of men to the enemy, both by land and water, from Windsor and Kingston; and it happened that Sir Charles Lloyd, or some other engineer, to blow up a barge laden with men and ammunition, which, as the fearful crack it gave, and the sad aspect upon it, struck such a terror into the rest of the recruits, that they all vanished, and we better satisfied with their room than their company.

Gwynne said less about Rupert's later activities in Brentford; as usual, the gallant Cavaliers were too fond of plunder: 'They have taken from the inhabitants all the linen, bedding furniture, pewter, brass, pots, pans, bread, meal, in a word all that they have . . . leaving them not a bed to lie on.'

This stupid greed motivated Londoners to defend themselves. On 12 November, the London trained bands turned out in Chelsea Fields, led by Major-General Philip Skippon, a man who had risen through the ranks in the Dutch wars by merit. He was a simple man, brave, soldierly, and passionate about religion. The poet and tutor John Milton was afraid, but hoped his literary skill would save him. He pinned a sonnet composed for the occasion to his door:

> Captain or colonel, or knight-in-arms,
> Whose chance on these defenceless doors may seize,
> If deed of honour did thee ever please,
> Guard them, and him within protect from harms . . .

With his usual sense that he was firmly at the centre of the known universe, Milton wasn't merely asking to be spared. He was asking to be kept under guard as a National Treasure. He uses some language that would have been familiar to Royalist officers: the language of honour, and also of client–patron relations; he promises that he will 'spread thy name o'er lands and seas/Whatever clime the sun's bright circle warms'. He flatteringly likens his future guard to Alexander, and diligently butters himself up as well by comparing himself to Pindar, whose house was the only one in Thebes that Alexander did not burn. It may be that all this rather extravagant language might have won the hearts of officers, but it may also have been fortunate that many of their men couldn't read; if ever someone was asking to be taken down a peg or two, it was the author of this sonnet.

The day after the battle, 13 November, being a Sunday, Essex and Skippon urged their men to pray, and then fight. 'Hey for old Robin!' shouted the soldiers, for Essex. There was almost a party atmosphere. The troops had a hot meal, recorded Bulstrode Whitelocke: 'The city goodwives, and others, mindful of their husbands and friends, sent many cartloads of provisions, and wines, and good things to Turnham-Green, with which the soldiers were refreshed, and made merry.'

The Royalists watched them eat, their own bellies empty. Charles was heavily outnumbered. His men were tired and ill-equipped. And his stomach may have turned at the idea of slaughtering the ordinary civilians that barred the way to London. He decided that there could be no battle: not then, not there. He withdrew to Hounslow, and then fell back on Reading, and then to Oxford. He could have swung south-east and come at the city from Kent. He could have re-formed and determined to take London. He didn't, and this decision was one of his worst.

John Gwynne thought they had done the best they could:

> Nor can anything of a soldier or an impartial man say that we might have advanced any further to the purpose towards London than we did, in regard of the thick enclosures, with strong hedges and ditches so lined with men as they could well stand by one another; and on the common road and other passes, were planted their artillery, with defensible works about them, that there was no coming at them any nearer, upon so great a disadvantage, to do any more than we did, and withal considering that they were more than double our number; therefore the King withdrew, and marched for Hampton Court, where, for my farther encouragement, I had the colours con- ferred upon me, to go on as I had begun. I cannot omit observ- ing, that Essex his right wing of horse, which stood on more ground than the king had horse to face them, wheeled to the left to join with the foot that came from Windsor, and Kingston, and fallen on the King's rear, he might have gone to London *nolens volens*.

Gwynne's words cast doubt on his own statement, for he stresses the extent of London's defences; natural ones such as ditches and hedges which could be used by snipers, and new siegeworks which had been hastily thrown up by the citizens. The Venetian ambassador recorded that 'they [Londoners] are working incessantly with a great number of pioneers', claiming that among the workers were 'women and little children'. The Lady Mayoress was one of them, carrying a spade; as Samuel Butler wrote disdainfully later, 'From ladies down to oyster wenches/Laboured like pioneers in trenches'. So urgent had the need been that work had continued even on Sundays; it was, said the clergy stoutly, the Lord's own work. These defences would be extended enor- mously later that same year and in early 1643, encircling the city with a ring of earthworks. Urged on by ministers, whole parishes turned out to dig. The Guilds had a friendly contest to see which could do the most. Even clerks and gentlemen got their hands dirty. The result was to make London look too big a mouthful for even the most voracious Royalist strategist.

The early campaigns had ended in military stalemate. But the war was not altogether about military objectives.

IX

Down with Bishops and Bells:
Iconoclasm

Nehemiah Wharton was an iconoclast. The Second Commandment insisted that there should be no 'graven image' made unto God. The iconoclasts set out to enforce it. For them, this was what the war was about.

Oxford was briefly occupied by Parliament in 1642, before the troops were forced to withdraw. As they did so, they struck a last blow:

> The London troopers went out about noon; and as they came along down the high street, the Mayor presented them with wine at his door freely; and passing by St Mary's church, one of them discharged a brace of bullets at the stone image of Our Lady over the church porch and at one shot struck off her head and the head of her child which she held in her right arm; another discharged at the image of our Saviour, over All Souls gate . . . some townsmen entreated them to forbear; they replying that they had not been so well entertained here at Oxford as they expected.

The mixture of religious motivation and vindictiveness is striking. It is the same mixture as in Wharton's letters. The porch statue the trooper's shot disfigured was not medieval, but brand-new. It was the work of Laud's chaplain Dr Morgan Owen. And it was a symbol not of medieval ideas that needed to be swept away, but of a terrifying novelty, a new cult.

Ideas varied on what an icon was: the vague notion was of something visual and symbolic that could be an object of worship or adoration, but individuals differed in where they drew the line. The cross, for example, was controversial. James I had complained about 'those that worship a piece of a stick', but the very Puritan Earl of Leicester kept one in his house. Later generations were stricter, debarring any attempt to bind God by making an image; the word and the word alone could be used to teach and explain. Consequently, even market crosses, which might not have been likely to provoke any actual worship, came under attack. The Civil War simply created opportunities for more widespread outbreaks of the strife which had been a constant of parish life since the Reformation. Nor were the iconoclasts always sanctioned by law and order; indeed, there was something of a tradition in some locales of icon-breaking as a bit of healthy political protest of an evening. Many churchyard crosses were destroyed in daring midnight raids by local youths. The famous Banbury Cross – to which one might once have ridden a cock horse – was demolished by workmen who began their task at dawn, but nevertheless attracted an angry crowd of objectors. 'I am glad for my part, they are scoured of their gay gazing', wrote a preacher to Parliament in 1645. The eye, said George Hakewill, 'is the instrument of wantonness, gluttony and covetousness' and especially the spectacle of 'the magnific and pompous fabric of churches'. Hakewill was writing to console a blind woman for her loss of sight. Conversely, iconoclasm was often presented as traditional; it united the image-breakers with their forefathers.

Just as some very dedicated Nazis saw their goal as the destruction of the Jews rather than the defeat of the Western allies, so some very godly Parliamentarians came to see the papists as their true target, and by this they meant not just Roman Catholics, recusants, or such groupings, but anyone or anything that violated their idea of true religion. Their aim was simple, spare and strict: a bare church room, with no stained glass, no altar, no hangings or paintings or any kind of colour or representation, a blank space in which to listen and receive. There could be no Laudian worship in such a space. For the strictest, even tomb monuments – especially the tombs of bishops and nobles – were a violation of this severity enjoined upon them by God. Anything outside this gauntness could be viewed with contempt as well as anxiety.

The reformers like Hugh Latimer had used ridicule and abuse to make people laugh at what they had once worshipped, but that laughter could easily turn into contemptuous violence. Like all violence, especially holy violence, iconoclasm could become a way of having a shamelessly good time doing something shocking while patting oneself on the back for holiness. Breaking things – when licensed – can be a considerable pleasure, especially when you are under stress.

What made all the resentment towards icons and symbols far more intense were the Laudian reforms that had overturned the Church of England in the 1630s. One of Parliament's main missions was to remedy all this. In Suffolk, William Dowsing led a campaign which destroyed decorations in 150 churches. Dowsing was careful, meticulous, a keeper of long lists and records. Though not a combatant, Dowsing believed his activities had a direct relation to the course of the war: he thought Fairfax was given victory at Nantwich because on that day images were destroyed at Orford, Snape and Saxmundham. Dowsing had removed the protective carapace of one side and thus strengthened the other. In Suffolk, Dowsing often arrived to find his work already done for him by parishioners eager to rid themselves of the hallmarks of Laud's reforms. At Haverhill, two hundred 'superstitious pictures' had been broken before Dowsing got there, and the same was true of altar-rails throughout the region.

'Images', writes Margaret Aston, 'were surrogates or dummies on which were vented some of the anger felt toward inaccessible human agents.' All iconoclasm was 'a process of scapegoating'. 'This present Parliament began, as the fruit of many prayers, for when the people of God in this land were full of fears and troubles, their hearts failing them . . . the Lord gave to them the spirit of supplication . . . The late lamentable Wars began, yet God was good to us in discovering many secret treacheries . . . And many superstitious relics were abolished, which neither we nor our godly fathers (as ye have heard) were able to bear.' There was an effort to make something new by cleansing, by destruction.

Iconoclasm also resembled atrocities, and was often described as if it were an atrocity; it offered the same chance to organize the terrified self by attacking the helplessly mysterious and powerful: soldiers attacking a figure of Christ might have been attacking any feminized target: 'another said "here is Christ", and swore that he would rip up his bowels: which they accordingly did, as far as the figures were capable thereof, besides many other villanies. And not content therewith, finding another statue of Christ in the frontispiece of the Southgate, they discharged against it forty shot at the least, triumphing much, when they did hit it in the head or face.'

Men overwhelmed by war and fighting against other men could vent their fear and rage on a helpless image that could not fight back. But to the soldiers, the image might not have seemed helpless: iconoclasts could hardly help endowing the statues they destroyed with the same power as combatants. If they were worth such destructive energy, then they almost had the kind of supernatural power ascribed to them by the superstitious.

The irony was that it was this Laudian increase in icons that provoked attacks on older works. When Henry Sherfield attacked and broke a stained-glass window in Salisbury Cathedral in 1633, he was especially affronted by its image of God the Father, 'a little old man in a blue and red coat'. Sherfield said he'd been motivated by the parish council's wish for more light to allow people to read their prayer books. But that was not good enough for Laud, who wanted to make the point that only bishops had the authority to enact reformation; it wasn't acceptable for every Tom, Dick and Harry to 'make batteries at glass windows in churches at their pleasure'. He was fined £500.

The violence makes more sense when we grasp the fact that the godly had every reason to feel themselves menaced. In the summer of 1637 Prynne, the most famous prisoner of his day, was being moved to Caernarvon Castle on charges related to his pamphlet *Newes from Ipswich*; his ears had already been cropped in London. The men of Chester had turned out to cheer for him, helped him on a shopping trip to palliate the austerity of his Welsh gaol, and (in supporter John Bruern's case) joined him in prayer. Prynne's pamphlet had attacked 'certain late detestable practices of some domineering lordly prelates' and 'their Romish innovations'. The crowd that cheered Prynne had seen the altar restored, 'used in times of Popery' which Laud 'caused to be digged up out of the ground where it was formerly buried'. The idea that Laudian clerics were literally digging up the buried past of popery was a powerful symbol.

So was Prynne himself; ironically, the man who condemned stage plays at voluminous length had himself a fine sense of drama. He first appeared as himself a kind of icon of anti-Laudian activism when the government ordered that his ears be cropped in the pillory and his book *Histrio-Mastix* burnt. This entirely excessive punishment was probably because of an entry in the index which said 'Women actors notorious whores', an equation taken rather personally by Henrietta Maria, but the general attack on theatricals was aimed squarely at the court and everybody knew it was, especially since Prynne also condemned almost everything else they enjoyed, including hunting, public festivals, Christmas-keeping, dances, and even the decking of a hall with green ivy.

It was Laud, however, who was most determined to prosecute Prynne and who combed his work for seditious ideas. The Star Chamber wanted to mark it as unusually awful: it 'is . . . to be burnt by the hangman, though not used in England. Yet I wish it may, in respect of the strangeness and heinousness of the matter contained in it, to have a strange manner of burning.' Prynne was also to be placed in the pillory at Westminster, with a paper on his head declaring the nature of his offence, and have one of his ears there cut off, and then to be held in Cheapside pillory, and have the other ear lopped. Prynne's punishment wasn't enough for some people; Lord Dorset thought he should also be branded in the forehead and have his nose slit. Others thought St Paul's pillory would be a better spot for it, as a warning to the London booktrade, but Laud said this would be a misuse of a consecrated place.

On 7 and 10 May 1634, Prynne was duly subjected to his ordeal. It made him an icon of godly martyrdom, a sign that Laud and his men were out to get the holy, the chosen. His supporters commented on his bravery. Nehemiah Wallington called him 'a harmless lamb' and godly people everywhere reached for Foxe's *Book of Martyrs* to help them understand the scene.

Such praise made it certain that Prynne would not be deterred. *Newes from Ipswich*, even more intemperate than *Histrio-Mastix*, denounced bishops for popish innovations and for 'tyrannising over bawdy thievish courts'. When Prynne and his fellow-authors Burton and Bastwick were sentenced to have their ears removed, the court asked whether

Prynne had any ears left, and ordered that the remaining stumps be cut off. This was duly done on 30 June 1637. Prynne was especially ill-treated, burned on both cheeks, and burnt twice on one because the letter had not come out well. One cheek bore an S, the other an L, for Seditious Libeller; Prynne said it stood for *stigmata laudis*, the mark of praise – or, alternatively, the Sign of Laud. And then he was hacked savagely about the ears, allegedly because he had promised the hangman the previous time that if treated well he would give him five shillings, and only gave five sixpences. This may be a cruel joke at the expense of godly meanness, though.

The hangman may have been hostile, but almost everyone else in London was on the side of the men being punished. As they came from the gatehouse towards the Palace of Westminster, the crowd threw herbs and flowers before them. Even people entirely hostile to their cause were impressed by their courage. All beholders, said a Dorset draper visiting London, shed tears. There were some ironies in all this hero-worship. According to the Catholic Sir Kenelm Digby, the godly were, hilariously, keen to gather relics of the martyrdom, the bloody sponges and handkerchiefs: 'you may see how nature leads men to respect relics of martyrs'. Prynne himself retold the story of those who dipped their handkerchiefs in his blood 'as a thing most precious' in *New Discovery*.

Horror at what had been done to Prynne as well as godly zeal inspired eagerness. Robert Harley's daughter Brilliana, named for her mother, wrote to her brother Edward in 1639, describing her father's zeal: 'My father had lately brought him a most horrible picture of the great God of heaven [and] earth which he broke all to pieces.'

Brilliana herself had thrown the dust of the picture 'upon the water'. She was ten years old. The picture was found in a stable on Harley's estate in Buckton. By now Harley was breaking into private houses he controlled to find ecclesiastical *objets d'art*. As in the days of Edward VI, people were buying and then squirrelling away religious art, some perhaps hoping that better times would allow them to bring it out. Harley was having none of that, as Brilliana explained in a later letter: 'The image that I writ you word of, it was found in Buckton in one Robert Mathiss's house, he plucking up a plank in his stable, he found it there and did keep it a quarter of a year in his house, and it should have been sold for 7 pounds. Then somebody told my father of it and then my father sent for it and broke it in pieces and flung the dust of it upon the water.'

This childish glee reflects what the young Brilliana had been taught. Meanwhile, any children Robert Mathis had might have been learning different lessons; the find points to the continued existence of devotional images in homes, though doubtless this one had once been in a church. Someone was willing to buy it, and for a substantial sum.

Meanwhile churches were being reformed. Altar-rails and communion tables began to come under attack in the summer of 1640, but it was when the House of Commons decided to outlaw them that many people got to work: in the church of St Thomas the Apostle, on 11 June 1641, John Blackwell, grocer to the king, told the congregation frankly that the altar-rails were popish innovations. Not everyone agreed, and the result was a tussle between traditionalists and the godly that was a microcosm of larger and bloodier conflicts to come. Blackwell's adherents won, and pulled down the rails, saying that the altar-rails were Dagon (the god of the Philistines) and should be burned like Dagon. The rector and eight others signed a petition asking the House of Lords to punish the wrongdoers.

You didn't have to be concealing works of art to be wary of those who came to be called 'the rooters', after the satirically named Root and Branch petition, signed by 15,000 London citizens on 10 December 1640, which urged the abolition of bishops, deans and chapters. The Commons didn't approve the bill that resulted from it, because some MPs were suspicious of its levelling tendencies. Similarly, when the House of Commons announced unilaterally that it was going to get rid of Laudian artefacts such as communion rails and altars, even some stoutly Puritan people like Sir Edward Dering became restive. 'Oh, you make an idol of a name. I beseech you, Sir, paint me a voice, make a sound visible if you can: when you have taught mine ears to see, and mine eyes to hear, I may then perhaps understand this subtle argument. In the mean time reduce this dainty species of new idolatry, under its proper head (the second commandment) if you can.' He went to gaol for ten days. But there were also plenty of people who leapt into a flurry of action. On 5 November in Chelmsford, there was an outbreak of violence: churchwardens had already taken down the Virgin and

Crucifixion, but the iconoclasts beat down the whole window with long poles and stones. London's parish churches also had their stained glass destroyed in October 1641. And the Harleys set to work personally, too; communion rails were removed and churchyard crosses destroyed. Harley personally crushed the cross at Wigmore with a sledgehammer, and threw the idols hammered out of church windows into the nearby River Teme at Leintwardine.

But the new rules still applied only to churches; the godly worked for their extension, and were rewarded by the ordinance of 28 August 1643, which allowed public crosses like Paul's Cross, Cheapside Cross and Charing Cross to be taken down. Thus in May 1644, all images came under scrutiny, public and private. There was nowhere left for the Virgin and saints to hide. The new order had finally arrived; Church and state were one, and the Church was a godly Church.

There was a tradition of turning objects loved by those deemed idolators to degrading secular use as a radical way of annihilating their sacred aura. Altars and holy water stoups became kitchen sinks, and (in a manner that looks forward chillingly to some Nazi practices) altar stones became pavements, so that those who had worshipped at them were forced to walk on them. Alternatively, the reformers could choose to burn idols, like Josiah and Jehu had in Biblical times. These were bonfires of the vanities of religion.

Nehemiah Wallington describes iconoclasm in Radwinter in Essex, one fast day in 1640; the soldiers were heading for Scotland, pressed into service, and probably angry: 'The Soldiers went into the church and pulled up the rails and pulled down the images (which as I hear cost the parson to set up thirty pounds) they tied the images to a tree and whipped them then they carried them 5 miles to Saffron Walden and burnt them and roasted the roast and heated the oven with it, and said if you be gods deliver yourselves.'

There's a faint, very uneasy echo of words said by the Jews of Christ: 'He trusted in the Lord, let him save him.' These soldiers are putting relics and icons to the test, a process that carried to extremes can call all religion into question. There are also echoes of anti-Semitic acts in all this: the despoliation of others' religion, forcing them to pray in order to prove that their God cannot help them. The one thing to be said in favour of the anti-popery hysteria is that it appears to have made anti-Semitism redundant. There are echoes of Isaiah and Baruch, but also of less elevated and authorized knowledge; fire was used to expurgate, to dispel miasmas caused by the Dog Star, and also to purify in the sight of the community, hence the burning of heretics. When heretics – or heretical books – were burned, crowds were present to see the errors turn into ashes. Conversely, legends told of objects so holy that they could not burn, such as the holy blood of Wilsnack, three hosts spattered with blood which survived a church fire in 1383. So burning the statues was a kind of anti-miracle, showing that *nothing* miraculous was happening. The Wilsnack hosts were themselves burned, successfully, in 1552. There was also something macho and defiant about the whole rite: it was saying to the icons, 'come on, show us what you've got!' and then celebrating when the answer turned out to be 'nothing'. And yet this very bravado suggests an underlying fear that the holy object might react. In the church at Hasselt, at midnight, a crucifix was being destroyed; suddenly, all the torches went out at once, as did the bonfire lit to burn it. Another factor was that the dead idol was being punished for its own lies, a practice that paradoxically endowed it with the very sensibility which the reformers wished to deny it.

If relics were not destroyed, they could be kept as souvenirs of this, the best of times. Nehemiah Wallington did this, saving bits of stained glass from the London iconoclasm of 1641 'to keep for a remembrance to show to the generations to come what God hath done for us, to give us such a reformation that our forefathers never saw the like'. Nehemiah's stained glass was a relic of attacks on relics; something sacred transformed into a curio, a memento, and thus robbed of its power.

Such things were also signs of the end, thought Richard Baxter: 'if you had seen the general dissolution of the world, and all the pomp and glory of it consumed to ashes, if you saw all on a fire about you, sumptuous buildings, cities, kingdoms, land, water, earth, heaven, all flaming about your ears, if you had seen all that men laboured for, and sold their souls for, gone . . . what would such a sight as this persuade you to do?' The world would end in a comparable fire that would burn away the false, a conflagration that only the righteous could survive. That made it vital to get rid of any idols that might incur God's wrath. It was not only Christ and the Virgin that were to be sent to the fires.

Maypoles were a target not only for the godly, but for God. Nehemiah Wallington punctiliously recorded God's acts against them. The more afraid people became, the more they attacked what they saw as objects of divine wrath. It was a way of making sure you were on God's side, and hoping that he was therefore on yours.

For some, images offered a chance to vent feelings that could not be poured out against the real person or power. As Charles's reign descended into violence, so his own image was no longer immune from assault. Hatred of religious icons overflowed into loathing for other kinds of icons. Statues and portraits of the king, once covered in flowers, were pulled down and destroyed.

In Oxford, during the brief Parliamentarian occupation, an alabaster and gilt image of the king at New College was destroyed by a Parliamentarian soldier; in the same year a picture of Charles in the house of Richard Mynshull in Buckinghamshire was destroyed, the soldiers ominously running it through with their swords. Of course, they may have had no idea who it was, though it seems unlikely that they picked that one painting for destruction and spared the rest by chance. If they did know who it was it is a sign that they had begun to see Charles himself as the enemy incarnate. In a more horrifying incident, a band of Parliamentary soldiers happened to capture one of their number who had gone over to the Royalists; they insisted on hanging him on the signboard of the King's Head tavern in Thame. The dying man's face was violently turned to face the king's portrait, and one of his murderers coolly said, 'Nay, sir, you must speak one word with the King before you go, you are blindfold, and he cannot see, and by and by you shall both come down together.' Iconoclasm, and the war itself, produced class beliefs that may not have existed before. Tombs could come under attack – though this was controversial – on the grounds that the rich were for the king. All rich men, said Wharton, were Royalists, and hence fair game – in part because it was thus obvious that they were not saved. It was acceptable in this mood to destroy every stick of furniture in the house of John Penruddock, a Catholic living in Ealing, leaving him not so much as a chair to sit on, and to rip up his small orchard.

At Winchester in 1642, the king's statue was attacked, and especially the crown, orb and sword, but this was in part because it adorned the hated roodscreen, and thus symbolized the king's sponsorship of the icons of Laud's regime. Fatally for the king, his own image was becoming entangled in the war against images, just as his regime was being called into question by dislike of Laud's innovations in religion and his perceived failure to protect the nation against Catholics. The destruction of the king's images suggests that religious rebellion was spilling over into political thinking and providing a model for it, and not just for a few ardent MPs, but for common soldiers.

Towns that were taken after a siege often suffered most. In Winchester, for example, it was the area around the castle which sustained most damage; as the Royalists retreated into it, they set fire to houses close by. During the sack of Winchester, unruly soldiers looted all the houses, and then 'found a great store of Popish books, pictures and crucifixes', which they carried through the streets to the marketplace, apparently in a drunken rage with all things iconic. Local legend has it that Parliamentarians rode into the cathedral on horseback, the better to reach its stained glass which they mainly destroyed. The town ultimately benefited from the destruction, as did Ludlow and Lichfield; brick and tile replaced flammable wood. But this was scarcely obvious at the time, and it is clear that the finding of popish books inspired the destruction of domestic property. Like the category of papist, the category of icons could expand to include anything, anyone. Which meant no one – no matter how elevated – was truly safe.

X

The Death of Dreams

So 1643 began with the sound of breaking glass and cracking stone, as people thought they were destroying the last traces of an old and haunted world in which saints stared from alcoves and windows.

But it was also the year a new world sprang into being, the world of newspapers, a squinting look at reality through black-and-white print. It was when the British press really began, the year weekly newsbooks first appeared. The first was *A Perfect Diurnall*, fairly impartial. Impartiality did not last long; it was succeeded by *Mercurius Aulicus*, edited in Oxford, and therefore Royalist, by *Mercurius Brittanicus*, edited in London and therefore Parliamentarian, and by various Presbyterian papers, some Royalist and some Parliamentarian. For the first time people could rely on someone outside their families and circle of acquaintants for news. It has been suggested that the newspaper is a kind of secular substitute for religious observance, that its regularity, the fact that everyone reads it on the same day, makes it an experience not unlike some great saint's festival. If so, the coincidence of the newspaper's emergence from the shards of Cheapside Cross is perhaps explicable. Newspapers helped to fill other kinds of gaps, too. Along with the emerging pamphlet-plays, they filled a drama-and-entertainment void left by the closure of the theatres.

Other certainties tumbled down. A young hothead named John Milton published a series of pamphlets arguing that men should be able to divorce their wives on grounds of mutual incompatibility. But some certainties remained; Thomas Browne's *Religio Medici*, published in an authorized edition for the first time, reasserted faith in the face of doubt induced by science. In France, Corneille's plays told the world of the death of proud Pompey at the hands of tasteless rebels, and a new king, Louis XIV, ascended the throne as a child-ruler. In the East, Japan had a new emperor. The Thirty Years War ground on miserably. The composer Claudio Monteverdi died, and in January, Isaac Newton was born.

1643 was also to be a year of bitter fighting, of many small and some great battles. Men of the king's army and Parliament's were to clash all over England, from Braddock Down in the west to Leeds in the north, and from Grantham in the east to Dorchester in the south. It was a year of many terrible deaths, and many failed plans. In Plymouth, for example, Prince Maurice's Royalist army ended the siege in defeat on Christmas Day, and when the defenders crept out to inspect their siegeworks, they found 'six hundred and sixty of the Cavaliers behind sick and maimed and not able to crawl out of their trenches'.

Was there a grand overall strategy, for either side? Military historians, ever eager to create order from chaos, like to think so, and they usually dub 1643 'the war for the centre'. Perhaps there was some such notion, though it's difficult to make it fit with Adwalton Moor or Winceby in the north, or even the siege of Plymouth (unless Devon is somehow 'the centre'). If so, though, just what either army thought it was doing to achieve its goal remained very dubious, and certainly unclear at local level. Rather, strategy tended to become reactive rather than proactive, with armies rushing here and there to cope with new threats or in response to sudden new ideas. Like ten-year-olds playing chess, the armies' commanders tended to argue for a long time, then suddenly do the first thing that came into their heads. The previous year had seen the failure of the king to take London and crush the rebellion quickly. Now no one was altogether sure what the military and strategic objectives should be. Foggy chains of command and lack of co-ordination meant armies raced in ratlike runs over ground covered before, pursuing the goal set by the commander of the moment. Rather like the Vietnam War, the English Civil War was mostly not fought in large Waterloo-like set-piece battles; many soldiers served for its entire duration without ever seeing a big engagement. Rather, it was fought in a series of skirmishes, guerrilla attacks, surprise encounters with rearguards, sudden cavalry swoops, and sieges, not only large sieges, but small ones, involving perhaps five hundred combatants. When we think of the Sealed Knot valiantly recreating Civil War battles, we think of Naseby or a big siege, as at Basing House. But if anyone really wanted to re-experience the Civil War battle in its most common form, they should walk down a long lane lined with a five-foot hedge, and suddenly come under musket fire from inside the hedge. Or they might stand drinking at a cattle trough, hear thundering hoofbeats, and be cut on the cheek with a cavalry sabre. Accounts of such fights rarely stress any military objective; once the action started, the goal was to stay alive.

The situation was far more confused even than the American Civil War, for no Mason-Dixon line divided Parliamentarian from Royalist. True, a line drawn down the middle of the country would show that the territory to its west was predominantly Royalist, the terrain to its east predominantly Parliamentarian. But there were exceptions: in the west Plymouth, Exeter, Gloucester and Bristol were all staunchly Parliamentarian, and a key Royalist war aim became the consolidation of their territory by the capture of these islands in the stream. Had they succeeded, the situation would have been more obviously and territorially two-sided. The division was also unbalanced by London, which had no equivalent and which was the very centre of Parliamentarianism. It should have been obvious that the Royalists' only hope was to capture it, but somehow it wasn't, and the rebuff at Brentford was allowed to harden into a southern limit on the king's activities. This effectively preserved Kent and the counties of the so-called Eastern Association from conflict.

Inside this ring-fence, Parliament set itself up as the true instrument of rule, and its members became used to the feeling of rule without, so to speak, a veto. Perhaps this sense of possibility was the most important outcome of Charles's failure to take London. Parliament was no longer a paranoid interloper; instead, like any new government, it produced too many ideas and too much legislation too quickly. Yet its rule was not yet accepted or inevitable. Committees multiplied examining Church and state with fresh and anxious eyes, and creating new ways to finance the increasingly expensive war. Of course, what this meant in practice was a rise in taxes. At a local level, something similar happened as the groups that controlled cities like Bristol, Exeter and Gloucester contended with the extraordinary circumstance of being besieged by their own countrymen. The burden of the war had now settled on men and women's shoulders. They tried to bear it gamely. But it grew heavier as the year went on, as taxes rose and supplies ran out.

Yet this was also the year in which peace negotiations faltered and petered out, despite the fact that both sides still hardly believed the enormity of what they were doing could go on. As the ground soaked up more and more blood on both sides, resolve hardened rather than weakened.

It was also to be a year when the relationship between England and Scotland was shifted by a new alliance. Yet all this hopeful expansion was checked when the leader of the Commons faltered, his own end marking the end of the war's first phase. Both sides were to lose key leaders who represented, too, the last best hope of compromise: a godly Royalist, and a moral member.

And it was a year that foreshadowed the uncompromising end of the war in the arraignment and trial of a man who had originally been one side's principal target.

The problem with Laud's acts is clear. But the man, too, was a problem, and something of an enigma. Archbishop William Laud had once been a man of many dreams. Of humble origins, son of a clothier and product of Reading Grammar School, he had winched himself irritably up by his own bootstraps to the highest archbishopric. Like many ambitious men, he exaggerated his father's status, claiming he had held all the offices in the corporation government, when in fact he had served briefly as a constable.

Laud was peppery, and he was detested. He minded – he was thin-skinned. And the minding came out in an inability to listen tolerantly to criticism, and also in disturbed nights, in which he was haunted by the desires he could not express or relieve in life.

Laud's dreams became public property in a curious manner, when his diary was exposed to the avid gaze of his enemies by his angry old foe William Prynne, and the juiciest bits published. When his dreams lay before the public, his whole heart seemed to lie exposed, as Hugh

Green's had been physically, and almost as painfully. Laud's dreams were mostly unpleasant, but the pleasant ones concerned his mother: 'I dreamed that my mother, long since dead stood by my bed and looked pleasantly upon me, and that I was glad to see her with so merry an aspect', he wrote in January 1627. This is actually remarkably close to the format of a benign apparition story. By contrast, Laud's reflections on death were usually grim: 'I dreamed of the burial of I know not whom, and that I stood by the grave. I awakened sad.' He often dreamed of the deaths of others; he dreamed that Lady Buckingham had had a miscarriage, that Sackville Crow, a gentleman of the bedchamber, had died of plague having been recently with the king. He also dreamed of his teeth falling out through scurvy; tooth loss, Freud tells us, is a castration dream. But there were everyday reasons why Laud might dream of illness and death; he himself nearly died as a child, and again while President of St John's College, Oxford, while in 1630 he suffered a fever so severe it nearly killed him. He managed to injure himself, too, by energetically swinging two hefty tomes over his head in his study to keep fit. In middle and old age, his pulled leg muscle hurt him.

All this sounds manic, obsessional, and faintly donnish. All his life Laud had plenty to be anxious about, and he was ultimately deserted by the king, impeached on trumped-up charges, and suffered the further indignity of having his diary rifled by Prynne. By 1642, his life's work was being destroyed by his enemies. While a prisoner in the Tower in November 1642, he dreamed 'that parliament was removed to Oxford, the church undone, some old courtiers came to see me and jeered. I went to St John's and found the roof of the old college ready to fall down. God be merciful.' This is an obvious anxiety dream. He also dreamed – terrifyingly – of conversion to Catholicism: 'this troubled me much'. Laud was not a Catholic, disliked Catholicism and especially the little queen whose fierce piety had pushed him out of Charles's circle, yet Rome, with its authority-figure, its rituals, appealed as much to Laud as it did to the leaders of the Oxford Movement two centuries later.

And his sensibility was certainly High Anglican. Laud had a significant dream about Buckingham: 'That night, in my sleep, it seemed to me that the Duke of Buckingham came into bed with me; where he behaved himself with great kindness towards me, after the rest, where-with wearied persons are apt to solace themselves. Many seemed to me to enter the chamber who saw this.'

When Prynne published this dream in his *Breviate of the Life of William Laud, Archbishop of Canterbury, extracted for the most part verbatim out of his diary*, in 1644, he suggested Laud was guilty of the sin of uncleanness. Laud replied angrily that 'there was never fastened on me the least suspicion of this sin in all my life'. But in reality matters were not so simple. Laud's diary is full of cryptic references to his 'unfortunateness' with T, SS, PB, Em, Ad, and EB. The pronouns show all of them were male, but none have been identified. 'Towards the morning [4 August 1635] I dreamed that LMSt came to see me the next day, and showed me all the kindness I could ask for.' 'I dreamed that KB sent to me in Westminster Church that he was desirous to see me.' Laud 'went with joy', but 'met another'. Like other diary references to KB, this one is enigmatic, but points to an intense and troubled relationship. He also expressed guilt and terror in a letter to Sir John Scudamore, 'One thing there is which I have many times feared, and still do, and yet I doubt it will fall upon me. I cannot trust my letters, but if it come I will take my solemn leave of all contentment. But in that way shall ever rest your loving friend.' This may simply be part of the consciousness of sin that endeared Laud even to his godly foes. He also had numerous dreams about his rival and political opponent Bishop Williams; having persuaded the king to banish him to Lincoln, Laud kept dreaming of Williams loosing himself from bonds, turning up at dinner and sitting above him. Perhaps this explains Laud's decision to have Williams taken before the Star Chamber and sentenced to be heavily fined. Awake and asleep, Laud saw Williams obsessively as the cause of problems within the Church.

When Charles threw Laud to his Parliamentarian enemies after the debacle of the Scottish Prayer Book, he replaced the Laudians with Williams and his friends. Charles, described by Laud as a king who 'knew not how to be or be made great' fulfilled a Laudian dream of betrayal.

He had longed, perhaps, for love. Now he would be killed by the country's burning and indignant hatred.

In London, there was a fresh casualty of war: Cheapside Cross was down, in spring 1643.

It had been the centre of commercial London, and also a place where heretical and seditious books were burnt, where their authors were punished. It was twelve yards high, three rich tiers of stone, like a wedding cake ornamented with statues of the Virgin and Child, and surmounted by a large brightly gilded cross and a dove to represent the Holy Ghost. Edmund Campion, racked savagely by Elizabeth I's torturers for his Jesuitical beliefs, nevertheless managed to bow to it as he passed on his way to the scaffold at Tyburn. This made the cross a guilty papist by association for some. People desecrated it throughout Elizabeth's reign; whether they were iconoclasts or simply vandals is not altogether clear. It was repaired after each attack, and 'marvellously beautified and adorned' for the entry of James I into London in 1603. A ballad celebrating its glory appeared in 1626, and the city turned a deaf ear to Robert Harley's efforts to persuade the Commons to pull it down as an idol. The Venetian ambassador thought especially well of it, admiring the 'exquisite workmanship' of the figures; high praise from a man of Venice. By the outbreak of war, it was still there, a little darkened by the soot deposits which bedevilled Stuart London's public spaces, but staunch as ever. People still sneaked the odd covert bow to it, though the godly were angry and accusing if they saw. The main threat to it was traffic; there were complaints that it hindered the passage of carts and carriages. But then Prynne, Burton and Bastwick came back to London, trailing clouds of sanctity, and Burton almost immediately urged London to get rid of 'the golden idol in Cheapside'. For him and his followers, the cross was female, a popish seductress.

On the morning of 25 January 1642, London awoke to find that the cross had been attacked again; crowds gathered, and heard that one unlucky iconoclast had fallen on the surrounding railings and spiked himself, and that the others had run away when they heard the Watch coming. London's civic leaders placed a guard on the poor old cross. But the maypole season of 1643 finished its chances; emboldened by the successful capture of Reading, the council gave orders for it to go. On Tuesday 2 May, a day 'calm, clear and fair', wrote Humphrey Mildmay, 'the cross in Cheape was taken down by the Jews [Mildmay's

name for the godly party], the town in much disorder'. Attacked by
the cross's passionate defenders, the demolition crew moved in, guarded
by none other than the reliable and stalwart men of the London trained
bands, who had also been protecting the cross until that moment. The
lead images were melted into bullets, to see off more papists. The bells
rang out, as if celebrating a famous victory. The waits sang, as if it
were Christmas, and the wine flowed. And on the spot where the cross
had stood, the very place where Prynne's *Histrio-Mastix* had been
burned, the Caroline *Book of Sports* – the one that allowed maypoles –
was also reduced to ashes.

Brilliana's husband Robert Harley was chairman of the committee
that supervised the smashing of stained glass and images in London's
churches and the chapels in the royal palaces around the capital during
the mid-1640s. Set up in April 1643, originally the committee was to
remove images from Westminster Abbey and 'any church or chapel in
or about London'. They duly destroyed stained glass in the Abbey,
St Margaret's Church, and the royal chapels at Whitehall, Greenwich
and Hampton Court. In Westminster Abbey, the committee broke up
carvings with axes and hammers, pulled down images of saints, and
tore out the high altar in the chapel of Henry VII. At Whitehall, they
plastered over pictures, smashed the windows, broke up the communion table, and cast out the pieces in the street. The Royalist newspaper *Mercurius Aulicus* reported that they went on 'until nothing was
left that was rich or glorious' (16–22 June 1644). Of course, Harley didn't
do most of the work himself; workmen's receipts survive, showing that,
for example, the east window at Whitehall was reglazed with 241 feet
of white glass, at a cost of £7. The committee also drew up lists of what
should be destroyed elsewhere; the first ordinance, of August 1643,
ordered the removal of all altars, rails, candles, crucifixes, and images
of the Trinity or saints; the second, dated May 1644, was directed at
copes, surplices, roods, fonts and church organs, and demanded the
use of plain church plate.

Over several months in 1643, Parliament managed to formalize what
had been all along an alliance, between itself and the ardently anti-
Laudian, Covenanting, godly Scots. Pym was the chief architect of the
Solemn League and Covenant, the treaty in which Parliament all but

hired an army of Scots in exchange for paying them £30,000 a month (which it didn't really have) and for establishing the Presbyterian Church in England and Ireland.

But not everyone in Scotland felt the alliance represented them. Some even began to see the Kirk as an enemy, the enemy of true Scots. When the Kirk and Scotland signed the Solemn League and Covenant, Montrose's position hardened still further. He had already written his *Discourse on Sovereignty*, a long letter in which he defended the sovereignty of the king under law and also condemned the once-hallowed Kirk. His reflections on loyalty and honour led him to join the king in 1643, and he offered to raise the king's friends in Scotland against the Kirk. It took a long time to persuade Charles to back him; the other Scots at the court at Oxford were against it, especially Hamilton. But at last Charles agreed, and Montrose rode out of Oxford as the king's lieutenant-general. He was ready to hurl himself into the midst of a country that loathed his king to raise an army. He entered Scotland disguised as a groom, collected a party of Irish troops from Antrim who had landed in the Highlands, picked up a few Highlanders as well, and began his campaign. At least he was on his own now; no court, no committee.

> My dear and only love, I pray
> That little world of thee
> Be governed by no other sway
> Than purest monarchy;
> For if confusion have a part,
> Which virtuous souls abhor,
> And hold a synod in thy heart
> I'll never love thee more.
>
> Or if Committees thou elect
> And goes on such a score,
> I'll sing and laugh at thy neglect
> And never love thee more.

His adventure was just beginning.

In 1643, the pressures on Brilliana Harley continued to grow as Hereford became more and more dominated by Royalist armies moving to attack

Gloucester and eager to pacify any pockets of resistance in their rear. Country houses like Brampton Bryan were always perceived as a threat, and Brilliana's case was by no means unique. It seemed inevitable that she would soon find herself besieged.

Hereford, which had been in the hands of Parliament, was occupied by the Royalists in January 1643. In February the commander Lord Herbert began preparing for a siege of Brampton, but his forces were diverted to attack Gloucester, where they were defeated by the Parliamentary army under Sir William Waller in March. In April, some Royalists entered Harley's estate at Brampton Park, took four oxen, beat up some workmen, and then opened fire, killing one man. Later in April Waller's forces took Hereford again for Parliament, but then had to march away to reinforce Bristol. It was then – May 1643 – that Ned Harley joined the army of Waller, and so did Robert (Robin), his brother, in June, after Ned had persuaded Brilliana to allow it.

The civilian refugee's lot is described by Ann Fanshawe: 'the perpetual discourse of losing and gaining towns and men; at the windows the sad spectacle of war'. And Brilliana's letters reflect her sadness. They also reflect her fear, the growing shortage of materials for life, and her loneliness:

> 13 December 1642: My heart has been in no rest since you went. I confess I was never so full of sorrow. I fear the provision of corn and malt will not hold out, if this continue; and they say they will burn my barns; and my fear is that they will place soldiers so near me that there will be no going out. My comfort is that you are not with me, lest they should take you, but I do most dearly miss you. I wish, if it had pleased God, that I were with your father. I would have written to him but I durst not write upon paper. Dear Ned, write to me, though you write upon a piece of cloth, as this is. I pray God bless you, as I desire my own soul should be blessed.

On Christmas Day 1642, Brilliana told Ned that she had been warned by a godly cleric that the people of Ludlow were against her: that 'they are in a mighty violence against me; they revenge all that was done upon me, so that I shall fear any more Parliament forces coming into the country. Dear Ned, when it is in your power, show kindness to them, for they must be overcome so. I pray you advise with your father whether he thinks it best that I should put away most of the men that are in my house, and whether it be best for me to go from Brampton, or by God's help to stand it out. I would be willing to do what he would have me do. I never was in such sorrows, as I have been since you left me. I hope the Lord will deliver me, but they are most cruelly bent against me.'

The king ordered Royalist leader Fitzwilliam Coningsby to prepare for an assault on Brampton in January 1643.

Brilliana was miserable, too, about the fate of her servants: on 28 January 1643 she wrote, 'Poor Griffiths was cruelly used, but he is now set at liberty. But the poor drummer is still in the dungeon [at Hereford], and Griffiths says he fears he will die. I cannot send to release him.' She was haunted by a sense of failure; naturally maternal, she felt she was supposed to protect her household as if they were her children, and the fact that she was prevented infuriated and shamed her. Her role as co-governor of a large household was collapsing: 'I know it will grieve you to know how I am used. It is with all the malice that can be. Mr Wigmore will not let the fowler bring me any fowl, nor will suffer any of my servants to pass. They have forbid my rents to be paid. They drove away the young horses at Wigmore, and none of my servants dare go scarce as far as the town. If God were not merciful to me, I should be in a very miserable condition. I am threatened every day to be beset with soldiers. My hope is, that the Lord will not deliver me or mine into their hands, for surely they would use all cruelty towards me. I am told they desire to leave your father neither root nor branch. You and I must forgive them.'

She was frightened, but by 14 February she was able to report, triumphantly, that 'we are still threatened and injured . . . but our God still takes care of us, and has exceedingly showed his power in preserving us'. She had heard of a Royalist plan to blow up Brampton Bryan, but the leader, Lord Herbert, was called away to the Forest of Dean. But the letter ends bleakly: 'Now they say, they will starve me out of my house; they have taken away all your father's rents, and they say they will drive away the cattle, and then I shall have nothing to live upon. All their aim is to enforce me to let those men I have go, that then they might seize upon my house and cut our throats by a few rogues, and then say, they know not who did it. For so they say, they knew not who drove away the six colts, but Mr Coningsby keeps them, though I have written to him for them.' She was genuinely afraid of being killed in her own home, as the Irish Protestants had been.

By 23 February she was having the moat filled with water. But she wanted instructions; though the soldiers had gone to Gloucester, she still received no rents, and knew that if she let her own men go, she would be 'every day plundered' (25 February 1643). What she hated most, though, was being cut off from letters: 'Dear Ned, find some way or other to write to me that I may know how the world goes, and how it is with your father and yourself; for it is death to be amongst my enemies, and not to hear from those I love so dearly.' Then she received a summons, demanding that she hand over her house, 'and what they would have', or be proceeded against as a traitor. 'It may be everyone's case to be made traitors, for I believe everyone will be as unwilling to part with their house as I am', she wrote (8 March 1643). 'I hear there are six hundred soldiers appointed to come against me', she added.

Things could only get worse. 'They sent for the trained bands and have taken away their arms; some say to give the arms to my Lord Herbert's soldiers that want. They say they gave half-a-crown to every soldier to look for enemies every day. They have taken More's lad, and he is in prison at Hereford, because he was with me [Samuel More, son of Richard More, MP, was at Brampton Bryan during the siege, and may have been released when Waller retook Hereford at the end of April]. If I had money to buy corn and meal and malt I should hope to hold out, but then I have three shires against me', she reported bitterly on 11 March 1643.

On 6 May, she lost her most trusted servant. 'Honest Petter is taken. Six set upon him, three shot at him as he was opening a gate not far from Mortimer's Cross. He fought with them valiantly and acquitted himself with courage; he hurt two of them, and if there had not been six to one, he would have escaped. He is wounded in the head and shoulder, but not mortally; he is in prison at Ludlow. I have done all that is possible to get him out, but it cannot be; but I hope the Lord will deliver him. I have found him very faithful to me, and he desired to have come to you.' Petter was still in prison on 9 May. Again,

Brilliana was unable to help someone who depended on her. The stress was almost crushing.

But she sent Ned off to the army with a glad heart: 'You may be confident my very soul goes along with you, and because I cannot be with you myself, I have sent you one, to be of your troop, and have furnished him with a horse which cost me £8. I hope it will come safe to your hand, with his rider.' Robin was still a problem teen: 'Your brother Robin goes about as if he were discontented, but I know not for what.' Brilliana had not lost her wry sense of humour.

By June things had calmed enough for Brilliana to be thinking about work on the court. But she knew this respite could not last. She sent to Lieutenant-Colonel Masscy in Gloucester for an able soldier to command and control the men she had, and he sent her 'one that was a sergeant, an honest man, and I think an able soldier; he was in the German wars'. To her joy, at last Petter was released: 'He was greviously used at Ludlow', wrote Brilliana indignantly. 'Turks could have used him no worse; a Lieutenant-Colonel Marrow would come every day and kick him up and down, and they laid him in a dungeon upon foul straw. In Shrewsbury he was used well for a prisoner, but he is very glad he is come home again, and so am I. I shall be full of doubts till the fair be passed.'

She was also delighted to receive at last a letter from Ned, telling her he had safely joined Waller's army:

> I received your letter dated the 17th of this month, which was dearly welcome to me, because it brought me word that you were safely come to Sir William Waller. My heart is with you, and I know you believe it, for my life is bound up with yours. My dear Ned, since you desire your brother to come to you, I cannot be unwilling that he should go to you, to whom I pray God make him a comfort. If Mr Hill be with you, and you would be free of him, you may if please you, tell him I desire he should come to me (June 1643).

And their closeness was revealed again in another June letter:

> That you left me with sorrow, when you went last from Brampton, I believe; for I think, with comfort I think of it, that you are not only a child, but one with childlike affections to

me, and I know you have so much understanding that you did well weigh the condition I was in. But I believe it, your leaving of me was more sorrow than my condition could be. I hope the Lord will in mercy give you to me again, for you are both a Joseph and a Benjamin to me, and dear Ned, long to see me.

She told him all her news, too, informing him that all the Herefordshire Cavaliers had returned, that Brereton had been surprised while plundering Hanmer in Shropshire, by Lord Capel's troops. She also reported triumphantly that 'all Lancashire is cleared; only Lathom House' (which was ironically held for the king by another woman, the Countess of Derby). She also sent the gardener and other servants to join Ned, irrespective of her own situation. It kept them safe, and it might help him. Writing to Ned on 11 July, she was more worried about him than about herself: 'I acknowledge the great mercy of my God that he preserved you in so sharp a fight, when your horse was killed.' She also worried about how to replace the horse.

Though Brilliana didn't always appreciate it, the local gentry had been restrained in not attacking Brampton sooner. They respected Brilliana and they were reluctant to sever the traditional class ties between gentry families.

But on 25 July 1643, the siege of Brampton started in earnest when the Royalists' commander William Vavasour found he had lost esteem in Hereford and the surrounding county because he had failed to reduce it. Then she could send Ned only a few lines: 'the gentlemen of this country have affected their desires in bringing an army against me'. It was like Brilliana to see this in personal terms. Inside the castle with her were her three smallest children, Thomas, Dorothy and Margaret; all were in their early teens. For six weeks the siege lasted, and during that time all Brilliana's surrounding buildings, the barns, the byres, were burnt and the livestock driven off and eaten. The Royalists kept up a steady barrage with cannon and a sporadic rain of musket fire. The cook was shot dead, and two other inhabitants wounded. Grain for bread had to be ground with a hand mill when the flour ran out. There were so many holes in the roof that no room was altogether dry or warm.

'The Lord in his mercy preserve me, that I fall not into their hands', she wrote, later referring to 'cruel and bloodthirsty enemies' (25 August) and adding that 'I long to hear of you, who are my great comfort in this life'. She began negotiating for an end to hostilities, and was offered a safe-conduct in early September, but she refused to abandon the castle to the Royalists because she was certain they would despoil it. On 9 September, the besiegers were forced to leave to fall on Essex's Parliamentarian army, which was marching to relieve besieged Gloucester. But again, Brilliana feared that the respite would not last. On 9 October she wrote: 'I am again threatened; there are some soldiers come to Lemster and 3 troops of horse to Hereford with Sir William Vavasour, and they say they mean to visit Brampton again.' Almost as an afterthought she added, 'I have taken a very great cold, which has made me very ill these 2 or 3 days, but I hope the Lord will be merciful to me, in giving me my health, for it is an ill time to be sick in.'

On 29 October 1643, one of Sir Robert's servants received a letter asking him to warn his master that Brilliana was seriously ill; she had the stone, then a cough, a fit, apoplexy, lethargy and convulsions. It was probably flu, complicated by stress. Her own servant Samuel More knew that she was dying, and advised that Ned should come to take over. Brilliana died two days later, managing to impress observers with her calm, courage and piety.

This story – of a brave woman alone in enemy territory, making the best of it, but terrified – was Brilliana's story, as she told it. But there was another way of seeing it; to try to keep the besiegers at bay, Brilliana could sometimes perform the role of the helpless woman, loyal subject of the king, ignorant of politics (which she certainly was not), stuck with defending her home on behalf of her husband as a good woman should. Before her death, in an effort to free her dependants she wrote to Viscount Scudamore for help; he was a Royalist commissioner, but she had some reason to hope that he might not be especially zealous. She expressed bewilderment about her ill-treatment, stressing the country loyalties that bound the gentry together. But by the time her letter reached him, Scudamore felt that those bonds had been severed. He wrote angrily to Robert Harley, saying he believed his wife was being held hostage against Brilliana's safety and he knew that Parliamentarian forces had plundered his estate at Llanthony, threatening to cut down the trees of Brampton if his trees were destroyed. Friendships and sociabilities of many years' standing could not withstand the outbreak of a shooting war.

Brilliana's house, Brampton Bryan, was damaged during two sieges, before the Parliamentarian garrison surrendered in March 1644. It was then 'slighted'; that is, razed to the ground so that it could never again be held as a stronghold against the government. But it was supposed to rise again. Brampton Bryan was given £2000 from the estates of Royalists in Montgomeryshire; the church of St Barnabas was rebuilt in 1656, largely funded by Sir Robert Harley, who was living in rented accommodation in Ludlow because he had no money to rebuild the castle. However, Brilliana's home was never rebuilt. The castle is a nub under thick turf today, with only a few broken and roofless walls to show where Brilliana struggled and suffered.

Brilliana Harley saw the Western wars from the point of view of a warm supporter of Parliament, and a civilian. They looked very different to Richard Atkyns, a soldier and a Royalist, who kept a diary to record his experiences and later transformed it into a memoir after the war.

Ironically, Richard, like Brilliana, felt isolated in hostile territory at the beginning of the conflict: 'As no cities nor counties were free from preparation for war as their affection inclined them, so the parts about Gloucester happened to be most unanimous for the Parliament, which was contrary to my judgement: for I am persuaded that none that heard the Lord Strafford's trial, and weighed the concessions of the King in Parliament, could conscientiously be against him.'

Also like Brilliana, Richard felt that he and his side were open to hostility as neighbourhoods broke into factions: he wrote that 'a man could hardly travel through any market town, but he should be asked whether he was for the King, or Parliament'. Having decided on the Royalist cause, Atkyns's next task was to organize himself to join the king. Like Brilliana's choice of sides, his had implications for his household:

> My servant Erwing . . . hearing of the war in England came over [from France] and proffered his services to me again, which I received as before, and being well known to his fidelity, I sent him to London to his brethren the Scots, to give me the best

intelligence he could; who did it most truly, and prophetically, and as an argument of his affection to me, refused a lieutenant's place of horse on the Parliament's side, to continue my servant. Him I employed to train up my horse, and make them bold; under one Forbes his countryman, who was then governor of Gloucester.

His diary shows what a long and tedious affair it could be to summon men and get permissions and make presentations. Atkyns was still sorting himself out after Edgehill:

And soon after the battle of Edgehill, I waited upon the Lord Chandos to Oxon [Oxford], not intending at that time, to stay any longer than to present myself to the King, and to assure him of my duty and affections, but while I stayed there I received intelligence that my being at Oxon was publicly known in Gloucester, so that I could not return in safety, but sent for the men and horses I left behind to come hither after me, and when the Lord Chandos had accepted of a commission to raise a regiment of horse, and mustered his own troop, he gave me a commission for a troop under him, which I raised with such success, that within one month, I mustered 60 men besides officers, and almost all of them well armed.

Edgehill made it all seem cut and dried, but Atkyns records cases of people changing their minds:

One Powell a cornet of the Parliament, with two troopers, all very well horsed and armed, came into my troop at Oxford; I carried him to the King, and begged his pardon, which the King graciously granted; and in token thereof gave him his hand to kiss; but asked him for his commission, which when he saw, he said, he never saw any of them before, desired to keep it, and put it up in his pocket, and gave him good counsel, with very great expressions of his grace and favour to me.

Meanwhile Atkyns had to finance his own men. But he was jaunty. He ended up serving under Prince Maurice, Rupert's brother, and recalled with delight the active role this gave him:

My troop I paid twice out of mine own purse, and about a fortnight after, at the siege of Bristol, I mustered 80 men besides officers; whereof 20 of them gentlemen that bore arms: (here the swearing captains put the name of the praying Captain upon me, having seen me sometimes upon my knees). The Lord Chandos afterward though I had the honour to be allied to him used my troop with that hardship that the gentlemen unanimously desired me to go into another regiment; which his Lordship understanding, I was thought to affix me to his by a council of war; but failing therein, I was admitted into Prince Maurice's regiment, which was accounted the most active regiment in the army, and most commonly placed in the out quarters, which gave me more proficiency as a soldier, in half a year's time, than generally in the Low Countries in 4 or 5 years; for there did hardly one week pass in the summer half year, in which there was not a battle or a skirmish fought, or beating up of quarters; which indeed lasted the whole year, insomuch as for three weeks at most, I commanded the forlorn hope thrice.

Honour motivated Richard Atkyns to try to get into the best regiments, the best parts of the army. But honour could also be menaced by the accidents of army life. In recalling skirmishes and battles, Atkyns remembered a series of struggles to stay alive and to preserve his reputation:

[11 April 1643] My charging horse fell a trembling and quaking so he could not be kept upon his legs, so that I must lose my honour by an excuse, or borrow another horse presently; which with much ado I did of the Lord Chandos his gentleman of the horse, leaving twice as much as he was worth with him. The charge was seemingly as desperate as any I was ever in; it being to beat the enemy from a wall which was a strong breastwork, with a gate in the middle; possessed by above 200 musketeers, besides horse; we were to charge down a steep plain hill, of above 12 score yards in length: as good a mark as they could wish: our party consisting of between two and three hundred horse, not a man of them would follow us, so the officers, about ten or 12 of us, agreed to gallop down in as good order as we could, and make a desperate charge upon them. The enemy, seeing our resolutions, never fired at us at all, but run away; and we (like young soldiers) after them, doing execution upon them, but one Captain Hanmer being better horsed than myself, in pursuit, fell upon their ambuscade and was killed horse and man; I had only time enough to turn my horse and run for my life. This party of ours, that would not be drawn on at first, by this time, seeing our success, came into the town after us, and stopped our retreat; and finding that we were pursued by the enemy, the horse in the front, fell back upon the rear, and they were so wedged together, that they routed themselves, so there was no passage for a long time: all this while the enemy were upon me, cutting my coat upon my armour in several places, and discharging pistols as they got up to me, being the outer-most man; which Major Sheldon declared to my very great advantage. But when they pursued to the town, Major Leighton had made good a stone house, and so prepared for them with musketeers, that one volley of shot made them retreat: they were so near me, that a musket ball from one of our own men took off one of the bars of my cap I charged with, and went through my hair and did me no hurt: but this was only a forlorn party of their army to face us while the rest of their army marched to Gloucester.

The king's decisions to try to control Gloucestershire from February 1643, and besiege Gloucester in August 1643 made sense, though military historians have never liked it much. If Gloucester had fallen, then the Royalists would have ruled the West. Atkyns's role was not to join the siege, however, but to mop up pockets of activity in the West. This led to the kind of vicious skirmishing that characterized the war. Atkyns could be critical of the way troops were wasted:

> Caversham Fight, 25 April 1643. The King always adventured gold against silver at the best, so now he adventured as gallant men as ever drew sword against mud walls; for the barn was as good a bulwark as art could invent. 'Twould grieve one's heart, to see men drop like ripe fruit in a strong wind, and never see their enemy; for they had made loopholes through the walls, that they had the full bodies of their assailants for their mark, as they came down a plain field; but the assailants saw nothing to shoot at but mud walls, and must hit them in the eye or lose their shot.

Historians today suggest the early modern musketeer was unlikely to hit his target at sixty metres or more, so this presented a challenge. In these conditions, and with more troopers lining the hedges, Atkyns had trouble rallying his men. He and his forces then left with Prince Maurice to join Ralph Hopton's army in the West and oppose Waller. Atkyns encountered Hopton's Cornish foot with some natural xenophobia, mixed with admiration:

> The Cornish foot could not well brook our horse ... but they would many times let fly at us: these were the very best foot I ever saw, for marching and fighting; but so mutinous withal, that nothing but an alarm could keep them from falling foul of their officers ... observing a hole in an elder hedge, I put in my hand and took out a bag of money; which if our foot had espied (who were also upon the search) they had certainly taken me for the enemy, and deprived me of both it and life.

Atkyns is brilliant at noticing what a mess the whole conflict is, as in his description of Chewton fight, which took place on 10 June 1643:

> When we came within 20 score of the enemy, we found about 200 dragoons half a musket shot before a regiment of horse of theirs in two divisions, both in order to receive us. At this punctilio of time, from as clear a sunshine day as could be seen, there fell a sudden mist, that we could not see ten yards off, but we still marched on; the dragoons amazed us with the mist, and hearing our horse come on, gave us a volley of shot out of distance, and disordered not one man of us, and before we came up to them, they took horse and away they run, and the mist immediately vanished. We had then the less work to do, but still we had enough; for there were six troops of horse in 2 divisions, and about three or four hundred dragoons more, lined the hedges on both sides of their horse; when we came within six score of them, we mended our pace, and fell into their left division, routing and killing several of them.

The chaotic engagement went on:

> [I] followed the chase of those that ran, within half a mile of their army; that when I came to rally, I found I had not thirty men; we had then three fresh troops to charge, which were in

our rear; but by reason of their marching through a wainshard [wagon yard] before they could be put in order; I told those of my party, that if we did not put a good face upon it, and charge them presently, before they were in order, that we were all dead men or prisoners; which they apprehending, we charged them; and they made as it were a lane for us, being as willing to be gone as we ourselves.

By now not only the troops, but Atkyns were spent.

When I came to Wells, the headquarters, I was so weary that I did not my duty to the Prince that night, but laid me down where I could get quarters; I was much unsatisfied for the loss of my lieutenant and colours, of which I had then no account. And laid all the guards to give me news of them, if they escaped. Early in the morning Mr Holmes my cornet brought my colours to me, which pleased me very well, but with this allay, that my lieutenant Mr Thomas Sandys my near kinsman was taken prisoner, and one more gentleman of my troop with him; and that he with some few troopers took such leaps that the enemy could not follow them, else they had been taken also. The next morning I waited upon Prince Maurice, and presented him with a case of pistols, which my uncle Sandys brought newly out of France; the neatest that I ever saw, which he then wanted [having lost his own when taken prisoner].

Atkyns identified the man who had rescued Maurice, and Maurice, unwisely, gave him many gold coins. The man promptly deserted, and Atkyns remarks that he saw him again about fifteen years later, 'begging in the streets of London with a muffler before his face, and spake inwardly, as if he had been eaten up by the foul disease [syphilis?]'. The incident shows how retrospective Atkyns's memoirs are, but his memory was vivid, if disorderly. He remembered the never-ending search for food. Once he found a house, 'a handsome case', he thought, 'but totally plundered, and neither beer nor bread in it', he wrote, putting first things first. He did find part of a Cheddar cheese, which he stole; this meant he was later in trouble for plundering. However, the cheese was misappropriated: 'I found my foot-boy giving it to my greyhounds, and reproving him for it; he cried, saying there was nothing else to give them.'

And he tried to recall anecdotes, cheerful and funny ones, writing of what he called A Mad Merry Saying. Atkyns had asked Dr John Cole, Prince Maurice's chaplain, 'to give me and my troop the sacrament, which he was willing to do'. The same morning, he was invited to dine with Maurice, who had evidently been given a whole buck-deer, and was hoping to feast his officers. Atkyns told the major who issued the invitation that he was about to go and receive the sacrament: '"Hang't, Hang't, bully," said he merrily, "thou mayst receive the sacrament anytime, but thou canst not eat venison at any time."' Atkyns, however, attributed to his own devotion and his men's their success in rescuing Prince Maurice and preventing the foot from being surprised.

This story contains a critique of Prince Maurice that is subtle but very noticeable. It is Atkyns, the praying captain, who saves the day by not eating venison, the result of hunting, but sharing in communion instead of in social success and ambition. By 1669, when he wrote the story down, Atkyns may have thought he knew why the Royalists lost the war.

But in fact the deer-fed men were winning in the far West. Ralph Hopton was now in command of a Royalist Cornish army which fought its way up and down Devon and Cornwall in the early months of 1643, then laid siege to Plymouth. It included Bevil Grenville, who wrote to his wife on 24 May 1643, making light of his injuries: 'You are doubtful lest my bruise stick by me. I thank you, but I hope it is prettily over, though I am something sore, & did spit blood two days, & bled at nose much . . . Our army is at Okehampton and what further will become of us I know not, we are sure of your good prayers as you are of mine.'

At the time Bevil Grenville wrote this letter, it would have been difficult for him or anyone else to summarize the situation in the West accurately; his uncertainty is entirely understandable. The Royalists had just been checked at Sourton Down, having been ambushed by the Parliament-men, but Hopton had then triumphed at Stratton, and the army was waiting for Prince Maurice and reinforcements from Oxford to arrive and assist. The ultimate goal was to leave the West secure so that Hopton's new army was free to join the king's forces further to the east, those trying to control Gloucester and the Severn Valley.

Bevil Grenville had always exemplified Royalist values: physical courage, honour, and leadership without calculation. They were expensive virtues. At Braddock Down in Cornwall, just outside Lostwithiel, on 19 January 1643, he led his men in a charge so wild that it 'struck a terror' in the enemy. At Stratton, near Bude, in May 1643, he led his men in an uphill charge with only swords and pikes. They were victorious, but the same reckless courage was to cost him his life at Lansdown on 5 July 1643. This engagement, fought a few miles north of Bath, was inconclusive. Atkyns gave an account of the whole battle:

> After we had refreshed ourselves about a week in quarters, we began to seek out the enemy, who were not far off; for four or five days, we skirmished by parties every day, and kept our body close together expecting battle daily. Each army consisting of about six thousand horse and foot, but theirs thought to be most; our headquarters were Marshfield, theirs Bath, within five miles of each other: very early in the morning, we sent out a party of horse, about 300, commanded by a Major, who did it so ill, that encouraged the enemy's forlorn hope to advance so far, as to give a strong alarm to our whole army, and we were forced to draw out in haste: the ground we stood in was like a straight horn ... on both sides enclosed with a hedge, and woods without that. They stood upon a high hill which commanded us, that opened to a large down, from whence they could discover our motions, but we could not theirs; both bodies within two miles of each other. For four or five hours, we sent parties out of each body to skirmish, where I think we had the better, but about three of the clock they (seeing their advantage) sent down a strong party of horse ... And this was the boldest thing I ever saw the enemy do, for a party of less than 1000 to charge an army of 6000 horse, foot and cannon, in their own ground, at least a mile and a half from their body.

At once several horses were killed by musket shots from the hedgerows:

> Their muskets playing very hard upon us, made us retreat so disorderly, that they fell foul upon our foot; and indeed there was not room enough for us to retreat in order, unless we had gone upon the very mouths of their muskets.

So Atkyns urges a charge:

The enemy, to encourage us to persecute this success, gave all
the symptoms of a flying army: as blowing up of powder, horse
and foot running distractedly on the edge of the hill, for we
could see no further: these signs made Sir Robert Welsh
importunately desire the Prince to have a party to follow the
chase, which he gave him the command of, and me of the
reserve; but when he came up the hill, and saw in what order
they lay, he soon quit his employment there, and desired he
might have my command and I his, which was ordered accordingly. As I went up the hill, which was very steep and hollow, I
met several dead and wounded officers brought off; besides
several running away; that I had much ado to get up by them.
When I came to the top of the hill, I saw Sir Bevil Grenville's
stand of pikes, which certainly preserved our army from a total
rout, with the loss of his most precious life: they stood as upon
the eaves of an house for steepness, but as unmovable as a rock;
on which side of this stand of pikes our horse were, I could not
discover; for the air was so darkened by the smoke of the
powder, that for a quarter of an hour together (I dare say) there
was no light seen, but what the fire of the volleys of shot gave,
and 'twas the greatest storm that ever I saw, in which though I
knew not whither to go, nor what to do, my Horse had two or
three musket bullets in him presently, which made him tremble
under me at the rate, that I could hardly with spurs keep him
from lying down; but he did me the service to carry me off to
a lead horse, and then died.

Atkyns's narrative collapses into incoherence as the battle explodes
around him into the hours of darkness: Walter Slingsby remarked, the
same night, that 'legs and arms were flying apace'. Once darkness fell,
'there was a great silence', and then, as Atkyns records:

By that time I came up to the hill again, the heat of the battle
was over, and the sun set, but still pelting at one another half
musket shot off: the enemy had a huge advantage of ground
upon our men, for their foot were in a large sheepcot, which
had a stone wall about it as good defence against any thing but
cannon as could be, and ours upon the edge of the hill, so steep
that they could hardly draw up, this true there were shelves near
the place like Romish works, where we quartered that night,

but so shallow that my horse had a bullet in his neck: we pelted at one another till half an hour before day, and then we heard not any noise, but saw light matches upon the wall, which our commanders observing, sent one to discover whether they had quit the field or not, who brought news that they were gone.

It was a miserable day.

Before the war, Bevil Grenville and Parliament's general in the West, William Waller, had been friends. Waller had once taken Grenville's son out to dinner in Oxford, like a kindly uncle. Giving Waller a horse before the war, Grenville called him 'my noblest friend'. Now his friend's army had shot him dead.

The odd thing was that the war violated such feelings and also allowed them their truest expression. As all soldiers know, on the battlefield wars are less about strategic objectives and master plans, and more about fighting for each other, fighting for the men who stood beside you last time your horse was shot under you. You don't want those men to see you run. Those simple feelings, well expressed by Atkyns, were complicated by the fact that you might, in this case, have similar loyalties to the men at whom you were firing. For many men, the war was no longer about the king or Parliament, personal rule or authority, even religion; it was about surviving today and saving one's friends. Atkyns came to live from action to action.

Of course, once Bevil Grenville was dead, his legend could begin and assume significance for the Cornish. The fact that he had frequently criticized the court before the war was not often mentioned. His suicidal charges, his personal charm, and his early death led to a collection of elegies, and later hagiographers were inspired by Bevil's son, one of Charles II's most trusted courtiers, created Earl of Bath and Viscount Lansdowne, a title specifically intended to evoke Bevil's heroic death. His loyalty became a symbol for Cornwall's own loyalty to the king. Bevil was an appealing figure for those inclined to see the Royalists as a bunch of godless tearaways, too, because he was and was known to be very religious, as diligent as the young Cromwell in making his men pray before battle, so he could be an apt figurehead of the piety and holiness of the Cornish army. By contrast, the darker and more ambivalent figure of his younger brother Richard Grenville received rather less attention, though he was to bring himself to everyone's notice later in the war.

Things did not improve next day for the Royalists, as Atkyns describes:

> The next morning was very clear, and about half an hour after sun rising, we rendezvoued our horse and foot upon Tog-Hill, between the hill where we quartered all night, and Marshfield; Major Sheldon and myself, went towards the Lord Hopton, who was then viewing the prisoners taken, some of which, were carried upon a cart wherein was our ammunition; and (as I heard) had match to light their tobacco; the Major desired me to go back to the regiment, whilst he received orders of his lordship; I had no sooner turned my horse, and was gone three horses lengths from him, but the ammunition was blown up, and the prisoners in the cart with it, together with the Lord Hopton, Major Sheldon, and Cornet Washnage, who was near the cart on horseback, and several others; it made a very great noise, and darkened the air for a time, and the hurt men made lamentable screeches. As soon as the air was clear, I went to see what the matter was, and there I found his lordship miserably burnt, his horse singed like parched leather, and Thomas Sheldon, that was a horse length further from the blast, com-planing that the fire was got within his breeches, which I tore off as soon as I could, and from as long a head of flaxen hair as ever I saw, in the twinkling of an eye his head was like a blackamoor; his horse was hurt, and run away like mad, so that I put him upon my horse, and got two troopers to hold him up on both sides, and bring him to the headquarters, whilst I marched after with the regiment.

Washnage died of his injuries. Sheldon was left behind as the enemy advanced, trying to take advantage of the confusion. Atkyns heard later that he too had died, 'by whose death I had lost my martial mistress, but had not time to bewail it'. His odd term should not necessarily be read as homoerotic; he means that his commanding officer ruled him, through love. For Atkyns, war was about this kind of love. And it was also about having to watch as the one he loved disintegrated before his eyes.

XI

The War over Christmas

One of the things everyone knows about the English Civil War is that Cromwell cancelled Christmas. In (very sober) fact, Christmas *was* cancelled, but not by Cromwell; it was cancelled by that transhistorical killjoy, a Parliamentary subcommittee exceeding its remit. All Cromwell did was enforce a policy agreed some years before his became an important voice in government.

When Parliament signed its treaty with Scotland, the Solemn League and Covenant, in September 1643, one of the promises it made was to reform the Church of England. No one had much idea what this meant – some kind of push in a more godly direction was expected, and a group of clergy and MPs was set up to draw up a report. The removal of saints' days from the calendar was expected, but the committee went much further. Led by Robert Harley, Brilliana's serious spouse, they reformed the Church calendar just as he had reformed Church décor. For Harley, paintings and stained glass were clutter that could obscure the simple truth of God, and the more beautiful they were, the more tempting and alluring they became, and therefore the more of an obstacle to true worship. The same stern aesthetic applied to the colourful festivals like Christmas, Easter, and saints' days; their very human appeal meant that they distracted believers from the motions of the spirit. As such, for Robert Harley the Church calendar too was to take less account of human needs for ritual, striving instead for an order which would allow the elect to approach the God of the Gospels without distraction. The committee therefore agreed that only the Lord's own day, Sunday, was a special day requiring special treatment.

All other festivals were to cease. The calendar would be marked only by fast days, and by days of national remembrance such as 5 November. The godly wanted to change for ever the way people thought about how they moved through time.

The old Church calendar that he wanted to erase mirrored the agricultural year, marking an annual cycle of birth, growth, death and resurrection. Christmas was an especially important feast for the idea of carnival. The incarnation and birth of Christ were reversals of the natural order of the universe; the king of the world born an outcast in a dirty stable. This encouraged symbols of paradox, transformation and the overturning of order to grow up around the feast. There was an implicit agreement: the labouring poor would share the life of the lords for whom they worked for the twelve days of Christmas, in exchange for quiescence for the rest of the year. Plum pottage was a kind of opiate of the masses. For this to work, symbolically, a number of things had to happen with clockwork regularity: the lord had to be present, sharing the feast; the feast had to be superabundant, symbolic of largesse; ideally, there must be games – ranging from mumming to cards and dice – in which extreme reversals of fortune featured. The most concrete expression of this was the Christmas Lord of Misrule, who presided over the feast; also linked were boy bishops, choirboys elevated to the mitre and crozier for Christmas from the feast of St Nicholas, 6 December. Battles between Christmas and Lent were sometimes staged on Shrove Tuesday; Christmas at Norwich in 1443 rode a horse decked in tinfoil while Lent was clad in herring skins, white and red, and his horse covered in oyster shells. The last night of Christmas, Twelfth Night, was especially associated with disorder and misrule through the lottery of the Twelfth Night cake. Whoever got the slice of cake with a bean hidden in it was king of the feast. The cake itself contained expensive spices: a 1620 Geneva tract gives the recipe as containing flour, honey, ginger and pepper. Hospitality was the goal of the season, and especially so tenants and poor neighbours could gain temporary access to the lord's hospitality, in return for the enforced gifts that marked their dependence: licensed openness with a careful structure. The poor may have got to eat in the hall, not by the gate. In exchange an acceptance of the hierarchical relationship was implied – and required.

The centrepiece was always food and drink, however; 'at Christmas we banquet, the rich with the poor/ who then (but the miser) but openeth his door?' asked Thomas Tusser. One of the main treats was a boar's head, and Tusser also lists brawn as an important element. He describes, too, a carnivorous feast of mutton, pork, veal, souse, and finally cheese and apples. He also mentions turkey, but stresses good bread, good drink, and above all a blazing fire in the hall; Christmas feasting might have represented the only real chance to be warm all winter for the very poorest guests. The other way to get warm – or not to mind about the cold – was of course huge quantities of alcohol, also central to Christmas. Wassailing – with a regional drink, sometimes cider, or the spiced beer called lambswool – involved a shared drinking and kissing ritual, sometimes involving a demand for money and food with menaces. (It was a struggle to get new wine for Christmas, as most of the previous year's wine was undrinkable by then.) People were menaced for money by mummers, too, and those who didn't give it, whether because they were godly or because they were mean, could be punished with a riding; on a staff to Chichester High Cross, for instance, in 1586. This was part of the general holiday fun of violence. Similarly, while gathered around the fire, more-or-less traditional and subversive songs could be sung, and stories could be told, the deeds of Hereward the Wake or Robin Hood, or of Tom Thumb. Christmas carols were promoted by the early Stuart Church; court preacher Lancelot Andrewes was an especial advocate.

That jovial man Humphrey Mildmay was always in search of a good Christmas, but his idea of what made Christmas good didn't altogether fit the model exhorted by the defenders of Yule. Mildmay was not enormously fond of the tradition of open-house hospitality. He noted, Ebenezer-like, that at New Year 'to dinner came rascal upon rascal without sending for'. Still, he did love food and drink; he made sure he ordered in hogsheads of wine, and like many a modern family he enjoyed walking off his excesses. 'I have been walking in the fields and woods so wide', he writes, 'on Danbury Hill.' Despite his reservations, he revelled in the sociability of the festival, and the contrast between indoor jollity and raging winter. In 1639/40, he noted that the weather at Christmas was especially nasty; it was clear and cold on 20 December, but it was also 'high winds, and dirty beyond measure, the floods mountain high'. Despite this, at Christmas everyone went to church, and the next day 'all night was a mighty storm'. On New Year's Day he wrote, 'to dinner; many here and the hall full of idle company'. During the Twelve Days, Humphrey Mildmay also enjoyed bull-baiting, and the indoor pleasures of cards, especially gleek and pink, also known as post and pair, and dice, and of course tables, and 'gammon', or backgammon. They all played for money, significant sums by the standards of the day, and women played as well as men. Dancing was also part of the festivities, to the music of fiddles and trumpeters.

Church was important too. In the old Roman Sarum rite, the devout were to attend three Christmas Masses; the most important was dawn vigil, after which the congregation could break their fast with the roasts, pies and puddings that had been forbidden in Advent. Churches were decorated with greenery – rosemary, bay, holly and ivy. Other customs included gifts exchanged at New Year: Christmas boxes for servants, tradesmen and the poor, and pastimes, which included singing, dancing, card games, stage plays, and the creation of a Lord of Misrule. Yet as with modern festivals, one person's cheer was another's noisy nuisance. The Elizabethan moralist Philip Stubbes complained that 'more mischief is at this time [Christmas] committed than in all the year besides', and he claimed that it incited robbery, whoredom and murder, dicing and carding, banqueting and feasting, 'to the great dishonour of God and the impoverishing of the realm'.

Complaints like this are the reason that Christmas was *always* under threat. It is true that the Edwardian and Elizabethan Church allowed it, along with St Stephen's Day and Holy Innocents' Day, because all could be found in the New Testament. Those eager to defend 'traditional' Christmas were also inclined to give it a much longer history than it actually possessed; Christmas didn't become a major Church festival until the high Middle Ages, though it was a minor one from early in Church history. No sooner was it established than it was criticized. From Henry VIII to Dickens, Christmas has always needed work to improve it, to endow it with the magic it possessed in the past. The Tudor Christmas among aristocrats was characterized by banquets, balls, plays, masques and mummings, coordinated by the Lord of Misrule; this replaced simpler, older open-house feasts for tenants. By the time the Civil War began, Christmas had again become controversial; as early as James's reign, the godly had objected to the king's masques and Christmas games as pagan survivals. Ben Jonson, author of *Christmas His Masque* in 1617, made his work an evocation of a traditional Christmas already seen as under threat, 'a right Christmas, as of old it was'. Like Dickens, Jonson castigates Londoners for their failure to bless the poor and keep Christmas. The poet Robert Herrick, too, insists that unless Christmas customs are kept up, the crops themselves will fail; 'Wassail the trees, that they may bear/ you many a plum and many a pear', he urges, referring to the custom of pouring wassail around fruit trees to make them bear, but using this as a metaphor for the relations between tenants and lords. Give hospitality, Herrick insists, or lose the loyalty of the poor. The connection was more obvious because, traditionally, the first Monday after the Twelve Days of Christmas was Plough Monday, when the ploughing began.

So Christmas was supposed to be a kind of dream-world, in which the rich could see themselves reflected as generous and hospitable, the poor as welcome and loved. But it was an illusion, and Parliament had no time nor place for illusions.

What helped to doom Christmas for the godly was the way Catholic Counter-Reformation clerics emphasized the cult of the Virgin and the Holy Family. Thus Christmas became more important to Catholics, and hence, dangerously, more associated with them: Dorothy Lawson, a staunch Catholic, celebrated Christmas 'in both kinds . . . corporally and spiritually', enjoying Christmas pies, dancing and gambling. In 1594, the imprisoned Catholic priests at Wisbech kept Christmas with a hobby horse and morris dances; at Douai, at the Benedictine school, they elected a Christmas King every year. The priest John Gerard reports that vigorous celebrations of Christmas made recusants conspicuous. And on the eve of the Civil War, Richard Carpenter, recently converted to Protestantism, reported that the recusant gentry were noted for their 'great Christmasses'. The result was that more and more Protestants viewed Christmas as one of the trappings of popery. The Protestant notion that 'all days are alike God's creatures', direct and simple, made Christmas seem a nonsense of noise and fuss. In December 1642, Thomas Fuller was delivering a fast sermon on Holy Innocents' Day, a sad note in the Twelve Days: he remarked that 'on this day a fast and feast do both jostle together, and the question is which should take place in our affections . . . [the young] may be so addicted to their toys and Christmas sports that they will not be weaned from them' and he advised the older generation not to be transported with their follies, but to 'mourn while they are in mirth'.

What encouraged the godly to try to shut down the entire festive calendar was the Solemn League and Covenant. Previously, even the most zealous godly had spoken only of abolishing saints' days, but now every feast was denounced by someone as superstition. So the Christmas Wars began, a reflection of the wars fought by the contending armies. Accordingly, in 1643, some shops opened on Christmas Day in London, and some churches, by contrast, were closed. Amazingly by modern standards, some MPs turned up for work. And some newsbooks attacked Christmas, pointing out that it contained the word 'mass', an 'idol', and tacitly urging Parliament to press forward with legislation. Eagerly Sir Robert Harley had been reforming the Sunday trading laws. All commerce, travel, labour, wakes, ales, dances and all pastimes whatever were to be banned on the Lord's Day, and maypoles were to be taken down.

The assembly of ministers convened to reform the Church decided in November that only the Lord's Day should be a holy day, and in December 1644 the crunch came when the monthly fast day clashed with Christmas; Parliament decisively backed the fast day. On 19 December, an ordinance was passed insisting that the fast day should continue as normal but 'with the more solemn humiliation because it may call to remembrance our sins, and the sins of our forefathers, who have turned this feast, pretending the memory of Christ, into an extreme forgetfulness of him, by giving liberty to carnal and sensual delights'. The sermon given to Parliament stressed the triumph of the monthly fast over the festival: 'the highest festival of all the year to meet with our monthly fast and be subdued by it'. Ironically, this used exactly the language of Christmas battles between villages. But preachers were told to secure some 'fire and plum pottage' for those who had missed the traditional fun.

Parliament kept up its offensive. On 4 January 1645 it issued the new *Directory for the Public Worship of God.* This reinforced the new status quo of Sunday-only holy days, fasts, and occasional celebrations of military triumphs. The last involved listening to long sermons, just like the others, but with something to eat beforehand. But of course all these directives could only be enforced in the parts of the country controlled by Parliament, and even there the *Directory* wasn't distributed till August 1645. The first real trial of strength was therefore over Christmas; Easter and Whitsun, being Sundays, could still be more-or-less observed, and no one seemed to mind much about the loss of saints' days. But Christmas most often fell on a weekday, in a calendar now centred on Sundays and fast days. A further ordinance in June 1647 abolished Christmas, Easter and Whitsun, and substituted as a regular holiday for students, apprentices and servants the second Tuesday of every month. The government rounded up a number of clergy for trying to preach on Christmas Day, including one who published his sermon under the provocative title *The Stillborn Nativity.*

The attack on Christmas actually licensed some popular violence. In 1643, mobs of apprentices in several towns forced any open shops to close, as they did in Bury St Edmunds in 1646, resulting in a scuffle and some injuries. The following year in Norwich, there were petitions from godly ministers trying to hurry reform through the mayor's office, and from apprentices angry that there had been any reform at all. In Ipswich, too, there was trouble when those who wanted to celebrate Christmas formed 'a great mutiny' and in 1647 there was trouble over the Christmas decorations that some city porters had draped around the conduit in Cornhill. The mayor and corporation assembled to take them down, and a crowd assembled to prevent them; one man ended up in Newgate. The shops in London continued, determinedly, to close, and the taverns were by contrast full. Godly Ezekiel Woodward admitted that 'the people go on holding fast to their heathenish customs and abominable idolatries, and think they do well'. Change was also strongly resisted; when a group of people violently attacked excisemen and their escort of soldiers at Chippenham in 1647, it was New Year's Eve; some of the attackers used disguise, suggesting a festive link.

The fiercest battles were in Kent. In Canterbury, the county committee outlawed Christmas in 1647, and in response a huge crowd gathered to demand a church service and to enforce the closure of shops and businesses. Predictably, fights broke out, and the mayor's house was

attacked. A crowd 'threw up and down the wares' of those few shopkeepers who obeyed the mayor's order to open for business, while
others set up holly in their doorways and gave out free drinks. They
also got out that ancient symbol of rebellion and misrule, the football.
For some weeks, the city was controlled by the rioters; they adopted
the slogan 'for God, King Charles and Kent', uniting a festive religious
calendar to Royalism. In early January they were forced to surrender,
but less than six months later Kent was thickly involved in the Second
Civil War.

As with any dispute, too, the press was active, and a pamphlet controversy developed. It began with a debate about the date of Christmas.
A Royalist pamphlet printed at Oxford, by Edward Fisher, entitled *The
Feast of Feasts*, asserted that 25 December was the right day; this was
part of an intellectual debate, and he also insisted that his readers
should 'hold the traditions which we have been taught, let us make
them known to our children'. In December 1647 came *A Ha Christmas*,
which stressed the charitable aspect of Christmas, 'those who God
almighty hath given a good share of the wealth of this world may wear
the best, eat and drink the best with moderation, so that they remember
God's poor members with mercy and charity, and this year requireth
more charity than ordinary because of the dearness of provision'. A
Canterbury cleric, Robert Palmer, wrote that continued opposition to
Christmas might create resentment which their enemies could harness
'as a fair cloak to put on for to begin a quarrel'. What he said was
plausible because some Kentish rioters the previous year had begun
their rebellion with a demonstration of Christmas tradition. Robert
Skinner, by contrast, argued on the other side that Christmas was just
the pagan festival of the Saturnalia and that customs like Yule games
and carols were relics of that pagan rite. Thomas Mockett argued the
same thing the following year, in his *Christmas, The Christian's Grand
Feast*: 'all the heathenish customs and pagan rites and ceremonies
that the idolatrous heathen used, as riotous drinking, health drinking,
gluttony, luxury, wantonness, dancing, dicing, stage-plays, interludes,
masques, mummeries, with all other pagan sports and profane practices
into the Church of God'. This was a fairly obvious attack on the court
in particular. In January 1649, Edward Fisher re-entered the debate,
republishing his old pamphlet under the title *A Christian Caveat to the*

Old and New Sabbatarians, defending Yule sports with a new appendix arguing that 'the body is God's as well as the spirit, and therefore why should not God be glorified by showing forth the strength, quickness and agility of our body ... to eat mince pies, plum pottage or brawn in December, to trim churches or private houses with holly or ivy about Christmas, to stick roasting pieces of beef with rosemary or to stick a sprig of rosemary in a collar of brawn, to play cards or bowls, to hawk or to hunt, to give money to servants or to apprentices a box [a gift], or to send a couple of capons or any other present to a friend during the twelve days'. It sold some 6000 copies, and was reissued five times. Later writers followed Fisher's lead, arguing that Christmas rituals were visual symbols of the sacred, especially for the illiterate. This was a conspicuously Laudian line, and so there was a predictably angry response; Ezekiel Woodward, the minister of Bray, wrote a pamphlet whose title summed up his thesis: *Christmas Day The Old Heathen's Feasting Day.* Less learned pamphlets, like *The Arraignment, Conviction and Imprisoning of Christmas, printed by Simon Minced-Pie for Cicely Plum Pottage,* took the form of a quarrel between a town-crier and a Royalist gentlewoman who was enquiring after Father Christmas's whereabouts. 'Since the Catholic liquor is taken from him, he is much wasted', says the crier, and 'is now constrained to remain in the Popish quarters'. The woman replies: 'If ever the Catholics or bishops rule again in England, they will set the church doors open on Christmas Day, and we shall have mass at the High Altar as was used when the day was first instituted, and not have the holy Eucharist barred out of school, as school boys do their masters against the festival. What, shall we have our mouths shut to welcome old Christmas. No, no, bid him come by night over the Thames, and we will have a back door open to let him in. I will myself give him his diet for one year to try his fortune, this time twelve months may prove better.'

John Taylor gloomily described the abandonment of Christmas festivities in the 'schismatical and rebellious towns' of London, Yarmouth, Newbury and Gloucester, where Christmas came and went with 'no sign or token of any holy day. The shops were open, the markets were full, the watermen rowing, the carmen were a loading and unloading ... all the liberty and harmless sports, with the merry gambols dances and friscals by which the toiling plowswain and labourer were wont to be recreated and their spirits and hopes revived for a whole twelve month are now extinct and put out of use in such a fashion as if they had never been.' Taylor especially saw Christmas as the festival of the poor; in a later pamphlet he wrote of the Devon people, 'the poor labouring hands and maid servants with the ploughboys went nimbly dancing; the poor toiling wretches'. A debate between Mistress Custom and Mistress NewCome over Christmas, by contrast, uses the language of misrule to describe the 'tatterdemallions' who have banned the festival.

But despite all this, the overall pattern of churchwardens' accounts suggests that most were willing to conform, albeit sulkily. True, many wistful pamphleteers and poets lamented the passing of the old ritual year. But they did think it *had* passed, at least in areas held by Parliament, a category that ultimately included everyone. True, the government had to keep insisting that Christmas should not be celebrated, but this was at least partly because celebrating Christmas had become a fine way of thumbing one's nose to the government. Many parishes in the West, East Anglia and Cheshire went on celebrating communion at Christmas, and at Easter and Whitsun too, but historian Ronald Hutton decisively shows that if the republic had lasted ten years longer, the old festive calendar would have been dead beyond recall. Christmas was killed at Naseby fight, mourned a popular ballad, 'The World is Turned Upside Down', to be sung to the tune of 'When the King Enjoys His Own Again'. John Taylor later sneered at those for whom 'Plum Pottage was mere Popery, that a collet of brawn was an abomination, that roast beef was anti-Christian, that mince pies were relics of the Whore of Babylon, and a goose or a turkey or capon were marks of the Beast'. But his very sneering recorded their triumph. Sir John Oglander complained that the Isle of Wight had become 'a melancholy, dejected, sad place – no company, no resort, no neighbours seeing one another'. Festivals and processions had been replaced by sermons and fasts. The new calendar would have wiped out all public traces of the old if the regime had survived longer. In this sense, Cromwell actually *saved* Christmas by dying opportunely.

Christmas returned with Charles II, and Samuel Pepys remarked on his London church, all decked with rosemary and bay, while the Verneys in 1664 were congratulated on the prospect of keeping 'the best Christmas in the shire', for which they had 'bought more fruit and spice than half the porters in London can weigh out in a day'. The war had left no trace, except perhaps a little extra excess, a little added relish for what is still the chief national holiday.

XII

The Queen's Tale: Henrietta Maria

On 30 March 1643, in a former palace in London, an act of iconoclasm was performed that seemed to condense the ferocity and misery of all of them.

The story begins before the war. In the spring of 1622, the Archduchess Isabella commissioned a large painting of the Crucifixion from Rubens to give to Sir George Calvert. He in turn presented it to the Duke of Buckingham. Finally it came to rest in Henrietta Maria's chapel at Somerset House, a move which sealed its doom.

In 1643, Parliament – or at any rate, sixty members of it – voted to arrest Henrietta's Capuchin friars, and also destroy the contents of her private chapel. Accordingly, on 30 March, Holy Thursday, Henry Marten and the half-mad Ulsterman John Clotworthy entered the Great Court of Somerset House. Two French aristocrats met them and insisted that the chapel was protected by the queen's marriage treaty, but Henry Marten was not the man to be troubled by this sort of consideration. He ordered his troops to batter down the doors of the friary and arrest any Capuchins. John Clotworthy and his troops burst into the chapel.

Clotworthy was a member of the Long Parliament, a fighting Ulsterman who had a sister married to John Pym. He was a passionate Presbyterian who had been working to cleanse Ireland from the taint of popery that for him disfigured it. He is said to have remarked that 'the conversion of the papists in Ireland was only to be effected by the Bible in one hand and the sword in the other'. Eagerly, this fierce man and his troops made straight for the altarpiece, a twenty-foot Rubens painting of the crucified Christ. Clotworthy clambered up the altar to reach it. He called for a halberd, and struck the painted image of Christ's face 'with terrible words', then struck the face of the Virgin, 'and then, thrusting the hook of his halberd under the feet of the crucified Christ, he ripped the painting to pieces'. The fragments were thrown into the Thames.

So perished the only picture of Christ's death on the cross that Rubens ever painted.

The Rubens altarpiece was singled out for special treatment. The careful Parliamentarian inventory of 1649 shows that over thirty paintings remained in the chapel, at that late date. Admittedly, the Rubens was large and obvious, and it was an image of Christ; these were particularly targeted by iconoclasts. But there was another, more subtle reason for its destruction. Two surviving works by Rubens might help us understand the impact this lost painting made. Rubens's *Crucifixion of St Peter* depicts the saint with brutal realism, all distended muscles and mouth gaping in agony. Furious soldiers, their bodies also bulging with power, are absorbed in their own ferocity, while the saint stares directly at us. The other relevant painting is Rubens's triptych of the elevation of the cross, depicting Christ with similar and extreme muscularity; even the gouts of blood which pour down his arms are powerful and exuberant, and the entire painting is dynamic, with the executioners wrestling the cross, struggling to make it upright; its muscular sadism is powerful and disturbing. It's influenced not only by Tintoretto, but by the Laocoön sculpture that was becoming one of the must-sees in Rome, and by Caravaggio's treatment of light. A muscular Christ like this seems hypermasculine compared with the slender, feminine Christs of the late Middle Ages.

The iconoclasts may have sensed the pagan overtones of Laocoön and the controversial homoeroticism of Caravaggio. What was especially disturbing was that Rubens had used both traditions to make religion and spirituality grossly *physical*, in a way that still intimidates us today. Rubens's Christ is very truly made flesh. It is his way of saying something about the place of art in religion, something defiant – he is insisting that it is through art – realist art – that the incarnation of Christ can be made *visible* – can almost be repeated by the artist. This was a direct and perhaps a conscious challenge to the Reformers' views.

There was a final reason for the iconoclasts' fury. Both Marten and Clotworthy were educated men, and the very name Rubens may have reminded them of what they hated, what they wanted to crush.

Henrietta Maria was especially associated with Rubens. Like her astute and very unpopular mother, Marie de Medici, she hired the best, the most showy and brilliant painters. In particular, she favoured Rubens's elegant combination of playful mythologizing with absolute and luminous reality. He had, after all, worked for Marie de Medici as well, creating a cycle of myth for her in 1625, which was ready for her daughter's wedding to Charles. And Henrietta copied the Rubens depiction of her mother's Amazonian costume in rich, carnation colours for one of her court masques, a masque at which her mother was present, the oddly ominous *Salmacida Spolia*.

It was probably in 1625 that Rubens met Buckingham, who had come to France to collect Henrietta; the painter sensibly loathed him, and wrote astutely, 'When I consider the caprice and arrogance of Buckingham I pity the young king, who, through false council, is needlessly throwing himself and his kingdom into such extremity. For anyone can start a war when he wishes, but he cannot so easily end it.'

However, Rubens's political views did mean he was happy to act as a peace envoy to try to broker what he himself called 'the English peace' with Spain. As a result, he came to London at the beginning of June, and lodged with the dubious Balthasar Gerbier, a portrait painter. Rubens's mission made him an unpopular figure in some court circles, especially the French Protestants and those eager to support the Elector Palatine against the Spanish. In return, Rubens noticed that many of the nobles had inadequate incomes, and were willing to sell themselves for ready money. Less sourly, he relished 'the beauty of the countryside, and the charm of the nation; not only for the splendour of the outward culture, which seems to be extreme, as of a people rich and happy in the lap of peace, but also for the incredible quantity of pictures, statues and ancient inscriptions which are to be found at this court' (August 1629). He was impressed by Buckingham's and Arundel's collections, but especially by Charles. In 1625, Rubens had hailed Charles as 'the greatest amateur of painting among the princes of the world', while Charles gave Rubens a knighthood. He also commissioned a painting of St George and the dragon from Rubens, in which the saint has Charles's features, and the princess those of Henrietta Maria.

The setting is the Thames Valley, with London visible in the distance. The Banqueting House can be seen clearly, so that Charles's role as innovator and sponsor of new styles is on display; this is also a kind of advertisement for Rubens's own panels, which adorned its ceiling. This suggests that the picture as a whole represents Charles as the defender of beauty against ugliness. Henrietta's glowing youth and beauty rise above images of darkness and destruction; for Rubens, Charles was rescuing Beauty itself from the wars of religion. It was eloquent of the baroque, the world of exceptional excess combined with odd restraint.

But if anyone remembered Rubens in the bleaker London of 1643, it was as Henrietta's hireling, ambassador for popery, keen demonizer of revolutionary energies. None of these memories was likely to inspire Marten and Clotworthy to be careful with his painting. They also wanted to wreck it not only because it was art, but because it was *good* art. That day, a master's work perished mostly because it *was* masterly, because it might actually influence people.

Clotworthy and his men proceeded to the side chapels, where they broke up two paintings of the Virgin and of St Francis, perhaps the iconoclasts' least favourite saint. In the vestry, they flung a large statue of the Virgin and Child to the floor, and then smashed the Virgin's face and the face of her child with feet and then with clubs. The sound of splintering stone spurred them on. In the chapel garden, they found another statue of St Francis, which they also destroyed, and another crucifix, ripe for breaking.

The crackling fires that the soldiers lit burned long into the night, consuming shreds of canvas, books, rich embroidered vestments. On Good Friday, the soldiers destroyed some minor masterpieces – Matthew Goodrich's and Thomas de Critz's oval ceiling painting of the Assumption of the Virgin, a work even larger than Rubens's *Crucifixion*. The remnants not burnt were again flung into the Thames.

Perhaps Charles's flight from London with the queen was not the stupid act historians have sometimes made it appear. For this passion of violence could as easily have been unleashed against Henrietta herself; not directly, but through Parliament, as it had been against

Strafford and Laud. By 1643, she had become the most hated queen in English history since Edward IV's wife, Elizabeth Woodville. And it was she and her influence that men like Marten and Clotworthy most wanted to destroy.

The queen was only too involved in affairs of state. The perception that she was involved itself helped to harden attitudes, because Henrietta was a troubling figure. The very closeness of her relationship with the king, their conjugal bliss, was a source of anxiety; a woman, a foreigner and a fervent Catholic at the heart of affairs exacerbated the dread of popery that Pym had been exploiting. Parliament's constant complaints about Jesuited papists lurking everywhere were directed squarely at her. One declaration actually said that Charles should stop listening to his wife. That was one reason why it seemed sensible to protect her – and defuse the tensions she aroused, too – by getting her right out of England, to Holland. So on 23 February 1642, she and Charles parted, in tears. Charles waved the ship out of sight.

But the queen's behaviour during the war upset people further. She sought help from overseas – from foreigners, and Romish foreigners at that; the sensible Dutch Protestants took little notice of her, though she managed to buy some guns from William of Orange after a lot of haggling. She was, thought one of her critics, on a kind of shopping spree: 'Who went to the Brokers with the Jewels of the crown, and the cupboard of gold plate? Who bought pocket-pistols, barrels of powder, and many such pretty toys to destroy the Protestants? Was it Queen Mary? The very same.'

Her activities contributed to her extreme unpopularity in the country at large. In the north, Thomas Beevers, a dyer of Thurleston, 'said he would lay ten pounds the Kings ears were stowled of within a month [i.e. that he was cuckolded], and that the queen was gone over into Holland to play the whore'. Going somewhere without your husband was itself whorish enough. But going off to buy weapons and raise money was not what the common people expected from a queen. Henrietta persevered, however, even though few of her weapons reached the king. She decided to go home. 'I need the air of England', she wrote. She sailed in early February 1643, but had to return to Holland after a terrible storm in which the ladies of the court had been forced to shout their sins at their confessors so as to plummet shriven to the bottom of the sea. Henrietta later remembered what interesting things she had heard. But she set out again in late February, and evading a Parliamentarian attempt to intercept her, reached Bridlington and began distributing her provisions to the king's armies of the north, thus ensuring that they would be regarded as even more darkly popish by their foes. She joined Charles near Edgehill, and the town of Kineton, scene of so much bloodshed and division, now witnessed a very happy reunion of the whole family, including the princes. Soon the royal family were all settled in Oxford, the king's new capital.

There she kept up a pasteboard version of the old life. In the midst of the sterner concerns of 1643, Henrietta wrote to Charles about a friend's woes:

> The Duchess of Buckingham [Lady Catherine Manners, Countess of Antrim, widow of Buckingham] has begged me to write to you that you would order secretary Nicholas to write on your behalf to her children to obey her, or else they will be lost; for they have no-one near them to take care of them, and they are becoming debauched. As to their concerns, she will not meddle with them in any fashion in the world, only let them believe what she says to them, that they may not be lost in this world. It would be a very small honour for you to see them ill brought up, after you have taken them under your care.

But the cultural project of change was faltering. On 26 October 1643 George Wither reported that 'it is there thought also by some of His Majesties Servants (as our Mercury verily believeth) that the queen will not have so many Masques at Christmas and Shrovetide this year as she was wont to have other years heretofore; because Inigo Jones cannot conveniently make such Heavens and paradises at Oxford as he did at White-hall, and because the Poets are dead, beggared, or run away who were wont in their late masques to make Gods and Goddesses of them, and shamefully to flatter them with attributes neither fitting to be ascribed or accepted of; and some are of the opinion that this is one of the innumerable vanities which hath made them and us become so miserable at this day'.

Once ensconced in Oxford, Henrietta had the same company as in

London; they brought their own furniture from home, while the queen took over the Warden's lodgings in Merton; he was a Parliament-man who had fled to London. The room a visitor was most likely to see was the presence chamber, with the queen seated on a raised dais to receive formal visitors, and this was also where she dined formally, attended by her cupbearer and her carver. It was large and light, and it was approached by an impressive carved oak staircase. It opened for business at nine, which meant that servants had to be up much earlier laying fires and cleaning the rooms. Then the queen would hear Mass in the college chapel, which had been given over to her, while the Anglican ladies-in-waiting attended prayers, often walking up to Trinity.

Behind lay the privy chamber, where the queen could enjoy privacy attended only by her own ladies of the bedchamber. Behind that was a still more private space, the withdrawing chamber, where Henrietta received only a very small and select circle – her confessor, the Countess of Denbigh and other chief favourites. It functioned as a parlour might in a less formal establishment. Behind this was the bedchamber itself.

The king liked to come and spend the time after midday dinner with the queen, if he wasn't playing tennis or going hunting in the woods around Oxford. This was when most people crowded into the queen's apartments. Prince Rupert might drop in; lodged in Laud's old college, St John's, he took no notice of any orders but the king's, and even the latter were interpreted fairly liberally. Rupert was always arguing energetically and vociferously for new and exotic campaign plans. Poets like Abraham Cowley or John Denham might present their barbed verses on the enemy, while Sir William Davenant might compose something more lyrical in praise of the queen. There were always French-speakers, papists, exotics such as Henrietta's dwarf Jeffrey Hudson and her eccentric lady-in-waiting, Margaret Lucas. The court was always overrun with dogs, not least Rupert's favourite Boy, but also Henrietta's many spaniels, especially her beloved Mitte who had been with her in Holland. The room could also be filled by the two tall princes, Charles and James. The godly still found it all scandalously arty. Henrietta liked walking in the college gardens, too, and Oxford had a warm summer that year. The ladies-in-waiting did a lot of waiting, in both senses; they ran to and fro delivering notes and picking up dropped items.

They played cards and gossiped and did embroideries and told each other romantic news. The men liked to play cards too, but also lost and won huge sums at dice, tennis and chess. Everyone struggled to keep up the smooth formal patina of pre-war life, to make the court – and especially the queen's court – a refuge from the conflict, a realm of normality.

But Oxford was not in a normal state. The effort to keep up appearances, to keep the court functioning, only exposed the changes besieging it. Normalcy was at best a cruel trick.

Henrietta and Charles had been reunited for only a month when Charles left for the siege of Gloucester, and Henrietta blamed Rupert. She suddenly felt isolated, the illusion of normality torn away. Merton's walls were part of the city's outer defences. Henrietta had only to open a window to see the sentries and their cannons. She knew, too, that if Parliament ever took the city then she would be in great danger. She was the one they blamed for everything. She was already charged with high treason, which meant that anyone who killed her would be rewarded, not hanged. Parliament had finally impeached her on 21 June 1643, though she was for the moment out of its reach; people reminded each other that she had never been crowned, and that she had pawned the Crown Jewels, and raised her 'popish army'. The only serious debate was about how to refer to the woman; some members didn't want her called queen, but this would mean referring to her by her maiden name, Bourbon, and thus offending the French royal family. Although Henrietta forgave the rebels, and although she had always been realistic about the seriousness of the situation, these new threats were daunting. The constant dread began to wear her down. And as summer turned to autumn, her situation grew worse.

XIII

Newbury Fight

In July 1643, the Royalists breached the outer line of Bristol's supposedly impregnable defences. This was to prove the high tide of their fortunes, the heroic climax of the war in the West; Rupert and his men had attacked impetuously rather than besiege Bristol steadily, but luck was with them. However, the godly people of Bristol were not welcoming. One of Bristol's citizens was Dorothy Hazzard, a devout woman who knew something had to be done. She gathered together two hundred women, and they ran to the city's vital Frome Gate. They worked with their own hands to strengthen its defences, blocking up the entrance with soil and woolsacks. Then she went to look for the governor, whose backbone was in need of stiffening, urging him to stand firm in the defence of the city, and promising him that she and her women would take their babes in their arms and stand in front of the defending soldiers, 'to keep off the shot from the soldiers, if they were afraid'. But it was all in vain; lack of ammunition forced the governor to surrender. The result was plunder on an almost apocalyptic scale. Shopkeepers were asked for protection money, and then found that paying one group of soldiers did nothing to prevent attacks by others. The garrison were stripped of all clothing and abused by the incoming Royalists. It was a sign that the rules of civilized warfare were beginning to crumble.

Every town in England could read the writing on the walls of Bristol. If Bristol could fall, nowhere was very safe. Shouting from its supposedly impregnable defences, the Royalists could not know that they had reached the height of their fortunes. Now, as the chilly autumn of 1643 began, things would get worse. They would fail to take Gloucester, and their armies would once again be driven back from London.

Battles are sometimes described as if seen by gods, but they are experienced sketchily, in zigzags of noise, light, hand-to-hand fights. The Battle of Newbury can be seen from the heavens, or from the earth. The dichotomy between the ideal straight line and the muddied, muddled reality existed for the Civil War soldier too. After putting on helmet, breastplate and buff-coat, after taking up pike or musket, after drilling, the infantryman was still a vulnerable soft human being.

Essex had hoped to occupy Newbury, but the Royalists blocked the London road, and occupied it themselves on 19 September 1643, a few hours before Essex and his Parliament-men arrived. The London trained bands and the rest of Essex's army were forced out into the fields. For the Royalists, Sir Jacob Astley commanded the foot; the king had a little over 14,000 men, and also had twenty guns, sixteen of them brass. He went to bed in Newbury on the night of 19 September in a cheerful frame of mind; he had ample supplies of food, and he had cut the rebels off from London. His troops were mainly comfortably bivouacked, but the Parliamentarians were cold, tired, footsore, homesick and short of food; they were also lying in the fields.

The Welsh Royalist John Gwynne remembered how tired he was before he reached quarters: 'we were like to drop down every step we made with want to sleep, yet notwithstandingly we marched on still, until the evening we overtook the enemy's army at Newbury town's end; then our quarter-masters, with their party, beat their quarter-masters and their parties of horse out of the town'.

Essex rode from camp to camp to warn his men of the Royalist advantages, but the army still cheered him as it had at Turnham Green with cries of 'Hey for Robin'. Their discomfort was a blessing in disguise because it allowed them to occupy the high ground, especially a hill called Round Hill that commanded an impressive field of fire. Skippon, occupying it, opened fire on the Royalists below in the plain to prove this at first light.

In the morning, one of the Royalist commanders, Lord Digby, realized that the Royalists had to take that hill 'or there was no holding of the field'; the task was given to the foot regiments of Sir Nicholas

Byron's brigade, but the hill was stoutly defended by Parliamentarians who lined every ditch and hedgerow. Young Edmund Verney was among those who fought with Byron up that stubborn little hill. At one point, Byron noted that his men would have to pass through a gap which allowed only one horseman at a time. He ordered it widened, but even as he did so his horse was wounded.

It was then that Lucius Cary, Lord Falkland spurred his horse through the gap. As they advanced against musketeers hidden in the hedgerows, a musketball hit him in the stomach and he toppled from his horse; he was dead before he hit the ground. Cary was a brave idealist and intellectual who represented the epitome of moderate Royalism. He was also the eldest son of Elizabeth Cary, Viscountess Falkland, the Catholic convert and friend to the queen who had also brought up all of her nine children as Catholics, except Lucius. Like his mother, he was physically short and unimpressive, with black eyes and black hair, but he had impressed everyone with his intelligence and idealism. Bulstrode Whitelocke described his actions on the morning of the battle:

> The Lord Falkland, secretary of state, in the morning of the fight called for a clean shirt, and being asked the reason of it, answered that if he were slain in the battle they should not find his body in foul linen. Being dissuaded by his friends to go into the fight, as having no call to it, and being no military officer, he said he was weary of the times, and foresaw much misery to his own country, and did believe he should be out of it ere night, and could not be persuaded to the contrary, but would enter into the battle, and was there slain (in the lanes about Round Hill). His death was much lamented by all that knew him, or heard of him, being a gentleman of great parts, ingenuity, and honour, courteous and just to all, a passionate promoter of all endeavours of peace betwixt the king and parliament.

Whitelocke may have been right that Falkland, like Sir Edmund Verney, was actively seeking a battlefield death. He had been reckless before at Gloucester, and he had volunteered for the front rank of Byron's regiment. For John Aubrey, Falkland threw his life away because he was overcome with remorse at having persuaded the king to besiege

Gloucester, which Aubrey thought so weakened the army that it lost the war. Falkland was also miserable about the loss of his mistress, Mrs Moray 'whom he loved above all creation'. His corpse was battered and mangled in the action, but Aubrey says it was recognized by a mole on the back of the neck.

Byron forced the gap himself, and found it deadly: '[the enemy] entertained us with a great salvo of musket shot, and discharged their two drakes upon us laden with case shot, which killed some and hurt many of my men'. The Royalists were blinded by smoke and obstructed by tall hedges, but they struggled on, working across farmland, one field at a time; as they approached Round Hill, the Parliamentarians opened fire with their muskets, and the hedgerows bristled with dragoons. More than a hundred men fell from Byron's own regiment alone. At one point Byron's horsemen reached the crest of the hill, and captured a few guns, but their success was to be shortlived.

What turned the tide was, once again, the London trained bands, commanded by the ever-reliable Philip Skippon, who threw them in to reinforce the tired lines, and they pushed the exhausted Royalists back down the long slope. They had good cannon and a field of fire which let them use it. The Royalists also managed to get fire up to the Parliamentarians, but the Parliament-men stood firm, holding back waves of cavalry with their pikes and muskets. Some Royalist troops lost their nerve completely. 'They found a hillock ... that sheltered them from the enemies' cannon', lay down behind it, 'and would not be drawn a foot from thence', wrote a disgusted observer. Sir John Byron said later that 'had not our foot played the poltroons extremely that day, we in all probability could have won the war'.

They had fought for twelve hours, and something like 3500 men lay dead on the field. The Royalists, who were down to their last ten barrels of powder, had no choice but to withdraw, leaving Essex in command of the field. They had been short of powder ever since the siege of Gloucester, in late summer, and had lost more when Essex captured their magazine at Cirencester. From there, Essex's army marched cheerfully on to Reading. The trained bands went on to London, reaching it on 25 September and receiving a heroes' welcome. They deserved it, but in their absence Essex could not hold Reading, which fell again to the Royalists. It still counted as a victory.

In John Gwynne's account, the Battle of Newbury looked far less coherent. He remembered the preliminaries more vividly than the battle itself:

> it proved to be a most miserable, tempestuous, rainy weather, that few or none could take little or no rest on the hills where they were; and the unceasing winds next morning soon dried up our through-wet clothes we lay pickled in all night (as a convenient washing of us at our coming from the trenches) and we made such haste in pursuit of Essex's army, that there was an account given of fifteen hundred foot quite tired and spent, not possible to come up to their colours before we engaged the enemy; and a night or two before [15 September] we lost two regiments of horse (Kentish men) and new raised regiments, which were surprised and taken prisoner in their quarters.

Of the battle he recalled only fragments, incidents, and one stark image:

> [I saw] a wing of Essex's horse moving gently towards us, made leave our execution upon the enemy and retreat gently into the next field, where were several gaps to get to it but not direct in my way; yet, with the colours in my hand, I jumped over hedge and ditch, or I had died by multitude of hands. We kept this field till midnight and until some intelligence came that Essex was marching away with a great part of his army; and that he had buried a great many of his great guns by two of the clock in the afternoon. Near unto this field, upon the heath, lay a whole file of men, six deep, with their heads struck off with one cannon shot of ours.

Sergeant Henry Foster's account of the battle is perhaps the best-known. Foster was a member of that crucial fighting-force, the Red Regiment of the London trained bands, the ones who had rallied to turn back the king at Turnham Green. His account, based on his own diaries, was probably sent as a letter originally, like Nehemiah Wharton's accounts. As always, letters were a good source of news. They were not always and altogether private; people handed them around. This still took place in the Second World War, despite the advent of censorship, which did not exist for Foster. The London press was quick to exploit letters and to rush them into print, often with

changes and deletions for propaganda purposes, but also often preserving wording and personal style. In this way news could circulate in a
familiar form, but more widely. Foster's letters were printed, and probably edited by the printer into a single document, because they were
so newsworthy.

To understand Foster's battle, he thinks, we have to go back several
weeks earlier. Foster's battle has a context; it is part of a continuum of
events. For Foster, the battle had begun in glory and adulation. But
already the glory was shadowed by hunger: '1 Sept. Great shouting and
triumph as he [Essex] passed by to take a view of our Regiments . . .
It was a goodly and a glorious sight to see the whole army of horse
and foot together [estimates 15,000] my lord general and the rest of
the army were quartered about a little mile from us, at a market-town
called Aynho, we were very much scanted of victuals in that place.'

On 2 September, there was a small skirmish at Hook Norton, and
on 3 September, Foster reported that 'our Red Regiment of the Trained
Band was constrained to march half a mile further to get quarter
[food], we were now in the Van of the whole army, having not so much
as one troop of horse quartered near us, but we were no sooner in our
quarters and set down our arms, intending a little to refresh our selves,
but presently there was an alarm beat up, and we being the frontier
regiment nearest the enemy were presently all drawn up into a body,
and stood upon our guard all the night, we were in a great distraction,
having not had any horse to send out as scouts, to give away any
intelligence . . . Our regiment stood in the open field all night, having
neither bread nor water to refresh ourselves, having also marched the
day before without any sustenance, neither durst we kindle any fire
though it was a very cold night.'

As the Little Ice Age held the autumnal countryside in its iron fist,
it was Essex's men who suffered most. However, they secured food next
day by foraging, and they needed it, for soon the enemy attacked the
end of the village where they were bivouacked. Keeping their heads, as
ever, the Reds sent off a messenger to Essex at top speed, and drew
themselves into a body, marching to the top of a nearby hill at the end
of the town. The Royalist horse manoeuvred to surround them. But
'we had lined the hedges with musketeers, which they perceiving did
not move towards our body, but only stood and faced us'. The Cavaliers

came up, firing their drakes, and 'I hope', said Foster, 'the mercy of that day will not be forgotten . . . we lost but one man, who was slain by our own cannon through his own negligence, and another sore burnt and hurt by the same piece.' It was the kind of rough, sharp little skirmish of which many men's war was made.

The Red Band were still being made to suffer in God's just cause: 'We lay out in the open field upon the ploughed land, without straw, having neither bread nor water, yet God enabled our soldiers to undergo it cheerfully.' 5 September found the Red Band isolated, without its supply-wagons, for they proved unable to tackle the steep slopes of Presbury Hill, 'we having neither hedge nor tree for shelter, nor any sustenance of food or fire', and 'it being a most terrible and tempestuous night of wind and rain, as ever men lay out in'. Deprivation on this scale led to trouble on the march. 'Our soldiers in their marching this day would run half a mile or a mile before, where they heard any water was.' There wasn't much to be had, or much of anything, Foster thought. A true Londoner, he was properly scornful of the 'poor little villages' through which they marched.

By now they were encamped on a hill outside Cheltenham. 'In the midst of all the storm and rain, which together with the darkness of the night made it so much the more dreadful, which also created a great distraction among our soldiers, every one standing on his guard, and fearing his fellow-soldier to be his enemy.' One man, who had just been summoned home, was shot by accident in the deluge and the dark.

On 6 September, the Red Band tried a little foraging in a nearby village. Soaked 'to the very skin', they found too many others ahead of them, and could get little. The Royalists were in Cheltenham, and Foster resented their more comfortable circumstances. Some men began to complain that they had had nothing to eat or drink for two days. They finally found provisions at Norton, three miles from Gloucester and four from Tewkesbury.

The following day they were ordered to march back five miles, 'but it being a very dark night, and our men worn out and spent with their former marchings, they refused to go'. This illustrates the difficulty often faced by commanders; discipline in the army was poor, and even trained men like Foster's would sometimes refuse to fight if they felt like it. But it illustrates, too, that even Foster's trained men fought without the disciplines considered so crucial to a modern army; they charged into fierce encounters naked, with their everyday selves alone to buoy them up, with no carapace of army identity to support their quaking humanity. At the siege of Gloucester, 'they shot many grandoes of great weight', Foster thought, 'which when they fell in the city were red as fire, yet blessed be God, killed not one man therewith, only tore up the ground', said Foster in wonder, 'as if a bear had been rooting up the earth'.

Foster's men then embarked on more long marches; on 15 September, they were in Cirencester, where they took 225 prisoners. Tying them together with match, a long woven cord used as a fuse to fire muskets and cannon, having no other rope, having to improvise, they marched the prisoners along in twos. They also captured substantial provisions at last, though this meant they were now encumbered with many wagons, '27', said Foster exultantly. By 16 September they were in Wiltshire, where they disturbed a group of wounded Cavaliers, 'ten cart-loads', 'who when they heard we were marching to this place, they then found their legs and ran away', said Foster, amused. The next day they were in Swindon when they heard that the Cavaliers had retaken Cirencester, 'and had taken and killed many of our men, who stayed behind drinking and neglecting to march with their colours, who are not much to be pitied'. Foster's tough scepticism contrasts with the hysterical reports of Rupert's atrocities in the London press.

In the meantime, the Red Band was tired of going hungry. Plainly, its men had worked off their feelings on the usual suspects, and the result was an interesting attempt at self-sufficiency. 'This day we drove along with our army about 1000 sheep and 60 head of cattle, which were taken from malignants and papists in the country for the maintenance of our army.' The Red Band had 87 sheep. 'But we afterwards lost them all, when we came to fight, it being every man's care then to secure himself and see to the safety of the army.' They were Londoners; perhaps they didn't know much about caring for sheep. There was another long march in the rain. 'We were much distressed for want of sleep, as also all other sustenance.'

On 19 September they reached a village on the outskirts of Newbury: 'the Lord General had intent to have quartered at Newbury that night, but the King got into the town that day before, and so we were prevented. This morning a trumpeter came from the king to the Lord General, to devise that Chirugeons and doctors might have free access from them to the Marquess that we had taken.' It was like Charles to worry so conscientiously about a noble prisoner, while consigning hundreds of men to mud, rain and hunger. 'But the messenger came too late; the Marquess [de la Veel] was past their care. That night our whole army quartered in the open field; we had no provision but what little everyone had in his knapsack; we had now marched many days with little food or any sustenance and little sleep. This night the King sent a challenge to the Lord General, to give him battle the next day; which accordingly was performed; and in the night our enemies gained the hills where they intended to give us battle, they planted their ordinance, got all advantages they could desire, before our Army marched up to them. Yet now we see there is neither wisdom, nor policy, nor strength against the Lord; yea, had not the Lord himself been on our side, they had swallowed us up quite, so great was their rage and fury stirred up against us, they being confident of the victory before we came to fight.' The almost endless propaganda and morale value of the godly world-view is especially apparent here. Anything terrifying done by the enemy can be transformed into proof of the godliness of Parliament's cause.

Foster's account of the battle, blurred by smoke and by his own individual perspective, is still useful. Some of it is anecdote, stories that would be good retold later, over a pint (and this may be where Foster heard them).

> When we were come up into the field, our two regiments of the trained bands were placed in open campania upon the right wing of the whole army. The enemy had there planted 8 pieces of ordinance, and stood in a great body of Horse and Foot, we being placed right opposite against them, and for less than twice musket-shot's distance from them. They began their battery against us with their great guns, about half an hour before we could get any of our guns up to us; our gunner dealt very ill with us, delaying to come up to us; our noble Colonel Tucker fired one piece of ordinance against the enemy, and aiming to give fire a second time was shot in the head with a cannon

bullet from the enemy. The blue regiment of the trained bands stood on our right wing, and behaved themselves most gallantly. Two regiments of the king's horse, which stood upon the right flank a far off, came fiercely upon them and charged them two or three times, but were beaten back with their musketeers, who gave them a most desperate charge and made them fly. This day our whole Army wore green boughs in their hats, to distinguish us from our enemies; which they perceiving, one regiment of their horse had got green boughs, and rode up to our regiment crying, 'friends, friends', but we let fly at them, and made many of them and their horses tumble, making them fly with a vengeance.

The note of glee is unmistakable. But Foster also recalls the horror of war:

The enemy's cannon did play most against the red regiment of trained bands, they did some execution amongst us at the first, and were somewhat dreadful when men's bowels and brains flew in our faces: But blessed be God that gave us courage, so that we kept our ground, and after a while feared them not; our ordinance did very good execution upon them: for we stood at so near a distance upon a plain field, that we could not lightly miss one another. We were not much above half our regiment in this place, for we had 60 files of musketeers drawn off for the forlorn hope, who were engaged against the enemy in the field upon our left flank. Where most of the regiments of the army were in sight, they had some small shelter of the hedges and banks, yet had a very hot fight with the enemy, and did good execution, and stood to it as bravely as ever men did. When our two regiments of the trained bands had thus played against the enemy for the space of three hours or thereabouts, our red regiments joined to the blue which stood a little distance from us upon our left flank, where we gained the advantage of a little hill, which we maintained against the enemy half an hour; two regiments of the enemy's foot fought against us all this while to gain the hill, but could not. Then two regiments of the enemy's horse, which stood upon our right flank, came fiercely upon us, and so surrounded us, that we were forced to charge upon them in the front and rear, and both flanks, which

was performed by us with a great deal of courage and
undauntedness of spirit, insomuch as we made a great slaughter
among them, and forced them to retreat; but presently the two
regiments of the enemy's foot in this time gained the hill, and
came upon us before we could well recover ourselves, that we
were glad to retreat a little way into the field, till we had rallied
up our men, and put them into their former posture, and then
came on again. If I should speak any thing in the praise and
high commendations of these two regiments of the trained
bands, I should rather obscure and darken the glory of that
courage and valour God gave unto them this day; they stood
like so many stakes against the shot of the cannon, quitting
themselves like men of undaunted spirits, even our enemies
themselves being judges. It might be expected that something
should be spoken of the noble and valiant service performed by
the rest of the regiments in the army both horse and foot, but
their courage and valour itself speaks, which was performed by
them that day, our men fighting like lions in every place, the
great slaughter made among the enemies testifies. My noble and
valiant Captain George Massie, who was with the forlorn hope,
received a shot in the back from the enemy, of which wound he
is since dead.

'This 26 of September – *hinc illae lachrimae*', adds the well-grammared
Foster: 'whence those tears' – 'we lost about sixty or seventy men in
our red regiment of the trained bands, besides wounded men'. The
Red Band was suffering disproportionately, he thought: 'we having the
hottest charge from the enemy's cannon of any regiment in the army'.
Dispassionately, he noted the aftermath: 'The next day I viewed the
dead bodies: there lay about one hundred stripped naked in that field
where our two regiments stood in battalia. This night the enemy conveyed away about thirty cart-loads of maimed and dead men, as the
town-people credibly reported to us, and I think they might have
carried away twenty cart load more of their dead men the next morning;
they buried thirty in one pit.' In a newsgiving vein, he reported the
deaths of officers: 'Also that worthy gentleman Captain Hunt was slain
in the battle, whose death is much lamented.' Foster also tried to reckon
up who ended with the advantage: 'It is conjectured by most that the
enemy lost four for one. 70 chief commanders were slain on their side.'

He also reported what was said about the king, showing that for him Charles was still an object of interest: 'It is credibly informed by those that were this day in the King's army, that the King himself brought up a regiment of foot and another of horse, gave fire to two pieces of ordinance, riding up and down all that day in a soldier's grey coat.' He also commented on what a long fight it had been: 'this battle continued long, it began about six a clock in the morning and continued till past 12 a clock at night: in the night the enemy retreated to the town of Newbury and drew away all their ordinance'.

He was conscious, as ever, of the sufferings of the army: 'We were in great distress for water, or any accommodation to refresh our poor soldiers, yet the Lord himself sustained us, that we did not faint under it; we were right glad to drink in the same water where our horses did drink, wandering up and down to seek for it.' He noted, too, that they survived because 'God fed us with the bread of our enemies, which we took at Cirencester.' His account breaks into incident, scattered recollections – responses to questions, or promptings from others. He jots down a few details, noting the armies' battle cries: 'Our word [battle cry] this day was religion; theirs was Queen Mary in the field.'

After the battle, Foster noted a further incident as the armies drew away. 'September 21 further skirmish in a lane near Aldermaston . . . Some that we took prisoners our men were so enraged at them that they knocked out their brains with the butt end of their muskets; in this great distraction and rout a wagon of powder lying in the way overthrown, some spark of fire or match fell among it, which did much hurt; seven men burnt and two killed: this enemy had got two of our drakes in the rear, had not our foot played the man and recovered them again: this was about four or five a clock in the afternoon, many of our men lost horses, and other things which they threw away in haste.'

This atrocity occurred after Foster's troop had been very much frightened by a sudden Royalist attack which routed their horse, leaving them exposed to the enemy. The retreating cavalry implored the infantry to join them, crying 'Away, away, let every man shift for his life, you are all dead men', which says Foster 'caused a most strange confusion amongst us'.

'Many men were killed on both sides', says the ardently Parliamentarian newsbook account of Newbury, 'but god be praised we won the
field of them . . . The fight was long and terrible, some talke of thousands slain on the king's side; I viewed the field, and cannot guess
above 500, but this the townsmen informed us, that they carried 60
cart loads of dead and wounded men into the Town before I came to
view the place, and much crying there was for Surgeons as never was
the like heard.' As never was the like heard: the pamphlet lamely tries
to record the misery and dread.

One Kentish man remembered Newbury with horror. His name was
George Robinson, a cobbler, a heelmaker. Later, in 1651, he petitioned
for a pension because of his injuries:

> Your worships' poor petitioner going in the Parliament's service,
> under the command of Colonel Springet and in the company
> whereof Mr William Jones was captain, at the first fight at
> Newbury was shot in one of his legs by means whereof he lay
> in the hospital of Bartholomew near Smithfield in London by
> the space of half a year lame and sore diseased in his body. And
> another half year after his departure thence in a chirurgeon's
> hand before he was able to work, having had above threescore
> splinters of the bone of his leg at several times taken out, to his
> great pains, and his own and his friends' great charge, whereby
> he is not alone disabled to follow his vocation, but is almost
> continually in intolerable pain thereof, of which he cannot hope
> of remedy during his life.

George's story shows that for those who were wounded, a battle never
ended. The Battle of Newbury lived on, vivid, ever-painful, in George's
shattered leg, his broken life. More hearteningly, the story also lets us
glimpse the beginnings of something resembling a system for caring
for the wounded.

If George's story seemed endless, the civilians around Newbury
might have said the same: 'that which exceedingly afflicts us', grumbled
the man sent to find out why the area was not keeping up its military
commitments, 'is the continual clamour of the soldiers of Newbury
and country people thereabouts, the soldiers having almost starved the
people where they quarter and are half-starved themselves, and for
want of pay are become very desperate, ranging about the county and

breaking and robbing houses, and passengers and driving away sheep and other cattle before the owners faces.' For many, the Battle of Newbury was to remain a tormenting reality for years to come.

XIV

Two Capitals:
Oxford and London

For Royalists, Oxford had become the nation's capital, because the capital was where the court did its business. The arrival of court and army meant that it was transformed from a comfortable, autonomous university city with run-down medieval walls to a crowded, bustling garrison town with stout defences, at the centre of a network of other fieldworks which reached as far as Faringdon in the west, twenty miles away, and to Islip in the north. Not everyone in Oxford welcomed the incoming Royalists and hangers-on. Not all the newcomers were glad to be there.

One of the displaced persons was Ann Harrison (later Fanshawe). Ann had always had trouble doing what was expected of her. She loved 'skipping and activity' and riding, and running, and 'was that which graver people call a hoyting [hoyden] girl'. She simmered down a bit when her mother instructed her. Ann remembered that her mother was 'kind to the poor' she 'drest many wounds of miserable people'. Ann's father was a rich merchant, and they lived 'with great plenty and hospitality, but no lavishness in the least, nor prodigality'. Her father invested heavily in the royal cause. Knowing his sympathies, the king's enemies arrested him at his house in Bishopgate Street, but he managed to escape his gaolers by pretending he had to go to fetch some writings they demanded. They sequestered his estate, and plundered the house. He fled to Oxford in 1643, and after that life became very difficult for the Harrison family, as Ann recorded:

We finding ourselves like fishes out of the water and the scene so changed that we knew not at all how to act any part but obedience: for from as good houses as any gentleman of England had we came to a baker's house in an obscure street, and from roomes well furnished to lye in a very bad bed in a garret, to one dish of meat and that not the best ordered; no money, for we were as poor as Job, nor clothes more than a man or two brought in their cloakbags. We had the perpetual discourse of losing and gaining of towns and men; at the windows the sad spectacle of war, sometimes plague, sometimes sickness of other kinds, by reason of so many people being packed together, as I believe there never was before of that quality; always want, yet I must needs say that most bore it with a martyrlike cheerfulness. For my own part I begun to think we should all like Abraham live in tents all the days of our lives.

Ann's family were not the only sufferers. The whole of Oxford was similarly crowded to the walls with a court that had overburdened the ampler palaces of London. The occupying forces needed billets. They swarmed into the half-empty colleges, taking rooms vacated by students who had 'fled home to their mothers'. But the colleges soon overflowed, and citizens' houses were requisitioned for the use of the king's men. It wasn't only the army that had to be accommodated. As well as refugee families like the Harrisons, the king and the princes brought their entire households with them. Many of the king's servants could hardly afford to stay behind. In January 1644, a listing of the inhabitants of houses showed five 'strangers' in each of seventy-four houses in St Aldate's. They included the king's seamstress, Mrs Julian Elliot, her barber Thomas Davies, his German apothecary John Wolfgang Rumler; there too was William White, poulterer to the king, the king's bakers Lawrence Ball and George Wild, William Langley, maker of wax lights, and Samuel Nurse, who was the royal coal-carrier. Just names, perhaps, but they hint at stories not unlike Ann's; these servants were unpaid or only partly paid for some or most of the war.

Townspeople suffered too; though some made money from the increased population, there were other kinds of difficulties. The godly Parliamentarian Unton Croke had some of the king's troops and servants billeted upon him; conversation at the dinner-table must have been lively. He absented himself, though we don't know exactly when, and was in high favour with the Lord Protector by the 1650s. By contrast, Abel Parne was a staunch Royalist, with what by·St Aldate's standards was a large house. He was a whitebaker, a baker of bread for the rich, and his house was also his workshop. His rooms do not all sound inviting, especially the dark room and the little room over the parlour, but every one was tenanted, with boarders who ranged from Mr Andrew Morrison, a 'very wanting man' who had been unable to pay the charge levied for the city defences, and the king's bakers Lawrence Ball and George Wild; perhaps they and Abel found they had much in common. But Abel was also host to Sir Henry Wood, the treasurer of the queen's household, and to a total of eleven other men and women, including the daughter of a local gentry family who had refugeed to Oxford to be away from the fighting. Unton Croke and Abel Parne had been neighbours for years in the crowded parish, with its hugger-mugger houses. There were no class divisions in Oxford town, no troubled estates glaring at leafy suburbs; rich and poor lived next door, used the same merchants.

Another source of housing was the residences of those who had fled to the cosy embraces of godly Abingdon; their houses were soon stripped and crammed with lodgers. The city's asylum, almshouses and prisons were bursting with visitors too. In the almshouses opposite Christ Church, thirty-one men brought in wounded from Edgehill died over the following weeks. Parliamentarian prisoners-of-war, locked in Oxford's churches, took the opportunity to perform a little godly iconoclasm.

What Oxford experienced was a combination of becoming a garrison town and taking in evacuees; the results were predictable. Like all overcrowded cities, Oxford saw many quarrels break out over lodging rights. Wealthy lodgers could expect to find the best rooms, with luxuries provided by the citizens; other households had to provide bed – and board – in time of war for guests in exchange only for paper 'tickets', redeemable at some future date, which were not even accepted as part-payment for the contributions laid on the citizens for the soldiers' upkeep.

The intense population pressure put a strain on the city, too. Its narrow streets became choked with rubbish and traffic, its simple drainage exploded into overflow under the strain. The king was far from happy with all this disorder. A royal edict complained of *horror abominalis* and cited pigsties and pigs crowding the highways, and dirt blocking the Northgate. Slaying Lane, now Brewer Street, where Abel Parne had his house, remained a mess. The water protecting the ditches was fouled with excrement and runoff from the teeming town. Animal carcasses rotted in the ditches, disturbed only when brewers went down to draw water to make beer.

Above all, the king needed money. Parliament had the advantage of drawing on London's much greater resources. The king, leaning on tiny Oxford and its hinterland, was more-or-less forced to extort money at a rate that almost all the citizenry found exceedingly heavy. Essentially, the occupying soldiers had to be paid to prevent them from burning the town. The size of the forced loans demanded was crushing. In spring 1643, £2390 had to be raised to pay for the fortifications and their weaponry; a large loan of £2000 went with this demand. Food stores had to be provided for every inhabitant in case of siege. All householders except the poorest and 'mere scholars' had to pay; the college servants who were usually exempt were included. The city also had to maintain a garrison, at £450 a month, a tax that had to be enforced by the military. Arrears were common despite this effort, though they could be worked off by ditch-digging, or by raising a regiment for home defence. The city borrowed desperately using its plate as collateral. The king ordered all adult males, even academics, to work one day a week or pay a shilling. The service was unpopular, and despite the efforts at enforcement, numbers declined to a point where only a small fraction of those who were expected appeared for duty. Despite the non-appearance of more than half the workforce, the fortifications proceeded, and decayed medieval walls became modern earthworks. The line of works enclosed the city, while its wet ditches and flooded fields helped to protect the fortifications, impressively surmounted by cannon.

The citizens had been deprived of money and time, and they had also had their arms taken; now they were asked to raise more regiments, and somehow six hundred new recruits were found, forming six companies; each came from a particular neighbourhood. There was a new gibbet at Carfax, where the farmers gathered to sell their wares, for military executions.

It was worse still for prisoners in Oxford Castle. One hundred men were taken by the Royalists at Marlborough in December 1642. Dragged through mud and ice to Oxford Castle, they were confronted by its brutal commander, William Smith, already known as a monster. One of the prisoners recalled that even the officers among the men of Marlborough were stripped to the skin and forced to don filthy rags, assigned small rooms which contained forty people, who at times were ankle-deep in their own excrement. But it was still worse for the men: 'On these poor souls did the viper Smith exercise his more than savage cruelties. He allowed them but five farthings a day, so that many of them grew very sick, all very weak . . . Now there began to be a great cry among them for bread and water, but Smith and his officers denied them both, though a river ran below the castle walls.'

Relatives tried to send food to them, but it was taken and eaten by the guards. Recalcitrant prisoners might be beaten, hogtied, or burnt with lit match. Smith was hoping that this reign of terror would induce the men to enlist in the Royalist army. The men could obtain their freedom by taking the protestation and then paying. But most of the men still sought other ways of escape. A group managed to creep through a hole in the wall and then to swim the river to safety. When they reported on conditions, the king himself dismissed Smith, and had him pilloried in the streets of Oxford.

But while some struggled and suffered, others found business was booming. Beer, bread, clothing, and even luxury goods were in demand as never before. The harvests continued to be good, and when the mayor bought in a supply of wheat for the public food store, he was able to do so at a good price. Another reason prices fell was that the king broke up some local monopolies, including the brewers' monopoly, with the result that it became impossible to regulate the supply of ale.

Amidst the mud and the smells, Ann Harrison contrived a life for herself. She liked to go to Trinity College with her friend Lady Isabella Thynne, daughter of the Earl of Holland (Lucy Hay's devotee), and tease its solemn head of house. Precisely because the world outside the colleges was smelly and crowded, the court liked to make theatrical and pretty pastorals, little islands of civility and prettiness under siege in a world stirred to unquietness. 'Our grove', Aubrey remarked, 'was the Daphne for the ladies and their gallants to walk in, and many times Lady Isabella Thynne, (who lay at Balliol College), would make her entry with a Theorbo or a lute played before her. I have heard her play upon it in the grove myself, which she did rarely; for which Mr Edmund Waller hath in his poems ever made her famous.' But Ann and her friends were young, and they also took refuge in fun. 'I remember one time this Lady and fine Mrs Fanshawe (her great and intimate friend, who lay at our college) would have a frolick to make a visit to the president. The old Dr Quickly perceived that they came to abuse him; he addressed his discourse to Mrs Fanshawe, saying, madam, your husband and father I bred up here, and I knew your grandfather. I know you to be a gentlewoman. I will not say you are a whore, but get you gone for a very woman.' Ann loved to shock him; she was still the hoyden, the one who loved to tease. She and Isabella Thynne liked to scandalize the elderly dons by coming to the chapel 'half-dressed, like angels [whores]'. The stress is said to have shortened the life of Ralph Kettell, one don more comfortable with books than with ladies.

Doubtless Ann also enjoyed the recreations that the queen brought with her. There was plenty of scandalous romping:

> Toward the evening of that day, Prince Rupert accompanied with some lords and other cavaliers danced through the streets openly with music before them, to one of the colleges where, after they had stayed about half an hour, they returned back again dancing, with the same music before them, and immediately there followed them a pack of women, or courtesans it may be supposed, for they were hooded and could not be known.

But Ann's life came very quickly to centre on Richard Fanshawe, the man with whom she had fallen happily and deeply in love. When she writes of Richard, she describes him so closely that it is clear she knew every inch of his face:

> He was of the highest size of men, strong, and of the best proportion, his complexion sanguine, his skin exceeding fair, his hair dark brown and very curling, but not very long, his eyes grey, and penetrating, his nose high, his countenance gracious, and wise, his motion good, his speech clear, and distinct,

he never used exercise but walking, and that generally with some book in his hand, which oftentimes was Poetry, in which he spent his idle hours. Sometimes he would ride out to take the air, but his most delight was to go only with me in a coach some miles, and there discourse of these things which then most pleased him of what nature soever. He was very obliging to all, and forward to serve his Mr, his country and friend ... He was the tenderest father imaginable, the carefullest and most generous Master I ever knew. He loved hospitality, and would often say it was wholly necessary for the constitution of England.

Writing for her children, Ann tried to find words which would help them understand the love she had found:

Now you will expect I should say something that may remain of us jointly, which I will do, though it makes my eyes gush out with tears, and cuts me to the soul, to remember and in part express our joys. I was blessed with, in him. Glory be to God we never had but one mind through out our lives. Our souls were wrapped up in each other, our aim and designs one, our loves one, and our resentments one. We so studied each other, that we knew each other's mind by our looks, what ever was real happiness God gave it me in him.

It was as if the mother Ann had lost as a young girl was found again, for Ann felt as safe and happy with Richard as a baby in its mother's arms. But as Royalists their lives would not be easy. They were married in Wolvercote Church, two miles from Oxford, on 18 May 1644. The choice of this obscure parish may point to Richard's relatively godly religious beliefs; the university was mostly Laudian. It was a war-wedding. Ann's father was present, and gave Ann her mother's wedding ring, with which she was married, and her sister Margaret and brother and sister Butler were also there. The other guest of note was Edward Hyde, later Earl of Clarendon and supreme historian of the Royalist cause. 'We might', said Ann, optimistic as ever, 'be truly called merchant adventurers.' With the twenty pounds they had between them, they bought pen, ink and paper, so that Fanshawe could ply his trade as a government secretary. At first he had trouble, Ann said, with Charles's

Secretary of State Windebank, who 'being a papist', said Ann, tartly, saw Richard Fanshawe as a Puritan enemy.

Richard missed a job as the Prince of Wales's secretary as a result. In 1645, he left for Bristol, leaving Ann in some difficulty, to say the least. All over England, couples were parting; those who had been together a week, and those who had been together for twenty years. Their grief was given voice by Richard Lovelace, in his famous lyric that captures both human plangency and very Royalist playfulness:

> Tell me not, sweet, I am unkind,
> That from the nunnery
> Of thy chaste breast and quiet mind
> To war and arms I fly.
>
> True, a new mistress now I chase,
> The first foe in the field;
> And with a stronger faith embrace
> A sword, a horse, a shield.
>
> Yet this inconstancy is such
> As thou too shall adore;
> I could not love thee, dear, so much,
> Loved I not honour more.

Lovelace and his own Lucy Sacheverell were parted for good; Lovelace was reported dead of wounds, and Lucy married someone else as a result. His lyric captures the anguished sense that a husband is deserting a wife, however good the reason. And this was what Ann felt, as Richard rode off to Bristol. She had particular reason for feeling bereft, and one can hear a wail in her first words:

> He left me behind him, I then lying in of my first son Harrison Fanshawe . . . as for that it was the first time we had parted a day since we were married, he was extremely afflicted even to tears, though passion was against his nature. But the sense of leaving me with a dying child, which did die two days after, in a garrison town, extreme weak and very poor, were such circumstances as he could not bear with, only the argument of necessity.

As Ann explains in the family notes attached to her memoir, Harrison Fanshawe was born at Oxford in Trinity College on Sunday 23 February 1644 'at 9 a clock at Night'. He was christened the next day, by Doctor Potter (Master of the College), so his health may have been a problem from birth. He lived 'but fifteen days & lies buried in the parish church of St John's College Oxford'. It may have been partly grief that dampened Ann's spirits and impaired her health:

> And for mine own part, it cost me so dear that it was 10 weeks before I could go alone, but he by all opportunities writ to me to fortify myself and to comfort me in the company of my father and sister, who were both with me, and that so soon as the Lords of the council had their wives come to them, I should come to him, and that I should receive the first money he got and hoped it would be suddenly. By the help of God, with these cordials, I recovered my former strength by little and little. Nor did I in my distressed condition lack the conversation of many of my relatives then in Oxford and kindnesses of very many of the nobility and gentry.

Despite her optimistic tone, Ann was really desperate for money. When she finally managed to struggle out to church, in May 1645, a messenger reached her from Richard, bringing fifty gold pieces and a letter saying she could come to him the following week. He sent word that he would find two of his men and that Lady Capel and Lady Brandford would meet her on the way. 'But that gold your father sent me when I was ready to perish did not so much revive me as his summons', wrote Ann loftily. Meanwhile, gold was not lying safe in Oxford, as the town was becoming more and more difficult to manage. One citizen was confronted by a party of Royalists who under threat of blowing up the house, took away plate and rings to the value of £300. The following week, Ann Fanshawe set out for Bristol. Perhaps it would be safer, she thought. In this she was doomed to disappointment. Ann's loving description of her husband was her gift to her son; for her daughters she had another book prepared, one which contained a different kind of knowledge acquired in the Civil War. This was her household receipt book.

Every woman who could read had a book of this kind; it contained everything from alchemical remedies for the Black Death to the secret of how to make a perfect cheesecake. Through its pages, one gets a strong glimpse of the way even a 'hoyting' girl who cared more for running than for housewifery might lead a life busy among the complexities of herbs, their gathering, growth and preparation, of cooking in a kitchen with servants, but without a reliable solid-fuel range; of sickrooms, with no medicines but with many, many remedies and much nursing and care; of nurseries, without inoculation but with great love and devotion. Each receipt is an act of maternal and housewifely earnestness. Ann's include recipes for curing 'melancholy and heaviness of spirits', something she must have seen often in the war; it sounds cheeringly warming: 'For Melancholy and Heaviness of spirits: Take Siena of Alexandria 4 ounces, of Salsaparilla 3 ounces, of Raisins of the Sun the stones being taken out one pound, of epthamum, of double camomile flowers . . . ½ an ounce of liquorice, 2 ounces and 2 drams of annyseeds.'

Ann did have plenty to make her sad. Like other women caught up in other wars, the men in her life began to die. Ann's brother William died at Oxford with a bruise on his side caused by the fall of his horse, shot out from under him against a party of the Earl of Essex in 1643. 'He was a very good and gallant young man, and those are the very words the King said when told of his death', she wrote.

Some of her other remedies suggest war experience too, a drink for a bruise, a way of staunching bleeding, a wound remedy that required over twenty plants, including avens, bugle, comfrey, dandelion, agrimony, honeysuckle, mugwort, five-leaved grass, violet leaves and wood betony. And above all her plague remedy refers to her time in Oxford:

> Dr Burger his directions in time of Plague:
> Take three pints of malmsey, boil in it a handful of sage, and handful of Rue, till a pinte be wasted, then straine it and set it over the fire again, and put thereto a penny worth of long Pepper, half an ounce of Ginger, quarter of an ounce of Nutmeg, all beaten together; then let it boil a little, and take it off the fire, and put to it a pennyworth of mithridate, a pennyworth of treacle, & a quarter of a pint of the best Angelica-water. Keep this as your life above all worldly treasure. Take it always warm both morning and Evening a spoonful or two if you be infected, and sweat thereupon, but if you be not infected then

one spoonful a day is sufficient, half a spoonful in the morning
and half at night. In all your Plague time under God trust to
this. For there was never none died of the Plague that took it.
This is not only good for the common plague, But for the meals,
Small Pox, Surfeits, and divers other kinds of diseases.

Perhaps Ann felt this had kept her and her family safe during the
terrible Oxford plague that struck the city like a great wave when it
was already reeling from the war. The struggling city first had to grapple
with a deadly disease in the army camps themselves in 1643, called gaol
fever; it may have been an outbreak of typhus. From this and other
causes, the death rate in the city climbed staggeringly, until by the end
of 1643 an eighth of the city had died. A fifth of the council lay in their
graves. And then the plague broke out afresh in the summer of 1644.
The city tried all the usual, ineffective measures – killing the cats and
dogs (thus ensuring skyrocketing numbers of rats), burials at night,
closing the churchyards, opening the pesthouses. Some plague huts for
victims were hastily set up in Holywell Street, just outside the city
walls; infected people were forcibly removed to them, dying at what
their neighbours hoped was a safe distance, but of course city walls did
nothing to stop the movements of rats or fleas. The dead were buried
in the wastes surrounding the old castle. A bill of mortality for a week
in October 1644 shows nineteen deaths. Smallpox broke out, too, and
typhus continued to rage. In neighbouring Berkshire, disease including
the plague was a particular problem. In 1643 alone, two parishes in
Reading had a total of 529 deaths, compared with an average of 152.
The close proximity of the worst-affected areas to military camps
suggests that the armies brought disease with them.

Law and order began to break down under all the pressure, and
some reports sound as if there were some atrocities: 'a woman shot –
lay dead three days', 'a soldiers grave that was murdered'. And Oxford
also had to face the scourge that follows plague. On the afternoon of
Sunday 6 October 1644, a fire began somewhere beyond the Northgate;
it raged through the city to the west, destroying some two to three
hundred badly-needed houses as it went, mostly in the poor parish of
St Ebbe's, melting the roof of St Peter's church, and wrecking many of
Oxford's key food industries.

Miserable as things were, some Oxonians managed a normal life for themselves. Anthony Wood – or Anthony à Wood, as he styled himself – was an Oxford type, a kind of person still to be found in the city's narrow streets. He liked to spend his afternoons picking up old ballads, broadsides, and pamphlets; he especially loved to acquire books that were not in the Bodleian Library. After the war he worked on the Bodleian catalogue. He catalogued his own collection, too, piling up pamphlets and listing them in categories. He had, for instance, 35 items on America, 21 on Astronomy, 413 on Catholic and Anti-Catholic, 105 on Conduct, and 660 on Armies, including battles, sieges and civil war. He also collected accounts of treason trials, crimes and murders (357), marvel tales (417), works on entertainment (including fishing, drinking, smoking, cards, feasting, progresses and sideshows) (56), and works on the radical sects – among whom he included Presbyterians (179) – and on witchcraft (42) and women (139). He was especially careful about cataloguing the last group, indexing them under 'Women's advocate; women's vindications, women virtuous; women hist of; Women's rhetoric; women history; Wom Parl. Of; Women modish and vanity; women excellent'.

'Wom Parl. Of': this cryptic entry refers to Parliaments of Women. There were of course no women MPs or voters, but there was a flourishing satirical genre which depicted women sitting in Parliament. It's fascinating that Wood should give this nonexistent body its own index entry. It's true that the Civil War produced a number of spoofs reporting on women's activities in a fantasy parliament; one of them, written by the satirist Henry Neville, attacked Ann's friend Isabella Thynne, and even more so Lucy Hay, Countess of Carlisle: '[The House] ordered that an English garrison be put into Carlisle, to prevent a foreign enemy from getting into possession thereof; as is to be feared by reason of some secret intelligence had by the French Ambassador in that place.'

In these satires, the women's powers are exercised in ensuring a supply of 'French commodities' without 'excise', and in retaining fashionable obstetricians 'to help them with their most pressing affairs'. It may not have seemed especially funny to Ann, after her sufferings in labour. But Wood might have found its cruelty ribtickling. He was a grump of heroic proportions, so irritable that not even Merton College's hospitable Senior Common Room could accommodate his quarrelsome nature. Describing his erstwhile friend and collaborator, the biographer John Aubrey, as 'a shiftless person, roving and maggoty-headed, and sometimes little better than crazed' was typical. Bodley's librarian Thomas Hearne responded gallantly that Wood himself was 'always looked upon in Oxford as a most egregious, illiterate, dull blockhead, a conceited impudent coxcomb'. The atmosphere in Oxford was becoming so tense that even the university was growing irritable.

If the king and his retinue had engulfed Oxford, they had left other places forlorn. Londoners could scarcely forbear to believe in change when they glanced at Whitehall Palace: 'A palace without a presence! A White-hall clad in sable vestments! A Court without a Court! Here are miseries, and miseries, and miseries which the silken ages of this peaceful island have not been acquainted with', mourned a London pamphleteer. But the lachrymose tone belies the pamphlet's subtle criticism of the vanished courtiers:

> To begin at the entrance into the Court, where there had wont to be a continual throng, either of gallants standing to ravish themselves with the sight of Ladies handsome Legs and insteps as they took coach, or of the tribe of guarded by whom you could scarce pass without a jeer or a fancy answer to your question; now if you would ask a question there is no body to make answer . . . You may walk into the Presence Chamber with your Hat, Spurs and Sword on.

Away from all the protocol, what was a palace but echoing rooms?

London was, as ever, curious. For months Whitehall Palace, once a Forbidden City, had stood unused and silent. No guards were posted, so there was nothing to prevent all London from drifting in, to look at the pictures, to prowl the state apartments like their modern tourist successors, to try out Charles's throne for size. Grass grew between the paving-stones, men said. A ballad mourned that 'we see Whitehall, with cobwebs hanging on the wall,/ Instead of silk and silver brave, which formerly it used to have,/ With rich perfume in every room, delightful to that princely train'. But not everyone was sad. London was, as always, opportunistic; people carted away the royal coal and the royal kindling, even the royal beer, for their own use. Londoners did not do these things because they supported Parliament and not the king; but when they had done them they could not feel the same way about the king, or the court. It was no longer a sacred mystery, but a place to play, to trade, to get some free winter fuel, not a sacred space any more. The connection between Laud's concern to rail off the altar and the king's tendency to rail himself off from his subjects now became obvious.

As London lost its sense that any space was forbidden, its idea of itself expanded. Now it was becoming the New Jerusalem. And in 1643, Londoners could feel that they had crossed a Rubicon. The year had begun frowningly, with rumours that Charles was planning to use his western armies eventually to encircle London in the hope that loyal Londoners would rise up from within the city and overthrow Parliamentarian rule. But by autumn Gloucester had held out stoutly, preventing the king's onward march, and soon a powerful new ally would help still more.

And yet not all change was welcome. By now some in London had had enough. They wanted peace.

One reason might have been Parliament's new demands for money. The search for revenue led to new powers which might well have made some recall the personal rule fondly. In January, County Committees were empowered to raise money by taxes from those who had not contributed voluntarily to Parliament's cause. A Weekly Assessment was established in February 1643. In May, Parliament passed an ordinance to sanction compulsory loans; it also created new duties on a wide range of goods, duties extended even to food by January 1644. There was, too, a peace party in Parliament, and due to its activities negotiations began with Charles at Oxford in February 1643. It was all over by April, agreement being impossible, but the talks had encouraged some to long for what they had proved incapable of providing. Another factor was Parliament's noticeable reluctance to forward the cause of godly revolution with sufficient rapidity. True, the promisingly Scots-sounding and entirely Calvinist Westminster Assembly was established in June to work out a religious settlement. Its one hundred and twenty divines had been hand-picked, but convening such a body meant that splits that were beginning to emerge between Presbyterians and Independents became more visible.

The same splits were echoed in Parliament. Convinced the war was unwinnable, and eager to save their skins from traitors' deaths, the earls of Holland, Bedford and Clare decided that Oxford looked healthier than Westminster. Denzil Holles began a long campaign of miserable inactivity. Other MPs were unenthusiastic about inviting a Scottish army onto English soil. But Pym did manage to coax the Solemn League and Covenant through the House in September 1643, in part because he won over the moderates by sending firebrand Henry Marten to gaol. And the taxes that were so little loved guaranteed that Parliament's finances were sounder than the king's could ever be. If the war went on long enough, Parliament would win it.

The peace protesters, like the defecting peers, failed to see this long view of Parliament's prospects. Some of them wanted the old world back. It was all many Parliamentarians had ever wanted; the king on his throne, Parliament acting as some kind of check or balance or remedy – never mind what kind – the social order firm, the Church properly good and godly, but not overrun by fanatical lecturers croaking about the onrush of Doomsday. Negotiations between king and Parliament stumbled, largely on bricks put in their path by Pym, with his keen eye for self-preservation, and the armies stumbled too.

Perhaps most importantly, London was running out of coal. The king controlled the coalfields of Newcastle and Durham, from which the city coal came by sea. He was willing to send supplies to London, but would also have collected enough tax revenue from it to hire foreign mercenaries – papists, as likely as not. So London shivered self-sacrificingly. The acrid aroma of coal-smoke had been the subject of complaint; people felt sure it was unhealthy. But now those who had complained the most cried out for the brightness and warmth of their fires. It was hard to feel hopeful when cooking, washing, and heating were all problematic.

The peace protests accordingly began with a women's peace petition outside the House of Commons on 8 August 1643. The protesters wore white ribbons in their hats. When a committee went out to try to appease them, they beat on the door of the committee-room to force it open, and threatened to cast Pym, Strode and others into the Thames. They threw brickbats, too. 'Some say they were Irish, servants and Queens [whores]; most of them came out of Southwark Westminster and other places without the city', said a news report. Other newsbooks called them 'the civil sisterhood of Oranges and Lemons'. Others called them 'army whores', 'of the poorest sort'. These were routine insults, but the women, like those protesting in Edinburgh five years earlier, were probably city traders' wives, fed up with the war. There had been an earlier demonstration, in January 1642, which had addressed loss of trade.

MPs thought it was impossible that women could have organized all that by themselves. The Parliamentary leaders of the peace party were suspected; men like Denzil Holles. 'They are put on and backed by some men of wealth and quality', thought MP Walter Yonge. On Wednesday, things deteriorated still further, and the demonstration was more violent: 'from words they fell to blows – troopers were called in, many were injured, and a woman was killed'. Newsbooks reported that the women 'are all of the poorer sort . . . oyster wives and dirty tattered sluts'. The Commons spent some time trying to find the ringleaders, but all of those proceeded against were men.

In fact, the faltering peace negotiations collapsed because no one – not Charles, not the Commons – wanted peace enough. Everyone was still hoping to win the war. And as the year wore on, Royalist hopes began to look more and more well-founded; battlefield successes combined with those Charles saw as the source of the trouble falling like birds from the sky. On 17 June 1643, John Hampden lay dead on Chalgrove field, after a short, sharp cavalry engagement in which Prince Rupert had personally led a charge by leaping a hedge that separated him from his enemy's cavalry forces. Hampden was a grievous loss, a possible commander-in-chief. Worse still, John Pym was ailing, racked by painful stomach cancer that left him too nauseated to eat. He died on 8 December 1643. His many enemies said he was eaten alive by lice, a traditional end for a usurping tyrant; his memorial pamphlet was obliged to deny the report strenuously. 'The man', wrote an elegist, 'was public good, and still his zeal/ Observed the king, and loved the commonweal.' Ambiguous words. In his gaping absence, fiery young Arthur Haselrig stepped to the fore, leading the bereft war party. No wonder Denzil Holles was now one of those most eager for a settlement.

Charles still had a few friends in London, and in the summer of 1642, several prominent Londoners had sent help to the king. But as they saw the kingdom's divisions deepen into war, the truly loyal left to join him. At Oxford they formed a band of embittered political exiles. By 1643, the king could form a company of horse from London citizens. Later, Basing House was garrisoned in part by escaped and 'resting' actors, since the London playhouses were closed in September 1642. Also present were artists, print-sellers and other members of the capital's cultured classes. Inigo Jones was captured there when it fell to Cromwell at the end of the war.

Humphrey Mildmay nevertheless managed to live as a Royalist in London. When the war broke out, he had fifteen children and a house in Clerkenwell, from which he liked to walk out to shop at Newgate Market or to buy books in Duck Lane. He liked to eat his dinner in taverns, with friends, which involved consuming a good deal of wine. He also liked his friends to visit him at home, and he liked to send them away 'mad, merry and late also'. He loved theatres, especially the Cockpit, the Globe, and Blackfriars; but they were closed, so he and others had to make do with printed playtexts and the odd clandestine performance. He hated November: 'frost, dry and hard, with a great mist for the thieves' and he hated it mainly because it kept him at home 'in a sad day of rain all day'. At times he hardly seemed to notice that the war was going on.

But for others the war was a sterner presence. John Milton called London 'the shop of war', with citizens flocking to the Guildhall to lend their silver and gold, arms and jewellery. Anna Trapnel was among them; she gave her jewels and plate to the army. They may not have been large or valuable, but she felt the gesture united her fortunes to the army's, made them almost one. Thousands of horses – even coach-horses – were brought in for the soldiers. It may have helped that the army was commanded by the Earl of Essex, popular in the capital, and resident just outside Temple Bar. He was also a symbol of the injustice of the court; three generations of his family were seen as its successive victims.

Having conspicuously failed to conquer London, the Royalists never gave up hope of subversion. Messengers, scouts and spies, including 'certain adventurous women' concealing secret dispatches in their voluminous skirts, passed to and fro, often using High Wycombe as their base. Money was sent to the king, and messages to London, including the crucial declaration of October 1642 that royal pardon was offered to any erring subjects who would lay down their arms. Lady D'Aubigny, widow of one of the glamorous and valiant Stuart brothers, cousins of the king, who had been killed at Edgehill, was taken to London to give official backing to the activities of the chief conspirators.

So Parliament's fear that the women peace protesters were female spies was not utterly without foundation. But were the merchant-women right to say the war was crushing them economically? Certainly the war disrupted London's coal supplies. There was a switch to wood, which was scarcer and more expensive, and this disrupted trades like glassmaking that needed fuel, and also – crucially – firearm manufacture. Things improved enormously when the Scots captured Newcastle in October 1644, agreeing to release the coal. This was fortunate, because the winter of 1645–6 was savagely cold, with the Thames frozen above London Bridge. Shipbuilding was affected too, so the pace of trade in Anna Trapnel's Poplar slowed catastrophically, with a decline in the production of East Indiamen and the river full of laid-up merchant ships. Other trades were affected by the absence of men at the war; Nehemiah Wharton was not the only apprentice to join the army. Trade routes were also badly affected, especially in 1643, by Royalist control of the west and south. Those particularly handicapped included the clothing and luxury trades, which had also lost the lucrative court market. On the other hand, Parliament sitting constantly boosted local economy and housing demands. With the suspension of the Licensing Act, print and newspapers flourished. Besides, refugees from towns that had declared for Parliament and been sacked by the Royalist armies began to arrive in London once the shooting war began.

With them, more godly folk arrived. London was full of preachers who felt themselves unsafe in hostile towns and villages. The united voice of anti-popery was dividing and multiplying into what would become a fan of radical sects. Nehemiah Wallington was bewildered by the sheer number of Puritan preachers flooding into London. As he galloped from Joseph Caryl to Hugh Peter, Wallington worried that he should really be somewhere else. Religious exiles who had emigrated during the Laudian years suddenly returned. More refugees flooded in after the fall of Bristol to the Royalists in 1643. London's godly tried to follow it all; the Bohemian intellectual Jan Comenius described Londoners listening to sermons and making shorthand notes so they could think about it hard afterwards. But at the same time many excuses for not leading a truly pious life were suddenly removed, and this increased the pressure on the godly. If the person Nehemiah had heard preaching did not inspire him, he blamed himself. At a prayer vigil on an all-day fast day, he lamented that 'Mr Roborough did pray so heavenly and preach so profitably, yet my heart would not yield . . . yet did I remain dead and drowsy, the day being very irksome and duties very tedious unto me, like unto one that never knew or heard of God'. One reason for his deadness might have been exhaustion, for Nehemiah Wallington was working man. He had an entire household to support by his trade, servants and children and wife. He was exactly the sort of man who had never met Charles Stuart, and was never likely to understand or be understood by him.

Nehemiah Wallington tended to see history in grand cosmic terms, as a struggle by the righteous against the deceits and plots of sinister and violent papists. For him and for many of his fellow-citizens, papists were fearsome and secretive. He recorded carefully what was said to be the speech made by the Catholic Lord Paulet to his soldiers at Sherborne, 'give no quarter to none that wears the sword . . . Deafen your ears and harden your hearts against all cries and prayers for mercy. But if you meet with any of their clergy, reserve them for more exquisite torments . . . I intend to have them flayed alive . . . [and] when you come to the Puritan towns – Taunton, Crewkerne, Bristol, Dorchester and Exeter – then let your swords cruel it without difference of age, sex or degree.' This kind of talk inflamed Nehemiah. Having begun the war with some faith in the king, he responded to propaganda, some of which consisted of the king's own unwise statements on religion. He faithfully transcribed a letter which claimed Charles 'hates the Puritan party' and diligently noted every single reported Royalist atrocity. 'The most savage cruelties at Bradford and Leeds', he wrote indignantly. By contrast he recorded the triumphs of 'our army'.

If Nehemiah wanted to get news, he could go out into London and buy it; some of the letters he copied diligently circulated from hand to hand, but such letters were being printed before long, and by 1643 many newspapers existed which could give opinionated accounts of the conflict, as well as news of other matters. With the lifting of censorship, all kinds of things could be said which would have been forbidden before the conflict. The sudden explosion of books, like the sudden explosion of preaching, was both heady and confusing. George Thomason, who tried to collect a copy of every book printed, amassed 2134 in 1642, and in the 1640s as a whole he collected 4044 newsbooks. (Not all of them were for Parliament; Royalist newspapers such as *Mercurius Aulicus* were smuggled into the city.)

The newsbooks were as vital to Parliament as any army or weapon, because they made men like Nehemiah Wallington believe in the cause. But Londoners also built a network of siege defences that became one of the largest urban defensive enclosures in early modern Europe. Men like Wallington, who followed the news, were anxious about a Royalist siege, because of the sack of Magdeburg in 1631, the news of which was still vivid in the 1640s. Especially the citizens feared Prince Rupert, called Prince Robber, who had served in Germany. The siege and capture of Bristol did nothing to reassure them. There was also fear of a Royalist uprising to seize the city; those living within the lines were asked to take an oath not to give intelligence of the defences to the enemy or to take part in any unlawful assemblies and tumults. The Venetian ambassador said 'the shape they [the forts] take betrays that they are not only for defence against the royal armies, but also against tumults of the citizens and to ensure a prompt obedience upon all occasions'. Despite these fears, Turnham Green was the only time the Royalists came within striking distance of the capital. A captured document used by Parliament for propaganda related that the queen believed the conquest of London would end the war, while the king's own propaganda stressed his intention to capture London, blockading the Thames below the city and occupying the Essex and Kent shores. Information like this meant that Nehemiah and others felt constantly on a war footing.

So did all the drilling and levying they could see around them. On 10 August 1642 'Directions for the defence of London' were issued. They contained a provision for the construction of fortifications, and for 'a good proportion of horse about the city and 4 or 500 young men trained and exercised in the city', and for men to go from house to house in London to discover the allegiance of the occupants. About the time of Edgehill, Parliament ordered the trained bands to ready themselves, and the posting of troops to defend the approaches to

London. During the initial stages of construction, that tirelessly curious Catholic gentleman Sir Kenelm Digby was discovered in disguise observing the building of works at Mile End and was arrested. He was not the only Royalist to investigate the new defences. John Webb, the Deputy Surveyor of Works, managed to take down details of the Parliamentarian fortifications and to send them to the king.

In December 1642 John Evelyn visited London to see 'that celebrated line of communication', but he left no description of what he saw. The Venetian ambassador saw the main forts completed in May 1643, and thought them admirably well designed, while in April 1643 the Scottish traveller William Lithgow toured the defences, and described them in detail; twenty-eight works with inner and outer defences. Extraordinarily, he was allowed to publish his description, but this may have been because the man known as 'lying Lithgow' would not have been regarded as a reliable source. Regrettably, his is the only detailed description to survive.

Several writers paint a picture of the enthusiastic willingness of Londoners to take part in the work on the fortifications; the Venetian ambassador said 20,000 people were working on them daily, without pay. He commented that 'the people do not even cease to work on a Sunday, which is so strictly observed by Puritans'. *A Perfect Diurnall* reported stirringly that even the great left their homes to toil on the building work: 'a great company of the common council and diverse other chief men of the city'. The autumn of 1642 was very cold, with early frosts, and there was snow in December, while the following months were very wet, with some flooding. The Royalists tried to suggest that all this digging was funny with a song called 'Roundheaded cuckolds come dig'. Rushworth thought the diggers were animated by 'terror of the citizens'; shops were ordered to shut in London and Westminster so people could help with the digging. The works nevertheless damaged farmland, and some buildings were destroyed to make way for the fortifications.

London was a city on the defensive, even though there was no enemy army in sight. Its citizens had begun the war believing they were under attack; from the king's counsellors, from papists at court and in the Church, from the king himself as his powers expanded. As the system of forts was completed, it was understandable that their defences did not make them feel safer, but confirmed their sense that they were under siege from without and within. The divisions created by their dread would ultimately splinter their side.

XV

The Bitterness of War

At the tiny village of Barthomley in Cheshire, at Christmastide in 1643, there was a massacre so notorious that it was used as part of Charles's eventual indictment for treason. Yet to this day no one is quite sure what happened or why. A bald newsbook account gives one version:

> The King's party coming to Barthomley Church, did set upon the same [the church]; wherein about twenty neighbours were gone for their safeguard. But Major Connaught, major to Colonel Snayde, (whom they in the Church did take for the Lord Brereton) with his forces by welcome entered the Church. The people within got up into the steeple; But the enemy burning forms, pews, rushes & the like, did smother them in the Steeple, that they were enforced to call for quarter, and yield themselves; which was granted them by the said Connaught, But when he had them in his power, he caused them all to be stripped stark naked; and most barbarously & contrary to the laws of arms, murdered, stabbed and cut the Throats of xii [12] of them, viz, Mr John Fowler (scholar), Henry Fowler, Mr Thomas Elcocke, James Boughey, Randall Hassall, Richard Steele, & Richard Steble, Willm Steele, George Burrowes, Thomas Hollins, James Butler, & Richard Cawel, & wounded all the reste, leaving many of them for dead. And on Christmas Day, and St Steven's day, they continued plundering & destroying all Barthomley, Crewe, Haslington, the places adjacent, taking all their goods, victuals, Clothes, and stripped many, both men and women, almost naked.

The fact that the people massacred were in a church, that there was no hotblooded battle, added to the horror. In other accounts, what happened at Barthomley is part of a campaign of destruction and plunder:

> The enemy, now drawing nearer to the town [Nantwich] spread themselves into Stoke, Hurleston, Brindley, Wrensbury, and all the country about, robbing and plundering everywhere, till December 22 [1643] . . . Connought cut the throat of Mr John Fowler, a hopeful [promising] young man, and a minor, and only three of them escaped miraculously the last being cruelly wounded. Christmas-day, and the day after, they plundered Barthomley, Crewe, Haslington and Sandbach, of goods and clothes, and stripped naked both men and women.

But was Barthomley really a massacre of unarmed villagers? In 1859, the local vicar recorded the memoirs of one of the village's oldest inhabitants, who remembered that his father had said that he had, in turn, heard from *his* grandfather that the massacre had a cause. 'The son of the rector fired from the steeple upon the troops marching past, and killed one of them; this so irritated the others, that they revenged themselves by butchering many within the church.' This man's great-grandfather was, he said, one of the three who escaped the slaughter.

A thrilling secret? Or a Royalist rector? For alas, the man who wrote the story down eagerly accuses the Barthomley victims of complicity and ultra-Puritanism. But the contemporary accounts are very plainly not especially godly, because they are using the old calendar, referring to Christmas and even St Stephen's Day. We may never learn what caused the atrocity, but it was not a simple matter of religion.

There is another source, too. Throughout the war, newspapers seized letters and printed them, from the letters of London wives begging their husbands to come home printed triumphantly by the Royalist *Mercurius Aulicus* to the reports of commanders. Lord John Byron's letter about the Barthomley massacre was intercepted and delivered into the hands of the Parliamentarians, where it was promptly printed in the newspaper *Mercurius Civicus*. The letter was to the Marquis of Newcastle, and in it Byron tries to justify his actions: 'the Rebels had possessed themselves of Church at Batumley, but we presently beat them forth of it. I put them all to the Sword; which I find to be the best way to proceed with these kinds of people, for mercy to them is cruelty.'

Editorial comment was militant: 'Such actions and resolutions were fitter for a Cannibal then a Christian, a Gentleman, or a Soldier, but I hope that now, when our men see what they must trust to from this new Lord, and the cost of the Popish party, they will resolve to run the greatest hazards rather than to fall into their hands.'

The deaths at Barthomley became, and remained, a recruiting poster, but that does not rob them of their tragic impact. To notice that we can never know the absolute truth of events there is to recognize that some of what we 'know' of this war is broken, fragmentary, and in some cases the result of 'spin' and propaganda. In Barthomley's case, we are lucky to know enough to be certain that we cannot be certain. How many other events, recounted with confidence, might appear just as blurry and unsatisfying if more rather than less evidence about them survived?

To understand the suffering created by the war, we have to be willing to enter the splinters of broken lives, to meet just for a few seconds people whose world was being destroyed.

Sometimes civilian suffering was so extreme that it induced madness. William Summers said that his wife 'hath been distracted' since their son died in the war and she lost all her possessions. A maid who witnessed the massacre of the garrison of Hopton Castle in Hereford-shire suffered from mental trauma all her life. Most pathetic was the case of Lady Jordan, who was caught in the siege of Cirencester in February 1643. There was a heavy bombardment with a large-calibre gun, and a terrible sack afterwards. Lady Jordan never recovered, but became childlike; she was happy only when playing with her dolls.

A sack was the most likely occasion for civilians to be terrorized. Rape was of course an obvious accompaniment. As early as the battle at Brentford in 1642 such events were reported: 'the divided pieces of a woman abused to death' were discovered, and acted as a kind of silent recruitment speech. 'Our soldiers are not so modest with ladies in their plundering, neither of the king's side nor the parliament's, when they are once at work', complained Edward Read in a letter to Sir John Coke. War 'enforceth the Mother to behold the ravishment of her own daughter', whereas peace 'shields the wife from Soldiers' force, keeps virgins undefiled', thought a pamphlet which urged the nation towards peace. Nehemiah Wallington noted that 'the virgins in Norwich, hearing of the Cavaliers' violent outrages committed upon their sex wheresoever they got the victory, are so sensible of their reputations, that they have readily contributed so much money as both raised and armed a goodly troop of horse for their defence, which is called the Maiden's Troop'. Wallington's comments may be a tribute to the effectiveness of propaganda rather than to the frequency of assault, but it does show how much rape was dreaded. It was also especially associated with Prince Rupert and his cavalry, perhaps part of a not altogether unfair sense that they were rather undisciplined.

In Bolton, for example, the wife of the captain of the garrison was allegedly raped in part because she would not reveal the location of her plate. The story appears in one of a number of pamphlets accusing Rupert's men of 'filthiness'. The title makes it clear that it is not exactly neutral in tone: *An Exact Relation of the bloody and barbarous massacre at Bolton in the Moors in Lancashire . . . by Prince Rupert.* Another news pamphlet told of how Rupert's men 'beastly assaulted many women's chastity, and impudently made their brags of it afterwards, how many they had ravished, glorying in their shame'. Assessing reports like this is impossible, because both sides tended to portray women and children as hapless victims because of their obvious propaganda value. Richard Baxter describes one particularly horrific and bizarre case, involving a miracle: 'When Prince Rupert put the inhabitants of Bolton in Lancashire to the sword (men, women and children) an infant escaped alive, and was found lying by her father and mother, who were slain in the streets: an old woman took up the child, and carried it home, and put it to her breast for warmth, (having not had a child her self for about 30 years) the child drew milk, and so much, that the woman nursed it up with her breast milk a good while.'

Most people are dimly familiar with the nineteenth-century painting of a boy being interrogated by sinister Puritans, and entitled *And when did you last see your father?* It was painted by W. F. Yeames, and is a nosegay of fresh errors, especially notable for its insistence that Royalists wore pale blue satin and lace while the Parliament-men wore dull black. Nonetheless, there may have been more than a grain of truth in the idea that children were sometimes interrogated about their families, and could certainly be victimized:

> On Monday 29 May 1643, a boy of five or six years of age attended by a youth, was coming to Oxford to his father an officer in the king's army, passing through Buckinghamshire, he fell into the hands of some troopers of Colonel Goodwin's regiment, who not only pillaged him of the clothes which he brought with him, but took his doublet off his back, and would have taken away his hat and boots . . . that night they came to the place where the child lay, and the poor soul being in bed fast asleep, his innocent rest not disturbed with the injuries of the day: they dived into his, and his attendant's pockets, robbed them of all their monies, and left them either to borrow more, or to beg for sustenance in their journey to Oxford.

This heartrending tale is told by Bruno Ryves, a man who specialized in compiling such stories and enfolding them in one gigantic anthology called *Mercurius Rusticus*, news from the country. Historians have tended to disbelieve Ryves. He was a passionate Royalist, and all the stories he recites have immense propaganda value. However, from accounts like the one above we can learn not about events, but about values. Ryves would not tell the story if the plunder of the innocent were not already what people feared. And we learn, too, that the pathetic figure of the sleeping child robbed was just as moving to the seventeenth century as it would be to the sentimentalists who gave us *And when did you last see your father?* We do learn, too, about events. The story would not be credible if it seemed impossible for a child to be journeying across England with only a servant for company.

Even if not all of Ryves's stories were true, they expressed and invoked, but also *described* the fears that people truly felt when their town was besieged and then occupied, when their family members were forced to travel the always-dangerous roads. Across England, stories of loss and death began to multiply. The idea was increasingly of the soldier as a brutal and indiscriminate eater, a waster: 'They have killed Ewes great with lamb, and one Ewe that was great with two lambs . . . whatsoever they cannot eat at any time, be their diet never so good, they throw away', mourned *A True Relation of Two Merchants of London, who were taken prisoners by the Cavaliers* in 1642. 'The soldiers having almost starved the people where they quarter and are half starved themselves, & for want of pay are become very desperate, ranging in about the county & breaking and robbing houses and passengers and driving away sheep and other cattle before the owners' faces.'

The figure of the Plundering Soldier was in any case almost all belly; woodcuts showed him with a great greedy Falstaffian girth. 'The Plunderer' fed on the entrails of the kingdom: the 'English-Irish soldier' 'had rather eat than fight', and was composed of all the goods he had plundered, a figure of someone without an identity who had deprived others of theirs in order to manufacture a specious one of his own. It was not only food that was taken or destroyed, but houses too. 'Miserable it is to see the multitude of inhabitants and their children flocking in the streets of the bordering towns and villages and have not a house to put their heads therein, whereby to exercise their calling.' After years of fighting, Joshua Sprigge described Banbury: 'scarce the one half standing gazing on the ruins of the other'. Towns were laid waste. This is Cirencester, taken by Rupert's men in 1643:

Our greater firemen, 'twere injustice to forget, for the terror and fury of the cannon much eased the victory. On one side the grenadoes were terrible, especially after they had fired one house ... the dying men in the very fight cried out, that Sir Robert Cook, Mr Stevens, Mr George, and their preachers, had undone them. Whereby you see that when God by affliction gives understanding, the justness of that cause cannot satisfy the conscience of the dying ... Some of the prisoners confessed, and others made it good, that the gentlemen and clothiers threatened them they should have no work. Others that they should be plundered. Others were violently fetched from their houses by dragooners, and made to get up behind them. Others were dragged from their ploughs, and others coming into the town about business were there detained, and threatened to be shot, if they offered to get out.

Thus spake the Royalist conquerers. But the Parliamentarian defenders told a different tale:

The enemy had fired some barns and ricks of corn and hay that lay quite beyond these hundred musketeers, so that the enemy

> being at the wall, and breaking of it down, and the fire so
> behind him, that it took away all possibility of retreating if they
> stayed any longer, and they being so few . . . our men were
> forced out of that works after two hours' valiant resistance of
> that furious charge of the enemy . . . the enemy killed without
> quarter those they met without or overtook . . . they stripped
> many of the prisoners, most of them of their utmost garments.
> They were all turned that night into the church, and though
> many of them were wounded, and weary, yet their friends were
> not suffered to bring them a cup of water into the church that
> night, but what they thrust in at the backside of the church.

One can feel the heat of indignation coming off both these newsbooks.
One other casualty of war was becoming visible: truth, and faith in
other men's tales. Ironically, just as men and women too became freer
to print their view of affairs, to discuss politics in London taverns with
less fear of repercussions, the stuff of such discussions, the news, was
corrupted.

The destruction of property, especially household property, continued to be painfully felt: 'Nay such was their barbarous carriage, that
many of the featherbeds which they could not bear away, they did cut
the ticks of them in pieces, and scattered the feathers abroad in the
fields and streets', reported *A True and Perfect Relation of the Barbarous
and Cruell Passages of the Kings Army, at Old Brainceford*. This pamphlet
also claimed that 'they left not unplundered the four alms-women in
the Spittle there, and took from them their wheel or rocks, by which
they got something towards a livelihood'.

This is a portrayal of men who have gone beyond law and order into
a realm of unmitigated violence. The siege and sack of Bolton in
Lancashire in 1643 introduced the inhabitants to such a world. It is a
recognizable world to us. It is the world of war:

> [the soldiers] spoiling all they could meet with, nothing regard-
> ing the doleful cries of women or children, but some they
> slashed as they were calling for quarter, others when they had
> given quarter, many hailed out of their houses to have their
> brains dashed out in the street, those that were not dead in the
> streets already, pistoled, slashed, brained, or trodden under their
> horses' feet, with many insolent blasphemous oaths, curses and

challenges to heaven itself (no doubt) hastening the filling up of their cup, and bringing that swift destruction upon them, which they shortly after tasted of . . . I forbear many sad things, which might be inserted, the usage of children crying for their fathers, of women crying out for their husbands, some of them brought on purpose to be slain before their wives faces, the rending, tearing and turning of people naked, the robbing and spoiling of all the people of all things that they could carry . . . the massacring, dismembering, cutting of dying or dead bodies, and boasting, with all new coined oaths, swearing how many Roundheads this sword, or they, had killed that day, some eight, some six, some more or less; arms, legs, yea, the brains themselves lying distant from their heads, bodies and other parts. Their treading under horse feet and prancing over half-dying poor Christians, who were so besmeared and tumbled in dust and blood that scarce any thing of men remained.

William Bolton was fetched out of his chamber with scorn, saying they had found a praying saint, and fetched him to kill him before his wife's face, who being great with child and ready to be delivered, fell on him to have saved him, but they pulled her off, without compassion, and had him call on his god to save him whilst they cut him in pieces . . . Elizabeth Horrocks [the wife of one of the commanders], a woman of good quality, after that they had killed her husband, took her in a rope, and dragged her up and down, after that they had robbed and spoiled her of all she had, and threatened to hang her unless she would tell them of her plate and money, who was yet wonderfully preserved, their inhumane using of her, and barbarous usages of other maids and wives of the town in private places, in fields, and in woods; the trees, the timbers, and the stones we hope will one day be a witness against them.

At their entrance, before, behind, to the right, and left, nothing heard, but kill dead, kill dead, was the word, in the town killing all before them without any respect, without the Town . . . pursuing the poor amazed people, killing, stripping and spoiling all they could meet with.

'To wreak ones fury upon a dead Carcass, is a most barbarous, cowardly, and impious thing', said Edward Symmonds sternly to the army of

Prince Rupert, in *A military Sermon*. Apparently he thought this needed saying. For its part, in 1644 Parliament passed a law prohibiting quarter for Irish soldiers and allowed their killing after capture: the Irish were outsiders, barbarians and Catholics. This could hardly help but encourage soldiers not to show mercy.

Atrocities did not only occur in sacks; because there was no 'front', soldiers could be encountered anywhere. It had always been dangerous to wander the roads alone; there were thieves, footpads, highwaymen. But now there were also the soldiers, some of whom might act in an unruly manner. So Richard Atkyns's wife discovered, to her cost:

> She adventur'd without a pass, which proved very unhappy, for at Nettlebed, a party of Sir Jacob Astley's Soldiers . . . took her prisoner, and carried her on to Reading, where the waters [of the Thames] being then overhigh, she took a great fright . . . When she came to London, she found her house full of soldiers, and could not be admitted there, but [found other lodging with a tenant next door]. Where seeing her goods carried away before her face . . . she fell ill and miscarried (as I understood) of three children, and was very near her death.

Nor were the outrages confined to the south-east. The north, too, was suffering. The war had been grim in Yorkshire, if not quite as deadly as in the south and west. In west Yorkshire, the woollen towns were for Parliament, but the whole area was dominated by Newcastle's huge Royalist army, and it was only when he left to escort the queen south in March 1643 that the Parliamentarians, led by a talented and dynamic father and son duo by the name of Fairfax, were able to retake a few strongholds, efforts that ended abruptly in the return of Newcastle and the crushing Royalist victory at Adwalton Moor on 30 June 1643. In north Yorkshire, York itself was a major Royalist stronghold, a kind of unofficial northern capital, and most of the surrounding area was also securely Royalist. Yorkshire exemplified a county where allegiance was divided by lifestyle and resulting religious conviction.

Large armies billeted in an area made for loss of law and order. Sometimes the gap between soldiers and highwaymen was very narrow. Soldiers and ex-soldiers ambushed trains of merchants and their pack animals, and were richly rewarded by the wealth from Yorkshire's

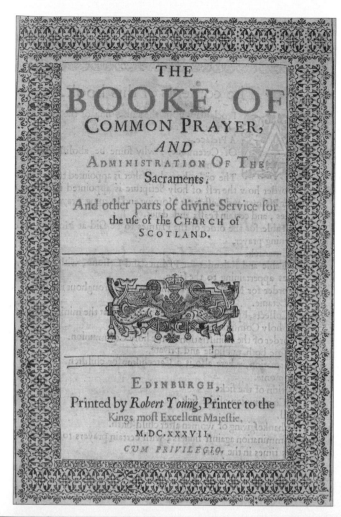

THE
BOOKE OF
COMMON PRAYER,
AND
ADMINISTRATION OF THE
Sacraments.

And other parts of divine Service for
the use of the CHURCH of
SCOTLAND.

EDINBURGH,
Printed by *Robert Young*, Printer to the
Kings most Excellent Majestie.
M.DC.XXXVII.
CUM PRIVILEGIO.

LEFT The title page of
the Scottish Prayer
Book of 1637, which
began the wars.
The book came to
symbolise the menace
of Popery and English
rule in Scotland.

BELOW Seventeenth-
century London,
showing one of the
city's landmarks,
London Bridge. Fifty
men a year died
trying to shoot the
bridge at ebb tide.

RIGHT Charles in 1605.
The long skirt was usual
for young boys, but may
also have helped hide
his disability.

BELOW William Laud in
a piece of propaganda
against the archbishop,
depicting atrocities and
immoral acts, and titled
'Laud's Dream'.

ABOVE Oliver Cromwell, aged two.

RIGHT John Hampden, tried for his refusal to pay Ship Money.

ABOVE Anna Trapnel, one of the many nobodies briefly given a voice by the war. This image is from a 1660 engraving designed to show her as a witch.

RIGHT The influential Lucy Percy Hay, in a portrait by court painter Anthony van Dyck. Lucy traded this portrait with that of her ally and admirer, Thomas Wentworth.

ABOVE Inigo Jones' sketch for the Queen's costume, designed for Henrietta Maria's lavish masque of *Chloridia*.

LEFT Henrietta Maria and her dwarf Jeffrey Hudson, one of the many 'exotics' the Queen used to keep up the patina of pre-war life.

The Short Parliament assembled at last, on 13 April 1640. After only a few
days it was evident to most that there was little hope of compromise.

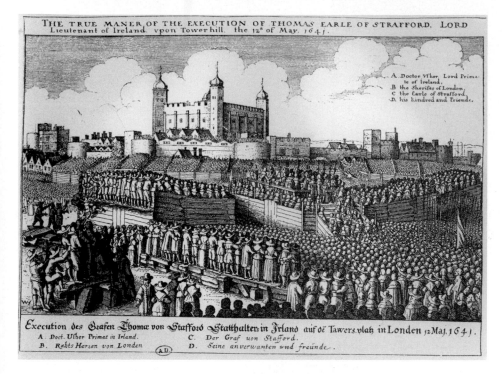

THE TRUE MANER OF THE EXECUTION OF THOMAS EARLE OF STRAFFORD. LORD Lieutenant of Ireland. vpon Towerhill. the 12ᵗʰ of May. 1641.

A. Doctor Vſher. Lord Prima-te of Ireland.
B. the Sheriſes of London,
C. the Earle of Strafford
D. his kindred and friende.

Execution des Grafen Thomæ von Stafford Statthalters in Jrland auf dē Tawers.platz in Londen 12 Maj. 1641.
A. Doct. Uſher Primet in Irland.   C. Der Graf uon Stafford.
B. Rahts Herzen von Londen   D. Seine anverwanten und freunde.

The execution of Thomas Wentworth, Earl of Strafford.

The nightmares of the Ulster rebellion: panics about Catholicism in England were fuelled by images like these.

At one Mr: Atkins house 7 Papiſtes brake in & beate out his braines, then riped upe his wife with Childe, after they had raviſhed her, & Nero like vewed natures bed of conception then tooke they the Childe & ſacrificed it in the fire

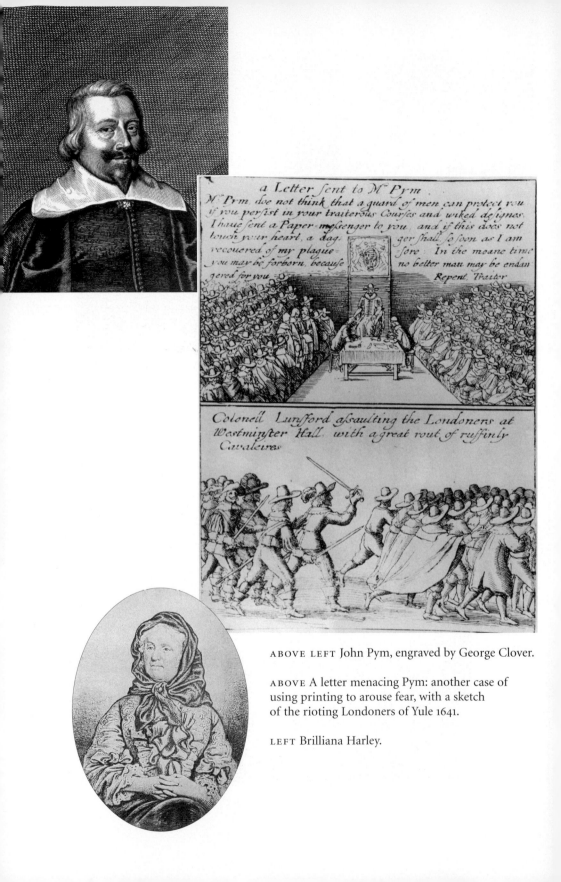

a Letter sent to Mr Pym

Mr Pym doe not think that a guard of men can protect you
if you persist in your traiterous Courses and wiked designes.
I haue sent a Paper messenger to you, and if this does not
touch your heart, a dagger shall so soon as I am
recouered of my plague sore. In the meane time
you may be forborn, because no better man may be endangered for you. Repent, Traiter

Colonell Lunsford assaulting the Londoners at
Westminster Hall with a great rout of ruffinly
Cavaleires

ABOVE LEFT John Pym, engraved by George Clover.

ABOVE A letter menacing Pym: another case of
using printing to arouse fear, with a sketch
of the rioting Londoners of Yule 1641.

LEFT Brilliana Harley.

LEFT James Graham, Marquess of Montrose.

BELOW Key figures of the Civil War depicted in a contemporary engraving. *Top row from left*: Robert, Earl of Essex; Alexander Leslie; Thomas Fairfax; Edward, Earl of Manchester. *Bottom row from left*: Philip Skippon; Oliver Cromwell; William Waller; William Brereton; Edward Massey; William Brown.

Robert Earle of Essex his Exellence etc: Generall of the Army

Alexander Lasley his Exellence Generall of the Scotch Army etc:

His Exellence S.r Thomas Fairfax Captain Generall of the Army etc.

Edward Earle of Manchester etc: Major Generall of the Asociation etc.

S.r Phlip Skipon Es.qr Major Generall of the Army etc:

Oliuer Cromwell Es.qr: Leiuten.t Generall of the Horse etc

S.r Will: Waller Ma.r Generall of Surry Sussex & Hampshire etc

S.r Will: Brereton Ma.r Generall of Chester Stafordsh. & Lancashire

Edw: Massey Es.qr: Major Generall of the Westerne Countyes

Rich. Brown Es.qr Major Generall of Oxon Berksh. & Buckingham

RIGHT Charles I in armour, after van Dyck. The armour is painted dark rather than silver, reflecting Charles's pose as intellectual and melancholic even in the midst of war.

BELOW *The Kingdom's Monster Uncloaked* a woodcut showing the many-headed beast unleashed by civil war – on the one side 'Papist Conspirators', on the other, 'malignant plotters' and in the middle, the 'bloody Irish'.

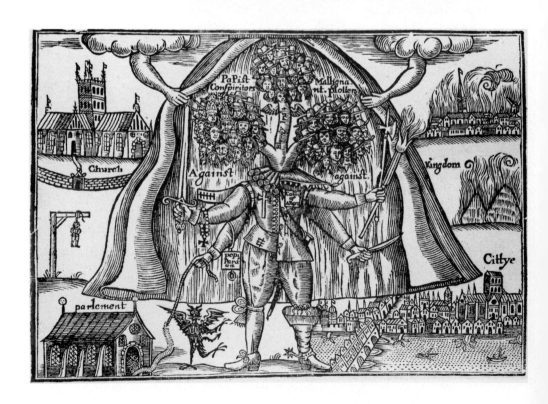

Oliver Cromwell in armour painted in 1649 after the execution
of Charles.

Civil war meant even dogs had taken sides by 1648.

Rubens' surviving *Descent from the Cross*, 1612, may give us some idea of what the Whitehall painting was like.

SIR RALPH VERNEY   C. JANSEN

ABOVE Ralph Verney, by the
sword divided from his
family.

RIGHT Ann Harrison
Fanshawe, sketched by one
of her descendents, perhaps
from an earlier painting or
engraving. She wrote of the
'perpetual discourse of losing
and gaining towns and men'.

LEFT Philip Skippon.

BELOW *Prince Rupert Hiding in a Field, July 1644*: a woodcut that clearly demonstrates that both sides used calumny.

OPPOSITE ABOVE *The Siege of Oxford*.

BELOW The battle of Naseby: a representation that illustrates military ideals rather than confused reality.

york

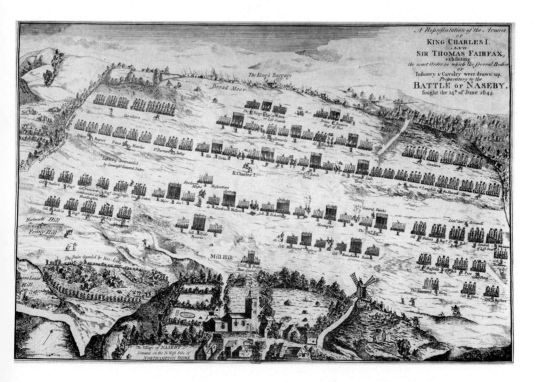

The Vindication of
CHRISTMAS,
OR,
His Twelve Yeares Observations upon the

Times, concerning the lamentable Game called Sweepstake ; acted by General *Plunder*, and Major General *Tax*;
With his Exhortation to the people ; a description of that
oppressing Ringworm called *Excize* ; and the manner how
our high and mighty Chriftmas-Ale that formerly would
knock down *Hercules*, & trip up the heels of a Giant, ftrook
into a deep Consumption with a blow from *Weftminster*.

Keep out, you come not here,

O Sir, I bring good cheere.

Old Chriftmas welcome ; Do not fear.

Imprinted at London for G. Horton, 1653.

'The Vindication of Christmas': by 1653, the years of being forced to do without the holiday
had not diminished some pamphleteers' enthusiasm for it.

LEFT John Milton as a young man. By 1639 he had published only one poem, but the experience of civil war would help make him one of the greatest poets in history

BELOW Milton's staggeringly electric pamphlet, *Areopagitica*, 'at once democratic and snobbish'.

AREOPAGITICA; 9
A
SPEECH
OF
Mr. JOHN MILTON
For the Liberty of VNLICENC'D PRINTING,
To the PARLAMENT of ENGLAND.

Τὸν δ' θεργν δ' ἐκεῖνο, εἰ τις θέλᾳ πόλᾳ
Χρηςόν τι βέλδ μ' εἰς μέσον φέρειν, ἔχᾳ.
Καὶ]αῦθ' ὁ χρήζων, λαμπρός ἐσθ', ὁ μὴ θέλων,
Σιγᾷ, τί τότων ἐςιν ἰσαίτερον πόλᾳ ;
Euripid, Hicetid.

This is true Liberty when free born men
Having to advise the public may speak free,
Which he who can, and will, deserv's high praise,
Who neither can nor will, may hold his peace;
What can be juster in a State then this ?
Euripid. Hicetid.

LONDON,
Printed in the Yeare, 1644.

Seventeenth-century cook-
books by Hannah Wolley
and Sir Kenelm Digby.

THE
CLOSET
Of the Eminently Learned
Sir *Kenelme Digbie* Kᵗ.
OPENED:
Whereby is DISCOVERED
Several ways for making of
Metheglin, Sider, Cherry-Wine, &c.
TOGETHER WITH
Excellent Directions
FOR
COOKERY:
As also for
Preserving, Conserving, Candying, &c.

Published by his Son's Consent.

London, Printed by *E. C.* for *H. Brome,* at
the Star in *Little Britain.* 1669.

A woodcut demonstrating Matthew Hopkins' skill in finding witches and the devil's emissaries. The Civil War was to bring about England's worst-ever witchcraft persecution.

THE
Declaration and Standard
Of the *Levellers* of *England*;
Delivered in a Speech to his Excellency the Lord Gen.*Fairfax*,
on *Friday* last at White-Hall, by Mr.*Everard*, a late Member of the
Army, and his Prophesie in reference thereunto; shewing what will
befall the Nobility and Gentry of this Nation, by their submitting to
community; With their invitation and promise unto the people, and
their proceedings in *Windsor* Park, *Oatlands* Park, and severall other
places; also, the Examination and confession of the said Mr.*Everard*
before his Excellency, the manner of his deportment with his Hat on,
and his severall speeches and expressions, when he was commanded
to put it off. Together with a List of the severall Regiments of Horse
and Foot that have cast Lots to go for *Ireland*.

Imprinted at *London*, for *G. Laurenson*, *Aprill* 23. 1649.

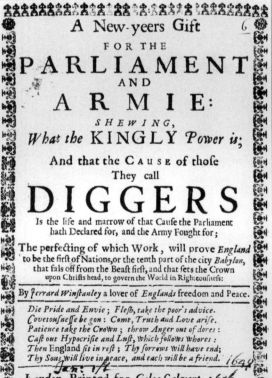

A New-yeers Gift   6
FOR THE
PARLIAMENT
AND
ARMIE:
SHEWING,
What the KINGLY *Power is;*
And that the CAUSE of those
They call
DIGGERS
Is the life and marrow of that Cause the Parliament
hath Declared for, and the Army Fought for;

The perfecting of which Work, will prove *England*
to be the first of Nations, or the tenth part of the city *Babylon*,
that fals off from the Beast first, and that sets the Crown
upon Chrifts head, to govern the World in Righteousness:

By *Jerrard Winstanley* a lover of *Englands* freedom and Peace.

Die Pride and Envie; Flesh, take the poor's advice.
Covetousnesse be gon: Come, Truth and Love arise.
Patience take the Crown; throw Anger out of dores:
Cast out Hypocrisie and Lust, which follows Whores:
Then England sit in rest; Thy sorrows will have end;
Thy Sons will live in peace, and each will be a friend. 1649
Jan: 1st
London, Printed for *Giles Calvert*, 1656.

The radical groups depended on the
press to spread their messages.
ABOVE Leveller pamphlet.
LEFT Digger pamphlet.

THE
World turn'd upside down:
OR
A briefe description of the ridiculous Fashions
of thefe dultacted Times.

By T. J. a well-willer to King, Parliament and Kingdom.

But the press could also be used to ridicule their ideals: *The World turned upside down*.

Pri Rupert with 3000 Horse to Chester advanced.
Knaresborough by the L. Fairfax besieged.
The L. Generall toward Plymouth removed.
The Marq. of Newcastle at Hamborow arrived.

Prince   Rupert.

Mercurius Civicus.
LONDONS
INTELLIGENCER:
OR,
Truth impartially related from
thence to the whole Kingdome,
to prevent mis-information.

From *Wednesday July 17 to Thursday 25 of July.* 1644.

N my last, I told you that after the taking and demolishing of Greenland-house, Major-generall
Browne advanced with his forces towards Reading, where he yet remaines with the London
Auxiliaries, which with his other forces make
him about 4000 strong; they are now fortifying
the Towne and making foure severall Redoubts or Batteries about

Ooo   the

The world of newspapers
sprang into being in 1643,
bringing drama and entertainment as well as propaganda to
people.
ABOVE: *Mercurius Civicus* from
1644.
RIGHT: *Mercurius Politicus*
from 1650.

Mercurius Politicus.

Comprising the Summe of all Intelligence, with the Affairs, and Designs
now on foot, in the three Nations
of *England*, *Ireland*, and *Scotland*.

In defence of the Common-wealth, and
for Information of the People.

——— *Ità vertere Seria Ludo.* {Hor. de
{Ar.Poet.

From *Thursday*,Septemb.5.to *Thursday*,Septemb.12.1650.

L A S, poore Tarquin, *whither wilt thou go!*
you know, in *Numb.* 5. I told you, all
my Feare was, that He and His *Jockies*
would never stand to it, and that one
Rout or *Retreat* would make Them not
worth a *Pamphlet*; and then I and my
man *Mercury* should be out of employ-
ment. I told you likewise, that the late rumor of a *Rout*
which came by the way of *Carlisle*, was as it were *the forestal-
ling of a Victory*, and that it would prove *a Propheticke piece of
Intelligence*; which being now fulfilled to the purpose, wee
must convert our *Satyrs* into *Praises*, our *Boastings* into *Humility*, our *wits* into *Admiration*, and imploy all our Facul-
ties to magnifie the good hand of God toward us; for *This
is his doing, and it is marvellous in our eyes*, and in the eyes of
our *Enemies*, Themselves being Judges.
E e   And

Carolus Magnæ Britanniæ Princeps, Caroli
Regis Duc, Cornubiæ et Rothsalæ &.
Natus anno Christi MDCXXXI.
P. de Iode excud.

ABOVE Prince Charles as a boy.
He fled to France in 1646, aged
fifteen.

LEFT Prince James in 1640, aged
just seven. Confined in London for
two years of the war, he escaped
England in disguise in 1648.

BELOW Two daughters of the King,
painted by van Dyck: Princess
Elizabeth cradles Princess Anne,
who was to die aged three in 1640.

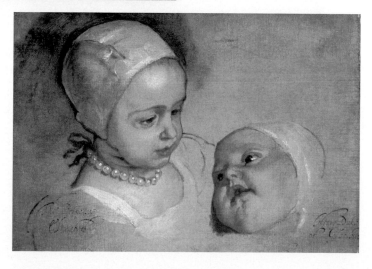

ABOVE LEFT John Bradshaw.

ABOVE A hat said to be Bradshaw's survives in the Ashmolean Museum in Oxford.

LEFT Like a lamb to the scaffold led: the execution of Charles I, reported in a contemporary broadsheet.

thriving wool trade. Bands of such soldier-highwaymen ranged over the countryside in the 1640s and 1650s, and ex-soldiers were also horse-stealers. In some cases this began as requisitioning, but it did not stop at it, and deserters were especially inclined to it, or those recently disbanded. Some soldiers also stole horses to get revenge; one man explained that he had taken his neighbour's horse because the latter had caused him to be put forward as a soldier. What this often meant was Royalist deserters and even army officers preying on those with Parliamentarian sympathies, exacerbating divisions. Henry Morton, a member of the Royalist garrison at Pontefract, became a well-known leader of a gang of highwaymen in south Yorkshire; he was caught in 1650 and hanged. His fellow-soldier at Pontefract, Captain Edward Holt, also turned highwayman; he was captured and hanged in 1648, having preyed on travellers between Lancashire and the West Riding.

The Yorkshire records for the war years show how the soldiers were beginning to be resented. At Holmefirth in an alehouse in 1648, John Oldfield extended a sarcastic greeting to a trooper: 'we must help winter you ... You are always oppressing us.' The trooper did not take it kindly, and Oldfield paid with his life. At Owram a pair of soldiers gatecrashed a wedding and helped themselves to drink, then killed the groom's father. One jealous husband was moved to kill his wife after 'she had drunk with a soldier all the day until the night', accompanied the soldier to a deserted house, and then returned home, drunk. A quarrel followed, and the man beat his wife to death. Soldiers often attacked villagers who tried to get their property back, and after one robbery the soldiers firmly told their pursuers that 'they would let their guts around their heels' rather than yield.

Ill-disciplined armies could turn the anger and aggression generated by battle onto the helpless: civilians, and also prisoners. An early pamphlet told Parliamentarians what to expect. Two London merchants were taken by the Cavaliers in 1642 in Thistlesworth, after getting lost in a sudden mist: 'It was a lamentable condition that these two gentle-men were in: they were not well acquainted with the way, the smoke had almost blinded their eyes, the night was as dark as cold, which were both then in extremes, they saw their lives at the mercy of the merciless men and to make their condition yet worse, there did arise a thick and swollen mist, which took from them the little knowledge of the way they had before.'

Asked about their allegiance, one of them tried the diplomatic answer 'the king and parliament', but the soldiers cut off their ears, repeating what had been done by the state to Prynne. The English countryside became a kind of underworld of black unfamiliarity and cruel torture to the poor lost Londoners; it was an experience which was repeated many times during the war. In Cirencester, 'they stripped many of the prisoners, most of them of their utmost garments. They were all turned that night into the church.' Similarly, after Hopton House in Hereford-shire surrendered to the Royalist troops of Sir Michael Woodhouse, an official order handed the naked, wounded prisoners over to the common soldiers, who attacked them savagely, driving them into a cellar full of water where they were massacred.

But of course most of those slain were killed in battle. The battlefields were unforgettable. Some employed apocalyptic language to describe what they saw:

> On both sides men were slain, whose carcasses bestrewed their mother's bosom, the earth wept in blood to see her native children foster cruelty, each trod the wine-press of rebellious wrath, Death triumphed in his colours, this bloody conflict made the earth appear a Marian Golgotha, the earth had changed its verdant livery, and put on scarlet, it was robed in blood, the sun did hide its glorious rays, the heavens were mantled in a dusky cloud mixed with some streaks of red, which seemed to express the blushing of the sky, to see men use such inhumanity. Death and destruction revelled in the fight, for each man there did strive, who first should die, thinking it base to live subject to fortune's scorn.

But the simplest words were often better at conveying the horror than flowery rhetoric. Henry Foster, who gave the account of the Battle of Newbury, described seeing his first corpse, a French mercenary who fought for the king called the Marquis de la Veil: 'I viewed his wounds, he received three shot in the body from us, one in the right pap, another in the face', he noted, struggling for a kind of clinical objectivity. 'The sight of so many, brought to Oxford, some dead, some wounded, since the battle [Newbury], would make any true English heart bleed.'

'That night we kept the field, where the bodies of the dead were stripped. In the morning these were a mortifying object to behold, when the naked bodies of thousands lay upon the ground and not altogether dead', wrote Simeon Ash, Parliamentarian chaplain, in horror. War itself was the worst atrocity.

XVI

Two Marriages

While the people of the three kingdoms fought, the world was changing. On the other side of the world, a Dutchman named Abel Tasman was exploring the northern coasts of what would turn out to be Australia. The Manchus invaded China and removed the Ming dynasty from power. And in Paris, René Descartes published his *Philosophical Principles*, written in Latin. From Virginia came news that the planters had fallen out among themselves, some supporting the king and others Parliament. They even began arming, but 'the Indians, perceiving this, took advantage of so fit an opportunity, and came suddenly upon them, and cruelly massacred about fifteen hundred'.

1644 was a year when England would be invaded, successfully, from the north, by a Scottish army. It was a year when an army of Englishmen would be destroyed in the West Country. It would see the rise of Montrose and the fall of Essex. And there were great set-piece battles, at Marston Moor and Lostwithiel and Second Newbury. John Milton would defend the free press with words sinewy and powerful enough to be still audible to the Founding Fathers. And it was a year when John Bunyan marched to war with his local militia, thus gaining the practical experience as a soldier that would help him to inspire those mired in the trenches of the First World War with his *Pilgrim's Progress*.

It was a year when the sound of organs vanished from churches when Parliament ordered them all destroyed, and the Globe theatre, once the home of Shakespeare's plays, was finally demolished on

15 April 1644, and much-needed houses were built on the site. William Lilly published his almanac, too. It stunned the nation with its brilliant predictions: Lilly saw a 'troubled and divided court' and 'an afflicted kingdom'.

It was the year when the Strand Maypole, the only place in London from which you could hail a cab, was pulled down as a pagan survival. Perhaps it was typical of London cabbies to adopt a pagan fertility symbol as their meeting-point. It was not only the old cabbies' mark that came down that year. At Canterbury the rich gold and silver embroidered cloth called the glory-cloth, recently made for the high altar, 'to usher in the breaden god of Rome, and idolatry', was burnt. Robert Harley's committee took evidence from the embroiderer, John Rowell. His life's work was gone.

It was a year in which many families suffered and some broke under the strain. The sound of the fabric of family life tearing was not necessarily audible in the House of Commons or at the court in Oxford, but after the war some people said that all the discontent had been caused by wives disobeying husbands or daughters defying fathers, that the fabric of society itself had unravelled. The story of Susan Denton's controversial marriage shows how the war could create opportunities for defiance and power that had not existed before its onset.

The Denton family was one of those torn by the war. John Denton was a colonel who served the king until he was killed, and William Denton was a court physician, and a keen Royalist, as was his sister, Elizabeth Isham. But their cousin John Hampden was one of the Five Members, and he was also a cousin of Mary Verney, Parliamentarian Ralph Verney's wife. So it was typical of the Dentons that one daughter should fall in love with her family's stoutest defender, and another with the man who had tried to destroy their home. The Dentons were about to experience war as the rupturing of their family solidarity and sense of identity.

Elizabeth Isham's ardent Royalism didn't make her enthusiastic about having soldiers quartered in her medieval manor, Hillesden House in Buckinghamshire. Strictly speaking, Hillesden was not her house. But with her husband imprisoned she had no other home, and her family took her in; all over the kingdoms, families were quietly bailing out homeless or helpless relatives in this way. Having been dispossessed already by the war, Elizabeth felt passionately possessive about Hillesden. The first soldiers to visit were Parliament-men. 'There is one hundred men', she wrote, desperately, 'in our one house, which me thinks is very hard to be put in one house, and we being almost 50 in the family.' The reason Elizabeth saw so many soldiers was that her home lay between the Royalist capital at Oxford, and Newport Pagnell, held by Parliament. In February 1644 Colonel Smith took command of it for the Royalists, and turned it into a makeshift fort, with barns for cavalry and a defensive trench. Smith's soldiers plundered the nearby countryside, and one day brought in cattle and horses which led to a violent quarrel and then a mutiny among the troops; one officer, Major Amnion, claimed all of the horses for himself. The owner of the cattle, a tenant of John Hampden, demanded payment; instead, he was himself made to pay for the return of his animals. This angry man went to the Parliamentary Committee in Aylesbury. Thus the Parliamentarians came to know that Royalist forces were gathering at Hillesden.

At first Sir Samuel Luke, in command at Newport Pagnell, tried a quick surprise assault on the house, and then prepared for a real attack. They amassed 2000 men under their tough, unsparing leader, Colonel Oliver Cromwell, a force which marched out on 4 March 1644. The Royalists at Hillesden dug in. They made a cannon, fetched some ordnance from Oxford. They also used labourers to dig the defensive ditch deeper. But before they could make much progress, the Parliamentarians under Cromwell were upon them. The ditches were only knee deep in most places, useless as protection against musket fire, let alone cannon, and the attackers pushed the defenders back to the church. The Royalist commander Smith surrendered, on promise of quarter. All the prisoners were marched off to Padbury, where they passed the night in some discomfort. Later reports, of questionable reliability, said they had been brutally used, some killed.

Then the victorious Parliamentarian soldiers began on the house. The morning after the surrender, a trooper struck the butt of his musket against the wainscot, and gold coins poured out. More treasure was found hidden under the roof. Later, though, the search was interrupted by news that more Royalist troops were coming, and with that Luke and his men set fire to the house. The town too was burned. 'We were not shamefully used by the soldiers,' Pen Verney wrote, 'but they took everything and I was not left scarce the clothes on my back.' Elizabeth said that everyone was talking about how 'Hillesden Park pales be every one up and burned or else carried away, and the Denton children like to beg'.

Susan Denton was no longer young, and a spinster, but something about her caught the eye and heart of one of the besiegers of Hillesden, a man called Jeremiah Abercrombie, a Covenanter, a foreigner, and a foe, and a captain in the army engaged in destroying what had been Susan's home. It was more *Persuasion* than *Pride and Prejudice* – two older, steadier people nonetheless carried away by passion. The courtship, the falling in love, can only have happened in the few hours in which the women of Hillesden walked across the sodden fields, crying as they went, to the refuge of Claydon. Only two days later, on 6 March 1644, John Denton, younger brother of Alexander the master, wrote, 'My sister Susan, her new husband [meaning fiancé] Capt. Abercrombie is quartered at Addington, and I fear to the endanger of bringing the house into the condition of Hillesdon.'

In June Jeremiah was still 'upon service', but Elizabeth could record, 'My sister Susan's marriage is to be accomplished very suddenly if her captain be not killed, it is him as did first plunder Hillesdon.' The two clauses, jammed together, show how amazed and horrified Elizabeth still was by the romance. But at least he was a good catch, Elizabeth thought. 'The captain his land is in Ireland, he is half Scots, half Irish. I think few of her friends like it, but if she hath not him she will never have any, it is gone so far.'

But their married happiness was shortlived. The following year, 1645, in a letter maddeningly devoid of specific dates, Henry Verney wrote that Jeremiah had been killed by a party from nearby Boarstall, and buried in the churchyard at Hillesden. He had by the time of his death become part of the family, church and landscape he had once tried to destroy.

Meanwhile Sir Alexander's son John was killed at Abingdon on 7 August 1645, in one of many unsuccessful attempts by the Royalists to retake the town and secure Oxford. Elizabeth described it: 'They came on so gallantly as there took the pikes out of the enemies' hands, and then a drake went off and killed him in the place, and seven bullets were found in his breast, and beside himself they was but 7 or 8 killed,

none of note but him, for they all retreated when they see him fall.' Sir
Ralph Verney tried to comfort Alexander: 'he lived and died most
gallantly, and questionless is now most happy; kings must pile up their
crowns at the gates of the grave, and lay down their sceptres at the feet
of Death, then let not us poor subjects think or desire to be exempted;
length of days doth oftener make our sins the greater than our lives
the better'.

Another romance was burgeoning in the ashes of Hillesden. Colonel
Smith, once the defender of the house, had begun to court one of the
two daughters of the house, Margaret Denton. 'One son is dead,' wrote
Elizabeth, with her usual bluntness, 'yet another son-in-law he hath
this month or five weeks, for Colonel Smith is married to his daughter
Margaret, and I think will be a happy match if these ill times do not
hinder it, but he is still a Prisoner. So you may think it a bold venture,
but if these times hold, I think they will be no men left for women.'
Later still, the romance took a new turn. Elizabeth, with the help of
Susan Verney, who was naturally sympathetic to the lovers, helped
Smith to escape from prison, and they found themselves imprisoned
on a charge of aiding and abetting him. Elizabeth hated prison. 'They
would not let me have so much as a pen and ink, but all of us were
innocent prisoners, and so came out without examining, for none
could have a word against us; your sister Susan and my nice niece were
my fellow prisoners, and for our own persons no hurt, only our purses
paid the fees.' Luckily, they were helped by Thomas Verney and his
wife. Elizabeth had heard, too, that they were to be moved, but she
said that for all she knew it might be to the Summer Islands. She
commented, too, that the guards read her letters. Susan wrote, too: 'I
make no doubt but you have heard that I was taken prisoner, for Bess
tells me that she wrote you word of it. I am now released, but this day
my keeper was with me to tell me the judge advocate was angry that I
was released . . . It was thought I had a hand in helping my new cousin
out of prison, but indeed I had not – I hope that I may never undertake
to do any such thing whereby I may bring myself in trouble,' she adds,
not especially nobly.

The Denton family's story was one of loss. John was gone and
Hillesden House was destroyed. Alexander was broken, and his family
soon lost him too. He finally died in prison, on New Year's Day 1646.

He was only forty-eight years old, but one of the many fevers that ran like fire through England's crowded gaols attacked his weakened body. He was buried near his family – and near Jeremiah Abercrombie, the man who was partial author of the turmoils that killed him. Sleeping in the quiet earth, their strife was at an end.

Another marriage that cut across the divisions made by the war was brewing for John Milton. Milton was the product of his turbulent age. Preoccupied as a young man with the Gunpowder Plot, he wrote four epigrams and a long and ambitious Latin epic on the subject early in his career. He was the oracular poet of the hard-working, godly, mercantile London citizenry, who saw themselves increasingly menaced by papists at court and abroad, and for him and his family and friends, the Gunpowder Plot was both the incarnation of their worst nightmares and solid proof that they were right to be afraid. All his life Milton would be preoccupied with the menace of Rome. There were two kinds of terror that stalked his world: the terror of sin, of becoming a reprobate oneself, and the terror of being overwhelmed by ungodly powers arrayed against the godly.

Milton feared for the nation and the Church, but not for himself. This seemed like arrogance; Milton felt sure he at least was elect, though he struggled to avoid saying so for fear of seeming presumptuous. He was haunted by a different dread, one that arose just as inexorably from the crowded and narrow street, the bustling city which bred him. He feared anonymity, being unheard, disappearing into a sea of chatter and hurrying people.

There were reasons for fear of early obliteration. The young Milton grew up in a family that saw itself as fighting on the front line of a faltering spiritual crusade, wrestling not against fellow-men, but against the rulers of the darkness of this world. The Milton family were squeezed into a house in crowded and narrow Bread Street. The house, variously called The Spread Eagle and The White Bear, stood in a street of similar buildings; London surveyor John Stow says they were mainly the homes of clothiers, but things had deteriorated since his survey and the street's population had rocketed due to the scarcity of London housing. The house did not belong solely to the Milton family; Milton's father leased the lower floors to some London tradesmen, and the upper floor to other lodgers. Milton's grandmother lived with the family until Milton was three, and there were apprentices and servants, too.

His father was a notary, financial adviser, moneylender and contract lawyer, and a member of the Company of Scriveners. He had grown up in a yeoman family in the Oxfordshire village of Stanton St John, and his own father, a devout Roman Catholic, had paid recusancy fines all his life. The family story ran that John Milton Senior converted to Protestantism in secret, and was disinherited and thrown out of home when his father caught him reading the Bible in English. John Milton was himself a veteran of the war against popery, having conducted his own secret guerrilla campaign while still a child. And yet Milton Senior was also more than a scrivener and a godly member of the congregation. He was a former choirboy and composer, and in 1611 he composed an *In Nomine* for a Polish prince visiting London, for which he was rewarded with a gold medal. Perhaps to make amends, Milton's new composition was *The Teares and Lamentations of a Sorrowful Soule*, published in 1613, a setting of some versions of the psalms produced by Sir William Leighton while languishing in debtor's prison.

John Milton was born on 9 December 1608, the child of an older mother, Sara, whose father had been a merchant tailor, another sturdy tradesman. We know very little about Sara Milton; biographers mostly content themselves with remarking that she was a good mother and a fine housewife. Milton himself calls her *probatissima*, most virtuous, and says she was known for her charity to the poor. But John Aubrey says she had very bad eyesight, and 'used spectacles presently after she was thirty years old'; he plainly thinks she bequeathed this affliction to her son. He had an older sister called Anne, and a younger brother, Christopher, baptized 1615. He also had two sisters who died in infancy: Sara, named after her mother, christened on 15 July 1612, and buried on 6 August, and Tabitha, baptized on 30 January 1615, and buried on 3 August. These losses may explain Milton's preoccupation with the menace of early death, his fear of being silenced before he had a chance to make his voice heard.

Bread Street opened onto at least two other worlds. One was All Hallows Church, with its community of merchant saints. The fathers were worthy, diligent, business-like. The rector, Richard Stock, was not a well-educated man, but rough, direct, sensible. He himself said he was slow to absorb what he read. He liked diatribes against Catholics, and he too was godly, eagerly cleansing the Church of England of any remaining traces of the years of popery. In 1606, in response to the Gunpowder Plot, he translated into English William Whitaker's *Answer to the Ten Reasons of Edmund Campion the Jesuit*, and the very fact that it was considered necessary to go on refuting Campion, who had been dead for almost thirty years, shows how immediate the threat of Jesuits seemed. John had his own copy of the Bible by the age of four.

The other was St Paul's Grammar School, to which John went when about twelve years old. The school was only a few streets away from Bread Street, but it was spacious in size and ample in learning, with a vast library. The pupils sat on benches along a great hall, which could be divided into two by a velvet curtain so the younger boys were separate from the older boys. The seating arrangements were as in church, and also like the House of Commons, which of course met in what had once been a church. But here, the most privileged seat was not accorded to rank, but to merit. The boy who did best in each form had a special privilege: his own tiny desk and chair, set apart from the others. This arrangement helped form Milton's belief in an English republic governed by the best minds, a meritocracy. Incredibly, the school was free, though boys had to be able to read and write in Latin and English to be admitted. Then as now, St Paul's was a pressure-cooker for the scrambling sons of the London merchants who hoped their children would do just a little better, rise just a little higher than they had. Competition to sit at that tiny desk set apart must have been ferocious.

John could walk to school past the booksellers' stalls in Paul's Yard, which were rather like the *bouquinistes* on the *Rive Gauche* in the early years of last century. He would also pass the preachers denouncing theatre and heresy at Paul's Cross. If he took the well-established short-cut through the cathedral itself, known as Paul's Walk, he might have tripped over the sleeping forms of the aspirant writers hunkered down there when short of business or patrons. The world of writing was open, but it had its dangers.

At St Paul's Milton was taught by Alexander Gill, an intelligent scholar of Latin and Greek, but irritable and prone to administering excessive beatings. Aubrey described him as given to 'whipping fits'. But Gill also loved English poetry, especially Spenser, whom he called 'our Homer', and Wither 'our Juvenal'. Milton made friends with Gill's son, a gifted Latin poet who wrote a joyful celebration of the death of over ninety Roman Catholics when the room in which they said Mass at Blackfriars collapsed in October 1623. This event became a major feature of anti-Catholic propaganda, and even on the afternoon in question the crowd that gathered mostly consisted of those eager to hurl curses at the victims rather than those eager to rescue them.

John's closest friend was a boy called Charles Diodati, whose father was a doctor and whose uncle was a Calvinist theologian. The problem with Diodati was that he was one of those boys who are outstandingly and precociously good at everything. He was awarded his Master's degree while Milton was still working on his Bachelor's, and published a long Latin poem while Milton was still at school. Two letters of his to Milton survive, both in Greek. He was also lively, witty, and charming. He was, in other words, exactly the kind of boy to induce an inferiority complex in his fellows. Perhaps he contributed to Milton's lifelong anxiety about whether he was doing enough, moving fast enough, developing enough. It began at Paul's, and soon John's father was instructing one of the maids to sit up with John while he read, determinedly, ecstatically, desperately – until midnight or later. His head ached and his eyes burned, but he was also on fire with his sense of God's mission for him and his family, a mission that went with and required worldly success.

The portrait of the ten-year-old Milton radiates candour, however. A large-eyed, delicate-faced boy, auburn-haired, closely cropped as a godly schoolboy should be, with rosy cheeks and full lips, he gazes directly at the viewer, smileless, with a trace of appeal, of anxiety in those huge eyes, so unwaveringly fixed on a distant vision. Commissioned by Milton's father from one of the many Dutch portrait painters working in London, Cornelius Janssen, it also radiates the Miltons' social ambitions. John is dressed in a black doublet trimmed with many lines of fine gold braid; he wears an immaculate collar, the lawn almost transparent, edged by a frill of fine lace.

Milton was admitted to Christ's College, Cambridge on 12 February 1625, and once again he was middle-class, neither a poor sizar forced to wait on others to pay for tuition, nor a rich fellow-commoner, but a lesser-commoner. Milton disliked Cambridge. It may have been the first time John had left London. All his little worlds were lost to him. Christ's was crowded, like Bread Street; most boys shared rooms and some even shared beds. The town was tiny, but it had churches and booksellers. The day was even more demanding than at Paul's: it began at five, with chapel, then work took up the morning, while after lunch there was recreation, and then vespers and supper. The Elizabethan curriculum stressed rhetoric in the first year, logic in the second and third, and metaphysics in the fourth. Some maths and Greek had been added. Milton would often spend a whole afternoon, three or four hours, walking – walking, that is, in the opposite direction from the young blades called the tulips, who wore outrageously bright garments and led outrageously bright lives. They liked gambling and drinking and sexual excess, and some of them, following in the wake of Kit Marlowe, scoffed at religion and behaved badly in chapel, not an atmosphere congenial to serious John Milton.

Milton's tutor was William Chappell, an erudite and godly man. And yet somehow, something went wrong between them. We don't know exactly what. Years later, John's brother Christopher told John Aubrey that Milton had received some unkindness from Mr Chappell; Aubrey adds that Chappell whipped him. Milton was rusticated, sent home briefly in 1626. George Orwell and Guy Burgess both claimed they had acquired a hatred of tyranny by passing through Eton. Milton's tyrannophobia might have begun with resistance to the little tyrant that is an Oxbridge tutor.

He certainly reacted by borrowing the rhetoric of a Stoic philosopher exiled from the court. This was a dignified role. It let him explain himself to Charles Diodati, who had been extremely successful at Oxford. He explained over and over again how happy he was, walking in the suburbs, and reading, of course. He kept insisting that it was all for the best. But for all his stoicism there's a note of real frustration. The world may be all before John, but he had to return to Cambridge – and try again to conform to a system he disliked. His father had requested a new tutor for his return, Nathaniel Tovey, and John worked hard to make amends. And yet he spent some of his vacation in 1628 composing a long, ostentatiously erudite poem to his former private tutor Thomas Young, who had just sent him a Hebrew Bible from Hamburg.

The plague outbreak in 1625 had increased the family's sense of embattlement. When his two-year-old niece Anne Phillips died in January 1628, Milton produced his first poem in English, addressed to his unlearned sister and perhaps also to his mother. It was a complete dud, mixing pompous consolations with a stark lack of interest in the personality of the lost baby. It showed off shamelessly; the infant came garbed in the heavy, stiff robes of classical myth. And yet all this overdressing might have made the poem seem a valuable commodity to the Milton-Phillips clan; it certainly looked expensive. Wasn't that the education they had been paying for?

His fellow-students at Cambridge were less accommodating. They just wouldn't do things his way, wouldn't admire him as he deserved. He himself confessed that he had 'a certain niceness of nature, and honest haughtiness, and self-esteem either of what I was or what I might be'. And he was a pretty boy, with the luminously fair skin that often goes with auburn hair. He was called 'The Lady' at Christ's. It stung. He was a little on the short side, too, as he himself recalled:

> I admit that I am not tall, but my stature is closer to the medium than to the small. Yet what if it were small, as is the case with so many men of the highest worth in both peace and war? (although why is that stature called small which is great enough for virtue?) But neither am I especially feeble, having indeed such spirit and such strength that when my age and manner of life required it, I was not ignorant of how to handle or unsheathe a sword.

Milton begins by saying he is 'not tall', then amends this to 'medium', then adds that even if he were small (which he isn't) there's no reason to despise him, because why should anyone despise small men if they are virtuous? Defensive indeed. But at least his talents were recognized by someone; he was invited to act as Master of Ceremonies for the Vacation Exercise, an official known as 'Father', whose many 'sons' presented a licentious, uproarious impromptu entertainment. 'Father' had to begin with a Latin oration, and this may have been why John was given the part. It is interesting that he took it. He complained later that some 'crabbed and surly' fellows were against such jollities. Cambridge's looser values were beginning to seep into London's godly son, but they still ran against the grain of his nature. Milton's surviving Vacation Exercise makes miserable reading; it's like the attempt of every shy nerd to be liked by the school's fast set. He makes joke after leaden joke, he flatters desperately. And all in a doomed bid to get them to listen and to like him. And he wanted them to listen to something particular, his first real burst of divine poetry: 'Such where the deep transported mind may soar/ Above the wheeling poles, and at Heaven's door/ Look in, and see each blissful deity.' 'Even of theology', he wrote, exasperated, of his fellows, 'they are satisfied with a mere smattering, if it seems enough to help them patch together a little sermon out of other men's scraps. It is so bad there is danger of our clergy gradually lapsing into the popish ignorance of bygone days.' As he took his BA exams, which in his day were oral exams in disputation, which prized arcane inventiveness and knowledge of sophisticated rules above common sense, Charles's Parliament was breaking; by the time Milton graduated in 1629, it had gone, and the king had vowed that it would not return.

Alongside Milton at Christ's were men who would take opposite sides in the coming conflict. To take just one example, Charles Lucas would raise a regiment of horse for the king, fight at Marston Moor, and be among those hanged after the siege of Colchester in 1648. That he and Milton could amicably inhabit the same halls only fifteen years before seems remarkable. Yet Milton pressed on with his MA, and continued with his friendship with Diodati, who wrote him an account of feasting and drinking deep at Christmas. Milton's first mature poem, produced in response, magnificently reshapes Christmas as a portent of angelic armies of the apocalypse. But it's also defensive, armouring a godly, militant Christ against the crib-images of popery, and the incarnate Christ's first act is to drive away pagan gods.

Milton's politics weren't yet formed, and he was willing to do odd literary jobs for aristocratic patrons, writing *Arcades* for the Dowager Countess of Derby and an epitaph for the Marchioness of Windsor. Since this lady was a Catholic, it might seem odd that Milton chose to mourn her, but fright may have outweighed politics: she was almost exactly his age when she died. Back at Cambridge, he marked his departure with a sizzling attack on the Cambridge system. He began, not especially winningly, by explaining that jobs like this are an unbearable interruption of his work. And after a high-minded and conventional defence of learning as a path to virtue, the nub is visible: 'to be the oracle of many nations, to have one's house become a shrine, to be a man whom kings and states invite to come to them, one whom men from far and near flock to see, while some consider it a point of pride if they but set eyes on him once'. The raw ambition here is startling. Milton doesn't just want to abolish saints' shrines; he wants to replace them, personally. He graduated *cum laude* in 1632.

He couldn't go back to Bread Street. His father had retired. His brother Christopher withdrew from Cambridge for the Inner Temple. Milton moved to Hammersmith with his father, then to Horton in Buckinghamshire. His father, however, didn't really approve of poetry as a way of life. John set out to convince him in another long Latin poem. Let others gather wealth; he, John Milton, has been given far greater gifts by the Muses. Eventually, he would be among the great – and then his father, too, will be remembered for ever. It's true that all this is conventional humanist praise of a patron, but its cheek is still astonishing. More audacious still was the brilliant, beautiful masque he composed for the Egerton family in September 1634. Milton had some trouble persuading his conscience that a masque was acceptable; to buttress his belief, he plied the audience with a fragile, lyrical but highly moral sermon against the dangers of excess. He was even less cautious when he had the masque printed in 1645. In that version, 'If every just man that now pines with want/ Had but a moderate and beseeming share/ Of that which lewdly-pampered luxury/ Now heaps upon some few with vast excess,/ Nature's full blessings would be well-dispensed', says the masque's heroine, indignantly, looking very hard at James and Lucy Hay and their deliberately wasteful antefeasts, with perhaps a sidelong glance at Henrietta Maria and her four-hour-long masques succeeded by the same rituals. It is a powerful critique of the growing excesses of the rich, though the fact that William Prynne had recently lost the tips of his ears for a similar swipe at the excesses of the court may have made Milton less inclined to give voice to all his views.

Perhaps John's repudiation of court extremes was violent because he sensed a faint, unwanted echo of them in himself. He was not so very different from the Hays in some respects. Himself ambitious, an excessive and desperate consumer of books and words, he channelled his urge to excel into learning. He set out to read the whole of ecclesiastical history; fairly early on, he found it very boring, speaking of the 'innumerable and therefore unnecessary and unmerciful volumes' of Athanasius, Basil and others. He gave up on comprehensiveness, and simply browsed. What he was looking for was the moment when the early Church lapsed from the purity God intended for it into the paganism of popery. He found the answer; it was, he thought, the fault of Constantine, who had taken 'a homely and yeomanly religion' and decorated it to excess, with 'a deluge of ceremonies'. It was almost as if the Church had become corrupt as soon as it ceased to be persecuted. He could hardly help connecting this flawed ruler's corruption of the early Church with the worrying activities of Charles and Laud in his own day. He also began to read Greek history, again searching for the moment of lapse: when did they cease to be the Greeks so admired by the humanists? As he read, he deepened his conviction that he alone knew, that Cambridge was full of ignorant fools, that most 'prelates' were 'ravenous and savage wolves threatening inroads and bloody incursions upon the flock of Christ'. Milton began to feel unable to join them. Laud had administered an oath designed to keep godly people like him out. But that wasn't his only reason. He had become convinced of the power of authorship as a way of ministry. When he came to write his extraordinary, brilliant and tense elegy for Edward King, Milton couldn't help thinking that he had done relatively little; like King, he might be all promise and no fulfilment, all flower and no fruit.

And there was another reminder of mortality. On 3 April 1637, his mother Sara Milton died. John wrote no elegy for her. But in that he did write for Edward King, 'Lycidas', mothers fail repeatedly to stand between their sons and premature death. The muse, John complains, can't save King, and couldn't save her beloved son Orpheus either. Instead, Orpheus is torn apart by the wild women who cannot understand or appreciate his song, and his severed head floats down to the shore alone. Elsewhere in the same poem Milton connects the maenads' silencing of Orpheus with the Laudian clergy, preying like wolves on the sheep entrusted to their care. If being a poet looked futile, being a cleric looked fatal.

He went abroad, to think. He passed quickly through France, which held few attractions for him. He wanted to get on to Italy. But in Paris he did meet the erudite Dutch theologian Hugo Grotius, Protestant Queen Christina of Sweden's ambassador to the French court. And then he rushed on to Nice, hastened to Genoa and took a small packet-boat to Leghorn. At last, his feet touched the ground in Tuscany.

And an astounding encounter took place. We don't know if Milton had read Galileo's banned book, *Dialogo sopra i due massimi sistemi del mondo*, which asserted his brilliant theory of planetary movement which the Vatican had been on the point of accepting until Galileo tactlessly insisted on putting a papal pronouncement into the mouth of an idiot. The pope, who shared Milton's own sense of enemies around every corner, took childish umbrage and turned his back on all Copernican discovery. Galileo, who had been forced to retract his views by an Inquisitorial court, must have seemed to John Milton a living symbol of the power of popes to deny the liberty of thought. Milton was to see the coming war as a fight for the greatness of the Renaissance, for curiosity and truth themselves.

We don't know what they talked about. Milton said later that 'there I found and visited the famous Galileo, grown old, a prisoner to the Inquisition for thinking in astronomy otherwise than the Franciscan and Dominican licensers thought'. For Milton, Galileo seemed largely a symbol. And yet there was something uncanny about the meeting. It was as if in Galileo John Milton unknowingly glimpsed the self he too would become; revered, but also alone, blind, virtually imprisoned, exiled from power and influence, a victim of a war against powers too mighty for the lone intellect to withstand.

John's views hardened in the warm Italian sun. He saw Siena and Rome and Naples. And in Naples he heard, at last, the news from England: that a war was beginning, initially against the Scots, and that his friend Charles Diodati was dead. He had been about to set sail for Sicily and Greece, but now he abruptly abandoned classical learning for present politics. He set out for home. By March 1639, Milton was back in Florence, and then he visited Geneva, capital of Protestant theology, centre of godly republicanism. Here was the border between the world God had meant and the corruptions of man.

But Milton was also still preoccupied with the border between life and death. Diodati's grave awaited him in England, and he mourned. However, it's hard to read the result of his mourning without a smile. Since Milton's relationship with Diodati naturally expressed itself in Latin and Greek, it was natural for him to mourn his friend in elegant Latin. But it may have been Milton's unspoken competition with his gifted friend that fettered him to a very strict use of Greek pastoral form, using a refrain which repeats a command to the sheep to go away and let the poet mourn. The sheep have to be thus dispersed no fewer than seventeen times. The poem betrays guilt, and there is also something anxious about it: was Diodati for ever the victor now, cut off in his prime? Guilt and dread can only be staved off by grand claims that Diodati was terribly lucky to have a gifted poet as a friend, who will ensure he is remembered for ever. The claim is no less irritating for being entirely justified. Humanist learning had always claimed to be a way to get on in society, but no one ever took this more literally or seriously than Milton.

He knew what he had to do: write a British epic – on King Arthur. But somehow he couldn't get on with it. Or he might write a tragedy, on Brutus. Or what about a Biblical subject? The Flood, perhaps? Or John the Baptist? He was indecisive, but he felt sure he was called upon to do it; he found an anecdote in Bede about Caedmon, called by God and 'suddenly made a poet by divine providence'. Meanwhile, in 1640 he moved back to central London, just beyond the old crowded city, to lodgings in Aldersgate Street. It was a quiet house, by London standards, set back from the road, with a garden. His nephews came to live with him, and were instructed by him.

But the peace was soon a victim of the developing conflict between the king and Parliament. He began to write anti-episcopal tracts, five of them, beginning with *Of Reformation*, composed between April and the first half of May 1641, which argued very learnedly against bishops and prelates in general, reserving particular criticism for social climbers like Laud. 'Coming from a mean and plebeian life, on a sudden to be lords of stately palaces, rich furniture, delicious fare, and princely attendance, thought the plain and homespun fare of Christ's gospel unfit any longer to hold their Lordships' acquaintance, unless the poor threadbare matron were put into better clothes.' There was something really personal at stake here, despite the pamphlet's scholarliness; what, after all, were bishops but functionaries who interfered, intolerably, with the rights of John Milton? They were like his Cambridge tutor; they cut across his proud, passionate, desperate ambition to invent his own glory. Salvation was personal and interior, plain and blank and unvarnished; it could not be managed by authorities outside the passionate self. Sincere as all this was, it was also risky for the poet. He had found a release outside art.

Milton sometimes portrayed himself as bravely sacrificing his poetic career to the cause of God, but it must have been reasonably easy to give up poetry when he wasn't writing any in the first place. Any blocked writer knows how gladly the kettle and the garden and even housework beckon one away from that terribly blank page. And while poetry that stubbornly refuses to work undermines confidence, sapping self-belief, becoming a controversialist at least means that you are talked about. And at last he could feel that he was enlisted in the ranks of the army of the saints: 'Should the church be brought under heavy oppression, and God have given me ability the while to reason against that man should be the author of so foul a deed, or should she by blessing from above on the industry and courage of faithful men change this her distracted estate into better days without the least furtherance or contribution of those few talents which God at that present had lent me, I forsee what stories I should hear within myself all my life after, of discourage and reproach.' For Milton, too, the Church was scarily like the nation; it was actually *more* important that the Church be governed justly than that the nation be well governed: 'quit yourselves like barons', he told the corrupt clergy. He had, too, ideas to replace the dreadful festivals of the vulgar:

> Because the spirit of man cannot demean itself lively in this body without some recreating intermission of labour and serious things, it were happy for the commonwealth if our magistrates, as in those famous governments of old, would take into their care . . . the managing of our public sports and festival pastimes, that they might be . . . Such as may inure and harden our bodies by martial exercises to all warlike skill and performance, and may civilise, adorn, and make discreet our minds by the learned and affable meeting of frequent academies, and the procurement of wise and artful recitations sweetened with

eloquent and graceful enticements to the love and practice of justice, temperance, and fortitude, instructing and bettering the nation at all opportunities ... Whether this may not be, not only in pulpits, but after another persuasive method, at set and solemn panegyrics, in theatres, porches, and what other place or way may win most upon the people to receive at once both recreation and instruction, let them in authority consult.

As ever, Milton did not exactly have his finger on the pulse of popular culture – or on the pulse of godly culture either, since this earnest programme was unlike what Harley and his committees eventually invented.

But Milton's new-found confidence was to be shattered, and in a wholly unexpected way. His father had made a loan to a Mr Richard Powell, of Forest Hill, Oxfordshire, a near neighbour of the estates of Milton's recusant grandfather at Stanton St John. The interest was due on 12 June 1642, but Powell couldn't pay it. His house was mortgaged; he'd already borrowed from others. Milton heard of it, and went up to talk things over in person. And there the thirty-three-year-old poet met Richard Powell's daughter Mary, just seventeen. It was June. The courtship took a month. They were married sometime in early July; John and Mary went back to the house in Aldersgate Street, along with some of Mary's relations, who stayed for the feasting. Finally, they left, and only Milton's nephews remained with the couple.

Mary was unused to grammar-school ways, and was upset when John beat the boys for disobedience. And she was hideously homesick for Forest Hill, for the life she had known. As the clouds of civil war descended, the Powell family began to panic. The king had ordered Oxford placed in readiness to defend itself. So Mary must come home. And John let her go. Before she left, he told her how disappointing he found her. And events provided her with the perfect excuse to stay away. By late summer of 1642, two armies lay between them. Nevertheless, John Milton was eager to join battle with his in-laws for possession of his wife; he sent a messenger demanding that Mary come back to him. The messenger was sent packing. And the war *was* closing the road to London; Parliament passed an order forbidding traffic with Oxford. The Battle of Edgehill was fought while the battle over Mary grew more intense. Forced, like every English family, to interpret and then to choose a side in the conflict, the Powells (with their notably Welsh name) had sided passionately with the king. And Milton had sided with Parliament, with equal ardour. The spear of war also divided him from his brother Christopher, Royal Commissioner of Seques-trations for three counties, active until 1646 on the king's behalf. Mean-while his wife and children, and the ailing John Milton Senior, fled to London after the siege of Reading. Milton wrote ruminatively that 'it was a strange time, when man and wife were often the fiercest enemies, he at home with the children, she the mother of the family in the camp of the enemy threatening death and destruction to her husband'. He began to think that the laws on divorce were actually just as unfair as the laws of Church government had been. Why not write a pamphlet to say so?

The resulting pamphlet is quite unconscious of its own courage. It doesn't seem to realize how wildly unconventional its ideas are. Milton had never been able to give up hope of infecting the world with his own glowing ambition to be better, quicker, more learned. He argued that incompatible people should be allowed to get divorced. He didn't use the word incompatible, and by people he meant men. He was only asking for simple justice, after all, for others, as well as himself. And the conscience of the husband, he felt, would always be the best arbiter of whether the couple were mismatched; he could simply state his decision in front of his minister and a few elders.

It amazed Milton that his sober pamphlet was reviled as libertinism. But it didn't deter him. He reprinted it, with some revisions, when the first edition sold out. His thinking about marriage was coming to affect his views of government. 'He who marries intends as little to conspire his own ruin as he that swears allegiance; and as a whole people is in proportion to an ill government, so is one man to an ill marriage . . . To resist the highest magistrate, though tyrannising, God never gave us express allowance.'

When Milton writes, with a shudder, that 'instead of being one flesh, they will be rather two carcasses chained unnaturally together; or as it may happen, a living soul bound to a dead corpse', he evokes a loneli-ness that goes beyond ordinary misery. The union that was supposed to confirm who he was actually threatened him with the oblivion he dreaded. This is one of many passages whose passion betrays an autobiographical ghost, flickering lightly and distortingly over the proclamations of reason and objectivity. He wrote: 'There is a peculiar comfort in the married state besides the genial bed ... We cannot therefore always be contemplative, or pragmatical abroad, but have need of some delightful intermissions, wherein the enlarged soul may leave off a while her severe schooling; and like a glad youth in wandering vacancy, may keep her holidays to joy and harmless pastime: which as she cannot well do without company, so in no company so well as where the different sex in most resembling unlikeness, and most unlike resemblance cannot but please best and be pleased in the aptitude of that variety.' Of course, what this meant (as the feminist Mary Astell pointed out sixty years later) was that he wanted someone to soothe his pride and flatter his vanity, but hers is a brutal way of putting it.

He never thought of blaming himself. He simply lamented his misery in terms designed to bring emotion to the aid of reason. 'When the mind hangs off in an unclosing disproportion, though the body be as it ought ... there all corporal delight will soon become unsavoury and contemptible.' Sex is no fun when you feel yourself hated. The embrace of someone who doesn't love you is the loneliest place imaginable. 'And the solitariness of man, which God had namely and principally ordered to prevent by marriage, has no remedy, but lies under a worse condition than the loneliest single life; for in single life the absence and remoteness of a helper might inure him to expect his own comforts out of himself ... but here the continual sight of his deluded thoughts without cure, must needs be to him ... a daily trouble and pain of loss in some degree like that which Reprobates feel.' Being married to the wrong person is hell, and damnation too. 'The aggrieved person shall do more manly, to be extraordinary and singular in claiming the due right whereof he is frustrated, than to piece up his lost contentment by visiting the Stews.'

If there was one thing Milton longed to be, it was extraordinary and singular. His life went on, despite the war; he took in more pupils. He wrote no poetry. He wrote a treatise on how future leaders should be educated; here Milton was able to revenge himself at last on unsatisfactory Cambridge by suggesting that all universities should be abolished. Instead, there should be a single academy, at least one in every city, where shepherds and gardeners would instruct the young, alongside other professionals. It was an attractive idea, but the main goal was actually to produce disciplined army regiments: two hours a day were to be spent on drill. It was just like Milton to publish yet another ideal a month before the heavy pragmatics of the Battle of Marston Moor.

And yet ideals were also and increasingly what the war was coming to be about. John Milton had been fighting his own little war against some Parliamentarians who were eager to censure his writings on divorce. In seeking to refute them, he wrote the most glorious of all his pamphlets, a learned and eloquent defence of the principle that all men should be given 'the liberty to know, to utter and to argue freely according to conscience, above all liberties'. Milton borrowed from his beloved Greeks to find a way of talking about freedom, about its dependence on books, and in doing so gave to prose in English something it has never lost: a way of speaking about human liberty. What also shines out is Milton's passion for books: books, he writes, 'are not absolutely dead things, but do contain a potency of life in them to be as active as that soul was whose progeny they are . . . As good almost kill a man as kill a good book.' As for books' power to corrupt, Milton will have none of it: he argues that someone already steeped in evil can find evil even in a good book, so a really eager censor will have to ban the works of the Church Fathers and the Bible, too. If you suppress works of learning, Milton argues passionately, the result will be to stop people from learning about argument itself, to take from them the tools by which they can tell truth from falsehood. Even a bad book can be useful to a good and intelligent reader: 'a wise man will make better use of an idle pamphlet than a fool will do of sacred Scripture'. 'I cannot praise a fugitive and cloistered virtue,' snorted Milton, glancing over his shoulder at monks and nuns, 'unexercised and unbreathed, that never sallies out and sees her adversary, but slinks out of that race where that immortal garland is to be run for, not without dust and heat. Assuredly we bring not innocence into the world; we bring impurity much rather; that which purifies us is trial, and trial is by what is contrary.'

Milton had stopped wanting the world to reflect him and his views in an admiring mirror. Instead, with this image he brilliantly turned his own passionate difference from it into proof of his own election, his own unique individuality. Now, as always, he wanted to find his own reflection in others again, by assigning to them the same glories of rationality and learning that he claimed for himself. *Areopagitica*, its rebarbative Greek title designed to put off the ignoramuses who had bought his pamphlets on divorce, at once holds out a hand to every man in the crowded London streets and soars above them on the wings of learning; it's both astoundingly democratic and unbearably snobbish. Both attitudes can be found in the prefaratory poem, translated from Euripides's *Suppliant Women*:

> This is true liberty when freeborn men
> Having to advise the public, may speak free:
> Which he who can and will, deserves high praise;
> Who neither can nor will may hold his peace.
> What can be juster in a state than this?

It was printed on or about 23 November 1644, after the second Battle of Newbury. It was electric and staggering. And it was followed all too soon by more pamphlets on divorce.

But there were limits to Milton's searing liberalism. Later, Milton commemorated a massacre of Protestants in Piedmont, called 'slaughter'd Saints', as opposed to 'our Fathers', who 'worship't Stocks and stones'. In *Of Civil Power*, Roman Catholics are chief among those that magistrates exist to suppress, along with blasphemers and idolators. Indeed, Roman Catholics, Milton explains, cannot claim toleration on the same grounds as Protestants, since the Catholic has placed himself in 'voluntary servitude to man's law' and hence his soul 'forfeits her Christian liberty'. Moreover, Catholicism is not *really* a religion at all, but the Roman political state seeking dominion over other men, and is therefore 'justly to be suspected, not tolerated, by the magistrate of another country'.

The divisions in John Milton's marriage were for him part of larger, more important divisions. He and his wife were parted, but that was part of a national fall, which would one day be righted by the triumph of the saints.

The astounding thing is that this fiercely competitive, neurotic, insecure, emotionally constipated man whose prose writings often bore and sometimes hector did truly have the mind of a genius. Milton's heart was not even as interesting as a foul rag-and-bone shop; it was more like a draper's store circa 1950, with flannel cloth in neatly wound bolts. Yet somehow the alchemy of war wrought upon this unpromising material and transformed its baseness into an avalanche of pure gold. From the dry wastes of Milton's egotism and emotional insensitivity somehow sprang skyrockets of bright angels, cascades of light, the mountains of Eden, and the bejewelled and velvet darkness of the most seductive Satan in Western literature. Of course we can catch glimpses of the splendours to come in the fugal sonorities of *Areopagitica*, in the starry courts of *Comus*, in the delicate fragile perfection of *Lycidas*. But Milton's great epic still takes away the breath, in part because it is astounding that such grandeur came from such a difficult man, but it could only have been produced by that war acting on that man. *Paradise Lost* is arguably among the war's greatest and most enduring consequences.

XVII

The Power of Heaven:
Marston Moor and Cromwell

The year 1644 ended some stories in silence and partings. When the ever-flexible friend the Earl of Holland had reappeared at the queen's side in 1643, eager to proclaim his repentance for his support of Parliament, she found his constant visits irritating. And then autumn began, with steady rain and cold, so that everyone was confined to their miserable Oxford lodgings, with plenty of unfilled leisure to notice their poverty and crowding.

Henrietta was pregnant again, miserably pregnant as she always was, ill and aching from what may have been rheumatism brought on by the pregnancy itself. Bad news began to trickle in, too; Montrose rode out of Oxford in March to raise Scotland for the king, but the king's enemies there were already on the move. As the army of the Scots crossed the border, it became obvious to everyone that Henrietta must leave for France, even though by now she didn't really know where to go. The islands of safety were being overwhelmed one by one. So in early summer of 1644, she began a journey into despair. Travelling hurt her terribly, jolting her on hard or muddy roads and aggravating her 'rheum', as she called it. Her physician called it hysteria, and it is hard for us to outguess him today. But she knew she had to go, to protect her unborn baby. She left Oxford on 17 April 1644. The king and the two princes, reluctant to say their goodbyes, went with her and shared the first night's halt with her in Abingdon. Next morning she said her goodbyes to her two sons. She then set out, westwards, into the Vale of the White Horse. But the king turned east, back to Oxford, while she made her way south to Exeter, where she had her baby, another tiny daughter. She left the new baby behind, in part because of the danger at sea. Then she sailed to France.

She and Charles had said their last goodbyes. They would never meet again.

For Henrietta, the war was over. She would go on intriguing for French backing for Charles, but she would not succeed.

Sometimes we get glimpses of the way the royal family appeared to ordinary citizens. A woman called Anne Smith, 'being diabolically affected towards our most serene Lady Mary now Queen of England and towards Prince Charles the Prince of Wales and the other children of the king and queen, publicly spoke and uttered these false and seditious words, to wit, "The King's children are bastards, And that the queen was delivered of a child at Oxford when the King had not been with her a twelvemonth before."' It was probably not the first time she had said it. By now the gap between the lived lives of the royal family and people's perceptions of them was cavernous. They had lost control of their images. They had lost control of London. Now they were to lose control of the nation as well.

Parliamentarians, too, had reason to despair. The Battle of Cropredy Bridge on 29 June 1644 dealt a crucial blow to their morale, because after it so many despaired of success that desertions from Waller's army became a haemorrhage. Even the trained bands had had enough, and slunk home quietly. The Tower Hamlets men, from Anna Trapnel's part of London, were among those who had been firm under fire. Now they may have begun to wonder why they had bothered.

It was from this desperate hour that the man emerged. When Oliver Cromwell's military career began, he was alongside men who lacked experience – most of the officers had never been in a battle. The main problem they faced at first was keeping their troops in order. Men who had not wanted to fight in the first place deserted at the first opportunity. If they couldn't get clean away, they would at least hope to while away the hours in plunder or drinking. Sickness in turn reduced the ranks, thinning them to paper.

Cromwell needed to be a good leader to manage men like that. He always excelled at staying close to the men under his command. His authority was based on tight military discipline, but also on real interest in his men and their welfare. He was relentless with soldiers who ran away or misbehaved. In his regiment 'no man swears but he pays his twelvepence; if he be drunk he is set in the stocks or worse; if one calls the other roundhead, he is cashiered; insomuch as the countries where they come leap for joy of them, and come in and join with them'. An exaggeration, perhaps, but after some of the disorderly forces led by others, the Eastern Counties had cause to rejoice that disciplined troops were in the area. Cromwell also supported his troops loyally if they kept the rules. He tried to make sure they were paid properly, and defended them if they were unjustly accused of plunder or other criminal activities. He also drilled his men, taking them into battle in close, tight formation. When they broke through, he made them re-form and attack again and he wouldn't allow them to rush off after plunder. 'I have a lovely company', he wrote in September 1643. 'They are no Anabaptists, they are sober Godfearing Christians.'

He also looked after their faith. He liked to recruit godly men, and he liked to promote them, especially. In abandoning promotion solely on grounds of social rank, Cromwell was breaking with tradition; he still preferred his officers to be gentlemen and godly to boot, but if he had to choose he put godliness before gentility. But he also needed supportive subordinates, and here he turned to the people he could trust most: his own family. His first Ironsides were led by his son Oliver, his nephew Valentine Walton, his cousin Edward Whalley, his brother-in-law John Desborough and his future son-in-law Henry Ireton. 'Better plain men than none,' he said, 'best to have men patient of wants, faithful and conscientious in the employment.'

Cromwell also needed to be a supportive subordinate himself. He served under William Waller for a time, who remembered that 'although he was blunt he did not bear himself with pride or disdain. As an officer he was obedient and did never dispute my orders nor argue upon them.' He also served under Thomas Fairfax for five years. Royalists liked to portray Fairfax as the dim-witted tool of scheming Cromwell, but this is nonsense; there is no reason for such a view.

Cromwell's first real job was given to him in early January 1643, when he was sent to East Anglia from London to support Lord Grey. In April Grey and a force of 5000 horse and foot left to join Essex in the Thames Valley, and Cromwell was left more-or-less in charge of the entire eastern area: Norfolk, Suffolk, Essex, Cambridgeshire and Hertfordshire. He had to suppress any insurgence, and to defend the area against Royalist attack. The Royalist garrison at Newark, just over the border in Nottinghamshire, was especially menacing, and Newcastle's army of papists was marching south.

Cromwell did his best to clean up the area. He and his troops swept through Norfolk intimidating and arresting anyone suspected of being none too firm for Parliament. The key towns were garrisoned. The northern border was secured after some sharp skirmishes. At Winceby, in October, Cromwell's Ironsides found themselves fighting desperately hand-to-hand against straggling outriders from Newcastle's army. It was then that his successes caught the attention of the London press, desperate to shore up the flagging morale of the capital. An image was born, but an image with substance.

Cromwell had to sustain a series of defeats and setbacks in 1643 that might have sunk a lesser man. In May 1643, for example, he was supposed to join forces with Lord Grey to stop a convoy of ammunition obtained by Henrietta Maria being sent south from Bridlington to Oxford. Another convoy led by the queen herself in June got through unopposed. By now Cromwell could offer little opposition because he was in such dire straits for money to pay his men. Local subscriptions were supposed to finance Parliament's army; they were inadequate, and by summer 1643 his men were on the point of mutiny. The situation was not helped by the fact that Royalist general Ralph Hopton was hammering William Waller's Parliamentarians in the West, while Essex was unable to drive the Royalists out of the Thames Valley. 'See how sadly your affairs stand', Cromwell wrote to the Cambridge committee on 6 August 1643. 'It's no longer disputing, but out instantly all you can. Raise all your hands; get up what volunteers you can; haste your horses.' To the Essex lieutenants he wrote, furiously, 'Lord Newcastle will advance into your bowels.' To Oliver St John he wrote that 'Weak counsels and weak actings undo all'. When he reached Boston and found no monies from Essex, he wept, and by the end of September 1643, his troops were on the verge of mutiny again. Desperate, he went to London and was there from mid-January to mid-February 1644.

Denzil Holles led a peace group of MPs who had given up all hope of winning the war, but he was opposed by a faction who felt equally strongly that the king must be defeated militarily before peace negotiations could begin. John Pym had been a key member of the latter, and had forced tough taxation legislation through. His death in late 1643 left a gap, but Oliver St John, Lord Saye and Sele and others took on his role. And it was this group that Cromwell initially joined. He pushed for a central committee to control money raised from the Eastern Counties at new levels, 50% higher. It was after a series of successful political moves that Cromwell was promoted in January to Lieutenant-General of the Eastern Association. So by the time the war moved north, he was poised for action.

The war in the north was a different story, a drama with a new cast of actors. What linked it to the events in the south was the dynamic Prince Rupert. Rupert's sheer speed and energy seemed to his enemies almost diabolical. His power to terrify was itself a weapon.

Rupert set out for the north on 16 May 1644; he had only a smallish force, about 2000 horse and 6000 foot, including the remnants of the Irish army that had been led to misery by Byron. He marched accordingly to Lancashire, hoping to pick up reinforcements. He took Stockport, and so alarmed the besiegers of Lathom House that they rushed to Bolton for shelter under their commander, Alexander Rigby.

Rigby had already been rather embarrassed by Lathom House. It was the Royalist equivalent of Brilliana Harley's Brampton Bryan, a besieged house defended by its mistress, in this case a Frenchwoman, Charlotte de la Tremoille, Countess of Derby. It had no strategic significance, but Rigby was determined to reduce it, despite its massive walls. Fairfax inspected it in February of 1644, but had decided it didn't matter much and couldn't be helped anyway. Rigby's cannons had made no impression on the walls, so he brought up a huge mortar, which fired an eighty-pound stone ball. He tried to get the Lord to help, too, holding a four-day prayer meeting. But his intercessions were met by a sortie from the castle, which captured the great gun and jammed it with rubbish, forcing Rigby to move his own artillery back. Maybe he was glad that Rupert's coming gave him an excuse to abandon the siege. In any case Rupert did his work for him; the prince gallantly ordered the countess to abandon the castle, and replaced her with one of his own captains, who surrendered in September 1645.

Rupert reached Bolton only the afternoon after Rigby arrived. The town fell after a short defence, and as rain poured down, the Royalists flooded in, and the streets were soon awash with something darker than rain. The notorious slaughter began: 1600 Parliament-men fell, some killed after they had surrendered. Rigby himself escaped by posing as a Royalist officer, having learnt the codeword of the day.

This was a clarion call for Royalist recruitment, and Lancashire men flocked to Rupert's banner. Reinforcements also arrived. He took Liverpool on 11 June, and Charles ordered him to relieve York at once. 'If York be lost,' he asserted on 14 July, 'I shall esteem my crown little less,' but he added, perhaps confusingly, 'but if that be lost ... you immediately march to Worcester, to assist me.' Rupert carried his uncle's letter till his dying day. He felt it proved he'd done as his king told him.

The locals in the north were paying lavish amounts of tax towards the upkeep of the Royalist army. They were not delighted to see more soldiers. York was a tough nut for Parliament to crack; it had stout walls, and behind them were Newcastle and a solid, resolute garrison of 4500 foot. Newcastle ran the town with a firm hand; all staple food went into a central store, and everyone got a pint of beans, an ounce of butter, and a penny loaf every day. In front of York was the large Scottish army of Alexander Leslie, Earl of Leven, and Fairfax's 5000, and the Earl of Manchester's forces, around 30,000 besiegers.

The cordon was so tight 'that a messenger could hardly pass'. Henry Slingsby wrote that 'they kept so strict guards, as I could not get any either in the night or day to go to Red House and bring me back word how my children did, but were taken either going or coming'. So the defenders used fire signals from the Minster. They didn't work very well, because the signallers remained unaware that Rupert was coming to their aid, and with his usual speed: by 30 June he was at Knaresborough, only fourteen miles from York. Parliament, on the other hand, was expecting reinforcements, but Rupert was, as always, quicker, so that the besiegers had to march away from their siege lines to face his oncoming army. They drew up on Marston Moor, about five miles west of the city.

But Rupert outmanoeuvred them again, crossing the rivers Ure and Swale and swinging around to the south-west to attack a detachment of Manchester's dragoons, who were guarding a bridge of boats; Rupert now held this bridge. He then dispatched dragoons under Goring to relieve York, and sent out scouts to find out where, exactly, the Parliamentarian army was. If he could destroy it – the next day! Rupert was in a hurry, as always – then the war in the north was as good as won.

But the Parliamentarians outnumbered Rupert by about 10,000 men. As often, haste was his glory and his undoing. As often, too, the other commanders were not overjoyed at being hastened along by an impatient young prince. Newcastle, who didn't appear until 9 a.m., five hours after Rupert's men had been on the move, tried to reason with the young man: why fight at once? The Parliamentarians and the Scots might divide if left to themselves, and in a few days more reinforcements would arrive. Rupert said, simply, that he had orders from the king: attack.

Newcastle gave way, and Marston Moor began to fill with armies. Eventually, about 46,000 men stood by, ready for battle.

Rupert's forces drew up on low flat country, guarded by a ditch that ran along the side of the road. Parliament and the Scots were deployed on rising ground, with a wide field of fire between the armies; there was a cornfield in front of the allied infantry, and it was July, so the corn was high, but otherwise it was open country.

Leven at once spotted that Rupert was outnumbered. He knew all about warfare; he had served under Gustavus Adolphus, just as Rupert had fought against him. He knew they must attack before Rupert could reinforce.

On the left of the allied army was the powerful cavalry, under Oliver Cromwell and another veteran of the Swedish wars, David Leslie. In the centre were the Scots and English infantry, which far outnumbered the Royalists, on the right more cavalry, Fairfax's men and the Scottish horse. Opposite Fairfax was the Royalist left, with cavalry led by Goring, a man who'd never been able to accept an order from above, or keep his troops in order below, and who was soon to be the most hated man in the West of England. And behind a low hedge were the Royalist musketeers, interspersed with the cavalry in Swedish style. Beside them were the foot, and beside them, facing Cromwell and his Ironsides, were Rupert's own cavalry; in front of them was Lord Byron – the poet's ancestor – with more musketeers, as a 'forlorn hope'.

The Royalist army's deployment was agonizingly slow for Rupert, who had hoped initially to launch an attack while the enemy was still forming up. Newcastle's men had finally arrived, having been persuaded grumblingly to leave York after a minor mutiny in which they insisted on being paid before going anywhere. The minutes crawled by. Lord Eythin arrived, too, and he was cranky; he dampingly reminded Rupert that 'your forwardness lost us the day in Germany, when yourself was taken prisoner'.

Rupert was not made more amiable by this sally. He fretted while the armies slowly drew up; the deployment took until four o'clock. There was an exchange of cannon fire at about two o'clock, but even over a short distance the guns were too feeble to throw their small three-pound balls with any accuracy.

The two armies were drawn up at very close range, with the extreme flanks within a musket-shot of each other, less than four hundred yards apart. Rupert could hear the Scots army singing their metrical psalms, across the lines. It was haunting; it was ominous. It was comforting for the Scots, though; they could remember the armies of the Hebrews as they stood in the grey twilight, exposed to their enemies' fire. It was by now so late that Rupert, perhaps influenced by the unenthusiastic responses of Newcastle and Eythin, decided not to attack until the following morning. It was plainly about to rain, and the field, clay soil, would be slippery when wet.

Newcastle sneaked off to his coach for a quiet smoke. Rupert sat down to his supper. He was 'set upon the earth at meat'. His army began to relax; his own men, who had been in the field since early morning, were tired. They dismounted and 'laid upon the ground'.

Leven noticed the Royalists relaxing. He at once gave the signal to attack, and the entire allied army, horse and foot, ran towards the Royalist position in the hedge. As they did so, the lowering storm broke. Thunder crashed, seven great peals. Rain put out the Royalist musketeers' matches, so some of their guns did not fire. The armies 'made such a noise with shot and clamour of shouts that we lost our ears, and the smoke of powder was so thick that we saw no light but what proceeded from the mouths of guns'. 'Our army', thought Simeon Ash, 'was like unto so many thick clouds.'

The allies broke through the cornfield, at a fast run; the Royalist drakes fired, but didn't stop the dead weight of Parliament-men, who pushed on into the centre. As he himself was later to describe, Fairfax charged on the right, but his progress was impeded by 'the whins [thorns] and ditches which we were to pass over before we could get to the enemy, which put us into great disorder'. The deadly fire of Goring's musketeers, interspersed with his cavalry, was a barrier too. Laconically, in good Yorkshire style, Fairfax notes his own refusal to quit; 'I was necessitated to charge them. We were a long time engaged with one another, but at last we routed that part of their wing.' He rallied his men, and managed to defeat the left wing of Goring's front line, which he pursued towards York.

Fairfax remembered that first charge as a bloody affair. His brother Charles had been mortally wounded, deserted by his men. Fairfax noted that he had 'at least thirty wounds'. Fairfax himself, rejoining the battle, had his face laid open by a sabre cut. The captain of the troop was shot in the arm, and Fairfax's cornet had both his hands cut 'that rendered him ever afterwards unserviceable'. So the second line broke, and Fairfax's third line, the Scots, were then routed by Goring's and Lucas's men.

The muddle and misery of the running cavalry battle are not always well conveyed by the orderly accounts of military history. Sir Philip Monckton, who saw it at first-hand, gives a much better idea of what it was like to be there:

> At the battle of Hessy Moor I had my horse shot under me as I caracoled at the head of the body I commanded, and so near the enemy that I could not be mounted again, but charged on foot, and beat Sir Hugh Bethell's regiment of horse, who was wounded and dismounted, and my servant brought me his horse. When I was mounted upon him the wind driving the smoke so I could not see what was become of the body I commanded, which went in pursuit of the enemy. I retired over the glen, where I saw a body of some two thousand horse that were broken, which as I endeavoured to rally I saw Sir John Hurrey, major general to the prince, come galloping through the glen. I rid to him and told him, that there were none in that great body, but they knew either himself or me, and that if he would help me to put them in order, we might regain the

field. He told me, broken horse would not fight, and galloped from me towards York. I returned to that body. By that time it was night, and Sir Marmaduke Langdale having had those bodies he commanded broken, came to me, and we stayed in the field until twelve a clock at night, when Sir John Hurrey came by order of the Prince to command me to retire to York.

Goring's men, notorious for their lack of discipline, went on to loot the baggage-train and to pursue the fugitives, but Lucas managed to get his men together and to launch an attack on the infantry's right flank, naked without Fairfax's defeated cavalry.

Cromwell had been luckier, on the left. He was opposed by Byron, who was in charge of a 'forlorn hope', the term for a group deployed in advance of the main army whose job was to harass and disrupt an enemy attack before it could reach the main body of the army. Byron understood the principle, but mistimed his counterattack, masking the fire of his own musketeers and floundering in a patch of marsh that should have been part of his defence. Rupert had positioned his army on rough ground with ditches and hedges. Byron's men had begun with a ditch in front and hedges on their flanks, lined (as always in this war) with musketeers. By advancing, Byron lost these advantages. Cromwell drove his first line from the field, and perhaps part of his second line too. Rupert mounted in haste, and at once saw that the centre was holding, but that Byron's left was in real trouble. So he set off, personally, to shore it up. As he rode forward, he was passed by scores of men running the other way. 'Do you run?' he cried. 'Follow me.' He charged Cromwell's horse.

By now Cromwell had been slightly wounded, perhaps by the sword of a colonel in Byron's front line (who later eagerly claimed to have done it), perhaps by the pistol of one of his own troopers, a not uncommon occurrence with the unreliable Civil War handguns. He may have left the field to get his wound dressed, though only those who didn't like him ever said so. But he came back into action later, when it was vital. 'Cromwell's own division', said Parliamentarian soldier Leonard Watson, 'had a hard pull of it, for they were charged by Rupert's bravest men both in front and flank; they stood at the sword's point a pretty while, hacking one another, but at last (it so pleased God) he brake through them.' Rupert cut down several of the foe in person, but his gallantry and dash ended ignominiously with him crouching at twilight in a beanfield while his routed forces crept back towards his own lines. The Royalist cavalry ran for York.

In the centre, Newcastle's Royalist Whitecoats – so called because of their woolly coats, undyed lambskin – had stood like rocks, while their stalwart opposition gave a cavalry brigade a chance to charge against the allied infantry; they ran right through them and reached the crest of the ridge. The allies, already dismayed, were then attacked by Lucas and his men, and the whole front almost caved in, with even Leven and Fairfax leaving the field, in something of a hurry. A Royalist victory seemed imminent.

In his memoirs, Parliamentarian Sir Arthur Trevor remembered how it felt to run:

> In the fire, smoke, and confusion of that day, the runaways on both sides were so many, so breathless, so speechless, and so full of fears, that I should not have taken them for men; both armies being mingled, both horse and foot; no side keeping their own posts. In this horrible distraction did I coast the country; here meeting with a shoal of Scots crying out 'Weys us, we are all undone' and so full of lamentation and mourning, as if the day of doom had overtaken, and from which they knew not whither to fly, and anon I met with a ragged troop reduced to four and a cornet; by and by with a little foot officer without hat, band, sword, or indeed anything but feet.

But for Parliament one brigade, under Lord Lindsey, stood like a bristling hedgehog, both flanks exposed, refusing to run, meeting charge after charge with an impenetrable phalanx of pikes, their butts set in the ground. They held their ground; they would not break, and they managed to take Sir Charles Lucas prisoner. They turned the tide.

For now, returning from having his wound dressed, still on the left, Cromwell managed to rally his men, helped by his second-in-command, Leslie. They charged again, and this time succeeded in putting Rupert's men to flight, down the long road to York. Cromwell sensibly kept his men together, refused to let them chase the fleeing enemy, and brought them back to the field, a feat which had proved to be beyond Goring or Rupert.

They were soon joined by Fairfax. Like all the allied troops, he had been wearing a field-sign, a white paper in his hat. He tore it off hastily. Without the field-sign he came right through the Royalist army to reach his own side. When he found Cromwell, he may have ordered him to attack; in any case they did so, and in the nick of time. His 'lovely company' struck at Goring from the rear. The combined cavalry moved around Wilstrop Wood, and began an attack on Goring's horse, who had thought the battle over and won. They broke and fled for York.

This left the footsoldiers entirely exposed to the Eastern Association cavalry, tough as iron, which wheeled and charged. There were few Royalist cavalry to oppose them, and the foot had no defence against their thunderous onslaught. At first Newcastle's Whitecoats inflicted heavy casualties on the Parliamentarian horse. They 'would have no quarter, but fought it out till there were not thirty of them living; whose hap it was to be beaten down upon the ground, as the troopers came near them, though they could not rise for their wounds, yet were so desperate as to get either pike or sword or a piece of them, and to gore the troopers' horses as they came over them'. This account, sent to the astrologer William Lilly by Colonel Camby, ends with a tribute: 'I never met such resolute brave fellows, or whom I pitied so much.' Newcastle's second wife Margaret Cavendish wrote that 'every man fell in the same order and rank wherein he had fought'. By then the moon had risen, illuminating the last hedge of pikes collapsing, the white coats of the 'Lambs', who had been led to this final slaughter. Only thirty of the four thousand Whitecoats survived the battle. 'They had brought their winding-sheets with them', said one observer. Their last act was to gouge desperately at the stomachs of their slayers' horses, like bulls in the Spanish bullring.

Why did they refuse quarter? When the attack on their position began, Royalist victory had seemed imminent. They may have thought that a firm stand would make it certain. After all, the resolute defiance of Lindsey's brigade had saved Parliament from total collapse only an hour earlier. Because the Lambs thought Royalist victory already won, they probably thought that their horse would come up – soon – and rescue them. As well, they were imbued with a military and chivalric ideal; stand and fight; don't run. Newcastle was partially responsible for this; he threw himself eagerly into the role of chevalier. He adored equitation, dancing, fencing, the arts of a gentleman. Sir Philip Warwick said 'he had a tincture of a romantic spirit and had the misfortune to have somewhat of the poet in him'. Clarendon noted later that while he liked the pomp and authority of being a general, he delegated military jobs to a professional officer, Lieutenant-General James King.

Why, then, did the Parliamentarians press on with the futile slaughter? Newcastle's northern army had been a particular object of dread since the beginning of the war. 'The Papist army in the North', it was called, and some Protestants actually deserted early in the war rather than fight alongside Catholics. Fairfax's troops, too, had been fighting a long, drawn-out guerrilla war against Newcastle's men. Fairfax, the rider on the white horse, was a crusader against this popish darkness.

Darkness was indeed enveloping them. By now it was about 9.30. With the Whitecoats died the last hopes of Rupert's shattered army. The battle had lasted only two hours.

It is always difficult to estimate Civil War battle casualties. According to the countrymen who interred the bodies, 4150 Royalists had been killed; others said 3500. Another 1500 were captured, along with many arms, colours and vital papers. Among the dead on the field was Rupert's celebrated white poodle, Boy, believed by some Parliamentarians to be a demon because of his supposed invulnerability to shot. He had slipped his collar at the beginning of the battle. Now he had proved all too vulnerable, like the army whose men he had cheered by his antics. He lay in the mud; 300 Parliamentarians lay dead, too, and many more were wounded. Edmund Ludlow's cousin Gabriel lay dying, 'with his belly broken and his bowels torn, his hip-bone broken, all the shivers and the bullet lodged in it'.

The allied troops, exhausted and hungry, held the field. They sang a psalm of victory. There they remained, too spent to move on, drinking from the puddles and ditches that were their only sources of water. When they were refreshed, they stripped the enemy dead, so that the morning light illuminated a field of naked bodies, a few still twitching in the last spasms of life. Battlefield scavengers followed, breaking fingers to get at rings. Relatives arrived, too. As Mary Towneley was rummaging frantically through corpses, searching for her husband's body, she met Oliver Cromwell. He asked her what she was doing 'in that vale of tears'. When she told him, he assigned her a bodyguard.

Sir Charles Lucas was taken around the sprawled bodies, to identify those of sufficient rank to merit burial in individual graves rather than the common pits which gaped for the majority. The sight was too much for him. He began to sob, exclaiming 'Alas for King Charles!' Around one soldier's wrist he saw a bracelet of bright hair; he asked that it be taken off and sent to 'an honourable lady'.

The Royalists staggered into York. Rupert's officers 'came dropping one by one, not knowing, but marvelling and doubting, what fortune might befall one another'. Micklegate Bar was crammed with wounded. More lay in the streets, crying out in pain. The governor had sensibly shut York's gates to stop the allied troops entering the town in the wake of the fleeing Royalists, but the fugitives struggled desperately for admission, panic-stricken. Rupert was among the last to reach the city. He had stopped to have a violent row with Newcastle. Each blamed the other for losing the battle.

Newcastle, his money gone, his forces destroyed, decided to call it a day; he took ship for Hamburg and did not return till after the Restoration. 'I will not endure the laughter of the court', he said.

Allied victory in the north was now only a matter of time. Victory in the war was still far away, though, and Marston Moor did not make it inevitable. It was, said Oliver Cromwell, accurately, crisply, 'an absolute victory, obtained by the Lord's blessing'. The Parliamentarians had taken enough colours, it was said, to furnish every cathedral in England. The Parliamentarians were jubilant: this was a victory 'such as the like never was since this war began', said Cromwell.

But Royalist troops, angry, muddled, still roamed the area. A remnant of Rupert's forces under Sir John Mayney clashed with some Parliamentarians near the village of North Scale in Lancashire. Mayney and his men were driven off, and Mayney fell embarrassingly from his horse in the process. The next day he and his troop returned and took out their feelings of angry defeat on the village. It had been abandoned by its frightened inhabitants, so they set it on fire, except for one house known to belong to a Royalist sympathizer.

York surrendered on 16 July, though some Royalist citadels held out until as late as 1646. The north came increasingly under Parliamentarian and Scottish control; which often meant Covenanters diligently sequestering the assets of 'delinquents' and anyone rumoured to be Catholic. A gentlewoman called Isabelle Hixton, for example, was deprived of her entire estate on the grounds that she was a Catholic; it was given holus-bolus to her former shepherd, Thomas Ellison, who had carried messages between Fairfax and the Scots, and so proved his good faith. Ellison was supposed to give Isabelle a pension of a third of the estate's profits, but he failed to do so, and also set about depleting the estate for quick profits, cutting down trees for timber and ploughing meadows; evidently he thought it unlikely that his good fortune would last long. Ellison said firmly that he was actually bringing wasted land under cultivation. He was eventually forced to pay Isabelle her allowance, but did not hand over the arrears until 1649.

Rupert, rallying himself, marched north with his straggling remnants, and was met by Montrose, searching for an army to attack Scotland. Rupert didn't have an army to give him, and instead crossed the Pennines, proceeding down to Bristol, where news of his uncle's far greater successes in the West awaited him.

Six days after the battle, London had a moderately accurate account of it, and four more detailed reports within the following four days. News was improving, and travelling faster. Nehemiah Wallington rejoiced in the news. There, he wrote, 'was God seen'.

There was some debate about exactly whom God had been trying to help, however; the Scots thought it was their Covenanting faith that the Almighty rewarded, while in London, their role was played down considerably in favour of exultant praise of Cromwell. One pamphlet by Lord Saye and Sele himself eagerly portrayed him as God's chosen instrument in winning the day; a newspaper called him 'one of the Saviours (as God has miraculously manifested him to be) of this Israel'. This praise of the very man who, they felt, was eager to obstruct their plans for settlement upset the Scots, who not unjustly felt that they were owed a meed of praise too. What had riled them was a perceived threat to their efforts to coax the Church of England into the Covenant. Cromwell had suggested that some Independents might be unable to submit to the common rule even then being debated by a committee of the Westminster Assembly. They angrily argued that Cromwell was 'an incendiary' who should be impeached for 'kindling coals of contention'. He wasn't. But he never forgot, and the event hardened his attitude to Presbyterians, whom he had previously tolerated. The little battle was over too.

After Marston Moor, the allied army dispersed, Leven and the Scots to Newcastle, Manchester to the Eastern Association, while Fairfax remained in Yorkshire. God would have to wait a few more months for final victory, particularly since Manchester was now so appalled by the quarrels and problems that he was seeking a negotiated peace. God's votary Oliver Cromwell was appalled in his turn.

One thing that overtook Cromwell was the death of a relative, a man on whom he relied. This is a letter to his brother-in-law on the loss of Walton's son Valentine Walton. It shows why he had become such a successful commander, why men had followed him to victory:

> Dear Sir,
>
> It's our duty to sympathise in all mercies; that we may praise the Lord together in chastisements or trials, that so we may sorrow together.
>
> Truly England and the church of God hath had a great favour from the Lord, in this great victory given to us, such as the like never was since this war began. It had all the evidences of an absolute victory obtained by the Lord's blessing upon the godly party principally. We never charged but we routed the enemy. The left wing, which I commanded, being our own horse, saving a few Scots in our rear, beat the Prince's horse. God made them as stubble to our swords, we charged their regiments of foot with our horse, routed all we charged. The particulars I cannot relate now, but I believe of twenty thousand the prince hath not four thousand left. Give glory, all the glory, to God.
>
> Sir, God has taken away your eldest son by a cannon-shot. It brake his leg. We were necessitate to have it cut off, whereof he died. Sir, you know my own trials in this way, but the Lord supported me with this, that the Lord took him into the happiness we all pant for and live for, never to know sin or sorrow anymore. He was a gallant young man, exceedingly gracious. God give you his comfort. Before his death he was as full of comfort that to Frank Russell and myself he could not express it, it was so great above his pain. Then he said to us, indeed it was admirable. A little while after he said one thing lay upon his spirit. I asked him what that was? He told me it was that God had not suffered him to be any more the

executioner of his enemies. At his fall, his horse being killed with the bullet . . . I am told he bid them open to the right and left that he might see the rogues run. Truly he was exceedingly beloved in the army by all that knew him. But few knew him, for he was a precious young man, fit for God. You have cause to bless the Lord. He is a glorious saint in Heaven, wherein you ought exceedingly to rejoice. Let this drink up your sorrow.

Cromwell's mixture of practical commonsense acceptance that beloved men die in battles, and his genuine regret at losing one, only seems odd to those of us who have been lucky enough not to be tried in the fires of war. The blend of strong, even passionate paternal love and tough truthtelling are typical not only of a good commander, but also of a godly commander, confident in God because from him comes victory.

William Waller noted Cromwell's way with words: 'He did, indeed, seem to have great cunning, and whilst he was cautious of his own words, not putting forth too many lest they should betray his thoughts, he made others talk, until he had as it were sifted them, and known their inmost designs.'

'God made them', Cromwell thought, 'as stubble to our swords.' They weren't men. They were stubble. Walton was a man.

Later, a group of Dutch artists suggested to the fledgling English republic that the Banqueting House might now be redecorated. (More Rubens masterworks destined for the Thames, like the *Crucifixion* from the queen's chapel . . . ?) What could be more appropriate than pictures of Marston Moor? Then the people could come and see for themselves a lasting record of the triumph of the saints. The proposal was rejected – too expensive, too flagrant, perhaps a little too Stuart – but in the nineteenth century schools and town halls were to fill up with copies of a later picture of the battle by James Ward, so that Marston Moor became a visual monument to Whiggishness.

XVIII

The Cookery Writers' Tales: General Hunger, Hannah Wolley, Kenelm Digby and the Deer of Corse Lawn

Armies trample, invade, destroy,
With guns roaring from earth and air.
I am more terrible than armies,
I am more feared than the cannon.
Kings and chancellors give commands;
I give no command to any;
But I am listened to more than kings
And more than passionate orators.
I unswear words, and undo deeds.
Naked things know me.
I am first and last to be felt of the living.
I am Hunger.

(LAURENCE BINYON, 1917)

By the time Marston Moor was fought, the men and women of England were fighting a grimmer battle, a battle to find enough food to stay alive. Not just the battered armies but the whole country was getting hungry. Harvests had been poor because of the cold, wet summers, and there were fewer men to get in the crops. The armies ate up household food supplies.

What made it especially hard was that most families lived precariously on the harvest of the year. Not only was there no refrigeration, but most households had few cooking facilities either. Few households had a range – most food was cooked in a cauldron, or on a girdle (where oat bread could be made). We tend to imagine an idyllic past of self-sufficient smallholdings, but it wasn't so. The poor in towns, then as now, did very little cooking; instead there were portable meals and pub foods available at the local alehouse, where the chef was usually a man, just as men were usually butchers, bakers and brewers. London's food came from swathes of countryside from hundreds of miles around; from medieval times grain-boats came from Henley and Faversham. The standard drink until the introduction of tea and coffee was beer, which provided a lot of quickly-absorbed calories. It also contained a considerable amount of alcohol; people sometimes imagine that it was weaker in the past, but slow fermentation made it likely to be stronger.

The rural majority ate a diet of deadly monotony. For the poor, bread, and various pulse-based foods called pottage, were the staples. Grain was still consumed as often in porridge or pottage as in bread, and for the very bottom rungs of society bread itself was a festive feast, linked with the saints' calendar that Robert Harley was keen to extirpate. Even for others, sweet fruit breads like Banbury cakes and soulcakes were linked to the ritual year. They provided sugar and longed-for fat, but they were generally abandoned with the saints' days they celebrated. This may actually have contributed to an ongoing nutritional crisis. What little variety vegetables could provide disappeared when the poor lost access to land of their own, and they were deprived of what little meat they had when common lands were enclosed for the wool trade. The poor in the seventeenth century may barely have eaten enough fat, or protein.

Just as everyone lived together, hugger-mugger, so there was a surprising degree of overlap in the food habits of rich and poor. But (as with houses) differences were widening. Breakfast was not taken until late morning, 9 a.m.; the more working-class you were, the earlier you ate it. Cold meat, with beer or ale, was usual; Henrietta Maria is said to have liked broth. Not until the eighteenth century did the English take to baked goods for breakfast. Bread was both a staple and an oddity. Soldiers refer to bread all the time, and with longing, as if it were at once central to meals and hard to come by. This is probably not as different as we might imagine from civilian life for those of lower socio-economic status; one effect of war is to force some of the gentry to live the lives of the worse-off. Baking would only occur once a week even in a large gentry household, and the goal would be to bake a huge quantity at once; this was because the fire required was so large and expensive. To heat a brick oven hot enough for breadbaking might consume more fuel than a modest family would use in a month. Some cheaper bread was made not from pure wheat, but from maslin, a mixture of rye and wheat grown and harvested together. For Gervase Markham, advocate of a self-sufficiency always rare and probably becoming rarer, baking was in the same chapter as brewing, and was slightly less important: 'forasmuch as drink is in every house more generally spent than bread . . . being made the very substance of all entertainment, I shall begin with it'. The two activities were bound together: both used grain transformed by yeast. For the noble or upper gentry household, the bread of every day was manchet bread, made with bolted (sieved) white flour, salted, leavened with ale barm, carefully shaped, and baked gently, said Markham. Cheat bread, made with coarser flour, was raised with sourdough, 'a piece of suchlike leaven saved from a former batch'. Food writers who know little of artisanal breadmaking often wrongly see this kind of leaven as a drawback; it *was* a cheap alternative, but it was more richly flavoured and if carefully kept, more reliable. Markham gives a recipe which works perfectly well, and which has the advantage of making the gentry household independent of the brewing and baking industries. And, says Markham proudly, with this 'you may bake any bread leavened or unleavened whatsoever, whether it be simple corn, as wheat or rye of itself, or compound grain as wheat and rye, or wheat, rye and barley, or rye and barley, or any other mixed white corn; only, because rye is a little stronger grain than wheat, it shall be good for you to put to your water a little hotter than you did to your wheat. For your brown bread, or bread for your hind servants, which is the coarsest bread for man's use, you shall take of barley two bushels, of pease two.' The combination of grains and legumes gives excellent protein value.

By contrast, the diet of the upper classes was becoming more and more unhealthy. This was partly due to the printing press, which began to make exciting and exotic recipes status symbols available to everyone. By the end of Elizabeth's reign, thrilling sugar confections had begun to be made by merchants' servants, not just aristocratic families. Thomas Tusser offered quince conserves to the countrywoman, while Partridge's *Treasurie of Commodious Conceits and Hidden Secrets* was not about sexual revelations, as its title implies to our ears, but about sugar: marchpanes and tarts, sugar and spice blended into blaunch powder, syrups, flowers, *Manus christi* (sugar work with gold leaf) lozenges, spiced wines and cordials. The *Queens Closet Opened*, first printed in 1655, incorporates medicine, sweetmaking and cooking. Marzipan bacon rashers that 'will deceive the curious, who cannot but take them for Bacon, unless you taste or smell them'. Or for the more ambitious, one could 'make the representation of a whole world in a glass'. Having mixed chemicals to make attractive vapours, she could 'close [the mixture] hermetically, and make a lamp fire under it, and you will see presented in it the sun, Moon, Stars, fountains, flowers, trees, fruits and indeed even all things'.

This was barely food at all. It was an installation, temporary art. Its pointlessness and excess are analogous to other court arts: the masque, the antefeast. Marzipan bacon is there to show off; it has no other purpose. This kind of etiolated aesthetic inventiveness was at odds with the concerns of health, which stressed both the need for moderation and the need for a balance of heat and cold, moisture and dryness.

But even what passed for food was not exactly a balanced diet. Take Charles I's menus when Prince of Wales; a record exists of exactly what he and his gentlemen and servants ate. There was manchet bread for Charles, and for the servants, cheat bread. There was beer and wine. These were the staples, the main calorie sources. But they also had mutton bone, chicken bone, beef, veal, capon, partridges, and larks. The lower servants ate collops, a kind of burger made from leftovers and fatty pork. There was some kind of tart or pie, unspecified, but probably containing more meat and some spices. On a fish day, all this would be displaced by carp, ling, pike and sometimes cod. No wonder Charles had rickets. He probably had stomach problems too, since there's very little vegetable or grain fibre. He may even have been short of crucial vitamins, minerals and trace elements because his diet so comprehensively lacked vegetables. But by the health standards of his own day, his meals were well-balanced: cold moist fish, heating inflaming meat.

The war brought such misguided consumption to an abrupt end. Even the court struggled to eat as well as it had before the war. Perhaps the new, festivity-free calendar's constant fast days were making a virtue of necessity.

Both tried to live off the countryside, with terrible results for those caught up in the plunder. Especially where households were viewed as 'malignants', soldiers could be extreme, working off deprivation, fear and rage. The common soldiers ate biscuit and cheese, supplied by themselves in most cases, sometimes by the army. The biscuit was the ancestor of ship's biscuit, a paste of flour and water beaten to make it flaky so it wouldn't get too hard to eat. Unrelieved by vegetables, the diet meant that many soldiers experienced the early signs of scurvy. They were saved only by foraging, but their foraging became others' starvation.

By 1644/5 desperate farmers joined forces to patrol their lands and keep them safe from soldiers; the governor of Berkeley Castle told Prince Rupert that he dare not send out soldiers to search for supplies, because 'the country people would knock them down'; they had already killed six cavalry.

A Somerset ballad expressed the feelings of those plundered:

> I had six oxen the other day
> And them the Roundheads stole away,
> I had six horse left me whole,
> And them the Cavaliers have stole
> God's sores they are both agreed . . .
> Here I do labour, toil and sweat
> Endure the cold, the dry and wet,
> But what dost think I get? . . .
> The garrisons have all the gains
> For thither all is vet
> They vet my corn, my beans, my peas,
> I dare no man to displease . . .
> Then to the Governor I come
> Desiring him to ease one zum
> Chave nothing but a paper.
> But dost thou think a paper will
> My back clothe nor my belly fill?

No, no, go take thy note.
If that another year may yield,
I may go cut my throat
And if all this be not grief enow
They have a thing called quarter too,
O! tis a vengeance waster.
A plague upon it, they call it free.
I'm sure they've made us slaves to be
And every man our master.

Even the regional dialect can't disguise the genuine indignation. John Taylor 'the water poet', a Thames waterman, made a similar complaint:

Tell me, experienced fools, did not your days
Glide smoothlier on . . .
When no grim saucy trooper did you harm,
No fiercer Dragon, when no stranger's Arm,
Did reach your yellow bacon, nor envy,
The richness of your chimney's tapestry?
When good Dame Ellen (your beloved spouse)
Bare to the elbow in the dairy-house
With fragrant leeks did eat the cheese she wrought,
Not sent it to the Garrison for nought . . .
Was not your ale as brown, as fat your beef
Ere plunderer was English for a thief?

Taylor is recording what may have been many women's feelings. The work of early modern housewifery was relentless, even heroic, when it came to food preparation. In towns, many things could be bought. In the countryside, even a woman with many servants had to be an expert cook, preserver, distiller and brewer, cheesemaker and baker, and also a gardener and small farmer, a doctor and nurse and pharmacist. The work of preserving the harvest was backbreaking – the simple labour of kneading up twenty-five pounds of flour in a wooden trough for long periods, of cutting up fruit and vegetables, of stirring cheese, of watching and waiting, balancing different tasks, directing servants . . . It could not be replaced. If the food thus created from raw materials was stolen, it wasn't possible to go out and buy more. Neighbours might have supplies, but if an army had been quartered on a small village, the larder of everyone you knew might be similarly depleted.

If the harvest was gone, or even part of it, the result was hunger, debilitating vitamin deficiencies and illness, and then susceptibility to infection and contagion. Early modern people knew nothing of vitamins and minerals, but they knew that if they didn't eat well they suffered.

In the area around a garrison, ordinary life was about survival as the soldiers sucked in every scrap of food and fuel to withstand a possible siege. Taunton, for instance, managed to hold out because it was well provisioned. Many commanders forgot to pay for the foods they requisitioned. Or they had no money, only the dreaded Royalist tickets. Or they had just their guns. Trees, too, were chopped down for siege equipment and fuel, and straw and furze faggots requisitioned for gun emplacements. This could leave villages dangerously short of fuel and feed for animals. When towns changed hands often, the soldiers defending would try to create an area of clear, open ground immediately inside their line of defences. This was essential to provide an unobstructed line of fire, to deny cover to attackers. But it involved tearing down people's houses and often destroying their means of making, preparing and storing food.

'They gave them whole great loaves', recalled Nehemiah Wharton in 1643, 'and cheeses, which they triumphantly carried away on the point of their swords.' However, 'they' were what Wharton termed 'papists', and 'they' were not generously supporting the army, but acting upon compulsion. The food was carried like a trophy because that is what it was.

Hunger such as that to be experienced by Essex's defeated army in the West or even by the trained bands before Newbury made the soldiers more likely to plunder, and so create extreme hunger in others. The effect of hunger on Civil War soldiers can be understood best through one crucial study, conducted in the United States immediately after the Second World War. Over six months, a group of men were restricted to approximately half their former food intake and lost, on average, 25% of their former weight. Although this was described as a study of 'semistarvation', this privation was less extreme than that experienced by Civil War armies, since the men were not marching across miles of rough terrain with pounds of kit on their backs at the same time as consuming a restricted diet.

The starved men in the American study began hoarding objects for which they had no need. According to the original report, hoarding even extended to non-food-related items. This general tendency to hoard has been observed in starved anorexic patients and even in rats deprived of food. Perhaps acts like the violent plundering of Lord Robartes's house in Cornwall were not always inspired by revenge, but by an obscure physiological response to prolonged hunger. The subjects of the experiment also became violent, and sometimes harmed themselves as well as others; and when the men regained access to food, they binged frantically, sometimes eating all day. Another hallmark was decreased ability to bear cold, a significant drawback in army conditions during the Little Ice Age, when average temperatures were an estimated two degrees lower than today, and the Thames froze in London every winter. It is notable that the diarists and letter-writers who complain of hunger almost always bewail the cold as well. In the US study, emotional disturbances persisted even after refeeding began; the men became progressively more withdrawn and isolated. This suggests that some at least of the army agitation that was to dominate the later years of the war was caused by two years or so of semi-starvation. English liberty was born wailing from an empty, aching belly, a body so depleted that its owner at last became too angry for social control.

As the men in the US study grew hungrier, they became obsessed with food; they dreamed about it, they began to read cookbooks. And the effects were so lasting that after the experiment two became chefs. This experience is reflected in the writings of Civil War soldiers; even when addressing loved ones, they write incessantly and obsessively about food; the loaf finally obtained, the hunger on the march. So it is not surprising that the English Civil War gave birth, among other things, to several cookbooks written by its survivors, testimony to a preoccupation with food born during the hungry years.

Hannah Wolley was the first English Delia Smith, the first Fannie Farmer, the first to instruct a nation in cooking and household arts. There had been cookbooks before, but Wolley was a general household guru. And – incongruous as it may seem – she and her enterprise were the results of the war. Not everyone was broken by its impact; some were elevated, and she was one example. She also represents a class of person whose historical significance is usually regarded as slight, but who lived and suffered through the war just as their more powerful contemporaries did: servants. Brilliana Harley was concerned for her servants, but their stories disappear from view when hers ends. Yet when Brampton Bryan was abandoned and then slighted, their lot must have been bitter; thrown out of work in an area of England hostile to them as servants of Parliament's supporters. The Harrisons, too, had servants, some of whom had to be dismissed when the war depleted the family coffers. These stories were repeated across England as the war continued. Hannah Wolley was in service with a Lady Anne Wroth before the war. Hannah, however, managed to turn her difficult experiences into a source of entrepreneurial ideas and initiative. Other cookbook authors were also trained in great households; Robert May, a chef who roamed from household to household during the war years, and William Rabisha.

Robert May learned to cook not from books, but from his father, whom he calls 'one of the ablest cooks of his time'. This method of learning was typical of pre-print culture. Everything from cobbling to ship design was taught from mouth to ear as a trade secret, often to family members only. Ann Fanshawe's receipt book, destined for her daughter, is a surviving example of this way of preserving and handing on knowledge; it was emphatically not for publication. However, the relaxation of censorship and the resulting expansion of print and reading during the war years did not only open the way for political discussion; it also allowed tradespeople to sell their once-secret knowhow to a wider reading public. It might seem odd to describe cookbooks as a product of political liberation, but Hannah Wolley's works were to open a new way of learning to those not born to the trade. They were part of a democratization of knowledge which in turn may have had political impact. Monarchy makes sense in a world where younger servants learn from older servants in a strict hierarchy. Once print made it possible to learn outside that hierarchy, the existence of privileged knowledge and even privilege itself could be called into question. Then, too, ordinary working people like cooks experienced the pressing weight of hierarchy less in terms of legislation and tax than in terms of trade guilds and the agonizingly slow transition from apprentice to master. Partridge's opening poem implies as much, claming 'to frame/ A happy common weale:/ And which at large reveals/

That time did long conceal?/ To pleasure everyone'. Has not the smallest he the same right to sweets as the greatest he? There is always something a trifle levelling about print. Partridge also says that the rich are not friendly to him for giving away their secrets.

As often with those below the gentry, our knowledge of Wolley's life is sketchy. We are not even sure how she liked her last name to be spelled; like Shakespeare she seems to like variety. We know she was born around 1622–3. Like most girls, she was instructed in domestic skills by her mother and sisters, especially in how to prepare medicines: 'my mother and my elder sisters were very well skilled in Physic and surgery from whom I learned a little', she writes. This allowed her to become a servant to a noblewoman; her first mistress was Lady Anne Wroth, wife of Sir Henry Wroth, to whom she dedicated her second book, *The Cook's Guide*. But Hannah was orphaned at the age of fourteen, so she depended on her domestic skills to survive. She had somehow learned fluent French, which might have allowed her to read French recipe books, then called receipt books, with profit. Many of her recipes have a French flavour, including French Bread, made with eggs and milk, a kind of rich *pain de mie*. The Wroths were Royalists, and Hannah says she once cooked a banquet for King Charles himself. It was exactly this kind of claim that made her cookbooks such a success. They represented a glorious vanished past, a golden age Before The War to which some of the nation longed to be restored.

She had a wartime wedding. In 1646 she married Benjamin Wolley, who taught at the Free Grammar School in Newport, near Saffron Walden. The war didn't stop their enterprises. They moved to Hackney in 1653, and opened a boarding school for boys. But Benjamin died in 1661, leaving Hannah without an income; she also suffered some kind of paralytic attack, a stroke, which left her lame. She decided to earn her living by sharing her domestic expertise with a Restoration world eager to recapture its past. Her writings were plainly prompted by Benjamin's death, since her first book, *The Ladies Directory*, appeared in the same year. It struck a nerve because it focused on preserving (a kind of hoarding?), a skill which the war had shown to be vital. Her next, *The Cook's Guide*, promised rarities, recipes 'never before printed'.

Wolley's books did not confine themselves to cookery. As Isabella Beeton was to do later, Wolley tried to advise women on every aspect of running a household, including the training of servants. In doing so, she gives us valuable insights into the lives of a group of women from whom we rarely hear. Washing plate, for example, involved a first rinse in warm water and soapsuds, rubbing any spots with salt and vinegar, then scouring the plate with vinegar and chalk, then drying it in the sun or before a fire, and a final polishing with warm linen cloths, an enormous amount of arm-aching work, all told. When Ralph Verney's aunt lamented the dire possibility of being forced to dine off pewter, she probably gave little thought to what plate meant to her household staff.

Wolley herself was keen to explain that as a servant she was not idle. 'I sit here sad while you are merry,' she wrote, 'Eating dainties, drinking perry;/ But I'm content you should so feed,/ So I may have to serve my need.' This servant's critique of the rich women she waited on shows that an awareness of injustice survived the war, along with cooking styles.

In *The Gentlewoman's Companion*, the Preface launches a swingeing critique of educational priorities: 'The right Education of the Female Sex as it is in a manner everywhere neglected, so it ought to be generally lamented. Most of this depraved late age think a woman learned and wise enough, if she can distinguish her husband's bed from another's. I cannot but complain of, and must condemn the great negligence of parents, in letting the fertile ground of their daughters lie fallow, yet send the barren noodles of their sons to the university.' This astringent remark shows that the critiques of the rich that were voiced by Civil War radicals could echo the feelings of ostensibly much more conservative members of the lower orders.

Wolley was also eager to explore new kinds of hobbies and crafts for women. The traditional pastime of embroidery, so enjoyed by Brilliana Harley, was supplemented by 'all kinds of bugle-works upon wires, all manner of pretty toys for closets, rocks made with shells, frames for looking glasses, pictures or the like, feathers of crewel for the corners of beds'. A skilled servant might contribute to the gentrification of a household through ornamentation. The 'moss work' and other skills Wolley claimed to teach offered a chance for a family to rise in status.

That styles of housekeeping were indicators of class is clear in another and much more scurrilous household manual, *The Court and Kitchen of Elizabeth Cromwell*. This rude satirical pamphlet portrayed Oliver Cromwell's wife Elizabeth as entertaining her court on a meagre diet of gruel and leftovers. Some modern cookery writers have missed the polemical intent, and diligently reprinted Elizabeth's 'recipes'. The satire shows that, then as now, you are what you eat.

It wasn't even that cookbooks began innocently and became political. They were always political. Even Gervase Markham, author of one of the oldest bestsellers, *The English Housewife* of 1615, couldn't quite maintain the self-sufficiency he preached without fairly frequent supplementations via cookbook writing, but he argued nevertheless for a traditional England of independent smallholders. This is not as far as all that from some of the ideas that would make Gerrard Winstanley and his followers significant political innovators in the late 1640s, in particular the notion that the poor could escape the power of the rich through self-sufficiency.

Somehow, receipts seemed a way of sustaining a vanishing past. Catholics had formed a habit of squirrelling the past away, for later use; perhaps that is why three out of the four bestselling cookbooks of the age were written by them. The most fascinating of all the cookbook writers was Sir Kenelm Digby, oddball and Catholic, that 'man of very extraordinary person and presence', as Clarendon called him. He loved to talk, in six languages. He was a bold, sexy pirate, a wide reader and an even wider knower, an experimenter and scientist who struggled to stop surgeons packing wounds with infection-bearing leaves and cloths, and one of the most handsome and seductive men of his time. Far more glamorous than today's celebrity chefs, his friends included the political philosopher Thomas Hobbes, and René Descartes. He did not only preserve receipts; he amassed a collection of 238 medieval manuscripts which he gave to the Bodleian Library in 1634, which included important texts by Chaucer, Langland and Lydgate. He also collected Arabic and Hebrew manuscripts, and presented a large library of these to the fledgling Harvard College in 1655.

And yet Digby was always an outsider. His father had been hanged, drawn and quartered in 1606, for complicity in the Gunpowder Plot. Because of his father's treason, Kenelm spent most of his early life overseas, in Spain, France and Italy. He claimed that Henrietta Maria's mother Marie de Medici pursued him amorously, but he was by then passionately in love with Venetia, illegitimate daughter of the Earl of Dorset. She was beautiful, 'a most lovely and sweet-turned face, with delicate dark brown hair', but a blot on any family's escutcheon. Kenelm Digby did not care; instead of making her his mistress, the normal course of action in such circumstances, he married her. He liked to tell everyone that 'a handsome lusty man might make a virtuous wife out of a brothel-house', which must have been tiresome for Venetia, as must the portrait painted by Van Dyck, which shows her trampling lust and deceit under her feet.

Digby was having breakfast one morning in May 1633 when Venetia suffered a cerebral haemorrhage. He was heartbroken; his beautiful, beloved wife was dead. He collected a few relics of her – hair, casts of her feet – and then summoned Van Dyck to paint her. It was an odd but entirely Catholic and courtly response. 'Sir Kenelm erected to her memory a sumptuous and stately monument at Friars near Newgate-Street, in the east end of the south aisle, where her body lies in a vault of brickwork, over which are three steps of black marble, on which was a stately altar of black marble . . . upon this altar her bust of copper-gilt, all of which is utterly destroyed by the great conflagration [the Great Fire].' He never remarried, but he remained curious and vital; he tried to resurrect a phoenix from ashes, and he visited the possessed nuns of Loudon in 1636, concluding that their malady was psychological; he did not believe in demonic possession. In 1640 he met and debated with Descartes. In 1641 he fought a duel to defend Charles I from an accusation of cowardice from a French nobleman. He was, however, imprisoned in November 1642 as a probable malevolent, and when released in June 1643, he left for France, where he went on to serve Henrietta Maria in her court in exile, and he remained in her household until his death in 1665.

And yet this romantic, spectacular figure was also the author of a cookbook, *The Closet of Sir Kenelm Digby Knight Opened*. It is no ordinary cookbook, admittedly, but something of a compromise between alchemical and scientific experimentation and cosmopolitan cuisine of Italian origin. A number of recipes are attributed to Henrietta Maria herself, by the Restoration era the fountain of all food goodness, and Digby's patron: 'the queen used to baste such meat with yolks of fresh eggs beaten thin', he says, apparently meaning that Henrietta did this personally. This seems unlikely, even for a queen in exile.

Digby's recipes cross the faultlines of the war, lacing together such stern political foes as Parliamentarians Lady Saye and Sele and Lady Robartes with Marie de Medici. Moreover, Digby's *Closet* isn't just a recipe book; it's a glimpse of high living. It unites everyone, as cook-books do, because everyone has to eat, everyone has to manage a household.

Digby's is the first English cookbook to recommend bacon and eggs for breakfast. He uses bread, and flour, but otherwise he offers meat dishes, rich, soft, delicately and formally spiced; they are often flavoured by reductions of stock, and by sauces that use cream, marrow, musk, ambergris, caraway and sugar. He was trying to introduce something like mortadella sausage. Queens like broth, Digby says, meat con-sommé, but Digby warns not to overdo herbs that will rob it of vitality. Chicken broth is also recommended as healthy, especially with orange juice added, but not too much lest it become too hot and dry. Creams are rich and soft, in cloudlike curds. Tough, gritty food was for the hungry poor, who still ate rough grain porridges and hard brown bread. The Digby recipes are the kind of protein-rich food eaten on feast days by those starving for enough fat and protein, but for the rich every day was a carnival. His venison is cooked until it can be cut with a spoon.

However, venison was not just any old meat – it was political. Even before the war, gifts of venison had been used to cement social net-works, much as an entrepreneur might use extravagant presents or dinner parties today. The Earl of Middlesex liked to give venison to people whose social status was too low to allow them to hunt them-selves, rather like giving a poorly-paid secretary a nice bottle of duty-free scent. Just as Digby's cookbook reeks of shared and enjoyed privilege, so did game announce status. But sometimes such announce-ments were unwelcome to those suffering the terrible pangs of hunger.

In early October 1642, a tract of forest and deer chase in the Severn Valley north-west of Gloucester, known as Corse Lawn, was trans-figured by the spectacle of six hundred dead and dying deer. 'A rising of neighbours' had killed them, wantonly, as some kind of protest against the Earl of Middlesex, who owned them. Oddly, Digby's cookbook can help us understand this curious affair through its sensuous evocation of the luxury of meat.

Hunting was fraught with significance. It was an expression of upper-class masculine values – courage, moral superiority over the animal and vegetable, knowledge of nature and endurance of nature's worst extremes, ownership of land, and generosity when the carcasses were divided. Hunting was, among other things, about rule. It was part of civilizing the countryside, striking a kind of unspoken bargain with it whereby its carnal largesse was at once consumed and contained by the hunters. And performing the role of hunter correctly created great honour for the performer. Hunting involved a body of knowledge hallowed by antiquity; Alexander the Great had hunted, and so had King Arthur. Hunting told king and nobles that they were part of an eternal order which would never be revoked or challenged. It trained body and mind for warfare: dens and setts suggested fortifications, and the twists and turns of a hare could remind hunters of the cunning of political enemies. The round of the year was marked by the chase rather than by arable activities for anyone in the greater gentry or above: Christmas was boar-hunting time, hare-hunting was midsummer. A seasonality marked by what beasts were on the table offered a savage pagan alternative to the Church calendar. Just as the indigenous peoples of Australia and the Americas, themselves great hunters, knew every hill and tussock on their hunting territory and recognized individual beasts of venery, so early modern hunters came to an intimate and passionate knowledge of every tree, every holt, every stag; hunting knitted the countryside to its owners and masters. The nobility of the deer, the courage of the boar: these were supposed to be matched, almost imbibed, by the hunters. Above all, the royal hunt was a micro-cosm of the state itself, a careful hierarchy of manners and classes, ordered as beads in a necklace, from king to huntsmen and hounds. Spending too much time in this challenging but richly arrayed and stratified world could easily lead a king to imagine that it *was* the entire world. But it was not, and the slaughter on Corse Lawn almost seemed designed to demonstrate the fact. Hunted deer were gralloched with care, according to a precise series of rules. These deer had simply been gutted, gracelessly, and left to bleed and rot.

It wasn't the first time the Middlesex deer herd had been illicitly attacked. Local men were not always willing to wait for Middlesex to send them a present of venison; sometimes – like the young Will Shakespeare, it is said – they liked to scrump a few deer and boast of their exploits. Some sold the venison to other local gentlemen. Woodcutters also came to the chase often, searching for kindling and scarce, precious, forbidden firewood. Usually, such poor men were left alone, but Middlesex made the mistake of lumping their trespass together with the much more serious offence of deer poaching in a single Star Chamber action.

He had actively supported the removal of royal forests in Worcestershire, Somerset and Wiltshire in the 1620s; they were cleared for enclosure and the dwellers on their margins, the very poorest of the poor, were cleared away too, turned off to starve. The forests were to belong solely to the Crown, and to work only as symbols for royal or noble power and control. But they were already enmeshed in politics. It was, as usual, a matter of religion. In the Forest of Dean, the Catholic magnates were said to be plotting to destroy the woodland, thus preventing England from defending itself at sea against the Spanish. The forest men saw themselves as defenders of the nation, as well as the trees. A man called Thomas Carpenter was hauled before the Star Chamber for cutting firewood. What's more, Forthampton Court, the residence of the earl, was coming under increased scrutiny. It had been owned by Tewkesbury Abbey once, and it had contained a chapel, built for the abbot. In 1540, the house had been granted to John Wakeham, the last abbot, and he had brought a few fragments of his ancient holy house with him: a crusader's tomb, and a few pieces of what had once been the Lady Chapel. When Parliament passed the ordinance against superstitious relics and images, it included objects not found in churches. It may be that in the tense atmosphere of late summer 1642 Middlesex's failure to remove all traces of popish relics from his property, together with his tyrannical behaviour, added up in the minds of local gentlemen and tenants to a suspicion of papistical leanings. Deer slaughter was a form of iconoclasm, like the covert attacks on suspected Catholics elsewhere.

The dead deer on Corse Lawn were as much an assault on the regime as any smashed statue of the king. They too had been icons. They too lay broken. It seems a long way from their bloody carcasses to Hannah

Wolley, but both are expressions of the feelings of servants, slighted, ignored, silently judging their masters. The conflict allowed those grievances and their cries of hunger to be heard.

XIX

Twenty Thousand Cornish Boys:
The Battle of Lostwithiel

'Sometimes we argued together, sometimes we scolded together like Fishwomen of Cheapside, and sometimes we fought very hot', wrote a member of Essex's Parliamentarian guard of the war in the West. Verbal abuse was a key part of Civil War tactics. 'The enemy calling ours "papist dogs", "Washington's bastards", "Russell's apes", "Where is the king of you rogues", "Where is your tettered king?", and ours replying and calling them "traitors", "villains", "rogues to your king and country", "the sons of a Puritan bitch", "bid you go preach in a crab-tree".'

This soldier plainly knew more about Cheapside than about Cornwall, and felt more at home there. To the Parliamentarian army invading it in 1644, Cornwall was a weird and hostile place, full of unfriendly locals who didn't even speak English. 'We are', thought one, 'among a people as far from humanity as they are from sanctities, for they will neither serve God nor man, but after the old fashion of their grandfathers.' Their Royalist soldier-opponents were by contrast more familiar. In the final campaign of the war in the West, the two armies were very close, for very long.

On 6 March 1644, Bevil Grenville's difficult brother Richard turned up in Oxford, with thirty-six of his troop, £600, and news of a Parliamentarian scheme to surprise Basing House. Colonel of Horse and Foot, Lieutenant-General to Ralph Hopton, Richard Grenville was born in 1600, a second son; he was knighted in 1627 and rose under Buckingham to be a baronet in 1630, 'a man who used to speak very bitterly of those he did not love'. As a result of a feud with the Earl of Suffolk, he fled to Ireland, where he held a command against the rebels from 1641 to 1643. Parliament liked the 'signal acts of cruelty which he did every day commit upon the Irish', and in 1643 he went to London and was expected to take up a command against the Royalists; he was appointed to be general under William Waller, but he underwent a change of heart, since, he said, he found 'religion concealing rebellion' and so declared that he would henceforward obey the king and that 'no fortune, no terror, nor cruelty' would make him change his mind again. He was sent to assist John Digby before Plymouth, and when Digby was wounded he assumed command.

Hopton was ordered to clear Dorset, Wiltshire and Hampshire, in October, and took Arundel Castle on 9 December. Waller destroyed a detachment in Alton on 13 December and on 6 January 1644 recaptured Arundel. Both armies reinforced and clashed in a pitched battle at Cheriton on 21 March. The battle was notable for the fact that both sides chose the same rallying cry, 'God with us'. It exemplified the war; both sides believed it. The Parliamentarians changed theirs to 'Jesus with us'. Perhaps he was, because the result was a Parliamentarian victory which opened the West to London. The king could see that something needed to be done. Why not combine the interests of heart and head? Henrietta Maria was already at Exeter, and Charles set out to join her on 12 July 1644. He just missed a reunion with his wife, but did manage to see his newborn baby daughter. Meanwhile, Essex had decided to march west as well, encouraged by Lord Robartes, who kept telling him how very godly and helpful the Cornish would be. Essex was personally brave, very popular, and the trump card in Parliament's pack because of his very high rank; his men adored him. But he was about to lead his admirers to disaster.

He raised the siege of Lyme on 15 June, however, and went on through Somerset into Devon. Grenville immediately fell back to hold a line along the banks of the Tamar. Lord Robartes urged Essex on, pointing to his own influence in the county. And Essex heeded him; he brushed the Royalists aside, reaching Bodmin on 28 July. But new forces began to gather against him. Maurice drew together around 12,000 men at Exeter, and was joined by the king with his 7000.

Meanwhile Essex was harried by the Cornish peasants, who starved his troops of food and information, while Grenville also harassed him, often preventing him from foraging. By contrast, the king was kept supplied and informed. A small boy told him on 4 August that 'there were many gay men in Lord Mohun's house at Boconnoc'. In the ensuing surprise many officers were captured, and Essex's quarter-master only escaped by disguising himself as a servant.

Parliament voted Essex fresh supplies and troops, to be sent by sea via Plymouth. Waller was supposed to reinforce him, but only got as far as Farnham, while the supply fleet was halted by contrary winds. Essex established himself in the ruined shell of Restormel Castle, but he failed to fortify the high ground above Lostwithiel.

What followed was perhaps the Royalists' greatest success, and it is to one of the victors that we owe our most detailed accounts of it. His name was Richard Symonds. Some of his family had declared for Parliament, including a first cousin, also named Richard, who died at Naseby in the New Model Army in 1645. But the diarist was a devout member of the Church who had welcomed the Laudian reforms eagerly. In 1641 he was aged just twenty-four. Introverted, solitary, he loved and admired the antiquity and orthodoxy of the Church, and as he travelled around Britain with the army he seized the chance to record what he saw in the village churches he passed. Imprisoned by Miles Corbett in March 1643, and with his assets sequestered, he escaped in October, and probably went to Oxford, where his younger brother died in October 1644. Symonds noticed everything. His war was also Brilliana Harley's war. On campaign, he was at Wigmore church, two miles from Brampton Bryan, and remarked the east window, 'very old and large', and a portrait of a man in armour, noting that 'Sir Gilly Merrick lived here in the castle. Sir Robert Harley was born here, and his father lived in it before Sir Gilly.' He reported eagerly on architecture, on duels, on a man who tried to hang himself. Everything was interesting. Richard's troop was called the 'show troop', the gilded, aristocratic Life Guards. He made sketches of Oxford colleges, and noted the remains of Osney Abbey.

Richard Symonds found time to make note of a sermon that had interested him, one against popery which had urged 'that one of the greatest arguments against them is the denial of reading the scriptures:

for how can that be an honest guardian that will not let the heir look into his father's will?'

As a lover of old churches, Symonds was especially dismayed by Parliamentarian disregard for them: 'One of their actions while they were in Lostwithiel must not be forgotten. In contempt of Christianity, religion and the church, they brought a horse to the font in the church, and there with their kind of ceremonies did as they called it Christian the horse, and called him by the name of Charles, in contempt of his sacred majesty.'

Symonds's source was probably a news-sheet – then as now, one of the ironies of war is that the frontline troops often find out what their foes or their army has been doing from journalists. Since Symonds was a Royalist, the news-sheet in question is likely to have been *Mercurius Aulicus*: 'When the earl of Essex was at Lostwithiel in Cornwall, one of the rebels brought a horse into that church, led him up to the font, and made another hold him while himself took water and sprinkled it on the horse's head and said "I sign thee with the sign of the cross, in token thou shalt not be ashamed to fight against the roundheads at London", with a deal more such horrid blasphemy.'

Mercurius, in turn, had heard the story from an East Anglian clergyman, returned from the wars, who had used it in a sermon. Such anecdotes fed a stereotyped view of the godly Parliamentarian: rough, blunt, harsh, and somehow a little vulgar. They may have been true, however. In summer 1644, another group of Civil War troops quartered at Yaxley in Huntingdonshire 'there being a child to be baptised, some of the soldiers would not suffer the child to be carried to church to be baptised, and the lieutenant of the troop drew out a part of the troop to hinder it, guarding the church that they should not bring out the child to be baptised; and instead of the child being baptised, in contempt of baptism, some of the soldiers got into the church, pissed in the font, and went to a gentleman's stable in the town, and took out a horse and brought it to the church and there baptised it'.

Thomas Edwardes, ever the chronicler of the madder kinds of godliness, cites several other examples: 'his soldiers fetched a bald horse out of Mr Finmore's stable . . . and in the church at the font, having pissed on it, did sprinkle it on the horse, and call him Bald Esau (because he was hairy) and crossed him in the forehead. They had soldiers [as] godfathers, and one widow Shropshire, a soldier so nicknamed, was the godmother.'

Apparently the same soldiers had baptized a pig on another occasion. This is a story about exceedingly transgressive bodily behaviour (pissing in the font). The extreme degradation is apparently required by the extreme situation; only really brazen impiety will demystify the mumbo-jumbo. But there is also an element of lads-on-the-razzle, shocking not just religious but social decorums. Once you have decided that there is nothing especially holy about a church, then its claims to sanctity appear comical. It is just another stone building stuffed with treasure to be looted.

Nehemiah Wallington, in far-off London, reported that he had seen an Anabaptist 'that did deride and mock of the ordinance of baptism in the baptising of a cat' and who subsequently suffered the judgement of God. A London woman was questioned in 1644; she had accused someone else of baptizing a cat; while William Dugdale mentioned Parliamentarian soldiers at Lichfield, who had brought a calf into the cathedral and sprinkled it with holy water from the font. There had been similar cases before the war: a man had ridden into a church in Devon demanding to have his horse christened, and there was another incident in Buckinghamshire, where dogs, a cockerel and horses also received the blessings of baptism, while in Eyam a cow underwent churching, though there, according to Wallington, the perpetrators were punished with all the plagues of Egypt. The war released these violent energies from the confinement of law. After the Restoration, cat baptisms continued at Henley; and at Ratcliffe in London, a hotbed of godliness during the war years, a horse was introduced to God in baptism, and also given communion.

Though lacking the careful arguments of the iconoclasts, these riotous souls were imbued with their energy, and Thomas Edwardes may have been right to imagine that they were influenced by the language of religious radicals. Or they may just have been groups of lads, having a bit of fun at the expense of more serious neighbours. And yet these ceremonies contain an odd recollection of the carnivals of the very medieval Church which they sought to destroy, in which dogs could be saints and boys were crowned with the mitre and robed in the cope, for one day of rule.

But the baptism was a sideshow to the real fight. The Battle of Lostwithiel was the end of a crushing war of attrition, and high jinks like those with the horse may have been a response to its asphyxiating pressure.

The Royalist forces began to close like a net around Essex's army, the tactics masterminded by Charles himself, leading general in the field, and in this campaign surprisingly competent. On 11 August Grenville secured Respryn Bridge, so that the Royalists now held both sides of Fowey. On 12 August Grenville occupied Lanhydrock, and the next day the ford at St Veep and the fort at Polruan were seized. The fort commanded the entrance to Fowey harbour. Essex was bottled up – and out of luck. Charles himself was viewing the Parliamentarian lines when he suddenly came under fire from across the river; a fisherman standing next to the king was killed.

Both armies had withstood an August so wet that crops rotted in the fields and the roads were rivulets. With no tents, and only limited food supplies, the weather made life very difficult. It helped – literally – to bog the army down. On 21 August, a misty morning, the Royalist guns on Becon Hill damaged the church in Lostwithiel. Essex had only small demi-culverins, little cannons with a short range, and could not return the fire. The bombardment stilled the town, and the Royalists even wondered if the king intended moving back to Fowey; when they realized he wasn't, they simply settled down to wait. Convoys reached them with food and powder, while Essex's powder ran short and food even shorter. The tight Royalist lines stopped his soldiers from foraging. Still, Essex had 10,000 men, and the king had 17,000 deployed along a fifteen-mile front.

On 30 August 1644, two deserters were brought to the king's headquarters at Boconnoc. They revealed that Essex intended to retire to the coast with his infantry and artillery, while Sir William Balfour was to break out with the cavalry. The king reacted promptly, sending warnings to St Blazey and St Veep, and a carrier to order Edward Waldegrave to break the Tamar bridges. The army stood to all night. And yet Balfour's cavalry did creep away, helped by the fog. At 3 a.m., Balfour passed the musketeers stationed on the Lostwithiel–Liskeard road, without a shot fired. Lord Cleveland scraped up 250 horse, but it wasn't enough to stop Balfour, and only at dawn did he muster a large enough force to offer a real pursuit. Balfour shrugged off the attack, crossed the Tamar, and made Plymouth with the loss of only a hundred men. This was a humiliation for the Royalists, and a testimony to the difficulty of holding a long line. 'They escaped only by our sloth and improvidence', thought Joseph Jane disgustedly. The army was actually roaming around looking for food in the ravaged countryside, having exhausted local supplies. But Symonds was undismayed: 'Sir Edward Walgrave took above 100 of the rebels' horse in the pursuit on Saturday, and told the King that if the country had brought in intelligence but an hour or two sooner, where and which way they went, he believed they might have cut off and taken all their horse, they were such cowards and so fearful that eight (said he) would make twenty cry for quarter.'

Meanwhile a group of Royalist prisoners managed to barricade themselves inside the belfry of St Bartholomew's church in Lostwithiel; they pulled up the ladder and refused to come down. Their captors tried to dislodge them with musket fire and smoke; when this failed they exploded a barrel of gunpowder, which lifted the roof.

The Parliamentarians began to move towards Fowey, as one of them recalled: 'The ways were so extreme, foul with excessive rain, and the harness for the draught horses so rotten, that in the marching off we lost three demiculverins and a brass piece, and yet the Major-general fought in the rear all day, he being loth to lose those pieces, thirty horses were put to each of them, but could not move them, the night was so foul and the soldiers so tired that they were hardly to be kept to their colours.' The confusion was so great that Royalist troops sometimes leapt eagerly into the midst of Parliamentarians, taking them for their own men.

'Daily skirmishes . . . kept them to continuall duty', said one Parliamentarian, tiredly. Essex was being slowly and inexorably confined to a narrow river valley, commanded by hills 400 feet high on either side, and terminating in an arm of the sea. Once Essex lost control of the hills around Lostwithiel or of Fowey harbour, he would be at the mercy of the enemy. There was little hope of relief arriving by sea because Waller had no troops to send. He had managed to push two thousand men as far as Farnham, but there he halted, complaining that his men were starving, 'the pictures of famine and poverty'. Parliament helpfully held a public fast on 9 August to support Essex's army. But not even a miracle could save Essex's men now. On that very day the Royalists had seized the ford at St Veep and a day later a relief column was defeated. The Royalists crept on, taking the hills to the north-east, the ruined castle of Restormil, confining Essex and his army to a strip only five miles long and two miles wide.

They had no supplies and no prospects. There were only the caves of Polkerris and Menabilly to serve as bases for communicating with the fleet. Essex wrote, not very surprisingly, of 'the fatigue of the soldiers, many of them not being relieved for eight days'. Parliament's munitions wagon was almost blown up with a lighted match, and the flame had crept to within only two inches of the powder when it was discovered. One Parliamentarian described the incident, and his letter was printed in London:

> We have been in skirmish a week tomorrow morning . . . many of our great pieces and theirs are within musket shot of each other, the enemy . . . The first morning they fell on us, I was sent out with a party of men to encounter them; we had very hot service all day.
>
> We were so near, that sometimes the kingmen would leap over the hedge into the midst of us, taking us for their own men . . . [the enemy] had procured one whom we have not found out, to blow up our train, and had so far affected it, that the wildfire and lighted matches were put into some wagons, one match (by the providence of God) went out of itself . . . Now stand still, and see the goodness of God: The first match burned clean out to the Powder, and there dies, doing no execution at all; the second match was burned within two inches of the powder. The Lord is good to us in providing for us in so barren a place. We were above a fortnight without beer, but now we have some sometimes from the Lord of Warwick, as also Biscuit, Butter and cheese, so that, blessed be god, we are in no great want.

The army was cut off from the outside world by an invisible wall of hostility from the locals: 'Intelligence have we none,' wrote Essex on 16 August, 'the country people being violent against us; if any of the scouts and soldiers fall into their hands they are more bloody than the enemy.'

On 31 August a more intense skirmish was fought, as Symonds told it: 'then about 11 of the clock Captain Brett led up the Queen's troop, and most gallantly in view of the King charged their foot and beat them from their hedge, killing many of them, notwithstanding their muskets made abundance of shot at his men . . . Shooting continued much on both sides, more on theirs, we still gaining ground.' Then Parliament charged 'very bold' to try to take the high ground, but were beaten off. The Royalists beat the tired foot from hedge to hedge. The Parliament-men made a last stand inside the shell of the old castle; they hung on, exhausted, till dusk fell, but as night drew on they broke at last. Symonds again: 'That night the King lay under the hedge with his servants in one field . . I saw 8 or 9 of the enemy's men dead under the hedges that day. Some shooting continued all night . . . That Sunday (1 September) the rebels being surrounded by we on three parts and our army on the land Skippon [who was in command] sent propositions of treaty.'

The next morning, very early, their general decided to leave them. Essex slid away in a fishing boat, with Lord Robartes. He neglected to inform his second-in-command, Philip Skippon, of his plans. 'I thought it fit', he said, afterwards, 'to look to myself, it being a greater terror to me to be a slave of their contempt than a thousand deaths', and he told Colonel Butler that 'I would rather fall into the hands of God than men, for if the enemy should take him, they would use him reproachfully'. In reply the Royalist newspaper *Mercurius Aulicus* asked, 'we desire to know the reason why the rebels voted to live and die with the Earl of Essex since the Earl of Essex hath declared he will not live and die with them'.

Sensible Philip Skippon was not flustered by Essex's sudden departure. He called his officers together, and told them the news without ado: 'That which I propound to you is this; that we having the same courage as our Horse, and the same God to assist us, may make the same trial of our fortunes and endeavours to make our way through our enemy as they have done and account it better to die with faithfulness than to live dishonourably.'

An ugly rumour ran through the desperate army; that 'by a counsel of war they had resolved, to put every man to the sword, and give quarter to none ... In the first assault having taken about 30 they put them to the sword, who asking quarter they answered God damme, not a man of you shall have quarter.' Of course this 'increased resolution and courage in our men ... who resolved to set their lives at a high rate, beyond what the enemy durst bid ... After Major-General Skippon had made a short speech to the army, they threw up their Hats and gave a great shout, resolving unanimously to fight it out to the last man, and to ask no quarter, and upon the enemy's approach, they gave them many fiery salutations, which much amazed the enemy, for by their great and small shot, sent with resolved courage, there fell of the enemy at least six for one.'

Alas, this was propaganda. The officers were not enthusiastic about a last stand. They knew the temper of the men: exhausted, miserable, shocked by Essex's departure. So they decided to surrender. The terms were good, because the Royalists too were short of supplies.

The defeated army was worth more than one glance for the ever-observant Symonds:

> They all except here and there an officer (and seriously I saw not above three or four that looked like a gentleman) were strucken with such a dismal fear, that as soon as their colour of the regiment was passed, (for every ensign had a horse and rode him and was so suffered) the rest of soldiers in that regiment pressed all of a heap like sheep, though not so innocent. So dirty and so dejected as was rare to see. None of them, except some few of the officers, that did look any of us in the face. Our foot would flout at them and bid them remember Reading, Greenland House (where others that did not condition with them took away all prisoners) and many other places, and then would pull their swords ... This was a happy day for his Majesty and his whole army, that without loss of much blood this great army of rascals that so triumphed and vaunted over the poor inhabitants of Cornwall, as if they had been invincible, and as if the King had not been able to follow them, that 'tis conceived very few will get safe to London, for the country people when they have in all the march so much plundered and robbed, that they will have their pennyworths out of them.

Later Bulstrode Whitelocke thought that Skippon 'carried his loss with a very good grace'. After the surrender, Charles pressed Skippon to join him. Skippon replied 'that he was fully resolved of those principles to which he stood to be for God and his glory, in which by God's assistance he would live and die'.

A Parliamentarian newsbook told the Lostwithiel surrender story very differently: the Royalists had cheated, hindering provisions. The pamphlet also cites a further letter from a participant:

> Then came our misery. For when we had laid down our arms, and came to march through the enemy's army, we were in- humanely dealt with: abused, reviled, scorned, torn, kicked, pillaged, and many stripped of all they had, quite contrary to the articles; for presently, even in the presence of the king, and of their general, they took away our cloaks, coats, and hats, calumniating us by reproachful words, and threats, if we would not desert the Parliament and turn to the King; And after a day or two march, they stripped many of our officers to their shirts, taking away their boots, shoes, hose, &c.

The nameless Parliamentarian remembered Philip Skippon keeping his head:

> Notwithstanding Major-General Skippon stoutly urged the con- dition several times . . . nor was this the worst, for they hindered us in all our march from provisions, and quarter, on purpose to destroy us: and truly the mercy and providence of God was wonderful to us, that we perished not in our march.

The defeated army had to endure a daily routine of humiliation from their Royalist foes: 'This was on the Monday, Septemb[er] 2. They made us, after we had laid down our arms, to march through the King's Army, where the soldiers came upon us in most lecherous manner, moiling our men in the dirt, and kicking them, pulling all from them, doublets, hose and shirts.' And the army did not suffer alone; the train of women who had followed them were also tormented. A woman who had given birth only three days before was thrown into the river, 'and there had almost drowned her; the woman died within twelve hours after'. This cruelty influriated the soldier, who wrote grimly that 'as their swords have made women childless, so shall their mothers be childless among women'.

As the broken army was forced to march on, divisions already present became violent: 'Also upon Lostwithiel Bridge there met three brethren; two were on the kings party and one for Parliament; the two laid hold on the other brother's throat; one of them would have killed him, but the other was more merciful; yet they stripped him and beat him, and swore if they ever caught him again, they would kill him.'

But the main torment was being harried on their forced march: 'It is not five sheets of paper that will contain the stories and tragedies of this kind. They so courted and hurried our soldiers, that many fell down under their merciless hands', wrote the anonymous Parliament-man. 'We marched about seven miles from Lostwithiel on Monday, that night we lay in the fields near to a spring, which was some refreshing, having no other provision. This night they stole away divers of our horses; my horse was stolen that night, and I was forced to foot it to Southampton.'

The next night found the captive army of Essex lying in the fields after another long march, 'it being a bitter rainy night'. A third day followed with no food. The army had not been well provisioned even before its defeat and it was hungry. 'The soldiers lay this night in the field, but they lay near the town, where you might have heard the saddest moans, and direful complaints for bread, that ever ear heard. That night a penny loaf would have been sold for half a crown, and many thanks besides; I myself offered twelve pence for three ounces of bread, at last I got about three ounces for six pence; I saw some of the soldiers pay six pence for a piece of poor cheese, not weighing three ounces.' But there was no real relief in sight: 'On the Thursday, we marched from Okehampton, forth of London Road, that we might avoid the king's forces, which always lay in our way, on purpose to eat up our provisions from us.' They were prevented by the Royalists from entering Tiverton, so they marched two more hungry miles to a village, only to find that the enemy was once again ahead of them. 'Next day, some of our soldiers mistook their way, and went a mile from the army, many of which were most miserably wounded; some were killed within a little of Tiverton . . . Many that escaped, came to us all blood, and wounded.'

It was not Napoleon's retreat from Moscow, but it was not much fun, either, and some reports said that of the ten thousand or so men that entered the West under Essex, only a thousand saw their homes and families again. What kept the soldiers going was the simple courage of their commander: 'In all this trouble I observed Major-General Skippon in his carriage, but never did I see any man so patient, so humble, and so truly wise, and valiant, in all his actions.'

But the West was now almost a Parliamentarian-free zone. In 1644 Exeter was taken on 6 September and Dartmouth on 5 October, under Prince Maurice. Then on 27 October 1644 came the second Battle of Newbury, and Philip Skippon had his revenge. Steady as ever, he was probably not thinking of vengeance. Sir Edward Walker saw Skippon's men advancing against his position singing psalms at Second Newbury. An unnerving sight: John Gwynne was certainly unnerved. In his account of the battle he is anxious to explain his own fear, and the defeat:

> The second Newbury fight at Dolman's House [Shaw House] and my going a volunteer with my worthy friend Major Richard Lloyd, who was upon a commanded party, as worth to my Lord Caulfield his life that day, for just as he came out of the mill, stripped and wounded, a lusty soldier was fetching of a desperate blow with the butt-end of his musket, to make an end of him, which of a sudden I prevented, and made him prisoner on the top of the hill by the windmill. He was examined before the King, and declared he was Lord Caulfield's son, of Ireland, and a cornet in the Parliamentarian service; and Wemes was severely rebuked by his Majesty for deserting his service, and to come in arms against him.
>
> The day before the second Newbury fight, when the King had made an end of his march, and was encamped about three or four of the clock in the afternoon, within a mile and half (or thereabouts) of Newbury, news came that Banbury was besieged; whereupon his Majesty was pleased to command the Earl of Northampton to go with his brigade of fifteen hundred horse to the relief of it; when, in the meantime, the King, for his own part, I dare swear, knew not in the least, nor did not in the least suspect, that on the other side of the town were three armies, drawn up upon the most advantageous ground

they could pitch and choose, to fight him; had his Majesty received but the least hint of this, certainly he would not have so much weakened his impaired harassed army, after the defeating of two armies, soon one after another, and after the loss of so many men killed and wounded, as to part with fifteen hundred of his best horse, when the very next day he was perforce to fight the three armies which waylaid him, and withal was conducted into a trap, which the enemy had laid to do it. Howsoever it came about, for when the King marched with his army fair and orderly through the town, into the spacious Speerham Land there, he drew up, as near as possible could be, in the centre of his enemies; for right before him were posted Essex and Waller's Armies, drawn up in the enclosures, and in ambushes of hedges and ditches, and fronted with cannon to maintain that pass. On his right wing was Manchester's army of seven thousand, to wheel and fall upon his rear. On his left wing was the deep river, as considerable as another army, to enclose and hem him in amongst them as he did. His Majesty, being then pinfolded with walls of armed men, every way ready to execute their fury upon him when he did but stir, advanced, with the major part of his army, against the cannon's mouth, to get to charge the two armies, which were so strongly linked together against him, and at their encounter, there was very hot fiery dispute, that the thundering peals and volleys of great and small guns, were sufficient sign for Manchester and Cromwell to fall on the King's rear with their army of seven thousand, as they did very boldly, desperately fought it, and were most wonderfully paid off by fourteen hundred commanded men out of his Majesty's army, as before mentioned. All this while the King was laying on with all eagerness imaginable, to beat through the two armies, which were so wickedly stubborn and obstinate, that they rather made to a head and forced him back further and further into Speenham lands, that both the enemy's armies were in the open field in close fight with the King and his army, and put them so hard to it, that his Majesty was engaged in his royal person. General Ruthven, wounded fighting by his side, and several persons of quality killed by them. This height of extremity the King was in, did so exasperate the great spirit of his approved brave cavaliers, that they fell on with

invincible courage, and pothered them back into their enclosures of hedges and ditches. Then the night drew on, and parted
us with a seeming joint consent on both sides, for we marched
away with our army all night by them, and they did not in the
least disturb us, nor we gave them no occasion in the least for
it; and so we came off to admiration. The next morning we
marched for Oxford, not without some skirmishing in the rear.

Gwynne's description is hopelessly inexact, but he fretted over this
battle and wrote about it several times: where had it all gone wrong?
He wasn't sure any more, but he hoped to show the world that it was
not the king's fault. The problem was that Gwynne didn't have the
kind of mind that remembered the details likely to convince others of
his own point of view.

The second Newbury fight, we drew up upon the same ground
which the enemy fought us upon the first battle. After our long
march from Cornwall, and great want of intelligence, we were
exposed unavoidably to fight three fresh armies, which waylaid
the King to oppose his march, whereupon a most remarkable
piece of service was done by the great contrivance of Major-
General Lord Astley . . . these fourteen hundred thus posted,
beat off twice Manchester's army of seven thousand horse and
foot; and at their third and last onset, beat them clear out of
the field, and stripped abundance of them. Some few hours
after, my Lord Astley marched away with us by moonshine, and
of necessity, through a narrow filthy pass of puddle and mire,
just by the hedge-side that parted us and the two armies, Essex's
and Waller's, who were as quiet as if they had taken the same
opportunity of drawing off too . . . the King commanded fifteen
hundred prime horse to the relief of Banbury, when it was too
late to call them back to our assistance, and for us to avoid
fighting, being so strangely surprised as we were: but, I presume,
that a forced putt [thrust] was never better managed, nor came
off with more honour, as to beat one army away, the other two
out of the way, and so cleared our way, lodged our artillery at
Donnington Castle, and marched for Oxford.

Gwynne was not thinking about strategy or tactics, but honour. Yards
more self-justification follows. We can also see the traces of many a
post-war conversation among old soldiers:

So when the King could have blocked up all the lane's end they were to march through with his artillery, face them with his army, and send such conditions as his Majesty should think expedient, which must needs be acceptable, considering his abundant goodness, and their own forlorn desperate condition at that present; they let them go by consent after their foot to recruit, which they did with so much haste and great perform- ance, that before the king, with his army, could march from Cornwall, within little more than a mile of Newbury, the enemy's armies, all three were come on the other side of the town, and there stayed, lurking in obscurity, till the King marched into their mouths, for he drew up within their arms of pikes and muskets, that he could not stir neither front, flank, or rear, but upon their fire; and had it not been for his great fighting, and more for the great providence that attended him in that imminent danger, he had not come off so well as he did.

XX

The Nation's Nightmares

After Second Newbury, the Royalists felt triumphant. They had managed to hold off a larger army on ground where they had lost many men the year before. On top of the Western campaign, the signs looked bright. Returning to Oxford for a winter pause in battles, the king had to believe in his success. But the victories had made little real difference to his position. While Parliament, immersed in gloom, argued over how the war could be prosecuted, some stories were ending hard and cold. Archbishop Laud was in the Tower, an old man, his Church now destroyed, other bishops impeached. He dreamed he had been released, but if this were so, his dreaming self knew he had nowhere to go; not back to Lambeth, but perhaps to a place of his own. He had been arrested in December 1640. Finally, in March 1644, he was brought to trial at the bar of the House of Lords. Pym had tried earlier to prove that he had discussed reconciliation with Rome, but no one had ever heard him do so. It was part of Laud's tragedy that by the time he was tried he was no longer part of the mainstream, his trial no longer a big event, but a sideshow, one death among thousands.

But Laud put up a gallant show. The government had a difficult time finding evidence against him; not surprising since most of the charges were of Catholic conspiracies and Laud had actually disliked the Catholic Church as much as anyone. He was tried under the notion of treason that he had himself used against Prynne, that treason included the creation of disunity in the kingdom. This involved a series of minor charges which together amounted to treason. This was a new and controversial legal hypothesis – cumulative treason. Laud's was made up of acts such as denying that the pope was the Whore of Babylon, and believing in the Real Presence in Holy Communion. Laud's defenders pointed to the lack of logic in 'cumulative treason': 'I crave your mercy, Master Sergeant,' said John Herne, 'for I never understood before this time that two hundred couple of black rabbits would make a black horse.' Still, everyone knew the outcome. William Lilly consulted the stars to see which day the old man would die. And after some hesitation, Commons and Lords passed the attainder.

Laud produced a pardon from the king. The Commons dismissed it, and wanted to hang, draw and quarter Laud, like a papist. But after repeated petitions, they agreed to have him beheaded on Tower Hill, like Strafford. 'I most willingly leave this world,' Laud wrote, 'being very weary at my very heart of the vanities of it, and my own sins many and great, and of the grievous destruction of the Church of Christ almost in all parts of Christendom, and particularly in this kingdom.'

But at least it boosted London's morale to see him die. It was a cold day, and the streets were thick with snow, but tens of thousands were there on 10 January 1645 to see him suffer. No one really listened to the old man rambling on about Charles as a true Protestant. One man asked for Laud's hat, pointing out that he couldn't take it with him. And Sir John Clotworthy, the indefatigable Ulsterman and destroyer of Rubens's *Crucifixion*, was on hand to taunt Laud, to tear the old man's spirit as he had torn paintings and smashed glass; he asked Laud what the most comforting words were for a dying man. And Laud replied *Cupito dissolve et esse cum Christo* (I long to dissolve and be with Christ). Clotworthy kept up his heckling. Others were crouched under the scaffold; Laud pointed out that they would get soaked in blood. Finally he laid his head on the block, and at just after twelve the headsman's axe swept down.

The next day Laud was buried at All Hallows, Barking by the Tower. Nehemiah Wallington wrote joyfully that 'his little grace the Bishop of Canterbury that great enemy of England, his head was cut off'. Laud's ghost was sighted in London. Eventually he was to be reburied at St John's College, Oxford.

His was not the only ominous death in London. On 22 October

1644, a man known as The King of the Beggars had been found dead 'against Whitehall'. He was a noted malignant, that is a Royalist, and the day before his death had been defying a fast day with a long drinking party. 'Let all drunkards and mockers that jeer at our fasting and make it their sport consider well of it', said Nehemiah Wallington, drawing a moral to illustrate God's providence. Charles might have noticed the omen too. London was willing to contemplate acts that had once been inconceivable.

By 1645, the men of both armies had been under nearly unbearable strain. They had been hungry and they had been cold; they had been under fire and they had been on the march for days. Some soldiers developed anxieties that were less rational than dread of Royalist cannon or sniper fire, less rational, even, than the dread of popery. For the anxious soldier, the worst moments were not the battles, but the days, sometimes weeks, before and after, when small bands would roam through hostile country, searching for food and plunder, likely to chance upon the enemy at any moment. They were isolated and lost in hostile lands. Perhaps those most prone to carry out such expeditions were the godly, who saw themselves as required not only to defeat armies, but to cleanse and renew the entire country.

For some of the civilians of the Eastern Association, a new nightmare was beginning. They had already been levied and taxed. If they were not godly enough they had been assailed, their property stolen and their churches systematically and methodically despoiled. If godly, they had felt engulfed by the forces of darkness, with deeper darknesses menacing: Newcastle's popish army, the queen and her arms. Now the terrors aroused by the war itself, and its suspension of normal central government, created an opportunity for a new kind of ideological strife. For the godly, it was both an extension and expression of the war they were already fighting; were they not wrestling already against princedoms, against the rulers of the darkness of this world? But now they saw that their enemies were all around them, and believed they were witches, women – and a few men – who were able supernaturally to channel the powers of the Devil to affect and afflict other people.

Both sides felt concerned about witchcraft as a weapon of war and rebellion. Many commentators interpreted the proliferation of witch-trials as a sign of increasing disorder. On the Royalist side, the text 'rebellion is as the sin of witchcraft' (1 Samuel 15: 23) was frequently quoted, while the Royalist newspaper *Mercurius Aulicus* observed that witchcraft is 'an usual attendant on former rebellions'. James Howell, while wearing his Royalist hat, remarked:

> we have also multitudes of *witches* among us, for in Essex and Suffolk there were above two hundred indicted within these two years, and above the one half of them executed. More, I may well say, than ever this Island bred since the Creation, I speak it with horror. God guard us from the Devil, for I think he was never so busy upon any part of the Earth that was enlightened with the beams of Christianity; nor do I wonder at it, for there's never a Cross left to fright him away.

Irritated by this kind of remark, *The Parliamentary Journal* of July 1645 reported that 'it is the ordinary mirth of the malignants of this city to discourse of the association of witches in the associated counties, but by this they shall understand the truth of the old proverb, which is that where God hath his church, the Devil hath his Chapel'. More ambiguously, a pamphlet entitled *Signs and Wonders from Heaven* bundles witches together with monsters, thunderstorms, wars, and other signs to argue that

> the Lord decreed a separation between the King and his Parliament before the wars began in England for the sins of the whole nation. That the Lord is angry with us every one; for our sin, doth appear in this ... have not a crew of wicked Witches, together with the Devil's assistance done many mischiefs in Norfolk, Suffolk, Essex, and other parts of our Kingdom, whereof some were executed at Chelmsford in Essex last to the number of fourteen, and many more imprisoned to this day, and by the voice of the people there are some in Stepney Parish now in question about witchcraft.

Stepney was Anna Trapnel's very godly parish, and it's barely possible that the pamphlet refers to her and to some of her fellow-sectarians; certainly she was to be formally accused of witchcraft in 1654, in Cornwall. But these views were not inevitable. For others it was superstitious belief in witches, and consequent witch-prosecutions, which represented the intellectual and social disorder of the Civil War years.

This was especially true in reports of witch-prosecutions in Scotland, which were generally hostile to the routine Scottish use of torture and contrasted this with the less tyrannical rule of England. Thomas Ady located belief in witchcraft in an ungodly reliance on the kind of superstition and ritual that Parliament was seeking to reform away. *The Moderate Intelligencer*, also a Parliamentarian journal, questioned Hopkins's activities in East Anglia, scornfully enquiring 'whence is it that the Devils should choose to be conversant with silly women that know not their right hands from their left, is the great wonder . . . They will meddle with none but poor old women, as appears by what we received this day from Bury.'

Both sides also used the figure of the witch as a propaganda weapon, taking up a series of prominent persons and trying to build up an association between those figures and witchcraft. Two examples, one from each side, are Oliver Cromwell and Prince Rupert. The imagery surrounding Rupert was far more lurid than that surrounding Cromwell. For instance, *Signs and Wonders From Heaven* reports that the arrest of some Norfolk witches was likely to impede Royalist fortunes. The witches, it seems, had been working for Rupert: 'It is likewise certified by many of good quality and worth that at the last Assizes in Norfolk there were 40 witches arraigned for their lives, and 20 executed : and that they have done very much harm in that country, and have prophesied of the downfall of the King and his army, and that Prince Robert [Rupert] shall be no longer shot-free: with many strange and unheard-of things that shall come to pass.'

James More of Halesworth, admitting making a covenant with the Devil, said he returned his imp to his sister Mary Everard, 'to send with others to Prince Rupert'. There were a number of more-or-less satirical portrayals of Prince Rupert's dog, Boy, eventually shot and killed at Marston Moor, as a familiar. 'Certainly he is some Lapland Lady', said one account which reported on but also parodied belief in Rupert's occult powers, 'who by nature was once a handsome white woman, and now by art is become a handsome white Dog, and hath vowed to follow the Prince to preserve him from mischief.' Among his other gifts, Boy can find hidden treasure (the Oxford plate, which could not be found before). Like a demon, the dog is proof against attack: 'once I gave him a very hearty stroke, with a confiding Dagger, but it slid off his skin as if it had been Armour of proof anointed over with Quicksilver', and he also catches bullets aimed at Rupert in his mouth. 'He prophesies as well as my lady Davis, or Mother Shipton', concludes the pamphlet ambiguously; plainly, Lady Eleanor Davies was not expected to feel complimented by the remark. The pamphlet tries to say that only the ignorant peasant would believe such tales, but it also implies that there are plenty of ignorant peasants about.

Cromwell too was likened to a witch, often metaphorically rather than literally. When Denzil Holles described Cromwell as a witch working to overthrow the realm, he was using witchcraft as a metaphor for a secret plot: 'your Sabbaths, when you have laid by your assumed shapes, with which you have cozened the world, and resumed your own; imparting to each other and both of you to your fellow-witches'. This notion of the witch as secret agent appeared in the Hopkins trials and elsewhere, taken entirely literally. Paranoia about double agents, secret agents, code and double meanings could easily shade into anxiety about witchcraft, as it had in the last decade or so of Elizabeth's reign. Thomas Ady told of a Suffolk minister who affirmed that one of the 'poor women that was hanged as a witch at Bury assizes in the year 1645 did send her imp into the Army to kill the Parliamentary soldiers and another sent her imps into the army to kill the king's soldiers'. The imps could work secretly, explaining losses on both sides. There is an eighteenth-century historiographical tradition that Cromwell had made a pact with the Devil before the Battle of Worcester, to run for seven years.

The result of all these pressures was numerous cases and reports of witchcraft as well as debates about its nature, existence and remedies. Many places experienced a peak of prosecutions in the 1640s and 1650s, and others saw a number of trials. In the summer of 1645, *The Parliaments Post* reported that 'There is an infection in wickedness; and the spirit of the Cavaliers because it could not prevail with our men, hath met with some of our women, and it hath turned them into Witches'. This statement encapsulates the relations between Civil War witch-trials and the war itself.

An egregious case of violence and aggression by soldiers attacking a woman they thought was a witch comes from Warminster. Anne

Warberton was attacked by a group of soldiers there, as she described:

> upon the feast day of the annunciation of the Blessed Virgin Mary last past [25 March 1644] was two years sithence one George Long of Warminster came to the house of your petitioner and two soldiers in arms with him and the said Long and one of the soldiers required the petitioner to open her door who answered she would not unless he was an officer. Then the said Long said he was as good as any officer whatsoever and immediately by force broke down a window leaf which fell into the house upon a pail of water whereby both window leaf and pail of water fell upon your petitioner and her child which did so bruise the child that it fell sick and shortly after died. Yet not being contented they also broke up the door and entered the house by force and then the said Long fell to biting, pinching, and scratching of your petitioner saying and swearing in most execrable and ignominious manner she was a witch and therefore he would have her blood which he drawed from her in great abundance.

Doughty Anne survived the attack to complain about her assailants in court.

In Wiltshire the Civil War was especially grim: largely Parliamentarian during the war's opening months, it was soon garrisoned by several Royalist groups, and the north-east came under the control of Royalist Oxfordshire. During 1643–4 most of the county fell to the king, and the Parliamentarians were isolated in scattered outposts to the north-west. Wiltshire was retaken by Parliament in 1645. This may have been the occasion for many minor acts of violence, as was the case elsewhere: the Civil War often allowed and enabled a range of behaviour ordinarily open to censure; like other wars, it both placed intolerable strain on male identity and allowed it full and destructive rein.

It was the areas on the fringes, or where the impact of conflict was less overwhelming, that outbursts of witch persecution occurred. That said, there was no special reason why a witchcraze of vast proportions should have started in Essex rather than in Wiltshire or Hertfordshire. What started it, enabled it, facilitated it at every turn, was the presence of a zealous witch-finder, a necessary though not a sufficient cause for the entire episode. The depositions collected from plaintiffs very closely resemble those from other trials, containing the usual popular pre-occupations with food preparation, the household economy, family tensions, and the stresses and strains imposed by the experiences of pregnancy, childbirth and maternity. Once it did start, however, the Witch-finder's own fantasies and the local depositions he collected were shaped and tinted by the particularities of the locale, the historical moment, the man himself.

Witches. The East was full of them. But one man planned to change all that, to remove the Devil's emissaries from God's own lands. His name was Matthew Hopkins, and he was able to use the Civil War to bring about England's worst-ever witchcraft persecution. It began in a small, local way. The first to be investigated was a one-legged, aged woman called Elizabeth Clarke, who lived in Matthew Hopkins's own village of Manningtree. On 25 March 1645 she confessed to keeping familiars. Familiars were servant-demon-pets; Satan sent them to witches in exchange for their souls. They could kill, cause illness, destroy animals or food supplies. The witch suckled them at her witchmark. So all a witch-finder had to do was to keep the witch in an enclosed room, under guard. Sooner or later her familiars would arrive, and then her guilt would be proved. Of course, what actually happened was that the woman in question was deprived of sleep, which inclined her to confess.

Using this method, Hopkins had soon secured thirty-six witches; about half of them were executed at Chelmsford in July 1645. By then, the hunt had spread – to Suffolk, Norfolk, Huntingdonshire, Cambridgeshire, Northamptonshire and Bedfordshire. The whole East burned with Hopkins's terrible light as witch-hunts sprang up every-where. We don't know exactly how many died; estimates vary from one hundred to three times that number. Hopkins's assistant John Stearne guessed two hundred. But regardless of numbers, everyone in the area was affected, or rather afflicted – by fear of witches, and by fear of being thought a witch. It began quickly, and gathered momentum. On 18 July 1645, fifteen women investigated by Hopkins were facing the gallows in Chelmsford. Elizabeth Clarke had to be helped up the scaf-fold because of her missing leg. Others from Manningtree were hanged a fortnight later, on 1 August. Many had already died in gaol, of disease and hunger – and this was not the end of it.

Numbers like this give us little sense of what it was like to be investigated by Hopkins or Stearne. What was distinctive about the Hopkins–Stearne cases was that both men asked more than the usual quota of questions about pacts with Satan. Interrogations often took the form of Hopkins asking some very leading questions, while the accused simply said 'yes'. As a result, the Hopkins cases are apt to be dully similar. The Devil appears, usually in the likeness of an animal or a black man, and requires soul. Sometimes he offers her wealth in exchange. Sometimes he demands that she lie with him. Then the Devil sends imps or familiars to do her bidding, which she has to suckle; these took the form of small animals, beetles and mice and spiders.

More distinctive is the amount of evidence Hopkins was able to amass from local people who disliked or feared the accused. What Hopkins did was to turn the interrogation of witches from a merely reactive affair to something proactive. Normally, villagers or towns-people might approach a local Justice of the Peace with a complaint about a neighbour. The JP could then choose to investigate by question-ing others in the area, or could tell the complainants to go home and stop bothering him with superstitions. The latter response was the more usual one in the 1630s. However, Hopkins actively sought out complainants by riding up and down East Anglia asking people if there were any witches in the locale and encouraging complainants to approach their own officials. He found fertile ground in the seething villages of the Association Counties. Fearful of the political and military menaces on all sides, and harbouring grudges against neighbours that went back years or even decades, many were willing and eager to testify. Religious divisions were a factor, where the godly were menaced both by Catholics and also by the new radical sects – Seekers, Anabapists and Familists – who were becoming a threat, too, in the eyes of the Commons in London. With Hopkins's encouragement, witch-hunting could also be old-fashioned papist-hunting under a newer and more fashionable name. Branches of the Rivers family, who had been savagely attacked in 1642, were located in and around the witch-hunting centre of St Osyth, while in nearby Hintlesham four witches with connections with the pro-Catholic Timperley family found themselves under interrogation. Similarly, in the Suffolk village of Wickham Skeith a woman who was 'a runner-after of the new sects' was accused. A minister named John Lowes who had been hostile to local godly people was accused; he was, said his parishioners, a 'reading parson', a Laudian, and therefore a malignant. He was duly hanged on 27 August 1645. But many of those rounded up came from families with a reputation for witchcraft, sometimes going back several generations. And the trials, imprisonments and hangings were an entertainment in themselves; the gaol in Ipswich was swamped with sightseers eager to encounter the witches.

In this sense, Matthew Hopkins was by the standards of his own times not a monster, but a product of his society. We know little of Hopkins's life before he dragged himself to prominence. He was a very minor gentleman, even more marginal to the gentry than Cromwell. He was born around 1619–22, and so was in his early to mid-twenties at the beginning of his witch-hunting activities. His mother, Marie Hopkins, was possibly a Huguenot refugee, and his father was the vicar of Great Wenham. Hopkins Senior uses godly language in his extant will: 'I shall be received to Mercy only through the Righteousness & Merits of the Lord Jesus Christ my Saviour.' His later associate John Stearne says of Hopkins that 'he was the son of a godly minister', and also names him as a Presbyterian 'and therefore without doubt within the covenant'. We also know little of his career before the witch persecutions. A manuscript now lost allegedly said Hopkins was 'a lawyer of but little note'. Since there is no record of him at the Inns of Court, or in other court records, he may have worked as a legal clerk, possibly for a ship-owner in Mistley. Suffolk Record Office contains a conveyance of a tenement in Bramford, only just outside Ipswich, dated 1641, bearing Hopkins's signature as a witness, which may imply a role as a lawyer's clerk.

Hopkins allegedly told Lady Jane Whorwood that he had 'studied maritime law in Amsterdam'. It is generally agreed that he did spend some time in the Netherlands, possibly with his Huguenot connections, but some suggest that this may mean the Essex village of Little Holland. We also know that Hopkins knew that other great self-fashioner of the Civil War years, William Lilly. There was iconoclasm in the areas of

Essex where Hopkins began his career: at St Mary's Church, Lawford, near Manningtree, the carved heads of the saints were hacked off during the 1640s. This may have provided a kind of mental model for Hopkins. Evil *could* be removed by determined destruction. It may not be a coincidence that Hopkins lived in the Stour Valley, scene of the violent demonstrations against 'papists' that marked the beginning of the war, or that his best-known victim was John Lowes, the vicar of Brandeston, thought by his parishioners to have papist leanings.

John Stearne was Hopkins's principal associate. He was proper gentry; Stearne was still paying hearth tax in Manningtree in 1666, despite apparently moving to Lawshall in 1648, which means he had two houses. In his writings, Stearne was heavily influenced by William Perkins's godly and influential *Discourse of the Damned Art of Witchcraft*, 1608, but he also borrowed at length from Richard Bernard, *A Guide to Grand Jurymen*, 1627; these may have been among Hopkins's intellectual antecedents too, but there is little trace of their influence in his writings. Hopkins drew more lavishly on the kind of thinking that had animated the Scottish witch-hunters since the sixteenth century: that witches were a sign of the Devil's activities in the world, and must be stamped out firmly. The English tradition of jurisprudence had always tended to see witches as sad and deluded, but in Scotland they were a genuine menace. The same channels that brought Scottish Presbyterianism into contact with the godly English might have carried Scottish witch-beliefs south as well, particularly since the Manningtree area was in constant contact with the north via its port. And in England too, attitudes to witchcraft hardened during periods of national crisis. The peak period for hangings for witchcraft had been the decade immediately following the Armada terror. If young John Pym fastened his fears to papists, others spied different kinds of diabolism at work in the kingdom. Now that another and far worse national crisis had ensued, those fears too were to be revived.

Hopkins lived in a vivid, narrow, frightened nightmare of a world where witches walked by night. It was said that Hopkins 'as a child', 'took affright at an apparition of the Devil, which he saw in the night'. As the child of a godly vicar, whose will insists firmly on salvation through faith alone, Hopkins was part of a godly discourse that could terrify through its vehement insistence on the gap between election and damnation. Although all his biographers have seen Hopkins as marked by this lineage, Hopkins himself invented alternative ancestries for himself, possibly grounded in family legend, but betokening a wish to make something of himself. He told William Lilly that he came from a line of schoolmasters in Suffolk, 'who had composed for the psalms of King David'. There was a John Hopkins, an English hymn-writer, a different godly father, perhaps, from his own. One less terrifying, more obviously a maker himself. By contrast, Hopkins told Lady Jane Whorwood that he was really named Hopequins and was the grandson of an English Catholic diplomat, Richard Hopequins. Lady Jane was a Royalist, so this may have been designed to create an identity acceptable to her, as well as to Hopkins. Being a witch-finder, with its money-making possibilities, was another way for Hopkins to reinvent himself.

Hopkins's fantasies of witches were part of his ruthless self-fashioning, a process which enabled him to flee from his family, to prove himself by making a place among the better sort, and also by piling up at least some personal wealth. This element of Hopkins's self-creation as Witch-Finder General is evident in his own account of his first encounter with witches in his self-defence. This account explains how he became involved in the process of discovery:

> The Discoverer [Hopkins] never travelled far for it, but in March 1644, he had some seven or eight of that horrible sect of witches living in the town where he lived, a town in Essex called Manningtree, with divers other adjacent witches of other towns, who every six weeks in the night (being always on the Friday night) had their meeting close by his house, and had their several solemn sacrifices there offered to the Devil, one of which this discoverer heard speaking to her Imps one night, and bid them go to another Witch, who was thereupon apprehended, and searched by women who had for many years known the Devil's marks, and found to have three teats about her, which honest women have not: so upon command from the Justice, they were to keep her from sleep two or three nights, expecting in that time to see her familiars, which the fourth night she called in by their several names, and told them what shapes a quarter of an hour before they came in, there being ten of us in the roome.

The people of East Anglian towns and villages called Hopkins in as a consultant, just as in less godly days or among less godly company they might have called in the local cunning man to finger the witch. Since for the godly a cunning person was culpable as a malicious witch, Hopkins opened himself to identification as supernaturally gifted when exposing such gifts in others. This interpretation may have occurred to no one but him, since there is no evidence for the tradition that he was himself swum as a witch and convicted (reported in Samuel Butler's satirical poem *Hudibras*), but the first question in *The Discovery of Witches* is a refutation of the idea that he must himself be 'the greatest Witch, Sorcerer and Wizard himself, else he could not do it'. Hopkins was of course aiming at a far more godly kind of identity, perhaps even at an *imitatio Christi*. Perhaps in a spirit of competitive envy, John Gaule wrote that 'country People talk already and that more frequently, more affectedly, of the infallible and wonderful power of the witch-finders, then they do of God, or Christ, or the Gospel preached'. Hopkins had certainly transcended his family.

Manningtree, where Hopkins lived and where his career began, was a curious place in the mid-seventeenth century because it was both a centre of activity and geographically marginal. It was a port and shipbuilding dockyard – Manningtree sent ships against the Armada. But it was peripheral because the Tendring Hundred is literally on the edge of Essex, and Manningtree and Mistley were themselves surrounded by the great and misty sea-marshes. The marshes and the Stour River were sites of a trade boom, but also of illegal activities: there was extensive smuggling up the Stour River, and over the marshes. The marshes and the river created opportunities for secret enterprises, for wealth creation neither sanctioned nor scrutinized by the authorities.

But these lawless terrains were stained in imagination by dread. Folktales from the East Anglian area prior to the drainage of fens and marshes stress the division between arable land and marsh. Regarded as unhealthy because of the miasmas associated with them, the marshes are given over to the supernatural activities of boggarts and others, including hags and other witches. The marshes were outside the law of the Church as well as state, and in the legends of the locale they are law-less, silent, pervasively misty. It was against this backward, gloomy background that the towns and their inhabitants defined themselves, just as the godly defined themselves against backward, hazy superstition.

This in turn was further exacerbated by fear of another kind of engulfment. Essex was one of the areas which quickly declared for Parliament, to the delight of its godly inhabitants. But throughout 1645–6, the Royalist army was still trying to break out into East Anglia and the whole territory was under threat of turning into a battlefield. Although Hopkins's activities began before the real military crisis, godly folk in Essex had heard of events in other counties, and knew (or feared) what might occur. For John Stearne, the war against witches was another way of fighting the Civil War: 'And so going ever well-armed against these rulers of darkness, devils and evil spirits, furnished with the heavenly furniture and spirituall weapons, of which the Apostle speaketh, Eph. 6.14.18, and being thus qualified, and armed, to trust in God only, who will keep thee under the shadow of his wings, Psal. 91.' What with one thing and another, the psychic pressures on a man like Hopkins, perhaps already warped by a hard Presbyterian father, reached unbearable levels in the mid-1640s, with the result that he produced a spate of fantasies to alleviate them.

Modern readers sometimes think Hopkins was motivated by simple lust. But his choice of victims suggests otherwise. He chose old women, not beautiful girls. He did strip his victims, but not erotically. For him, horror seems to have swallowed eroticism. It was to avoid the erotic and its entanglement, its power to implicate, that he took pleasure from seeing the elderly witch naked and hearing her disclose her sexual relations with the Devil. Far from seeking otherwise forbidden pleasures, Hopkins seems to have sought to distance himself from the eroticized female body by conjuring it up in a repulsively aged form. Nor did they desire him, as Stearne mischievously reports: 'Then said Mr Hopkin, in what manner and likeness came he to you? she said, like a tall, proper, blackhaired gentleman, a properer man then you self, and being asked which she had rather lie withal, she said the Devil.' In this case, the witch used her sharp tongue to get her own back, but such levity was probably fatal to her.

Hopkins also thought of himself as a kind of scientist, trying to prove the existence of witches and find forensic tests to check on whether they were real. He stripped women to search for the witchmark, supposedly the place where their familiars suckled them. But he also thought he was a kind of clergyman, helping to save these women's souls. Godly confession and testimony, wrung from sinners by violent speaking and questioning, were part of ordinary Protestant life. Stearne explains that watching is 'not to use violence, or extremity to force them to confess, but only the keeping is, first, to see whether any of their spirits, or familiars come to or near them', and 'that Godly Divines and others might discourse with them, and idle persons be kept from them, for if any of their society come to them . . . they will never confess'. He tells the story of a group of witches who all kept together in a barn and made a pact not to confess, except one who made the pact known. 'But if honest godly people discourse with them, laying the heinousness of their sins to them, and in what condition they are in without Repentance, and telling them the subtleties of the Devil, and the mercies of god, these ways will bring them to Confession without extremity, it will make them break into Confession hoping for mercy.'

Heroism is also uppermost in Hopkins's understanding of his role as interrogator. Godly preachers and congregations did not see interrogation and confession in quite the secular light in which they appear to us. Rather than forcing an unwilling admission from a suspect in violation of their personal integrity and civil liberties, he was actually heroically venturing into hell itself to help her, despite the menaces that surrounded him: '29 were condemned at once, 4 brought 25 miles to be hanged, where this Discoverer lives, for sending the Devil like a Bear to kill him in his garden, so by seeing diverse of the mens [sic] Papps, and trying ways with hundreds of them, he gained this experience, and for aught he knows any man else may find them as well as he and his company, if they had the same skill and experience.'

Finally, Hopkins may have been motivated by money. He made as much as £23 from Stowmarket and £15 from King's Lynn, with promises for more after the next sessions. His inn bill was also paid in Stowmarket. But he got only £6 in Aldeburgh – £2 from each visit, three visits – suggesting that the rate was decidedly variable. Hopkins himself denies that he made much money. What seems most likely is that both Hopkins and his victims were caught in the swirling emotions of the time. Hopkins was by no means alone in seeing witches everywhere. In fact, his 'discoveries' impressed many as a sign of the times.

There is a comforting historiographical tradition that Hopkins was hanged as a witch, but in fact – like Pym – he fell ill early, and died of consumption: 'he died peaceably at Manningtree, after a long sickness of a Consumption, as many of his generation had done before him, without any trouble of conscience for what he had done, as was falsely reported of him'. He was buried on 12 August 1647 at Mistley.

Hopkins and his reign of terror were products of the war. Sometimes, most heartrendingly, 'the Devil' spoke to witches in the voice of a dead husband or, worse, in the voice of a dead child. Such voices might be identified as a Devil's only later, under interrogation. In this way, what women had already lost was turned against them. Their dead family members, their poverty, their vanished youth and prettiness – these losses might have made them seem like walking reminders of the ache of war, like the embodiments of its pain. Perhaps those already half-mad with Calvinism, anti-popery and violence could not bear to look upon their own griefs, and believed that exterminating the symbol would relieve the feeling. As with iconoclasm, the idea spread, and the painful process of cleansing went on, into Kent, into the north, so that many areas had their own witchcrazes, a series of brutal wars on a different front.

XXI

Th' Easy Earth That Covers Her:
The Children's Tales

In 1643 the Royalists were besieging Wardour Castle in Wiltshire. The defending Parliamentarians were surprised when a twelve-year-old boy arrived at the gate. Like Sir Gareth in Arthurian legend, the youth begged for the lowliest employment, turning the spit. Edward Ludlow, who had probably read the same romances, agreed. But almost at once mysterious ill-luck began to dog the garrison. A gun exploded as it was being fired, and the boy had been seen near it. The guards on duty became suspicious, and the boy was interrogated; the soldiers, angry and frightened, threatened to hang him. He remained silent, so they tied a piece of match around his neck and began to hoist him on a halberd. He confessed at once that he had been ordered to assess the strength of the garrison, and then to poison the water supply (and, worse, the beer), blow up any gunpowder, and destroy any ordnance. He had been offered the lavish wages of half a crown for all this diligent sabotage. They let him go.

The war bore hard on children. They lost their fathers and brothers. Some lost both parents to disease. Thousands more lost their homes and were forced onto the teeming roads, while still others were forced into temporary exile, like the young Ann Harrison (later Fanshawe), and the royal children. But there were opportunities for fun, too; they were not always victims. Schools were closed, as their schoolmasters joined the opposing armies. In Southampton, and in Plymouth, the boys formed themselves into rival gangs, the Roundheads and the Cavaliers, and staged mock battles; one such gang inadvertently broke up a church service by shouting 'Arms!' The men, nervous, rushed outside, to find that the alarm was just part of a game. Boys will be boys, and it was sport in Exeter, as in Oxford, to see the prisoners brought in, and to vent some rage and fear by throwing dirt at them and shouting abuse. In both cities, boys and girls worked alongside parents on the town defences. It was the same in London, as Samuel Pepys recalled: 'I was a great roundhead when I was a boy', he boasted.

If Pepys's father had been in Essex's army, Pepys himself might have followed it in the baggage-train, as many boys did. They were there to be with fathers, or occasionally brothers, but they were useful too: they could be 'horseboys', or act as servants. With very little encouragement, they could join in the fighting. During the siege of Plymouth, a Parliamentarian remarked that many of the defenders were 'poor little boys', boys from London.

To console ourselves against the thought that people who lost a quarter of their children felt about it much as we would if it happened to us, historians have sometimes argued that the high death rate somehow led people to mind the deaths of their children less than modern parents do. Ann Fanshawe's daughter died of smallpox at the age of nine. Ann wrote that she and her husband 'both wished to have gone into the grave with her'. Ann's journeys meant that she buried children in Lisbon, Madrid, Paris, and in Oxford, Yorkshire, Hertfordshire and Kent.

Mary Verney was forced to leave her husband, Ralph, in France, and to travel alone to London to try to persuade the Parliamentary committee for compounding to let the family keep something from its once-great estates, now sequestered. She was pregnant, and she may have hoped that this would help to persuade them. But it meant that she was without Ralph and her other children during the long, stressful business of lying-in, and she wrote that 'to lie without thee is a greater affliction than I fear I shall be able to bear'.

Mary worried about all her children, especially Jack, now seven, whom we have already met; his rickety legs were a health concern, and Mary blamed his wartime carers for his condition. But she also defended him lovingly and stoutly against any who might criticize him. 'Jack is a very gallant boy ... but truly if he stay there a little longer he will be utterly spoiled . . . he hath no fault in him beside his legs, for though 'tis mine own I must needs say he is an extremely witty child.' They agreed that Jack should go to France with her in 1647. Meanwhile, Ralph, her baby son, born in June 1647, was on his way to Claydon, and his mother worried about him too. 'I wish myself heartily there too', she wrote. 'I pray speak to Mrs Allcock to let the nurse have a Cradle; one of the worst will serve her turn, and a hard pillow.' This was probably to make sure the nurse didn't go to sleep and lie on Ralph, something every mother dreaded. Ralph was not very healthy, but he did recover at Claydon, and Mary searched desperately for a new wetnurse. All she could find was 'Raph Rodes Wife, and I fear they are but poor and she looks like a slattern, but she sayeth if she takes the child she will have a mighty care of it, and truly she has two as fine children of her own as ever I saw'. The nurse was paid four shillings a week, and two loads of vital, scarce wood. Nurses, Mary noted, were getting more expensive. 'He thrives well,' she wrote, 'and is a lovely baby.' At three months she wrote, 'I mean to coat him this week.' The nurse insisted on it. So Mary felt happy about leaving Jack and Ralph at Claydon and going back to London: 'I am so weary that 'tis a pain to me to hold the pen, but yet I cannot conclude, until I have chid thee that thou dost never give me an account how thyself and boy and girl have your healths, and yet I have entreated it of ye before now; 'tis a duty I weekly perform to thee.' She went on worrying about the other children in France: 'I cannot now express to thee how sad a heart I have to think how long 'twill be before I come to thee.' She sent them clothes, but in the wrong sizes; children grow so fast. Edmund, called Mun, was eleven years old. 'Mun's grey stockings', Ralph complained, 'are about a handful too short and almost an inch too little, so I have laid them up for Jack.' She sent Ralph reams of advice, orders even: no more dancing lessons, for instance, since '2 or 3 months in the year is enough to learn that'. 'Mun', she added, 'must learn to play the guitar and sing.' She would like Peg to learn the lute, too, but the main thing was to correct her deportment: 'I am sorry to hear that she holds her head so, but I hope it will not be very long before I am with thee, and then I hope to break her of it.'

But before long, small eight-year-old Peg was ill with dysentery and fever. Ralph could not bear to tell Mary she was ill. As Mary asked him for news, her little girl was already dead. 'I am so full of affliction', he wrote to a friend, 'that I can say no more but pray for us . . . My poor Peg is happy but I am your most afflicted and unfortunate servant. Tell me how and when this shall be made known to her mother.'

By the time Dr Denton had decided to break the news of Peg's death to Mary, she had been overtaken by a different grief; her little son Ralph had died of sudden convulsions. She was in bed at Claydon when Denton told her, as gently as he could, that she had lost Peg too. She was beside herself. 'She spake idly for two nights, and sometimes did not know her friends.' But she recovered and went to London. It was Ralph whose reason seemed more comprehensively overthrown. He longed for Mary, whose company 'I desire above all earthly things, but if that cannot be and that for the good of your self, and those few Babes that are left us, we must still be kept asunder, I tell you true, I have not a heart to stay here without you . . . It hath pleased God to provide for my poor sweet girl and I hope he will so direct me in the disposing of my boy that this shall not be for his disadvantage.'

He planned to run away. To Italy, and then to Turkey. He would change his name. Then his family would be able to enjoy his sequestered estates. But of course Mary was horrified. Ralph gave way and they struggled on with their burden of grief.

They were not alone. There are no complete records, but the war caused the deaths of many children, and not only in sieges and battles. The war spread disease, especially water-borne infections. When troops moved into new areas, they brought with them enteric disorders to which locals may not have built up immunity. The overstretched and never-reliable sewage and water systems, strained further by the exig-encies of quartering and besieging, often became poisonous, especially to young children, then as now vulnerable to dysentery. The same risks arose when fleeing families themselves moved to new areas – such as Paris, in the Verneys' case. The war also brought the dangers of chronic malnutrition as armies plundered local food reserves, leaving families more exposed to infection and less able to fight it. It also disrupted care arrangements, with children more vulnerable to accidents. 'Many parents,' wrote Thomas Fuller, 'which otherwise would have been loving pelicans, are by these unnatural wars forced to be ostriches to their own children, leaving them to the narrow mercy of the wide world.' He was thinking of plunder and sequestration, bad enough, but many children were orphaned by the war, deprived of care and nurture as well as sustenance. Children were often cared for by relatives after fathers and sometimes mothers too had been killed, executed or driven into exile.

Childhood deaths from diseases were common before – and after – the war, but it made them more frequent. Sir John Gibson lamented the loss of an entire family:

> Twelve sons my wife Penelope
> And three fair daughters had.
> Which then a comfort was to me
> And made my heart full glad.
> Death took away my children dear
> And at the last my joy,
> And left me full of care and fear,
> My only hope a boy.

Alice Thornton, who had suffered in the Ulster Rising, thought that her sister, Lady Danby, had died in childbed because of the war:

> The troubles and distractions of those sad times did much afflict and grieve her, who was of a tender and sweet disposition, wanting the company of her husband Sir Thomas, to manage his estate and other concerns. But he, being engaged in his king's service, was not permitted to leave it, nor come to Thorpe but seldom, till she fell sick. These things, added to the horrid rudeness of the soldiers and Scots quartered then among them which, vexing and troubling her much with frights, caused her to fall into travail sooner than she expected, nor could she get her old midwife, being then in Richmond, which was shut up, for the plague was exceeding great there.

Some believed the war had encouraged children to be unruly. A godly minister who fled to New England thought so: children were much more disrespectful to their parents than in days of yore. They 'carry it proudly, disdainfully and scornfully towards parents, and it's well if their very parents escape their flouts'. In Clarendon's opinion youthful manners were in decline as well: 'young women conversed without any circumspection or modesty . . . Parents had no manner of authority over their children, nor children any Obedience.' The wargames children played in Plymouth were typical, for children imitated the behaviour of adults. Surrounded by soldiers who plundered, ravished and destroyed, they were hardly likely to grow up bursting with respect for adult authority. Yet parents themselves often drew the opposite conclusions, finding it more than ever necessary to insist on authority. Henry Slingsby, himself destined to become a victim of authority when he was executed in the late 1650s, wrote an advice book for his son, in which he gave detailed instructions about how to behave after his death. 'Subjection to superiors' was an important duty. And yet Henry Slingsby's very insistence suggests that this duty was felt to be neglected.

Certainly Mary Verney thought so. When she reached Claydon, she found that not only was her son's health in danger, but also her two sisters-in-law had enjoyed rather a lot of freedom in the absence of their father, slain at Edgehill, and Ralph, exiled in France. The place was a mess. 'The house is most lamentably furnished,' she wrote, 'all the linen is quite worn out, the feather beds that were walled up are much eaten with rats . . . The spits and other odd things are so extremely eaten with rust that they cannot be ever of any use again . . . And the dining room chairs in rags.' All the new, fashionable upholstery had suffered during the war years, because soldiers had been quartered in the houses. She could hardly find a horse to ride. And yet the roads were dangerous for a woman on foot, and Mary dreaded the unruly soldiery. 'I left them a fighting at 4 a clock this morning,' she wrote, 'but I trust in God they are appeased by this time.' Just as she got things straight, a new detachment arrived. 'I fear they will make us very poor as beggars', she wrote despairingly. Mary was a brave and unhappy woman. Perhaps she felt the terrible losses of the war more than most because her own childhood had been lonely. She was an orphan with a large fortune. She had been forcibly married at the age of ten to a cousin by relatives hoping to secure her fortune for themselves. Luckily, one of Mary's uncles objected to these not unusual proceedings, and managed to win custody of her. Instead, she was married to Ralph Verney on 31 May 1629, at the age of thirteen.

Hester Pulter, a passionate Royalist, inveterate reader of romances, and talented poet, was cut off from her children by the war, too. She tried to express her anger and frustration in a poem which borrows from the legend of the Pied Piper of Hamelin:

Now see how breach of promise is accurst
The fellow piping went away again
A hundred and thirty children in his train
Into a hill he led those pretty boys,
And thus their parents lost their hopes and joys
Which with sad hearts they now too late deplore
For they neer be were never heard of more.
By these their grievous sufferings you may see,
That breech of promise punished sure will be.

For women like Hester, the war itself was interpreted as an event that affected the family. Anne Temple wrote to her daughter in the tense winter of 1641, and her thoughts, too, were fixed on the nation as a place to bring up children: 'Dear Daughter, I am in reasonable health I praise God, and so I hope are all the rest at Hanwell and little Sara, only I am troubled with a cold and so are some of them, for it is a general disease I think, yet Sara is free for aught I know, God is exceeding good to us every way, both for Bodies and souls; and hath done wonderful things among us already', she wrote pellmell. For her, thinking of her children's safety prompted a longing to reform the Church: 'we shall see idolatry and superstition rooted out, and God's ordinances set up in the purity and power of them; altars begin to go down apace and rails in many places, and yours must follow if it be not down already'. But she also longed for a visit from the grandchildren: 'if we live till spring I hope we may see my son and you here, and that he will give you leave once more to come and see me, and bring pretty Nan and Moll with you, I should be very glad to have them both here that they might go to church, which they cannot do with you especially in winter, they shall be most welcome to us, but if I may not have both, I pray you to let Nan come'. She commented lovingly on her granddaughter Sarah, already living with her: 'Sara goes daily and will remember her doctrines, one is that God is the giver of all grace, and she will set me of it, and her other also, she is a pretty child and I hope you will have much comfort of her, she is so loving to me and enquires after me and sends to me to come home'. The letter was dated 'Broughton this day 16 January 1641'.

Love tried to bridge the gaps the war made. As a world was smashed, a grandmother tried to gather in her grandchildren. For all parents, to experience the war was also to experience love and fear. Children were the future for which the war was fought.

XXII

God with Us! Montrose's Campaign

After months of hanging miserably around Oxford in 1644, Montrose had been granted his wish; he was to raise the Highlands for Charles. He managed to reach his own lands in August 1644 after a dangerous journey through the Covenanting Lowlands. Word of the king's defeat at Marston Moor made his task more difficult. But he did find willing recruits among the traditional enemies of the Campbells – MacDonalds and Camerons. Crucially, he found the Roman Catholic battleaxe of a tribesman, Alasdair MacColla, a man who knew how to use a Highland charge and had done so in Ireland. The Civil War was Highland rivalry by other means, and that was how Montrose managed to raise an army. It was a bit short of weapons; some of its men carried bows and arrows and axes. But they were tough Highlanders and Irish MacDonnells.

At Tippermuir, in August 1644, he effortlessly defeated an army twice the size of his, and entered Perth. At Aberdeen in September he fought and won again. His old foe Argyll was sent in pursuit. Montrose led him on a wild goose chase through the snow-covered mountains. At the beginning of December, his army set out for Inverary through Breadalbane to Loch Awe. Within a fortnight they were in Campbell heartland. Houses were burned and livestock eaten. Any man named Campbell died. The MacDonalds under Montrose pillaged the Campbell countryside while Argyll hid in his castle at Inverary. By the end of January they were in the Great Glen, bound by a new Covenant, to 'stand to the maintenance of the power of our sacred and native sovereign, contrary to this present perverse and infamous faction of desperate rebels now in fury against him'.

On 31 January 1645, Montrose led his 1500 men in a flank movement through bitter weather, over the trackless mountains of Monadliath, covering thirty miles in just a day and a half. His followers were outnumbered, but they were willing to fight Campbells anywhere, anytime. So on 1 February they charged ferociously, over frozen ground, and another 1500 Campbells fell in battle at Inverlochy. Again, it was tribal, savage, but immensely impressive, and in Edinburgh the Covenanters began wondering if Montrose had been sent by a wrathful God to chastise them. Montrose also raided Dundee, and crushed three armies at Auldearn in May. This battle involved an especially effective and impressive tactic: Montrose's force was actually perilously small, but he drew it up so that it appeared to be massed well forward, while actually the bulk of the troops were stationed in the rear. The plan almost went wrong when the MacDonalds noticed that among the advancing troops were some Campbells, but although they attacked too early enough of the Covenanters had been lured into the trap, and the hidden army fell on them. Even Sir John Hurry, the Covenanters' commander, threw in his lot with Montrose, though admittedly he had changed sides before. He was not alone: Montrose at last had an army of respectable size. At Alford in June, he lured his pursuers onto boggy ground and attacked. As ever, the clansmen's charge was decisive and terrifying. They pursued and destroyed their enemies. More Covenanters came; Montrose fought them, too, and in the heart of Covenanting country, at Kilsyth on 14 August. The Highlanders won again, cutting down the Covenanters as they fled. Over 6000 men died, and the Highlanders were relentless because the Covenanters had massacred their women camp-followers a few weeks earlier, at Methven. (As at Naseby, this massacre seems to have been sparked by some sense of the women's foreignness; they were probably all Gaelic-speaking.) But this was tribal warfare, clan fighting on a grand and bloody scale: now the Highlands and the Irish, the *gaeltacht*, would have revenge. Along the line of the Antonine wall they heaped the bodies high. Bones were still being discovered in the area in the late eighteenth century, including a pitiful heap of the small bones of drummers and fife-players, boys. As a Gaelic poem had it: 'Like the short-lived web of the

spider when facing tempest, not more enduring is that host laid low
on knolls; thousands are slain./ Bodies like clothes a-bleaching are
stretched on hillsides, ignoble of aspect.'

Standing atop this heap of dead, Montrose was master of Scotland.

> But I must rule and govern still,
> And always give the law,
> And have each subject at my will,
> And all to stand in awe.
> But 'gainst my battery, if I find
> Thou shunnest the prize so sore
> As that thou settst me up a blind,
> I'll never love thee more.

Montrose was received eagerly, fulsomely in Glasgow, and Edinburgh
set free its Royalist prisoners. Drummond of Hawthornden, Ben
Jonson's friend, wrote eagerly to Montrose: 'the golden Age is returned,
his Majesty's crown established, the many-headed monster is near
quelled'. Here was the Gaelic culture of the Highlands in triumph.

> But if thou wilt be constant then,
> And faithful by thy word,
> I'll make thee glorious by my pen
> And famous by my sword.

But by now events further south had freed David Leslie to move north
with his experienced army. Now Charles had only Oxford and the
Celts. And they could not stand long. Nonetheless, the king decided to
march north, to join Montrose. Leslie managed to keep him away,
however, and Montrose was soon himself pursued. Leslie, who was a
clever, careful, well-trained soldier, may not have seemed a threat
precisely because of these professional attributes. He lacked authority
to a Highland noble. And Montrose was at heart a fatalist, a gambler:

> Some friends as shadows are
> And fortune as the sun;
> They never proffer any help
> Till fortune hath begun:
> But if in any case
> Fortune shall first decay

Then they, as shadows of the sun
With fortune run away.

In writing this, Montrose was defying Calvin, who had said emphatically that since everything – good and bad – came from God, none of
it could be seen as 'chance'. Like his fondness for gambling, Montrose's
passion for Fortune was a weakness, and yet he also felt God might
have had a hand in it all: 'it may be sensibly seen to be the Lord's
doing', he wrote, 'in making a handful to overthrow multitudes'. This
was part of his ongoing adherence to the Kirk and to the Covenant; he
felt sure the Lowlands would eventually go over to the king. They must.

The trouble was that Lowland Scotland remained unconvinced. How
could Montrose be a proper Covenanter when his army was full of
Irish, the people who had unleashed what Lowland Scotland saw as a
bloody reign of terror?

As Montrose moved south, his Highlanders began to go home, laden
with loot. Their leaders defected; they fell out among themselves.
Montrose, despite his charm and ability as a commander, was powerless
to prevent the desertions. There was a lesson here for Bonnie Prince
Charlie, had he possessed enough sense to see it. By this time Montrose
seems to have parted company with reality, speaking as if he were
pursuing Leslie, not the other way about. He even hoped to supplement
his forces in the Lowlands. But there is a Highland legend that when
Montrose stopped at Selkirk a local woman was boiling a sheep's head,
vowing that if it had been Montrose's head she would have held the
lid down. So by the time he met Leslie at Philiphaugh, Montrose had
only 600 men. They were taken by surprise; the result was a massacre,
not a battle – Montrose's men were mostly still trying to catch their
horses as Leslie advanced. The Irish infantry fought frantically, fiercely,
but were overwhelmed and persuaded to surrender. The Covenanting
ministers who accompanied Leslie convinced him that he had granted
quarter only to the actual officers who had met him to agree the truce.
The Irish were butchered, and so were their wives and families: 'the
boys, cooks, and a rabble of rascals and women with their children in
their arms . . . were cut in pieces with such savage and inhuman cruelty
as neither Turk nor Scythian was ever heard to have done the like'.
There was a rash of trials and executions.

> Now let us a' for Leslie pray
> And his brave company
> For they have vanquished great Montrose
> Our cruel enemy.

Montrose wanted to die fighting, but his followers convinced him that he could serve the king best by escaping. He cut his way out of the press with a small remnant of his men. Those who tried to follow on foot were cut down as they fled. He took to the heather and the hills once more, managed to raise another force in the Highlands, and conducted a guerrilla war for some months. He was still a terror to the Lowlanders, who dreaded what he might do in summer, with another Highland army.

But finally he had no choice but to flee when Charles surrendered to the Scots. Charles urged him to accept the peace, but this was made difficult for Montrose by his own explicit exclusion from it; he was not to be pardoned except for safe-conduct to a ship waiting to take him overseas. So he disbanded his small remaining force, as ordered: 'His soldiers fell at his knees, and besought him with tears, if the king's safety required him to quit the kingdom altogether to take them with him where he would. They were ready to live, to fight, and if it pleased God, to die under his command.'

Sensible, as usual, he left for the Continent. But he almost missed the boat; it didn't arrive until 31 August, and the shipmaster, a Covenanter, refused to sail on the grounds that the ship needed caulking and rigging. Montrose smelt a rat; his agents found another ship, a small Norwegian vessel, whose master agreed to take on passengers.

And so that night, a small cock-boat brought the Reverend James Wood (Montrose in disguise) aboard. With him was his shabby, poorly-clad manservant. Montrose had not given up, after all; his love of tricks was as active as ever.

> I'll serve thee in such noble ways;
> Was never heard before,
> I'll crown and deck thee all with bays
> And love thee evermore.

Despite his disappointments, Montrose was still full of burning zeal, and the execution of Charles only made him more determined. He escaped to Sweden and began trying to raise Scandinavian levies. He racketed around Europe – Paris, Geneva – being offered high military office by an admiring Mazarin, corresponding in ebullient Cavalier style with Rupert. He received Charles II's commission to raise Scotland in April 1650, and landed with a handful of Danes and seven hundred men from the Orkneys. But within three weeks the Covenanters annihilated him at Carbisdale. He was betrayed into his enemies' hands, and also by Charles II, who signed an agreement with Argyll without bothering to secure Montrose's fate. He was executed at the Mercat Cross, and his head was placed on a spike at the Tolbooth.

He was, said Clarendon, the man of 'clearest spirit and honour' among all the royal advisers. He was no politician, but a fine soldier, and a magnificent leader of men, fighting in primitive country, with wild followers. Exactly one hundred years later, a Highland army would again leap the border and then melt away, this time under Bonnie Prince Charlie. Ironically, the fate of the House of Stuart was fore-shadowed by the fate of the man they abandoned. But to the Lowland Scots, he was a brigand, a pirate who had let loose wild Catholic Irish on their farms and homes, a man who had sacked and destroyed estates and towns, and had set the Scottish nation itself at naught in pursuit of personal pride.

Ann Fanshawe, too, was discovering new worlds. While some marriages broke, hers held firm:

> And next week [May 1645] we were all on our journey for Bristol, very merry and thought that now all things would mend and the worst of my misfortunes past, but little thought I to leap into that sea that would toss me until it racked me, but we were to ride all night by agreement for fear of the enemy's surprising us as we passed, they quartering in the way. About nightfall, having travelled about twenty miles, we discovered a troop of horse coming towards us, which proved Sir Marmaduke Roydon, a worthy commander and my countryman. He told me that hearing I was to pass by his garrison, he was come out to conduct me, he hoped, as far as there was danger, which

was about 12 miles. With many thanks we parted, and having refreshed ourselves and horses we set forth for Bristol, where we arrived the 20th of May.

Ann's cheerfulness emerges clearly, as ever. 'My husband had provided very good lodgings for us, and as soon as he could come home from the council . . . he with all expressions of joy received me in his arms and gave me a hundred pieces of gold, saying "I know that thou that keeps my heart so well will keep my fortune, which from this time I will ever put into thy hands as God shall bless me with increase." And now I thought myself a queen, and my husband so glorious a crown that I more valued myself to be called by his name than born a princess, for I knew him very wise and very good, and his soul doted on me.'

And yet it was in Bristol that Ann and Richard had a kind of quarrel. Ann's friend Lady Rivers ('a brave woman and one that had suffered very many thousand pounds lost for the king', Ann said, thinking of the riots inspired by the Rivers family) commended the 'knowledge of state affairs' that some women had, including Ann's friend Isabella Thynne and Lady Aubigny. She added that she knew that the queen had recently sent a post from Paris to the king, and that she longed to know what was in it. Ann was young, and 'to that day had ever in my mouth, "What news?"' She thought perhaps it would be fashionable, and that perhaps it would please Richard, if she found out more. So when Richard came home she greeted him as usual; then he disappeared into his study. She followed him, and she asked him what the queen had said.

Richard reacted like a parent. 'My love,' he said, 'I will immediately come to thee.' Then he went on with his work, then came out of his closet, kissed her, and spoke of other things. Ann failed to take the hint. She asked him again. He talked still more of other things. Ann was put out; at supper she ate nothing. Richard was firm, like a parent with a nagging child. 'He as usually sat by me and drunk often to me, which was his custom', and he talked to the others at the table, guests. At bedtime, Ann asked him again. And now she applied some pressure, saying she could not believe he loved her if he would not tell her. Richard knew his Shakespeare: 'he stopped my mouth with kisses, so we went to bed'. 'I cried,' Ann remembered, 'and he went to sleep.' The next morning, Ann still wasn't speaking to him. He kissed her, and went to court. Then he came home for dinner, and Ann burst out, angrily, 'Thou dost not care to see me troubled.' Now Richard took her in his arms and spoke to her gently, saying, 'My dearest soul, nothing upon earth can afflict me like that, and when you asked of me my business, it was wholly out of my power to satisfy thee. For my life and fortune shall be thine, and every thought of my heart, in which the trust I am in may not be revealed, but my honour is my own, which I can not preserve if I communicate the Prince's affairs, and pray thee with this answer rest satisfied.' Ann was instantly repentant. Richard's courtesy and reason made her think twice, in a way an order might not have done. So 'from that day until the day of his death, I never thought fit to ask him any business, but that he communicated freely to me, in order to his estate or family'.

Events were now moving swiftly, and they were about to carry away Richard's master the Prince of Wales, and the Royalist cause too. Ann, Richard and the prince were forced to flee Bristol by that great general King Plague, whose mighty armies raged in its streets. Prince Charles and his retinue went to Barnstaple, where Ann, ever the cook and housewife, noticed a curious new kind of cherry, a massard, 'and makes the best pies, with their sort of cream, I ever eat'. Her comment shows that for her Devon was almost as exotic as Istanbul might be today. Once Rupert had surrendered, Prince Charles had no choice but to flee. Charles wanted his heir safely in France, and so did Henrietta, but the council sensibly pointed out that Charles would then be seen as a foreign, French papistical foe. For now, he moved slowly into Cornwall. He, Ann, and Richard reached Truro.

By then the war in Devon was all but over. Cromwell had beaten Hopton in a fierce engagement in deep snow in January 1646. Hopton hardly had a man left to fight him. Fairfax, who was active in Devon too, wrote to his father that he had reached Totnes, a lonely outpost of godliness that was especially glad to see him. Ann was anxious to leave Truro anyway. She had been attacked by robbers because she had in her keeping a small trunk of jewels. She and her servants put up a typically stout defence until help came. Next day the prince sent her a guard. She met the Grenvilles – John, son of Bevil, of whom Ann wrote that 'his father was a very honest gentleman who lost his life in the king's service, and his uncle, Sir Richard, was a good commander, but a little too severe'.

Now the prince decided to head for the Scilly Isles. Not France, but far enough away. So on 4 March 1646, in the first real darkness of the night, Charles and his entourage crept onto the frigate *Phoenix*, moored at Land's End. He was only just in time. Hopton signed the surrender ten days later at Exeter. Ann and Richard packed up their entire estate in two trunks and boarded another ship, where Richard was forced to pay the sailors extra to get them to sail at all, and once on board the crew rifled their trunk and made off with some gold lace, all Ann's combs, gloves and ribbons, and all their best clothes. Now she had none of the stuff from which a woman of her time fashioned an image. To add to her misery, Ann was violently seasick; no wonder, since she was also heavily pregnant.

Now the prince was king of just these islands. The legendary lost lands of Lyonesse were said to lie beneath the Scillies like a haunting remembrance of that other kingdom Charles had lost, drowned under the flood of war.

'I was set ashore almost dead in the Isles of Scilly', Ann reported, and 'when we had got to our quarters near the castle where the Prince lay, I went immediately to bed, which was so vile that my footmen ever lay in a better, and we had but three in the whole house, which consisted of four rooms, or rather partitions, 2 low rooms, and 2 little lofts, with a ladder to go up. In one of these they kept dry fish, which was his trade, and in this my husband's two clerks lay; one there was for my sister, and one for myself, and one among the rest of our servants. But when I awoke in the morning, I was so cold I knew not what to do, but the daylight discovered that our bed was near swimming with the sea, which, the owner told us afterwards, it never did so but at spring tides. With this we were destitute of clothes, and meat or fuel for half the court, to serve them a month, was not to be had in the whole island. And truly we begged our daily bread of God, for we thought every meal our last. The council sent for provisions into France, which served us, but they were bad, and little of them.'

Then 'after three weeks and odd days', the prince and his dwindling court set out again, this time for Jersey. The pilot did not know the safe channel into the harbour and simply sailed over the rocks, but somehow they survived. Ann found Jersey much more to her taste; there were avenues of trees leading to castles, grassy pastureland. And her daughter was born, and christened Anne.

But where should Prince Charles go next? The queen still wanted him in France; she was lonely and she hoped his presence would help her raise support. At last he went, reaching Paris in July 1646. Richard followed, but he sent Ann back to England to try to recover his revenues. Ann left the baby with a nurse on Jersey, and took a boat to Caen and then another to Southampton. She was pleased to be entrusted with a mission, and managed to extract some money from the Commons. When Richard too reached England, however, he had to hide. Ann is almost silent about these years of eclipse. But she had one more part to play, before their bitter end.

XXIII

New Professions:
Parliament Joan and Richard Wiseman

The year 1645 began in bitter cold, and the future was bone-cold, too, for the Royalists. In this year, the astrologer William Lilly's prophecy *The Starry Messenger* predicted stunning and sweeping victory for Parliament, and it was printed on the very day of the war's most astounding and resounding victory, the Battle of Naseby. In the north, Montrose was to offer the Royalists the cruel hope of success before he too was engulfed by the tidal wave of failure that was sweeping the king's cause away. Even the remaining Royalist sandcastles – Hereford, Basing House – were soon swallowed up.

This year, too, the poems that John Milton had allowed to appear slowly and obscurely were brought together in a single volume, and republished with notes pointing out their prophetic relevance. In using his poems, especially 'Lycidas', as a kind of pamphlet, Milton was responding eagerly to the spirit of a time that had no leisure for the lyric. But he was also withdrawing, disappointed, from affairs of state. He was having trouble with his sight, too:

> I noticed my sight becoming weak and growing dim, and that the same time my spleen and all my viscera burdened and shaken with flatulence. And even in the morning, if I began as usual to read, I noticed that my eyes felt immediate pain deep within and turned from reading, though later refreshed after moderate bodily exercise; as often as I looked at a lamp, a sort of rainbow seemed to obscure it. Soon a mist appearing in the

left part of the left eye (for that eye became clouded some years
before the other) removed from my sight everything on that
side.

He dreaded blindness. He dosed himself with medicines. He hoped.
But the darkness closed in, slow and unstoppable, cutting him off from
the books he needed and loved. No one is sure what caused his blindness, but whatever it was, it made him less certain as a pamphleteer,
keen not to waste the dying light on controversies that didn't matter.
From now on he would stick to poetry, and to the really important
political causes. And after all, Homer had been blind.

At Oxford, the days of the court were numbered. While Paris had
its first taste of Italian opera, the English court was collapsing. Soon
there would be no court at all to entertain the languors of pastoral;
only brisk hard-headed satire and bitter songs. The masque house at
Whitehall was pulled down; now theatre had no place in London life.
Yet the violent, macho Cavalier spirit refused to die. The Church of
England was stripped to its essentials, plain and simple. By now there
were no organs, no prayer book, none but ordained clergy preaching
in the English churches. People who had committed crimes were not
to be allowed to receive the sacraments. But in that bleakness, many
strange things were to flower, and perhaps the most important was a
group of men who began to meet at Gresham College to think about
the physical world and how it worked. After the war, they were to
become the founders of the Royal Society.

Parliament might be winning the war, but the battle for hearts and
minds was still in the balance. One factor that was helping to decide it
even then was the newly freed press. The London print trade, liberated
by the absence of the Licensing Act, was mushrooming, fuelling hectic
political discussion and religious innovation, deflating the pompous
and setting up new pomposities of its own. As well, there was an
overlap between the print trade and the world of politics: print traders
were ideal informers. Hawkers and chapmen sold broadsides and pamphlets in the streets of London. They brought in news while they also
spread it about. They tramped all day from the Exchange to Westminster, from Westminster to the Old Bailey, from the Old Bailey to
St Paul's Churchyard, then back to Westminster again. In so doing,

they also passed the booksellers' stalls, and they stopped at inns and ordinaries, hostelries and lodgings to pick up gossip, listening especially to any carriers who transported goods to and from the country along a fixed route. As they handed out their pamphlets, people expressed their views on the latest news, even though the hawkers might remember, and might tell the authorities.

Some of what they found to say would have been sedition even hundreds of years later. Early modern London had a salty tongue. When she saw two sheep's heads together for sale, Alice Jackson said 'she wished the King and Prince Rupert's heads were there instead of them, and then the Kingdom would be settled, and the Queen had not a foot of land in England and the King was an evil and an unlawfull King, and better to be without a King than to have him King.'

In 1646 Ansell Powlten said 'that the King was run away from his Parliament, and that he was no king, neither had he foot of land but what he must win by the sword, and being asked of one why the state did not impress in the king and parliament name, for answering that they did that to cozen the subject'. But the king was not the only one to be attacked. Verbal assaults on Parliament were common too. Men and women who might quarrel over the ownership of a pair of shears and exchange lavish insults would use the same language for the government. One man thought 'The Parliament nothing but a Company of Robin Hoods and Little Jacks', while in Somerset the Parliamentarian candidate was known as Robin Hood. People also knew about the leaders of the Peasants' Revolt, Jack Cade and Wat Tyler; in 1642 a pamphlet was published about them, which in turn was based on an old Tudor drama. The penitent ghost of Jack Straw appeared to proclaim the need to obey the king.

Bookshops and printing houses were also places where books and pamphlets could be discussed; a Jesuit debated with a godly minister in Thomas Bates's shop in Bishop's Court near the Old Bailey in 1641. Religious lecturers might perform outside or nearby, and on days when they did the canny booksellers would crowd their window displays with religious satires criticizing bishops. Bates, however, was eclectic, and sold anti-Puritan satires alongside godly books, Royalist squibs alongside anti-episcopalian theology. Other booksellers specialized in particular kinds of books. Francis Grove's shop sold the latest ballads and jestbooks; he sold scandalously satirical ballads celebrating Marie de Medici's departure in 1641. You could buy pamphlets about whale-sightings, a pool in Lancashire that had turned to blood, children born with horns, with two heads, about Oliver Cromwell's adultery with Mrs Lambert, and Anne Fairfax's wish to be queen.

Early modern people often greeted each other by asking, 'What's the news?' At work, in alehouses, at ordinaries, men and women discussed the whole range of contemporary issues: Charles I's religious policy, the influence of Henrietta Maria, the designs of the king's evil councillors, Laud's secret allegiance to Rome, Catholic plots in London. They were often overheard and reported on, which is how their views have been recorded and preserved. In the crowded streets, privacy could be hard to find. This could be either an advantage or a drawback for radicals, depending on how you chose to look at it. Katherine Hadley, a spinster and servant to John Lilburne, was sentenced to seven months' imprisonment on suspicion of 'having thrown abroad in Moor Fields copies of Lilburne's pamphlet *A Cry for Justice* in the Whitsun holidays in 1640'. She was arrested, yes, but she managed to get the pamphlet out too.

Other agents were working among the crowds. Elizabeth Alkin, or Parliament Joan, was born about the turn of the seventeenth century, and died in 1654. As befits a spy, she remains a shadowy figure. The Committee for the Advancement of Money gave her two pounds in March 1645 'for several discoveries', and forty shillings later, for discovering the delinquency of George Mynne. Mynne, an ironmaster of Surrey, was supplying the king with the raw materials for warfare, storing iron and wire in caches around the country. Parliament Joan discovered one such cache. Her husband was a spy, too; he was caught by the Royalists early in the war, and hanged at Oxford.

Both capitals were haunted by spies. Sir Samuel Luke had an intelligence network in Oxford which supplied Parliament with information. In July 1643, Nehemiah Wallington recorded that 'there was a she-spy who was in Oxford on the Lord's day last. She relates that on the Monday morning, about five of the clock, there were three executed there for spies.' Joan petitioned the Committee for Compositions, trying to claim a sequestered house whose owner had fought against

Parliament and had also worked for the very man who had hanged Joan's husband. She had also searched for unlicensed or seditious presses for the authorities. A printer warned his friends to 'have care of a fat woman, aged about fifty, her name I know not, she is called by many Parliament Joan'. She had discovered four presses in the custody of a man called Dugard, in the Merchant Taylor's School. Joan herself said that she'd been employed as a spy by Essex, Waller and Fairfax, but found spying didn't pay well enough, and eventually became a printer of newsbooks herself. After a hectic career as a printer, she became a naval nurse, continuing to petition Parliament for the money she felt they owed her for 'my continual watchings day and night'.

Joan's story shows how the apparent liberalization of politics through print was countered by government agents. She was a printer, exposing news to the eager eyes of a nation hungry for it. But when her neighbours expressed their views or acted on their opinions, they did so knowing that someone like Joan might be listening.

The new times created opportunities for other professions, too. An army surgeon was paid only four shillings a day, and most relied on private practice to eke out a decent living. As a result, there was a chronic shortage of surgeons, and those left to the army were often frighteningly incompetent. Surgical techniques were also at an early stage; one self-deprecating practitioner, Edward Coke, admitted that 'one Death, who doth and will prevail' had carried off most of his patients to 'the great God of heaven'. There were facilities for the sick and wounded; at the Savoy, for instance, for the Parliamentarian casualties, and in 1648 Ely House became a hospital. These took 350 patients between them. Nurses were employed – chiefly the widows of soldiers, one for every twelve patients.

There were also attempts to support wounded soldiers. Old clothes, linen and wool were gathered, and a tax was levied. After the Restoration, 1840 disabled veterans and 1500 widows were given twelve weeks' pay each, but after that they had only the uncertain mercy of their parishes to rely on. Sometimes instead of transporting patients to a town, officers would commandeer a large building as a hospital. On 18 September 1645, George Blagrave recorded:

John Bullock, of Captain Barron's, a very sore cut in the fore part of his head, which caused a piece of his skull the breadth of a half-crown piece to be taken forth, also a very sore cut over his head, £1 10s 0d. For curing the cavaliers taken at the fight at Ashe, whereof one was shot in the arme at the elbow joint and the bullet taken forth, in the wrist near the hand. The rest were sore cut in their heads and thrust in the back. £5.

The best accounts of what war did to the bodies of men can be found in the writings of surgeons like Richard Wiseman, whose treatise *Of Wounds* was widely used in surgical practice. Wiseman was born in 1621 near London, and apprenticed in 1637 to Richard Smith, surgeon. He was present at the siege of Weymouth in February 1645, as a surgeon to a battalion commanded by a Colonel Ballard of the Royalist army. He was also at Taunton and Truro, and finally was among those who escaped with the Prince of Wales to the Scilly Isles. He observed carefully and dispassionately the rending of human flesh, on and off the battlefield: 'I have known pieces of splinters, etc, sometimes stick so fast in the inward parts, or to have been so inclosed, that they could by no means get them out, yet at length, upon Apostumation of the part, they have thrust forth . . .' Wiseman was endlessly curious about the human body: 'If the parts be grown stiff with cold, as when the party hath been left in the field all night, which after a battle hath often happened (and particularly to a merry fellow, a common soldier, that used to wear an iron scull under a cap, and from thence was called by a nickname; his wounds were large, and the lips hardened with the cold, and it was well for him, his bleeding was thereby stayed)'.

Some of what he noticed was horrible. 'Sometimes a weapon sticketh so fast, that by no art it can be extracted', he wrote grimly. When the weapon had been drawn out, he said, the wound must be cleansed from rags 'and aught else', and allowed to bleed. He knew perfectly the importance of removing every scrap of fabric to prevent infection, and describes numerous cases where musketballs carried small pieces of torn cloth into a wound and infected it. He insisted that if necessary a surgeon should enlarge the wound to clean it. When gangrene set in – and Wiseman gives descriptions of several different sorts of gangrene – he suggests scarification, then the pouring in of salt and vinegar, which might have had some antiseptic impact on gas gangrene. He also knew how to stop bleeding: 'bring the lips of the wound together by suture, and by applying such medicaments to them as have a drying and agglutinative faculty'. He also did amputations, 'then with a good knife I cut off the flesh by a quick turn of my hand, Mr Murry putting up the flesh while I sawed the bones. After which with a few motions of my saw I separated the bone, the patient not so much as whimpering the while.' He did at least want to spare his patients pain. But he also thought – oddly – that pain might help in the healing process.

He noticed that in war sword-wounds are frequent, 'especially when the Horse-men fall in among the Infantry, and cruelly hack them; the poor soldiers the while sheltering their heads with their arms, sometime with the one, sometime with the other, until they be both most cruelly mangled; and yet the head fareth little the better for their defence, many of them not escaping with less than two or three wounds through the skull to the membrane, and often into the Brain. And if the men fly, and the enemy pursue, his hinder parts meet with great wounds, as over the thighs, back, shoulders, and neck . . . At Stirling in Scotland . . . one of the soldiers had such a gash thwart the nape of his neck that it was a wonder to us he lived. His wound was full of maggots; and so were those of all the rest that were inflicted on the hinder parts, they having been some days undressed.'

He turned a cold and precise eye, too, on the damage done by musketballs: 'The figure of [musket wounds] is always round; the bullet furrows the flesh in with it, and the place by which it enters presently contracts closer, but its going out is more lax. A common soldier, shot in the breast through the sternum, lay roaring very grievously, complaining of a pain in his back. I was fetched to him, and turning him on his side I saw the bullet lie like a small wen or scrofule . . . the soldier ceased his crying, and acknowledged before us his pain was from the bullet in the skin. For indeed the lungs and other internal parts are seldom so sensible of pain, though wounded through.' He died, Wiseman reports sadly.

He gave helpful advice on how to diagnose injuries to the organs: lung wounds would cause a cough and frequent sighing, while intestinal wounds – almost always fatal – were revealed by excrements and filthy discharges. After stories like this, it's not surprising that Wiseman also records cases of madness; one man hurls himself in front of a coach, believing himself pursued by demons.

Working with primitive Civil War ordnance presented extra hazards. Ralph Hopton's mishap with the exploding ammunition cart was not unusual. Nicholas Small of Taunton was injured when a musket he was cleaning went off by accident, tearing off most of his hand. In his petition for a pension years later he claimed he could not work. Many such petitions were received from those whose right hands had been shot away or whose arms had been torn off. Musketballs often shattered bone, creating wounds which rarely healed well, full of splinters of bone, ripe for infection; such wounds could sometimes kill months later. Sword cuts healed better.

Another problem was disease. 'Camp fever' ravaged both sets of armies. It may have been a type of malaria, and seems to have been brought on by exposure. The plague flared up in towns like Bristol and Oxford, and there were typhus-like diseases. Pneumonia and other fevers complicated healing.

Multiple injuries were common too. At Cropredy Bridge John Middlewick was felled by a sword cut in the face, and while he lay in the mud a horse stood on him, 'trod out his bowels', then a passing soldier ran him through. Unsurprisingly, he claimed after the war that his wounds had incapacitated him.

When Richard Wiseman was present at the siege of Taunton, he recorded a case so horribly graphic that it acts as a kind of summary of what must have happened to thousands of the men who fought. Written on one man's body were all the powers of war: 'One of Colonel Arundel's men, in storming the works, was shot in the face by case-shot. He fell down and, in the retreat, was carried off among the dead; and laid in an empty house by the way until the next day: when, in the morning early, the colonel marching by that house heard a knocking within against the door.'

So the wounded man arose like a dreadful spectre of war:

> Some of the officers, desiring to know what it was, looked in and saw this man standing by the door without eye, face, nose or mouth. The colonel sent to me . . . to dress the man. I went but was somewhat troubled where to begin. The door consisted of two hatches: the uppermost was open and the man stood leaning upon the other part of the door, which was shut. His face, with its eyes, nose, mouth and foremost part of the jaw,

with the chin, was shot away and the remaining parts of them driven in. One part of the jaw hung down by his throat and the other part pushed into it. I saw the brain working out underneath the lacerated scalp on both sides between his ears and brows.

Wiseman's scientific exactitude applies to his own feelings as well. He knew his limitations: 'I could not see any advantage he could have by my dressing. But I helped him to clear his throat, where was remaining the root of his tongue. He seemed to approve of my endeavours and implored my help by the signs he made with his hands.'

Courtesy must stand in for knowledge where there was none to be had:

I asked him if he would drink, making a sign by the holding up of a finger. He presently did the like and immediately after held up both his hands, expressing his thirst. A soldier fetched some milk and brought a little wooden dish to pour some of it down his throat; but part of it running on both sides, he reached out his hands to take the dish. They gave it him full of milk. He held the root of his tongue down with one hand and with the other poured it down his throat (carrying his head backwards) and so got down more than a quart. After that I bound his wounds up.

It was all he could do. War had erased this man, as it had so many.

XXIV

The World is Turned Upside Down:
The New Model Army and Naseby Fight

D uring the early months of 1645, Parliament's commitment to
holy war intensified. Any captured Irishman or Catholic from
Ireland could be condemned to death at once. When Abingdon was attacked and five officers captured, Major-General Browne
hanged them immediately. Rupert and his Parliamentarian opposite
number Mytton swapped atrocities in the north, taking revenge on
each other in a parody of the honour culture. Only the Earl of Essex
seemed to think that he was still engaged in a gentlemanly pursuit,
returning the Prince of Wales's hawk and its falconer when they were
captured. And his gentlemanliness had recently shown his profound
limitations for leadership in war.

The New Model Army was both part of the trend towards holy war,
and a form of resistance to it. Its building was one of the bravest acts
Parliament performed in the entire war, and meant surrendering the
military initiative for months at a time while it was formed. It also
meant putting up with almost constant mutterings from the peace
party in Parliament. From the moment the legislation to create it was
passed, it was obvious that the New Model would have to succeed
quickly in the field or be voted out of existence.

Recruitment was by now so difficult as to be virtually impossible.
Most of what had been Waller's army had simply gone home when it
had had enough. Though it was still possible to find those of enough
substance to join the cavalry and bring their own horses, the infantry

was far less attractive. Elevenpence a day was a day-labourer's wage, and even the meagre sum of eightpence a day was by no means regularly paid. Conditions were tough and rations very basic; men were expected to march and fight after meals of biscuit and cheese. Like pay, even this poor fare was by no means always available. The result was a steady stream of desertions, and plenty of mutinies; those left in what had been Waller's army were vehemently mutinous, while Essex's regiments had only been prevented from mutiny by prompt action on the part of that soldier's favourite Philip Skippon, who promised them their arrears of pay.

The New Model was supposed to have 14,400 infantry, and needed to recruit 8460 new men to meet this target. The Parliamentarian heartlands of London and the south-east were given targets to levy, and few fulfilled them on time. The French ambassador saw men being rounded up in the streets of London, and then sent to Maidenhead by boat to stop them from escaping at once. Even when a rough bunch of unwilling troopers could be rounded up, they often deserted immediately. The men from Kent mutinied as soon as they had been impressed, barricading themselves into a mansion near Wrotham, and had to be put down by a full-scale military operation by the trained bands. When the Kentish levies got to Windsor they deserted and headed for home once more. It didn't help that some of the initial conscripts were ex-Royalists. Richard Baxter thought that 'the greatest part of the common soldiers, especially of the Foot', were 'ignorant men, of little religion', and 'the abundance of them such as had been taken prisoners, or turned out of Garrisons under the king, and had been soldiers in his army. And these would do anything to please their officers.' But he also wrote with eloquent affection of those who served with him in Colonel Whalley's regiment: 'Many of my dearest friends were there, whose society had formerly been delightful to me, and whose welfare I was tender of, being men that had a deeper interest in my affections than any in the world had before those times . . . It was they that stuck to me, and I to them . . . My faithful people that purposedly went through with me so many wars and dangers.'

Baxter had begun the war by thinking that all armies were vanity, which partially explained his reluctance to join up. Now he came to see them as the Lord's chosen people. Later, he saw them as deluded idiots. One thing that helped change his mind was his mother's experience of war. She was in a town that was stormed, and burned, and she saw men killed before her eyes, and survivors stripped to their shifts and plundered. She was a timid woman and she never recovered. But Baxter felt certain that his own men were not capable of acts like this. He was in a crack corps: Whalley's horse, half of Cromwell's old Ironsides. Somehow it was those old Ironsides who set the tone for the new army.

Each of the New Model infantry regiments consisted of 1200 men arranged in ten companies. Pikemen were interfiled with musketeers. The pikemen had to be tall and strong to manage their hefty weapons, and they gave themselves a few airs as a result. There is a myth that the people of early modern England were much shorter than those of today because of poor nutrition. Archaeology suggests not: the average Londoner in 1700 was only about an inch shorter than his counterpart today, but differently shaped, with bow legs, and beefy arms, a physique suited to use of the pike, which had a heavy iron head; by the time they'd picked up their sleeping gear and rations, the pikemen had to abandon any armour or fail to move at all. The muskets were hefty affairs too. Musketeers had swords as well as guns to carry, but these were often fragile, cheap affairs that gave way in battle, so in close combat they learned to use their muskets as clubs.

Arguably they were more useful as clubs than they were as guns. The Civil War musket was both cumbersome and unreliable. It was fired by match, a long woven cord, which had to be lit and kept alight whenever there was a chance of action. In the wet and miserable weather of the Little Ice Age that chilled England in the seventeenth century, this was virtually impossible. To fire, the soldier had to ram the powder charge down the length of the muzzle, and then ram in the heavy lead ball. Then a short length of lighted match had to be fixed in the cock, which then had to be primed with a small pinch of powder; too much would make the gun explode. To do all this in a surprise attack, like the Parliamentarian charge on Byron's 'forlorn hope' at Marston Moor, was very difficult indeed. Reloading was also very slow. Given the closeness with which the armies usually drew up, musketeers would often only fire one round before hand-to-hand clubbing began. To cope with this, Civil War armies usually placed musketeers six deep, so each front rank could be replaced by others with pieces primed and ready. The New Model, however, was trained in the Swedish method where three ranks fired at once; the first kneeling and the second stooping while the last rank stood. The massed fire-power proved decisive.

There were other problems with the musket which Swedish methods couldn't solve. Since soldiers carried their charges in bandoliers, any kind of wind made it likely that a spark from someone else's match might set them all off. It had a wide barrel, four feet long, which made it exceptionally heavy. Its range was limited; it could kill at 400 yards, but this was due to luck rather than judgement; to have any hope of accuracy, musketeers had to withhold fire until the enemy was within 150 yards. There were flintlock firing mechanisms, but they were far too expensive for the infantry; the New Model had a company of flintlock-armed men guarding artillery.

The cavalry had iron headpieces, buff-coats of thick leather, and were armed with a sword and a pair of pistols; only officers carried the lighter flintlock-fired gun, called a carbine. They had been completely won over by Rupert's ruthless, terrifying cavalry tactics, inspired by Gustavus Adolphus. And yet Sir Charles Firth was sure that Cromwell and his men never mastered Rupert's express speeds, relying more on perseverance than on shock tactics. But Rupert sacrificed discipline to speed; Cromwell's men were better controlled.

What the New Model lacked was artillery. It did have fifty or so field guns, including the culverin, with its twelve-pound balls, and the tiny drakes which could fire three-pound balls. Most guns could fire only around fifteen shots an hour. They couldn't be relied on to hit anything they were aimed at beyond around 300 paces, and were only effective against tightly-massed troops at close range. But in a battle they could be devastating.

As well as guns, the army needed food. There was an initial shipment of Suffolk cheese and bread, the meal of what John Evelyn called an honest laborious countryman, but otherwise the soldiers were supposed to buy their food locally out of their wages. The cavalry had to feed their horses as well. Since the ordinary soldier got only eightpence a day – with Fairfax himself on ten pounds a day – this allowed only for biscuit or bread, cheese and beer. Occasionally there might be meat, as a treat. There were regimental surgeons, paid about the same as ensigns, seldom properly trained or qualified, each one aided by two surgeons' mates.

But the New Model wasn't only about food and guns and tactics. It was about ideas. Initially, only the Eastern Association cavalry and probably a few infantry, especially those in Skippon's regiments, were really committed to what later became the ideology and spirit of the entire army: the idea that they were God's saints fighting the Lord's battles, as the ancient Hebrews had done before them. Banal though it sounds, one of the first things to begin to unite these men was the adoption of a uniform, the red coats worn in the Eastern Association troops. This was so inspirational that it survived as the standard dress of the British soldier long after the New Model's other ideals had been abandoned. The Eastern Association cavalry had of course been portrayed in every Parliamentarian newsbook as the great God-given victors of Marston Moor. In putting on their uniform, the New Model was conceding that they were its models. It was as if they donned its ideology with its red jackets.

And just as Cromwell had been forced away from the peace party by what he took to be the unacceptable behaviour of the peacemakers, so the New Model Army more and more conflated the war with religious struggle because their opponents said they were doing so; as always, Civil War politics were often about heated reactions to propaganda. The other force driving this view of the New Model was the London radical sectarians, especially the Baptists, who volunteered for military service in the army precisely because they saw it as God's instrument for the destruction of popery.

The creation of the New Model meant a fresh emphasis on merit which allowed for the removal of Essex, and of Manchester, Cromwell's *bête noire*. Admittedly, Essex didn't go quietly even when decisively pushed by Parliament, producing a long moan about how ill-used he felt before resigning; not for the last time, Parliament was being savaged by a dead sheep. By contrast, Cromwell was quickly recommissioned by an eager Fairfax, who wanted him to be Lieutenant-General of the Horse. By now, Cromwell had some friends and many enemies. He was becoming one of the leaders of the independent faction, with Sir Henry Vane. But Essex and Manchester, and their supporters in the Lords, were furiously resentful, and Manchester insisted that Cromwell was a base, levelling fellow who was filling the ranks of officers with plebeians – doubly mendacious, because it was Fairfax and not Cromwell who was picking the officers. Denzil Holles and the Presbyterians in both England and Scotland were also his foes, Lucy Hay's allies, who wanted peace and a restrained but still potent monarch ruling a Protestant but not Independent England. Denzil Holles thought the New Model officers distinctly beneath him – 'most of the colonels', he wrote, 'are tradesmen, tailors, goldsmiths, shoemakers, and the like'. The list sent up to the Commons was eventually pruned of those suspected of radicalism: both Rainsborough and Okey were excluded, and so was Major Richard Cromwell. Others, however, were excluded for duller reasons: keeping existing officers happy, patronage, clientage. And yet by no means all radicals were shut out, and the Lords may have made some attempt to balance religious views within regiments. One of those promoted when a number of Scottish colonels left in a huff was Ned Harley.

But this was a moral and class panic generated by a very small change in style. Only seven of the new colonels were not gentlemen, and nine of them were from noble families. Cromwell's well-known 'plain russet-coated captain' was actually able to pay for the creation of his own troop. You could look at them and see no difference from Royalist officers, as Fairfax's feat of walking through Royalist lines at Marston Moor shows. Yet internally the New Model began to make a difference. Once the amended Self-Denying Ordinance had been passed, on 3 April 1645, the officers were chosen on grounds of professional ability. The Ordinance demanded the resignation of members of both Houses from all military or civil offices held since 1640; a rider added that individuals might be reappointed later, as Cromwell was. Effectively, Parliament sacked its entire command and administrative staff, and reappointed those whose performance was thought to merit it. On these toughly meritocratic grounds, nobles like Essex and Manchester were ousted by minor gentlemen like Cromwell. Scarcely egalitarian, this nonetheless installed a notion that merit was not the same as rank. Of course, most of those who voted for the Ordinance did not see themselves as ushering in democracy, or the rule of the saints either. They simply wanted to win the war. But the remodelling was able to generate an *experience* of meritocracy which had a powerful impact.

That impact was heightened by the New Model's ancillary 'army' of preachers. There were a few regimental chaplains, but most preaching was done by ministers from army headquarters, who were especially eager to offer sermons just before battles. Hugh Peter preached on 20 July 1645, to encourage the soldiers to go on during the siege of Bridgewater. There was another homily, this time from the Reverend Bowle. Then the drums beat, the troops attacked, and with Peter exhorting them to do their utmost, they managed to take the town. But when they were not available, the Eastern Association cavalry were used to officers and even men taking over the pulpit, and they continued the practice. It spread to the rest of the army.

The New Model could also consult the Bible for further advice. One publication, *The Soldier's Pocket Bible*, was created especially for the army in 1643, but became progressively more popular as the war dragged on. It contained special prayers, mainly from militant psalms, and it dealt extensively with issues like courage in battle; most of it came from the Old Testament. It was full of exhortations: the first page began 'A soldier must not do wickedly' and 'A soldier must be valiant for God's cause'. Soldiers were reminded to pray before battles, in case they were killed. The *Pocket Bible* also interpreted the war as a holy one, in which the Lord might first afflict and then save his people: 'For the iniquities of Gods people are delivered into the hands of their enemies . . . Then shall all nations cry, wherefore hath the Lord done this unto this land, how fierce is his great wrath.' Such quotations were also an attempt to explain misfortune and to comfort.

Also consoling were images of the powerful God of the Hebrews: 'The Lord is a man of war; his name is JEHOVAH.' The last entries promised uprightness and integrity: 'I have vowed and I will perform it, that I will keep thy righteous judgement' (1644 edition). Civil War bullets were fired so feebly that even quite small Bibles could stop them, and Richard Baxter said that this happened so often that it was hardly worth recording. Some soldiers also had a catechism, which claimed that the Royalists 'were for the most part Papists and Atheists . . . generally the most horrible cursers and blasphemers in the world . . . for the most part inhumane, barbarous and cruel'. It was realistic, though; it also asked why morals were not higher in the army of Parliament. 'Because', it explained smoothly, 'honest religious men are not more forward to put forth themselves.' It added that 'officers in towns and countries aim to press the scum and refuse of men, and so by easing themselves pester our armies with base conditioned people'.

The New Model Army is associated in the popular mind with Cromwell, but its supreme commander was Thomas Fairfax, the man who had struggled back through hostile lines at Marston Moor to snatch victory from the jaws of defeat. And in its lifetime the New Model was not called the New Model; in official documents it was always described as the 'army under Sir Thomas Fairfax'. Fairfax was small, slight and self-effacing. When appointed to supreme command, he was just thirty-three years old. Yet despite these handicaps his authority over the army he helped to create was absolute, and unquestioned. Certainly Cromwell himself never questioned it. Fairfax was a man whose straightforwardness and integrity defeated even his willing detractors; the worst thing Royalists could find to say of him was that he was stupid and easily influenced. The last was the reverse of the truth; Bulstrode Whitelocke says that he would sit listening to the council discussing something, endlessly, and then go straight out and do the opposite of what they had decided upon. He was not stupid, either, but as a general there was a simplicity about him that anticipates Ulysses Simpson Grant. He didn't flank or encircle. He liked a good direct simple frontal assault, well sustained, and didn't mind if it cost a lot of men. By contrast, we have William Waller's description of Cromwell:

> And here I cannot but mention the wonder which I have oft times had to see this eagle in his eyrie. He at this time had never shown extraordinary parts, nor do I think that he did himself believe he had them. For although he was blunt, he did not bear himself with pride or disdain. As an officer he was obedient and did never dispute my orders nor argue upon them. He did indeed seem to have great cunning, and while he was cautious of his own words, not putting forth too many lest they should betray his thoughts, he made others talk, until he had as it were sifted them, and known their inmost designs. A notable instance was his discovering in one short conversation with one Captain Giles, a great favourite with the Lord General,

that although his words were full of zeal and his actions seemingly brave, that his heart was not with the cause. And in fine
this man did soon after join the enemy at Oxford, with three
and twenty stout fellows. One other instance I will here set
down, being of the same sort, as to his cunning: When I took
the Lord Percy at Andover, having at that time an inconvenient
distemper, I desired Colonel Cromwell to entertain him with
some civility; who did afterwards tell me, that amongst those
whom we took with him (being about thirty) there was a youth
of so fair a countenance that he doubted of his condition; and
to confirm himself willed him to sing; which he did with such
a daintiness that Cromwell scrupled not to say to Lord Percy
that 'being a warrior he did wisely to be accompanied by
Amazons.' On which the Lord in some confusion did acknowledge that she was a damsel. This afterwards gave some cause
for scoff at the King's party, as that they were loose and wanton,
and minded their pleasure more than their country's service or
their master's good.

One of the chaplains of the New Model was Richard Baxter, who left
a detailed record of his experiences. 'Oh the sad and heart-piercing
spectacles that mine eyes have seen in four years' space . . . scarce a
month, scarce a week without the sight or noise of blood . . . So hearing
such sad news on one side or the other was our daily work insomuch
that as duly as I was awakened in the morning I expected to hear one
come and tell me such a garrison is won or lost, or such a defeat is
recorded or given. And "do you hear the news?" was commonly the
first word I heard. So miserable were those bloody days, in which he
was most honourable that could kill most of his enemies.' He added,
'It must be a very extraordinary army that is not constituted of wolves
and tigers, and is not unto common honesty and piety the same that
a stews or whorehouse is to chastity.' Baxter had been Cromwell's choice
as chaplain for his troop as early as 1642, but despite being nearly
lynched by his own people in Kidderminster at the start of the war, he
decided to sit it out until 1645. This was in part because he expected
the war to be over quickly: 'so wise in the ways of war was I, and all
the country beside, that we commonly supposed that in a very few
days or weeks one battle would end the war'. He was wrong.

The campaign that was to end at Naseby fight began in early 1645 as an attempt to check Montrose. It was an integral part of the War of Three Kingdoms. Scottish commander Leven was afraid that if Montrose managed to join the king he would be unstoppable.

Meanwhile Fairfax was sitting idle before Oxford. He complained. 'We should spend our time unprofitably before a town, whilst the King hath time to strengthen himself and by terror to enforce obedience of all places where he comes.' Parliament's army under Massey managed to take Evesham, cutting the king off from Worcester. Meanwhile, the king too was unenthusiastic about the New Model sitting outside Oxford. He thought the city's provisions inadequate for a long siege. So to draw off the New Model, the Royalists under Rupert attacked Leicester, which had only a small garrison and stout walls to defend it. The walls weren't stout enough to withstand Rupert's guns, and within a day they had taken and sacked the town.

It was a terrible sack, as those involving Rupert's men generally were. They took the mayor's mace, and no soldier, it was said, left with less than forty shillings. Two hundred men were killed and 1200 more imprisoned. The news sent London into a panic. The Leicester garrison, it was reported with some exaggeration, had been butchered to a man. 'All these things will seem like dreams for many men, but they must understand we will be no more a-dreaming; the business of Leicester hath awakened us.'

The Committee of Both Houses met, even though it was the Sabbath. At once it ordered Fairfax and Sir Samuel Luke to act, telling Fairfax simply to follow the king. Cromwell went to defend the Eastern Association. But London felt no reassurance. 'Never hardly did an army go off to war who had less the confidence of their own friends or were more the objects of the contempt of their enemies.' Rupert argued passionately that the king should continue to harass Midland towns, thus drawing off Fairfax and relieving Oxford. But Rupert by now had enemies who would not have voted for his plans even if he had been leading an army of angels. The Royalist army simply hung about the Midlands, doing nothing, and some of its men deserted, the Yorkshire levies because they would not march south and others because they were already rich enough with plunder. But Charles was happy because Fairfax had duly left Oxford, marching to Newport Pagnell and asking that Cromwell be released to serve under him. There were plenty of hearty jokes about the 'New Noddle' Army.

But the smiles vanished when Charles heard that Fairfax and his forces were only five miles away from his own position at Burrow Hill, not far from Daventry. He had slipped easily through the Royalist scouts, and the king's army was scattered. Charles was out hunting when he heard the news, on 12 June. Fairfax's arrival was only recognized when the Royalist pickets were driven in. There was immediate confusion. Many soldiers, as always, were out foraging, and horses were foraging too, grazing on the slopes of Burrow Hill.

Fairfax, on the other hand, was well briefed. He had intercepted a letter from Goring to the king, explaining that he was not able to bring his troops to the Midlands. The king's forces had been depleted by the war and by desertion: some of his twenty-six regiments of infantry contained only about eighty men, and the proportion of officers to soldiers was very high because some regiments had all but disappeared. Estimates vary, but perhaps the Royalists had about 4000 foot and about 5000 horse. The New Model, however, had 13,000 even before Cromwell's horse arrived on 13 June. It may have been this disparity that prompted the king to begin moving back towards Market Harborough. Fairfax pursued him, and by night had reached Gainsborough, with his vanguard entering Naseby and capturing a Cavalier patrol, who had stopped at a local inn for a feast. Hearing of Fairfax's pursuit, the king immediately summoned a council of war, which met in the dark of night on 14 June. Some sensibly argued for withdrawal, but the Royalist honour code generated its usual appetite for battle, whatever the odds, and soon they had decided to turn and face the enemy on the long, high ridge south of Market Harborough. It blocked the road between Fairfax's camp and the town, and if Fairfax tried to use the road, the Royalists could sweep down onto his left flank. If he tried to flank the position, he would expose his own flank to attack.

The army was on the ridge, waiting, by 8 a.m. In the centre was the Royalist foot, commanded by Sir Jacob Astley, with 800 horse to protect it. To the right were another 2000 horse under Rupert, while on the left Sir Marmaduke Langdale commanded the northern horse. Its ranks were decidedly thin without Goring's support.

The New Model had been moving since 3 a.m. But Fairfax couldn't see the enemy, and didn't want to stumble into them in the thick morning mist. He too stopped, outside Naseby.

Then each army sent out scouts looking for the other. Rupert's reported that they couldn't find the New Model. Irritably, Rupert decided to go and look himself. Fairfax, on the other hand, knew where the Royalists were; he rode forward, wondering about occupying some boggy ground that could make a Royalist cavalry charge difficult. But Cromwell argued urgently against it. Rupert could, he maintained, turn the position, or simply sit on the high ground and decline battle. It would be much better to occupy the ridge to the rear, which would tempt Rupert across the valley and force him to charge uphill at them. Fairfax showed his good sense and leadership ability: he saw at once that his subordinate was right. The New Model was strung out along the line of march, gradually closing up to the village, where the front ranks had stopped.

At this moment Rupert cantered up and saw the army withdrawing, it seemed, and about to occupy the ridge. Like Cromwell, he didn't like the idea of fighting a cavalry battle on the boggy ground, but he could see another, better possibility; why not flank them? Go around to the right, keep the windward position so his men would not be too blind with black smoke to charge? He sent the army an urgent message to follow, and struck off to the right. The Royalists responded, though Rupert's artillery couldn't keep up and he ended by opening hostilities with only a few sakers, small cannon, in place.

As the Royalist army followed Rupert, with the king himself in front on horseback, bearing his drawn sword aloft, Fairfax saw its movement from the ridge. The New Model prepared for action; Skippon drew up the foot, and Cromwell was on the right. Whalley's horse, so loved by Richard Baxter, stood ready to plunge into action. They were on terrible ground, broken, thick with furze, pitted with rabbit holes. On the other wing, the left, were more cavalry under Cromwell's capable future son-in-law Henry Ireton. Cromwell placed some dragoons to line the hedges so as to take any Royalist advance in enfilade. This was always sound strategy, but it bore heavily on the dragoons, who were exhausted from constant outpost duty while the army was on the move, and who were now vulnerable. There was a forlorn hope, too.

At about ten in the morning, the Royalist advance began, heavy and slow, the officers clad in velvet and taffeta, with silk colours flying. Cromwell later remembered that 'when I saw the enemy draw up and march in gallant order towards us, and we a company of poor ignorant men, to seek how to order our battle . . . I could not riding alone about my business but smile out to God in praises, in assurance of victory, because God would, by things that are not, bring to naught things that are.'

The forlorn hope fired, and as if it were a signal, the New Model moved over the crest, as the Parliamentarian artillery got off a round of fire. As Rupert's cavalry trotted forward and caught up the infantry, the musketeers in the hedgerows fired, but it did little to slow the charge. Rupert's forces swept up the hill and collided with Ireton's cavalry; the attack was fierce enough to break one of the regiments, which was saved by the musketry of Okey's tired dragoons. The survivors faced Rupert's second line, which pushed Ireton's men from the field.

But then, as ever, Rupert couldn't get his men to re-form and charge again. On they rode, pursuing the fleeing New Model stragglers, until they galloped right into the New Model baggage-train. They were eager, but the camp guard was determined, and made a genuine attempt to see them off. An hour went by before Rupert could get his men back to the main business of the day. And he himself, supposedly the commanding general, was absent too.

The Royalist foot pressed forward, 'falling in with their swords and the butt end of their muskets'. Skippon had taken a musket bullet that had pierced his armour under the ribs. He reeled in the saddle, but refused to retire. Yet news of his wound spread, and his men wavered; his front line crumpled, though it did not break. Ireton, who had re-formed his men, crashed into the right of the Royalist foot, but they managed to hold off his attack with pikes and muskets, and his horse was shot out from under him. Dismounted, he was vulnerable; a pikeman ran him through the thigh. A halberd gashed him in the face. Finally, he was captured. His counterattack had hindered the Royalists, but now they broke through to Skippon's second line.

Only half an hour after the battle had begun, a Royalist victory seemed imminent. But the New Model was saved by the clash between Cromwell and Langdale on the left. Cromwell, seeing Langdale advancing, trotted to meet him, his flank protected by the bad ground on his right. Whalley's troops, doubtless filled with holy thoughts by Richard Baxter, had the advantage of moving down the hill, and the advantage of numbers too.

Joshua Sprigge, a chaplain like Baxter, gave an eyewitness account of the battle: 'Colonel Whalley being the left hand on the right wing, charged first two divisions of Langdale's horse, who made a very gallant resistance, and firing at a very close charge, they came to the sword; wherein Colonel Whalley's division, routed those two divisions, driving them back.'

Before Langdale's men could get to the top of the hill, Clarendon later wrote, they gave back, 'and fled farther and faster than became them'. Cromwell did not lose an instant. He sent two regiments to stop Langdale's men from rallying, and the rest of his men attacked the Royalist foot's flank and rear. Astley's men, already tired, pushing at the New Model pikemen, could do little to oppose Cromwell's thundering horsemen, who drove hard against them, swords and pistols out. Now Okey ordered his dragoons to mount, and they charged into Astley's men on the other flank, who gave way, and began to fling their weapons down, crying out for quarter. Cromwell's two regiments chased Langdale off the field.

Watching from a nearby hill, Charles was horrified, shamed. He turned his horse, and prepared to charge Cromwell's men himself. Beside him, the Earl of Carnwath seized his bridle as if the king were a naughty little boy, and with 'two or three full-mouthed Scottish oaths', said, angrily, 'Will you go upon your death in an instant?' This may have been Charles's idea; he knew of Richard III's final charge. But the result was chaotic. As Carnwath swung Charles's horse around, to the right, it was misinterpreted as a signal. Someone shouted that they must march right, away from Cromwell's pursuing cavalry, and the whole body of horse galloped frantically rightwards. Thus the mounted reserve never came to the aid of the infantry. One infantry brigade hung on against the relentless pressure; Fairfax eventually charged against it personally, cutting down an ensign, taking his colours, wielding his sabre like any other cavalryman. Rupert finally arrived back at the battlefield, and was greeted by the spectacle of the Royalist foot surrendering their arms. Only the cavalry reserves were still on their feet, and the king was trying uselessly to rally them for a last charge. They were menaced by Cromwell's horse, and Fairfax was assembling his infantry and horse, too, for a last attack.

The Royalist cavalry did not charge. It fled. And it left behind the king's foot, men who had fought for him at Edgehill, at Newbury, at Lostwithiel when Essex's army had been defeated and captured. The army which had been close to winning now stood like grass, waiting for the scythe.

The New Model had already overrun the Royalist baggage-train. There were hundreds of women there, soldiers' wives who came to cook and wash for them, and the less respectable women who followed the army too, some of them richly dressed, with money. 'They [the Royalist army] carried along with them many strumpets, who they term "leaguer Ladies"', noted the Lancastrian diarist Edward Robinson. 'These they made use of in places where they lay in a very uncivil and unbecoming way.' Prim and godly responses to such scenes might lie behind the outrage which followed. The New Model men attacked every woman there; all of them were branded as whores, by having their noses slit or their faces slashed. A hundred were simply murdered. Only the previous week, a newsbook had reported that a thousand Irish women followed the king's camp. Well, said the soldiers, they were *Irish*. And they didn't even speak English, some of them – and they had knives. Whores and camp-sluts, attending a wicked army.

Probably they were from the king's Welsh levies, and the knives were being used to get midday dinner for their partners. Now they lay in their blood.

In London, the newsbooks reported the massacre. No one condemned it, and Cromwell and Fairfax left the perpetrators unpunished.

The New Model captured all the king's guns, a huge quantity of arms and ammunition, and the king's coach, perhaps the most important prize of all. Sprigge gloated: 'all their ordinance, being brass guns, whereof two were demi-cannon, besides two more mortar pieces, the enemy got away not one carriage, eight thousand arms and more, forty barrels of powder, two hundred horse, with their riders, the King's colours, the duke of York's standard, and six of his colours, four of the Queen's white colours, with double crosses on each of them, and near one hundred other colours both of horse and foot; the King's cabinet, the King's sumpter, many coaches, with store of wealth in them'. The king's coach contained his correspondence, and once it was published under the sensational title *The Kings Cabinet Opened*, it seemed to confirm what his enemies had said about him all along; he had been treating with papists, raising a force of Irish and French Catholic mercenaries, menacing England with popery ... 'the cabinet letters, which discover so much to satisfy all honest men of the intention of the adverse party, fell likewise into our hands', reported Sprigge.

Victory came at a price:

> I saw the field so bestrewed with the carcasses of men and horses as was most sad to behold, because subjects under one government, but most happy in this because they were most of them professed enemies of God and his Son. The field was about a mile wide when the battle was fought. The bodies lay slain about four miles in length, the most thick on the hill where the King stood. I cannot think there were less than four hundred men slain there, and truly I think not many more, and three hundred horse.

But for now the New Model sat down in the field to enjoy the bread, cheese and biscuits that had been won. It had fought hungry. Its hunger would become more and more of a feature of the years ahead.

London rejoiced at the news; its low expectations made the surprise even more joyful. The first newsbooks gloated, 'For the glorious victory that it hath pleased God to give our army under the command of that Heroic General Sir Thomas Fairfax, deserves to be taken notice of in an extraordinary manner.' 'I should be much to blame', wrote one instantly published correspondent, 'if I should not acquaint so public a spirit as yourself with what God hath done for this kingdom by our poor, despised and contemptible army.' The army's low reputation meant that the hand of God in the victory seemed even plainer. And the good performance of the army was stressed, too: 'All our officers and soldiers did as bravely as could be: the former performed all points of soldiery well, though envy hath frequently bespattered them, as not able to command, and therefore deserted by so many out of fear.' The newsbooks also reported every rumour: 'Lieutenant General Cromwell with a gallant party of horse is in the pursuit [of the king].' Some of them were too optimistic: 'some of our scouts have just now brought intelligence that Prince Rupert is taken'. The wounding of General Skippon and fears for his health were also reported. This was of particular interest to Londoners; he had been their general too. Londoners were later to enjoy the spectacle of the prisoners of Naseby paraded through their streets. 'The common soldiers were put into the Artillery Garden in Tothill Fields, the Officers into the Lord Peters house in Aldersgate street.' In Tothill Fields, the soldiers were treated to sermons by divines eager to convert them to Parliament's cause.

Other places heard the news too. Royalist strongholds began to surrender. Carlisle on 2 July, its garrison starved, Pontefract on 21 July, Scarborough on the following day. The king hurried to South Wales, and took refuge in Raglan Castle. He still had a force of sorts – 4000 horse, 2500 foot. 'There his Majesty stayed three weeks, and as if the genius of the place had conspired with our fates, we were there all lulled to sleep with sports and entertainments; as if no crown had been at stake, or in any danger to be lost': Sir Edward Walker was baffled, but the king was hiding from reality.

And all over the three kingdoms, people noted the news. Isabella Twysden did, though she was preoccupied with more personal matters. Naseby and its outcome crowds its way into her book, jostling for room with entries that describe her dealings with her baby's nurse:

> The 24 Nurse Jane went to London
>
> The 21st Sr Mills brought troops came into Kent to barrack for their pay
>
> The first of April Nurse Jane had 12d for a month nursing of Charles the month was not up till 2 days after
>
> The 14 of June Sir Tho Fairfax had a great victory at Nasby where he took 12 pieces of ordinance 4000 foot soldiers and the Sc letters.

Some of Isabella's family eventually responded to Naseby and its implications with flight: 'The first or 2 of July 1647 my sister Ann Waler lay at Tunbridge, next day when she was gone Sir Will her husband went through that town, all went tis said for France, 2 horses went with him heavy loaded though little to come to, and she carried a heavy box in her coach, this I was told, they went not to France but back to London.'

Like Ann Fanshawe, Isabella was both interested in political events and inclined to see them as disruptions of normal family life: 'The 5 of August my husband came to Peckham where he has not been in 5 years before.' This sounds bald, but they had a very tender marriage. 'Never man had a better wife, never children a better mother', he wrote of Isabella. Before the war, he wrote: 'I enquire by you of what state the deer are, and wonder much they are so backward, they thriving most in such weather. I thank thee for thy sugar cakes my good heart, which will be very useful to me . . . Farewell again and again my own dear heart whom I never knew what it was to be parted from till now.'

Roger Twysden was a moderate in an age of extremists. He was staunchly Church of England, but disliked episcopacy. His response to Naseby was therefore neither dread nor delight.

In Scotland, the consequences would be more far-reaching than anywhere. From the Scottish point of view, Naseby represented the triumph of Independency, an Independency that was to insist, vehemently, on rule from Westminster, on the same prerogatives as the king had. Independency was a radical extension of Presbyterianism, one which extended the ideas of Presbyterians to an extent that alarmed the Kirk's most ardent spirits. Independents wanted freedom of conscience, freedom for congregations to choose their own forms of worship. They did not even want the Church to be nationally organized, for *any* structure might impede the workings of the Holy Spirit among them. Even church buildings came to be suspect, and Independent sects – Baptists, Congregationalists – came to prefer meeting in places that were not called places of worship, assembly rooms and warehouses, to show that they were not bound to any order or hierarchy. Godly John Pym would not have stood it for a moment. It is impossible to be sure how many Independents there were, but there were enough to cause considerable anxiety. Their individualistic radicalism frightened many, for it came to be loosely allied with the party in Parliament and in the army which stood for the prosecution of the war to the last ditch and the outright defeat of the king. From Naseby on, Scotland was fighting against being absorbed into an England run by the Independents, fighting against them just as it had against Charles and Laud.

XXV

Ashes: The Siege of Taunton and the Clubmen

By early 1645, in other parts of England, the opposing sides so laboriously drawn up had collapsed into victims and perpetrators, the hungry and the full, the homeless and the housed. The struggle to hold on to house and home diminished the importance of abstract political ideas. In the spring of 1645, tired apathy suddenly burst into vehement resistance; true, there had been protests before, but not on such a wide and ferocious scale. Soldiers on both sides were attacked sporadically, as the exhausted civilians vented their rage. Peacekeeping associations began to appear across the south, whose members eventually came to be called Clubmen – because they carried clubs. Courted by both sides, in Dorset and Wiltshire they slightly preferred the king to his foes; in Somerset, they took the opposite line.

The root of the problem was the Royalist troops that occupied Somerset, who were unpaid and almost entirely out of hand. They were a problem even for the Royalist high command, and those under George Goring were an especial headache. Goring was a man capable of brilliant individual action, but he was also feckless and irresponsible. Consistently putting his personal ambition to be in charge of the western campaign ahead of the king's cause, he was also notoriously undisciplined, engaging in drunken bacchanals in which his staff were expected to join. Though Goring's men were to become notorious for 'continual butcheries, rapes and robberies', the trouble started with one of Ralph Hopton's better-disciplined regiments. Troops from Colonel John Tynte's regiment quartered in a Somerset village called South Brent early in March, and returned in larger numbers around 24 March. They rode in from Bristol, passing through Axbridge during the fair. Bystanders abused them in the street, and eventually a maddened soldier drew his sword against a Cheddar man, who defended himself with a staff, broke the soldier's sword, but was then beaten savagely around the head. Next, the soldiers robbed a butcher who was on his way home from the fair, and killed a poor labourer they met on the highway. When they finally reached South Brent they seized the fat bullock of a farmer, bought at the fair, beat the servant who tried to deny it to them, put a rope around his neck and pretended to hang him, threatening to do so unless he gave them money. The tithingman gave them what money he had, but they said they would come back tomorrow and tie his neck and heels together if he could not do more to satisfy them.

Moving to Lympsham, they ordered the citizens out of bed, telling them to lie upon straw while they had the beds, while at Berrow they wrecked William Lush's house, stole clothes and bedding, and told him they would burn his house and kill his wife if he did not keep quiet. Others threatened to burn the whole village if the inhabitants did not cooperate. The commander John Tynte was a local from near Nailsea, but most of the thugs were not, and some were Irish; John Tynte's brother, Henry, announced that 'most of the country were fools, and good for nothing but to be made idiots'. When ordered into action by Hopton, the regiment refused to move until the villages produced more tribute. This was enough for a local gentleman called 'John Somerset' and his followers, who promptly took up pikes and staves, and attacked the soldiers on Good Friday, 4 April 1645.

This was by no means the only incident of its kind; elsewhere too, troops in search of plunder were set upon by locals who had had enough – or rather, by locals who had *not* had enough or very much of anything for a long time. The Clubmen were not solely a Somerset phenomenon. There had been Clubmen in Shropshire, Worcestershire and Herefordshire in early spring, and nearer Somerset there were risings in surrounding counties – Wiltshire, Dorset – and rather later in the summer further disturbances occurred in South Wales. In autumn,

Berkshire, Hampshire and Sussex saw Clubmen risings; in Berkshire, some 16,000 men were said to be involved. Evidence – sparse, and contradictory – suggests that the first Clubmen were probably ordinary farmers and peasants who were tired of the likes of Goring, and whose discontent was then exploited or harnessed by gentlemen and professional men.

Many began by valuing tradition and the rule of law, especially in matters of religion; many greatly disliked the Directory for Worship which had in March 1645 ousted the prayer book. The Clubmen, said one of their critics, wanted 'the old vanities and superstitions of their forefathers, the old necromantic order of prelacy, and the wondrous old heathen customs of Sunday pipings and dancings'. These aims seemed most likely to be fulfilled by the Royalists for some – perhaps most – but by Parliament for others, and none of the above for still others. Some surviving evidence about their grievances survives in a petition sent to the king by the Wiltshire Clubmen in 1644 and also read in the House of Lords. The Clubmen said that they had 'more deeply than many other parts of the kingdom tasted the miseries of this unnatural intestine war', and complained explicitly about the 'pressures of many garrisons', while also insisting that their aim was to maintain true religion. Other petitions called for the return of 'the ancient ways'. All this diversity means that the Clubmen's aims have become a matter of debate between historians; some argue that they were like French peasant organizations, hierarchically arranged and led by gentlemen followed by peasants, in defence of that very hierarchy. Others argue that some Clubmen at least had more radical aims. What is clear is that ordinary people were trying to enter the political decision-making process, and that some were already familiar with self-government; the Somerset Clubmen elected their officers, suggesting an allegiance to democratic process, which made it even harder to be subject to the demands of the Royalist armies and their undisciplined men.

The miseries of Taunton were especially acute. It had been garrisoned by the Royalists for fourteen months from May 1643 and was retaken in July 1644 for Parliament, and placed under the leadership of Colonel Robert Blake. It managed to hold out against a Royalist siege earlier that year. By Christmas of that year, it had been under siege for three months, and the civilians and garrison were both hungry. The Royalist besiegers reported that a sortie from the town had failed when those in the party had stopped chasing the Royalists in order to look for bread in surrounding houses. Many men died this way, ambushed by the Royalists as they rushed out of the houses 'with the bread in their mouths'.

It was again besieged from April 1645. Royalist commander Richard Grenville, Bevil Grenville's younger brother, began pouring musket and cannon fire into the town from new siegeworks on 10 April. Grenville's efforts were hampered by Goring. Ordered to send his foot and guns to Grenville, he did send the foot, but himself went sulkily off to Bath, thinking he should have been given command. After Grenville was wounded, he took care to ensure his officers would dislike the new interim commander, Sir John Berkeley. Once again, the Royalist commanders were thinking about personal honour rather than about the conduct of the war. At times it was hard to be sure who was in overall command; all three men behaved as if they were, though only Hopton had royal authority. Meanwhile, in Taunton the streets were blockaded and the town entrances blocked by earthworks, so that it could only be taken in pieces. It was a little Stalingrad.

The New Model Army under Fairfax had been told that its first task was to relieve Taunton. Goring and his cavalry were ordered back to Oxford to join the king and Rupert for a new northern campaign, and without his cavalry to act as scouts Hopton was surprised by the speed of the New Model's advance, hearing nothing until Fairfax was at Salisbury. Then Fairfax was himself recalled to respond to Charles's movements, leaving a force of around 6000 men under Colonel Ralph Weldon to relieve Taunton. Before he left, however, Fairfax bluffed Hopton with a clever feint; on 8 May he swung west, which made Hopton think that he was about to face the whole of the New Model. Then Fairfax turned east again while Weldon continued towards Taunton. By now the town was suffering terribly from Hopton's artillery; two days before, the Royalists had captured an outwork to the east but then next day were driven back by musket fire, and also stones and boiling water. Baffled, Hopton staged a sham fight between two parts of his force firing blanks, hoping that Blake would think the fighting caused by the relief and send out a sortie. It was then that he heard that Fairfax was moving west, and he reacted by making one last all-out effort to storm and burn the stubborn town.

The successive sieges caused great hardship in the town. Sieges almost always began with a cannon bombardment designed to terrify the people and also to tire them into surrender. In Taunton, it felt as if they were being besieged by a wall of fire. The civilian population could only hide as the assailants swarmed through every street in bitter house-to-house fighting. At seven in the evening a general assault began; in the east, it succeeded in breaching the defences, and the soldiers immediately tried to light fires that would burn the entire town. Thwarted by a change of wind, the Royalists were nevertheless cheered to hear that Fairfax had turned east, and that Goring was on his way back from Oxford; they attacked again on Friday 9 May, and now they fought their way through barricaded streets and against frantic house-to-house resistance. By evening, half the town was burning. The defenders held only the castle, St Mary Magdalen's church, Maiden's Fort, and an entrenchment in the marketplace. Ironically, for a war at least in part about religion, churches were key points in armed conflict because they could be fortified as strongholds. Weldon's relief force advanced slowly, seeing the flames of Taunton against the night sky; Weldon sent word to Blake that he would signal his coming with ten cannon shots.

On Saturday morning, the Royalists made a last attempt to fire the small part of the town that still held out. Three were caught and lynched; one, a woman, was hanged by the women of Taunton. Hopton sent in a final demand for surrender; Blake replied that he would eat three of his last four pairs of boots first, an engaging mixture of determination and common sense. Weldon's advance guard arrived that afternoon, and Blake, who had always felt God was with him, was triumphantly vindicated. By four o'clock, the Royalists were retreating, felling trees as they went to hamper pursuit.

So on Sunday 11 May, Weldon entered what were almost the ruins of Taunton. The townspeople were starving. Two-thirds of the houses had been destroyed, while the rest had been stripped of their thatch to feed the horses, and their bedcords to make match for muskets. More than a hundred defenders were killed, and twice that many lay wounded. But the men began to creep out of hiding, and the slow work of clearing up began. Next day, the people from the surrounding countryside crept in too, and stood around, with 'broad eyes of wonder'. On the first anniversary of the relief, the godly minister preached a sermon which recalled the day. 'You may read it in the ruins of this place', he said, meaning the story of other towns that had actually fallen to the enemy. 'Look about her and tell her heaps of rubbish, her consumed houses, a multitude of which are raked in their own ashes. Here a poor forsaken chimney, and there a little fragment of a wall that have escaped to tell what barbarous and monstrous wretches there have been.'

Goring's forces remained, in part because Goring himself could not seem to decide what to do instead. By now, however, he faced real, organized resistance. In Herefordshire, there had been a great Club outbreak, a throng demanding compensation for their losses. But the Clubmen centred on Dorset, Wiltshire and Somerset, a poor area with a long history of riots against enclosure. Like modern Countryside Alliance protesters, many Clubmen were people who had managed to claw something together, but not a lot, and who had seen it taken away. There was a huge assembly at Gussage Corner, near Wimborne St Giles, on 25 May, and a 'peacekeeping' force was formed, its principal aim being to preserve its members from violence and plunder. A Clubmen banner proclaimed: 'If you offer to plunder or take our cattle/ Be assured we will bid you battle.' It intended to petition both king and Parliament for peace. Bands of farmers wearing white ribbons in their hats were soon demonstrating against both sides; church bells were rung to warn villages farther afield if marauding soldiers were sighted. Armed with pikes and clubs, men interposed between Royalist and Parliamentarian forces and made them stop fighting and drink together instead. On 2 June a group of 5000 men gathered near Castle Cary and the Prince of Wales received a delegation denouncing Goring's activities. There were various attempts to convert them to Royalism, to which the Somerset men turned a deaf ear.

They were deaf because the war had cost so much, more than they could afford; not only sons, brothers, fathers, but livelihoods and food and above all housing, especially in the towns. All over England, buildings that had once stood stalwart against rain and wind lay in crumpled heaps or were reduced to ash and rubble. Faringdon, close to the

Berkshire–Wiltshire border, saw 'the whole town almost pulled down, demolished and wilfully consumed by fire' as the last desperate battles for Oxford were fought in and through its narrow streets. Here 236 families were made homeless. Bridgewater lost all its suburbs, including an entire parish, Eastover; the loss was estimated at 120 houses, around a third of the entire housing stock. In the north, too, there were losses; the garrison towns often lost almost everything that stood outside the city walls. In York, 'all the houses in some streets . . . burnt and broken down to the ground' testified mutely to the homelessness of their former residents. About one-sixth of York's houses lay outside the walls. Carlisle, which suffered similar destruction, was 'a model of misery and desolation'. England was to see nothing on this scale again until 1940; for the purposes of comparison, the German raid on Coventry was to destroy about half the houses in that city.

There were bitter human costs, too. After the war, the widows of Somerset petitioned the local authorities for pensions. The petitions reveal the extent of the suffering the war caused. Only those who had fought for Parliament were eligible. Joan Burt, of Durlenge, wrote that she was of a 'great age', and hence could not support the children of her son Jeffrey, who had been cruelly hanged at Taunton after imprisonment; nor could she care for the two children of her daughter, or her son-in-law John Abbott, killed at Bridgewater. Alice Drummond of Horningsham had lost her husband Colonel Edmund Ludlow at the siege of Wardour Castle, leaving her with three small children and nothing to keep them; she was subsequently the victim of Goring's plundering Royalists. The whole family then succumbed to leprosy, so that they were likely to die 'for want of food and to be turned out of door naked for want of house room'. Her case, too, was referred to the parish overseers of the poor for relief. The exhausted countryside embarked on a long, cold voyage to recovery.

XXVI

The Birds in the Greenwoods
are Mated Together: Anne Halkett
and the Escape of James II

After Naseby in June 1645, the Royalist armies crumpled. Charles rode away, first to the Scots, eventually to captivity. His fate would be decided later. His pasteboard capital, Oxford, finally surrendered to the new and hard reality on 24 June 1646. Among the loot gathered in was a little prince, the future James II, now Duke of York. Like the royal art collection, the royal family were now in the hands of their enemies.

Yet culture did not stand still. John Suckling's poems, *Fragmenta Aurea*, appeared; the title summed up the tattered but still surviving Caroline ideals. John Donne's witty justification of suicide saw print for the first time; perhaps it seemed topical, for it argued that Jesus Christ was a suicide, too. Thomas Browne tried to correct numerous vulgar errors in *Pseudodoxia Epidemica*. The Catholic poet Crashaw produced his devotional *Steps To The Temple*. And the poems of an unknown Welshman called Vaughan appeared. Edward Hyde, his royal master defeated, began writing his own history of how it had all happened.

There was a sense of ending. Some were certain that they were living through the Last Days. In Leicestershire, a great pond of water turned to blood under the shocked eyes of locals. It signified that all men were of one blood, and that the wars should stop, so its chronicler thought. In Shoe Lane, in London, a woman gave birth to a child without head or feet, and out of its neck was born another, smaller baby. Above Newmarket, there were strange apparitions: 'three men in the air struggling, and tugging together, one of them having a drawn sword in his hand, from which judgement God in mercy preserve those three kingdoms of England, Scotland and Ireland from further conflicts and effusion of blood'. It may have been the Northern Lights, not usually seen so far south; they were to haunt the American Civil War battlefields in the cold hard winter of 1863, as far south as Fredericksburg in Virginia, so perhaps the heavens were really eager to deliver a message to humanity about kin-strife and fratricide.

Under their glare, one woman would find a way to help the stricken royal family look towards the future. Anne Halkett had the same kind of education as her contemporaries Ann Harrison Fanshawe and Lucy Hutchinson. She learnt to write, speak French, play an instrument and dance, and she also learnt needlework, 'which shows I was brought up in an idle life'. She got up every morning for divine service, at five in summer and six in winter. She also loved plays, and to walk in the Spring Gardens ('before it grew something scandalous by the abuse of some', she adds hastily), and declared proudly that when she went to the theatre she paid for her own ticket.

But then Anne fell in love, and in doing so disobeyed her parents, committing exactly the crime later thought to have been a cause of the war itself. Her private love life was inextricably intertwined with affairs of state, and it proved impossible for Anne to live and love outside the political concerns that swept the nation into war. This was in part because her love crossed the bounds of class. Her suitor, Thomas Howard, was related to a patron to her father. In the 1640s and 1650s, Edward, first Lord Howard of Escrick, was a prominent Parliamentarian. He joined the Commons when the Lords were abolished. Thomas's younger brother William was an even more controversial figure. Involved in a Leveller plot to overthrow the Protectorate in the 1650s, he accepted Charles II, but then when sent on a spying mission to the Netherlands swapped sides, and served William of Orange; later his enthusiasm for William led him to Whig politics and ardent support for James's exclusion from the succession. This might explain Anne's eagerness to tell what at first glance seems a private story, unrelated to the war.

Thomas Howard, it seems, was a seducer. He used a hard-to-resist romantic approach, assuring Anne that 'he had endeavoured all this time to smother his passion which he said had begun the first time that ever he saw me, and . . . if I did not give him some hopes of favour he was resolved to go back again into France . . . and turn Capucin'. He was menacing Anne with popery. Anne 'did yield so far to comply with his desire to give him liberty one day when I was walking in the gallery to come there and speak to me . . . his hand trembled when he took mine to lead me, and with a great sigh said, "If I loved you less, I could say more."' Anne replied under the constraint of propriety: 'I told him I could not but think myself much obliged to him for his good opinion of me, but it would be a higher obligation to confirm his esteem of me by following my advice.' He was undeterred. 'Madam', said he. 'What I love in you may well increase, but I am sure it can never decay.' He proposed a private marriage. Anne refused. She wanted her mother's consent, and his father's. They got neither, and so had to part; it was an emotional encounter. Thomas 'fell down in a chair that was behind him, but as one without all sense, which I must confess did so much move me that laying aside all former distance I had kept him at, I sat down upon his knee, and laying my head near his I suffered him to kiss me, which was a liberty I never gave before'. Later Anne's faithful maid Miriam managed to reach her with the urgent message that Thomas was at the back gate hoping for a few final words with her. Anne steadfastly refused to see him, but then Miriam came up with an alarming report. 'I believe you are the most unfortunate person living,' she said, 'for I think Mr H is killed.' Miriam had been speaking to him, when 'there came a fellow with a great club behind him and struck him down dead'.

Anne was frantic. For her, the Civil War had in that moment become a sudden, criminal, violent disruption of normality. Her lover had been mugged. 'The reason for this was from what there was too many sad examples of at that time, when the division was between the King and Parliament, for to betray a master or friend was looked upon as doing God good service.' The attack was not, however, a piece of random violence. There was a story behind it, though Anne didn't work it out fully until later. Anne's brother-in-law's estates had been sequestered, that 'with much difficulty my sister got leave to live in her own house and had the fifth part to live upon'. After that the family was spied on by one of her brother's tenants, a man named Musgrove, 'who was a very great rogue', and who saw Thomas and mistook him for Anne's brother-in-law Thomas Newton. Perhaps the stalker heard the name Thomas. Anne wasn't interested in Musgrove's story, and we don't know enough to reconstruct it, but it was an example of the ripple effect of war, how one event might overwhelm many caught in its consequences.

Thomas survived, and Anne managed a final meeting, blindfolding herself so that she could keep her promise never to see Thomas again. It was the night of 10 October 1644. Anne waited. Then one day she heard the news. A letter came from a female friend. He was married. Married. To an earl's daughter. Anne flung herself down on the bed. She thought, 'Is this the man for whom I have suffered so much? Since he has made himself unworthy my love, he is unworthy my anger or concern.' And rising, she immediately went out and ate her supper as if nothing had happened. Her loyal maid Miriam shared her rage, and voiced it in sturdy terms that Anne couldn't use. 'Give her, O Lord, dry breasts and a miscarrying womb', she cried. Anne reproached her decorously, but noted that the Lord had apparently accepted her request, for 'that lady miscarried of several children before she brought one to the full time, and that one died presently after it was born'. She added, with poorly restrained glee, that 'not only was this couple unfortunate in the children, but in one another, for it was too well-known how short a time continued the satisfaction they had in one another'. The stubbornness that had made her a trial to her mother now helped her. But Anne's story goes on, and it takes a darker turn.

Anne's mother died in 1647, and Anne went to live with her brother and his wife. It was at their house that she met a much darker and more dubious man than Thomas Howard, the Irish adventurer and Royalist spy, Colonel Joseph Bampfield. Anne was attracted to him almost at once. 'His discourse was serious, handsome, and tending to impress the advantages of piety, loyalty, and virtue; and these subjects were so agreeable to my own inclination that I could not but give them a good reception.' This sounds demure enough – but Bampfield was married, though he explained that it was the king's service that had led him to London while his wife remained in the country.

Bampfield was born in 1622 or 3, so he was only in his twenties when Anne met him. He had joined the king's army at the age of seventeen, and had risen through the ranks to become a colonel. Indeed, he had been charged with helping the thirteen-year-old Duke of York to escape from St James's Palace. Charles was especially eager that his son should get away. 'I look upon James's escape as Charles's preservation', he told Bampfield, meaning that he could live on through hope and through his son.

Bampfield needed Anne's help, because his plan involved dressing James as a girl. Thirteen-year-old boys were regarded as girlish in this period, and James at this age was fair-haired, blue-eyed, pale, small and slight. Anne sensibly pointed out that the imposture would be more convincing if James's female clothes fitted him perfectly. At Anne's urging, Bampfield arranged to see James alone. Anne told him to take a ribbon and to bring back measurements for the prince's waist and height. Her tailor thought the measurements odd:

> When I gave the measure to my tailor to inquire how much mohair would serve to make a petticoat and waistcoat to a young gentlewoman of that bigness and stature, he considered it a long time and said he had made many gowns and suits, but had never made any to such a person in his life . . . he had never seen any woman of so low a stature have so big a waist.

However, the tailor went ahead and produced a mix of light and dark mohair, with a crimson underskirt. The scarlet skirt was a kind of in-joke, a royal robe reused.

Meanwhile, James had intelligently arranged a routine of playing hide-and-seek with his brother and sister, Prince Henry and Princess Elizabeth, after supper, 'and sometimes he would hide himself so well that in half an hour's time they could not find him. His Highness had so used them to this that when he went really away they thought he was but at the usual sport.' James had also persuaded one of the still-loyal gardeners to lend him the key to the gate which led out into St James's Park. Both Charles's elder sons were much better at getting around useful people than their father, as one of Henrietta Maria's French ladies noticed: 'having observed often the great defects of the late king's breeding and the stiff roughness that was in him, by which he disobliged very many and did often prejudice his affairs very much', Henrietta had insisted that her sons 'should be bred to a wonderful civility'. James's childhood uncannily paralleled his father's; like his father, he was always the second son, the less important one, beached, bereft. And like Charles I himself, James was lumbered with a handsome, clever, older, *taller* brother with whom half the world was in love. He grew up quarrelsome, requiring proofs of love. And like his father, it was to doom him.

But he was intelligent. Immediately after supper, under cover of the hide-and-seek game, he slipped down the privy stairs to where Bampfield waited at the garden gate. He clapped a periwig on James's head, swathed him in a cloak, and they set off.

Anne was waiting for them in a house Bampfield had rented, on the river by London Bridge. Bampfield told her not to wait after ten o'clock; if they had not arrived by then, it would mean they had been discovered, and she must fly.

Ten o'clock struck, and Anne was still alone. Bampfield's servant began to urge flight, but Anne refused to leave. 'I had come with a resolution to serve His Highness and I was fully determined not to leave that place till I was out of hopes of doing what I came there for.'

Then she heard 'a great noise of many as I thought coming upstairs, which I expected to be soldiers come to take me'. But it was James; he burst in, shouting eagerly, 'Quickly, quickly, dress me.' Anne did so, and admired his prettiness. Her warm and motherly heart had a snack ready for him, and a Woodstreet cake, which she knew he loved, to take on his journey. Then there was no more time, and Bampfield led the strange young gentlewoman in his awkward skirts to the barge which was to take them to Gravesend, and then to Holland.

As soon as they had gone, Anne and her faithful maid Miriam had to face the long walk back through the dark streets to Anne's brother's house. But the streets seemed deserted; they could detect no sign of hue and cry, and they reached home in safety.

The next day, the escape was discovered, and Parliament moved to close the Cinque Ports, and to search every ship, but before the orders had even reached the wardens, James was safely at sea. Bampfield delivered James to his sister Mary at The Hague, and then returned to England to lie low. As soon as he arrived, he made contact with Anne, who continued to work for him and for the king, which necessitated frequent visits to his rooms. She knew the risk she was running; she knew that she could be exposed as his mistress, but she herself said that everything she did was justified by her wish to serve the king.

But one day Anne found Bampfield lying on his bed, staring at the ceiling. She asked him what was wrong. He told her his wife was dead. He had heard this from a faithful servant – but they must keep it a secret, he warned, or her estates might be sequestered by Parliament. After carefully working out their joint income, he invited Anne to marry him, and after some hesitation she accepted, agreeing to postpone the wedding until they knew whether the king's affairs would prosper.

Was Anne his mistress? Some of her family probably thought so, and there is a leaf missing from her memoirs, which were themselves written fifteen years after the fact by a lady now both widowed and pious. She was later anxious about marrying someone else; there may have been some kind of secret ceremony, one that permitted intimacy. For Anne, the Civil War did not break down the family structure, but it dissolved enough of Bampfield's social identity to allow him to reinvent himself in her eyes. But like many an adventurer, Bampfield had been economical with the truth. Anne heard he was in prison, and the same day, she also heard that his wife was still alive, that he had 'abused' her. Anne immediately fell very sick. Bampfield had other things on his mind.

He wrote to the king, suggesting that a rescue operation might be launched. The Prince of Wales, he thought, might lead a force which could storm Carisbrooke and carry the king away. The Prince of Wales had other, saner ideas, but Bampfield's plan made him feel guilty. Seeing the mad but stalwart colonel became unwelcome; it is hard to act as a Royalist when the leading royal doesn't relish your company.

What could Bampfield do? Turncoat that he was, the best option seemed to be working for his former enemies, and he acted as a spy for the Protectorate, fleeing England at the Restoration. In his new home, the Dutch republic, he was again active in public service, but retired to a small town in the far north, a place he later described as 'this Egyptian darkness', 'this dead calm'; his metaphors illustrate the eloquence which made him so attractive to witty, clever Anne. There he wrote his memoirs, eager to defend himself. This was necessary because tensions generated by the Rye House plot of 1683 against

Charles II, and specifically James's conversion to Catholicism, threatened to spiral out and involve him.

Like many another broken-hearted woman, Anne found some solace in nursing soldiers. She went to Scotland to tend the sick and wounded of the wars: 'She became very famous and helpful to many,' wrote her biographer, 'both poor and rich, though it was mainly with respect to the poor that she undertook that practice.' She had her own special home-made medicines, balms and plasters. 'In the summer season she vied with the bee or ant in gathering herbs, flowers, worms, snails etc.' and she treated sixty men in one day, many riddled with rot, stinking, dying. She saw a man whose brain was exposed and bubbling with what she called water, and a boy of sixteen who had been run through with a tuck, and was swarming with 'creatures', maggots. She noted that very few of the soldiers had their wounds dressed on the field, so that 'it may be imagined that they were very noisome, but one particularly was in that degree who was shot through the arm that none was able to stay in the room, but all left me. Accidentally a gentleman came in, who seeing me (not without reluctancy) cutting off the man's sleeve of his doublet, which was hardly fit to be touched, he was so charitable as to take a knife and cut it off and fling it into the fire.'

Later, Anne married her employer while working as his governess. Before they were united, however, Colonel Bampfield made a final appearance. Seductive as ever, he tried to persuade Anne that he was honest. Anne told him that she was already married to Sir James Halkett. He asked her if she was wedded. 'I am', she said boldly. She breathed the word 'not' under her breath so she would not be forsworn. At least she had the satisfaction of lying to a liar.

Later, Anne met the future Charles II in Dunfermline. He congratulated her and gave her a purse of gold. Not for rescuing his brother, but for her work among the wounded. Later still, James II gave her a pension himself, though by now his religious beliefs had made him an embarrassment to devoutly Protestant Anne, who wrote of her 'greatest abhorrence to the mischevious designs of the Roman Church, whose pernicious counsels and violent methods had threatened the total subversion of religion and Liberties, and had actually sacrificed the King and Three Kingdoms, to promote their interests'. There was an irony in the fact that the prince who brought the three kingdoms closest to

Rome had been helped to escape by a devoutly Protestant woman. She had played a crucial part in a cunning, dramatic rescue, one that was a foreshadowing of the escapes of later, lonelier Stuart princes.

XXVII

Nor Iron Bars a Cage:
The Capture of Charles I

On 27 April 1646, just before dawn, King Charles I left Oxford. He rode over Magdalen Bridge and up Headington Hill, following the road to the south. He had no clear idea of where he was going or what he would do. The little party headed for Henley. Then they went on to Hillingdon and stopped for a meal. Then they waited for three or four hours.

No one knew what Charles was waiting for. Some thought he was hoping to slip somehow into the backstreets of London, to lead a revolt of loyal citizens. His advisers urged him to abandon any such idea. The little party set out again, for St Albans. And there they were accosted by an old man with a halberd, who asked them who they were. 'From Parliament', they said, but a horseman galloped up out of the gathering darkness; the king's party nearly jumped out of their skins with fright. But it was only a drunk, a bore, whose company they had to bear as far as Wheathampstead. They decided to cut their hair, but as they only had knives, the result was untidy.

They travelled on, through the outskirts of the Fens, to Downham Market. By now word had travelled fast and far that the king had escaped. Charles attracted suspicion by burning papers in his room at the inn. The town barber, too, could not help but suspect when invited to trim the royal party's frayed locks. Charles waited for word from the Scots, and it came; they would not compel him to anything against his conscience. He had to be satisfied with that. He rode on, but by a leisurely route, through Huntingdon, past places where he had hunted in happier days, to sleep on the floor of an alehouse at Coppingford, with the alehouse keeper and his family snoring beside him. The Scots accepted his surrender at once, as soon as he reached Newark. They could hardly believe their luck. With Charles in their custody, they felt sure they could make peace for all the kingdoms; they felt confident that Charles would accept their proposals in religion.

But it took only days for these hopes to sour. Charles entered Newcastle, and found that his entry lacked the ceremonial due a monarch. He was lodged in the mayor's house, guarded by musketeers. His long imprisonment had begun, and he knew it. He urged his followers to flee before the Scots could hand them over to Parliament. Now began his religious instruction, but Charles steadfastly stood by his Anglican faith. He knew, he said, that the Church needed bishops, because he had been instructed to believe it by his royal father James VI – of Scotland.

But, said his Presbyterian opponents, kings had to break with the past to bring about the Reformation in the first place. If Henry VIII had believed what his father taught him, there could be no reform. And anyway, James would have welcomed the sweeping away of bishops. Charles was icy. It touched a raw nerve, this assumption of knowledge about his father. He claimed identity with his father: 'I had the happiness to know him much better than you.' The little boy once bullied and neglected by his father was now his defender. Even when rows of Covenanters begged him to convert on their bended knees, he refused. Their bullying induced an aching melancholy: 'I never knew what it was to be barbarously baited before,' he wrote to Henrietta Maria, 'there was never man so alone as I . . . no living soul to help me . . . all the comfort I have is thy love and a clear conscience.' Mazarin's envoy Jean de Montreuil was impressed with his dignity, and his 'kindly demeanour' to those who 'treat him with very little civility'.

Charles had rational reasons for opposing Presbyterians and their Covenant, too, but for him rationality was always mixed with passionate feeling. The Church, he thought, could never flourish without the protection of the Crown, and therefore the Church's dependence on the Crown was 'the chiefest support of regal authority'. Presbyterianism, he felt, could only 'bring anarchy into any country'.

But for the Scots who had signed the Covenant, Presbyterianism had become a matter of national identity. The Covenanters were not sourbellies who wanted to spoil everyone's fun, but men and women who believed that they, low-born, and ordinary, could bring Scotland closer to God. They didn't have to wait for bishops to say they could do it. They could do it themselves. Covenanting gave them what social theorists now call 'agency', the sense that they were shaping great events. They remembered the passionate and apocalyptic fervour of the prayer book riots. They knew that was what power felt like. They were not going to give in.

At an individual level, the Covenanters and Charles shared a close, passionate and personal relationship with God. God was important in a way we in the twenty-first century can hardly begin to grasp. He was endowed with a mixture of the qualities of a beloved but powerful boss, a father, and a best friend, and he could fulfil all of those roles in turn. His worshippers did not only kneel to him out of fear of hellfire; they spent hours every day trying to put themselves in his presence. Everything that Covenanters did was filtered through the frighteningly tight-meshed sieve of Calvinism, which required that the believer constantly ask himself if he were saved. This was not unlike very strict dieting – rules were made, and then appetites revived and they were broken, and then self-loathing set in, leading to more and harsher rules. Those who are thus strict with themselves can hardly be lenient with others.

The king worried about his crown, his children and his own safety. And he worried most of all about religion. In a letter, he pointed out that 'this is a right way to make me a Papist, for if I follow your present advices concerning religion, I foresee such a necessity for it, that the time will come you will persuade me with more earnestness to submit to the Pope, than now you do for my concession to Presbyterian government; for, questionless, it is less ill, in many respects, to submit to one than many Popes'. He worried desperately about preserving the rights of his son. 'I have already cast up what I am like to suffer, which I shall meet (by the grace of God) with that constancy that befits me. Only I desire that consolation, that assurance from you, as I may justly hope my cause shall not end with my misfortunes, by assuring me that misplaced pity to me do not prejudice my son's right.'

It is as if Charles was foreseeing his execution; certainly he wanted to get away. But Henrietta Maria was against it. She told him that all his friends abroad disliked the idea. 'I conjure you, that till the Scots shall declare that they will not protect you, you do not think of making any escape from England . . . You would destroy all our hopes, besides the danger of the attempt', she wrote.

Contemporaries said she took this view because she was having an affair with her courtier and confidant Henry Jermyn. It wasn't true, but the rumour might have increased her husband's melancholy. Charles wrote to her abjectly, pleadingly, as once he'd written to his brother: 'I assure thee, both I and my children are ruined, if thou shouldst retire from my business: for God's sake leave off threatening me with the desire to meddle no more with business . . . As thou lovest me give me so much comfort (and God knows I have but little, and that little must come from thee) as to assure me that thou wilt think no more of any such thing.' He still hated to feel himself alone.

The Scots handed Charles over to Parliament in January 1647. After living with him for a while, they had despaired of a quick peace. They were going home with 100,000 pounds. Among the commissioners sent by Parliament were Pembroke and Denbigh, old friends of the king's. They agreed to Charles's suggestion of moving to Holdenby House in Northamptonshire, the largest private house in England, built by Queen Elizabeth I's favourite Christopher Hatton. For the men of Parliament, Holdenby had the advantage of being firmly in godly territory, in the east.

The journey south was a progress in all but name. In Durham, in Leeds, in Nottingham and Leicester, people flocked to see him, pressed him to touch them for the king's evil, prayed for him, cheered him. As Sir Thomas Herbert dryly noted, some were there out of curiosity, but others out of love. At Holdenby itself, he found his chaplains, and more crowds hoping for the royal touch. He did have to accept Parliament's appointees as personal servants (and hence spies); the gentle and civil Thomas Herbert as Groom of the Bedchamber alongside the stalwart Harrington. Otherwise, it was almost like old times. Charles spent a few hours reading every day, enjoyed walking, games of chess, the occasional game of bowls in Althorp. Not the life of a king, perhaps, but the life of a civil and sober gentleman. And Charles's pious love of the Church of England was unquenched; he resumed his pre-war Sunday acts of devotion. On Sundays he sequestered himself.

And he managed to get news, too; one day when he was out riding a supporter named Boswell, a Royalist spy, dressed as a labourer, thrust a parcel of letters from the queen into his hands. Charles hastily told the commissioners that the man had a personal suit for preferment. Another time, one of his visitors was seized and searched. This was Lady Jane Whorwood, who later tried to help Charles escape. She was the daughter of a man who had surveyed James I's stables; the king's most loyal supporters often came from such families, loyal tradesmen or professionals whose lives had been bound up with the court. Jane married at nineteen, and her husband, Brome Whorwood, came of a minor gentry family from Holton. Like Mary Milton, Jane's political sympathies remained with her birth family, and the marriage collapsed. Again like Mary, Jane was attractive, and at twenty-seven she had a magnificent head of fire-red hair, though an ungallant Parliamentarian also noted that she had 'pock-holes in her face'. Anthony à Wood said that she was 'the most loyal person to King Charles I in his miseries, as any woman in England'.

Charles wrote to her in the romantic terms of the court of love which he and Henrietta had created before the war, calling her 'sweet Jane Whorwood', and signing himself 'your most loving Charles' and 'your best Platonick lover and servant'. She adopted the *nom de plume* Helen: Helen of Troy, who deserted her husband for her true love, Paris, for whose beauty a war was fought. Separated from Henrietta, and also badgered and nagged by her, perhaps doubtful of her fidelity, Charles enjoyed Lady Jane's devotion. He never once mentioned her to the queen.

While the king did little, the soldiers were electing representatives or agitators, and formed the Army Council to take charge of their own affairs. Before long, the Army was at odds with Parliament. The analogy of continuing the work of reformation slid over from Church thinking into political thinking. It was true – or was it? – that Charles had been neutralized, but was Parliament turning out just as tyrannical? 'King Charles his seventeen years misgovernment before this parliament . . . was but a flea-biting, or as a molehill to a mountain, in comparison of what this everlasting Parliament already is', complained one newsbook.

Like any good and sane officer, Cromwell was disturbed by the rise of radical opinion within the New Model Army. Certainly, he did not want to see the victors deprived of their wages, and he was keen to represent them thus far against timid men of Parliament. It occurred to him to make use of the captive king. In secret, a man called Joyce appeared at Holdenby, at dead of night, and asked to speak to the king. Charles said he wasn't going to speak with anyone at that hour and Joyce had to cool his heels till morning. But Charles did get up before his usual time, performed his morning devotions, and sent for Joyce. 'What', he asked, 'are your instructions?'

'There they are, sir', said Joyce, pointing to his troop of horse.

'Your instructions', said Charles, 'are in fair Character, legible without spelling.' He made plans for departure. Before long, he was at Newmarket, where Cromwell and Henry Ireton waited for him. There was an offer on the table – later to be known stolidly as the Heads of the Proposals – and it was generous. Ireton was offering almost complete religious toleration – no obligation to take the Covenant, no Presbyterian Church. The existing Parliament would be dismissed and new Parliaments summoned every two years; these would not sit for long, for no more than 240 days. A Council of State would participate in foreign affairs, and there would be a general amnesty.

It sounded good, but Charles still hoped for more. As recently as March, he had written ingenuously, 'I am endeavouring to draw either the Presbyterians or the Independents to side with me for extirpating the other so I shall be really king again.' His hope to be 'really king again' evidently meant no compromise. He had also told Henrietta Maria that he planned to drive a wedge between Parliament and the Scots, and he had heard intelligence reports of unrest in Scotland and in London which made him unduly hopeful. He rejected the Heads of the Proposals summarily. His counsellor Sir John Berkeley asked him tartly if he had some secret weapon for winning the war that he had failed to inform his advisers about. And like many people, he didn't take to Ireton. Ireton was far too frank, not deferential enough. But for the Army, Charles had ceased to be a person, or a king. He was a criminal, a man of blood, 'over head and ears in the blood of your dearest friends and fellow commoners'. Cromwell and Ireton were, increasingly, taking a risk in treating with Charles at all.

Cromwell had to deal with the Army, who were threatening a march on London unless their demands for pay and rights were met. On 2 August they drew up on Hounslow Heath, and members of both Houses rode out to meet them. There were great cries of 'Lords and Commons and a free Parliament!' Six leading Presbyterians, including Denzil Holles, left the House to the Independents; more Presbyterians withdrew when Cromwell and a regiment of horse arrived in Westminster.

Charles too was heading for London, at a more leisurely pace than the Army, being escorted, but lightly; no question of iron bars or a cage. He saw his younger children again at Maidenhead. They had been left behind, pathetically, when the king and queen had fled London, and had been prisoners of Parliament, first at St James's, then at a house in the city from 1642. Parliament had had thoughts of using them as hostages, and although it never came to anything, they couldn't help knowing that they were powerless prisoners. Henry, who was seven, could hardly remember his father, whom he had last seen at the age of two, and didn't recognize him. Charles spoke gently to him: 'I am your father, child, and it is not the least of my misfortunes that I have brought you and your brothers and sisters into the world to share my miseries.'

After that, Charles met his two small children much more often, and they may well have had an impact on his thinking, planning, plotting. His occasional hesitancy about escape plans may have been partly due to a reluctance to abandon them, even for good reason – to abandon them as he had been abandoned, as he had already abandoned them once.

He usually saw them at Syon House, once Lucy Hay's home, and he also met his nephew the Elector Palatine. And there were a few halcyon days at Hampton Court; Sir Thomas Herbert remembered it as a last golden age, in which the king was attended by chaplains, accompanied by nobles, sustained by the visits of his children.

Charles's visitors knew they were seeing the end of something they loved, the presence chamber, the monarchy as itself. Warm-hearted Ann Fanshawe was in tears when she paid her third and last visit to the king at Hampton Court. Charles's farewell to her showed an awareness of both possible endings of his small story: the romantic and the tragic. Ann wished him a long and happy life, and Charles affectionately stroked her cheek, saying, 'Child, if God pleases, it shall be so, but both you and I must submit to God's will, and you know in what hands I am in.' He gave Richard a bundle of letters for Henrietta Maria, and promised that 'if ever I am restored to my dignity, I will bountifully reward you for your service and sufferings'.

The problem was that this last golden era made Charles feel happy and relaxed and confident and blessed. Everything was just the way it ought to be. Who could ever imagine that it could be truly different? So he felt able to reject the Parliament peace terms in September. He tried to string them along by telling them that the Heads of the Proposals could be the basis for peace. But then he forgot to suggest further concessions. While negotiations were paralysed, the Army radicals improved the time, addressing their growing congregations, disseminating their new and exciting ideas to an audience primed for change.

Charles was frightened by what he heard of the debates within the Army, especially when they were formalized at Putney and the Army commanders actually listened to what the radical elements had to say. Everyone was talking about *An Agreement of the People*, the astounding series of demands made by the Army radicals which sought to give ordinary men a voice in government. The world it sought to create was one Charles could hardly imagine. At this point Charles was not alone in failure of the imagination. No one could feel confident, now, about the ending of what was being acted out, or who was writing the play. Perhaps, Charles thought, he was caught in a tragedy, with himself as black-clad melancholy hero, a role he had enjoyed when young. He felt sure he would be poisoned if he stayed at Hampton Court. He had already received a mysterious warning letter. Could he convert a tragedy to a romance? He made a plan to be a romantic hero – he would escape.

Knowing Charles's hopes, Jane Whorwood consulted William Lilly, the London astrologer and Royalist, to learn where Charles should go to be safe. At first, Lilly would not let her in, because a member of his household had plague. Resolutely, wittily, Jane made a joke of her own scarred face: 'It is not plague I fear,' she said, 'but pox.' Lilly let her in after all, and carefully casting a horoscope, he calculated that the safest and best place for Charles was in Essex, twenty miles from London.

'She liked my judgement very well,' he wrote afterwards, 'and being herself of a sharp judgement, remembered a place in Essex about that distance, where was an excellent house, and all conveniences to be acted upon.'

Charles's daughter Princess Elizabeth had come to stay for a few days. She had always been a delicate little girl. Born on the ill-omened Feast of the Holy Innocents, in 1635, she is a serious little creature in Van Dyck's portrait of the royal children. She was one of the fair-haired and blue-eyed members of the family, like James, and unlike the swarthy, gipsy Prince of Wales. She had huge eyes in a face made elfin by illness. She was clever, learning Latin, Greek and Hebrew, and she was pious too; she and her sister Mary enjoyed the Catholic regalia their mother gave them; Mary had a tiny rosary which she would whip out when she thought no one was looking. But although clever, Elizabeth was a pawn, to be pushed about by the powerful. Now, none too scrupulously, Charles himself used his daughter's visit to further his own plans for escape. He told Colonel Edward Whalley, captain of the guard, that the thudding footfalls of his men walking their beats at night was keeping the nervous young Elizabeth awake. So the guards were moved away. Charles always went to his room early to write letters on Thursday and Friday; leaving by a back stairway, he slipped out of Hampton Court on 11 November 1647. It was raining, it was cold. A boat was waiting to take Charles across the river to Thames Ditton; his servant stood by on the opposite bank, with horses. They rode off into the gathering darkness.

Then next morning, Charles's Groom of the Bedchamber tried to keep Whalley out, saying that the king was still asleep. When Whalley eventually forced his way in, he found the bed empty. Charles's dog whimpered in a corner; his master had abandoned him. He had also left two letters, one of which was a simple thank-you note to his gaolers, the other explaining to Parliament his reasons for going. Charles had seen pastoral plays, and had read romances like Sir Philip Sidney's *Arcadia*, in which aristocrats are forced to take to the forest in disguise, but then break out gloriously to the joy of their people. 'Let me be heard with Freedom, Honour and Safety, and I shall instantly break through the clouds of retirement, and show myself ready to be *Pater Patriae*', he wrote.

First, though, he became lost in Windsor Forest. He wandered through it for hours, baffled, angry, defeated by his own terrain. He hadn't meant to become the hero of a *roman d'aventure*, but the protagonist of a pastoral, something smooth and civilized, providential. When Charles and his servant finally reached the inn at Bishop Sutton, where they were to change horses, they found that the local Parliamentarians were using it as a meeting-place. Where should he go? To Essex, as Jane Whorwood had suggested, and thence to the Continent? Or to London, to place himself at the head of the moderates?

Both might have worked. Either might have changed the course of history; would the former have prevented the Restoration or enabled it sooner? Would the second have brought the Civil War to the streets of London? Led by Charles in person, might an alliance of Royalists and Presbyterians have succeeded in controlling events?

Probably not. But the potentialities were never tested. Charles, who had always hated London, but who couldn't bring himself to give up his kingdom, chose neither London nor France. Instead he decided on the Isle of Wight, an emblem of his indecision rather than a way of resolving it. He could go to the Continent from there, or to London. This may have been his worst mistake, worse even than fleeing London at the beginning of the war, worse even than rejecting Ireton's terms. Ann Fanshawe knew he was not in a romance plot, but in the plot of a tragedy – among plotters, in fact. For her, the servants who helped Charles were guilty of folly ('to give it no worse name'), drawn in by 'the cursed crew' of the Army. She meant the Army rebels; she too found them terrifying.

Charles waited at Titchfield, across the Solent from the Isle of Wight. The king sent his servants to feel out the governor of the island, Colonel Robert Hammond. Charles felt sure he'd be sympathetic, but it is hard to see why. Hammond was a veteran of Essex's army, one of the men to whom things seemed clear in 1642 and opaque by 1646. He wasn't comfortable in the New Model Army as he had been under the earl. He had asked for the job on the Isle of Wight in the hope that he might stay out of the mess he felt sure would follow the war. But Hammond was no Royalist. He had fought for three years with Essex and seen many a good fellow die. Given Hammond's hostility, it was fatal that Charles sent Sir John Berkeley as his messenger to him, for

Berkeley bungled it badly. Asking Hammond whether he knew who was near him, Berkeley rushed into speech: 'Even good King Charles, who is come from Hampton Court for fear of being murdered privately.' Hammond, astonished, pulled himself together, and suggested that they should go to the king together. He promised to treat him with 'honour and honesty'.

Charles had been restless and anxious, and had begun looking for a boat to France, but the ports had been closed on news of his escape. When he heard that Hammond himself was at his door, he panicked. 'Oh, Jack!' he cried, 'thou hast undone me! For I am by this means made fast from stirring.'

Now he had no choice but to travel to the island. He reached Cowes the same day, and stayed the night at the Feathers Inn. Above the king's bed hung a text. 'Remember thy end', it said. He went on to Carisbrooke Castle in the centre of the island. A woman thrust a damask rose into his hand, plucked from her own garden in midwinter; she promised him her prayers.

Sir John Oglander was most impressed. He was a staunch Royalist and feared that the island would be a trap for the king, but he was also delighted when Charles was able to visit his house. There were a few odd little signs that Charles was being pushed into closer relations with his subjects than ever before. One day Charles's coach passed a funeral procession, and the king asked whose it was. It turned out to be Sir James Chamberlain, a Royalist who had died of his war-wounds. Charles dismounted at once, and joined the mourners. In a letter, he praised the islanders, 'very good, peaceable and quiet people'.

Hammond had at once got in touch with the Army Command's search parties.

The Army Command had found the note Charles had left, and the letter warning him that he might be murdered if he stayed in their custody. Who had sent it? What if Cromwell and his supporters had done so, to drive a wedge between Charles and the Army? Could Charles have forged it himself? Or was the note from a genuine Royalist? Charles had succeeded in giving his enemies a divisive mystery to solve.

In any case, Charles soon settled in at Carisbrooke, and in due course reopened negotiations with both Parliament and the Scots, reaching a

secret agreement with the latter almost at once; three years of Presbyterianism in exchange for another army. The agreement was so secret
that it was buried in lead in the castle grounds by the end of December.
Charles tried to avoid giving Parliament a firm no, but the commissioners wouldn't leave the island without knowing his mind. By
this time, Charles had more-or-less abandoned any façade of hoping
for peace by negotiation, and had set his face for more war.

XXVIII

A New Heaven and a New Earth:
Anna Trapnel and the Levellers

Looking around them, the people of England in particular could see what the war had cost them: the ruined houses, the empty food stores, and the uncounted dead, killed in battle or by disease. There was now to be a breathing-space for those tired of battles, though it was to prove brief.

By 1647, it seemed to many that the genie of change could not now be forced back into the bottle. Little as anyone liked it, the world had changed, truly changed, and no one could change it back. But others kept trying to bring back the old days, because *they* had not changed. Robert Herrick's lyric collection *Hesperides* staunchly refused the floodtide of war and change. Herrick wrote about maypoles and weddings, church ales and hock-carts; he evoked the lavish, decorated, customary world that had now been obscured by the simple elegant black pall of Presbyterianism. Royalists were learning what the press could do. They created rough, robust jest-playlets, about *Mistress Parliament* vomiting up stupid laws in the throes of childbirth, about Cromwell smuggling his mistress into the palace, thus cuckolding General Lambert, about the Devil persuading Parliament to do his will. These were signs that people missed the theatres, and in 1647 a group of London actors formed and began acting plays at the old Cockpit and at the Red Bull. They were told to stop, but begged the House of Lords for permission to carry on. They were refused. But they did not stop, performing in secret. They were actors; what else could they do? The main result was a spate of raids on theatres; seats were broken and spectators fined for attendance at renegade performances. The old days could not come back; some would not allow them to. When the Earl of Essex died unexpectedly from a stroke in September of 1646, Parliament had given him a handsome and expensive funeral, and a funeral effigy which portrayed him in his buff-coat and scarlet. Just five short weeks later, a poor farmer from Dorset hacked the statue to pieces. He gave as his reason that an angel had ordered him to destroy a statue which insulted God by bringing the image of a man into a place of worship. This stoutly Independent act was hardly reassuring for those Presbyterians for whom Essex had represented moderation. Moderation was not the theme of the moment.

These two acts of iconoclasm, the destruction of theatres and the smashing of the Essex statue, were representative of the ascendancy of the Independents. They were not a majority in any institution or organization except the Army. Perhaps they were not even a majority in any town or city. But they made their views known through a bold willingness to challenge anything that ran up against their opinions. They were immeasurably strengthened because they had now achieved their aim of winning the war. True, they did not quite command the Commons, but they were more numerous than they had been. While the Long Parliament had been sitting, its members had been reduced by old age and illness, forcing elections, some of which were contested, and some of these resulted in the installation of MPs more radical in their opinions than those chosen when Parliament was first summoned. Men like Henry Marten, now restored to the House, and also republicans like Edmund Ludlow and Thomas Chaloner. Ideas that had once been unthinkable and certainly unsayable were now held by a significant, vocal and very active minority, which could reasonably credit itself with having won the war.

While the Army was in ferment, London's godly churchgoers were in uproar; and the two groups of agitators were intimately connected, though they did not altogether overlap. Victory brought the New Model Army to God. William Dell, preaching to the New Model in June 1646, claimed that 'I have seen more of the presence of God in that army, than in amongst any people that I have ever conversed with in my life

. . . For he hath dwelt among us, and marched at the head of us, and counselled us, and led us, and hath gone along with us step by step from Naseby.' Even a captured Royalist opined that 'God was turned roundhead'. The same confidence inspired the radical churchgoers of London, who had suffered so under Laud, and they rapidly became more radical still. Presbyterianism was no longer enough for the Independents. They removed ecclesiastical authority altogether. Learning – and especially an Oxford degree, once a passport to a clerical living – became hated signs of Royalist sympathies. Priests and vicars were replaced by preachers and lecturers – 'mechanick' preachers, as Presbyterians said in horror, meaning that they came from artisanal backgrounds. These unqualified people would address congregations – not in churches, but in meeting halls, since it was icon-worship to think any building especially holy – for hours at a time, or as the spirit moved them. The same Holy Spirit might motivate listeners to reply at equal length; this usually involved a detailed account of the speaker's dreadful sins, then an account of how salvation had come through the direct promptings of the Spirit. Through this process, it came to seem normal to many members of London radical sects to be addressed by people who had no particular qualifications, people who would not get a hearing in the Commons, in town meetings, or in trade guilds. It even came to seem meritorious that a speaker had no qualifications: a sign of purity and even of election. The Bible said that 'the last shall be first, and the first last'. The London sectarian congregations were the template for all the radical politics that were to follow. They too were inspired by Biblical promises that distinctions would disappear in the presence of Christ. They were defending themselves against the Presbyterians, those compromisers who wanted to let the king exercise the powers that had, in Independent eyes, brought the nation to bloody ruin. They had an open structure, too, which itself served as a model for the removal of layers of hierarchy in other arenas. If bishops and priests could very well be abolished, why did anyone need kings and magistrates?

It was from this culture of radical religion that the agitators appeared in the spring of 1647, and their activities in turn reinforced the radical religious sects' sense that the world was indeed ripe to be turned upside down. The agitators were representatives of the New Model regiments elected by the men to discuss political issues with the officers. From them came the General Council of the Army in July, the debates, and ultimately radicals like the Levellers, who sought rights for men without substantial property.

Though the radical Independent sects and the agitators appeared to be riding the zeitgeist, most people feared them, and that included moderate opinion on the Parliamentarian side. Nobody hated them all more than New Model Army chaplain Richard Baxter, who had seen his men charge the Royalists at Naseby. He hated them all even more after the war than he had before; he felt that they were to blame for the plight of godly people like himself. To defend his party from charges of revolution, he tried to open up a visible gap between the godly and the revolutionaries. But along the way, he did try to describe the ferment in the army, and while his panic may have exaggerated, he did not lie:

> A great part of the mischief they did among the soldiers was by pamphlets, which they abundantly dispersed, such as R Overton's *Martin Mar-Priest*, and more of his; and some of J Lilburn's, who was one of them . . . And soldiers being usually dispersed in their quarters, they had such books to read when they had none to contradict them. And all their disputing was with as much fierceness, as if they had been ready to draw their swords upon those against whom they disputed . . . I thought they were principled by the Jesuits, and acted for their interest and in their way.

This seems an odd idea, but shows how Catholics could still be seen in everything disliked, because of course these men were not Catholics. They were the Levellers. For Baxter, the Levellers were like the Jesuits because they had abandoned belief in predestination for faith in free will. He connects this ungluing of religion with their social beliefs, and perhaps he was not altogether wrong. Discontent like his soon found an active outlet. Those not enthusiastic about the radical sects or the Army radicals were beginning to be active; there were signs of a Royalist rising in the capital. This opposition only cemented determination to reform the state thoroughly. The New Model declared its intention of marching on and occupying London to put down what increasingly looked like Royalist insurgents, and was only restrained by Fairfax's efforts. On 23 July 1647, the committee had its first meeting at the Guildhall, and its members were assaulted by some young men with Royalist sympathies, who said 'that if they came here again they would hang their guts about their ears. And never left them till they had compelled them to rise, and, as they went, followed them with ill language.' On 26 July a violent mob assaulted Parliament itself; it included some Cavaliers, and disrupted voting. Besieged on all sides, Parliament prepared to defend London against the New Model, and even though ten thousand men in arms were produced, the New Model occupied the capital on 6 August, handily assuming a role as protector of Parliament. The lord mayor was replaced by a radical Independent, John Warner, and the Royalists among the aldermen found themselves in the Tower.

The Cavalier and Royalist agents among the rioters had presented the New Model as a ravening horde of plunderers and rapists, but in fact London couldn't help but notice how disciplined and orderly the New Model was in comparison with its supposed defenders, the reformadoes; Thomas Juxon noted that 'there was not so much as an apple took . . . by any of them'. It was so obviously an agent of law and order that it sold itself to people otherwise doubtful, and the city began to simmer down. But the radical sects were heartened by its presence, which allowed vital cross-communication between radical Independent leaders and the Army agitators. The result was to reinforce the radical tendencies of both groups. What went on in the churches and meeting houses was the engine that was to drive the astonishing political demands made by the Army's more militant agitators.

Part of what inspired these demands was the heady personal experience of meeting houses, of seeing the power to speak in public vested not in those appointed by still higher powers, but in those customarily silenced. There could be no apter symbol of the lowly and the silenced than women, and in some congregations women began to speak with greater and greater frequency. They took as their text the Magnificat, in which the Lord, said Mary, 'has put down the mighty from his throne/And exalted the lowly'. The speech Mary makes is overtly about the very myth England's godly loved best, the myth of themselves as a great exiled people surrounded by ungodly enemies, fighting for God against the unholy armies of darkness. In this way, the speech of women like the prophets Sarah Wight and Anna Trapnel was not incidental to the Army reformers' quest, but part and parcel of the same activist movement.

Yet women who spoke did face opposition, just as the Army radicals did. In his first epistle to Timothy, St Paul had declared roundly that women should not be suffered to teach, but to be in silence; if they were baffled by anything they might ask their husbands for elucidation at home. And yet the Civil War and Independency made it possible for some women to ignore this injunction. Anna Trapnel was famous for her fasts and prophecies, but she was not the only woman speaking out in London churches and meeting halls. Even before the war, Mrs Attaway had denied that 'any in the world this day living had any commission to preach', by which she meant that ministers had no special rights. It was this idea which could be read as a licence for women to speak. Katherine Chidley, for example, had been involved in political and religious struggles on behalf of the Independent sects from as early as the late 1620s, and she also had links with radical Levellers in the New Model Army. It may have been the liberty allowed them that attracted many women to the radical and Independent sects.

The role of prophet, in particular, allowed women to wriggle around the Pauline prohibition. A prophet was chosen by God, not by men; he or she was proof that the Holy Spirit 'bloweth where it listeth', as people said. And she could argue that she was not, herself, speaking, only allowing God to speak through her. The idea that God might choose someone unimportant, weak, 'low', reinforced the idea of the last being first and the first last that was dear to the Independents' millenarianism. Finally, there were women prophets in both the Old and New Testaments who could be cited as examples of God choosing to speak through the vessel of a woman.

But women prophets and preachers could find themselves open to severe criticism and even savage punishment unless they were careful. A woman named Mary Gadbury, for example, emerged in the late 1640s from the radical sectarian groups of St Stephen's Coleman Street in London. She had been deserted by her husband, and she was unilaterally blamed for this by her critics. She was assumed to be sexually entangled with her fellow-missionary William Franklin, a charge she denied; for a woman to open her mouth in public was to court charges of sexual immorality and even whoredom, and thus the condign punishments that accompanied them. She was whipped at Winchester, and then sent to Bridewell. Admittedly, her belief that Franklin was the Messiah cast especial doubt on her claims to have seen him transfigured by a bright light, but she was punished more severely than he was.

In this fraught context, London responded with various kinds of passion to women like Anna Trapnel. By the late 1640s there were, at least, many of them. Anne Hempstall is said to have spoken for two hours to women who came from far away, but the author says they stayed only because they had been promised 'a good fat pig' after the sermon. This suggests the women can't rise above their bodily appetites, but also implies that those concerned are poor, perhaps hungry. One critic wrote with feigned amusement that 'Thus I have declared some of the female Academies, but where their University is I cannot tell, but I suppose that Bedlam or Bridwell would be two convenient places for them'. The misogyny evident here is not the point. It is assumed to be widely shared, but uses that prejudice to discredit the Independent sects, whose ministers lacked Oxford and Cambridge training.

Others claimed that women used religion to cover up their sexual longings: 'of all WHORES there is no WHORE to a holy WHORE, which when she turns up the white of her eye, and the black of her tail when she falls flat on her back, according as the spirit moves her, the fire of her Zeal, kindles such a Flame, that the Devil cannot withstand her, Besides she can fit a man with such a cloak for her knavery that she can cover her lust with Religion, O! these lasses that can rise and get them ready by Six a Clock in the morning to go to Christ church, And then in the Afternoon to go to Saint Amholing O! how they listen for that Tinkle Tinkle bell that raises them in a morning to a stirring exercise'.

This is anxious about women, but also bothered by the radical sects in general, and it uses the oldest image of trouble in the book to discredit them, the image of the sexually voracious woman. But Trapnel and dozens of other women were not deterred by abuse. Rather they were powerfully motivated by seeing themselves as part of a larger political cause that extended to heaven itself, a cause so holy that it was bound to attract the attention of diabolical foes. And for Trapnel it was especially significant that her career as a prophet derived from her mother, who was one of those to die in the war (Trapnel doesn't tell us how she died). Nine years later, as the Independent sects of which she was a part became dominant in London, Anna remembered her death: 'The last words she uttered upon her deathbed were these to the Lord for her daughter: "Lord! Double thy spirit upon my child." These words she uttered with as much eagerness three times, and spoke no more.'

These words suggest that Trapnel's mother was not only godly, but actively Independent. Trapnel quotes them because they help to prove the authenticity of the prophecies she was to utter. But they also point to the bereavements of the war years, bereavements that might cause those prophecies to seem worthwhile, even urgently necessary. Because of her mother's death, Trapnel was an orphan in the roughest, most lawless of London suburbs. An aunt took her in, but often such care meant a life of fairly robust servitude, being a kind of unpaid servant. However, Trapnel's training in her aunt's household included the vital literacy skills that would allow her to absorb the political pamphlets of the day, along with the Bible; she notes 'I was trained up to my book and writing'. Basic literacy was often seen as a necessity for godly children. Reading allowed her to discover in the psalms and in the prophecies of her namesakes Hannah and Anna intimations of a new age when poor women like herself would be advanced by God ahead of rich and powerful men. She believed that God would himself select those to whom power would be extended, and she strove to be in their number.

Like others, she found the 1640s a time of material struggle. Starting in 1645, she 'kept house with the means my mother left me'. After selling her plate and rings to support the army further (she had already paid taxes for them) she 'wrought many nights hard to get money', though she does not say at what. There were trades open to women in Poplar and its environs, usually connected with the shipbuilding industry: sailmaking, for example, and laundry work. There were also all the usual businesses, from turners to bakers. Any of these would have brought her into further contact with the world of Poplar, a world outside the staid laws of the City and passionately pro-Parliament and inclined to Independency. She moved in with a minister's widow, then with one of her daughters. This makes it sound as if she sold her house as well, also for the army; some did do this, but also because there was little point in home ownership if the Second Coming was imminent.

It was after the military victories of the New Model that she began speaking out in assemblies: in May 1646 her first discourse appeared, published later as *A Legacy for Saints*. In June 1646 she suffered her first 'distemper of body', the rigours of some illness intimately connected with her spiritual growth.

In 1647, Anna visited Sarah Wight, a girl who had fasted for fifty-three days, between 6 April and 11 June with short respites: 'her drink being only fair water for about twenty days: and since that, some small beer: and both these only at once in two, three or four days', wrote her spiritual adviser Henry Jessey. A few weeks later, Anna Trapnel began her own fast, on 1 July. Just as eating disorders spread now in girls' boarding schools, so fasting became a competition for holiness in Anna's circles. The new calendar of the Church year was about fasting rather than feasting. Parliament used fast days as if they were magical, holding them to help Essex's stricken Western army in 1644. The army was itself hungry, so it was partly a matter of solidarity. But food had private as well as public significance. In the modern world, anorexics are often stereotyped as those who want to regress to childhood, avoid maturity. Of course, fasts like Wight's and Trapnel's were not about the body in the mirror; they were about the body as *felt*, roaring with hunger and need. Refusing the powerful call of that screaming body made the faster feel powerful: the fiercer the hunger, the greater the power. To fast is to be entirely autonomous, to need nothing and no one. Modern anorexic Marya Hornbacher writes that 'the anorectic is attempting to demonstrate – badly, ineffectively, narcissistically – a total independence from the helpless state of childhood, from the infinite needs that she recognises in herself, and will annihilate in any way she can'. Fasting may have stood for independency in more ways than one. A girl who had spent her childhood uncomfortably part of households not properly her own might have felt an especial longing to renounce need, and with it mastery. She could do this best by choosing Jesus as her master. She sang:

> I could not eat of anything
> Nothing will now go down,
> For I have tasted other meat
> In viewing of the crown.

Her hunger allowed her to critcize the greed of others. Addressing the army, she rebukes it for plundering, and asserts that God will:

> . . . welcome all of you
> And say, oh here is that,
> Which is more costly food for thee,
> And far more delicate
> Then all thou hast of that thou stolst
> From the Commonweal poor,
> For to feast thy carcass withall,
> Which is to be no more.

This is itself a kind of declaration of independence. Fasting also allowed Trapnel to pull away from those trying to manage her:

> I was judged by diverse friends . . . to be under a temptation for not eating; I took that Scripture, Neglect not the body, and went to the Lord and enquired whether I had been so, or had any self-end in it to be singular beyond what was meet; it was answered me, No, for thou shalt every way be supplied in body and spirit, and I found a continual fullness in my stomach, and the taste of diverse sweetmeats and delicious foods therein, which satisfied me.

It also shows how much attention her fasting won for her, even as she denied any needs. And yet like all girls who refuse to eat, she said she was not hungry. To be hungry is to admit a need, and there can be none. The fullness of which she speaks is probably the euphoria of fasting. After several days, the body compensates for hunger by producing chemicals which make for a rush of joyful and liberating energy. To someone like Trapnel, always waiting for the Holy Spirit, this euphoria might have seemed like encouraging proof that he had come to her at last.

Her fasts were also the last extreme of iconoclasm, and just as violent. First the new Laudian reservations in churches had been broken down, so that no space was more sacred than any other. Then statues and stained glass had been destroyed. Then had come the Independent sects, which revolted against the idea of the very building of the church, and liked to hold their meetings here, there and everywhere. The last remaining icon was the body of the believer, the body as temple of the

Holy Ghost, and it too must be destroyed to allow the Spirit to blow freely. But her fasts were controversial, as her defence of herself shows. Some people thought the body at least should be kept intact, and those who sensed the power of her rebellion were understandably a little afraid.

Anna also had a new audience to impress. She had moved from outlaw Poplar, and was now living in the Minories, another suburb with a heterogeneous population, exempt from city craft and trade regulations and so attractive to immigrants. Among those arrivals there were strong Calvinist leanings – and many preachers had strong Independent tendencies. The role of leader of reform was ultimately taken up by All Hallows the Great, and Anna was determined to march in the vanguard of the saints. Here is what Anna Trapnel saw as the New Model Army approached:

> After this there was a day of thanksgiving that I kept with the church of Allhallows in Lime Street [sic], for the army that was then drawing up towards the city, in which I had a little discovery of the presence of the Lord with them, in which day I had a glorious vision of the New Jerusalem, which melted me into rivers of tears, that I shrunk down in the room, and cried out in my heart, 'Lord, what is this?' It was answered me, 'A discovery of the glorious state of whole Sion, in the reign of the Lord Jesus, in the midst of them, and of it thou shalt have more visions hereafter.' So then when the day was ended, I retired to my chamber, at that time lying in the Minories in Aldgate parish, where I conversed with God by prayer, and reading of the scriptures, which were excellently opened to me touching the proceedings of the army.

Anna tells us about her church. For her, 'church' was not a place but a congregation of people. She also tells us about where she lived; the Minories runs from Aldgate High Street to Tower Hill, and she may mention it because it was itself evidence of the redemption of London; the Minories took its name from the *Sorores Minores*, or the Poor Clares, an order of nuns established in the thirteenth century by St Clare. Like Trapnel they were devoted to praying, fasting and helping the poor. But all this locality matters less to her than the meaning of the army's approach; for her it is the first footfalls of the Second Coming. She is excited by being offered the chance to know what is happening through the Holy Spirit, but she also gives us a portrait of a London woman trying to get news:

> It was first said to me that they were drawing up toward the city (I not knowing anything of it before) and that there was a great hubbub in the city, the shops commanded to be shut up. Upon this I went down, and enquired of the maid of the house whether there was any stir in the city. She answered me, 'You confine yourself to your chamber, and take no notice of what is done abroad. We are commanded', said she, 'to shut up our shops, and there are great fears among the citizens, what will be the issue, they know not.'

It was unusual for a servant-maid to address a gentlewoman in this way, and it implies that she thought of Anna as either a child or a fellow-servant. No maid would speak that way to a lady. And Anna's response implies some annoyance at being so addressed:

> With that I answered, 'Blessed be the Lord that hath made it known to so low a servant as I'; then repairing to my chamber again, I looked out at the window, where I saw a flag, at the end of the street. This word I had presently upon it, 'Thou seest the flag, the flag of defiance is with the army, the king of Salem is on their side, he marcheth before them, he is the captain of their salvation.'

Evidently, too, Anna did not stay indoors, because: 'I looking saw a hill (it was Blackheath); it was said to me, "Thou seest the hill, not one but many hills rising up against Hermon Hill, they shall fall down and become valleys before it."'

What Trapnel was seeing was the arrival of the Kentish Royalist troops on Blackheath, and she also 'saw' their downfall. For Trapnel, the landscape of London had become the landscape of the Holy Land:

> It was then said unto me, 'Go into the city and see what is done there.' Where I saw various things from the Lord in order to his appearance with the army. As I was going, hearing of a trumpeter say to a citizen these words: 'We have many consultations about our coming up, but nothing yet goes on'; presently it was said to me, 'The counsels of men shall fall, but the counsel of

the Lord stands sure, and his works shall prosper.' So repairing home, I had many visions, that the Lord was doing great things for this nation.

This inspires a ferocious outburst of fasting and prophecy, the first of many until the final one in 1654 brought Anna Trapnel to the attention of Cromwell: 'And having fasted nine days, nothing coming within my lips, I had upon the ninth day the vision of horns; first I saw in the vision the army coming in Southwark-way, marching through the city with a great deal of silence and quietness, and that there should be little or no blood spilt; this was some weeks before their coming in.'

Such extreme fasting is grounded in a surprisingly Catholic-sounding belief in penance on behalf of others. Rather like the IRA hunger strikers of the 1980s, the Londoners who engaged in these fasts made them into political as well as religious events. Anna's fasts were extreme even by the standards of her day; she writes that she was seen as 'under a temptation' for 'not eating'. Her local preacher warned her that this might be inspired by vanity, 'to be singular beyond what was meet'. But Anna Trapnel was not going to be directed now, except by the Bible itself and the Spirit, which informed her that 'thou shalt in every way be supplied in body and spirit'. Inspired by eating nothing, she had a vision of the horns: its rich symbolism is drawn from the Book of Daniel:

> Then broke forth another vision as to the horns: I saw four horns, which were four powers, the first was that of the bishops, that I saw was broken in two and thrown aside; the second horn more white, had joined to it a head, endeavouring to get up a mount, and suddenly it was pushed down, and broken to pieces; the third horn had many splinters joined to it, like to the scales on the back of a fish, and this was presented to be a power or representative consisting of many men, having fair pretences of love to all under all forms; this I saw broken and scattered, that not as much as any bit of it was left.

Plainly, Anna is not just reporting events, but interpreting them in the light of scripture. For many Independent religious thinkers, the 'little horn' of Daniel was Charles I. But Trapnel's vision seems more complex, and there are many horns, not merely one; the third certainly sounds like Parliament. Because the Book of Daniel was about the rule of God becoming incarnate in the world, it was a guide to saints who were hoping to achieve the same thing. By now Anna was moving headily through those revolutionary circles in London that believed they were sent to bring about the end of the world. It was probably a longing to be in the thick of things, and to hear more sermons, meet more saints, that led Trapnel to move from the Minories to the house of a relative in Fenchurch Street, in the City. She was moving to the centre of political ferment, where other women were now taking their political demands to the Parliamentary government, and not always bothering to justify their claims in the name of religion.

In the first days of January 1647, Mary Overton and her brother-in-law Thomas were working, sewing together the leaves of a pamphlet. Mary was running a small printing press, trying to support herself and her three children while her husband Richard was in prison. Since he was one of the leading Levellers in the country, most of what was offered to Mary's press was extreme in content, potent – and illegal.

What made it illegal was its Leveller content. The term 'Leveller movement' used by historians is misleading, suggesting the existence of a single group with an agreed manifesto. There were saints and socialists, radicals who believed in reason and radicals who thought they were bringing about the Second Coming. On any issue there were likely to be more than three opinions. Some saints – Independent church congregations – hated the Levellers for spoiling a moment of godly triumph with their carping. Others saw them as the spearhead of the ever-ongoing process of ecclesiastical reformation. So the Levellers were not a party or a group, and in retrospect the extent to which they even held common views seems doubtful; certainly they did not have any kind of simple programme. But the name was and is still given to those who held a certain set of very radical opinions. At various points, those claiming to be Levellers demanded such previously unthinkable reforms as manhood suffrage for all freemen, the abolition of the monarchy and the House of Lords, complete religious toleration for Protestants and the equality of all men before the law. Some of their views are still, so to speak, to the left of the British polity.

The Levellers' cause was hopeless from the start. They never stood the slightest chance of winning over those with the power to grant their demands, or even of winning over a majority of the population for whom they claimed to speak. But somehow they broke through an encrusted order of thought, if not of power, releasing desires and possibilities that would only be translated into action hundreds of years in the future.

'Leveller' is a term created by the enemies of those thus named. There is something of destruction in the name: to level is to raze, to erase, to sow every acre with salt, to obliterate civilization as we know it, and this signifies the origins of the movement in an era which was beginning to believe itself on the verge of apocalypse. The end of the world was the only vision of truly radical, permanent change that Christian thought allowed. Political ideas of change were imagined through its rhetoric of the annihilation of difference; if the lion could lie down with the lamb, then the rich and the poor might also one day be reconciled. The Levellers grew out of three things: the experiences of the godly members of the Parliamentarian army, the experience of Independent churchgoing and the unfolding story of the times. All these made change seem thinkable, along certain lines. The Levellers' leaders could assemble their ideas like patchwork, putting together a fragment of an idea from here, an original thought from there. What they made was a new map of how the world might look. But to most people it just looked like a misdrawn map, or even a big mess without rhyme or reason.

The congregations were also a little world, a gathering-place for innovation, and full of the excitement of newness and the hopes it brought. Among those who must have met in the seething, gasping crowds were the men who became the Leveller leaders: Richard Overton, William Walwyn and John Lilburne, for their pronouncements began to appear coordinated, or at least similar. But the Levellers and the sectarians were also increasingly at odds, because *The Case of the Army* and later Leveller documents granted equality to all, and the more radical godly congregations were beginning to think that the war had been allowed to bring about the rule of the saints unencumbered by sinners.

What the Levellers wanted was a just state. They wanted to call themselves 'freeborn Englishmen' and to extend the reformation of the Church to the reformation of the state, and along similar lines. They wanted a new constitution and a new simplified legal system: no imprisonment for debt, capital punishment only for murder and treason. Legal procedures should be in English, as church services were. Just as the monasteries had been dissolved, so tithes should go. There should be no beggars, free trade would replace closed shops, and there should be freedom of worship. What about an assembly, a single legislature that could consist of representatives elected by every adult male? And local magistrates, also elected?

They said, emphatically, that they didn't want men's property, or to make all things common. However, they were a threat to property ownership precisely because they were no longer willing to see it as a distinguishing characteristic in other spheres. For the Levellers, legitimate authority could only come from an agreement of the people. Then where did Cromwell's authority come from? From what did Henry Ireton's derive? And how, in any case, could the people decide anything?

In the cold winter of 1647, Mary was stitching a pamphlet so seditious that even now its contents would be shocking, a pamphlet which argued that every king since the Norman conquest was nothing but a usurping tyrant, that the power of Parliament derived from those it governed: *Regall Tyrannie Discovered*. Mary may have agreed with every word, or she may not have liked the pamphlet, but she was running a business. She and her brother-in-law went on sewing, surrounded by drying sheets of treason. The heavy printing press stood in the corner. The searchers arrived while Mary was still working on the pamphlet. The searchers found loose leaves of it, and other 'scandalous pamphlets'. Mary, and her brother-in-law Thomas, who was stitching sheets, were arrested. This is Mary's account of what Parliamentary arrest was like. She already knew, for Richard had been arrested in August:

> though your Petitioner's husband hath constantly adhered to the Parliament, and hath given ample testimony of his sincere and upright affections to the Honourable House, to the just laws and freedoms of England, in general, and to the rights and properties of all and every commoner in particular . . . upon the 11 of August 1646 had his house surrounded with diverse

armed men with swords and muskets, under the conduct of one
Robert Eales, and by the said Robert Eales with his Sword drawn
in his hand, and by one Mr Eveling (dweller at the Green Dragon
in the Strand) with his pistol ready cocked, was suddenly and
violently entered, and his person laid hold of.

Now it was her turn to suffer the some injustice. Brought before the
Lords on the afternoon of 6 January 1647, and asked by the Speaker
who had brought the 'scandalous pamphlets called *Regal tyranny discovered* to her Shop, and of whom she had them', Mary refused to
answer. Thomas, too, would say no more than that he had found them
there. She was dragged to prison 'on two cudgels . . . headlong upon
the stones through all the dirt and mire of the streets,' with her small
'tender infant', her six-month-old baby clutched in her arms, and
pregnant once more. All the way there, the officers of the law abused
her, calling her 'the scandalous, wicked names of whore, strumpet etc.'
Finally she arrived at 'the most reproachful gaol' of Bridewell, where
Mary miscarried her baby. There she was to remain until July of that
year. Neighbours took in her older children, in the informal scramble
of kindness which was early modernity's version of social services, and
her house was shut up. Mary was indignant on her own behalf; she
felt certain that her treatment had been outrageous: she says her impris-
oners are 'parallel'd by none but by the Spanish or Romish inquisitors'
and she concludes that if they don't give all of the accused fair and
speedy trials, then '. . . you have absolutely resolved . . . To inslave the
commons [i.e. the common people] of England to a Lordly arbitrary
vassalage and bondage, to conquer and destroy their laws, rights, Liberties and Freedoms, and to turn co-Usurpers and joint Tyrants with
that Norman brood of insolent dominating tyrants and usurpers, the
House of Lords.'

In his account, Richard Overton described the scene in similar
pathetic detail: 'their 3 small children (as helpless Orphans bereft of a
father and mother) exposed to the mercy of the wide world', and he
also writes passionately of his wife's mistreatment: 'with the poor infant
still crying and mourning in her arms, whose life they spared not to
hazard by that inhuman barbarous usage . . . calling her strumpet and
wild whore'.

Unlike earlier generations victimized by repressive governments,

Overton was able to articulate his horrified sense that this outrage was a violation of privacy and of his wife's good name, and hence a violation of his masculinity. Therefore he saw it as a sign of tyranny – a tyrant is that which cannot allow privacy and the right to privacy to ordinary men. A wife and children are markers and guarantors of that private male identity. The public shaming of Mary Overton – being dragged through the streets, the shouts of 'whore', her literal circulation in the mud and mire – is a violation of Richard's identity as well as hers.

Mary also complains that the officials have stolen goods 'which were then her present livelihood for her imprisoned husband, herself, and three small children, her brother and sister; and to bring your petitioner, with Thomas Overton her husband's brother'. This was cheek, for she meant the printing press, which had been confiscated. But it may have been true all the same. It was an established custom that when men were killed or imprisoned, their wives and daughters were expected to keep their businesses going. Thus women ran ale-houses, farms, mills, cobblers – and printshops. Mary was referring to this tradition obliquely in defending herself.

Richard Overton was no ignoramus, no 'mechanick preacher'. He matriculated as a sizar at Queens' College, Cambridge, while Milton was still at Christ's. The record of his matriculation means that he had had to pledge allegiance to the king and to the Church of England to enter the university. And yet Queens' in Overton's day was riven by faction; of the thirty-four fellows, twelve were expelled for their Catholic sympathies. There was also the powerful godly preacher Preston. Overton was something of a wit, whose first literary effort was a pamphlet-play which featured Archbishop Laud feasting on the ears of William Prynne. Later, Laud is punished by having his nose pressed to the grindstone. Overton's carnivalesque humour appeared, too, in *Articles of High Treason Exhibited Against Cheap-Side Cross* (1642). The cross is tried by the people for treason and found guilty of being a cause of civil war. And yet the predominance of iconoclasm in the war's opening years suggests he may have had a valid point to make. When the same carnivalesque tactics were used against his family, Overton drew the line.

He could be an astoundingly scandalous critic of government. In *The Baiting of the Great Bull of Bashan*, for example, he portrays the

Levellers as bulldogs attacking the genitals of Oliver Cromwell as a bull. The genitals are pox-ridden, so they come away easily. The Levellers were not always solemn sectarians; they could be bawdy pamphleteers too.

But Mary's less amusing experience of what it was like to be a Leveller was more typical. The Levellers formulated their ideas under the hammer of surveillance and oppression. Those eager to silence them could hardly have done more to make them want to speak. No one knew this better than Elizabeth Lilburne (or Dewell, as she was at first), who seems to have met her future husband John through his political fame, which was considerable. John Lilburne had been an ardent follower of John Bastwick, and cut his political teeth distributing one of Burton's satirical pamphlets. This made it natural that he should become a distinguished member of the Parliamentarian forces defending Brentford, and later a radical and religious pamphleteer in his own right. His wife, he said, was 'an object dear in my affections several years before she knew anything of it'. She seems to have begun in the role of comforter of the afflicted: 'when [he] was more like Job upon the dunghill by his sufferings than a man at that time fit for her society', that is, when he was in the Fleet Prison. She may have been the woman who visited him immediately after his whipping. John always spoke very tenderly of his wife, but that was partly to bolster his self-image as an honest father and husband.

When Lilburne was captured at Brentford, and imprisoned in Oxford Castle awaiting trial for taking up arms against the king, he smuggled out a letter to his Elizabeth. She was pregnant, but had been following the army, as the wives of poorer men did. She had not been idle, daily and hourly petitioning the House of Commons to help her husband. She managed to reach the Royalist headquarters, after 'so many sad and difficult accidents to a woman in her condition as would force tears from the hardest heart'. She contrived to get Lilburne released as an exchange, and he was greeted as a hero on his return to London.

Like many businesses, Lilburne's brewery had all but collapsed in its master's absence, and John sold it almost at once. Elizabeth had obtained a government position for him at a generous salary, but he turned it down, declaring that he would rather fight for eightpence a day, and he re-enlisted at once, recruited by Cromwell. Elizabeth set off to follow him again, with the baby.

Nevertheless, he left the army in the spring of 1645 because he would not take the Covenant, and he was soon imprisoned again, this time by Parliament, for insulting the Speaker. Elizabeth went with him to Newgate Prison in the late summer of 1645, until his release in October. She was again pregnant, so it was especially miserable that when the Lilburnes reached Half-Moon Alley, they discovered that the officers who had ransacked their house had stolen the carefully stored childbed linen. Like Ann Fanshawe, Elizabeth had lost the household stuff that was important to her, the valuable household linen which defined a wife's identity and often constituted her wealth. There were public quarrels, too, between husband and wife. She tried – desperately – to persuade him to give up the cause, to take care of his wife and children.

But by then John Lilburne was politically articulate, and there was no holding him. He wanted the Commons elected and meeting annually; the Self-Denying Ordinance should be enforced, and payment given to poor MPs for attendance. He wanted an end to the Solemn League and Covenant, to church tithes, to excise, to laws in tongues other than English. Between the spring of 1646 and late September 1649, he produced almost forty pamphlets. Hardly anyone escaped uncriticized. Lilburne saw his own imprisonment as the first proof of injustice and the loss of ancient liberties, and from that it followed that he and every other right-thinking person was engaged in a battle to defend liberty – against the Long Parliament, Commons and Lords both, the judiciary. Some titles reveal Lilburne's vitality, but also his debt to the ferocious pit-bulls of the wartime London press: *Liberty Vindicated Against Slavery* (1646); *Jonah's Cry out of the Whale's Belly and The Juglers Discovered* (1647); *A Whip for the Present House of Lords, or the Levellers Levelled*, and *The Prisoners Mournful Cry* (1648). It was less that Lilburne had a coherent ideology than that he was relentlessly against all those in power, whether acquired recently or long ago. And he was an icon, like his masters Bastwick and Burton.

A month after Mary Overton's arrest, Elizabeth found her home too was being ransacked by the Stationers' Company, and the following day (8 February 1647) she was arrested for distributing the books John had written. She and her husband found themselves before the Committee of Examinations. John read them a paper he had prepared demanding a public hearing, but was interrupted so many times that finally Elizabeth lost her temper. 'I told thee often enough long since, that thou would serve the Parliament, and venture thy life so long for them, till they would hang thee for thy pains, and give thee Tyburn for thy recompense, and I told thee besides, thou shouldst in conclusion find them a company of unjust and unrighteous judges, that more sought themselves, and their own ends, than the public good of the kingdom, or any of those that faithfully adventured their lives therefore.' John managed to get the committee to agree to discharge his wife, on the conventional grounds that she could not be held responsible for his actions.

When the army reached London, Lilburne was in the Tower once more, with the Overtons and other Levellers. The newswriters expected the army to free him, but nothing happened. Elizabeth, as always, had to make it happen; she was constantly petitioning army headquarters to press for his release. More turmoils followed; ordered from Westminster Hall, Lilburne was preparing to fight for his freedom in the most literal fashion, but Elizabeth hurled herself against him to protect him from his foes' drawn swords. She adored him, but she hardly ever had him at her side. Finally, he was hauled off to the Tower again – one of his children was even named Tower to commemorate his absence. Elizabeth got him back for a while during the Second Civil War, but by then everything that made for household calm had collapsed, including all visible means of financial support. He had no estates, no income, no business and no trade. (Eventually, he became a soap-boiler.) And soon he was back in the Tower again. Commentators noted that he had become thin and haggard in gaol, but his family may also have suffered, for shortly after the Burford mutiny, Elizabeth and all three children fell sick with smallpox. The eldest boy called desperately for his father, and the authorities allowed Lilburne to visit his family, but both his sons died. Elizabeth and his daughter young Elizabeth slowly recovered, but Lilburne thought his sons' death a worse trial from God than years in gaol, and wrote that he was 'weary of any thing I might see abroad'. The political conflict had been one long ordeal for an honest, decent family man who longed only to live in peace:

> Parties of horse and foot are sent at unreasonable hours to hale
> and pull people out of their beds and houses, from their wives
> and children, without so much as ever summoning of them and
> without any crime or accusation shown or accuser appearing

or the least pretence or shadow of law produced – some sent into remote garrisons, where they have been most barbarously used and endeavoured to be starved and tossed from garrison to garrison, others locked up close prisoners with sentinels night and day upon their doors, and all due trials and help at law stopped and denied, and no remedy to be obtained.

Lilburne's proper place, he says, is quietly at home with his wife and children. Yet he rarely chose to occupy it. Like Overton, he tried to defend his wife. Lilburne complained that Elizabeth was 'attacked at the very Parliament-door, when she was peaceably waiting there with eight Gentlewomen more, for an Answer to her late Petition, and for Justice from the House, about my illegal sufferings . . . a piece of unmanlike cruelty and barbarism . . . which renders him to be one of the malicious, basest, unworthiest, and cowardliest of men, to use a gentlewoman in such a manner'. Lilburne excused Elizabeth by saying that 'she is my wife, and set at work to do what she did at the earnest desire of me her (unjust imprisoned) husband, and truly I appeal to every one of your own consciences, whether you would not have taken it very ill at the hands of any of your wives, if you were in my case, and she should refuse at your earnest desire to do that for you'. Overton went further, claiming to have written his wife's petition, and indeed its language is extremely close to one of his own. Lilburne claimed that 'I was led presently to take care, to do something for my wife as the weaker vessel . . . and for that end I drew her presently up a few lines, which I read unto her, and gave her instructions . . . unto which she readily assented, and set her name to it, which verbatim thus followeth'. The women's petitions were also republished in pamphlets written by their husbands, as if taken under the protective embrace of marital ideology. 'We, our husbands, brethren, friends, and servants, contrary to all law, severally, and in a forced and unjust separation from our husbands, are kept and mewed up in your several starving, stinking, murdering prison houses.'

The Levellers' moment came when they made contacts in the increasingly dissatisfied New Model Army in the spring of 1647. Parliament, the Army thought, seemed determined to dismantle it for the most part – its disbandment was ordered formally on 27 May 1647 – and (worse) to send the remaining remnants to Ireland. The Army radicals suspected Parliament of Presbyterian leanings. Some in the Army were Presbyterian too, but many were not, and no one was keen to be forced to choose between being sent home without pay and being posted to Ireland.

The Army was also unpaid, and had petitioned Parliament repeatedly for its earnings. Lilburne and others seized the chance to begin organizing the election of 'agitators', as they were termed by their foes, a process that began in April 1647. Leveller ideas spread fast from cavalry to foot regiments, and soon the officers were as unhappy as the men had been.

The soldiers had also experienced authority more directly and frustratingly than they might have as smallholders or bakers or husbandmen. Faith in Parliament was weakened when they came to feel that it was not protecting them; not considering them, not paying them. The soldiers were starved: of pay, of care, of attention. Like shambling unwanted children, too, they were about to be thrown out of home, sent to Ireland, as if the Army had no stake in England but was merely a band of mercenaries. Fearful, angry, longing to be acknowledged, the Army wanted, at least, to be heard. But their foes in Parliament were deaf. Denzil Holles and the Presbyterians expressed Parliament's 'high dislike' of the Army's petition for indemnity for acts committed in war, security for arrears, provision for the maimed and for the widows and children of the dead, and no service in Ireland. The Army showed its wounded feelings when it called this the Declaration of Dislike. Its sense of honour was affronted, and its sensible, blunt commander was offended too. Fairfax and his council of war, who had been fighting for Parliament all this time, decided, momentously, not to disband the Army on Parliament's orders.

In June 1647, the New Model Army acted. It became a political entity – almost like the Roman army – when it stole the king from Parliament's custody at Holmby House, and began marching in sweeps towards London and Westminster. As the Army moved, it communicated: a series of declarations were produced. One claimed that they 'were not a mere mercenary army, hired to serve any arbitrary power of state, but called forth and conjured by the several declarations of parliament to the defence of our own and the people's just rights and liberties.

And so we took up arms in judgement and conscience to those ends.'
These declarations came not from the Army's commanders, but from
its ranks.

But the Levellers could scarcely hope to gain what they wanted
by petitioning Parliament. The House of Commons, to which they
addressed their pleas, was a cosy club for portly gentlemen and
merchants, who had no enthusiasm for what they called 'the meaner
sort'. Those who had begun the war – men like the Five Members –
had never had the slightest intention of changing the social order
fundamentally, only of protecting what was theirs as members of the
gentry, and preserving – not radicalizing – the Church. Rebuffed, the
Levellers began to think that the New Model Army was more to be
relied on.

The Army swept down on London, and terrified its Presbyterian MP
opponents into hasty flight, and in this situation the Levellers saw an
opportunity to enter the world of national politics. They united with
newly elected Army agitators to produce *The Case of the Army Truly
Stated*, a long and miserable grizzle, but at its heart lay *An Agreement
of the People*, the key text for the exciting debates held at Putney between
the Army and its commanders from 28 October until 9 November 1647.

The press was not supposed to report the proceedings, but a few writers
managed to leak terse remarks. 'Not fit to be presented to the public
view', said the newspapers coyly. But copies of *An Agreement of the
People* were in wide circulation, in two editions, and the newspapers
gave summaries of it. It was an astounding wish-list for political change.
It called for the dissolution of both houses of Parliament on the grounds
that they had been there for long enough to grow corrupt. They were
to be replaced by a sovereign body of 400 men, which would be elected
by manhood franchise, a principle embodied in a swingeing critique
of the seventeenth-century system of rotten boroughs: 'That the people
of England being at this day very unequally distributed by counties,
cities and boroughs for the election of their deputies in parliament,
ought to be more indifferently proportioned according to the number
of the inhabitants: the circumstances whereof, for number, place, and
manner, are to be set down before the end of this present parliament.'
This body was to have absolute authority over monies and foreign

policy, and was to safeguard freedom of conscience in matters of religion: 'We do not empower or entrust our said representatives to continue in force, or to make any Laws, Oaths, or Covenants, whereby to compell by penalties or otherwise any person to any thing in or about matters of faith, Religion or God's worship or to restrain any person from the profession of his faith, or to exercise of Religion according to his Conscience, nothing having caused more distractions, and heart burnings in all ages, then persecution and molestation for matters of Conscience in and about Religion.' They also demanded one law for rich and poor alike: 'That in all laws made or to be made, every person may be bound alike; and that no tenure, estate, charter, degree, birth, or place do confer any exemption from the ordinary course of legal proceedings whereunto others are subjected.' These things, they said, we declare to be our native rights.

All the time, however, a man named William Clarke was trying to make notes that summarized what was said at Putney, in a newfangled shorthand system. After the Restoration, he set out to write up his notes, though historians didn't discover their existence until the nineteenth century. Thus for two hundred and fifty years, the Putney debates were a secret at the heart of Civil War history; when they were uncovered, they changed our sense of the possibilities of the age.

The Putney debates provided an arena in which the Levellers and the grandees of the Army struggled to win the minds and hearts of junior officers and common footsoldiers.

To Cromwell and Ireton, the debates might have seemed an infuriating interruption to the process of reforming the state and negotiating with the king. Sensible officers, they knew that mutineers could be pacified only if officers were willing to hear their grievances. But like most busy people, they probably resented the leisurely pace of democratic process. And yet the very fact that the debates were held at all – that the grandees thought such things could be *debated* – was astounding. The debates themselves undermined the certainty of the very system the Army grandees wanted to defend. It was even more extraordinary that such debates could be held – and could only be understood – inside the Army. This was a result of the army's own experience, and not just in the New Model. War offers an atypical experience, and thus provokes ideas of further change. The New Model Army felt itself victorious. In the very first paragraph of *An Agreement*, it presents itself as the protector of liberty:

> Having by our late labours and hazards made it appear to the world at how high a rate we value our just freedom, and God having so far owned our cause as to deliver the enemies thereof into our hands, we do now hold ourselves bound in mutual duty to each other to take the best care we can for the future to avoid both the danger of returning into a slavish condition and the chargeable remedy of another war. For as it cannot be imagined that so many of our countrymen would have opposed us in this quarrel if they had understood their own good, so may we safely promise to ourselves that when our common rights and liberties shall be cleared, their endeavours will be disappointed that seek to make themselves our masters.

The Army radicals saw themselves as martyrs for the liberties of the people: 'For your safety and freedom we have cheerfully endured hard labours and run most desperate hazards. And in comparison to your peace and freedom we neither do nor ever shall value our dearest blood; and we profess our bowels are and have been troubled and our hearts pained within us in seeing and considering that you have been so long bereaved of these fruits and ends of all our labours and hazards.' What they meant was that the Army commanders did not appreciate the cause for which they had fought. It was in this attitude of intransigence that they came to Putney.

Not all MPs turned a deaf ear to the Army radicals. Thomas Rainborough was a member of the tiny republican group of MPs led by Henry Marten. He was the son of a naval commander, brought up to be a sailor, and served for a short spell at sea as a vice-admiral. Then he became a colonel and raised a regiment under Manchester, officered mainly by men who had emigrated to New England but come home. He managed to capture Crowland Abbey, which made his name; he was given command of a regiment in the New Model Army, and fought at Naseby and Bristol; at Bristol he took Prior's Hill Fort, and put everyone in it to the sword. He was tall and hefty, strong, intimidating, known both for his daring and for the very strict discipline he imposed on his men. He was especially gifted at siegecraft, and he liked to use the pike, a weapon suited to his great size and strength. He had pikeman values, too: stand together or fall apart.

But he was hotheaded, and always went just a little further than other people. He became more radical as the 1640s wore on. Disgusted especially by Charles's intransigence in rejecting the Heads of the Proposals, he spread the story of his stubbornness through the army. His dislike of the king meant that he distrusted Cromwell and Ireton for continuing to talk to Charles. In his ardent republicanism he was influenced by Henry Marten and hence by the political philosophies of the ancients, but it was also the outcome of his experience and his reading. He was also angry that Cromwell had opposed his appointment as vice-admiral. Cromwell saw him not only as a personal enemy, but as 'endeavouring to have no other power to rule but the sword'.

Other MPs were more equivocal. Henry Ireton was a man whose name begins with the word 'ire', and sounds like 'iron'; both are suggestive and relevant. He was the intellectual star of the Putney debates: their head, if Rainborough is their heart. Ireton was a hard man who insisted that property in land or a freehold of trading rights was the foundation of civil society, but he left no writings behind him save one letter. At Putney he was also relatively young, just thirty-six years old. He had been at Trinity College, Cambridge and at the Inns of Court, and he knew how debates were supposed to go. He was fresh from commanding the left at Naseby, from accepting the surrender of Bristol, from overseeing the surrender of Oxford, and from marrying Oliver Cromwell's daughter Bridget, a young woman of twenty-two. He was the man of the moment, the man in form.

Ireton had had a difficult adolescence; he lost his father when he was only thirteen, and after that he was the oldest male, with four brothers and three sisters to protect and instruct. Being with Cromwell was a relief and also a source of tension; Ireton was used to being in the lead, but also liked being fathered. Lucy Hutchinson was married to his cousin, and she took note of him. 'A very grave, serious, religious person', she thought. Zealous in promoting the godly interest, Ireton was modest, prudent, 'very active, industrious, and stiff in his ways and purposes', thought Bulstrode Whitelocke. Until the war he had lived quietly, believing himself accountable only to God. He raised a troop of horse for Parliament in 1642, prompt to declare that the king had violated its powers. Himself elected MP in 1645, he sat in silence. Like Margaret Thatcher in our time, he was disliked even by people who admired his abilities, and admired even by those who disliked him and his ideas.

His peace terms to Charles (the Heads of the Proposals) were the best and sanest offer Charles could have expected, and only Charles would have refused them. They show what Ireton too might have wanted: biennial Parliaments, Parliamentary control of the militia for ten years, the exclusion of leading Royalists from office. There would be religious toleration of everyone except Catholics, and neither the Book of Common Prayer nor the Covenant was to be compulsory.

Clever, and a powerful influence on Cromwell's slower mind, Ireton could also seem too certain of everything, sure that absolute truth could be got at. This silent, intense, inward man was to speak for the grandees at Putney, who opposed the Army agitators and Rainborough. 'Proud self-ended fellows', John Lilburne thought them. The grandees wanted reform of the existing system: a king restrained by a Parliament that represented men of property. *An Agreement of the People* called for something completely different from anything seen in England before, an assembly elected by all men.

The debate began when leading agitator Edward Sexby, outrageously blunt, told Cromwell and Ireton that their reputations had been damaged both by their attempts to placate Charles and by their service to a 'rotten' Parliament. Cromwell then gave a response to *The Case of the Army Truly Stated*. A man recorded as 'Buff-coat', but actually Robert Everard, replied with his own account of the purpose of the meeting: 'we have [here met] according to my engagement, that whatsoever may be thought to be necessary for our satisfaction, for the right understanding one of another, that we might go on together. For though our ends and aims be the same, if one thinks this way, another way, that way which is best for the subject is that they may be hearkened unto.'

Immediately Cromwell began grilling him about *The Case of the Army*, which he called a paper:

Truly this paper does contain in it very great alterations of the very government of this kingdom ... although the pretensions in it, and the expressions in it, are very plausible, and if we could leap out of one condition into another that had so specious things in it as this hath ... How do we know if, whilst we are disputing these things, another company of men shall gather together, and put out a paper as plausible perhaps as this? ... And not only another, but another, and another, but many of this kind. And if so, what do you think the consequence of this would be? Would it not be confusion? Would it not be utter confusion?

He went on to declare his faith in the workings of providence: 'God will manifest to us to be the thing that he would have us prosecute', he asserted. He also argued fiercely that everyone must consider any engagements they already had, any pledges to others. Ireton agreed. But Rainborough said, 'I shall speak my mind', and responded that it was true that every honest man was bound in duty to God and to his conscience, let him be engaged in what he will. He also responded to Cromwell's point on division and difficulty by alluding to the war they had just fought, pointing out that the kind of conservatism Cromwell now appeared to be advocating would have meant that it was never fought at all. When Cromwell and others said of the constitution proposed in *An Agreement of the People*, 'It's a huge alteration, it's a bringing in of New Laws' (Rainborough's scathing summary), Rainborough commented, 'if writings be true there hath been many scufflings between the honest men of England and those that have tyrannized over them'.

Crucially, Cromwell argued that the Army was committed to what it had itself said about its intentions. A long wrangle ensued about what exactly was binding on the Army. But it was not dully bureaucratic; it was shot through with the language of the Bible, of the coming of God in glory. William Goffe, for example, spoke of God 'throwing down the glory of all flesh', by which he meant that no one could rise above being God's instrument. One reason the debates are eloquent is that most of the participants were more used to hearing issues discussed theologically than in committee. John Wildman broke up a consensual interchange between Goffe and Ireton on the centrality of God to debate, reminding everyone sharply that the people's grievances were not being redressed by Parliament. He also pointed out that the army wanted to be heard at once, not after weeks had gone by. Wildman exemplified the fervour of the committed Levellers. To them – as, perhaps to us – what they wanted was so obviously just and right that they couldn't see why they shouldn't have it at once.

This roused Ireton's ire. He explained:

> If you will resort only to the law of nature, by the law of nature you have no more right to this land, or anything else, than I have. I have as much right to take hold of anything that is I have a desire to for my satisfaction, as you. But here comes the foundation of all right that I understand to be betwixt men, as to the enjoying of one thing or not enjoying of it; we are under a contract, and, we are under an agreement, and that agreement is what a man has for a matter of land that he hath received by a traduction from his ancestors, which according to the law does fall upon him to be his right.

In other words, he interpreted the Levellers within the Army as a potential threat to the right to own property. Wildman responded by asking whether an engagement to do an unjust thing could be binding, and explained that he meant the plan to bring in the king 'in such a way as he may be in a capacity to destroy the people'. This point was expressed still more bluntly by Captain Lewis Audley: 'if we tarry long, if we stay but three days before you satisfy one another, the king will come and say who will be hanged first'. Despite robust assertions of the rights of the Commons, the ghost of monarchical terror sometimes seemed to haunt the Putney debaters. Like John Pym in the early 1640s, they knew that if they did not win they were doomed. What they feared was that the moderates in Parliament would make an agreement with the king that excluded them.

Cromwell and Ireton were groping for a starting-point that might create consensus, and that might also prevent a march on London and an Army coup. It was as part of the drive for consensus that the commanders established a committee to look into the Army's declarations. Of course, a committee is also a way of not doing something, but this was not Cromwell's intention. He wanted a resolution.

*   *   *

The key debate on Friday 29 October took place by accident, almost in private. Everyone agreed to hold a prayer meeting originally suggested by William Goffe, feeling uneasily that God hadn't so far blessed anyone with a comfortable compromise. At the house of a Mr Chamberlain, every godly man and officer gathered, and after several hours of prayers and testimonies, the Levellers arrived to confer with the committee. Noticing that a large and sympathetic audience was already present, they immediately wanted to launch a debate on the *Agreement*. Cromwell was against it, pointing out that everyone was tired after a late-night debate and five hours or so of prayer, but Rainborough (who had skipped the prayer meeting) seized his chance and supported the Levellers. Rainborough's right to be there at all was debatable, since he was by now a vice-admiral and not a colonel; Cromwell had approved his appointment after all, as a way of getting rid of him. It hadn't worked.

The debate began to turn on property, in response to some of what Ireton had said the day before. Maximilian Petty said that so far from the paper destroying property, it preserved it. 'For', he said, 'I judge every man is naturally free, and I judge the reason why men chose representatives when they were in so great numbers that every man could not give his voice was that they who were chosen might preserve property for all ... and I would fain know, if we were to begin a government, [whether you would say] "You have not forty shillings a year, therefore you shall not have a voice." Whereas before there was a government every man had such a voice.'

Ireton responded:

> If a man be an inhabitant upon a rack rent for a year, for two years, or twenty years, you cannot think that man hath any fixed or permanent interest. That man, if he pay the rent that his land is worth, and hath no advantage but what he hath by his land, is as good a man, may have as much interest, in another kingdom as here. I do not speak of not enlarging this representation at all, but of keeping this to the most fundamental constitution in the kingdom, that is, that no person that hath not a local and permanent interest in the kingdom should have an equal dependence in election.

What Ireton meant was that property-owning landlords had a stake in the nation, and that those without land didn't. This was common sense to most educated men, but it was precisely this link between power and ownership that the Levellers were questioning. Colonel Nathaniel Rich worried that an assembly of such men would vote in equivalency of goods and estate. And, he added, thinking of ancient Rome, 'if we strain too far to avoid a monarchy in kings, [let us take care] that we do not call for emperors to deliver us from more than one tyrant'.

But Rainborough was not satisfied. He kept asking how it came about that some freeborn Englishmen had property and its rights, while others did not. Another Leveller, Cowling, pointed out that the law worked absurdly, so that 'there is a tanner in Staines worth three thousand pounds, and another in Reading worth three horseskins'. But only the first 'has a voice'. Ireton clung determinedly to the idea that the identity of electors had been established long ago, intelligently appealing to the dread of foreigners intervening in government in defence of the interests of the landed gentry. But Sexby was having none of it: 'We have engaged in this kingdom and ventured our lives, we have had little property in the kingdom as to our estates, yet we have had a birthright. But it seems now, except a man has a fixed estate in his kingdom, he hath no right in this kingdom . . . I do think the poor and mean of this kingdom . . . have been the means of preservation of this kingdom.'

Powerfully, he argued that the Army at least had proved its interest in the kingdom by shedding its blood. Rainborough took up the theme: 'I would fain know what the soldier hath fought for all this while? He hath fought to enslave himself, to give power to men of riches, men of estates, to make him a perpetual slave.'

Ireton was determined to carry the debate back to the origins of rights rather than their results: 'I will tell you what the soldier of the kingdom hath fought for. First, the danger that we stood in was that one's man's will must be a law . . . they thought it [the law] was better to be concluded by the common consent of those that were fixed men, and settled men, that had the interests of the kingdoms in them.'

And he kept on saying this, and kept on repeating that only these fixed and settled men could be counted on. For Ireton, the right to choose representatives was not a natural right, but a constitutional right, available because property ownership conferred 'a permanent fixed interest in the kingdom'. For Ireton this part of the constitution safeguarded property; without it, property was under threat. If a man has the right to elect by right of nature, then he has exactly the same right to any goods he sees. It's hard to believe Ireton's anxiety wasn't motivated by the experience of how the soldiers had actually behaved during the war, picking up anything not red-hot or nailed down, and arguing that its ownership by 'malignants' gave them a title to it. Men fought, he said, 'that the will of one man should not be a law, but that the law should be by a choice of persons who were chosen by fixed men and settled men that had the interest of this kingdom in them'. Sexby, for the Levelling party, retorted that the soldiers had fought to 'recover our birthrights and privileges as Englishmen'. Note that the soldiers were not demanding new rights, but claiming that the rights they had always enjoyed were being taken away. If Ireton was correct, he said, 'we have fought all this time for nothing', and he added that had they known, 'I believe you would have had fewer under your command to have commanded.'

And it was in this obscure, odd, highly religious context, and in response to this iron obduracy in Ireton, that Rainborough produced the ringing statements for which he will be remembered for ever.

> I do not find anything in the law of God that a lord shall choose twenty burgesses and a gentleman but two, or a poor man shall choose none.
>
> I am a poor man, therefore I must be pressed [conscripted]: if I have no interest in the kingdom, I must suffer by all their laws, be they right or wrong ... gentlemen with three or four lordships (God knows how they got them) can always get into Parliament and evict the poor from their homes. I would fain know whether the potency of rich men do not this, and so keep them [poor men] under the greatest tyranny that was ever thought of in the world.
>
> Really I think the poorest he that is in England hath a life to live as the greatest he; and therefore, truly sir, I think it's clear that every man that is to live under a government ought first by his own consent to put himself under that government, and I do think that the poorest man in England is not at all bound

in a strict sense to that government that he hath not had a voice
to put himself under.

Though the Levellers didn't use the word democracy in this sense,
Rainborough's final statement is democratic in that it imagined people
making decisions who had previously been shut out of all choice.

Now Cromwell groped for compromise and tolerance. Perhaps, he
said, everyone could at least agree that suffrage might be improved,
and he suggested that great and inevitable solution to the breakdown
of political consensus, the formation of a committee. Ireton agreed and
pointed out that he had been among the first to press for the dissolution
of the present Parliament and the introduction of regular elections. He
too agreed to a committee that would consider extending the franchise
to 'freemen, and men not given up to the wills of others'. Another
Leveller, Petty, responded that he now saw the reason for the exclusion
of servants and apprentices, but this may not mean all Levellers were
convinced, since Petty was not a leader among them. It was meant to
remind the Levellers that they too felt franchise had its limits, and to
move towards compromise.

A committee was duly created, and both Rainborough and Ireton
sat on it. It met several times, though we have no records of what was
discussed; the proposals it prepared, though, show that the battle lines
remained the same as before.

And here everyone not already keenly interested must prepare to be
just as excited as one usually is by political committees and their work;
they are not unimportant, but the longueurs are considerable. There
was redrafting, no end of redrafting, negotiation, compromise. Ireton
thought kings and lords should have veto powers over laws affecting
their persons or estates. Rainborough and Wildman rejected the idea,
Rainborough expressing surprise that Ireton was keen to preserve a
constitution broken repeatedly by the Commons since the beginning
of the war. The committee did end up recommending a package in
which the king's reserve powers were almost invisible and in which the
Commons was firmly sovereign, but the grandees continued to be
dismayed by its radical elements.

There were in the end four drafts of the laboured-over *Agreement of
the People*: the First Agreement, the one debated at Putney; the Second

Agreement, drafted by the committee; the Officers' Agreement, a rewriting of the Second by the Council of Officers; and the Third Agreement, published by the imprisoned Levellers in May 1649, who felt that the Officers' Agreement should have been submitted to the people and not to Parliament.

Historians have usually admired Ireton's arguments more than Rainborough's, but in fact Ireton won the battle and lost the war. It was his fate to be clever, but unpersuasive to his audience. When he defended the provisions he himself had made for the king, he did so high-handedly, dismissing the idea that the Army might be sovereign. Debate rumbled on for months, and slow piecemeal progress was made towards acknowledging the Levellers' position. Under the committee's proposals, explicit rights were reserved to the people: the representative body could not press for war; interfere with religion; arraign men for acts committed during the war (unless for being Royalists); punish contrary to law; or 'take away any of the foundations of common right, liberty or safety contained in the Agreement'.

Ireton opposed the clause on religion, arguing strongly for judgement in moral as well as civil matters, and he succeeded in ensuring that toleration did not extend to Catholics or prelacy. He also fought hard against the clause on punishment, and yet the result was a compromise in which no one really believed.

Now the Levellers adopted a new and startling strategy. Rainborough and Lilburne finally met on 31 October 1647, when Rainborough went to visit Lilburne in the Tower. It seems Rainborough was hoping to get Lilburne's agreement to treating with the king; if so he was knocking at an open door, because Lilburne had no republican ideas, and may already have been in touch with Charles through his fellow-prisoner Lewis Dyve; Lilburne may have promised the king the Army's devotion. At first it may seem odd that the Levellers, keen to abolish monarchy, were willing to develop a working alliance with Charles. It was in part a case of 'the enemy of my enemy is my friend', and it also made a kind of metaphorical sense in the light of early Leveller tracts, which almost identified with the king on the grounds that he too had been scorned and dishonoured by Parliament, who 'make the king their scorn and us their slaves'. 'Remember the end of your taking up arms was to defend the king's majesty and to bring offenders to trial, let them be of what side they will', said another, and a third proposed that reform must begin with 'his Majesty invested in his just power'.

But if Lilburne made the offer he was promising something he couldn't deliver, because the Army was turning against the king. People like Goffe had begun to wonder if God had withdrawn himself from the Army because they had been treating with his enemy. We are all distracted in council, the Army said, because we have been complicit in preserving the man of blood. By now it was depressingly clear even to the most eager spirits that the debates were opening up fresh divisions rather than healing them. By 8 November, Fairfax and Cromwell could see that it was all going nowhere. They also knew the king was about to bolt. They wound things up.

Because they had failed at Putney, leading Levellers argued for a rendezvous of the whole Army where they hoped to present *An Agreement of the People* to the soldiers. Fairfax and Cromwell ordered three separate assemblies rather than one, so the Levellers tried to persuade everyone to attend the first meeting, held on 15 November 1647, at Corkbush Field, Ware.

The atmosphere was tense. No one knew where the king was. He had escaped from Hampton Court only four days earlier. There was a rumour that he would join the Army on Monday. Would he appear at Ware? The officers knew by Sunday night that Charles had reached the Isle of Wight, but the soldiers had heard many rumours and no facts: would the war begin all over again?

The soldiers drew up. Fairfax arrived, and was met by Rainborough, who handed him a copy of the Agreement as an official petition from the Army. Fairfax reviewed each regiment and asked each to subscribe to the Agreement. Seven regiments had been ordered to the field, and two more came with them, parading with copies of the Agreement in their hats, a kind of 'field sign'. In black letters, the papers were superscribed, **ENGLANDS FREEDOMS, SOLDIERS RIGHTS.** One was Thomas Harrison's regiment, which had managed to discard its officers; the other was Robert Lilburne's men. This was not only a mutinous act, but a flagrant and disruptive attempt to turn the tables on Fairfax and Cromwell on a day which was supposed to demonstrate the unity of the Army in the face of its foes.

There was a moment when history trembled on the verge of radical alteration.

Then Cromwell acted: he plunged into the ranks of the two regiments, drawn sword in hand, and managed to cow them. The papers were torn from their caps, and a number of the Leveller leaders were rounded up. They were ordered to draw lots for their lives. The three losers then diced, and the loser this time, Private Richard Arnold, was shot in front of his regiment by his two reprieved companions. The field was littered with discarded, trampled copies of the Agreement. Clarke, shorthand notebook ever at the ready, noted that John Lilburne was there, incognito: 'things not succeeding at the rendez-vous according to expectation, came not further'. The officers, the Levellers felt sure, were the problem; they had betrayed their trusts.

But in reality the problem they faced lay deeper. Most people went on believing in inequality; they saw it all around them, and they found it hard to make the imaginative leap the Levellers had made; it was hard to understand how things could be *as* different as the Levellers wanted.

Even while the debates were going on, the seeds of disaster were being sown. Mutiny broke out in the Army, independently of the Levellers. The Second Civil War saw the Army gather itself together, but by spring and summer 1649 the officers had rid themselves of their enemies in the Commons, and abolished both kingship and the House of Lords. Their only remaining enemies were the leaders of Army mutinies. In March 1649, Cromwell was heard to strike the Council table and cry out, 'I tell you, you have no other way to deal with these men but to break them in pieces.'

There had been a mutiny – yet another – in April. A group of people were sent to one place and stayed put; these had the sense to barricade themselves into an inn, the Bull. They hung on to their colours, too. They were complaining that they had no money to pay for their quarters; their critics said if they'd managed their money better they'd have plenty left. Their commander, Whalley – again – promised them money, but they wanted their arrears guaranteed, and Whalley couldn't promise that, so when a soldier called Lockyer disobeyed a direct order he arrested him instead. In the end only Lockyer was executed, because Fairfax decided that he was the ringleader. Some Leveller women told the authorities that they were about to murder a saint, but they pressed ahead. He was executed in Paul's Yard. He was smiling.

Thousands attended his funeral; a newsbook reported, 'every one having a Black ribbon and a small one fastened to it of a sea green colour . . . It is said so called not of the sea but of the republic, for the People in many places of scripture are compared to the great waters, the sea or ocean, which was signified by sea green.' The coffin was decorated with rosemary, dipped in blood, for remembrance. Lockyer was buried in Moorfields.

There were two kinds of honour in early modern England, and historians have labelled them vertical honour and horizontal honour. Vertical honour involved showing special respect to superiors: cap-doffing, forelock-tugging, saluting, loyal toasts. The Levellers often flouted vertical honour, in part because it was supposed to be a reciprocal system and they felt that it had broken down. Broadly, the implicit contract was that social superiority had to flow from hospitality, generosity, and courtesy to inferiors. The Levellers thought that these things had broken down during the war. Moreover, social hierarchies had been called into question by the emergence of an alternative system, election, being part of God's elite. But they all still believed in horizontal honour, the respect for equals, and inasmuch as they came to think that even officers were equal in some respects, though not in all, they came to feel slighted. A courtesy manual said that to be interrupted, contradicted, pre-empted, or simply ignored, was to be dishonoured. The Army rank-and-file felt all these things about its officers. They understood their plight in terms of the past. Like the Saxon peasants, they felt, they were now living under rulers who were exploiting them rather than providing for them in fatherly fashion. The only choice in such circumstances was to turn outlaw.

So in May 1649, in Oxfordshire, a group of men, armed and mounted, were assembling. They were led by William Thompson: hot-tempered, brave, and eagerly concerned for the poor groaning under the Norman Yoke, following the Robin Hood code of honour that animated so many. Thompson wasn't entitled to any Army rank. He was a corporal who had been cashiered from Whalley's regiment because he had been on a drinking and gambling binge so excessive that it went beyond the usual soldierly excesses. He had been at Ware; had been, in fact, one of the ringleaders. He called himself 'Captain', perhaps less as a usurpation of an army rank to which he was not entitled than because it was what food-riot leaders often called themselves.

The men with Thompson were mutineers. They were also Levellers. They wanted to stop the payment of all taxes. Thompson wrote and published a manifesto: 'Through an unavoidable necessity, no other means left under heaven, we are enforced to betake ourselves to the law of nature, to defend and preserve ourselves and native rights . . . Gathered and associated together on the bare account of Englishmen, to redeem ourselves and the land of our nativity, from slavery and oppression, to avenge the blood of war shed in time of peace, to have justice for the blood of Mr Arnold shot to death at Ware, and for the blood of Mr Robert Lockyer, and divers others who of late by martial law were murdered at London.' The language of honour is clear and strong.

But this feisty band proved reluctant to fight against their old comrades-in-arms. After a parley, some even enlisted with their pursuers, while Thompson and a small party shot and cut their way free. While they gathered, army mutineers had been rioting for pay in Salisbury and Thompson thought that if he could join up with them they would be unstoppable. While this was happening, Fairfax and Cromwell were assembling a force in Hyde Park to quell the mutinies. Many of those summoned came to the rendezvous with green ribbons on their hats symbolizing their support for the Levellers. Cromwell wasn't having that: angrily, he pulled out the sea-green men. But he had plenty of sense, as ever; he had secured ten thousand pounds to cover their back pay, subtracting it from the navy.

Meanwhile the Wiltshire mutineers were marching north, from Salisbury to Marlborough, to Wantage and godly Abingdon, where they joined up with Thompson's men. Cromwell and Fairfax were hoping to overtake them before they could all unite. The combined Levellers and mutineers left Abingdon and turned west, then ran into Reynolds's horse, which held the Thames at Newbridge Crossing against them. This time no one felt any scruples about attacking 'a mercenary damn crew', made up mainly of Royalist prisoners from Colchester: 'a company of blood-thirsty rogues, murderers, thieves, highwaymen, and

some that were taken in Colchester'. But the Levellers were persuaded
to avoid bloodshed and to use a nearby ford instead: 'having marched
through the ford into the marsh on the other side, we called our council
together'. On the evening of 14 May 1649 they came to Burford, a town
so traditional in outlook that it still paraded its giant and dragon
through the streets once a year, at midsummer. That mythical battle
would be displaced by a real one.

During the day Cromwell and his troops had covered forty-five
miles. At midnight his tired but numerically far superior forces arrived
in Burford. Despite the pacific efforts of Major White, one man on
each side was killed. At the Crowne Inn, where Sheep Street joins the
High Street, a man called Eyres, a friend of Henry Marten, fought on
bravely against hopeless odds. These were, after all, men of the New
Model Army. Both sides were used to winning, but Cromwell had far
more soldiers. Three hundred and forty prisoners were taken from
among the mutineers, and placed under guard in the church. The rest
escaped, but without their horses, which fell as booty to the loyalists.

Next day the prisoners were relieved of the threat of decimation –
the Roman practice of taking out one in ten mutineers and killing
them – that hung over them, but had to listen to reproachful sermons.
Most of them decided to show due penitence – perhaps they
remembered the fate of the rebels at Ware. Nonetheless, there was a
court martial and four victims were chosen. Cornet Denne, the chaplain; Cornet Thompson, the younger brother of the hot-tempered
Captain; and Corporals Church and Perkins. Denne had brought a
winding-sheet and sat wrapped in it, like John Donne. He rejoiced, he
said, to suffer under so righteous a sentence. All this did the trick; he
was pardoned and sent off to preach to his fellow-prisoners.

The other three were shot outside the church. Cornet Thompson
was terrified – ironic, since he was being punished for his brother's
derring-do. An eager contemporary reported:

> This day Cornet Thompson was brought into the churchyard
> (the place of execution). Death was a great terror to him, as
> unto most. Some say he had hopes of a pardon, and therefore
> delivered something reflecting upon the legality of his engage-
> ment, and the just hand of God; but if so, they failed him.
> Corporal Perkins was the next; the place of death, and the sight

of his executioners, was so far from altering his countenance, or daunting his spirit, that he seemed to smile upon both, and account it a great mercy that he was to die for this quarrel, and casting his eyes up to his Father and afterwards to his fellow prisoners, who stood upon church leads to see the execution, set his back against the wall, and bid the executioners shoot: and so died as gallantly as he lived religiously. After him Master John Church was brought to the stake, he was as much supported by God in this great agony as the latter; for after he pulled off his doublet, he stretched out his arms, and bid the soldiers do their duties, looking them in the face, till they gave fire upon him, without the least kind of fear or terror.

Church's demeanour was a deliberate imitation of Christ's death on the cross: meek, resigned, self-sacrificing. This wasn't weakness, but a kind of passive protest, like lying down in front of a tank. The phrase of which the modern political left is fond, the 'massacre at Burford church', makes it sound as if it was a kind of early modern Peterloo. It was far from that; just the routine punishment of a few mutineers to discourage the others, sad, unjust, but not worth the pilgrimages it has inspired – unless, perhaps, it is when authority is understood by almost everyone to be in the right that it is most tyrannical. A disappointment about the 'English revolution' is its lack of real martyrs, their hearts' blood dyed in every fold of a Red Flag. (Indeed, martyrdom was to be the Royalists' trump card.) The Levellers' courage means that they deserve respect for what they were, not for what we would like them to have been.

Meanwhile, Captain Thompson and a small band had escaped in the night to look for more trouble. They managed to storm a gaol in Northampton and release its Leveller prisoners – Robin Hood again – and scattered money from the excisemen's tills among the poor. At Wellingborough on 17 May, a troop of Oxfordshire horse overtook them. Characteristically, Thompson retreated to a wood, scorned quarter, and chose to fight. He charged three times though wounded, killing one of his pursuers and injuring another, before falling himself. When she heard of his death, his wife, who was pregnant, miscarried and died.

Thompson's Robin Hood mien and defiant last stand were inspiring, and it may be no coincidence that Wellingborough became the site of a new Digger community. A Royalist newspaper, only half-joking, called him 'that Alexander of the Levellers'. Its half-hearted support was due to the fact that Cromwell was hoping to use the crushing of the mutiny as proof that he was on the side of law and order, as a way of wooing moderate and conservative opinion. He did a lot of table-thumping, announcing (honour again) that either he or Lilburne must die for it. Then he went off to spend the night in comfort at Burford Priory, before moving on to Oxford. With its usual agility, the university was keen to confer honorary degrees on the Army leaders. Anthony à Wood said the speeches were 'bad, but good enough for soldiers'. Cromwell confounded this snobbish response by making a very good speech himself, in which he declared that no commonwealth could ever flourish without learning. Then he went off for dinner at Magdalen and bowling on the green after dinner, Charles's own favourite game in captivity, pursuits which marked his new status as a ruler, if not (yet?) a monarch.

The Levellers lost their sectarian followers to the new policy of tolerance, but more importantly, the Army came to see itself more and more as soldiers, distinct from the London citizens. The Levellers didn't disappear, but they were reduced to pamphleteering and complaining, attacked by other pamphleteers. In the end they were creatures of paper. Despite this, history has loved them because they are thought to have led to us, to liberal democracy. The Levellers' independency, their longing for the rights of men who scrabbled in dirty jobs to be noticed, are like the yearning of blue-collar voters everywhere to be truly enfranchised; to this day, they know that governments are not run by people like them, and can therefore not be run for people like them. Representation, they know, is about seeing yourself mirrored in government. That vision is still not reality.

When the Levellers talked about representation and suffrage, they meant for the English. But some among them had genuine sympathy for the people of all the kingdoms, even for the feared Irish. William Walwyn, one of the Levellers' most active pamphleteers, is supposed to have said that 'the Irish did no more but what we would have done our selves, if it had been our case . . . That they were a better-natured people than we . . . why should they not enjoy the liberty of their consciences?' Common sense is always something that has to be worked for strenuously when the subject is Ireland. The book that reported Walwyn's words thought it likely to damn him in everyone's eyes. How could anyone say such things? It was an outrage. But did Walwyn really say them? A Leveller leaflet, now lost, entitled *Certain queries propounded to the consideration of those who are intended for the service of Ireland* asked some very pertinent questions:

> Whether Julius Caesar, Alexander the Great, William Duke of Normandy [the usual radical villain] or any other the great conquerers of the world, were any other than so many great and lawless thieves; and whether it be not as unjust to take our Neighbouring Nations Lands, and liberties from them, as our neighbour's goods of our own nation?
>
> Whether the condition of the conquered be not Ireland, and the condition of the conquerers be not England, and Ireland unjustly termed rebels, and their cause just, and England a thieving usurping tyranny, and their cause altogether unjust, being against God and nature?

It went on to propose an Irish Free State, though not toleration for English Catholics. What gave all this urgency was that the Army mutineers were refusing, specifically, to go to Ireland. The Ulster Presbyterians declared for Charles II and moved towards open rebellion, while the Irish Catholics tried for a separate peace. But *The English Souldiers Standard*, often attributed to Walwyn, advised the Army not to go and settle matters. What's wrong with negotiation? it asked. John Harris, another Leveller, wrote that Cromwell and Ireton must be possessed; 'the good soul of Philip the Second is got into them'. *The Souldiers Demand*, too, was sceptical about the grandees' motivation:

> What have we to do with Ireland, to fight, and murder a people and nation (for indeed they are set upon cruelty, and murdering poor people, which they glory in) which have done us no harm, only deeper to put our hands in blood with their own? We have waded too far in that crimson stream already of innocent and Christian blood . . . And if they could but get us once over into Ireland (they think) they have us sure enough: either we shall have our throats cut, or be famished, for they are sure we cannot get back again over the Great Pond.

Scepticism about the horror stories used to whip up anti-Irish feeling had at last set in. How just was this war? *The Souldiers Demand* is not a Leveller pamphlet; it expresses doubt about executing Charles: 'poor simple men' who had believed they were fighting for liberty are simply deluded. Other publications tried to restore the panicky heat of 1641 by reminding the soldiers of the outrages of a barbarous and bloody people, the murder of women and children. But the attempt to play an anti-popery card was vain; eager arguments for religious toleration had finally begun to impact on anti-Catholic feeling. Overton remarked imaginatively that a Protestant sermon would strike a papist as heretical, while a popish Mass would seem so to a Protestant. One of the most vehement Leveller pamphlets denounced anti-popery: 'When I think how worse then barbarians the French men dealt with the Waldences, and so did the Spainiards with the Moorians, and how the English hunted the poor Irish: and how Duke d'Alba persecuted the Belgians . . . When I consider these, and many more cruel changes, and no bettering, but all to establish tyranny in other forms and fashions, then I think O white Devil, O Tyranipocrit, how impious art thou.'

Henry Parker had tried to get around this kind of argument by claiming that Catholicism was not a religion at all, but an international political conspiracy to conquer Europe. A subtler move was to argue that Irish barbarity required the civilizing influence of the English, so that their conversion to Protestantism could be achieved. Cromwell, too, thought of the Irish as barbarous: 'they will make this the most miserable people in the earth, for all the world knows their barbarism – not of any religion, almost nay of them, but in a manner as bad as papists'. It would have been well for the three kingdoms if the voices of toleration had been heard. But for others, toleration was far less important than retaliation. Cromwell went to Ireland with their voices ringing in his ears.

The Levellers had their limits. One of them was the question of women's political rights. The activities of Elizabeth Lilburne and Mary Overton must be understood in the context of women's role in politics. It is true that women could be citizens in the sense of inhabitants of the land, but they could not defend the state in arms, so they were excluded from one of the most powerful – and most levelling – definitions of citizenship. Women could, however, be subjects of the Crown, and could petition the monarch, or Parliament, and they could and did participate in informal, unlicensed protest.

It was possible for a woman to live through the war years without ever smelling powder. However, in other locations – sometimes just up the road – there could be long-felt repercussions. Women did do war work on occasion: in Coventry they filled in quarries 'that they might not shelter the enemy'. And we've seen how women were crucial at Turnham Green. Others nursed the wounded, or were camp-followers, cooking and washing for their men. Even more dramatically, as we have seen, women like Brilliana Harley commanded siege defences. Still others acted as spies, intelligence-gatherers; a woman known only as 'Mary the scout' was rewarded by Fairfax himself after the fall of Taunton, and we have met Parliament Joan. Other women were involved in political intrigue: Ann Fanshawe, Anne Halkett, Henrietta Maria and Lucy Hay amongst them. Some women, too, had the experience of seeing their houses despoiled, their husbands and sons killed, their bedlinen burned, their children hungry. Some were stripped, others raped during sacks of towns. The women cooking dinner for their husbands at Naseby probably had no idea why they were being slaughtered. Women had to fight for pensions, for subsistence. They had to take on men's work in farms and businesses. Women got involved in the print trade, as we have seen. Perhaps all these experiences made them feel they had a stake in the commonwealth just as the experience of the New Model Army and its victories gave confidence to its Leveller minority. For in traditional ways, but in larger numbers than ever before, women were active in wartime politics. They began as peace petitioners, and went on to become participants in the excitement and danger of radical politics.

On 11 September 1648, a group of women staked a claim to the political process not very different from the one articulated by the Leveller men. They had begun to imagine equality through their experiences in Independent churches. Now they translated that vision of entitlement into the political sphere. They told the Commons that:

> since we are assured of our creation in the image of God, and of an interest in Christ, equal unto men, as also of a

proportionable share in the Freedoms of this commonwealth, we cannot but wonder and grieve that we should appear so despicable in your eyes, as to be thought unworthy to petition or represent our grievances to this honourable house. Have we not an equal interest with the men of this Nation, in those liberties and securities, contained in the Petition of right, and other the good Laws of the Land?

But the House of Commons wasn't ready for women in politics, just as it had not been ready for lower-class men. The Leveller women petitioners were active in April 1649, on behalf of the imprisoned Leveller leaders: 'We are so over-pressed, so overwhelmed in afflictions, that we are not able to keep in our compass, to be bounded in the custom of our sex, for indeed we confess it is not our custom to address our selves to this house in the public behalf.' But on 25 April Parliament refused the women's petition. MPs reacted intolerantly, telling the women that 'it was not for women to petition; they might stay at home and wash their dishes'. The Journal of the House reported that they had not been answered directly, but had been told through the Serjeant that 'the matter you petition about, is of a higher concernment than you understand, that the House gave an answer to your Husbands, and therefore that you are desired to go home, and look after your own business, and meddle with your housewifery'. The women went home only when dispersed by troops. Perhaps they did housewifery for ten days or so, but they also found time to meet and write. Then they returned on 5 May with a more strongly worded petition. This used the figure of hungry children already exploited by the Overtons: 'we are not able to see our children hang upon us, and cry out for bread, and not have the wherewithal to feed them, we had rather die than see that day'. They also used historical women as examples: 'By the British women this land was delivered from the tyranny of the Danes . . . And the overthrow of episcopal tyranny in Scotland was first begun by the women of that Nation.'

They described their contributions to the war effort, too: 'our money, plate, jewels, rings, bodkins &c. have been offered at your feet'. Their petitions were surprisingly like another kind of women's petition produced in large numbers by the war, the pleas of the wives of prisoners for their release, and of war widows for financial help. One

Cheshire widow, for example, sounded very like the Levellers when she wrote:

> Though I have been in hopes every day to be dispatched, yet such is the hardness of the hearts of men that nothing is brought to perfection as yet, but as soon as it shall please God to put an end to this miserable bondage and that I may have the money which I have so dearly bought I intend . . . to return again. Wherefore genteel men I entreat you that you will consider my distressed condition and the great loss I had with you and the great charge [of children] upon my hand and nothing to support them but what was bought with the blood of my dear husband.

Left alone after the imprisonment of their men, the Leveller women were claiming that it was impossible for them to manage, and thus asking for their men's return.

The Royalists thought it was all terribly funny. 'Hannah Jenks, Ruth Turn-Up, Doll Burn-It and Sister Wagrayle have petitioned the supreme authority for their man John, and Mr Overton . . . Holofernes Fairfax look to thy head, for Judith is a coming, the women are up in arms, and vow they will tickle your members.'

No woman's voice was heard in the Putney debates of October and November 1647. Rainborough spoke for 'the poorest he', but no one had a word to say for 'the poorest she'. This was in part because freemen – as opposed to slaves or bondmen – were the only ones discussed. As Ireton had said, the dependent couldn't be relied upon to vote with independence. Though everyone agreed that Englishwomen were born free, they lost their liberty upon marriage.

The Levellers, men and women, were eventually to be overtaken by events. Said Ireton, 'If the generality of the people could see the end of the Parliament, [they] would . . . look for a succession of new Parliaments in the old way and old form of a King again.' Perhaps it was Ireton's good luck that he never knew how right he was. The restored government he predicted was to dig up his decomposing corpse and hang it from Tyburn Tree. Thus the man who had fought to preserve what he thought of as tradition became a symbol of its destruction. He died of fever, tired out, in 1651.

It seemed that 'primitive' and Edenic native societies understood what the leading Levellers wanted better than their own countrymen. A Leveller newsbook in *The Kingdomes Faithfull and Impartiall Scout* described two American Indians displayed in France by merchants as objects of curiosity. But the Indians are not only observed; they also do their own observing, and they are 'stood amazed':

> That so many gallant men which seemed to have stout and generous spirits should all stand bare, and be subject to the will and pleasure of a Child [Louis XIV]. Secondly, that some in the city were clad in very rich and costly apparel, and others so extreme poor, that they were ready to famish for hunger; that he conceived them to be all equalised in the balance of nature, and not one to be exalted above another.

So said *A worthy expression of two heathen levellers.* Perhaps the New World would be more hospitable to their ideas than the old world had been.

XXIX

Stand Up Now, Stand Up Now:
Gerrard Winstanley and the Diggers

If the Digger leader Gerrard Winstanley is remembered at all, it is as a voice crying for liberation in an age that did not understand. The Diggers were not like the Levellers except in their concern for the ordinary men of the British kingdoms. Winstanley was a critic of the economic as well as the political division of the kingdoms: his reading of the Bible, like Trapnel's, led him to censure the injustice of the rich to the poor. Influenced by the general godly spirit of a return to essentials, he took the Garden of Eden as a model for the way God wanted human affairs to work. He wrote that 'in the beginning of time God made the earth. Not one word was spoken at the beginning that one branch of mankind should rule over another, but selfish imaginations did set up one man to teach and rule over another.' He particularly disliked enclosures, the process in which common lands given over to the use of the poor because they were not easy to cultivate – fens, marshes, moors and other uninhabited places – were reclaimed and converted to new private plots. Winstanley wrote: 'The power of enclosing land and owning property was brought into the creation by your ancestors by the sword; which first did murder their fellow creatures, men, and after plunder or steal away their land, and left this land successively to you, their children. And therefore, though you did not kill or thieve, yet you hold that cursed thing in your hand by the power of the sword; and so you justify the wicked deeds of your fathers, and that sin of your fathers shall be visited upon the head of you and your children to the third and fourth generation, and longer too, till your bloody and thieving power be rooted out of the land.' But in fact his views were not unique. Long before the war, they had been expressed helplessly by people who had no hope of being heard. In 1629, the cloth industry in Essex was hit hard by a slump in European trade and clothworkers lost their jobs. In the meantime, the price of grain rose, and more and more of it was shipped from the Eastern ports to the Low Countries while people in the streets of Maldon went hungry. The women of the town boarded Flemish ships and took the grain themselves, just enough for their own families. The unrest had been going on since just after Christmas. Bands of men and women armed with staves and pitchforks seized grain that would otherwise be exported. They intended to meet their own needs, then sell the surplus – but at their own price, not the inflated amounts being charged by merchants, and they threatened to kill the factors who might arrange more grain shipments.

The rioters mostly came from Maldon's poorest parish, St Mary's, 'much overcharged with poor'; most of them were married to men who had to juggle three or four jobs in a vain effort to make ends meet. They were also already known to the law for a number of petty offences: drunkenness and absence from church, trying to keep animals in the streets, assault and violence in the case of Ann Spearman's husband. Dorothy Berry had been placed in the stocks for six hours at Easter for being drunk. When hauled before the magistrates for the same crime only a few months later, Dorothy was unable to provide surety, but sarcastically offered 'her dog for one of her sureties and her cat for the other'. Anne Carter was equally willing to use the language of insult against the magistrates, calling one of them 'a bloodsucker', and telling another who complained about her absence from church that she would go if he would send round someone to do her work for her. She added that she served God just as well as he did. When a third tried to arrest her husband, John Carter, Anne attacked him with a cudgel and rescued her husband. All this suggests simmering anger that could find expression in the usual early modern language of insult and accusation. Such outbursts became political when they found a suitable cause or grievance, like grain exports and magistrates who favoured foreign merchants.

The town magistrates decided not to prosecute this time. But things went on getting worse. The cloth trade fell into more severe decline, and the workers, dependent on wages that were repeatedly cut from small beginnings, began to starve: 'many hundreds of them have no beds to lie, nor food, but from hand to mouth to maintain themselves their wives and children', recorded a contemporary pamphlet. Even the Venetian ambassador was moved to remark on the probability that many would starve. The workers begged the local authorities for relief, and then addressed the king, telling him that they were forced to sell their beds to buy bread, and to lie in straw. They warned him that 'many wretched people' would mutiny if he did nothing. The king made a few sporadic efforts to organize local relief; when nothing came of them in a system never designed to relieve want on this kind of scale, there was a second riot at Burrow Hills. Anne Carter led the mob; illiterate, she hired a local baker, John Gardner, to act as her secretary and had written letters, signing herself Captain and drumming up support. 'Come, my brave lads of Maldon,' she cried, Robin Hood like, 'I will be your leader, for we will not starve.'

Once authority had been petitioned and had failed, what was the point of it? Ominously, some of the rioters had attacked the local magnates; Francis Cousen found himself in gaol in Colchester; he too had gathered grain from ships, but had also urged the crowd of poor people to go to the Earl Rivers's house, 'saying there was gold and silver enough'. Crowds have memories; did someone recall this eleven years later, when equally angry crowds, differently composed, attacked Lady Rivers?

Riots – including the ones that began the Civil War – were not expressions of panic or loss of control so much as carefully staged and disciplined demonstrations of dissatisfaction. Part of a culture of punishment, shaming, bullying and communal rudeness, they could be violent: some anti-drainage rioters actually stoned the workers, beat them, and even erected mock-gallows on which to hang them. If the king was there, some said, they would kill him too. Rioters often tried threats, blackmail, communal disapproval and bullying before resorting to mass demonstrations. Rhymes and songs, libellous, scabrous, anticipated those that circulated in the Civil War: if they urged people on to protest, they also expressed a rage that could detonate in violence. 'The corn is so dear', went a rhyme circulating in Kent in the 1630s, 'I fear many will starve this year,/ If you see not to this/ Some of you will speed amiss/ Our souls they are dear/ For our bodies have some care/ Before we arise/ Less will suffice.'

Riots were usually about a small local matter, viewed as a departure from normality, rather than about sweeping changes in Church and state. Food rioters were affirming the right to eat, to buy corn at a price they could afford and not be cheated by middlemen and merchants. These rights were seen not as novel, but as traditional, stemming from the good world, under the old religion, when prices were low, not like now. Protests were often very organized, with demonstrators marching in companies like small armies. In the same way, men and women would riot to defend a right to use common land. In many places freeholders had fewer than five acres of land, while some had only a cottage and garden, so without common rights such smallholders could not survive. There was often a theatrical element – rioters could be led by Captain Alice, a man dressed as a woman, or the Midland Revolt's Captain Pouch, who claimed to carry in his pouch authority from the king himself to destroy enclosures (actually it contained nothing but a piece of green cheese). Part of this ritual context was a language of insult which included a kind of eat-the-rich rhetoric, 'for reformation of those late enclosures which made them of the poorest sort ready to pine for want', and 'rich men had all in their hands and would starve the poor'. Such statements made each riot into a drama of poor but plucky leaders versus rich evildoers, a drama like *The Seven Champions of Christendom* or *Bevis of Hampden*.

Woodland commons in particular were vital to the poor for fuel and building materials as well as game, for grazing geese, pigs and sheep, for collecting herbs and nuts and mushrooms and berries, and catching fish in brooks. In the Forest of Dean, thousands eked out a living from the woods and wastes, while earning a little more in coal and iron mines, or as day labourers, or with a bit of fishing and waterfowling, or quarrying for grindstones and millstones. In the fens there were many such people, living in turf huts, burning turf fires. Marshes also provided reeds, turf for fuel, rushes for basket-making, which might bring in a bit of cash; hemp and flax for spinning; alders and willows for more baskets. Birds provided feathers as well as meat. When their woods were enclosed or their fens drained, the best they could hope for was usually a small plot of one or two acres.

For these people, the Civil War represented not a chance to claim their rights at last, but an opportunity for outbreaks of lawless destruction of the fencing and drainage systems they hated while authority was looking elsewhere. They did not want a new world. They wanted their old world back. And sometimes it was taken from them by the war. During the siege of Lydney House, near the Forest of Dean, Princes Rupert and Maurice raided parishes, looting property and burning every building (mostly humble cottages) that could give shelter to their enemies. The people fled deep into the mines, but came back to find smoking ruins where their huts had been.

And if they were not interested in political radicals, the radicals were not interested in them; the Levellers did have a couple of sentences about reopening common land, but it was scarcely a central plank of their platform. Only the Diggers were concerned at all with the rural labouring poor, and they wanted to bring more land under the plough, not free use of unimproved land. In this they may have sounded to their would-be beneficiaries rather like the white settlers in Botany Bay did to the Aborigines. Repeatedly exhorted to farm, the Koori people kept asking why on earth they should, when they had always had abundant food without having to do more than a few hours' work a day? The near-hunter-gatherer economy of the forest edges and fens was similarly autonomous and unruly; grazing pigs stuffed themselves with acorns from Michaelmas to Martinmas, and could then be deliciously barbecued. As with the indigenous peoples of Australia, this rough pastoral was jeopardized because it no longer fitted anyone's idea of how people might live. Charles I diligently sold off royal forests to nobles, who then enthusiastically cut them down.

Paradoxically, the eighteenth century was to revive the idea of living wild in the greenwood as the quintessence of English liberty, but the gentlemen who dreamed of riding with Robin Hood, Prince of Thieves, might have found it difficult to manage on the diet of the poor of the seventeenth century. But Robin and his forest pals Clym of the Clough and Adam Bell remained popular with the poor too. *The True Tale of Robin Hood* of 1632 survives in Pepys's collection:

Poor men might safely pass by him
And some that way would choose,
For well they knew that to help them
He evermore did use
But when he knew a Miser rich
That did the poor oppress,
To feel his coin his hands did itch
He'd have it, more or less.

Ballads of Robin Hood went on being produced throughout the Civil War and English Republic years, ten in 1656–7 alone; indeed, most of the surviving Robin Hood ballads are sixteenth- or seventeenth-century compositions. Like fairy stories, they described a lost world of abbots, vast forests and vaster feasts, crusading kings and lying nuns. Wicked men meet a thoroughly deserved downfall, while the good are rewarded. The wicked are always rich, and the innocent always poor through no fault of their own. Especially, the wicked are often rich churchmen: they are not only greedy, but oppressive, music to the ears of Presbyterians and Independents alike: 'These bishops and these archbishops/ Ye shall them bite and bind.' The death of Laud on the scaffold was foreshadowed not only by the beheading of Simon of Sudbury, Archbishop of Canterbury, by Wat Tyler's men; it was also a story men knew from Robin Hood's fleecing of the corrupt clerks. And yet these stories are also conservative, like enclosure protests: Robin's aim is never to unsettle the social order, and particularly not the class structure, but to restore it after some disruption has made it malfunction. This logic of fixing something broken also animated the Diggers, but with a difference: they lacked the insistent loyalism of Robin and his outlaws, or of other medieval rebels. The convention of rebellion on behalf of monarchs who only needed to free themselves from evil counsellors was entirely absent.

The Levellers' temporary alliance with the king illustrated the separation of economic issues and Leveller claims for political rights. Said William Walwyn, 'Who ever heard me speak either in behalf of butchers or cobblers as to places of government? I profess I know not where, or when.' But the belly of the state could still ache with hunger, and its owner could find a voice as a result. There were elements of such traditions in apparently diverse rebellions that centred on food, from

Anna Trapnel's fasts to Gerrard Winstanley's Digging. Yet the Diggers were inspired by Leveller ideas, as expressed eloquently at Putney and in pamphlets: 'Therefore we are resolved to be cheated no longer, nor be held under the slavish fear of you no longer, seeing the earth was made for us as well as you . . . If we lie still and let you steal away our birthrights, we perish; if we petition we perish also, though we have paid taxes, given free quarter and ventured our lives as much as you.' Or, 'Stop not your ears against the secret mourning of the oppressed . . . lest the Lord see it and be offended and shut his ears against your cries, and work a deliverance for his waiting people some other way than by you.'

Or as Leveller William Walwyn put it:

> Look about you and you will find . . . thousands of miserable, distressed, starved . . . Christians . . . see how pale and wan they look, how coldly, raggedly and unwholesomely they are clothed; live one week with them in their poor houses, lodge as they lodge, eat as they eat, and no oftener, and be at the same pass to get that wretched food for a sickly wife, and hunger-starved children (if you dare do this for fear of death and diseases).

The war made people hungrier. Food production broke down: fields were untilled, grain unmilled. Poor relief collapsed. The transportation of food was hit by the destruction of roads and bridges. Fields were trampled flat by many boots, neglected, weed-filled. When Hugh Wolcott was forced to give up his farm, he said it was because of the war: 'men have almost been at their wit's end, for no Turkish slavery can be worse than hath been inflicted over us. We have been robbed and stripped of all our goods, both within doors and without, and led away captive from house to harbour, and like to suffer death.'

Winstanley thought poverty no bar to enlightenment: 'The poorest man, that sees his maker, and lives in the light, though he could never read a letter in the book, dares throw the glove to all the human learning in the world, and declare the deceit of it.' This light was an inner vision of God:

> As I was in a trance not long since, diverse matters were present to my sight, which must not be here related. Likewise I heard these words: work together. Eat bread together. Declare this all

abroad. Likewise I heard these words: Whosoever it is that labours in the earth, for any person or persons, that lifts up themselves as lords and rulers over others, and that doth not look upon themselves equal to others in the creation, The hand of the Lord shall be upon that labourer; I the Lord have spake it and I will do it; Declare this all abroad.

For Winstanley the regaining of this vision was redemption, for this was the vision Adam had lost at the Fall, which was a fall into covetousness. The Beasts of Revelation were kingly power, 'which . . . makes way to rule over others thereby, dividing the creation, one part from another; setting up the conquerer to rule, making the conquered a slave, giving the Earth to some, denying the earth to others'; other beasts were the power of 'the selfish laws', 'hanging, pressing, burning', the 'thieving art of buying and selling', an art to which Winstanley had himself unsuccessfully aspired, and clergy-power. The people can be saved from these terrible powers through the spirit of Christ welling up inside them, bringing back within them the natural sense of justice which existed before the Fall.

The Bible was full of cheering accounts of the rich confounded by the poor. The Magnificat is firm that the Lord will cast down the mighty from their thrones, and exalt the lowly, fill the hungry with good things, and send the rich away empty. Or as godly Digger Everard put it, 'to make the barren ground fruitful . . . To renew the ancient community of the enjoying of the fruits of the earth and to distribute the benefit thereof to the poor and needy, and to feed the hungry, and to clothe the naked.' The Psalms, so popular with the New Model Army, are full of similar reversals. In Biblical language, then, Winstanley could write that 'some are lifted up into the chair of tyranny, and others trod under the footstool of misery, as if the earth was made for a few, not for all men'. He had more careful ideas, too: a local government electorate of all men aged twenty and upwards, not excluding servants and those receiving alms, as the Levellers did.

However, the Diggers intended synergy; God's grace could only act redemptively if they began the process. 'When the earth becomes a common treasury as it was in the beginning, and the King of righteousness comes to rule in every one's heart, then he kills the first Adam: for covetousness thereby is killed.' The idea was to seize a moment. But like many such visionary plans to reform human society radically, it broke down in the face of opposition and grinding practicalities.

The leader of the Diggers, Gerrard Winstanley, came to national prominence and published all his work in a tiny span of four years, 1648–51; his was a brief if shining moment. He was baptized in Wigan, in Lancashire, and was the son of a mercer. Like many others, the parish was riven by religious differences. There was a local grammar, and Winstanley probably went there, since he did know some Latin. The schoolmaster was a notorious figure: John Lewis, who was described by his own patron as a haunter of alehouses, a gambler, a blasphemer and a fighter. On 25 March 1630, Gerrard Winstanley was apprenticed to a woman, Sarah Gater, in London, of the Merchant Taylors' Company. Sarah was a widow, devout and powerfully learned, with a small, carefully chosen library of her own on medicine and religion, including a thick receipt book. Her deceased husband had been a lecturer at St Andrew Undershaft. She was distantly connected with his family. Sarah managed to carry on in independent trade until her death in 1656. Gerrard shared the house with her, her infant son William, a journeyman called Henry Mason, and one or two female servants. There were two other apprentices, too. It sounds cosy, but Gerrard was the only apprentice to whom Sarah left nothing in her will. Maybe it was religion that divided them, for Sarah was a fan of Isaak Walton, biographer of Donne and writer of the first manual of angling in English, who had himself begun in the cloth trade. Sarah also favoured the Arminian writings of Henry Mason.

Whatever their differences, Gerrard stayed with her until 1638. He established himself as a shopkeeper in the parish of St Olave, Old Jewry. He was probably a cloth trader, rather than a weaver, buying up cloth for resale. In September 1640 he married Susan King, daughter of a barber-surgeon, resident in St Lawrence Jewry. They had a servant called Jane Williams, and an apprentice, and they also had a lodger, as the Miltons did, to help make ends meet.

The vicar at St Olave was Thomas Tuke, removed in 1643 because he was 'superstitious in practising and pressing the late innovations'. And yet Winstanley was an active parishioner here, apparently never abandoning the established Church. He didn't even show up to elect the lecturers his parish appointed. But he did take the Solemn League and Covenant on 8 October 1643. Unlike other wives, Susan Winstanley did not sign below Gerrard's signature.

He never was much of a businessman. When he set up his shop in 1638/9, he was among the poorer members of his household, and from 1641 he was operating on credit. By early 1642, the business had serious difficulties with cash flow. Bad debts and undercapitalization were the causes; he had shipped cloth to Ireland, and now the 1641 rising made it impossible to collect payments. From early 1643, the little enterprise teetered on the brink of bankruptcy. Later in 1643, there was nothing for it but to wind up the business, and on 30 November he divided his remaining stock among his creditors. By 20 December 1643, he had settled his affairs and moved to Cobham, near Susan's family. London had beaten him. 'Beaten', he wrote, 'out of both estate and trade, and forced to accept the goodwill of friends crediting of me, to live a country-life.'

His business failure may have taught him about the unreliability of trade. The whole clothing industry was in recession, with cloth workers hard hit; little people who had moved off their scrabbled livings on poor land to the even more uncertain rewards of waged labour. Like Gerrard's, their hopes had crashed around them.

Gerrard was now living 'a country-life', and he became a cattle entrepreneur. He bought up cattle, fattened them, and sold them at market. He worked hard, and by 1646 he was a householder again. He at once began pressing for the right to dig peat and turf for fuel on the manorial estate. He lived in an area dominated by the middling sort, dominated by passing trade on the old Portsmouth Road rather than by manors.

Then he was hit by another wave of economic disasters, which crushed another fledgling business: the harvest of 1647 was poor and grain and hay prices rose; there was a drought and a dearth of livestock; the Parliamentarian army began eating Surrey out of house and home. It was at some point in this difficult period of economic floundering that Winstanley underwent the kind of religious transformation which had overtaken Cromwell and Anna Trapnel earlier. He became a Baptist, and then made friends with a man named John Fielder, a future Quaker, and a former army radical called William Everard, who had been blooded at Burford Church and knew just how menacing new ideas could seem. He also became acquainted with Lawrence Clarkson, and with Samuel Highland, a Leveller who led an Independent church in Southwark. This powerful mix of influences turned him into the man who inspired and led the Diggers.

The Diggers were men who wanted to perform something close to an act of Christian magic: on themselves and on the land. Their acts were both practical and symbolic. They were at St George's Hill – a magical name, recalling holiness triumphant over evil – from April to August 1649. And they began on April Fools' Day. Aubrey calls this 'Fools holy day', and ascribes it to German influence. It was a Robin Hood day in which the poor took from the rich, a day of tricksterdom, of ritual reversals, like the spectacle of enclosure protesters dressed as women. Their starting-date was a sign that they were trying for an almost magical transformation; had they been trying for legitimacy they could have chosen Plough Monday.

Their first step was to cut turf on the heath, a perfectly conventional exercise of commons rights. But then they did something astonishing. They treated common land as arable land. They dug, they manured, and they planted.

There were never more than fifty of them at most. But they were terrifying – to London newsbook writers, at any rate:

> The new fangled people that began to dig on St George's Hill in Surrey, say, they are like Adam, they expect a general restoration of the Earth to its first condition, that themselves were called to seek and begin this great work, which will shortly go on throughout the whole world: and therefore they begin to dig and dress the Earth: One of them getting up a great burden of thorns and briars: thrust them into the pulpit at the church at Walton, to stop out the Parson. They profess a great deal of mildness and would have the world believe, they have dreamt Dreams, seen visions, heard strange voices, and have dictates beyond man's teaching. They profess they will not fight, knowing that not to be good for them. They would have none to work for hire, or be servants to other men, and say there is no need of money: yet they offer, that if any gentleman, & c., that hath not been brought up to labour, shall bring a stock, and put it into their hand, he shall have a part with them; a pure

contradiction of themselves. They allege, that the Prophesy in Ezek[iel] is to be made good at this time, where is promised so great a change, that the travellers which pass by, shall take notice, and say, This land which was barren and waste is now become fruitful and pleasant like the Garden of Eden.

Or as the Diggers put it:

Rich men receive all they have from the labourer's hand, and what they give, they give away other men's labours, not their own. Therefore they are not righteous actors on the earth.

The poor would go with cap in hand and bended knee to gentlemen or farmers, begging and entreating to work with them for 8d or 10d a day, which doth give them occasion to tyrannise over poor people.

Later, 'labouring poor men who in times of scarcity pine and murmur for want of bread, cursing the rich behind his back and before his face, cap and knee and a whining countenance'. Once, the unrighteous had been the papists; then it was the turn of witches. Now the rich were those not blessed by God.

So the poor were to withdraw their labour. All labourers were called on to stop working for large farms. 'What', Winstanley asked, 'would you do if you had not such labouring men to work for you?' 'For what is the reason that great gentlemen covet after so much land? Is it not because farmers and others creep to them in a slavish manner, proffering them great sums of money for such and such parcels of it, which does give them an occasion to tyrannise over their fellow creatures which they call their inferiors?' wrote Robert Coster. Yet the goal was never to destroy hierarchy – and it was they who were persecuted. The local landlords and lesser freeholders were determined to be rid of them. The Diggers' crops were trampled, their animals driven away, their houses pulled down, and their safety menaced.

After they were forced out, they moved to Little Heath, probably in late summer of 1649; not an ideal moment to move a community dependent on what it grew. There they stayed for eight months, until a local minister set some parishioners on to set fire to their houses and burn, too, their clothes and household stuff, 'up and down the Common', wrote Winstanley, 'not pitying the cries of many little children and their frighted Mothers'. In the meantime, other Digger groups had mushroomed, at Iver in Buckinghamshire, Wellingborough in Northamptonshire, elsewhere too. They were mere scrapings, easily erased as if they had never been.

The Diggers' opponents portrayed them as harmless lunatics at best, 'feeble souls and empty bellies'. 'Their actions hitherto have been only ridiculous', said the Council of State. The first army officer sent to investigate said it was 'not worth the writing nor yet taking notice of'. Only Henry Saunders, a paid informer who may have been hoping for more cash in exchange for more important information, thought the Diggers were a menace, and pointed out that numbers were continuing to rise while the Diggers were also firing the heath, thus threatening the town.

Less liked by eager left-of-centre history than the Diggers, the locals at Walton were equally representative of the poor. They didn't like a mob of strange people moving onto their common land and wanted to ship them out. They were used to having to do so, and they were good at it. On 11 June, the new traditionalism of the Diggers clashed head-on with an older kind of rural protest against the misappropriation of common land when four Diggers were badly beaten by a group of men dressed in women's clothes. It was meant to mock and shame. The Diggers' foes were not big landlords; one was a carpenter, and another a sheep farmer, though one was a freeholder whose lands near St George's Hill were perhaps most directly affected, and who had been attacked in the past by one of the Diggers in front of his ten-year-old son.

In Cobham it was no better. In 1646 Winstanley himself had been fined for digging peat on waste ground. But at least the Diggers had some friends there. Other Diggers in Northamptonshire had some local support, while Winstanley's more moderate stance on private property must have been reassuring. People might even have hoped that the Diggers' methods would really relieve the poor.

But somehow it all went sour. Winstanley thought the gentry were to blame, and as a result his own views became more extreme, which aroused his opponents to further efforts. It was also far from reassuring for the regime that Winstanley was arguing for civilians' rights; soldiers, he said, should not have all common land at the expense of the people whose taxes and produce had sustained the army. Magpie-like, as ever, Winstanley had picked up another bright glitter of popular protest with which to bedizen his own ideas, and was now channelling the Clubmen.

All the time he was at the Digger colony, he maintained a separate residence. He had grazing land still, on which he kept his own cattle and pastured others for a fee. He contracted with a local landlord to purchase and reap the harvest from several local fields. Though he described himself as a labourer in 1649, all the Diggers were thus described.

What were women to do among the Diggers? Girls were to be taught to read. Boys were to learn skills through apprenticeships, though Winstanley added, perhaps tellingly, that if a boy proved to have different skills from the ones in which he was being trained, then 'the spirit of knowledge may have his full growth in man, to find out the secret in every art'. Girls were simply consigned to 'easy neat works' like needlework and spinning. And what did the Diggers actually do all day, when not fighting off their irate neighbours? They refer to ploughing, but may not have had any ploughs. Their land was unproductive because their goal was to farm areas that were waste or common. Scratching at unyielding soil with primitive tools, they were returning to the Iron Age, not a golden age.

The leadership was caught up in what they hoped were higher channels. Winstanley and William Everard met Fairfax in London on 20 April 1649, but refused to remove their hats. Fairfax, they said firmly, was but their fellow-creature. Besides, they said, they brought their hats to wear on their heads, not to hold in their hands. A newspaper reported that 'they were asked the meaning of the phrase "Give honour where honour is due", they seemed to be offended, and said, that their mouths should be stopped who gave them that offence'. These menacing words alarmed everyone, although Fairfax paid the Diggers a personal visit in Surrey, and seems to have found them harmless and mad.

Whatever the Diggers did, it proved fundamentally unattractive to most people. They were not joined by the labouring poor because the majority didn't know Winstanley was there, or because they thought that the authorities would probably shut it all down, and thought themselves better off in their own villages. A fourth reason might be that emigration offered a better alternative. Winstanley's belief that the state would uphold him and his followers against the landlords was manifestly millenarian rather than pragmatic. The landowners soon called in the army, and Winstanley was in no position to criticize them, since by the end he too had come to believe state power might be needed to support and control his ideal society.

Winstanley imagined a world where a hardworking labour force created abundant food that could be given out free from huge communal warehouses, given to anyone who came as long as they worked: 'for those that come in and work, they shall have meat, drink, and clothes, which is all that is necessary for the life of man; and that for money, there was not any need of it, nor of any clothes more than to cover their nakedness'. It was to be like the pleasant land of Cockaigne, a dreamland of sausage houses and bacon trees, but different, too, because that was a fantasy of endless, abundant meat. Winstanley didn't like the idea of eating huge quantities of meat; he linked it with the wastefulness of the diet of the rich. Having worked with cows, he thought of them as rational beings. They were, as Winstanley explained to Fairfax, to provide only milk and cheese; they were not to be killed for meat. This showed, Winstanley thought, that he was different from the army, who, he felt sure, would have eaten the cows, cashed them in, consumed them rather than making them produce.

Winstanley hated waste. His loathing extended even to what he called 'seed-spilling', something he associated with too much commerce with women: too much sex, in other words, which he links with the Biblical sin of Onan; such seed-spilling 'produces weakness and much infirmness through immoderate heat', and hence spawns 'sickly weakly' children. Seed, Winstanley felt, should be carefully husbanded. He was only voicing the common belief of his day that too much sex was a menace to men's health and fertility, but it chimed ideally with his dislike of commerce and throwaway commodity culture, his loathing of waste. Because of his transformation of the struggle between good and evil from a war between men to a war within men, Winstanley saw the Devil as an interior force, King Flesh, ruling within man, and creating a corrupt social order. 'Gaffer dragon', as Winstanley called him, was both inside men and outside them. 'That everlasting covetous kingly power, is corrupt blood, that runs in every man, more or less, till reason the spirit of burning cast it out.'

Winstanley had identified the problem; now he provided an answer:

> And the common people, consisting of soldiers, and such as paid taxes and free-quarter, ought to have the freedom of all waste and common land, and crown-land equally among them; the soldiery ought not in equity to have all, nor the other people that paid them to have all, but the spoil ought to be divided between them that stayed at home, and them that went to war; for the victory is for the whole nation.

In *The True Levellers' Standard Advanced*, the land is a mother who cannot provide milk because she is shut away from her baby: 'Thy Mother, which is the earth, that brought us all forth: That as a true Mother, loves all her children. Therefore do not thou hinder the mother Earth, from giving all her children suck, by thy enclosing it into particular hands, and holding up that cursed bondage of enclosure by thy power.'

At a time when nobles were constantly splattering the greenwood with the blood of expertly gralloched deer, when gifts of game implied aristocratic status, Winstanley's moderation was a criticism of the bloodiness and bloodthirstiness of the upper classes.

The tiny community was bedevilled by what Winstanley called the 'snapsack boys', soldiers, hungry plunderers who hoped to carry food away in their snapsacks without working for it, and by 'ammunition drabs', army camp-followers, also hungry. For Winstanley did not welcome everyone, it seems. His ideal community was about locality, especially ironic since he was himself an incomer to Cobham.

But Winstanley wasn't a farmer, and he wasn't a woodsman. Like so many who were desperate, he was a small tradesman, a cloth trader, urban rather than rural. When he thought about ploughs and their dignity he did so as a townie. He knew about grazing, perhaps, but he may not have known anything about how to grow food. However, he knew the romance of the greenwood, the waste land as a place that could be home to those who were outsiders. When he wrote about oppressive landlords, he thought of them in Robin Hoodish terms, as Normans: 'now if they get their foot fast in the stirrup, they will lift themselves again into the Norman saddle'. The Army, too, was

'Norman'. When Winstanley and Everard met with Fairfax, Everard expressed the whole story clearly and fully, straight from John Foxe and *The Gest of Robin Hood*:

> Everard said, All the liberties of the people were lost by the coming in of William the Conquerer, and that ever since, the people of God had lived under tyranny and oppression worse than that of our forefathers under the Egyptians. But now the time of deliverance was at hand, and God would bring his people out of this slavery, and restore them to their freedom, in enjoying the fruits and benefits of the earth. And that there had lately appeared to him a vision, which bade him arise, and dig and plough the earth, and receive the fruits thereof, that their intent is, to restore the creation to its former condition.

He thought of the new English republic as a new kind of enclosure, cutting people off from the land. By contrast, he thought of himself and the Diggers as returning to an Edenic state of oneness with the land. In Winstanley, the search for a New Jerusalem collides headlong with the fleeing figure of Robin Hood. His work is the ultimate expression of woodland food protest, conservative and theatrical. It seems remarkable to us only because the voices that speak through it are usually inaudible above the roar of history. But there were many of them, people who lived the life and people who only dreamed of it.

Winstanley was above all a writer, an early modern Upton Sinclair, an Orwell with a powerful sense of the pain and misery of the poor. Like Orwell, he had experienced those miseries, that sense of failure that gnawed at the heart every time hunger gnawed the belly. He knew. What he made was like what Defoe would make later on; a new world inhabited imaginatively, through words. And like Defoe, he was grappling with how to be godly in an age of trade, and like him his answer was to make a paradise inside himself where everything could be lit up and resolved. For centuries, people have felt they *knew* the Diggers, knew their ideals. Winstanley is the author of himself, himself as Robin Crusoe, bridging the Middle Ages and the coming of the modern capitalism he so hated.

> Then they came privately by day to Gerrard Winstanley's house, and drove away four cows, I not knowing of it; and some of the

lord's tenants rode to the next town shouting the diggers were conquered, the diggers were conquered. Truly it is an easy thing to beat a man and cry conquest over him, after his hands are tied as they tied ours. But if their cause be so good, why will they not suffer us to speak?

I feel myself now like a man in a storm, standing under shelter upon a hill in peace, waiting till the storm be over to see the end of it.

Winstanley's co-leader William Everard described himself, oddly, as 'of the race of the Jews'. He didn't mean he was, literally, Jewish; he meant that he was like the Chosen People, enslaved, persecuted, about to be redeemed. The new and powerful image of Jewishness was on the political agenda for the fledgling English republic. The Jews had of course been excluded from England by Edward I in 1290. A few crept in unacknowledged, after the Sephardim had been expelled from Iberia by Ferdinand and Isabella in 1492; one Jewish family, the Bassanos, were noted court musicians from Venice, and their daughter Aemilia Lanyer became a published poet. None of these Jews practised their religion openly, and many may really have been Christians.

And yet there was an enthusiastic philo-Semitic element in English godliness that kept Jewishness on the agenda. Humanists had eagerly studied Hebrew to try to understand the Old Testament better. But above all, the godly expected the millennium soon, very soon, and believed it would be preceded by the Jews' conversion. Some people wanted to readmit the Jews to England for the precise purpose of converting them and bringing about the Second Coming. The Baptists Joanna and Ebenezer Cartwright petitioned Fairfax for the readmission of the Jews as early as 1648/9. Richard Overton was another who favoured the cause of toleration; in *The Arraignment of Mr Persecution*, he wrote passionately: 'How then can we complain of the vengeance that is at this time upon us and our children, that have been so cruel, so hateful, so bloody-minded to them and their children? We have given them the cup of trembling, surely we must taste of the dregs: Hearken therefore no longer to those which teach this bloody doctrine of persecution.'

In the autumn of 1650, Gerrard found employment for himself and some of the other 'poor brethren' on the estate of Lady Eleanor Davies at Pirton in Hertfordshire, apparently serving as her estate steward. She was a woman with a powerful reputation. The daughter of Baron Audeley, later the Earl of Castlehaven, she spent hours every day studying the Bible. Any man who tried to silence her by the weight of his authority was, she thought, doomed. By the time she hired Winstanley she was famous for her accurate prophecies. These, interpreted variously as brilliance or madness by her contemporaries, were a way of recounting a terrible story which explained and justified the life and death of a little boy who couldn't speak. Eleanor had a son, Jack, who was an anxiety – he was mute. 'It is certain he understands everything that is spoken to him, without making any signs, so the defect must be in his tongue.' Jack drowned in an accident when he was still a child. Eleanor never wrote about her feelings when Jack died, but one can catch a glimpse of them in her warm response to her daughter Lucy's loss of a child. Eleanor had a vivid dream, of a child's severed head, crying inconsolably. Shortly after Jack died, Eleanor found a boy of thirteen called George Carr, and she took him into her home in the spring of 1625. He was dumb, as Jack had been. In George, Eleanor had rediscovered her lost son, and thus found a way to begin her life again. But George also made claims to mystical knowledge. People tested him; they opened the Bible and asked him to act out its contents, they made loud noises to check if he could hear. He was asked to guess the number of items in a sealed box or bag. And then there was another miracle, the one for which Eleanor had probably hoped years ago, with another small speechless boy. George began to talk.

And somehow that unlocked Eleanor too; she too began to speak, to prophesy. It was as if her identity had merged with George's. Her pleasure in George was shortlived, though. He grew terrified, 'and provoked to speak, lost the wonderful gift [of prophecy] for that time and after went beyond sea'. Eleanor herself soon became even more famous than George had been. On 25 July 1625 she had her first vision, in the early morning. She was awakened by a voice, which said, 'there is nineteen years and a half to the day of Judgement, and you as the meek virgin'. (Eleanor had a fine aristocratic disdain for laws of grammar and syntax.) The voice belonged to the prophet Daniel. She was at Englefield, which she called Angelfield, the Berkshire manor she felt was especially blessed. (When she did leave home, Eleanor always chose to stay at inns called The Angel.) Later, it would be engulfed by the war; already there was a field nearby which Eleanor called Hell, where the old, the blind, the lame would gather to beg. And later still, Eleanor would re-imagine the name as 'England's bloody field'; the second Battle of Newbury was fought very close to her house. As the meek virgin, Eleanor was also the Virgin Mary, pregnant with the Word. Her prophecies replaced her lost children; they filled her empty arms. All those dead sons . . . It was as if Eleanor could only tell her own story over and over and over, a story of the death of a dumb son, a story of a dumb son who learned to speak and so was saved.

In May of 1609 she was married to the thirty-six-year-old Sir John Davies. He was clever, but also difficult to like. It was a quarrelsome marriage. At one point she told him that he would be dead in three years; to bear out her words, she began wearing mourning dress for him. Eleanor kept it up with the perseverance of an angry toddler. They were dining with friends some months after this quarrel, in early December 1626. Suddenly, Eleanor began crying loudly. Trying to carry off the awkward situation, John said, jokily, 'I pray weep not while I am alive, and I will give you leave to laugh while I am dead.' Three days later, on 7 December, he did die. Eleanor married again after just three months, this time choosing Sir Archibald Douglas, whom she saw as the true heir to the throne, since he was James I's bastard son. Soon people were consulting her. Lady Berkshire invited Eleanor to her son's christening, and Eleanor declined. Lady Berkshire was worried, and pressed for an explanation. Finally, Eleanor told her that the baby would die. He did. Henrietta Maria, like many another insecure wife to a member of England's royal family, was anxious and keen to get advice from those who knew of the beyond. Eleanor met her one day coming from Mass. It was 1627, and Henrietta asked Eleanor when she would be with child, and also 'what success the Duke would have'. Eleanor reassured the queen; she predicted the death of the glittering, sinuous, unpopular favourite George Villiers, Duke of Buckingham before the end of August 1628. When he *did* die – and in August – her reputation was confirmed. By the time the Diggers were active, Eleanor had been confined in the Gatehouse and in Bedlam on the orders of the Privy Council. Between May 1641 and January 1645, she produced twelve tracts, seven in 1644 alone.

Winstanley and Eleanor had a good deal in common. Both wanted to recreate earth in the image of heaven through their writings. But perhaps rivalry developed, for in December 1650 she sacked him. There was a dispute. He had approached her, asking for pay for his men, who had helped with the harvest. It may not have appeased him that she confronted him angrily in the barn and told him, in response, that she was the prophetess Melchisedecke, the Queen of Peace, using the Bible in her customary creative way.

She accused him of faking the invoice. Winstanley was unmoved, and wrote to her bluntly: 'What's the reason', he asked, 'that divers men call upon you for money, which you truly owe them, and you either put them off, by long delays, or else make them spend 10 times more to it in suits of law, whereas you have estate sufficient that you might pay all?' She wrote across it: 'He is mistaken.' She cited Matthew 25:19: 'After a long time the Lord of those servants cometh and reckoneth with them.' How long, O Lord, how long? Winstanley might have retorted. He claimed not only reaping, but also arranging to have the sequestration taken from her estate, leaving her with plenty of funds. She still claimed to be 'destitute'. His letter was also a jibe at her sex: 'you have lost the Breeches which is indeed true reason, the strength of a man. And you must wear the long coat's tail [a fool's coat] till you know yourself.' This astringent misogyny was his last hurrah.

Winstanley went back to Cobham. He stopped Digging, either with his spade or with his pen, refusing to sanction violence or to denounce all authority. He bent to the regime, dedicating *The Law of Freedom* to Cromwell. It is less polished than his earlier writings, as if he himself were giving up. His wife Susan died, without children, and he married again to a woman called Elizabeth Stanley who bore him two sons. They died in their teens. He became a corn chandler, re-entering the world of trade which he had fought to destroy. The great experiment was over, the light had gone out. Only the passionately dreamed writings survived.

XXX

The Second Civil War

Extremists now held the floor; some of them had been moderate once, but had become convinced that they were seeing the last days of Antichrist. Nehemiah Wallington had once hoped that the Lord would change the heart of the king, but it was his own heart that had been changed by endless reading of atrocity stories, and by the ongoing dread of popery. He had heard of papists ordering massacres of the godly, and of Prince Robber, as he called Rupert, and his deeds in the Midlands; but he was also worried by the very kind of sectarians whom Trapnel saw as the true children of God. He was fiercely loyal to the emerging republic, and eager to see the Scots beaten by Cromwell, yet he also feared that the falling out among the godly was a sign that the judgement was not far off. God, he felt, had stopped listening. Like John Milton, he might have thought that 'license they mean when they cry liberty', for he believed passionately in parish discipline; if men did not whip each other, then God would send judgements, fires, swords, plagues, and wars. Were these the Last Days, now?

Anna Trapnel was not the only one stimulated to produce a flood of prophecies. There were many others. London often seemed to be drowning in a sea of prophets. Among them was Eleanor Davies, who had been predicting Charles's downfall since well before the war began, the woman who had briefly and querulously employed Winstanley.

While the Army debated and the Diggers sought to change the world, the captive Charles had decided to try to reconquer his kingdom. The conflict that resulted was far worse than the First Civil War had been, and there was no more talk of 'war without an enemy'. Both sides had been brutalized by the first war, and now found themselves capable of doing things more dreadful than they had imagined. There was now a cadre of very experienced soldiers, who saw themselves as separate from civilians. And the War of Three Kingdoms became the divisive, bitter War *Between* Three Kingdoms, so xenophobia could heighten cruelty further.

The Second Civil War was begun in confusion, in the last week of March 1648. The Parliamentarian commander of Pembroke Castle refused to hand over authority to his rival. He declared for the king, and South Wales did the same. Then Berwick and Carlisle were surprised in late April by Royalist insurrectionaries. Most of Kent and much of Essex had risen for the king in the second half of May. Montrose's enemy Argyll had managed to prevent the Scots from setting out in support of southern Royalists. They finally crossed the border in July.

There was plenty of plotting, but little order. Among the plotters was Lucy Hay, Countess of Carlisle, the woman who had helped to trigger the First Civil War by betraying the king's plan to arrest the Five Members to Pym. She had, of course, remained with Parliament on the outbreak of war, but she exemplified those who were increasingly alarmed by the Army radicals, and by the rise of commanders like Fairfax and Cromwell rather than the more reliable gentry of the House of Commons. She had always wanted to reform rather than abolish the court. Her contacts there were used in 1646–7 by the Parliamentarians seeking a compromise peace with the king. During the Second Civil War she conspired with the Scots, London Presbyterians, and her old ally the Earl of Holland, one of the Royalist commanders, to raise men and money for Charles I. It was typical of Lucy to detect the nation's mood, but she seriously overestimated the efficiency and intelligence of her confederates. Like other women, she had to confine herself to intrigue rather than command, when she might have done a better job than her male allies. She could hardly have done worse. Just as energetic Prince Rupert had begun almost every battle waiting for his Royalist colleagues to get themselves onto the field, so now Royalist insurrectionists stood about waiting for each other.

This hopelessly sporadic timetable meant that Fairfax and Cromwell could attack each rising as if it were a little local difficulty. Cromwell went off to Wales, and Fairfax sent John Lambert to the north to intercept the Scots, while he himself headed for Kent, where things seemed most menacing. Kent had not forgotten the riots over Christmas. 'Their rage is all against godly men', wrote a terrified news-sheet journalist. Fairfax's soldiers marched for three days without rest, and reached Maidstone on 2 June; by midnight Fairfax was master of the town, after some sharp fighting.

The commander of the Royalists in Kent was George Goring's aged father, the Earl of Norwich, who had little except longevity to recommend him for the job. He decided to march to London, hoping the city would rise for Charles. His supporters, who had been soundly beaten in Maidstone, thought they could smell defeat; they began to creep home, so that Norwich had only three thousand men left when they emerged onto the hill of Blackheath on 3 June 1648, after an all-night march.

Despite Norwich's shrunken army, the situation in London looked promising for Royalists, as Fairfax had left only a small garrison in the capital, commanded by the ever-reliable Philip Skippon. Cromwell was still tied down outside Pembroke Castle, where a group of former Parliamentarians had dug in, and were resisting the siege Cromwell had started on 24 May. The rebellion in Essex had begun on time. The ever-loyal Cornish, like the rest of the Celtic nations, were up in arms for the king, believing the Scots were coming from the north.

But then it fell apart. In London it did so thanks to the indefatigable, sturdy Philip Skippon. As always, Skippon kept his head when all about were losing theirs. He shut the city gates and manned its defences. Norwich's hoped-for rebellion within the City of London never materialized, so he left Blackheath for Chelmsford, crossing the river. Few of his Kentishmen followed him (most went home). Five hundred or so swam their horses across the Thames, using the Isle of Dogs as a base, and landing near Poplar docks. They were glimpsed by Anna Trapnel as harbingers of a storm of apocalyptic proportions.

But Trapnel's fears were well in excess of reality; Fairfax had already mopped up the remnants of the Kentish rising, and in Cornwall, too, the insurrection had collapsed. The only remaining area of revolt left unsubdued was Essex. The Royalists occupied Colchester on 12 June, and there was a ferocious encounter, in which the Parliamentarians attacked Sir Charles Lucas's infantry, who resisted stoutly. They were 'like mad men killing and slaying them [the Royalists] even in the cannon mouths', thought one observer. A cavalry sally by Lucas's men enabled their infantry fellows to escape the Parliament-men and take refuge within Colchester's walls. The town's only hope lay with the king's old commander among the Scots, James Duke of Hamilton, and his promised Scottish invasion in support of the king. Fairfax was tied down in the south, and Lambert alone could not have held the north. But Hamilton delayed, wanting the war as good as won before he would move. This gave Fairfax time to move his forces into Essex from Kent.

So in June 1648, the siege of Colchester began, one of the bitterest of all the conflicts of the Civil War years. Each side accused the other of terrible deeds. The Royalists inside the town were said to use soft-tip and poisoned bullets. Fairfax cut off the town's water supply, and also melted down its lead pipes for bullets of his own. The defenders did the same, but their roughly made bullets were interpreted as a deliberate attempt to inflict serious wounds, and the Parliament-men shot twenty prisoners found carrying them. When the Parliamentarians captured the house of Sir Charles Lucas, just south of Colchester, they broke open the family vault and tore apart the bodies of Lucas's mother and sister, cutting off their hair to wear in their hats as scalps. This was no longer iconoclasm, but a kind of tribal magic.

It was another hideously wet summer, even worse than 1644. The fields were awash; there were storms, floods, and the weather was appallingly cold. Inside the town, the food supply ran out quickly. The defenders said at first that they would hold on until they had gnawed their own fingers to the bone. Soon everyone was eating horsemeat and then dogmeat, at twelve shillings a carcass, and by the end of the siege, every cat in Colchester had been eaten. Prices mushroomed; soon cheese was five shillings – half a week's wages – a pound. The ration dropped to seven ounces of bread, made from oats, malt and salt water; it may have been a kind of improvised salt-leaven bread, and like the bean bread being eaten by Lambert's men it was a triumph of ingenuity, but the officers didn't think much of it. 'Let them eat horsemeat and maggots', suggested Parliamentarians, gloatingly. The townspeople, though, who were loyal Parliamentarians and had been so throughout the last war, were starving too. Desperate women petitioned to leave town with their families – no wonder, when a Royalist soldier was heard to comment that one crying, hungry baby 'would make a good deal of meat, well boiled'.

The garrison's commander Lucas, 'more intolerable than the siege', thought Clarendon, was unbearably determined to hang on, hoping for the Scots to arrive under Hamilton, for Holland's forces in Surrey, for the young Duke of Buckingham to march on London and thus draw Fairfax off, for the Prince of Wales and the fleet, now anchored off Holland. London newsbooks reported the Royalist forces as barbarians, some all but incoherent with horror:

> Much filthiness might be named of women, attempted some, forced others, shrieking, crying, flying and sometime scaping; sending their husbands out forcibly, and fall on their wives in their absence ... The most memorable is the answer of a gentlewoman, who if she did not yield had a pistol set to her breast, yes, says she, I shall cheerfully embrace your pistol and my death, but not you ... Women, some presently upon their delivery, some ready to be delivered, Infants in their mothers' laps, and some hanging on their mothers' breasts, all turned out of harbour, and left helpless to lie upon cold ground.

A group of women tried to escape. Startled, Fairfax ordered the men to fire blanks at them. When this failed to deter them, the besiegers used more drastic measures. The Parliamentarians stripped four of them naked and sent them back. Lucas's men refused to admit them and they had to sit disconsolately outside the walls.

And meanwhile, Lucas's hopes began, one by one, to fail. On 11 July 1648, Pembroke fell to Cromwell, so Lucas knew he would be arriving soon. Holland managed to raise only five hundred men for the king. There was no hope now of surprising London and drawing Fairfax away from Colchester. All Holland could do was wander about England until overhauled. He tried to take Reigate Castle, but was prevented, and his men routed; on his retreat through Surrey, he was surprised by a Parliamentarian force, and in the encounter, Francis Villiers, the younger brother of the Duke of Buckingham, was killed, a man who had possessed, it seemed, much of the beauty and charm of his notorious father, the first Duke, and an equal measure of military incompetence. His death was due to Cupid rather than Mars: he sent his company on ahead in order to make a night of it with Mary Kirk, daughter of the poet Aurelian Townshend. The Parliamentarians cut and mangled his body after his death. Andrew Marvell was asked to write an elegy, and did, revealing an enthusiasm for the king's cause surprising in a friend of John Milton. After Villiers's death, the Royalist soldiers began to melt away, and soon there were only two hundred, effortlessly rounded up by the Parliamentarians sent in pursuit of them. Holland was soon on his way to London to be tried.

Although the Second Civil War was largely fought over the territories that had escaped the first, Devon and Cornwall were unlucky enough to be central to both. In May 1648 a group of Cornishmen who had rebelled against Parliament in the name of Charles I met with comprehensive defeat at a place called 'the Gear', near Helford, and were pursued back across the Lizard peninsula to the seacoast beyond; surrender seemed inevitable, but some of them refused it. They joined hand to hand and hurled themselves bodily into the water, a desperate expedient on that rocky coast, as one later writer noted. Cornwall had been occupied by Parliamentarian troops, mostly from London and the south-east, who had attacked the Cornish churches, demolishing the chapels and ornamental stones which formed part of the landscape, and trying to close down Cornish sports and games. The locals reacted angrily, and the rebellions of the Second Civil War were especially fierce in Cornish-speaking areas. On the Land's End peninsula, still almost entirely Cornish-speaking, a force of three to five hundred men occupied Penzance in the name of the king. They called to other Cornishmen for assistance, and in St Ives and Helston they found some support.

The Cornish county committee were warned of the imminent Penzance rising by a merchant called Anthony Gubbs, but they took no notice, and Gubbs was sent home profitless. To his horror, his house was already surrounded by the rebels when he reached it. That very night a force began gathering, and by dawn it was ready, marching on St Michael's Mount. The rebels had hoped for surprise, but the garrison had been warned. The Cornish insurgents hurried back to Penzance, and Gubbs immediately galloped to St Ives, where he sent his son Joseph straight to the military commander of the West, Sir Hardress

Waller, for help. Returning to Penzance, Gubbs was seized by his angry countrymen; his goods were confiscated, and he was ordered to pay £300 to supply them further. He refused, and they imprisoned him under sentence of death.

The insurgents dug in, establishing a gunpowder magazine. They hoped for support from Helston, but a rising there was pre-empted when a force of thirty Parliamentarian soldiers arrived the afternoon before, on their way to the Mount. Nevertheless, the Penzance rebels' ranks were swollen by men from the western parishes, and they had also sent a message to the Lizard. They put up fortifications and lined the hedges with musketeers against the Parliament forces. The Parliamentarian leader Bennett called on them to surrender, but those in Penzance refused to listen. So Bennett attacked, and after two hours of fighting at the barricades, the Royalists were scattered, losing 'about 60 or 70 slain, some drowned, and sixty taken'. The survivors ran for it along the narrow maze of ancient field-boundaries that surrounded Penzance. When one local Parliamentarian tried to ride into Penzance to congratulate Bennett, he was confronted by 'a bloody soldier, who held up his musket to knock me on the head'.

The chief hope of the rebels lay in the Lizard peninsula, the traditional home of Cornish rebellion, and the only other part of Cornwall with a majority of Cornish-speakers; an emissary was sent there and managed to raise 120 men at once; they immediately made for St Keverne, hoping to draw on a tradition of riot in order to gain support for their cause; and it worked, since their number increased to 350, setting off to join the Penzance rebels. Did they dream of 1497, when they had tried to throw off the English? But before they even reached Penzance, the rebels there had been crushed, and no one else had joined them, so Parliament could spare all its troops to attack the men from the Lizard. The result was the rout at 'the Gear'.

Meanwhile, brilliant young John Lambert, a major-general at only twenty-eight, had not been idle. Managing to rally and unite the once-discontented Northern Association troops, he had enough men to keep Royalists like Sir Marmaduke Langdale contained while he waited for Fairfax and Cromwell to intercept any Scottish invasion. And worst of all, the Scots were defeated when they finally crept across the border. There were nothing like as many of them as Hamilton had hoped to raise. Denounced as wickedness from many a pulpit, on the grounds that the terms of The Engagement (the deal the Scots offered to Charles) offered far too little to the Kirk, the enterprise had little chance, and good commanders like David Leslie bowed to Kirk pressure and withheld their services. What chance the Scottish invasion had was lost when a Covenanting protest against the war was broken up violently; the two sides actually skirmished, Scot against Scot, and it was the Royalists who were forced to flee, making their cause seem both feeble and immoral. Recruits from Ulster were slow to arrive; landing in fishing boats, the Ulstermen were set upon by the Scots, so that only about fifteen hundred ever reached Hamilton. Eventually, he had a force of around nine thousand, many so raw that they didn't know how to use the pikes they carried.

They joined up with Marmaduke Langdale at Carlisle, and set off after Lambert, now outnumbering him. After a failure to engage early in the summer, Hamilton, with characteristic indecisiveness, decided to wait for the rest of his forces, which dribbled in, including the few Ulstermen who had managed the journey. The delay was fatal, as help was on its way for Lambert, who was just over the Pennines. His men were subsisting on bean bread, eaten only by the poorest. But Cromwell, after taking Pembroke Castle, was moving north, having paused only for a thanksgiving service in a Pembroke church. He sent his cavalry in advance, with typical boldness. His infantry were almost barefoot in the thick mud, so he had to divert to Leicester to pick up new shoes for them, but this also enabled him to collect fresh troops in the Midlands. He was anxious to join forces with Lambert before either of them met the Scots, and he did so successfully on 12 August 1648.

Still Hamilton did not move, except against the local inhabitants; his army spent its time plundering the countryside. At last he managed to collect his troops and to advance, along the Lancashire borders, hoping to join up with men from Wales. His disorganized forces marched towards Preston, strung out and blind to Cromwell, who had already reached Skipton, and who knew perfectly where Hamilton's army was. Cromwell decided to attack and the battle that followed, usually called Preston, was arguably Cromwell's masterpiece. Outnumbered, almost swamped, he managed to destroy Hamilton's much larger forces in an engagement that was less a single set-piece than a series of piecemeal fights in which the Scots and their Royalist allies were picked off at Cromwell's leisure.

First, he surprised a substantial body of straggling Royalists; they fought all day up a long, deep, muddy lane which was soon full of trampled dead. The Royalists had forgotten to secure their retreat, too, and when they tried to cross the Ribble, were trapped by Cromwell's troops.

At the end of that first day, Hamilton still had more men than Cromwell, but the Royalists were so tired that they lay down in the mud, exhausted. The next day, the Scots managed to get away, pursued by Cromwell. The Royalists had little powder left, and what they had was wet. They spent the night in Wigan. Cromwell's men spent the night in a field, 'very dirty and weary', he recalled. Next day the pursuit continued. The Royalists decided on a last stand; they made themselves a stronghold, a bank, where they managed to force Cromwell's vanguard back. But some local men – who had probably been plundered by the Scots – showed Cromwell a way around the flank, and from then on it was a slaughter, with Cromwell estimating a thousand dead and two thousand prisoners. The Royalist remnants surrendered next day, soaked in mud, sleepless, starving. Some of the leaders fled, but eventually even Marmaduke Langdale was unearthed in a Nottingham alehouse, and Hamilton in Stafford on 23 August. In Scotland, Argyll had the Engagement declared a sin, and anti-Engagement Covenanters began throwing out the remaining cavalry troops, and then triumphantly marched on Edinburgh. They were poor, and they were poorly armed, but they were supported by Cromwell, who brought his victorious troops to the border, and demanded the surrender of the remaining garrisons in Carlisle and Berwick. Over dinner in Edinburgh, Argyll and Cromwell struck a deal which shut the Engagers and Montrose's followers out of public office.

Lancashire was a ruin, with hardly a horse or a cow left. Penzance was so 'exquisitely plundered' food prices rose 50%, and the price of wheat doubled.

Cromwell reported to Parliament: 'Surely this is nothing but the hand of God, and wherever anything in the world is exalted, or exalts itself, God will pull it down, for this is the day wherein he alone will be exalted. It is not fit for me to give advice, nor to say a word what use should be made of this, more than to pray you, and all that acknowledge God, that they would exalt him, and not hate his people, who are the apple of his eye, and for whom even kings shall be reproved.' This was disingenuous. Cromwell was actually giving plenty of advice. But despite the Army's views, Parliament went on trying to treat with Charles.

Now only Colchester was left in Royalist hands. Conditions in the town were desperate, but the commander, Lucas, had no intention of surrender. The Parliamentarians decided to call upon a siege expert, the Leveller Thomas Rainborough, who was to be another victim of the Second Civil War, though indirectly. He had faced a naval mutiny which coincided with the Royalist uprisings, but had managed to get ashore because his own men liked and trusted him. It was unwise; out of the navy, he re-enlisted in the army and ended up facing the Royalists across the walls of Colchester; Rainborough the siege expert was vital, and Colchester duly fell.

After months of bitter siege, the starving town wanted to surrender. Lucas and Norwich refused, but the desperate townspeople eventually forced them to give in, and the town was in Fairfax's hands once more by 28 August 1648.

The stubbornness of the Royalist commanders made Fairfax more determined to punish them, and when negotiations began, his steely attitude was only too evident. Both the commanders Lucas and Lisle had promised never to take up arms against Parliament when captured before, at Stow and Faringdon. Moreover, Lucas had killed two men himself when the garrison at Stinchcombe in Gloucestershire surrendered. But what really motivated the Army was the besieged troops' use of poisoned bullets. Fairfax sent Norwich and Capel to London, but immediately sentenced Lucas, Lisle and the third leader, Gascoigne, to death, that same night in the castle yard. As Lucas was led forward, he asked Ireton on what grounds he was being killed, in a manner eerily proleptic of what Charles himself would say later at his trial. Ireton, cold as ever, replied tersely that he was a rebel who had committed high treason. Lucas went on defending himself; he was only fighting for his king, he said. As a soldier, how could that be treason?

He was silenced by a bullet. Lisle was next, and he asked the firing squad to move closer for a cleaner kill. They said, grumpily, that they would not miss, and Lisle, with a ghostly grin, suggested they had missed him at closer range before. Finally, they moved in, and it was a clean kill. Then Gascoigne was suddenly reprieved – he was actually a Tuscan mercenary, Bernardo Guasconi, fighting under an English name. Later, Capel too was to be executed.

Rainborough himself was killed in the same year at Pontefract. He was murdered by two Royalists who found him unarmed in his room. His funeral, at the Independent chapel in Wapping, was a last rallying point for the Levellers. 'Rainborough, the just, the valiant and the true', said his epitaph.

And the garrisons who had fought against Parliament, at Colchester and in the north? Sent to Bristol, sold into slavery in Barbados. The war might have begun on Pym's and Lord Saye's colonial committee; for some it ended in the sugar-fields. Or forced into European exile on condition that they fought for the Republic of Venice. For some, the war began in admiration for La Serenissima; for others, it ended in fighting for her.

XXXI

To Carisbrooke's Narrow Case:
Charles I in Captivity

By now Charles was spoken of by his foes as 'Charles Stuart, the man of blood'. If he had been blamed for the first war, he was excoriated for the second. Understandably, the king was thinking about escape again. He found conditions intolerable. The bedlinen wasn't changed often enough for a king and the wine was simply dreadful. But at least there was a miniature golf course within the grounds of the castle, and Governor Hammond also built him a bowling green. His coach was shipped to the island, and he used it to visit the sharp jutting rocks of the Needles. He liked to go for walks around the castle walls, and he kept up his reading. He made translations of Latin, but also devoured volumes of Lancelot Andrewes's sermons and Herbert's *Divine Poems*. He still loved romance, though, and read Spenser's *Faerie Queene* and Tasso's *Godfrey of Bulloigne*. Bacon's *Advancement of Learning* was always at his side, and he liked to annotate it as he read. He also wrote, pouring out his own reactions to everything that had happened to him. Reams of self-justification flowed from his pen. He had no choice but to flee London, he explained, in order 'not to prostitute the Majesty of my Place and Person, the safety of my Wife and Children'. Henrietta's departure had hurt him most, not because he missed her, but because of 'the scandal of that necessity'. Brooding on his life, measuring himself by the common standards of manliness, Charles could see that he'd fallen short; he'd failed to protect his female

dependant. He was equally upset by the publication of his letters after
Naseby. He couldn't understand why they had given offence; all they
showed was 'my constancy to my wife, the laws, and religion'. But he
was not without real remorse for signing Strafford's death warrant.
Strafford, he felt, had abilities which 'might make a Prince rather afraid
than ashamed to employ him in the great affairs of state'. Like everyone
involved in the wars, Charles hoped most of all to advise his son, to
help avoid a repetition. He had many hopes for his son. Perhaps
adversity might even help him, 'as trees set in winter, then in warmth
and serenity of time' grow faster. Be Charles the Good, he told him,
don't try to be Charles the Great. In reaching out to the future, the
king tried to allay his feeling of solitude, even abandonment.

He was scarcely alone, however; he was still attended by loyal servants, by his by-now-grown page; he had his tailor, David Murray; his
barber, his butler (who was a spy, and conveyed letters in Charles's
gloves) and his laundress, Mrs Wheeler, with her assistant Mary, as
well as an aged retainer who carted coals. There were other helpful
people in attendance, too, including the indefatigably loyal Jane Whorwood, and a range of go-betweens, including Major Bosville, who like
Lear's Kent managed to stay near his sovereign by disguising himself
as a rustic. Charles was not the only one whose pre-war theatregoing
seeped into his wartime thinking. One veteran of the king's army,
Captain Burly, staged a rising, marching on the castle accompanied
only by a drummerboy and a few women. Parliament hanged Burly,
and drew and quartered him too, for treason.

Mrs Dowcett, the kitchen clerk's wife, sent her king a cheerful note
to tell him that she had not been punished for smuggling his letters to
the queen. Mary, the assistant laundress, was critical. She would enter
his rooms during the day, when they were open and empty, bearing a
load of clean linen. In it she would have concealed a letter, which could
be hidden under a tapestry or carpet. 'I know that nothing will come
amiss when it comes in thy hand', Charles wrote. In this way, the king's
confederates hatched a plan to make a hole in his ceiling through which
he could make his way to an upper storey of the castle, one only lightly
guarded. It was ingenious, but Hammond was a match for the plotters,
and they were discovered. Hammond sacked Mrs Wheeler, and Mary
too, and also Charles's barber, who had nothing to do with the plot.

Charles refused to let a Parliamentarian gambol about him with a razor; he let his hair and beard grow. He knew there was a boat waiting to take him to Southampton. He was ready to embark, leaning out the window, when he saw the castle weathervane swing around to the north. Now he was trapped on the island once more.

Charles learnt his lesson. From now on, he wrote his plans on tiny scraps of paper, some no more than one inch across; he also disguised his handwriting and used a cipher for key parts of his messages. Charles still loved disguise, play, theatre, and he was still fearful of being found out, scrutinized. Hammond searched his room, but Charles managed to hurl his papers on the fire. And when the thaw began, when the buds broke on the trees, Charles's hopes too began to unfurl. The Scots were ready to cross the border and come to his aid, and in South Wales, troops under Colonel Poyer declared for the king; an Irish force was ready. Why should he compromise now? What he should do was escape.

He was communicating with Henry Firebrace, the slightly super-annuated page, through a hole Firebrace had made in the wall of Charles's bedroom; it was hidden by the hangings. Charles knew where to surmount the castle walls, and had been told that two horsemen would be waiting for him with three fast horses beyond the outer defences. He knew there was a boat waiting at the port to take him to the mainland. He knew too that he could easily get out of his bedchamber window; he'd tried the space with his head.

On the night of Monday 20 March 1648, Charles began his escape. His head went comfortably through the bars – but his rickety, inflexible body would not follow. For moments which seemed like hours, he was actually stuck, unable to withdraw his head or get his body further. Eventually, he was relieved to be back in his room.

He wrote to thank all those who had tried to help, and began to think about how he might weaken the bars. Perhaps nitric acid would do the trick. Jane Whorwood attempted to supply some, but it spilt on the long and rough journey from London. A fat plain man gave Charles equipment that let him turn two knifeblades into a saw, with which he did succeed in cutting one of his window bars, and more nitric acid was obtained locally. But by now so many people were in the know that it was almost inevitable that Hammond would become one of them. He acted promptly; he informed Parliament.

Charles's faithful servants thought of setting the castle on fire, and smuggling him out in the confusion. But in the end they decided instead to hide one of their number on the island. Firebrace was indefatigable; he suggested bringing to Carisbrooke a servant, Henry Chapman, dressed as a country gentleman, with a bushy false beard and a wig, white stockings and a big hat. The guards would remember this outlandish garb, and would forget to look at the face; then Charles could assume the same disguise and sidle out.

Charles loved the idea because it involved the theatrics and masquerading he adored. It was like the good old days of the Spanish Match. He called it 'the most practicable' of all Firebrace's schemes. But Chapman couldn't get past the guards. Other schemes foundered, or were uncovered by Hammond, or betrayed by those involved for sums of money that seemed trifling to the king, but handsome to servants. The fact that Charles insisted on writing letters to everyone, sometimes two a day to the same person, made secrecy impossible to sustain. Then the king heard the news of James's escape, masterminded by Anne Halkett and her lover. Charles felt relieved, but his thirteen-year-old son's success demeaned him; James had done what he could not.

The hot fires of rebellion had been lit everywhere, but they burned out quickly, leaving a deathly taste of ash. After this, there was real hatred, and it showed in the behaviour of both sides. For example, when Woodcroft House surrendered, the victorious Parliamentarians had thrown its master over the battlements, but Michael Hudson managed to grasp a drainage spout, and he hung on desperately kicking air. They hacked off his hands, and he plunged into the moat. Then they recovered his body, made sure he was dead with a musket blow to the head, and cut out his tongue. After that, what forgiveness could there be? Men who acted thus could only forgive themselves by blaming someone else; Charles had rejected what to the Army was the judgement of providence, given clearly in the First Civil War. Now his hands were incarnadine with the blood of his people.

Charles's powerful position in spring had withered by the end of the summer of 1648, and he was transferred to a prison in Newport. On his last day on the island, he met the nine-year-old son of the master gunner, who was marching up and down the walls. Charles stopped his restless pacing to speak to the child; what are you doing, he asked the boy. Defending your majesty, the child replied. Charles patted his head, touched, but awkwardly patronizing, and gave the boy the ruby ring from his cravat.

A commission was sent to Newport, dominated by Charles's sympathizers, the Presbyterians. It seemed a fine opportunity for compromise; the Army was away, fighting. But despite the weakness of his position, Charles still refused to take negotiation seriously. His friends worried that he was throwing away a last chance; they feared that the Independents were hanging on until Cromwell and Fairfax had finished their work in the field, and that once the Army was in control, they would break off the negotiations.

Charles too seemed to be playing for time, though no one was sure why. He made concessions, sometimes far-reaching ones, and then withdrew them the next day after discussions with his secretary, Sir Philip Warwick. One night he had to turn away from his staff to hide the tears which flowed from his eyes. When the commissioners left, he made a speech in which he became the protagonist of a tragedy once more, this time a *de casibus* morality tale about the fall of the mighty: 'My Lords, you are come to take your leave of me, and I believe that we shall surely never see one another again. But God's will be done. I thank God I shall make my peace with him, and shall not fear whatsoever he shall suffer men to do unto me. You cannot but know that in my fall and ruin you see your own, and that also of those near to you. I pray you God sends you better friends than I have found.'

This penultimate remark shows that Charles was thinking of the Army. He was reasoning like any educated seventeenth-century man: 'Take but degree away, untune that string/And hark what discord follows!' By their refusal of his authority, Parliament had condemned themselves to the abrogation of their own by the Army. But in the king's final remark his sense of isolation, his loneliness, are inscribed in large letters. Despite the brave devotion of his servants and helpers, Charles felt himself friendless.

His main hope was for an Irish rising, and he warned the queen not to be deceived by anything she might hear about concessions on Ireland. Perhaps he should escape? But Charles was again advised not to by Henrietta. He dreaded her anger, and stayed. He conceded Presbyterianism for three years, though he still refused utterly to take the Covenant, and continued to oppose the death penalty for any of his supporters, perhaps with the hangings of Capel, and most recently Holland, fresh in his mind. But he did concede that they should be punished and their estates reduced. By now he wasn't even sure what he was trying to achieve, writing confusedly that he was so desperate to avoid returning to gaol that he was making concessions in the hope that he might escape, but now only escape and success could justify the concessions . . . 'My only hope', he wrote, despairingly, 'is that now they believe I dare deny them nothing, and so be less careful of their guards.' But Charles continued to deny them episcopacy, and the negotiations foundered quickly. He tried again to escape, but Hammond was two steps ahead of him at every moment. By now he had been warned that the Army wanted to put him on trial. He grew sadder and sadder.

His daughter Elizabeth was even more alone. She was twelve years old, and it was half a year since she had seen her father. She had been staying at Syon House, cared for by the Earl of Northumberland, Lucy Hay's nephew. Charles wrote lovingly to her on 27 October 1648:

> Dear daughter,
>   It is not want of affection that makes me write so seldom to you, but want of matter, such as I could wish; and indeed am I loath to write to those I love when I am out of humour (as I have been these days by past), lest my letters should trouble those I desire to please. But having this opportunity, I would not lose it, though at this time I have nothing to say, but God bless you! So I rest, Your loving father, Charles R. Give your brother my blessing with a kiss, and commend me kindly to my Lady Northumberland, by the same token.

Like a modern father calling his daughter on a mobile phone from far away, Charles knew he urgently wanted to make contact with his little girl, but he didn't know enough about her world to know what to say.

The Army wanted Charles tried. Lilburne kept up his complaints, warning anyone who would listen that a trial would hand power to the Army grandees and lead to arbitrary government. But most soldiers wanted a trial. For them the former king was now Charles Stuart, the man of blood. They had bled. They wanted something that would make it clear that they had fought for change, for betterment – it would be truly unbearable if nothing were to change. The Army could not trust Parliament; Parliament might make peace with Charles or let him escape.

The Army took action. The king's Parliamentarian gaoler Hammond was removed from the Isle of Wight and placed in custody, and on 30 November 1648 Colonel Cobbett arrived at Newport with a detachment. Charles's friends begged him to escape. There were horses ready, and a boat. But at the last minute Charles refused to go. His excuse was that he had given his word to Parliament, but in reality it was to Henrietta he had given it; if he did escape, he would have to face her reproaches. His friends pointed out that it was no longer Parliament with whom he had to deal, but the Army. Charles ignored them, and retreated to bed.

Next morning he was woken at daybreak by soldiers, who hurried him away without his hot breakfast, and prevented his servants from kissing his hand in farewell. The Leveller Major Rolph tried to climb into the carriage with the king, who forcibly removed him, saying that it had not yet come to that; Charles had always been reluctant to share air with commoners.

Across the Solent stood Hurst Castle, surrounded on three sides by sea. It was Charles's new prison. His rooms were so dark he needed candles all through the day. There was no golf course and his daily exercise was reduced to a walk along the pebbly strand. So Pride purged the Commons while Charles enjoyed watching his ships – his fatal ships – sailing up the Solent. While he was there he managed to smuggle out a letter to Firebrace, sending good wishes to his friends – Jane Whorwood, and Lucy Hay. 'I do expect the worst', he wrote. Charles was terrified that he had been brought to Hurst Castle to be murdered, like many another deposed English king. It was a relief when he was moved again, to Windsor, across happily familiar lands, and some people in the town even cried out 'God bless the king'. And there was plenty of company; Hamilton was a prisoner in the castle too, and so were Elizabeth and Henry, two of the royal children. But as Charles paced up and down the terrace, his change of situation was only too painfully apparent. Now he was not even allowed his own servants, and letters no longer reached him. It was but 'the husk and shell' of

life, he thought. 'That I must die as a Man, is certain, that I may die a
King, by the hands of My own subjects, a violent, sudden and barbarous
death, in the strength of my years, in the midst of my kingdoms,
my friends and loving subjects being helpless spectators, my enemies
insolent Revilers and Triumphers over me . . . is so probable in human
reason, that God hath taught me not to hope otherwise.' His hair grew
grey, he lost weight, his face looked more haggard. His personal servant,
assigned by Parliament, was however all but converted by the Stuart
charm that Charles could still wield. When Thomas Herbert's bedstraw
caught alight one night – a common enough occurrence in the seventeenth century – Charles put the fire out himself. When the man
overslept, Charles reassured him, and promised him an alarm clock.
He could still be a benign father.

Events in London were to show that Charles's advisers were right
about who held power. On the morning of 3 December 1648, the House
of Commons had agreed to accept the king's answers, given at Newport.
But the Army leaders noted who had voted in its favour; as the House
rose, a group of officers and their allies decided that the Commons
must be purged of anyone even faintly supportive of a negotiated
settlement with Charles. Suspicion fell on any member who had implic-
itly or explicitly denied that supporters of the Scots were traitors,
anyone who had wanted to settle with the king, any who had voted to
repeal the Vote of No Addresses in which Parliament had agreed to
halt approaches to the king, and on those who had shown that they
were too eager to treat with Charles Stuart, that man of blood.

A war that had begun when Charles had tried to remove unruly
MPs ended with the Army deciding to do the same. Colonel Thomas
Pride, with a group of musketeers, forcibly removed one hundred and
forty-five Presbyterian MPs, leaving a group of fifty who supported
the Army. This was an extraordinary event, an armed coup. It was the
end of 'Parliament' as a cause, the end of law and order, but also the
beginning of true populism. After all its moderates had been forcibly
expelled, the House of Commons was transformed into a kind of
kangaroo court. Its purpose was to emerge almost at once: try the king
for high treason. Its opponents were to christen it the Rump Parliament,
which made for a lot of bitter jokes. Among those excluded were the
Harleys, new widower Robert and Brilliana's beloved Ned; Robert had

been among those who had pushed hardest for a treaty with the king. Some of those excluded were imprisoned for the night in a tavern called Hell, and they spent the night singing psalms and talking. Ned Harley tried to write to Fairfax about the king's trial; everyone knew Fairfax was not in favour of killing the king, but he did not take any open action against the regicides. Ned urged him to do just that:

> Neither God nor man can be satisfied with any passive dislikes of what is done amiss by your army. Their evils for want of your prohibition will become your guilt, which I beseech your excellency seriously to consider. I hope God has given your excellency this command for such a time as this. But if you altogether hold your peace – and a General's words cannot be other than commands – at this time, then shall there enlargement and deliverance arise from another place ... they [the Army] are hastily digging a miserable sepulchre for all the beauty and strength of our native kingdom, if God be not pleased wonderfully to deliver.

Still Fairfax did not act, or did not act directly, although Ned Harley was not the only one to beg him to involve himself. John Milton, too, addressed him, in a sonnet subtitled 'at the siege of Colchester':

> Thy firm unshaken virtue ever brings
> Victory home, though new rebellions raise
> Their hydra heads ...
> O yet a nobler task awaits thy hand;
> For what can war, but endless war still breed,
> Till truth and right from violence be freed,
> And public faith cleared from the shameful brand
> Of public fraud. In vain doth valour bleed
> While avarice and rapine share the land.

But Milton's new friend Andrew Marvell, who was at this time tutor to Fairfax's daughter Mary, praised him for his decision to retire. And Fairfax may also have repudiated Royalist overtures to lead troops to rescue the king. He spent the rest of the war out of politics, raising horses and collecting books at his house Nunappleton. His war was all but over.

XXXII

Oh, He is Gone,
and Now hath Left Us Here:
The Trial and Execution of Charles I

On Saturday 20 January 1649, Charles travelled from St James's Palace in an enclosed sedan chair to Whitehall Steps; the river mists made it cold that day. There he boarded a barge, also heavily curtained. He was accompanied on the river by boats of musketeers. There was a chilly half-mile journey to the steps of Sir Robert Cotton's house on the Thames. Cotton, the great librarian, had no reason to love Charles, who had seized some of his antiquarian treasures twenty or so years earlier. And the guards were hostile, keeping their hats on even in his presence.

Charles's trial was about to begin. A king of England was being openly and publicly tried for high treason. It was to be held in Westminster Hall. At one end sat John Bradshaw, the Lord President, on a velvet chair, with a desk in front of him and judges behind him. On a nearby table rested his sword and mace of office. The dock walls were so high that the audience could see only the top of Charles's head. Tickets had been sold weeks in advance. Everyone saw Charles walk in, and refuse, in his turn, to take off his hat for his judges. But revenge was what the whole day was about. The indictment was read aloud to the court by the prosecutor, ardent republican and godly zealot John Cook, who accused Charles of having 'traitorously and maliciously waged war against his people'.

But Charles was eager to interrupt the reading of the indictment. He still had no idea that things had changed, in ways almost too fundamental for him to grasp. He tapped Cook on the shoulder with his silver-topped cane. 'Hold a little', he said. Cook read on. Charles tapped again. Finally, the silver tip fell from his cane with a loud thud, and rolled noisily across the wooden floor. Everyone stood frozen, watching it.

Charles waited. No one picked it up.

It was then that Charles realized that he was entirely alone. 'It made a great impression on me', he remarked, a few days later. But he could at least take refuge in the person he had been, the one who didn't understand – it became a mask to hide behind. When Cook called him 'a tyrant and traitor', Charles laughed.

Now Bradshaw asked him how he wished to plead.

The king refused to respond. 'I would know', he said, 'by what power I am called hither ... There are many unlawful authorities in the world,' he added, 'there are robbers and highwaymen.' He clung to what he knew. 'Remember I am your king, your lawful king, and what sins you bring upon your hand, and the judgement of God upon this land.' Bradshaw explained that he was brought to trial 'in the name of the people of England, of which you are elected king'.

This gave Charles his opening. 'England', he pointed out, had never been an elective kingdom, 'but a hereditary kingdom for these thousand years.' He added: 'I do stand more for the liberty of my people than any here that come to be my pretended Judges.' What he meant was that it was he who was refusing to submit 'to a tyrannical or any other ways unlawful authority'. Like his grandmother, Mary Queen of Scots, Charles's responses to his accusers were both intelligent and stupid. He was displaying bright legal manoeuvring, but his recalcitrance was also a tactically dim way of getting everybody's goat. He underestimated how much he was now blamed for those bloody fields, those empty beds. As he left, people shouted 'Justice! Justice!' A few others cried 'God save the king!'

Charles added a little extra touch of Stuart bravura. Walking past the sword, he said: 'I have no fear of that.'

The second day was like the first – Charles still refused to plead. If, he said, power without law may make laws, may alter the fundamental laws of the kingdom, 'I do not know what subject he is in England that can be sure of his life.'

This was Charles's most telling point, and he knew it. And it was not without substance. But he also disputed the court's authority. 'I do not know', he said, coldly, 'how a king may become a delinquent.' He insisted that 'the Commons of England was never a court of judicature. I would know how that came to be so.' Bradshaw stonewalled, insisting that Charles make a plea; Charles continued to refuse. Finally he said, 'I do require that you give me my reasons.'

'Sir,' said Bradshaw, still trying, 'it is not for prisoners to require.'

'*Prisoner, sir! I am not an ordinary prisoner!*' So assured was Charles's tone that the trial recorders wrote his words in italics.

Charles was returned to Cotton's house, and on his way someone in the street cried out 'God bless you, sir'. This consoled him, and he also prayed for a while, then told Herbert that he felt sure the common people only shouted 'Justice!' because their officers had told them to; for Charles, common people still had nothing in their heads but what was put there by their betters. And, he said, how insignificant the judges were; he could only recognize eight of them. This was a commonplace Royalist jibe; the Royalist newsbooks still appearing commented on the low birth and mechanic origins of the justices. It was embarrassing for Parliament and for the committee that drew up the list of judges – a body led by Cromwell and Ireton, helped by eager republican Henry Marten – that all of the senior justices originally nominated had refused to serve, including Oliver St John, one of the most consistent critics of the king.

Henry Vane had been unable to accept Pride's Purge, which for him violated the Commons, and he too was absent, as was Algernon Sidney, who disliked the legal basis for the Commons trying the king. This did leave the justices looking like second- or third-choice men. Although some of them were indeed former tradesmen drawn from the ranks of the New Model Army – Colonel Pride himself was said to have been a brewer's drayman – most of the hundred-and-thirty-five men called to try the king for treason were solid mayors and gentlemen.

Charles again refused to plead on the third day. Finally, Bradshaw moved the trial to the Painted Room and the judges heard evidence without the king. The old tales were told: how the king had raised his standard at Nottingham, how he had been at Edgehill, at Newbury, at Cropredy Bridge, Lostwithiel, Naseby. There were thirty-three witnesses, barber-surgeons and soldiers, from north and south. They all told the same story – Charles Stuart was a man of blood, and the judges decided that blood must have blood; their verdict came on 27 January: that 'Charles Stuart as a tyrant, traitor, murderer and public enemy to the good people of this nation shall be put to death by the severing of his head from his body'.

Decapitation is an ancient practice; Neolithic peoples posted the heads of their enemies around their gates. So did Stuart kings. It is an adaptation of ancient rituals of sacrifice, in which the blood of the accused must spurt – the Greeks even have a word for it, *sparge* – from the great vessels of the neck. The blood is redemptive, fertilizing; it gives life to the nation on whose soil it is spilt. It is also analogous to hanging, and in Stuart England an upper-class felon was beheaded, a lower-class one hanged; in each case the head was symbolically separated from the lower body. Charles's blood was to inaugurate a new republic, and his head was to adorn it; it symbolized the new state's resolution. It also meant Charles's blood would be spilt to cleanse the land of the blood he had spilt. And it meant, too, that Charles would follow in the footsteps of Strafford and Laud, he would be just another traitor. The sky had not fallen in when they died.

So the justices reassembled in Westminster Hall for sentencing. Bradshaw wore scarlet, the colour of blood, and a black hat.

Charles insisted on being allowed to address the court. He knew the law, and he knew that once the sentence of death was pronounced, he would be legally dead and unable to speak. Bradshaw tried to stop him, telling him he must hear the court first. Charles persisted. Bradshaw continued reading '. . . Crimes exhibited against him in the name of the people of England . . .'

Suddenly Charles was supported from a most unexpected quarter. From the ladies' gallery, a masked woman cried out, 'Not half, not a quarter of the people of England. Oliver Cromwell is a traitor.' The musketeers levelled their arms at her and Colonel Axtell shouted 'Down with the whores!' She was hustled out by her friends.

The intervention came from Anne, Lady Fairfax, Thomas Fairfax's wife. Was she acting without his knowledge? Or was she intervening on behalf of them both, their consciences made increasingly uneasy? No one knew then, nor do they know now. But we do know that it was not Anne's first intervention, not her first piece of barracking. When the names of the judges had been read out, there had been a notable absence from the commissioners empowering the court to act. Fairfax, the man who above all had won the war for Parliament, was not there. A masked woman had cried out, 'He has more wit than to be here!' And the fact that Fairfax himself was heard to ask after Charles's health on the evening of the day he had been executed suggests a determination to be out of the loop. At any rate, Anne's cry just before the sentencing was itself a kind of verdict – Charles was winning this war. Finally Bradshaw promised that he would be heard before sentence was passed, and again the charges were read.

Now Charles tried a new tactic; he proposed that his case be transferred to a joint session of Parliament. Bradshaw was against it, but others rather favoured the idea; later, Justice John Downes was to make a great deal of his support for the king's request. Cromwell ordered him to be quiet in an angry whisper, but Downes insisted they deliberate. They did. Half an hour later, they were back, with nothing achieved but a short delay. Bradshaw spoke for forty minutes. And now he told the clerk to read the sentence. The clerk did so: 'that the said Charles Stuart, as a tyrant, traitor, murderer and a public enemy, shall be put to death by the severing of his head from his body'.

Charles burst in again: 'Will you hear me a word, sir?'

'Sir, you are not to be heard after sentence', Bradshaw replied.

'I may speak after the sentence. By your favour, I may speak after the sentence ever', Charles insisted. But the guards began to hustle him out. 'I am not suffered to speak. Expect what justice other people will have', he exclaimed. By now the atmosphere was so disorderly, so contemptuous that the king was spat on, and tobacco smoke blown in his face. 'Poor souls,' said Charles, as ever closing his eyes to his people's opinion of him, 'for a piece of money they would do so for their commanders.' It was like Charles to blur the lucidity of martyrdom with such reflections. Legally, he had a case; the Rump did lack power to try him. But morally and practically, it had become brutally clear that kings depended on the consent of the governed for their continuance in office.

And now Charles had only to wait. He went back to Whitehall Palace for the night, where he said he wanted to see only his children and his chaplain William Juxon. Some of his supporters appeared, desperate to find a way of saving him. Charles turned them away at the door.

On Monday, he burned all his papers, and then his children came. There had been a letter from the Prince of Wales, borne by a weeping servant. Now Princess Elizabeth and Prince Henry were brought in to say goodbye.

They came in crying, bewildered. Charles tried to help them face the future; he told them they must obey their brother, the prince, who would now be king in his place. Elizabeth went on crying and crying, and her constant sobs began to tear at Charles's self-mastery. 'Sweet heart,' he said desperately, visibly upset, 'you will forget this.' 'No, I shall never forget it while I live', she swore. Charles on his last day on earth was worried about Elizabeth's future religious beliefs, suggesting various books 'which would ground me against Popery'. Charles tried to help her see him as a martyr to true religion, calling it 'a glorious death', and urging her to read Hooker, and Lancelot Andrewes, and Laud. He did not forget Henrietta Maria, either, far away in France, and urged Elizabeth to tell the queen that he had never strayed from her.

Later Elizabeth remembered:

> He wished me not to grieve and torment myself for him, for that it would be a glorious death that he should die, it being for the laws and liberties of this land, and for maintaining the true Protestant religion ... He told me he had forgiven all his enemies, and hoped God would forgive them also, and commanded us and all the rest of my brothers and sisters to forgive them. He bid me tell my mother that his thoughts had never strayed from her, and that his love should be the same to the last. Withal he commanded me and my brother to be obedient to her, and bid me send his blessing to the rest of my brothers and sisters, with a commendation to all his friends.

He tried to give Elizabeth a picture of the better life towards which they were moving: one day, he said, Christ's kingdom would come, 'and we shall all be happier than we could have expected to have been, had I lived'.

Charles had a practical message for his eight-year-old son Henry. Seeing conspiracy everywhere – the very mindset that had inspired others to rebel against him – he saw it closing around his son, and he feared some might make him a puppet king. It shows Charles's difficulty in imagining any regime other than a monarchy. He sat Henry on his knee – good child psychology – and looked into his son's eyes.

'Now they will cut off thy father's head', he said, matter-of-factly. 'Mark what I say. You must not be a king, so long as your brothers Charles and James so live, for they will cut off your brothers' heads (when they catch them), and cut off thy head too at last. And therefore I charge thee do not be made a king by them.' Charles's reported speech, with its repeated fierce words of beheading, is an effort to protect his little son by frightening him thoroughly.

Henry played his role with the thespian ability of a true Stuart. He struck exactly the right note. 'I will be torn in pieces first', he vowed. Elizabeth reports that Charles 'rejoiced exceedingly' at this declaration. Then Henry burst into tears, as did the guards. Charles turned his back hastily and moved towards his bedroom before he too could be seen crying. He gave the children a few remaining pieces of jewellery in an effort to send them away smiling. But when the moment of farewell came, Elizabeth was crying once more. Charles urged her not to weep, 'for I shall die a martyr', he said. He kissed the children and blessed them. Elizabeth's desperate misery, drowning in sobs, made some observers break down too. As his children were being ushered away for the last time, he turned back for one final fierce hug. Then they were gone, and he was alone, facing the end. His accusers spent the day trying to find people willing to sign his death warrant.

That evening, Charles took communion, prayed, read. His guards were persuaded to leave him alone. He told his servant to put out his best clothes, saying he must be up early, having important work to do. He was determined to put on two shirts; it was still bitter January weather, the Thames frozen in London, and he worried that his shivers from cold might be attributed to fear. He finally fell asleep at around two in the morning.

The next day was 30 January 1649. Charles woke before dawn, because his servant Herbert was in the noisy throes of a nightmare about William Laud, an appropriate dream. On this icy day, Charles was calm. 'This is my second marriage day', he said. 'I will be as trim today as may be, for before night I hope to be espoused to my blessed Jesus.' Then Juxon arrived, and together they read Matthew's account of the Passion of Jesus Christ. It happened to be the lesson for that day. Charles knew it was an omen, and it made him happier.

There was a knock at the door. 'Come, let us go', said Charles, taking Juxon's hand. It was ten o'clock. They were marched across St James's Park, to the drumming of dozens of soldiers. Charles's dog Rogue tried to follow his master, but was turned back. They entered Whitehall Palace by the Tiltyard steps and made their way to Charles's old bedroom. The walls were bare. The king prayed, and – on Juxon's urging – ate a loaf of bread and drank a small glass of claret. Bread and wine: the Last Supper.

So they waited. A little after two, Charles was summoned, and Juxon went with him to the end. They were led into the Banqueting Hall, its Rubens splendours shrouded in darkness. They had proclaimed the divine protection afforded sovereignty. Now the sovereign himself was led through one of the first-floor windows out onto the scaffold, which had been built in the street. It was draped in black. On it stood the executioner and his assistant, and the very small block Parliament had ordered, perhaps an unkind response to Charles's height. It was so low that he had to lie on the floor, and had large straps to bind him if he fought.

There was a great silence. Most – though not all – shops were closed. The crowd – in the street, on the roofs – waited in bitter cold for Charles to speak. But the guards had kept the people so far back that none could hear his words.

Charles felt his death was justice, not for the war, but for his acquiescence in the fate of Strafford, and he returned to the argument he had used at his trial. 'A subject and a sovereign', he insisted, at this last, 'are clear different things.' He remembered to declare his faith only when Juxon prompted it, not because it was not central to his thoughts, but because it was so central that he had forgotten to confide in those around him.

And now there was a prick of fear. Someone tried the edge of the axe, and Charles's anxiety surfaced: 'Hurt not the axe that will hurt me', he urged, and then asked Colonel Francis Hacker, in command of the King's Guard, 'Take care they do not put me in pain.' He remembered accounts of bungled beheadings. He tucked his hair carefully under his white satin nightcap, to make sure his neck was clear.

'I go from a corruptible to an incorruptible crown, where no disturb-ances can be, no disturbances, in the world', he said. He gave Juxon his Garter insignia, and said 'remember' to him. No one has ever been sure of what it meant. The last words of the ghost in *Hamlet* to his son are 'Adieu. Remember me.' The son is supposed to remember, and avenge.

Charles now prayed a little. He had been on the scaffold for fifteen minutes or so. Then he lay down on the block. He thrust out his arms. The axe swung down, and severed his head in one clean blow. There was a sigh from the crowd – no cheering, no laughter, just a long-breathed sigh, a collective groan.

At once, two troops of horse dispersed the crowds, though not before some had managed to dip handkerchiefs in the king's blood; they would sell them later as remedies for scrofula, for now there was in the Three Kingdoms no king left to touch for it.

XXXIII

Into Another Mould? The Aftermath

The men who had fought in the Civil War gave it various names; 'the war of King Charles the First', 'the troubles', 'the late unnatural and uncivil wars', 'the civil wars', 'the late deplored war', 'the late unhappy wars'. Historians have been equally uncertain: 'the great rebellion', said Clarendon stoutly, but few have followed him; 'the English Revolution', said the late Christopher Hill, and many agreed, but the term was Hill's invention, not that of contemporaries. Whether or not there had been a revolution, the regicides were men who had done the unthinkable and survived. But after Charles's death, no one quite knew what came next.

Charles himself lay in state in a lead coffin under a black velvet pall, with his head resewn to his body, a seemly denial of the violence done to his person and the state. He was embalmed, and laid in the chapel at St James's. It was said that Oliver Cromwell visited the body, to pay his last respects. 'Cruel necessity', he is supposed to have told it. Charles was eventually interred at a good safe distance from London, in St George's Chapel, Windsor. As the body was borne from the castle hall to its vault, thick flakes of snow began to fall, and the heavy black pall turned white. Now he was the White King of prophecy and legend. The day he was buried, Charles was at last heard; his meditations – considerably embellished – were printed as *Eikon Basilike*, and the loving image was created of gentle Charles king and martyr, destroyed by tyranny. John Milton rushed out a refutation, *Eikonoklastes*, but no one really attended to it. As the title implied, Milton was eager to align Charles's death with the iconoclasm that for some had been the whole point of the war. But the moment was over by the time it was printed, and new winds were blowing.

Prince Charles heard the news of his father's execution on 4 February – no one told him in person; no one wrote; it came as part of the general newspapers. Charles's chaplain addressed him, stammeringly, as 'Your Majesty'. Charles asked to be left alone. He was proclaimed king by the Scots at the Mercat Cross, and in Ireland, and in the Scilly Isles. Not in England, however.

Henrietta Maria had heard a different tale: Charles had been rescued by an eager crowd, who had mobbed the scaffold. But invention was soon overtaken by chill truth; she heard the news in silence, and remained sitting silently for some time. Finally, she broke into tears when a friend embraced her. With Charles, she had lost her part in affairs of state; her son did not heed her advice. She was never to play an active part in politics again.

After the war, four of Princess Elizabeth's rockers, the nursemaids who rocked her cradle, turned up at her brother's court in exile, and asked for money. The princess herself met a cruel fate, and a lonely one. A sensitive girl, prone to illness, just reaching adolescence, she was terrified when her brother's landing in Scotland in 1650 led to her own removal to the Isle of Wight. Always dressed in black as a sign of deep mourning for her father, she looked a washed-out little ghost of the old regime. She was unreconciled to her circumstances, and after one piece of teenage defiance, her captors threatened to apprentice her to some nearby glover or button-maker at Newport. Within a week of her arrival, she caught a cold playing bowls with her brother Henry. Her head ached, she refused to eat; perhaps she half-intended to starve herself, one of the only ways left to her of displaying her anger. She developed a high fever, and she died of it, her head resting on a Bible which lay open at the text 'Come unto me, all ye that labour and are heavy laden, and I will ease you'. Her mother, helplessly sad at the loss of another family member without so much as a farewell, thought she had died of grief. Ironically, the day before, Parliament had decided to allow her to join her sister Mary in Holland. Queen Victoria, who had been another lonely princess, visited her grave and is said to have cried over it. Prince Henry survived in captivity until soon after the Restoration.

What fell with Charles's head was the possibility of restoring anything like the pre-war status quo. In the face of Charles's blood on the straw, not even the most determined ostrich could deny that there had been a change, and therefore that the constitution might need some rethinking.

There was the Rump, less an idea than a body of people sitting, *de facto*, governing, *de facto*. Now ideas had to race to catch up with *actualité*. The learned turned to ancient Rome and to the ideal of the Roman Republic for a model of greatness that excluded a king, and that was founded on the removal of a wicked tyrant. The liberty of the individual was guaranteed by the liberty of the free commonwealth. For the state as well as the individual, the loss of liberty was enslavement. But this blissful state of affairs depended on the individual citizen's willingness to maintain virtue, and for some people this meant a world of constant warfare in which citizen-soldiers were knitted into units by the experience of shedding their blood for the state. For others, like Marchamont Nedham, it meant that freedom was enshrined in fairly commonsense laws: private property, a system of justice, and free elections – all very much more sturdy. But as it happened, neither point of view would last, nor would either entirely vanish.

What was also slow to fade was the cruelty the war had unleashed, its violence, best glimpsed in the admirably upright person of Oliver Cromwell. While the English had been fighting the two Civil Wars, a separate but related conflict had been going on in Ireland. The upshot was that the fledgling English republic was forced to send over an army to pacify those areas of Ireland still unsubdued by forces friendly to it. On 10 September 1649, Cromwell and his army arrived at Drogheda, which controlled the mouth of the Boyne. He who could take Drogheda could take hell, thought its governor, former Royalist commander Sir Arthur Aston. The Cromwellian cannon opened fire, breaching the walls to the south. The next day, there were two terrible assaults, marked by the Pythonesque black comedy of Colonel Warren, who tried to go on fighting when both his legs had been shot off. The breach was in the end closed up with English dead. Finally, the English fell back, but Cromwell had no intention of going home. He led a new assault, in person, and his fresh courage broke through the stack of bodies. The town fell.

Perhaps Cromwell could have taken hell indeed; he certainly proceeded to make Drogheda into a close imitation of it. He ordered that
no quarter be given. In its way, this was the last act of the Second Civil
War, and partook of its cruelty. The English beat Sir Arthur Aston to
death with his own wooden leg. Survivors tried taking refuge in
St Peter's church, and in an uncanny replication of what the Royalists
had done at Barthomley, Cromwell set fire to the pews to smoke out
those who had hidden in the steeple. The fire spread upwards, and
some of the fugitives were burned to death, screaming. Cromwell himself reported that in the midst of the flames one was heard to say 'God
damn me, God confound me, I burn'. As always, he interpreted this
providentially: the man was clearly a reprobate, and would be burning
soon anyway. The captured garrison was decimated – literally – and
the rest sent to Barbados. Cromwell reported coolly, 'I believe we put
to the sword the whole number of the defendants.' All the officers were
bludgeoned to death.

Among those slain was young Sir Edmund Verney, heir to the father
who had died at Edgehill, who had been fighting against Cromwell's
forces: 'As he was walking with Cromwell by way of protection [having
been given quarter] one Ropier who is brother to Lord Ropier called
him aside in a pretence to speak with him, being formerly of acquaintance, and instead of some friendly office which Sir Edmund might
expect from him, he barbarously ran him through with a tuck.'

At Wexford, things were even worse. Two boatloads of desperate
refugees 'being overpressed with numbers sank', said Cromwell, cool
as ever, 'whereby were drowned near three hundred of them'. The
Cromwellian troops killed any priests or friars they found. Two hundred
women were butchered at the Market Cross, while they begged for
mercy. Cromwell saw himself as acting in the name of God, and God,
he thought, was acting through his soldiers. With him on campaign
was the tirelessly violent Clotworthy, the man who had destroyed the
Rubens *Crucifixion* in Henrietta Maria's chapel; now he annihilated
human Catholics with the ferocity he had learned there. By May
Clotworthy was back in Bristol, and Cromwell was about to turn his
lightning bolts on Scotland.

The military campaign went on and on. Oliver Cromwell rose to
become England's greatest military leader to date, and ultimately to be

Lord Protector, ousting the republican regime he had done so much to create. He refused the crown three times, and his death in 1658 ended his era and his ideas more finally than Charles's had ended his ten years earlier. Charles II dug up his body and hung it on a gibbet to show his treason.

Anna Trapnel never forgave Cromwell's betrayal. For a brief and glorious moment, he had inaugurated what she and others had dreamed of: the rule of the saints, a Parliament chosen entirely by the Independent congregations from among the godly and headed by Praise-God Barebone. It ruled for five months, but then dissolved itself, and Cromwell became Protector, usurping, in Trapnel's eyes, the power that should belong to those God had chosen. So in 1654 she denounced him as a dark minion of Satan. Falling into an eleven-day prophetic trance at Whitehall, she proclaimed the coming of the kingdom of God, then went on an ill-starred tour of Cornwall to try to preach God's word. The Cornish, unregenerate as ever, charged her with witch-craft, but she managed to escape conviction. She is last heard of in Bridewell Prison in 1654.

Thomas Fairfax retired to build his garden and collect books, which he left to the Bodleian Library in his will. He later emerged to invite Charles II to return. He had chosen the winning side, but its actions in displaying the bodies of his old comrades Cromwell and Ireton disgusted him, and he turned back to his books and garden.

Lucy Hay, Countess of Carlisle, was interrogated about her part in Presbyterian elements of the 1648 risings; she was taken to the Tower, the place where she had lived as a girl, and shown the rack and other instruments of torture, to encourage her to tell all. For her involvement in the Second Civil War, she spent eighteen months in the Tower and under house arrest, but she was active again on the Presbyterian side in 1659–60. She remained strongly Presbyterian all her life, and arguably pursued a consistent set of political goals, in her own stylish manner.

Anne Halkett survived, and saw her son with Sir James Halkett grow to maturity; he was given fifty pounds by the Duke of York, but the new king denied her many petitions. She opened a school to make ends meet, dying in 1699. Her son Robert was to serve in Ireland under the prince she had rescued, and to go to gaol for his pains.

Charles, Prince of Wales, invaded Scotland in an effort to regain the throne in 1650; his forces were defeated and he was obliged to flee. After that, the first of many Stuart re-invasions, he tried to raise foreign aid, but was only successful when recalled by Parliament itself. He rode in triumph into London in 1660. His brother James succeeded him, though his reign was marked by a continuation of the bitter religious strife of the wars. Bevil Grenville's sons both became close friends of Charles II, and the elder became Earl of Bath.

Ann Fanshawe eventually made her way back to England and to her estates in Yorkshire and Huntingdon. After the Restoration, Richard became a knight and an MP, and then ambassador to Spain in 1664; Ann went with him to Madrid. He died in 1666, and she in 1680; they were buried side by side.

Artemisia Gentileschi returned to Italy and settled in Naples, where her new works suggested the influence of English classicists. She died in 1652. That same year, Eleanor Davies died – or, as her epitaph put it, entered immortality – in July, mourned by her daughter Lucy.

Hannah Wolley became the cookbook and household-science guru of Restoration England, an early Isabella Beeton. After the Restoration, she married again, and did more cooking and less writing.

John Milton also married again after his recalcitrant Mary died, and then again when his Katherine too proved mortal. He wrote his epic, or rather composed it in his head since he was entirely blind by 1652. It was sombre and ringing, it was *Paradise Lost*, and with it Milton really had entered earthly immortality. Put on a government blacklist at the Restoration, he was talked off it by his friend Marvell, who sensibly argued that the regime would not cover itself with glory by persecuting an old, blind poet. He died in 1674, of that Royalist-sounding malady, gout.

Humphrey Mildmay survived the republican regime almost intact, despite his mounting debts, sympathy with Royalism, and enthusiastic Christmas merrymaking. By 1650 he was his old self: 'I put on a new suit and am easy in it', he said. Somehow this seems a metaphor for his adaptability. His collection of newsbooks reminded him of the stirring times, but his own life went on much as before the war. He died shortly after the Restoration brought England into line with what he had always thought.

Sir Kenelm Digby invented a salve that was supposed to prevent wounds from becoming infected; unfortunately, his idea was that the salve be rubbed on the blade that had caused the wound. He died in 1665. Poignantly, his tomb was destroyed the following year in the Great Fire.

Gerrard Winstanley became a gentleman, and he married the daughter of another gentleman when his first wife died. He could not beat them, but he did at least manage to join them. He also became a corn-chandler and a Quaker, a chief constable and a churchwarden – respectability incarnate. When his countrymen failed to respond to his calls, he settled back into the old order, and began searching for that light only in himself.

John and Elizabeth Lilburne kept on fighting, and were frequently sent to gaol for their pains. John died in 1657 while on parole.

We do not know what became of Sergeant Henry Foster.

After the war ended, Richard Symonds pursued his artistic quest by embarking on the Grand Tour. He met Poussin in Paris, and was the source for the allegation that Caravaggio slept with his models; his acquaintance with the Caravaggists might explain how he knew about Nicholas Lanier and Artemisia Gentileschi. He was the origin of the famous anecdote that Cromwell visited the corpse of the dead Charles I. He died in June 1660 at the age of forty-three.

Richard Atkyns's marriage did not survive the war. After a complicated dispute with the Stationers' Company, Atkyns was imprisoned for debt in the Marshalsea, where he died in 1677.

John Gwynne remained a soldier, ending his career in Monmouth's army in 1679–80.

Philip Skippon refused to have anything to do with the regicides. He became an MP, and later tried to persuade Cromwell to take the crown; in his simple way, he saw it as a simple solution. He died just before the Restoration, still in command of his beloved London militia.

Brilliana's dearly loved son Ned Harley never wielded the politcal influence of his father. He refused to recognize the republic, and the whole family were barred from local office until 1654, when Robert and Ned were engaged in removing 'scandalous ministers'. Ned managed to get back onto the Herefordshire bench, and became an MP in 1656, though he was excluded from the chamber. He died in 1700.

Ralph and Mary Verney resettled in Buckinghamshire. Their family still holds the estates they held during the wars.

Nehemiah Wallington went on thinking and going to sermons and praying. He also carried on turning wood. He wrote down everything that happened to him in his spiritual journals, because he knew that he had lived through the beginning of the end. He reread them all in the weeks before his death, hoping to understand himself and the part his prayers and thoughts had played in events. But he stopped, defeated, because 'I am very ill in body'. He died in 1658.

Richard Wiseman escaped to the Scilly Isles at the same time as Ann Fanshawe, as part of the Prince of Wales's entourage. During Charles's exile, he became one of his closest and most trusted confidants, and was rewarded with royal appointments.

The English republic was finding its shape through all this blood, this iron. It had already broken up the Crown Jewels. Those one sees today were carefully reassembled – or faked, really, since most of the original stones were not recovered – after the Restoration, all but the spoon for the holy oil used to anoint the king during the coronation service. All the other clotted metal magnificence was melted into common coin, the jewels sold. Henry Marten, who had helped John Clotworthy tear up Henrietta's Rubens masterpiece, had uncovered the Crown Jewels in a cupboard at Westminster:

> and having forced open a great iron chest, he took out the Crowns, the robes, the Swords, and Scepter, belonging anciently to K Edward the Confessor, and used by all our kings at their inaugurations with a scorn greater than his Lusts and all the rest of his vices, he openly declares, That there would be no further use of these toys and trifles. And in the jollity of that humour, invests George Wither [an old Puritan satirist] in the Royal habiliments Who being thus Crowned and arrayed (as right well became him) first marched about the room with a stately garb, and afterwards with a thousand apish and ridiculous actions exposed those sacred ornaments to contempt and laughter.

After that they were locked up for six years. The plate in the Tower had already gone to fund Essex's ill-fated attempt to conquer the West. And by January 1650, the Crown Jewels and other regalia were sold, but not intact; they were to be 'totally broken and defaced'. One buyer got the sapphires from the State Crown, another the pearls, and another the emeralds. Only the spoon, dating from the twelfth century, was bought by a member of the royal household, who returned it so it could be used in Charles II's coronation ceremony. A new St Edward's Crown had already been made, albeit with hired stones.

As well as beheading Charles, the republic also beheaded his statue at the Old Exchange. The place where the statue had once stood bore an inscription, '*Exit tyrannus, Regum Ultimus Anno Libertatis Angliae Restitutae Primo*' (Exit the tyrant, last of the kings, in the first year of England's restored freedom). Inns quietly took down loyal signs. 'Here *was* the King's Head', said one tactful pub. Parliament had captured the Great Seal of the kings of England with Oxford. It was broken to pieces by a blacksmith, to the sound of cheering, as was the old Parliament-seal, which had the king's picture on it. The new seal bore a motto, 'In the first year of freedom by God's Blessing Restored'. Other people fought against this rebranding of the nation. A ballad wrote: 'Oh Charles, that exit which they put, up o'er thy statue's head, was but/ An entrance to our woe;/ That fatal Axe which thee divorced from us, our happiness hath forc'd/ Into the grave to go.' 'From fools and knaves in our parliament free/ *Libera nos, Domine*' (Lord, deliver us), ran another, cheekily using church Latin.

Another magical act of restitution and inauguration performed by the republic and protectorate was the readmission of the Jews to England. Jews had been forbidden to enter the country since the reign of Edward I, but the godly had become accustomed to identifying with them as God's chosen elect, and had also come to have great respect for Hebrew Old Testament scholarship. The idea behind their readmission was also to convert them and thus bring about the Second Coming, but in reality it was they who converted England to more civilized ways. With them came the very spirit of cosmopolitan urbanity – things would never again be quite so crude, so raw. The very first coffee house in England opened in that most Royalist of cities, Oxford; its proprietor was one Jacob, a Jew. They became intelligent alternatives to the alehouse, replacing shouted ballads with intellectual discussion.

But the ambivalence of what the republic made and broke can be glimpsed best in the fate of Charles's cherished art collection. The finest art collection ever assembled by an English monarch was also a casualty of war. The king had left a legacy of debts, and his servants begged

Parliament to pay them. Accordingly, the king's creditors and the amounts he owed them were listed. But the works of art found few buyers. Some of the finest paintings in Europe were sold off cheaply, or offered to servants and claimants in lieu of money.

So a London goldsmith called John Bolton bought Van Dyck's equestrian portrait of Charles for £40, probably the one that now hangs in the National Gallery. The future artist Sir Peter Lely snapped up pictures. Colonel John Hutchinson, Lucy Hutchinson's husband, bought two Titians, one for £600, the other for £165. One, *Venus of Pardoe*, now hangs in the Louvre. Giorgione's *Holy Family* went to John Linchbeck, merchant, for £114. Brueghel's *Massacre of the Innocents* was bought by Captain Robert Mallory, a serving officer who might have found its subject-matter sadly consonant with the times. A tavern-keeper named William Proctor bought Correggio's *Holy Family* for £58. Colonel William Webb bought a number of Van Dycks, including his portrait of *The King's Three Eldest Children*, and also acquired Titian's *The Entombment*. The king's own plumber, John Emery, got a Titian, *St Margaret Triumphing over the Devil*. Jerome Lanier, Keeper of the Queen's Music, acquired a Raphael and a Tintoretto, while Nicholas Lanier bought back his own portrait by Van Dyck for £10, along with a Bellini. The king's glazier got a Correggio. Edmund Morrison, embroiderer, received Rubens's *Peace and War*, Mantegna's *Dead Christ* (now in Milan), two Titians, and Van Dyck's portrait of Prince Henry. Edward Bass was rewarded with some Raphaels for telling Parliament where some of the king's plate had been hidden.

In one sense, this was a tragedy for the nation, for the collection was dispersed, and many of its finest pieces ended up in France, in Russia, in Spain. In another sense, it was a great and astonishing democratization of art. For one brief moment, the walls of relatively ordinary tradespeople were hung with masterpieces. They had managed, suddenly, and a little uneasily, to lay hands on what had never been meant for them.

And they would never forget how it felt. Never again.

'Remember', said Charles, as the axe swung down.

FURTHER READING

·

GENERAL
Many of the chapter titles are taken from ballads of the day, many found in *Cavalier and puritan: ballads and broadsides illustrating the period of the Great Rebellion, 1640–1660*, edited with an introduction and notes by Hyder E. Rollins, New York: New York University Press, 1923. A few are from contemporary poems, particularly Milton's. The Diggers' Song ('Stand Up Now, Stand Up Now') is from *The Penguin book of Renaissance Verse: 1509–1659*, selected and with an introduction by David Norbrook; edited by H. R. Woudhuysen, London: Allen Lane, The Penguin Press, 1992.

The industrious production of books and articles on the English Civil War began during the war itself, as I hope to have shown here, and has continued apace ever since. The result is a large, bewilderingly rich and hence unwieldy body of literature, much of it deeply and sometimes overtly political, much of it also deliberately and polemically in disagreement with what has just been said by another expert. This fractiousness has characterized the field since Clarendon's time, but taken together with the sheer number of materials makes it impossible for the amateur to approach the topic with confidence. The Civil War – or perhaps the English Revolution, the Great Rebellion, and latterly the Wars of Three Kingdoms, each title politically correct to some and anathema to others – cannot even be named with certainty. That is natural, for it is also the first major historical turning-point for which really substantial numbers of disputing sources survive for many though not all events. Rival newspapers and polemical pamphlets contend for who shall authoritatively describe particular battles with the memoirs of soldiers and generals. All this sounds daunting, and it is; my principal motive for writing this book was to try to tell the stories of the war to people who didn't already know most of the main events well, and so make it less daunting. Those who now feel well prepared can launch themselves into the additional reading below.

The plethora of previous work is by no means all bad news, however. It also indicates that any work of scholarship on the English Civil War must reveal that it is a mere mouse, standing on the shoulders of an elephant, for this book would not have been possible or even conceivable were it not supported by generations of patient and intelligent historians, and companioned by others who offer different and even adversarial accounts.

This means, however, that it would not be practical to list here all the sources I have consulted. What I offer instead is some suggestions for what primary and secondary sources may be most central to the matter I discuss and to my own text. My focus has been on the impact of the war on people – key players, but also those who were less central to determining its course: the human face of the war. This bibliography is similarly focused.

The historiography and its battles is canvassed in *The debate on the English revolution revisited* by R. C. Richardson, 2nd edn, London: Routledge, 1998. See also Ronald Hutton's recent vivid summation, 'Revisionism in Britain', in Bentley, Michael (ed.), *Companion to historiography*, London and New York: Routledge, 1997, 377–91. The history of some at least of those papery and inky battles has been eloquently and wittily described in Blair Worden, *Roundhead reputations: the English Civil War and the passions of posterity*, London: Allen Lane, 2001.

Anyone keen to read a single traditional top-down history of the Civil War can find magisterial and readable single-authored accounts by Samuel R. Gardiner, and by C. V. Wedgwood, neither of whom has yet been surpassed for style and scholarship, though many of their interpretations have been challenged.

ISABELLA TWYSDEN

Isabella Twysden's diary comes from BL Add MS 34169–72, and is printed in *Archaeologia Cantiana*, 51, 1939. For women's diaries in the Stuart era, see Sara Mendelson, in Mary Prior, ed., *Women in English Society*, London: Methuen, 1987.

CHARLES I

Our principal sources for Charles's childhood include the surviving letters of the physicians who examined him and the memoirs of his foster-father Robert Carey, ed. G H. Powell, 1905. Fyvie's reports: *Letters and State Papers of James VI*, ed. Adam Anderson, 1838, 46–7. The Fyvie/Seton household: George Seton, *Memoirs of Alexander Seton*, 1882. Atkins's letters: 13/5/04 Hertfordshire Record office MS 65447, and SP 14/14/8. On James's upbringing and tutoring, Alan Stewart, 'Boys' buttocks revisited: James VI and the myth of the sovereign schoolmaster', in Tom Betteridge, ed., *Sodomy in early modern Europe*, Manchester and New York: Manchester University Press, 2002, 131–47. Charles's boyhood: Letter to King James from Dunfermline, County Record Office Hertford MS 65447; CSP Venetian 1623–3, 592, and Robert Carey, *Memoirs*, 1975, 25–6 and 66–9. On rickets, Audrey Eccles, 'The dissemination of medical thought in the 17th century – a case of rickets in Westmorland', *Transactions of the Cumberland & Westmorland Antiquarian & Archaeological Society*, ns, 83, 1983, 101–5, and *De Morbo Puerili Anglorum*, 1645; Charles as not erect but repandous is from the hostile and anonymous *Reign of King Charles*, 1655, but it seems unlikely that even a hostile source would insist that a man seen by thousands was deformed if it were untrue; 'A Declaration of the Diet and particular fare of King Charles the first, when duke of York', *Archaeologia*, 1806, vol. 15, 1–12. Valerie Fildes; '"The English disease": infantile rickets and scurvy in pre-industrial England', in J. Cule and T. Turner, eds, *Child care through the centuries*, Cardiff, 1986, 121–34; *The Childrens Disease of the English*, by Daniel Whistler, 1620; Arnold Boate's chapter on what he called *Tabes pectora*, and Gerard Boot, physician in ordinary to Charles I and brother of Boate (or Boot), *Ireland's Natural History*, 1645; *The Secret History of the Court of James I*, 1811; F. Osborne, *Historical Memoirs of the Reigns of Elizabeth and of James*, vol. 2; Anon, *Reign of King Charles*, 1655; Henry Cornwallis, *A Briefe Life of Henry Prince of Wales*, 1641; Anderson, *Letters and State Papers James Sixth*, 1838; Alex Macdonald, *Letters to King James VI*, Edinburgh, 1835, xxxviii; BL MS Harl. 6986, 151; Simonds D'Ewes Autobiog; William Lilly; Philip Warwick; Carlton; Sherborn to DC, 31 May 1616; CSPD 1611–1618, 370; PRO SP 14/86/95, and 14/87/40, cit. Lockyer, *Buckingham*, 33–4; James Howell, *Epistolae Ho-Elianae*, ed. Joseph Jacobs, 1892, I, 164; cf. Chamberlain, letter, II 32, *Calendar of State Papers Domestic 1619–23*, p. 4. Relations with Henry: among others CSPV (the Venetian ambassador) 1603–7, 739; BL MS Harl. 6986, 174. Buckingham: Roger Lockyer, *Buckingham, the life and political career of George Villiers, first Duke of Buckingham, 1592–1628*, 1981; Charles on the Isle of Wight: *A royalist's notebook: the commonplace book of Sir John Oglander, Kt., of Nunwell*, transcribed and edited by Francis Bamford with an introduction by C. F. Aspinall-Oglander, London: Constable, 1936; *The letters, speeches and proclamations of King Charles I*, edited by Sir Charles Petrie, London: Cassell, 1935.

Charles I has been the subject of innumerable works; the most readable biography is Charles Carlton, *Charles I: The Personal Monarch*, London: Routledge, 1983 which also brings a welcome freshness to considerations of his character. Pauline Gregg, *Charles I*, London, 1984, is solid and reliable on context. Richard Cust's biography *Charles I: A Political Life*, is excellent and up-to-date. On the personal rule Kevin Sharpe, *The personal rule of Charles I*, New Haven and London: Yale University Press, 1992, is indispensable, though not all of its conclusions have found general acceptance. Conrad Russell uses Charles's own ideas to explain the war in the final chapter of *The Causes of the English Civil War: the Ford Lectures delivered in the University of Oxford, 1987–1988*, Oxford, 1990.

On the personal rule and the Forced Loan and Ship Money, see Sharpe, above, and also Richard Cust, 'Charles I, the Privy Council and the parliament of 1628', *Transactions of the Royal Historical Society*, 6th ser., 2 (1992), 25–50, and his *The Forced Loan and English Politics 1626–1628*, Oxford, 1987. On Ship Money a great deal of local history has carefully tracked returns. Some general works include Russell Conrad, 'England in 1637', in Todd, Margo (ed.), *Reformation to revolution: politics and religion in early modern England*, London and New York: Routledge, 1995, 116–41; Peter Lake, 'The collection of ship money in Cheshire during the sixteen-thirties: a case study of relations between central and local government', *Northern History*, 17, (1981), 44–71; Nelson P. Bard, 'The ship money case and William Fiennes, Viscount Saye and Sele', *Bulletin of the Institute of Historical Research*, 50, 1977, 177–84. Some contemporary reactions survive in journals and in *An humble remonstrance to his majesty against the tax of ship-money imposed*,

1641; *The arguments of Sir Richard Hutton . . . and Sir George Croke . . . upon a scire facias brought . . . in the court of exchequer against John Hampden esquire*, 1641; Oliver St John, *The speech . . . of Mr. St. John . . . 1640 . . . concerning ship-money*, 1641. On the contemporary idea that Charles was the cause of the war, see Patricia Crawford, 'Charles Stuart, That Man of Blood', *Journal of British Studies*, 16, 1977, 58. On Charles's actual reactions to events, see the sources and studies mentioned earlier.

On Charles's trial and execution: among other sources, see *The Articles and Charge of the Army exhibited in Parliament against the Kings Majesty*, 1648; *The Charge of the Army, and Counsel of War, against the King. With a brief Answer thereunto by some of the Loyall Party*, 1648; *Articles exhibited against the King, and the Charge of the Army against his Majesty; Drawn up by the Generall Councell of Officers*, 1648; *His Majesties Declaration concerning the Charge of the Army; And his Resolution to die like a Martyr*, 1649; *The manner of the Deposition of Charles Stewart, King of England, by the Parliament, and Generall Councell of the Armie*, 1649; for Fairfax's objection the British Library Thomason copy of *A Remonstrance of his Excellency Thomas Lord Fairfax; King Charles His Speech made upon the Scaffold at Whitehall-Gate, Immediately before his Execution . . . published by special Authority*, 1649; *Eikon Basilike*, 1649; Amos Tubb, 'Mixed Messages: Royalist Newsbook Reports of Charles I's Execution and of the Leveller Uprising', *Huntington Library Quarterly*, 67:1, 2004, 59–74; Joad Raymond, 'Popular representations of Charles I', in Thomas N. Corns, ed., *The royal image: representations of Charles I*, Cambridge: Cambridge University Press, 1999, 47–73; Jason Peacey, ed., *The regicides and the execution of Charles I*, Basingstoke and New York: Palgrave, 2001; Sean Kelsey, 'The Trial of Charles I', *English Historical Review*, 118, 2003, 583–616, and his 'The Death of Charles I', *Historical Journal*, 45, 2002, 727–54.

OLIVER CROMWELL

On the young Cromwell, there are a number of angry Restoration slanders, but fewer reliable sources; Cromwell's own remarks can be found in *The letters and speeches of Oliver Cromwell*, ed. Thomas Carlyle and S. C. Lomas, 3 vols, 1904 and in *Speeches of Oliver Cromwell*, ed. Ivan Roots, 1989 there are also uncollected letters. Thomas Beard's *Theater of God's Judgements*, 1597, provides an insight into his world-view. On godly education in general, see John Morgan, *Godly learning: Puritan attitudes towards reason, learning, and education, 1560–1640*, Cambridge: Cambridge University Press, 1986. We await the magisterial biography of Cromwell promised by Blair Worden; in the meantime, the best discussion is John Morrill, 'The making of Oliver Cromwell', in *Oliver Cromwell and the English revolution*, London: Longman, 1990. It is still worth reading two older studies, Thomas Carlyle's introduction and notes to his edition of Cromwell's writings, ably summarized and contextualized by Blair Worden in his *Roundhead reputations*, London: Allen Lane, 2001; and Christopher Hill's *God's Englishman: Oliver Cromwell and the English revolution*, London: Weidenfeld & Nicolson, 1970. See also **Afterwards**.

LONDON

On London, see Valerie Pearl, *London and the outbreak of the Puritan revolution*, Oxford: Oxford University Press, 1961; Jeremy Boulton, *Neighbourhood and society: a London suburb in the seventeenth century*, Cambridge: Cambridge University Press, 1987; and Paul Griffiths, and Mark S. R. Jenner, eds, *Londinopolis: essays in the cultural and social history of early modern London*, Manchester and New York: Manchester University Press, 2000, which is especially rewarding on food. Lindley, Keith, 'London's citizenry in the English revolution', in Roger Charles Richardson, ed., *Town and countryside in the English revolution*, Manchester, 1992, 19–45. Weinstein in Porter, *London and the Civil War*. Bardsley, M. and Hamm, J., *London's Health; Key Facts and figures*, 1995; M. Bardsley, and D. Morgan, *Deprivation and Health in London*, 1996; D. Gainster and P. Stamper, *The Age of transition: the archaeology of English culture 1400–1600*, 1997; J. Landers, *Death and the Metropolis, 1670–1830*, 1993; anthropological research is summarized in *London bodies: the changing shape of Londoners from prehistoric times to the present day*, compiled by Alex Werner introduction by Roy Porter, London: Museum of London, 1998; on deserted Whitehall see *A deep sigh breath'd through the lodgings at White-hall, deploring the absence of the court, and the miseries of the palace*, 1642.

LUCY HAY, COUNTESS OF CARLISLE

On Lucy Hay Countess of Carlisle, see 'Report on the manuscripts of Lord De L'Isle and Dudley', 6, HMC, 77, 1966; *The letters of John Chamberlain*, ed. N. E. McClure, 2, 1939. Ironically Lucy's husband James has received his own biography: R. E. Schreiber, *The first Carlisle: Sir James Hay, first earl of Carlisle as courtier, diplomat and entrepreneur, 1580–1636*, 1984. Lucy's follower Holland is discussed in Barbara Donagan, 'A courtier's progress: greed and consistency in the life of the earl of Holland', *Historical Journal*, 19, 1976, 317–53.

HENRIETTA MARIA

Letters of Queen Henrietta Maria, including her private correspondence with Charles the First, ed. M. A. E. Green, London, 1857 [1856.] *The Queens Majesties letter to the Parliament of England, concerning her dread soveraign lord the King, and her proposals and desires, touching his royall person.* H. Ferrero, *Lettres de Henriette-Marie de France . . . à sa soeur Christine, Duchesse de Savoie* [Letters of Henrietta Maria of France . . . to her sister, Christine, Duchess of Savoy], Turin, 1881. The memoir of Madame de Motteville, one of Henrietta's ladies-in-waiting, is fascinating if used cautiously. *The court and times of Charles the first; illustrated by letters, incl. Memoirs of the mission in England of the Capuchin friars*, by C. de Gamache, T. Birch. R. A. Beddard, 'Six Unpublished Letters of Queen Henrietta Maria', *British Library Journal*, 25, no. 2, Autumn 1999, 129–43; Susan Field Senneff, *Some Neglected Writings on Contemplation by Walter Montagu (c. 1603–77), the English Recusant Chaplain to Queen Henrietta Maria; Neglected English Literature: Recusant Writings of the 16th–17th Centuries*; Dorothy L. Latz, 1997. On the queen's court, N. R. R. Fisher, 'The queenes courte in her councell chamber at Westminster',

English Historical Review, 108, 1993, 314–37; on the court servants see Aylmer, Gerald Edward, *The King's servants: the civil service of Charles I, 1625–42*, London and New York: Routledge & Kegan Paul, 1961. On women at court and on the queen, there have been numerous studies; a new biography of Henrietta Maria and assessment of her role would be welcome, but in the meantime there are biographies by Alison Plowden and Quentin Bone, the latter annoyingly sceptical and patronizing; more satisfying is Malcolm Smuts, 'The puritan followers of Henrietta Maria in the 1630s', *English Historical Review*, 93, 1978, 26–45. *Court culture and the origins of a Royalist tradition in Early Stuart England*, Philadelphia: University of Pennsylvania Press, 1987 and Erica Veevers, *Images of Love and Religion*, Cambridge: Cambridge University Press, 1989, give the best idea of the atmosphere. On Artemisia Gentileschi in England, see Mary Garrard, *Artemisia Gentileschi*, Princeton, NJ: Princeton University Press, 1991, and on her relationship with Nicholas Lanier, musician and art buyer, see Richard Symonds's Diary, BL MS Harleian 991 f. 34. On Rubens see Fiona Donovan, *Rubens and England*, New Haven, CT: Yale University Press, 2004. On Davenant, *The shorter poems*, ed. by A. M. Gibbs, Oxford: Clarendon Press, 1972. On the royal palaces, Sir Geoffrey Callender, *The Queen's House, Greenwich: a short history, 1617–1937*, National Maritime Museum, 1964; Susan Alexandra Sykes, 'Henrietta Maria's "house of delight": French influence and iconography in the Queen's House, Greenwich', *Apollo*, 132, 1991, 332–6; *An act for sale of the goods and personal estate of the late King, queen & prince*, London, 1649; on struggles to overthrow her, Conrad Russell, 'The first army plot of 1641', *Transactions of the Royal Historical Society*, 5th ser., 38, 1988, 85–106. On the ongoing royal marriage see *Charles I in 1646: letters of King Charles the first to Queen Henrietta Maria*, ed. J. Bruce, Camden Society, 63, 1856.

VERNEY FAMILY

The principal source is *Memoirs of the Verney family compiled from the letters and illustrated by the portraits at Claydon House*, London: Longmans, Green, 1892–1899, in four volumes. Margaret Eure, letter to Ralph Verney, 4 August 1642 is from *Memoirs of the Verney family*, I, 258; John Broad, 'The Verneys as Enclosing Landlords 1600–1800', in *English rural society, 1500–1800: essays in honour of Joan Thirsk*, edited by John Chartres and David Hey, Cambridge: Cambridge University Press, 1990; Susan E. Whyman, *Sociability and power in late-Stuart England: the cultural worlds of the Verneys 1660–1720*, Oxford: Oxford University Press, 1999 is a superb analysis with relevance to the Verneys' Civil War concerns.

WOMEN

The role of women is itself one of the biggest growth areas in Civil War studies: see also under the individual women here, and **Matthew Hopkins** and **Levellers**. See also S. L. Arnoult, 'The sovereignties of body and soul: women's political and religious actions in the English civil war', in L. O. Fradenburg ed., *Women and Sovereignty* (Yearbook of the Traditional Cosmology Soc., 7), Edinburgh, 1992, 228–49; ; Keith Thomas, 'Women and the Civil War sects', *Past & Present*, 13, 1958,

42–62; Georgia Wilder, 'The weamen of Middlesex: faux female voices in the English Revolution', in Mark Crane, Richard Raiswell, and Margaret Reeves, (eds) *Shell games: studies in scams, frauds, and deceits (1300–1650)* (Essays and studies, Victoria University, Toronto, Ont.), Centre for Reformation and Renaissance Studies, 2004, 163–84; on camp-followers Griffin, Margaret, *Regulating religion and morality in the King's armies 1639–1646* (*History of Warfare*, 22), Leiden: Brill, 2003; on fighting women Katharine A. Walker, 'The military activities of Charlotte de la Tremouille, Countess of Derby, during the Civil War and Interregnum', *Northern History*, 38:1, 2001, 47–64; *Annals of Bristol* by John Latimer, Bath: Kingsmead Reprints, 1970, p. 179, for Dorothy Hazzard. Good general studies of women's position include the readable *The prospect before her: a history of women in Western Europe*, by Olwen Hufton, London: HarperCollins, 1995; *Women and religion in England 1500–1720*, by Patricia Crawford, London: Routledge, 1993; and above all *Domestic dangers: women, words, and sex in early modern London* by Laura Gowing, Oxford: Clarendon Press, 1996, which does away with the myth that Stuart women were silent and modest while accepting that their society was far from eager to acknowledge their power.

PARLIAMENT

Important sources include Parliamentarian diaries, such as that of Simonds D'Ewes and Judith D. Maltby, *The Short Parliament (1640) diary of Sir Thomas Aston* (Camden Society, 4th ser., 35), 1988, and Esther S. Cope 'John Rushworth and the Short Parliament of 1640', *Bulletin of the Institute of Historical Research*, 51:123, 1978, 94–8; W. H. Coates, V. F. Snow, and A. S. Young (eds), *Private journals of the Long Parliament*, [1]: 3 January to 5 March 1642; [2]: 7 March to 1 June 1642; [3]: 2 June to 17 September 1642, 3+ vols, New Haven, CT, and London, 1982–. Other key documents have been recently edited in Maija Jansson, ed., *Proceedings in the opening session of the Long Parliament*: 1, House of Commons, 3 November–19 December 1640; 2, House of Commons, 21 December 1640–20 March 1641; 3, 21 March–17 April 1641; 4, 19 April–5 June 1641, Woodbridge: Boydell & Brewer, 2000–2004, 4 vols. Crucial debates are analysed in Sheila Lambert, 'The opening of the Long Parliament', *Historical Journal*, 27, 1984, 265–87; David Cressy, 'The Protestation protested, 1641 and 1642', *Historical Journal*, 45:2, 2002, 251–79; Jack H. Hexter, 'Power struggle, parliament and liberty in early Stuart England', *Journal of Modern History*, 50, 1978, 1–50; and the crucial refutation in John Morrill, 'The unweariableness of Mr Pym: influence and eloquence in the Long Parliament', in Susan Dwyer Amussen and Mark A. Kishlansky, eds, *Political culture and cultural politics in early modern England: essays presented to David Underdown*, Manchester and New York: Manchester University Press, 1995, 19–54. Pennington, D. H., 'Tuesday, November 16, 1641: a day in the life of the Long Parliament', *History Today*, 3, 1953, 681–8. J. Forster, ed., *The debates on the Grand Remonstrance* (Nov.–Dec. 1641), with an introductory essay, 1860. On Henry Marten, *A revolutionary rogue: Henry Marten and the English republic*, by Sarah Barber, Thrupp, Stroud: Sutton Publishing, 2000; on the Long Parliament see Mary Frear Keeler, *The Long Parliament,*

1640–1641: a biographical study of its members, Philadelphia: American Philosophical Society, 1954. For a different view, see also Christopher Hill, 'Parliament and
people in seventeenth-century England', *Past & Present* 92, 1981. On elections, *The
representative of the people?: voters and voting in England under the early Stuarts* by
Derek Hirst, Cambridge: Cambridge University Press, 1975 is in disagreement with
Parliamentary selection: social and political choice in early modern England, by Mark
A. Kishlansky, Cambridge: Cambridge University Press, 1986; as often in such
disputes, both have helpful things to say. On the eventual fate of the Long Parlia-
ment see David Underdown, *Pride's Purge: politics in the Puritan Revolution*,
Oxford, 1971.

LAUD AND THE LAUDIAN REFORMS

On Laud himself, Hugh Trevor-Roper, *Archbishop Laud, 1573–1645*, 2nd edn,
London: Macmillan, 1962; Charles Carlton, *Archbishop William Laud*, London:
Routledge & Kegan Paul, 1987, and 'The dream life of Archbishop Laud', *History
Today*, 36:12, 1986, 9–14, which draws on Prynne's *Breviate of the Life of William
Laud, Archbishop of Canterbury, extracted for the most part verbatim out of his diary*,
in 1644; Kevin Sharpe, 'Archbishop Laud', *History Today*, 33:8, 1983, 26–30. For his
execution, *The Archbishop of Canterbury's speech: or his funerall sermon, preacht by
himself on the scaffold on Tower-Hill, on Friday the 10. of Ianuary, 1644. Upon
Hebrews 12. 1, 2. Also, the prayers which he used at the same time and place before
his execution. All faithfully written by John Hinde, whom the Archbishop beseeched
that he would not let any wrong be done him by any phrase in false copies*, 1645, and
*A briefe relation of the death and sufferings of the most reverend and renowned
prelate the L. Archbishop of Canterbury: with, a more perfect copy of his speech, and
other passages on the scaffold, than hath beene hitherto imprinted*, 1645.

On the Laudian reforms, see above all *The booke of common prayer, and administration of the sacraments. And other parts of divine service for the use of the Church
of Scotland*, 1637, which also gives clues about the English reforms. On Laud's own
reasons for the reforms, William Scott and James Bliss, *The works of . . . William
Laud, . . . Archbishop of Canterbury*, 7 vols in 9, Oxford, 1847–60, IV, p. 283; but
also Kenneth Fincham, 'The restoration of altars in the 1630s', *Historical Journal*,
44:4, 2001, 919–40; Peter Lake, 'The Laudian style: order, uniformity and the
pursuit of the beauty of holiness in the 1630s', in Kenneth Fincham, ed., *The
early Stuart Church, 1603–1642*, Basingstoke: Macmillan, 1993, 161–85; John Walter,
'Popular iconoclasm and the politics of the parish in eastern England, 1640–1642',
Historical Journal, 47:2, 2004, 261–90; David R. Como, 'Predestination and political
conflict in Laud's London', *Historical Journal*, 46:2, 2003, 263–94; Jacqueline Eales,
'The rise of ideological politics in Kent, 1558–1640', in Michael L. Zell, ed., *Early
modern Kent 1540–1640* (Kent History Project, 5), Woodbridge: Boydell and Kent
County Council, 2000, 279–313; David R. Como and Peter Lake, 'Puritans, Anti-
nomians and Laudians in Caroline London: the strange case of Peter Shaw and
its contexts', *Journal of Ecclesiastical History*, 50:4, 1999, 684–715; David Cressy,

'Conflict, consensus, and the willingness to wink: the erosion of community in Charles I's England', *Huntington Library Quarterly*, 61:2 (2000 for 1998), 131–49; Peter Lake, '"A charitable Christian hatred": the godly and their enemies in the 1630s', in Christopher Durston and Jacqueline Eales, eds, *The culture of English Puritanism, 1560–1700*, Basingstoke: Macmillan, 1996, 145–83.

JOHN HAMPDEN

E. S. Cope and W. H. Coates eds, *Proceedings of the Short Parliament of 1640*, Camden Society, 4th ser., 19, 1977; *The Short Parliament (1640) diary of Sir Thomas Aston*, ed. J. D. Maltby, Camden Society, 4th ser., 35, 1988; *JHL*, 3–4 (1620–42); *The journal of Sir Simonds D'Ewes from the first recess of the Long Parliament to the withdrawal of King Charles from London*, ed. W. H. Coates, 1942; W. H. Coates, A. Steele Young and V. F. Snow (eds), *The private journals of the Long Parliament*, 3 vols, 1982–92; *De jure majestatis, or, Political treatise of government (1628–30), and the letter-book of Sir John Eliot (1625–1632)*, ed. A. B. Grosart, 1882; C. Russell, 'The ship-money judgments of Bramston and Davenport', *English Historical Review*, 77, 1962, 312–18; *State trials*; R. P. Cust, *The forced loan and English politics, 1626–1628*, 1987; J. T. Cliffe, *The puritan gentry: the great puritan families of early Stuart England*, 1984.

JOHN PYM

A key early source for Pym's parliamentary and administrative career is Wallace Notestein, Frances Helen Relf and Hartley Simpson, eds, *Commons Debates, 1621*, 4: *A diary by John Pym*; 7 vols, New Haven, CT and London, 1935. Many of Pym's speeches survive in the form in which they were originally printed between 1641 and 1643, including his vital speeches on the Grand Remonstrance and the Remonstrance itself. On Pym's career see *The reign of King Pym*, by J. H. Hexter, Cambridge, Mass: Harvard University Press; Oxford: Oxford University Press, 1941, challenged by Morrill, John, 'The unweariableness of Mr Pym: influence and eloquence in the Long Parliament', in Susan Dwyer Amussen and Mark A. Kishlansky, eds, *Political culture and cultural politics in early modern England: essays presented to David Underdown*, Manchester and New York: Manchester University Press, 1995, 19–54. Important discussions can also be found in Perez Zagorin, 'The political beliefs of John Pym to 1629', *English Historical Review*, 109, 1994, 867–90. Conrad Russell, 'The Scottish party in English parliaments, 1640–1642', *Historical Research*, 66, 1993, 35–52. W. H. Coates, V. F. Snow and A. S. Young, eds, *Private journals of the Long Parliament*, [1]: 3 January to 5 March 1642; [2]: 7 March to 1 June 1642; [3]: 2 June to 17 September 1642, 3+ vols, New Haven, CT and London, 1982–. Anthony Fletcher, *The Outbreak of the English Civil War*, 1981. Conrad Russell 'The parliamentary career of John Pym, 1621–9', in Peter Clark, Alan Gordon Rae Smith and Nicholas Tyacke, eds, *The English Commonwealth 1547–1640: essays in politics and society presented to Joel Hurstfield*, Leicester, 1979, 147–65, 248–53, and in the books listed in the section on the outbreak of hostilities. Keen to emphasize the role of the aristocracy rather than the Commons is J. S. A.

Adamson, 'Parliamentary management, men-of-business and the House of Lords, 1640–1649', in *A pillar of the constitution: the House of Lords in British politics, 1640–1784,* ed. C. Jones, 1989, 21–50. Reactions to Pym's death can be found in *A narrative of the disease and death of the noble gentleman John Pym esquire,* 1643; *Threnodia: The churches lamentation for the good man his losse: delivered in a sermon to the Right Honourable the two Houses of Parliament, and the Reverend Assembly of Divines, at the funerall of that excellent man John Pym, Esquire, late a member of the Honourable House of Commons. Preached in the Abbey-Church of Westminster, by Stephen Marshall, B. D. Minister of Gods word at Finching-field in Essex.; Published by order of the House of Commons,* 1644, and in Ian Gentles, 'Political funerals during the English Revolution', in Stephen Porter ed., *London and the Civil War,* Basingstoke and London: Macmillan, 1996, 205–24.

ANTI-POPERY
See also **Iconoclasm**, below
Cornelius Burgess, *The First Sermon,* 40, 67, 68–9. *Trust a Papist and Trust the Devil.* For the Catholic side of the story, see R. Challoner, *Memoirs of the Missionary Priests,* ed. J. H. Poller, London, 1924, 378–491. The source for Hugh Green's death is a letter by Elizabeth Willoughby, in Challoner, op. cit. 421–8. See also Edwin H. Burton and Thomas L. Williams, *The Douay College Diaries 1598–1654,* II, 437, 477, and Joseph Gillow, *Literary and Biographical History of the English Catholics,* III, 18–23.

On anti-Catholic panics Fran Dolan, *Whores of Babylon: Catholicism, gender, and seventeenth-century print culture,* Ithaca, NY and London: Cornell University Press, 1999, and Peter Lake, *The Anti-Christ's Lewd Hat: Protestants, Papists and players in post-Reformation England,* New Haven, CT: Yale University Press, 2002; R. Clifton, 'The popular fear of Catholicism during the English Civil War', *Past & Present,* 52, p. 29; Morrill, in *Public duty and private conscience,* ed. D. Woolf, 1993. *Iconoclasm vs Art and drama,* ed. A E. Nicholas and C. Davidson, 1989. *The Month,* 175, 1941, 348–57; M. J. Havran, *The Catholics in Caroline England,* 1962. Andrew J. Hopper, '"The popish army of the north": Anti-Catholicism and Parliamentarian allegiance in civil war Yorkshire, 1642–46', *Recusant History,* 25:1, 2000, 12–28. Marotti, Arthur F., 'Southwell's remains: Catholicism and anti-Catholicism in early modern England', in Cedric C. Brown and Arthur F. Marotti, eds, *Texts and cultural change in early modern England,* Basingstoke: Macmillan, 1997, 37–65; Alexandra Walsham, '"The fatall vesper": providentialism and anti-Popery in late Jacobean London', *Past & Present,* 144, 1994, 36–87; Caroline Hibbard, *Charles I and the Popish Plot,* Chapel Hill, NC, 1983; Hibbard, in *Princes, Patronage and Nobility,* 1991. The description of Henrietta's pilgrimage to Tyburn is from John Pory's letter to Joseph Mead on 1 July 1626, in Thomas Birch, *Court and Times of Charles I,* 1, 119–23; the description of her chapel is from the memoirs of Cyprien de Ganache, 432–3.

ANNA TRAPNEL

On Poplar see among others *Poplar, Blackwall and the Isle of Dogs: the parish of All Saints*, ed. Stephen Porter, Athlone, 1994. On Stepney see *Memorials of Stepney parish, the vestry minutes from 1579 to 1662*, with an intr. and notes, ed. by G. W. Hill and W. H. Frere. I am grateful to Richard Channon, of the Shipwrights Company, for a helpful e-mail on shipbuilding and shipwrights. The probate inventory is Guildhall MS 9174/4 Probate inventory for Daniel Jeames, Chaundler, Middlesex, 1663. Primary sources on Trapnel include A. Trapnel, *The cry of a stone, or, A relation of something spoken in Whitehall*, 1654; A. Trapnel, *A legacy for saints*, 1654; Anna Trapnel's '*Report and plea, or, A narrative of her journey from London into Cornwall*', 1654; A. Trapnel, *A voice for the king of saints and nations*, 1658; A. Trapnel, '*Poetical addresses and discourses*', Bodleian, Oxford, MS Rawl. A. 21, 325. While there has been a flurry of work on Trapnel's writings, there have been few biographical discoveries. The best accounts are James Holstun, *Ehud's dagger: class struggle and the English Revolution*, London: Verso, 2000 and Diane Watt, *Secretaries of God: women prophets in late medieval and early modern England*, Cambridge: D. S. Brewer, 1997. On the rise of the radical sects, see Nigel Smith, *Perfection Proclaimed*, Oxford: Clarendon Press, 1989. On women's role in the radical sects see Rachel Trubowitz, 'Female preachers and male wives: gender and authority in civil war England', in James Holstun, ed., *Pamphlet wars: prose in the English revolution*, 1992, 112–33; M. Claire Cross, '"He-goats before the flocks": a note on the part played by women in the founding of some Civil War churches', in *Popular belief and practice* (Studies in Church History, 8), eds G. J. Cuming and D. Baker, Cambridge, 1972, 195–202; and Patricia Crawford, 'Historians, women and the civil war sects 1640–1660', *Parergon*, ns, 6, 1988, 19–32. On anorexia Marya Hornbacher, *Wasted: A Memoir of Anorexia and Bulimia*, London: HarperCollins, 1998 and on eating and fasting as protest Maud Ellman, *The hunger artists: starving, writing & imprisonment*, London: Virago, 1993.

THE BISHOPS' WARS, THE THREE KINGDOMS, AND MONTROSE

The outbreak of the conflict in Scotland has become perhaps the hottest topic in Civil War studies. Indispensable are *The Scottish National Covenant in its British context*, ed. John Morrill, Edinburgh, 1990, 134–54, and David Stevenson, *The Scottish Revolution, 1637–44: the triumph of the Covenanters*, Newton Abbot: David & Charles, 1973. A recent survey is David A. Scott, *Politics and war in the three Stuart kingdoms, 1637–49* (*British History in Perspective*), Houndmills, Basingstoke: Palgrave Macmillan, 2004.

On Montrose there has been a large, patriotic and sometimes romantic literature. Sources include Mark Napier, *Memoirs of the marquis Montrose and his times*, 2 vols, Edinburgh, 1856; Robert de Salmonet Menteth, *The History of the Troubles of Great Britain, containing a particular account of the most remarkable passages in Scotland from 1633 to 1650, with an exact relation of the wars carried on . . . by the Marquis of Montrose. Written in French by R. Mentet. To which is added, the true causes . . . which contributed to the Restoration of King Charles II. Written in French* by D. Riordan de Musery. Translated into English by Capt. J. Ogilvie, L.P., 1735; George Wishart, Later Bishop of Edinburgh, *The memoirs of James, marquis of Montrose, 1639–50*, Amsterdam, 1647. Biographies include Wedgwood, Cicely Veronica, *Montrose*, new edn, Stroud: Sutton, 1995; E. J. Cowan, *Montrose. For Covenant and King*, 1977; McNeill, W. A., *Montrose before 1700: from original documents* (Abertay Historical Society publications, 8), Dundee, 1961, and for fans of the legend, John Buchan, Baron Tweedsmuir, 'Montrose and leadership', in *Men and deeds*, 1935. For the poetry, *Civil warrior: the extraordinary life and complete poetical works of James Graham, First Marquis of Montrose, warrior and poet, 1612– 1650*; edited with a commentary by Robin Bell, Edinburgh: Luath Press, 2002; helpful military histories include Stuart Reid, *The campaigns of Montrose: a military history of the civil war in Scotland, 1639–1646*, Edinburgh, 1990, and *Auldearn, 1645: the Marquis of Montrose's Scottish campaign*, Oxford: Osprey, 2003.

THE ULSTER RISING AND IRELAND, AND ANTI-PAPIST PANICS IN ENGLAND

There is an enormous pamphlet and diary literature on the rising. HMC Seventh report Pt 1 appendix, London, 1879, Verney MSS, 435–7; Richard Love, *The Watchmans watchword*, 1642; *The Earl of Straffords Ghost*, 1644; Baxter, *Reliquae Baxterianae*, p. 46; *The autobiography of Mrs Alice Thornton of East Newton, Co. York, 1875*. Durham; Marie Hickson, *Ireland in the Seventeenth Century*, 1884, I, p. 152; deposition dated 25 May 1653; K. M. Noonan, ' "The cruell pressure of an enraged barbarous people": Irish and English identity in seventeenth-century policy and propaganda', *Historical Journal*, XLI, 1998; Kathleen M. Noonan, ' "Martyrs in Flames": Sir John Temple and the Conception of the Irish in English Martyrologies', *Albion*, 36:2, 2004, 223–55; K. J. Lindley, 'The impact of the 1641 rebellion upon England and Wales, 1641–5', *Irish Historical Studies*, XVIII, 1972, 143–76; N. Canny, 'Ireland in the first British empire', in *Strangers within the realm: cultural margins of the first British empire*, ed. B. Bailyn and P. D. Morgan, Chapel Hill, NC and London, 1991, 58–9; on the pamphlets the key text is E. H. Shagan, 'Constructing discord: ideology, propaganda and English responses to the Irish rebellion of 1641', *Journal of British Studies*, XXXVI, 1997, 4–34; N. Canny, *From Reformation to Restoration: Ireland, 1534–1660*, 1987.

On the anti-papist panics in England: *A True Relation of the putting to death one Master Boys, a citizen of London, at Redding, by . . . Colonell Aston . . . Of the great danger the Protestant Religion is in, if this Army of Papists grow to a great body, etc*, 1642; Henry Sawyer on the Catholic menace, CSPD 1633–4, p. 2; 'Kneeling to the cross on the shilling', Coke MS 58, 9 July 1638, Sharpe, p. 844; *A damnable treason, by a contagious plaster of a plague-sore: wrapt up in a letter, and sent to Mr. Pym: wherein is discovered a divellish, and unchristian plot against the High Court of Parliament, October 25, 1641*. 1641. Many others could be cited; see **Anti-popery** above.

THE OUTBREAK OF WAR IN ENGLAND

This is perhaps the most bloodstained historiographical arena because the answer to the question 'what caused the war?' is taken to bear directly on the politically charged question of what the war was about. This book's goal is to separate those questions; the war's cause was not always visible to the majority of those who fought and suffered in it. Ann Hughes, *The causes of the English Civil War*, Basingstoke: Macmillan, 1991, tries to reconcile the competing claims of leftist treatments such as *Society and Puritanism in pre-Revolutionary England*, by Christopher Hill, London: Secker & Warburg, 1964, and revisionist accounts such as *The revolt of the provinces: conservatives and radicals in the English Civil War, 1630–1650*, by J. S. Morrill, London: Longman, 1980. Most detailed and still most satisfying is *The Outbreak of the English Civil War*, by Anthony Fletcher, New York: New York University Press, 1981. Also on the outbreak is *The English people and the English revolution*, by Brian Manning, with a new introduction, 2nd edn, London: Bookmarks, 1991, whose ideas have been challenged by revisionists. Regional studies of the war and the choosing of sides include John Morrill, *Cheshire, 1630–60: County Government and Society during the English Revolution*, Oxford, 1974; Ann Hughes, *Politics, Society and Civil War in Warwickshire, 1620–1660*, Cambridge, 1987; John Morrill, *The nature of the English revolution*, London: Longman, 1993, 1–29; Ronald Hutton, *The royalist war effort, 1642–1646*, 1981; Clive Holmes, *The Eastern Association in the English civil war*, Cambridge, 1974; B. G. Blackwood, *The Lancashire gentry and the great rebellion*, Manchester, 1978; Roy Sherwood, *Civil strife in the Midlands, 1642–51*, 1974.

THE FIGHTING

Civil War battles are recorded by many participants: I have used especially the memoirs of Richard Atkyns and John Gwynne, printed as *The Civil War: Richard Atkyns*, edited by Peter Young, and *John Gwyn* edited by Norman Tucker, Hamden, CT.: Archon Books, 1968; the memoirs of James Duke of York, *The memoirs of James II: his campaigns as Duke of York, 1652–1660*, ed. A. Lytton Sells, Bloomington, Indiana; 1962; Jacob Astley in R. W. Ketton-Cremer, *Three generations: based on letters of the Astley family during the civil war*, 1992; Henry Foster, *A true and exact relation of the marching of the trained bands of the city of London*, 1643, repr. in James Washbourne, *Bibliotheca Gloucesterinsis*, Gloucester, 1828, I 253–71; Richard Symonds's diary of the marches of the royal army, BL MS Harleian 991 edited by Ian Roy, Cambridge: Cambridge University Press, 1997 ; Henry Slingsby, *The diary of Sir Henry Slingsby, of Scriven, Bart.: Now first published entire from the ms. A reprint of Sir Henry Slingsby's trial, his rare tract, 'A father's legacy' written in the Tower immediately before his death, and extracts from family correspondence and papers, with notices, and a genealogical memoir. By the Rev. Daniel Parsons* . . . London: Longman; 1836. Nehemiah Wharton, 'Letters of a subaltern officer'; ed. Sir H. Ellis, *Archaeologia*, 35, 1853, 310–34. *A relation of the rare exploits of the London Souldiers*, 1642. Peachey, Stuart ed., *The Edgehill campaign and the letters of Nehemiah Wharton*, Leigh-on-Sea, 1989; not all such accounts can be attributed to a named soldier: a newsbook telling of Marston Moor does not identify its source: *W. H. A relation of the good successe of the Parliaments forces under . . . Generall Lesly, the Earl of Manchester, and the Lord Fairfax, against the forces commanded by Prince Rupert and the Earl of Newcastle, on Hesham-Moore . . . July 2. 1644. Sent by way of letter from a captain there present, to a friend in London*, [Cambridge] 1644; *Memoirs of Edmund Ludlow Esq; Lieutenant General of the Horse, Commander in Chief of the forces in Ireland, one of the Council of State, and a member of the Parliament which began on November 3, 1640.: In two volumes Switzerland, printed at Vivay in the canton of Bern.* [s.n.], 1699. I have also read memoirs on which I have chosen not to draw in detail: J. Lister, *A Genuine Account of the Taking of Bradford, A Description of the Memorable Sieges and Battles in the North of England . . . during the Civil War*, ed. J. Drake (Bolton, 1785), 87–108; S. Porter, 'The Biography of a Parliamentarian Soldier', *Transactions of the Bristol and Gloucestershire Archaeological Society*, CVIII, 1990, 131–4; and J. Priestly, 'Some Memoirs Concerning the Family of the Priestlys', Surtees Society, LXXVII, 1883, 18–19, 23, 26–7. Contemporary military textbooks are useful too: Richard Elton's *The compleat body of the art military . . . for the foot*, London, 1650, is especially useful for the ordinary soldier. For accounts of Lostwithiel, see **Devon and Cornwall**.

The first historian to make memoirs and experience the focus is Charles Carlton, *Going to the wars: the experience of the British civil wars, 1638–1651*, London: Routledge, 1992; more straightforward military history is provided clearly and vividly by Peter Young and Richard Holmes, *The English Civil War: a military history of the three civil wars, 1642–1651*, London: Eyre Methuen, 1974, and Trevor Royle, *Civil War: the wars of the three kingdoms 1638–1660*, London: Little, Brown, 2004.

On Edgehill, Peter Young, *Edgehill 1642: the campaign and the battle*, Kineton: Roundwood Press, 1967, reprints most of the key sources. On Marston Moor see Peter Young, *Marston Moor, 1644: the campaign and the battle*, Moreton-in-Marsh: Windrush Press, 1998, and Austin Woolrych, *Battles of the English Civil War: Marston Moor, Naseby, Preston*, London: B. T. Batsford, 1961. The battlefield ghosts of Edgehill are described in 'The Diary of John Greene 1635–59', ed. E. M. Symonds, *English Historical Review*, 43, 1928, p. 391, and in *The New Yeares Wonder*, p. 5. Soldiers suffering in the aftermath of battle are described in many surviving petitions, such as those of the Kentishman from Newbury fight in Kent County Record Office Q/Sb2/66.

THOMAS SALUSBURY AND WALES

W. J. Smith (ed.), *Calendar of Salusbury correspondence, 1553–circa 1700*, 1954. I am grateful to Lloyd Bowen for lending me his transcription of Salusbury's letter, NL Wales, MS 5390D, 251–3; T. Jones Pierce, *Clennen Letters and Papers from the Brogynton collection*, Aberystwyth, 1947, item 444. On Wales and the Welsh see

Lloyd Bowen, 'Representations of Wales and the Welsh during the civil wars and Interregnum', *Historical Research*, 77:197, 2004, 358–76, and his 'Wales at Westminster: Parliament, Principality and pressure groups, 1542–1601', *Parliamentary History*, 22:2, 2003, 107–20, as well as Ronald Hutton, 'The Royalist War Effort', and Jason Peacey. 'The Outbreak of the Civil Wars in the Three Kingdoms', in Barry Coward, ed., *A companion to Stuart Britain* (Blackwell Companions to British History), Oxford: Blackwell, 2003, 290–308; and Stephen K. Roberts, 'How the West was Won: Parliamentary Politics, Religion and the Military in South Wales, 1642–9', *Welsh History Review*, 21:4, 2003, 646–74; Philip Jenkins, 'Anti-Popery on the Welsh Marches in the Seventeenth Century', *Historical Journal*, 23, no. 2, 1980, 275–93; Mark Stoyle, 'Caricaturing Cymru: images of the Welsh in the London press, 1642–46', in *War and society in medieval and early modern Britain*, ed. D. Dunn, Liverpool, 2000, 162–79. C. Hill, 'Puritans and the "dark corners of the land"', *Transactions of the Royal Historical Society*, 5th ser., XIII, 1963, 77–102; see also the section on **The Outbreak of War**.

COUNTESS RIVERS AND THE RIOTS IN EASTERN ENGLAND

Bruno Ryves, *Mercurius Rusticus, containing news from the severall Counties of England*, I, 1–6. CUL Hengrave MSS 88, vol. 2, no. 150, Penelope Gage's letter. CUL MS Add 33, fos 19–21; Francis Peck, *Desiderata Curiosa*, 1735, op. cit. II, Bk XII, 23–5. See also Ryves, *Mercurius Rusticus*, I, 1–6. The Stour riots in general: HMC 10th report Appendix VI (1887), p. 147; CUL MS Patrick 33ff., 19–21; *An Exact and True Diurnall 23–30 August 1642; A Perrfect diurnall of the passages in parliament no 14, sub 14 September; Speciall Passages*, no. 3, p. 22; Cf also John Rous, Diary, Camden Society, 1st series, 66, 1856, 121–2. Clive Holmes, *The eastern association in the Civil War*, 43–5, 52, 58; B. Sharp, *In contempt of all authority*, 45–50, 262–5; Anthony Fletcher, *Outbreak of the English Civil War*, 1981, 374–9; John Walter, *Understanding popular violence in the English Revolution*, CUP, 1999; 39, 43, 44, 48, 55, 152–3, 233, 260, 286, 305, 333; and Brian Manning, *The English People and the English Revolution, 1640–1649*, 1976, 175–6.

PHILIP SKIPPON

Letter from a Gentleman; Rushworth VI 43; E 288 (38); *Englands Worthies* 55–7; Bulstrode Whitelocke, *Memoirs*, 150, 151; *Harleian Miscellany* 3, p. 136; *The names, dignities and places of all the collonells, lieutenant-collonels, serjant majors, captaines, quarter-masters, lieutenants and ensignes of the city of London: vvith the captaines names according to their seniority and places. The Major Generall is the right worshipll. Philip Skippon Esquire, Serjant Major Generall of all the forces of London: one of the committee for the militia and captain of that ancient and worthy society exercising armes in the artillery garden of the same city. London: printed for Richard Thrale, 1642; Divers papers from the army: viz. 1. Marshall Generall Skippons speech to the army, May the 15th. 2. The answer of the army: wherein they set downe their grievances. Whereunto are added other papers of concernment. London: Printed for Hanna Allen, at the Crowne in Popes-head-Alley*, 1647; Skippon's own works: *True treasure: or, Thirty holy vowes*, 1644; *The Christian centurians observations, advices, and resolutions*, 1645; *A salve for every sore or, A collection of promises out of the whole book of God, by P. Skippon*, 1643; *A pearle of price in a collection of promises out of the whole book of God*, 1649. *Skippon's brave boys: the origins, development and Civil War service of London's Trained Bands*, Buckingham, 1984. C. E. L. Phillips, 'Phillip Skippon', *Cromwell's captains*, London and Toronto: W. Heinemann, 1938.

ICONOCLASM

Like everything else in Civil War historiography, iconoclasm is politicized; stressing it is often seen as a sign of Royalist allegiance in the wake of T. S. Eliot's conservative anxieties about disassociated sensibilities. However, it is impossible to understand the period unless we are willing to see that religion in this period could generate genuine political radicalism, in a manner difficult for the twenty-first century to grasp; opposing 'politics' and 'religion' is alien to the Civil War era. Thus Richard Overton had a point when he said half-satirically that Cheapside Cross had caused the war. Much of the most startling material on iconoclasm comes from Parliamentarian sources, though Royalists like Bruno Ryves certainly made use of it. The following primary texts are useful:

Trevor Cooper, ed., *The Journal of William Dowsing*, Woodbridge: The Boydell Press, 2001; Thomas Thorowgood, *Moderation Justified*, 1645, p. 16; *Cathedrall Newes from Canterbury*, 1644, by Richard Culmer; 'Original Account of the Springett family', *Gentleman's Magazine*, October 1851, p. 372; George Hakewill, *The Vanitie of the Eye*, 1608; *The Crosses Case in Cheapside*, 1642; Nehemiah Wallington on the army on its way to Scotland, BL MS Sloane 1457, fol. 60R; see also Harold Smith, *The ecclesiastical history of Essex*, 1932, 69, 77–8, 82–4, 180; *Sermo Secularis*, 1643; *The copy of a letter sent to an honourable Lord, by Doctor Paske*, 1642, repr. *Mercurius Rusticus*, 2, 119–20.

Margaret Aston, 'Puritans and iconoclasm, 1560–1660', in Christopher Durston and Jacqueline Eales, eds, *The culture of English Puritanism, 1560–1700*, Basingstoke: Macmillan, 1996; John Morrill, 'William Dowsing, the beaurocratic Puritan', in *Public Duty and Private conscience in seventeenth-century England*, ed. John Morrill, Paul Slack and Daniel Woolf, Oxford: Oxford University Press, 1992, esp. p. 206; David Cressy, 'The downfall of Cheapside Cross: vandalism, ridicule, and iconoclasm', in David Cressy, *Agnes Bowker's cat: travesties and transgressions in Tudor and Stuart England*, Oxford: Oxford University Press, 2001, 234–50; Cressy, David, 'Different kinds of speaking: symbolic violence and secular iconoclasm in early modern England', in Muriel C. McClendon, Joseph P. Ward, and Michael MacDonald, eds, *Protestant identities: religion, society, and self-fashioning in post-Reformation England*, Stanford, CA: Stanford University Press, 1999, 19–42. Spraggon, Julie, *Puritan iconoclasm during the English Civil War*, Woodbridge: Boydell, 2003; John Marcus Blatchly 'In search of bells: iconoclasm in Norfolk, 1644', in Trevor Cooper, ed., *The journal of William Dowsing: iconoclasm in East Anglia during the English Civil War*, Woodbridge: Boydell for the Ecclesiological Society, 2001, 107–22.

PRYNNE, BURTON, BASTWICK

For Prynne sources include his own writings, especially William Prynne, *Histriomastix. The players scourge or actors tragedie, divided into two parts*, 1633, and Laud's speech against him; William Laud, *A speech delivered in the Star-Chamber . . . at the Censure of J. Bastwick, H. Burton & W. Prinn, concerning pretented innovations in the Church*, 1637; William Prynne, ed., *The popish royall favourite or a full discovery of his majesties extraordinary favour to . . . Papists, priests, Jesuits . . .*, 1643. *Newes from Ipswich*, sigs A3V-A4R; Wallington is cited in Kirby, *William Prynne*, p. 30; *Gathering Prynne's blood*: Kenelm Digby in CSPD 1637, 332, 334; *Soldiers cropping ears of Parliament-men: A True relation of Two Merchants of London*, 1642; Clarendon also describes their entry into London; III, p. 264, 1888 edn. There are remarkably few modern studies of any of the three, but there is W. M. Lamont, *Marginal Prynne, 1600–69*, London and Toronto, 1963, and W. M. Lamont, 'Prynne, Burton, and the Puritan triumph', *Huntington Library Quarterly*, 27:2, 1963–4, 103–13.

THOMAS WENTWORTH, EARL OF STRAFFORD

Sources include G. Radcliffe, *The earl of Strafforde's letters and dispatches, with an essay towards his life*, ed. W. Knowler, 2 vols, 1739; C. V. Wedgwood, *Thomas Wentworth, first earl of Strafford, 1593–1641: a revaluation*, 1961; repr. 1964; J. P. Cooper ed., *Wentworth papers, 1597–1628*, Camden Society, 4th ser., 12, 1973; J. F. Merritt ed., *The political world of Thomas Wentworth, earl of Strafford, 1621–1641*, 1996; R. C. Johnson et. al. eds, *Proceedings in parliament, 1628*, 6 vols, 1977–83; J. Watts, 'Thomas Wentworth, earl of Strafford', *Statesmen and politicians of the Stuart age*, ed. T. Eustace, 1985, 83–114; H. Kearney, *Strafford in Ireland, 1633–41: a study in absolutism*, 2nd edn, 1989; S. P. Salt, 'Sir Thomas Wentworth and the parliamentary representation of Yorkshire, 1614–1628', *Northern History*, 16, 1980, 130–68; J. P. Cooper, 'The fortune of Thomas Wentworth, earl of Strafford', in *Land, men and beliefs: studies in early-modern history*, ed. G. E. Aylmer and J. S. Morrill, 1983, 148–75; P. Little, 'The earl of Cork and the fall of Strafford, 1638–41', *Historical Journal*, 39, 1996, 619–35; M. Jansson and W. B. Bidwell eds, *Proceedings in parliament, 1625*, 1987; J. P. Kenyon ed., *The Stuart constitution: documents and commentary*, 2nd edn, 1986; F. Pogson, 'Making and maintaining political alliances during the personal rule of Charles I: Wentworth's associations with Laud and Cottington', *History*, new ser., 84, 1999, 52–73; C. Russell, 'The theory of treason in the trial of Strafford', *English Historical Review*, 80, 1965, 30–50; W. Notestein, F. H. Relf and H. Simpson eds, *Commons debates, 1621*, 7 vols, 1935; W. R. Stacy, 'Matter of fact, matter of law, and the attainder of the earl of Strafford', *American Journal of Legal History*, 29, 1985, 323–47; J. Rushworth, *The tryall of Thomas earl of Strafford*, 1680; J. H. Timmis, *Thine is the kingdom: the trial for treason of Thomas Wentworth, earl of Strafford*, 1974; M. Perceval-Maxwell, *The outbreak of the Irish rebellion of 1641*, 1994; Charles I, *Eikon basilike*, 1649; *The autobiography and corre-spondence of Sir Simonds D'Ewes*, ed. J. O. Halliwell, 2 vols, 1845; *The remarkable speech of John Pym, Esq; in the House of Lords, upon the impeachment of Thomas Earl of Strafford for high treason., London: Printed for A. Dodd, at the Peacock without Temple Bar*, 1642. Speech made on 23 March 1641.

BRILLIANA HARLEY

The key sources are BL MS Add 70110 Portland Papers, vol. CX, 29/72; Letters to Sir Robert Harley from his third wife, Brilliana; 1626–1643, n.d. BL Loan 29/174 ff. 278r-v. HMC MS Duke of Portland, III, 92; Gower, Loan 29/273 f. 9r, and Harley 29/173 f 62r. Lewis, T. T. (ed.), *Letters of the Lady Brilliana Harley, wife of Sir Robert Harley, of Brampton Bryan, Knight of the Bath*, Camden Society, 58, 1854. Young Brilliana's letter: BL MS Add 70002, f. 206r, 213r; Eales, *Puritans*, p. 47; Jacqueline Eales, 'Patriarchy, puritanism and politics: the letters of Lady Brilliana Harley (1598–1643)', in James Daybell, ed., *Early modern women's letter writing, 1450–1700*, Basingstoke: Palgrave, 2001, 143–58; Jacqueline Eales, *Puritans and Roundheads: The Harleys of Brampton Bryan and the Outbreak of the English Civil War*, Cambridge, 1990, the best book to date on an individual family of the period. On Lathom House, see *Warwick, Robert, Earl of. An Exact and True Relation in Relieving, 1644*, T Tracts E 50 (23); E. Chisenhall, *A Journal of the Siege of Latham-House, defended by Charlotte de la Tremouille*, 1823. For Robert Harley's iconoclasm and the formation in April 1643 of the Orwellian-sounding Committee for the Demolition of Monuments of Superstition and Idolatry, see Julie Spraggon, *Puritan Iconoclasm in the English Civil War*, Woodbridge: The Boydell Press, 2003.

WILLIAM, SUSAN AND BASIL FEILDING

DNB; Rushworth's Historical Collections; Historical Manuscripts Commission, 4th rep.; Lodge's *Portraits of Illustrious Persons*, ed. 1850, IV, 113–19; Gardiner's *Hist. of England*; Feilding, Cecilia Mary Countess of Denbigh, *Royalist Father and Roundhead Son, the memoir of the first and second earls of Denbigh, 1600–1675*, London, 1915.

JOHN MILTON

Primary sources include *The early lives of Milton*, edited with introduction and notes by Helen Darbishire, London: Constable, 1932; *Original papers illustrative of the life and writings of John Milton, including 16 letters of State written by him*, ed. by W. D. Hamilton, London, 1859, and Milton's own poetry, judiciously selected in *John Milton*, edited by Stephen Orgel and Jonathan Goldberg, Oxford: Oxford University Press, 1991 and his voluminous prose, in eight volumes, *Complete prose works of John Milton*, D. M. Wolfe, general editor, New Haven, CT: Yale University Press; London: Oxford University Press, 1953–1982. The best recent biography is Barbara Lewalski's *The life of John Milton: a critical biography*, Oxford: Blackwell Publishers, 2000, though it is dense and scholarly; the more accessible efforts of A. N. Wilson and Christopher Hill are lively but often wrong-headed. David

Norbrook's *Writing the English Republic: poetry, rhetoric and politics, 1627–1660*, Cambridge: Cambridge University Press, 1999 places Milton's work in political context.

MATTHEW HOPKINS

On Matthew Hopkins, Hopkins's own *Discovery of witches* and his colleague John Stearne's far longer *A Confirmation and Discovery of Witch-craft*, 1648; John Gaule's *Select Cases of Conscience touching Witches and Witchcrafts*, 1646; *The Magastromancer*, 1652, p. 207; BL Add MS 27402, fol. 114v; *A True and Exact Relation*, p. 5; Cambridge UL EDR 12/19, 11, 2; *Howell's Letters*, 1726, 405, 441 (letters of 3 Feb. 1646 and 20 Feb. 1647); Clarke's *Lives*, 1683, p. 172 b (Fairclough); Baxter's *Certainty of the World of Spirits (1691)*, 1834, p. 20 sq.; Hutchinson's *Historical Essay Concerning Witchcraft*, 1720, p. 50 sq.; *Anthologia Hibernica*, June 1793, p. 424 sq.; Granger's *Biographical History of England*, 1824, III, 255; *Notes and Queries*, 16 Nov. 1850, p. 413; information from the Rev. W. H. Barlee, Brandeston. Secondary works include Richard Deacon, *Matthew Hopkins: Witchfinder General*, London: Frederick Muller, 1976; *Instruments of darkness: witchcraft in England 1550–1750* by James Sharpe, London: Hamish Hamilton, 1996; Malcolm Gaskill, *Witchfinders: a seventeenth-century English tragedy*, London: John Murray, 2005, arrived too late for me to assimilate its findings entirely, but is a readable treatment which is masterly on locale.

On witch-panics in the Civil War, see *A most certain, strange and true discovery of a witch, being taken by some of the parliament forces*, 1643; *Mercurius Civicus*, 21–28 September 1643; *Epistolae Ho-Elianae: The Familiar Letters of James Howell*, ed. J. Jacobs, 1890, p. 506, 3 Feb. 1646; *The Parliaments Post*, 13: 29 July–5 August 1645 on Rupert's dog; *Observations Upon Prince Rupert's White Dogge Called Boy*, 1643, pp. 4–9; *Prince Rupert's Disguises*, 1642; *A Dog's Elegy*, 1644; S. Everard, 'Oliver Cromwell and Black Magic', *Occult Review*, April 1936, 84–92; PRO ASSI 45, which contains a number of records from the Northern Circuit; these are partially transcribed in James Raine ed., *Depositions from York Castle*, Surtees Society, 40, 1860. See also his *Depositions and other Ecclesiastical Proceedings from the courts of Durham*, Surtees Society, 21, 1845; pamphlet accounts include *An account of the trial, confession, and condemnation of six witches at Maidstone at the assizes held there . . . to which is added The trial, examination, and execution of three witches executed at Faversham*, 1645; *The Divel's Delusions or a faithful relation of John Palmer and Elizabeth Knott, two notorious witches lately condemned at the sessions of Oyer and Terminer in St Albans*, 1649.

PRINCE RUPERT

Abingtons and Alisburies Present Miseries, Prince Robert, 4–7; R. Andrewes, *A Perfect Declaration of the Barbarous and cruel Practices Committed by Prince Robert*, 1642; *Observations Upon Prince Rupert's White Dogge Called Boy*, 1643, 4–9; *Prince Rupert's Disguises*, 1642; *A Dog's Elegy*, 1644; E. Warburton, *Memoirs of Prince*

Rupert and the cavaliers, 3 vols, 1849; *The letters of Elizabeth, queen of Bohemia*, ed. L. M. Baker, 1953; G. Bromley (ed.), *A collection of original royal letters (1787)*; C. H. Firth (ed.), 'The journal of Prince Rupert's marches, 5 Sept 1642 to 4 July 1646', *English Historical Review*, 13, 1898, 729–41; G. Martin, 'Prince Rupert and the surgeons', *History Today*, 40, 1990; *A collection of original letters and papers, concerning the affairs of England from the year 1641 to 1660. Found among the duke of Ormonde's papers*, ed. T. Carte, 2 vols, 1739 ; R. Symonds, *Diary of the marches of the royal army*, ed. C. E. Long and I. Roy, Camden Society Reprints, 3, 1997; C. Petrie (ed.), *King Charles, Prince Rupert, and the civil war from original letters*, 1974; *Memoirs of the life and death of Prince Rupert*, 1683; G. Davies, 'The battle of Edgehill', *English Historical Review*, 36, 1921, 30–45; *A true relation of prince Robert his forces, coming to one m. Purslins neere Coventry, and burning downe all his out-houses [&c.]. Also the manner of the cavaliers coming to Oxford, and how they were entertained*, 1642.

THE KING'S PICTURES AND THEIR FATE

The Inventories and valuations of the King's goods 1649–1651, ed. Oliver Millar, Walpole Society, 43, 1970–2, XI, XIII, n. 5; Claude Phillips, *The Picture Gallery of Charles I*, 1896, p. 47; C. Thomas-Stanford, *Sussex in the Great Civil War*, 1910, 153–4; Michalski S., *The reformation and the visual arts*, 1993, 90–1; W. L. F. Nuttall, 'King Charles I's pictures and the commonwealth sale', *Apollo*, 82, October 1965, 306. *the Late king's goods: collections, possessions and patronage of Charles I in the light of the Commonwealth sale inventories*, edited by Arthur MacGregor in association with Oxford University Press, c1989.

WAR IN WINCHESTER

News indeed: Winchester taken. Together with a fuller relation [signed E. A.] of the great victory obtained ... at Alsford ... March 28, 1644, by the Parliaments forces under ... sir W. Waller, etc; A True Relation of the putting to death one Master Boys, a citizen of London, at Redding, by ... Colonell Aston ... 2. A Relation of the Battel at Tadcaster, between the Army of Protestants under ... the Lo. Fairfax, and an Army of Papists under the ... Earle of Newcastle ... 3. A list of the prisoners that were Officers, taken at the Battell at Winchester by the Parliament forces ... 4. Of the great danger the Protestant Religion is in, if this Army of Papists grow to a great body, etc, 1642; *A letter from Captain Jones ... being a more full and exacter relation of the particular proceedings of Sir W. Waller's Armie, than any ... yet published ... With a true relation of the taking of Winchester by the Parliament's forces; A true and exact relation of a great overthrow given to the Cavalliers in Winchester by Colonell Hurrey, Colonell Browne, and some others of the Parliaments forces, on Tuesday last ... Also certaine votes agreed upon by the House of Commons, of great consequence, and delivered to the Lords ... for their assent.*

ANN FANSHAWE AND OXFORD

BL MS Add 41161; Wellcome Institute MS. 7113; John Loftis, ed., *The memoirs of Anne, Lady Halkett, and Ann, Lady Fanshawe*, Oxford, 1979; Civil War Oxford: HMC Portland, 1, pp. 56–8, HMC House of Lords, XI, pp. 324, 326, 329; *A Full and True Relation, 1 July 1646*, BL E 342 (9); Bodleian Library MS Add D 114, ff. 17, 24–6, 46–9, 81. Basis for Toynbee study; Bodleian, Twyne-Langbourne MS 2, ff. 37–8, 47; Oxford Protestation Returns, ed. C. Dobson, B. Dunham, et al., 'Oxford's northern defences', *Oxoniensia*, 48, 1983, 13–40; David Eddershaw and Eleanor Roberts, *The Civil War in Oxfordshire*, Stroud: Sutton, 1995; Firth, C. H., 'The mutiny of Colonel Ingoldsby's regiment at Oxford in September 1649', *Proceedings of the Oxford Architectural and Historical Society*, n.s. IV, 1884, 235–46; *History of Oxford University*, volume IV; Christopher John Kitching, 'Probate during the Civil War and Interregnum; 1: the survival of the prerogative court in the 1640s; 2: The Court for Probate, 1653–1660', *Journal of the Society of Archivists*, 5:5, 1976, 283–93; 5:6, 1976, 346–56; F. Madan, *Oxford Books*, 1693; P. Manning, 'Sport and pastime in Stuart Oxford', in *Surveys and Tokens*, ed. H. E. Salter, Oxford Historical Society, LXXV, 1920, 109–23; R. R. Martin, *The church and Parish of St Michael's*, 1967; Oxford Council Acts, 1626–1665, ed. M. G. Hobson and H. Salter, 1933; Oxford Life in Oxford Archives, 1972; Steven Porter, 'The Oxford fire of 1644', *Oxoniensia*, 49, 1984, 289–300, and see also his *Destruction*, notes above; Ruth Spalding, ed., *The diary of Bulstrode Whitelocke, 1605–1675* (Records of Social and Economic History, ns, 13), Oxford, 1990; John Stevenson, and Andrew Carter, 'The raid on Chinnor and the fight at Chalgrove Field, June 17th and 18th 1643', *Oxoniensia*, 38 (1974 for 1973), 346–56; A. Taylor, 'The royal visit to Oxford 1636', *Oxoniensia* I, 1936, 151–8; P. E. Tennant, 'Parish and people: South Warwickshire and the Banbury area in the Civil War', *Cake and Cockhorse*, 11:6, 1990, 122–52; M. Toynbee, and P. Young, *Strangers in Oxford: A Sidelight on the first Civil War*, 1973; F. J. Varley, ed., *Mercurius Aulicus: a diurnall communicating, the intelligence and affaires of the court to the rest of the kingdome*. Oxford: 1948; Jonathan P. Wainwright, 'Images of virtue and war: music in civil war Oxford', in Andrew Ashbee, ed., *William Lawes (1602–1645): essays on his life, times and work*, Aldershot: Ashgate, 1998, 121–42; Ian Roy, 'The city of Oxford, 1640–1660', in Roger Charles Richardson, ed., *Town and countryside in the English revolution*, Manchester, 1992, 130–68; Wood, *City of Oxford*, Wood, *Life and Times*, ed. A. Clark, 1895, esp. I, p. 63 for destruction of images by Parliamentarian troops; see also *Mercurius Rusticus*, 112, 212–13. On Anthony Wood himself, see Llewellyn Powys, *The Life and times of Antony a Wood*, OUP, 1961; Andrew Clark, *The Life and times of Anthony a Wood*, 1891–1900; Nicolas K. Kiessling, *The Library of Anthony Wood*, 2002, Appendix VII, 702–10; John Barnard and D. F. McKenzie, *The Cambridge History of the Book in Britain, 1557–1695*, 2002; Gabriel Naude, *Instructions concerning the erection of a Library*.

NEHEMIAH WALLINGTON

Wallington's writings survive in BL Sloane 1457, *A memorial of God's judgment against the rebels from 1628 to 1655, by Nehemiah Wallington*, ff. 1–107. The following note is prefixed: 'Nehemiah Wallington, 1632. May the XXIV 1658. Folger MS V a 436, fol. 151. BL Add 40883 *The Growth of a Christian, The Second booke consarning the fruit and Bennifeet y (through the marcy of God) I gaine by the Sacrament'* a spiritual diary of Nehemiah Wallington, puritan, of London, 3 Jan. 1641–31 Dec. 1643; BL Add 21935, Historical notes and meditations, by Nehemiah Wallington, printed as *Historical Notices of Events Occurring chiefly in the Reign of Charles I*, 2 volumes, London, 1869; Richard Baxter, *The Saints Everlasting Rest*, 1653, pt II, p. 124. The main modern study is P. S. Seaver, *Wallington's world: a puritan artisan in seventeenth-century London*, 1985.

ATROCITIES

Here the pamphlet and newsbook literature is really too extensive to be properly documented in a general study, but it is vital to note that the English Civil War was a paper war in which print was used not just to convey rational argument but to inflame feeling. The following have been especially suggestive for this book: for diverse accounts of the fall of Burton-on-Trent: *Journal of Sir Samuel Luke*, ed. I. G. Philip, Oxfordshire Record Society, 1947, p. 117; R. E. Sherwood, *Civil Strife in the Midlands 1642–51*, London: Phillimore, 1974, p. 69; *Mercurius Aulicus*, 18 July 1643; *A True Relation of Two Merchants of London, who were taken prisoners by the Cavaliers*, 1642; John Morrill, 'Discontent in Provincial Armies 1645–7', *Past & Present*, 56, 1972, p. 51; *A Particular Relation of the Action before Cyrencester (or Cycester)*, 1642, and *A relation of the taking of Cicester, in the countie of Glocester, on Thursday February 2 1642*, 1642; *A True and Perfect Relation of the Barbarous and Cruell Passages of the Kings Army, at Old Brainceford*, 1642, p. 6; *An exact relation of the bloody and barbarous Massacre at Bolton in the Moors in Lancashire*, 1644, pp. 2–3; *A military Sermon*, Oxford, 1644, p. 35; the story of the wife who goes mad is from Aubrey, on William Summers. The following document rapes: Rape: HMC *Cowper*, vol. 2, p. 327.; *Scourge of Civil War, The Blessing of Peace*, 1645, unpaginated. On general atrocity, 'to wreake ones fury upon a dead Carkasse, is a most barbarous, cowardly, and impious thing' is Edward Symmonds, *A military Sermon*, Oxford, 1644, p. 35. On Barthomley *A breefe and true relacon of the all such passages and things as happened and weire donne in and about Namptwich*, by Thomas Malbon, ed. James Hall, Lancashire and Cheshire Record Society, 19, 1889, 94–6. Edward Burghall, *Providence Improved*; *Mercurius Civicus*, 35, Thursday January 18–25 1643/4.; *A true relation of two great victories obtained of the Enemy, the one by Sir William Brereton in Cheshire, the other by sir John Meldrum in Lancashire*, 1644, p. 4. On the damage of war, see Stephen Porter; Barbara Donagan, 'Atrocity, War Crime and Treason in the English Civil War', *American Historical Review*, 99, 1994, 1137–66. There have been many recent attempts to assess the impact of the war on the ordinary man and woman: Mark Stoyle's work is exemplary, as are P. Tennant, *Edgehill and Beyond: The People's War in the south Midlands*,

Stroud: 1992; J. Wroughton, *A Community at War: The Civil War in Bath and Somerset*, Bath, 1992; S. Ward, *Excavations at Chester: The Civil War siege works*, 1987; M. Atkin, *Gloucester in the Civil War: A City Under Siege*, 1992; P. Harrington, *Archaeology of the English Civil War*.

CHRISTMAS

Sources include BL E 422 (6), E 540 (20); *The Moderate*, 29 (23–30 Jan. 1648/9); Humphrey Mildmay, *Diary*, MS Harleian 454 fol. 50; Stubbes, *Anatomie*; Ben Jonson, author of *Christmas His Masque* in 1616; in December 1642, Thomas Fuller, Edward Fisher, *The Feast of Feasts; came A Ha Christmas*; Thomas Mockett, *Christmas, The Christian's grand Feast*; January 1649, Edward Fisher, *A Christian Caveat to the Old and New Sabbatarians*; Ezekial Woodward, *Christmas Day The Old Heathen's Feasting Day*, 1656; *The Arraignment, Conviction and Imprisoning of Christmas, printed by Simon Minced-Pie for Cicely Plum Pottage*; John Taylor, *The Vindication of Christmas, or, his Twelve years Observations upon the Times, concerning the general game called Sweepstake, acted by General Plunder and Major-General Tax*, 1653; *Women Will Have their Will, or, Give christmas His Due, in a Dialogue between Mrs Custome a Victuallers wife neere cripplegate, and Mrs Newcome*, 1648. *Christmas In and Out*, p. 9; cf. Bl TT 669 f. 10 (47); *The World is Turned Upside Down; The Commonplace Book of Sir John Oglander Kt*, 1936; Evelyn, *Diary*. The important secondary source is Ronald Hutton's impressive, readable *The rise and fall of merry England: the ritual year, 1400–1700*, Oxford: Oxford University Press, 1994; an outline of events is given in Christopher Durston, 'Lords of misrule: the Puritan war on Christmas 1642–60', *History Today*, 35:12, 1985, 7–14.

DEVON AND CORNWALL

On Exeter: Exeter Quarter Sessions Order Book 62, f. 152r; *Loyalty and locality: popular allegiance in Devon during the English Civil War*, by Mark Stoyle, Exeter: University of Exeter Press, 1994; Mark Stoyle, 'Whole Streets Converted Into Ashes: Property destruction in Exeter during the english civil War', *Southern History*, 16, 1994, 67–84.

On the beginnings of the conflict in the West, see Stoyle, *Loyalty*, 232–5, 241, and see *New News from Cornwall*, 27 October 1642, pp. 3–5; on the Western rising and its relation to the war, see Joyce Youings, 'The south-western rebellion of 1549', *Southern History*, 1, 1979, 99–122, and Anthony Fletcher, *Tudor rebellions*, 47–63.

On Bevil Grenville: 'Verses on the death of the right valiant Sr Bevill Grenvill, Knight.: Who was slaine by the rebels, on Landsdown hill neare Bath, Iuly. 5. 1643, s.n., Printed in the yeare, 1644'; 'Some original letters of sir Bevill Grenvile, with others relating to members of his family' [ed. by St D. M. Kemeys-Tynte], Exeter, 1893; A. Duffin, *Faction and faith: politics and religion of the Cornish gentry before the civil war*, 1996; M. Coate, *Cornwall in the great civil war and interregnum, 1642–1660*, 1933; R. Granville, *History of the Granville family*, Exeter, 1895; B. Grenville, letters; *Bellum civile: Hopton's narrative of his campaign in the West, 1642–1644*, ed.

C. E. H. Chadwyck Healey, Somerset RS, 18, 1902; John Stucley, *Sir Bevill Grenvile and his times, 1596–1643*, 1983; *The Vindication of Richard Atkyns esquire*, 1669, p. 32; Jerrilyn Greene Marston, 'Gentry Honor and Royalism in Early Stuart England', *The Journal of British Studies*, vol. 13, no. 1, Nov. 1973, 21–43. On general perceptions of the Cornish, see Mark J. Stoyle, '"Pagans or paragons?": images of the Cornish during the English Civil War', *English Historical Review*, 111, 1996, 299–323. See also the brilliant vignette in Ronald Hutton, 'The experience of the Civil War in the west', *Somerset Archaeology and Natural History*, 138, 1995, 1–6.

On the fight at Lostwithiel: Thomas Edwardes, *The Third Part of Gangraena*, p. 17 (on the baptism of animals); *A Second Powder-Plot discovered in his excellency the Lord Generall's Armie: truly relating the manner of this . . . malignant plot: in two severall letters, etc.* 5 September 1644; Rushworth V 702–5; *Mercurius Aulicus*, 21 September 1644; *Kingdoms Weekly Intelligencer*, 10–17 September 1644; CSPD, 16 August 1644; Rushworth V 303; G. S., *A True Relation of the Sad Passages Between the Two Armies*, 1644; *New News from Cornwall*, 27 October 1642, 3–5; Symonds, *Diary*, as above (military history); on the Cornish rising, *A Letter from the Isle of Wight* [dated 30 May 1648], *of the design to have gotten the King from the Isle of Wight . . . And a great victory against the Cavaliers that rise in the West . . . certified in a letter to a Member of the House of Commons*; Mark J. Stoyle, '"The Gear rout": the Cornish rising of 1648 and the second Civil War', *Albion*, 32:1, 2000, 37–58, and his *West Britons: Cornish identities and the early modern British state*, Exeter, 2002; on Somerset and on the Clubmen, David Underdown, *Somerset in the Civil War and Interregnum*, Newton Abbot: David & Charles, 1973; Andrew J. Hopper, 'The Clubmen of the West Riding of Yorkshire during the First Civil War: "Bradford club-law"', *Northern History*, 36, 2000, 59–72; G. D. Gilbert, 'The Worcestershire clubmen of 1645', *Transactions of the Worcestershire Archaeological Society*, 3rd ser., 15, 1996, 211–18; Simon Osborne, 'The war, the people and the absence of the Clubmen in the midlands, 1642–1646', *Midland History*, 19, 1994, 85–104; David Underdown, 'The Chalk and the Cheese: contrasts among the English clubmen', *Past & Present*, 85, 1979, 25–48. On destruction, *The civil wars experienced: Britain and Ireland, 1638–61*, by Martyn Bennett, London: Routledge, 2000, and *Destruction in the English Civil Wars*, Stephen Porter, Stroud: Alan Sutton, 1994.

FAIRFAX

Essential sources include W. Johnson ed., *The Fairfax correspondence: memoirs of the reign of Charles the First*, 2 vols, 1848. There are also numerous surviving letters in manuscript, and all significant memoirists and correspondents comment on Fairfax; especially useful are the Thurloe papers and Whitelocke, and there are of course many newsbooks and countless satirical portrayals. See also R. Bell ed., *Memorials of the civil war . . . forming the concluding volumes of the Fairfax correspondence*, 2 vols, 1849; T. Fairfax, 'Short memorials', BL Harley MS 2315; C. R. Markham, *A life of the great Lord Fairfax*, 1870; J. Sprigge, *Anglia rediviva*, 1647; Anon, *The siege of Bradford: an account of Bradford in the Civil War, together with the text of The rider of the white horse a rare pamphlet of 1643*, compiled and edited by staff of the Bradford Libraries and Information Service, Bradford, 1989. Crucial historical studies include Ian Gentles, *The New Model Army in England, Ireland, and Scotland, 1645–1653*, 1992; John Wilson, *Fairfax: a life of Thomas, Lord Fairfax, Captain-General of all the Parliament's forces in the English civil war, creator and commander of the New Model Army*, London and New York, 1985; David Underdown, *Pride's Purge: politics in the puritan revolution*, 1971; Hopper, A. J., 'The readiness of the people: the formation and emergence of the army of the Fairfaxes, 1642–3' (Borthwick paper, 92), York: University of York, Borthwick Institute of Historical Research, 1997.

FOOD AND COOKERY WRITERS

Dan Beaver, 'The Great Deer Massacre: Animals, Honor, and Communication in Early Modern England', *The Journal of British Studies*, vol. 38, no. 3, April 1999, 187–216; John Walter, 'Public transcripts, popular agency and the politics of subsistence in early modern England', in Michael J. Braddick, and John Walter, eds, *Negotiating power in early modern society: order, hierarchy and subordination in Britain and Ireland*, Cambridge: Cambridge University Press, 2001, 123–48, 272–8; Roger B. Manning, *Hunters and poachers: a social and cultural history of unlawful hunting in England, 1485–1640*, Oxford: Clarendon Press, 1993; *The noble arte of venerie or hunting [by G. Gascoigne]*, 1611; *A short treatise of hunting / compyled for the delight of noblemen and gentlemen by Sir Thomas Cockaine, knight, 1591. Presented to the Roxburghe Club by G. E. Cokayne*, facsimile edition, London: Nichols, 1897; Gilly Lehmann, *The British housewife: cookery-books, cooking and society in eighteenth-century Britain*, Totnes: Prospect Books, 2003. Colin Spencer, *British food: an extraordinary thousand years of history*, London: Grub Street, 2002. Judy Gerjuoy, 'The Middle to Late Sixteenth-Century English Upper-Class Meal', in Walker, Harlan (ed.), *The meal: proceedings of the Oxford Symposium on Food and Cookery, 2001*, Totnes: Prospect Books, 2002; D. E. Williams, 'Were "hunger" rioters really hungry? – some demographic evidence', *Past & Present*, 71, 1976, 70–5 (but this is on an eighteenth-century riot). On hunger and plunder: *A True Relation of Two Merchants of London, who were taken prisoners by the Cavaliers*, 1642; MS Tanner 60, fol. 491; *A Particular Relation of the Action before Cyrencester (or Cycester)*, 1642, and *A relation of the taking of Cicester, in the countie of Glocester, on Thursday February 2 1642*, 1642; *Wits Interpreter*, 1655, 143; John Taylor, *Ad populam, or a letter to the people*, 1644; John Morrill, 'Discontent in Provincial Armies 1645–7', *Past & Present*, 56, 1972, p. 51; A. P. Phillips, 'The diet of the Savile household in the 17th century', *Transactions of the Thoroton Society of Nottinghamshire*, 63, 1960, 57–71. On the US hunger study, see the summary in *Hunger: An Unnatural History*, by Sharman Apt Russell, Basic Books, 2005. On cookbooks and politics: *The Court & Kitchen of Elizabeth, commonly called Joan Cromwel the wife of the late usurper, truly described and represented, etc.* [With a portrait.], London, 1664, and 'Elizabeth Cromwell's Kitchen Court: Republicanism and the Consort' by Katharine Gillespie, *Genders*, 33, 2001, *http://www.genders.org/g33/g33_gillespie.html*;

on Hannah Wolley see *The compleat servant-maid: or the Young Maidens Tutor,* 1685; *The Accomplished Lady's delight in preserving, physick, beautifying and cookery,* 1677, and *The Queen-like Closet, or rich cabinet, stored in all manner and more receipts for preserving, candying and cookery,* 1670; Hannah Wolley, *Cook's guide,* 1664; Jennifer Summit, 'Writing home: Hannah Wolley, the Oxinden letters, and household epistolary practice', in Nancy E. Wright, Margaret W. Ferguson and A. R. Buck (eds), *Women, property and the letters of the law in early modern England,* Toronto: University of Toronto Press, 2004, 2001–18; Elaine Hobby, 'A woman's best setting out is silence: the writings of Hannah Wolley', in Gerald M. MacLean, ed., *Culture and society in the Stuart Restoration,* Cambridge: Cambridge University Press, 1995, 179–200; on Kenelm Digby see *The closet of the eminently learned Sir Kenelme Digbie Kt. opened,* 1669, edited from the first edition, with introduction, notes and appendices by Jane Stevenson and Peter Davidson, Black-awton, Totnes, Devon: Prospect Books, 1997; Jackson I. Cope, 'Sir Kenelm Digby's rewritings of his life', in Derek Hirst and Richard Strier, eds, *Writing and political engagement in seventeenth-century England,* Cambridge: Cambridge University Press, 1999, 52–68, 200–2.

NEWS AND THE PRINTING PRESS

Levy, Fritz, 'The decorum of news', in Joad Raymond, ed., *News, newspapers and society in early modern Britain,* London: Cass, 1999; Peacey, Jason, *Politicians and pamphleteers: propaganda during the English civil wars and interregnum,* Aldershot: Ashgate, 2004. On women and the press in particular, see Marcus Nevitt, 'Women in the business of revolutionary news: Elizabeth Alkin, "Parliament Joan," and the Commonwealth newsbook', *Prose Studies,* 21:2, 1998, 84–108, in Joad Raymond, ed., *News, newspapers and society in early modern Britain;* Mary Westwood, Quaker Publisher, Publishing History: *The Social, Economic and Literary History of Book, Newspaper and Magazine Publishing,* 23, 1988, 5–66; David L. Cole, 'Mistresses of the Household: Distaff Publishing in London, 1588–1700', *CEA Critic: An Official Journal of the College English Association,* 56, no. 2, Winter 1994, 20–30; David Underdown, 'The Man in the Moon: Loyalty and Libel in Popular Politics', in *A freeborn people: politics and the nation in seventeenth-century England,* Oxford: Clarendon Press, 1996.

RICHARD WISEMAN AND THE WOUNDED SOLDIER

On Richard Wiseman, see his own *Severall chirurgicall treatises. / By Richard Wiseman, serjeant-chirurgeon,* London, 1676, and the modern fascsimile *Of wounds, of gun-shot wounds, of fractures and luxations / by Richard Wiseman, Sergeant Surgeon to Charles II,* with introduction, appendix and glossary by John Kirkup, Bath: Kingsmead, 1977. See also T. Longmore, *Richard Wiseman . . . a biographical study,* 1891; J. Dixon, 'Contributions towards a memoir of Richard Wiseman', *Medical Times and Gazette,* 19 Oct. 1872, 441–3; J. R. Kirkup, 'The tercentenary of Richard Wiseman's "Severall chirurgicall treatises"', *Annals of the Royal College of Surgeons of England,* 59, 1977, 271–83; D. A. Power, 'Richard Wiseman and his times', *St Bartholomew's Hospital Journal*, 19, 1911–12, 198–201; A. D. Smith, 'Richard Wiseman: his contribution to English surgery', *Bulletin of the New York Academy of Medicine*, 46, 1970, 167–82; John Woodhall's *The surgeon's mate*, reprinted in 1639; John Steer's 1643 translation of Fabricius Hildanus's *Experiments in Chyrurgerie*; H. A. L. Howell, 'The story of the Army Surgeon and the Care of the sick and wounded in the Great Civil War', *Journal of the Royal Army Medical Corps*, 3, 1904, esp. p. 430; W. B. Richardson, 'Richard Wiseman and the surgery of the Commonwealth', *The Asclepiad*, 3, 1889, 231–55; Mark Stoyle, '"Memories of the Maimed": The Testimony of Charles I's Former Soldiers, 1660–1730', *History*, 88 (2), April 2003; E. G. von Arni, *Justice to the Maimed Soldier: Nursing, Medical Care and Welfare for Sick and Wounded Soldiers and their Families during the English Civil Wars and Interregnum, 1642–60*, Aldershot, 2001.

THE LEVELLERS

The remarkable and fascinating Levellers had the ill luck to become icons of the Left, which meant a stream of eager, beautifully written misinterpretations has been their fate; Christopher Hill's writings are brilliant and often misguided examples. On the conceptual link between the Levellers and iconoclasm, see Overton's *Articles of high treason exhibited against Cheap-side crosse. With the last will and testament of the said crosse*, London, 1642. Other important Leveller writings and the vital Agreement of the People are available in *The English Levellers*, edited by Andrew Sharp, Cambridge: Cambridge University Press, 1998, and in *Leveller manifestoes of the Puritan Revolution*, edited, with introduction and commentaries, by Don M. Wolfe, foreword by Charles A. Beard, New York and London: Nelson, 1944. Mary Overton's arrest is described in *To the right honourable the knights, citizens and burgesses, the parliament of England . . . the . . . petition of Mary Overton* [against the continued imprisonment of herself, her husband and brother], London, 1647. See also Andrew Hopton, ed., *Tyranipocrit discovered*, [1649], Aporia Press, 1990, and J. R. McMichael and Barbara Taft, eds, *The writings of William Walwyn*, Athens, GA, 1989. On the army mutineers at Burford and Ware, see *A Full Narrative of Proceedings between Lord Fairfax and the Mutineers*, 10 May 1649; *A Declaration of the Proceedings of the Lord General in May*, 23 May 1649; *Sea Green and Blue*, 6 June 1649; *The Levellers, falsely so called, vindicated*, 14 August 1649; *A true relation of the Proceedings Burford*, 17 September 1649; *The Justice of the Army Against Evildoers Vindicated*, 1649; *The Same Hand Again*, 1649; *The Kingdoms Weekly Intelligencer*, 8–15 May 1649; *Moderate Intelligencer*, 24–31 May 1649; and R. H. Gretton, 'The Levellers at Burford', *Burford History*, 233–56.

Of the vast literature on the subject, the following are especially helpful: Pauline Gregg, *Free-born John: a biography of John Lilburne*, 1961; David Wootton, 'Leveller democracy and the Puritan revolution', in J. H. Burns and Mark Goldie, eds, *The Cambridge history of political thought, 1450–1700*, Cambridge, 1991, 412–42; Jason Peacey, 'John Lilburne and the Long Parliament', *Historical Journal*, 43:3, 2000, 625–46; Patricia Crawford, '"The poorest she": women and citizenship in early modern England', in Michael J. Mendle, ed., *The Putney debates of 1647: the army, the levellers and the English state*, Cambridge: Cambridge University Press, 2001, 197–218; and McEntee, A. M., '"The [un]civill-sisterhood of oranges and lemons": female petitioners and demonstrators, 1642–1653', in James Holstun, ed., *Pamphlet wars: prose in the English revolution*, 1992, 92–111; Lesley Le Claire, 'The survival of the manuscript' [of the Putney debates of 1647], in Michael J. Mendle, ed., *The Putney debates of 1647: the army, the levellers and the English state*, 19–35; Brian Manning, *The far left in the English revolution 1640 to 1660*, London: Bookmarks, 1999; Alan Thomson, *The Ware Mutiny 1647: order restored or revolution defeated?*, Ware: Rockingham, 1996; Ann Hughes, 'Gender and politics in Leveller literature', in Susan Dwyer Amussen and Mark A. Kishlansky, eds, *Political culture and cultural politics in early modern England: essays presented to David Underdown*, Manchester and New York: Manchester University Press, 1995, 162–88; Mark A. Kishlansky, 'What happened at Ware?', *Historical Journal*, 25, 1982, 827–39; Keith Lindley, *Fenland riots and the English Revolution*, 1982; R. B. Seaberg, 'The Norman Conquest and the common law: the Levellers and the argument from continuity', *Historical Journal*, 24, 1981, 791–806; Mark A. Kishlansky, *The Rise of the New Model Army*, Cambridge, 1979; C. M. Williams, 'The Anatomy of a Radical Gentleman: Henry Marten', in D. H. Pennington, and K. V. Thomas, eds, *Puritans and revolutionaries: essays in seventeenth-century history presented to Christopher Hill*, Oxford, 1978, 118–38; Brian, Manning, *The English People and the English Revolution, 1640–1649*, 1976, though its conclusions have been challenged repeatedly; Jason Peacey, 'The hunting of the Leveller: the sophistication of parliamentarian propaganda, 1647–53', *Historical Research*, 78:199, 2005, 15–42.

WINSTANLEY AND THE DIGGERS

The Law of Freedom and Other Writings, Christopher Hill, ed., London: Cambridge University Press, 1983; David Loewenstein, 'The Powers of the Beast: Gerrard Winstanley and Visionary Prose of the English Revolution', in Neil Rhodes, ed. and introd., *English Renaissance Prose: History, Language, and Politics*, Tempe, AZ: Arizona State University, 227–46; *Winstanley and the Diggers, 1649–1999*, edited by Andrew Bradstock, London: Frank Cass, 2000, especially Alsop's essay on his life; James Holstun, *Ehud's dagger: class struggle in the English revolution*, London: Verso, 2000; G E. Aylmer, 'The Religion of Gerrard Winstanley', in J. F. McGregor and B. Reay, *Radical Religion in the English Revolution*, Oxford: Oxford University Press, 91–119. On Robin Hood and outlawry, see especially Stephen Knight, *Robin Hood: a mythic biography*, Ithaca, NY: Cornell University Press, 2003, and on the difficulty in defining 'popular' culture, see Adam Fox, *Oral and literate culture in England, 1500–1700*, Oxford: Clarendon Press, 2001. On the wild foresters and miners of Dean, see Alf Webb, *Civil War in Dean: the history and archaeology of the English Civil War in the Forest of Dean and west Gloucestershire*, Dean Archaeological Group occasional publication, 7, Lydney: Dean Archaeological Group, 2001, and Buchanan Sharp, 'Popular Protest in Seventeenth-Century England', in Barry Reay, ed., *Popular culture in seventeenth-century England*, 1985, 271–308; Buchanan

Sharp, *In contempt of all authority: rural artisans and riot in the west of England, 1586–1660*, Berkeley, CA and London, 1980.

SECOND CIVIL WAR

Colchesters Teares: Affecting and Afflicting City and Country, 1648; *A true and exact relation of the taking of Colchester*, 1648; *Diary of the siege of Colchester*, 1648; Sheppard, S., *The Years of Jubile: or, Englands releasement purchased by Gods Immediate assistance*, 1646; Rushworth, VII, 1179, 1298; Matthew Carter, *A true relation of the . . . expedition of Kent, Essex, and Colchester, in 1648*, 1650; J. Morrill, *Revolt in the provinces: the English people and the tragedies of war*, 2nd edn, Harlow, 1999, 175–6; Robert Ashton, *Counter-revolution: the second civil war and its origins, 1646–1648*, London: Yale University Press, 1994; B. Lyndon, 'The South of England and the start of the Second Civil War, 1648', *History*, 71, 1986, 393–407; Brian Lyndon, 'Essex and the King's cause in 1648', *Historical Journal*, 29, 1986, 17–39; Ian Gentles, 'The struggle for London in the second Civil War', *Historical Journal*, 26, 1983, 277–305; D. T. D. Clarke, *The Siege of Colchester, 1648*, Colchester, 1975. On London and the New Model, Thomas Juxon, *Dr Williams' Library* MS 24.50, ff. 118v–19v; for other accounts see TT e 438 (10), and E 404 (34); less favourable is e 419 (6) and E 422 (9), and Clement Walker, *The History of Independency*, 1648.

CHILDREN

The story of the boy pillaged on his way to Oxford is Ryves, *Mercurius Rusticus*, 113–14. There is little work on children during the Civil War; typically, even Charles I's own children have been neglected. On Princess Elizabeth, so loved by Queen Victoria, see M. A. E. Green, *Lives of the princesses of England*, 6 vols, 1849–55, vol. 6, 335–92; J. Granger, *A biographical history of England, from Egbert the Great to the revolution*, 2nd edn, 4 vols, 1775; on James Duke of York see *The memoirs of James II: his campaigns as duke of York, 1652–1660*, ed. A. Lytton Sells, Bloomington, Indiana, 1962; *The life of James the Second, king of England*, ed. J. S. Clarke, 2 vols, 1816, and on children in general see *The family in the English Revolution*, by Christopher Durston, Oxford: Basil Blackwell, 1989, and Linda A. Pollock, *Forgotten children: parent–child relations from 1500 to 1900*, Cambridge: Cambridge University Press, 1983, which shows, as the Verney letters demonstrate, that early modern parents cared just as much for their children as modern parents do. On Hester Pulter, see Mark Robson, 'Swansongs: Reading Voice in the Poetry of Lady Hester Pulter', *English Manuscript Studies 1100–1700*, 9, 2000, 238–56; I am grateful to Elizabeth Clarke of the magnificent Perdita Project for making me aware of Pulter and for lending me her transcript of her heartbreaking poem. On the history of parent–child relations, see also Claire M. Busse, 'Profitable children: children as commodities in early modern England', in McBride, Kari Boyd (ed.), *Domestic arrangements in early modern England*, Medieval & Renaissance literary studies, Pittsburgh, PA: Duquesne University Press, 2002, 209–43, 314–17; Elizabeth A. Foyster, 'Silent witnesses? Children and the breakdown of domestic and social order in early modern England', in Anthony Fletcher and Stephen Hussey, eds,

Childhood in question: children, parents and the state, Manchester: Manchester University Press, 1999, 57–73.

ANNE HALKETT

Halkett's autobiography has been edited in John Loftis, ed., *The memoirs of Anne, Lady Halkett, and Ann, Lady Fanshawe*, Oxford, 1979. Her numerous and neglected devotional writings are currently being edited by Suzanne Trill. *Colonel Joseph Bampfield's apology: 'written by himself and printed at his desire' 1685*, edited by John Loftis and Paul H. Hardacre; and *Bampfield's later career: a biographical supplement*, by John Loftis, Lewisburg, PA: Bucknell University Press; London: Associated University Presses, c1993. Ezell, Margaret J. M., 'Ann Halkett's Morning Devotions: posthumous publication and the culture of writing in late seventeenth-century Britain', in Arthur F. Marotti and Michael D. Bristol, eds, *Print, manuscript & performance: the changing relations of the media in early modern England*, Columbus, OH: Ohio State University Press, 2000, 215–31. Susan Wiseman, ' "The Most Considerable of My Troubles": Anne Halkett and the Writing of Civil War Conspiracy,' in Jo Wallwork, ed., and Paul Salzman, ed. and introd., *Women Writing, 1550–1750*,Meridian, Bundoora: Australia Pagination, 25–45; Ottway, Sheila, 'They Only Lived Twice: Public and Private Selfhood in the Autobiographies of Anne, Lady Halkett and Colonel Joseph Bampfield', in Henk Dragstra, ed. and introd., Sheila Ottway, ed. and introd. and Helen Wilcox, ed. and introd., *Betraying Our Selves: Forms of Self-Representation in Early Modern English Texts*, Houndmills, England: Macmillan; New York: St Martin's Press, NY Pagination, 136–47; Gabriele Rippi, ' "The Conflict Betwixt Love and Honor" – The Autobiography of Anne, Lady Halkett', in Susanne Fendler, ed., *Feminist Contributions to the Literary Canon: Setting Standards of Taste*; Lewiston, NY, 7–29.

AFTERWARDS

A good general account of the shortlived English republic can be found in Ronald Hutton, *The British Republic 1649–1660*, 2nd edn, Basingstoke: Palgrave, 2000, and the same author's *The Restoration: A Political and Religious History of England and Wales, 1658–1667*, Oxford, 1985, is also a good account, with Tim Harris, *Restoration. Charles II and His Kingdoms, 1660–1685*, London: Penguin, 2005. For more on Parliament, see Blair Worden, *The Rump Parliament, 1648–1653*, 1974. Most work on Cromwell focuses on his acts during the republic and Protectorate; see especially John Morrill, ed., *Oliver Cromwell and the English revolution*, 1990; J. C. Davis, *Oliver Cromwell*, London: Arnold, 2001; David L. Smith, *Cromwell and the Interregnum*, Blackwell Essential Readings in History, Oxford: Blackwell, 2003; for Cromwell in Ireland see J. McElligott, 'Cromwell, Drogheda, and the abuse of Irish history', *Bullán*, an Irish Studies Review, 6:1, 2001, 109–132. The trend at the moment is towards accounts that question the black legend of Cromwell in Ireland. For his readmission of the Jews to England, see *Philo-semitism and the readmission of the Jews to England, 1603–1655*, by David S. Katz, Oxford: Clarendon Press, 1982. The religious conflicts which characterized the war continued to dog the Stuart monarchy: see John Coffey, *Persecution and toleration in Protestant England, 1558–1689*, Harlow: Longman, 2000, and the ensuing *Popish Plot and Glorious Revolution*.

REMEMBERING THE WAR

The story of the Last Cavalier comes from British Library MS Harl. 986 f. 94, and Bodleian MS Eng. Hist. E. 309 f. 14; see also Newman, *Royalist officers in England and Wales, 1642–1660: a biographical dictionary*, Garland Reference Library of the Social Sciences, 72, New York: Garland, 1981, p. 272. On the war and memory, see Mark Stoyle, ' "Memories of the Maimed": The Testimony of Charles I's Former Soldiers, 1660–1730', *History*, 88, 2, April 2003; Maija Jansson, 'Remembering Marston Moor: the politics of culture', in Susan Dwyer Amussen and Mark A. Kishlansky, eds, *Political culture and cultural politics in early modern England: essays presented to David Underdown*, Manchester and New York: Manchester University Press, 1995, 255–76; Andrew Hopper, 'The Farnley Wood Plot and the Memory of the Civil Wars in Yorkshire', *Historical Journal*, 45, 2002, and in a Welsh context, Philip Jenkins's 'The Old Leaven: The Welsh Roundheads After 1660', *Historical Journal*, 24, 1981; John Miller, *After the Civil Wars: English politics and government in the reign of Charles II*, Harlow: Longman, 2000; Burke W. Griggs, 'Remembering the Puritan past: John Walker and Anglican memories of the English civil war', in Muriel C. McClendon, Joseph P. Ward and Michael MacDonald, eds, *Protestant identities: religion, society, and self-fashioning in post-Reformation England*, Stanford, CA: Stanford University Press, 1999, 158–91.

INDEX

Charles I, King – *contd.*
33, 36–7, 75, 107, 113–14, 116, 146, 431; statues, 27; opposes conversions to Catholicism, 36–7; attends Lucy Hay's wedding, 54; court and protocol, 56–7; art collection, 57–8, 60; gardening, 58; and Lucy Hay, 63; attempts uniformity of religions between kingdoms, 72, 75, 78; status in Scotland, 72–3; and Scots threat, 83; marches against Scots (1639), 84–5; returns from Scottish war, 87; and Parliamentary function, 93; relations with Parliament, 95–6; joins Northern Army (August 1640), 96; calls Parliament (April 1640), 89, 96; (November 1640), 97; and Irish rebellion, 113–14; signs Strafford's death warrant, 117, 544, 559; and passing of Grand Remonstrance, 120; enters Commons to charge Pym and colleagues, 122–3, 126; moves from London to Hampton Court, 126–7, 131; attitude to London, 127–8; refuses to sanction hanging of priests, 139; raises standard (August 1642), 140–1, 158; popular hostility to, 172–3; petitions to, 173; threatens then withdraws from London, 194, 209, 279; images vandalised, 205–6; commissions painting from Rubens, 246–7; Rubens praises, 246; at siege of Gloucester, 251; and first battle of Newbury (1643), 260, 263; financial difficulties, 269; Parliamentary peace party negotiates with, 279–81, 541; controls coalfields, 280; loyal Londoners send help to, 281; Milton satirizes, 312; and Henrietta's departure for France, 323–4; and fate of York, 328; food and diet, 343; at Lostwithiel, 362; at second battle of Newbury, 369–72; attempts to join Montrose in Scotland, 399; surrenders to Scots, 401, 452; pursued and harassed by Fairfax, 425–6; threatened by New Model Army in Oxford, 425; army weakened, 426; at Naseby, 427, 429; coach captured, 431; withdraws to Raglan Castle, 432; leaves Oxford for Scotland, 442, 451; correspondence

with Henrietta Maria during imprisonment, 452, 454–6, 544; rejects religious conversion, 452; in custody of Parliament, 454–8; Scots hand over to Parliament, 454; rejects Heads of Proposals, 456, 489; meets younger children, 457; rejects Parliament's peace terms, 458, 460, 462, 490; escape to Isle of Wight, 459–61, 498; Levellers propose alliance with, 497, 516; plays bowls in captivity, 504; execution questioned by *The Souldiers Demand*, 506; sells royal forests, 515; in Second Civil War, 532–3, 543; captivity at Carisbrooke, 543–6; reading, 543; escape plans and attempts, 545–6, 548; transferred to prison in Newport, 546; negotiates while prisoner, 547; promises Henrietta Maria not to attempt escape, 547, 549; writes to daughter Elizabeth, 548; moved to Hurst Castle, 549; physical decline, 550; trial and sentence, 552–8; awaits execution, 558–9; beheaded, 560; lying-in-state and burial, 561; art collection dispersed, 569–70; statue beheaded, 569; *Eikon Basilike*, 561
Charles II, King (*earlier* Prince of Wales): stature and appearance, 14, 459; introduces 1662 Prayer Book, 71; at Edgehill, 176, 179; reintroduces Christmas, 242; in Oxford, 250; flees Bristol for Scilly Isles and France, 404–6; receives delegation of Clubmen, 440; Bampfield proposes escape attempt on Charles I at Carisbrooke, 448; rewards Anne Halkett, 449; Ulster Presbyterians declare for, 505; and Second Civil War, 536; writes to Charles before execution, 557; learns of father's execution, 562; disinters and hangs Cromwell's corpse, 565; invades Scotland (1650), 565–6; Restoration (1660), 566
Chaucer, Geoffrey, 142–3, 172
Cheapside Cross: demolished, 213–14
Cheltenham, 258
Cheriton, Hampshire, 358
Chester, 141

Mokena Community
Public Library District

3 1985 00160 4037